Searching for
George Gordon
Meade

Searching for

George Gordon Meade

The Forgotten Victor of Gettysburg

Tom Huntington

STACKPOLE BOOKS

Paperback edition published in 2015 by
STACKPOLE BOOKS
5067 Ritter Road
Mechanicsburg, PA 17055
www.stackpolebooks.com

Printed in the United States of America

First paperback edition

10 9 8 7 6 5 4 3 2 1

Portions of this book have appeared in modified form in *Civil War Times* and *America's Civil War* magazines.

Cover design by Wendy A. Reynolds
Cover photo of George Gordon Meade, courtesy of Library of Congress

ISBN 978-0-8117-1498-3 (paperback)

Library of Congress has cataloged the hardcover edition as follows:

Huntington, Tom.
    Searching for George Gordon Meade : the forgotten victor of Gettysburg /
Tom Huntington. — First edition.
        pages   cm
    Includes bibliographical references and index.
    ISBN 978-0-8117-0813-5 (hardcover)
    1. Meade, George Gordon, 1815–1872. 2. Generals—United States—Biography.
3. United States—History—Civil War, 1861–1865—Biography. 4. United States—History—Civil War, 1861–1865—Campaigns. 5. United States. Army—Biography. I. Title.
    E467.1.M38H95   2013
    355.0092—dc23
    [B]
                                                                    2012034362

Contents

Maps

Preface

I came to the Civil War somewhat late. I was born and bred in Maine but did not know that Maine provided more Union troops, per capita, than any other Northern state. I had seen the memorials many Maine towns had erected to their Civil War dead, each crowned by a soldier statue, holding a musket and looking stalwartly northward, but I never thought much about them. When I was very young my parents had the board game Gettysburg. I bet they got it sometime around 1963, when I was three years old and the nation was commemorating the battle's one hundredth anniversary. I never knew anyone to play the game, although sometimes I would unfold the game board and study the names written on it, the various woods and orchards and farms. I remember seeing the words "Pickett's Charge," and that made me think of soldiers running in a blind rush to overcome their enemies.

For two years I attended Bowdoin College in Brunswick, Maine. I even lived next door to the former residence of Joshua Lawrence Chamberlain, who commanded the 20th Maine at Gettysburg. At the time his home served as student housing. There was a bronze plaque on the front of the building, but I didn't pay it much thought.

I first began to get interested in the American Civil War after I moved to Washington, D.C., in 1985. Driving around the countryside outside the city one day I drove past the split-rail fences that marked the boundaries of the Bull Run Battlefield. I parked the car and wandered around, reading some of the historical markers—a mass of undifferentiated names and dates to me at the time—and I felt excited that an actual battle had taken place where I was standing. Americans had killed Americans here. History had been made. Around this time I joined the History Book Club and bought *Battle Cry of Freedom*, James McPherson's classic one-volume history of the Civil War. Like millions of others, I watched Ken Burns's *The Civil War* on television and found it engrossing.

Still, I remained pretty ignorant about the war even after I began editing some history magazines. One time I was looking at the illustrations for an article that noted Lincoln scholar Harold Holzer had written. It was about how painters and printmakers depicted the room where Lincoln died, and how each successive artist squeezed more and more important people into the scene. Holzer called his article "Lincoln's Rubber Room." When a painter named Alonzo Chapel finished his version, an epic work he called *The Last Hours of Lincoln*, he had shoehorned a remarkable forty-seven people into the tiny room, making the dying president's final moments look like an especially awkward cocktail party. Chapel had taken great pains to paint realistic portrayals of each personage he included. "He even got Henry Halleck in there," remarked one of the magazine's editors as he gazed at the guest list. To which I replied, "Who?"

They say it is a wise man who knows his own ignorance, so I must be a wise man indeed. I have since learned a lot about Halleck, but I remain uncomfortably aware that there are people who forget more about the Civil War as they brush their teeth with a historically accurate toothbrush than I will ever know.

I do know, though, that the Civil War remains a fascinating and compelling period of American history for many people. Why is that? My guess is that the war is distant enough to seem strange and exotic, yet not so far away that it appears off-puttingly foreign. It was also a war captured in photographs. The people who stare out from the old daguerreotypes and cartes de visite don't seem that different from us—except maybe for the weird facial hair. The Civil War may not be quite close enough to touch, but it hasn't slipped completely out of reach either.

The fact that this was a civil war—sometimes literally a war between brothers—means the passions it aroused still linger. I remember arguing with a Virginian of my acquaintance who avowed that the war had nothing to do with slavery. He may have even called it the War of Northern Aggression. I've had similar discussions with people while working on this book. When I interviewed Barbara Franco, then the executive director of the Pennsylvania Historical and Museum Commission, for a magazine article I was writing about the war's sesquicentennial, she pointed out that civil wars are different from other conflicts. "They never end," she said. "The Civil War is an ongoing conversation that we have with ourselves about ourselves," she added.

Sometimes that conversation gets a little heated, even after 150 years. The war left scars that have not fully healed. Those scars reveal themselves when people protest the display of the Confederate flag—or in the spring of 2010, when Virginia's governor sparked outrage by declaring April to be Confederate History Month, without mentioning that slavery played a role in the war's outbreak. Every January brings discussion about Virginia's recognition of Lee-Jackson Day, which commemorates two of the Confederacy's generals. Civil War–related discussions about race and the role of government can still spark spirited discussion.

So obviously the Civil War interests a lot of people. But what prompted me to write a book about Gen. George Gordon Meade? I first started considering it after *Civil War Times* magazine ran an article about the figures from the war who hadn't received the attention they deserved. That article didn't mention Meade, but the next issue had a letter from a reader who pointed out that Meade hadn't received a major biography since Freeman Cleaves's *Meade of Gettysburg* appeared in 1960. That struck me as wrong.

So I began to look into Meade a little bit. I found out that he had fought in almost all the major battles in the Eastern Theater, with the exception of First Bull Run. He had been badly wounded at the Battle of Glendale during George Mc-

Clellan's Peninsula Campaign and had steadily risen from command of a brigade to head of the Army of the Potomac. And he did that without conniving against his superiors, as other generals had done. He seemed truly to believe that he would be justly rewarded for doing his duty and behaving honestly and conscientiously.

But Meade was no paragon. Paragons are boring. He could be petty and peevish, and he had a legendary temper, described by one contemporary as "a rage so magnificent that it seemed capable of moving mountains."[1] Where did that come from? And why didn't the general who won the Battle of Gettysburg receive more attention from historians?

So consider this book to be a journey of discovery. I did not set out to write the great Meade biography. Somebody else will have to do that, and maybe it will be Christopher Stowe, whom I met in Petersburg to talk about Meade. I set out to write what I started to call a "participatory biography." I wanted to tell the narrative of Meade's life, but I also wanted to visit the places Meade knew and the battlefields where he fought so I could find out what's there today. I wanted to talk to historians, curators, park rangers, and various experts and enthusiasts to get their insights on Meade and the Civil War. As I explored the battlefields and interviewed people, I began to think of the project as a documentary in print, bouncing between the color footage and the talking heads to the slow pans over sepia-toned photos and the historical narration. I wanted to mix past and present, to find out what happened then but also what's happened since. In a way, I became a ghost hunter.

There are at least two ways of looking at the past. "The past is a foreign country; they do things differently there," wrote English novelist L. P. Hartley. Indeed they do. Reading about the Civil War makes you realize how foreign the 1860s are for modern visitors. The clothing, the weapons, the medical techniques, and the social codes all clearly belong to another era, and it's one I'm happy to visit in books, but I'm glad I do not have to live there. On the other hand, as William Faulkner once observed, "The past is never dead. It's not even past." History is like the cosmic background radiation from the Big Bang that permeates everything. It's the ether in which we live. The past is always present.

That's one reason why I decided to braid today and yesterday together in this book. It's not just about what happened then, it's about the history we can find now. Before you can ask, "Why isn't Meade better remembered today?" you have to find out how we remember him in the first place.

◆ ◆ ◆

I'd like to extend my heartfelt thanks to everyone who took the time to talk with me and share their thoughts on George Gordon Meade and the Civil War. Even those individuals who didn't make it into the book directly are here one way or another, for they helped me build the knowledge base I needed. I'd especially like to thank Andy Waskie and the General Meade Society of Philadelphia, not only for what they do to preserve Meade's memory but also for not treating me like an interloper on their turf. In fact, Andy and everyone else welcomed the opportunity to see their favorite general receive some attention. I am proud to say I am a member of the General Meade Society of Philadelphia.

I'd like to express my gratitude to Christopher Stowe for showing me around Petersburg. Chris has been researching Meade for years but, like the members of the Meade Society, he did not treat me like a trespasser—in fact, he shared some of his writings on Meade with me. Reading his stuff made me realize that I had to work all that much harder. I also spent an enjoyable afternoon with Jim Hessler at the Gettysburg battlefield and I thank him for his time and expertise. Charlie Smithgall arranged for me to visit the North-South Skirmish Association's fall nationals and invited me right up on the front lines with his crew. John Cummings III guided me on a fascinating afternoon around Spotsylvania, and Mike Block generously took me to sites around Culpeper and Brandy Station. Thanks also to Peter Palumbo, who loaned me his three volumes of John Bachelder's correspondence about Gettysburg. I probably held on to them a lot longer than he expected I would!

The National Park Service deserves my thanks—and the thanks of people everywhere—for the work they do to preserve and share the many battlefields I visited in the course of writing this book. I always left impressed by the friendly and knowledgeable people I encountered on my visits. Thanks to Donna Schorr of the Greater Philadelphia Tourism Marketing Council for arranging accommodations for me when I was in town, and to Felix Espinoza of the Brownsville Convention & Visitors Bureau for driving me all over the place in the colorful Wow! van.

Libraries are having a tough time of it in today's economy but I couldn't have written this book without their help, especially the Cumberland County Library System and the State Library of Pennsylvania. Meade's papers are in the collections of the Historical Society of Pennsylvania in Philadelphia but I was also able to rely on the microfilmed versions at the Army Heritage Center in Carlisle, Pennsylvania, a wonderful research facility with a knowledgeable and helpful staff.

I'd also like to thank Google Books. I found dozens of important works online through them, which saved me from having to travel to far-off libraries. As much as I love libraries (and real, ink-on-paper books), I couldn't have done this without Google.

Thanks to everyone at Stackpole Books for getting behind this project, and special thanks to Kyle Weaver, my editor. This is the third book I've done with Kyle and he's always a source of help and encouragement. Thanks also to Brett Keener for helping whip the manuscript into shape and to Joyce Bond for her copyediting.

Dana Shoaf and Tamela Baker at *Civil War Times* and *America's Civil War* magazines ran portions of the work-in-progress in their excellent publications. That made me feel that maybe there was something of value in what I was doing, after all, and I thank them for it.

I'd like to thank my parents, Milton and Lillian Huntington, for a lifetime of encouragement. Not to state the obvious, but I wouldn't be here without them. Most of all, my love and thanks to my wife, Beth Ann, who is a constant source of encouragement and a great companion on my Civil War travels. And to my kids, Katie and Sam, who make me proud even if they don't (yet) share my interest in the Civil War. Someday they may torment their own children with visits to historical sites.

INTRODUCTION

Searching for Meade

George Gordon Meade
LIBRARY OF CONGRESS

• • •

The near-cloudless July skies promise a day of relentless sun for the people who have gathered at this large field near Gettysburg, Pennsylvania. Even the faint notes of "When Johnny Comes Marching Home" sound as though they're wilting in the heat. The scents of fresh hay and wood smoke fill the air, and the loud crump of a mortar sounds from the nearby pasture. Men—and a few women—in Union blue and Confederate gray make their way through the crowds moving among the twin rows of white tents alongside the road. Their wool uniforms look unbearably hot. A few of them display beet-red complexions that don't bode well for their health.

This annual reenactment of the Battle of Gettysburg, the pivotal Civil War clash from July 1863, offers a surreal mix of past and present, like a steampunk novel sprung from the page. As I enter the reenactment grounds I'm confronted by a mounted Confederate cavalryman who brandishes a saber in front of neat rows of Porta-Potties. A helicopter hovers high overhead, while golf carts, tractors, and all-terrain vehicles dart here and there. People wearing Harley-Davidson and Homer Simpson T-shirts mingle with generals clad in blue and gray. A period brass band adds to the nineteenth-century atmosphere. The music is stirring but I almost expect it to fade out and provide background for narration by David McCullough.

The sutlers who sell their wares from the tents offer an astonishing array of merchandise, from brass uniform buttons at $1.50 to an elaborate Confederate officer's frock coat, sleeves emblazoned with gold braid, for $278. Civil War soldiers or period civilians can find everything they need—hats, socks, shoes, boots, buttons, and snoods, as well as swords, pistols, and rifles. A new Colt signature 1860 army .44 caliber will cost you $675, or you can get a replica 1861 Springfield rifle for $850. At the Miller Wagon & Cannon Company tent, Dan Miller will sell you a wheel that will set you back $825.

Joe Sodomin bakes in the hot sun while dressed in Union blue and clutching a rifle. The deer tail in his hat identifies him as a member of the 13th Pennsylvania Reserves, a unit that called themselves the Bucktails. Sodomin has been reenacting for about ten years, but he says he's still a relative novice.

Douglas McReynolds of Tom's River, New Jersey, is here, too, his big, droopy mustache and Union uniform making him instantly recognizable as Col. Joshua Lawrence Chamberlain. On the second day at Gettysburg, Chamberlain and his men of the 20th Maine valiantly defended the flank of Little Round Top against a Confederate assault. McReynolds tells me about the time he visited Brunswick, Maine, where the real Chamberlain once taught at Bowdoin College. Wearing his full uniform, McReynolds walked into the small Chamberlain museum there. "A woman came in and just stared," he says, "then reached out and gave me a push on the shoulder." Satisfied that he was real, the woman turned and walked away.

Later in the day, people line up to enter the observation area to watch the battle reenactments. They have paid an additional $10 for a seat in the long ranks of bleachers alongside a field. The field slopes down to a small creek, then rises to a low ridgeline. There's a farm complex on the ridge to the left and a parking lot

2

for reenactors beyond that. A line of cannons at the bleachers' right promises some loud noise. Spectators too frugal to pay the extra ten bucks have set up folding chairs beyond the bleachers.

On the opposite side of the field, a line of soldiers in Confederate gray moves past the farm buildings. I estimate there are about 250 of them. Union horsemen wait in the shade of the trees way off to the left. An artillery piece fires in the distance, then another. White smoke rises against the trees. I can almost imagine this must have been what it was like back in 1863, although the golf carts and tractor-towed hay wagons behind the reenactors distract from the illusion. And so do the trucks and SUVs parked out in the field where they have towed the cannons and limber boxes.

The modern vehicles soon depart, and the Confederate artillerists advance to their weapons. I hear shouted commands, and then the guns fire. They are loud, and I feel the concussion waves pass over me. Union guns return fire from across the field. They're pointed in my direction, and I can only wonder what it must have been like when the Confederate soldiers of George Pickett's division watched Union cannonballs emerge from the smoke, black dots that got bigger and bigger until they tore off limbs, smashed torsos, and left soldiers splattered with their comrades' blood and brains. Unless something goes horribly awry, that won't happen today. This is just a homeopathic taste of war.

Now Union soldiers advance to meet the Confederates, flags streaming. A smoke ring from a Confederate cannon races across the sky and dissolves. The sun beats down mercilessly. "Fire at will!" shouts a Confederate officer. The muskets discharge with a loud ripping sound. A second line of Union troops moves forward amid the rattle of beating drums.

The two sides are now blasting away at each other—but no soldier falls. Finally two Union combatants lie down and remain reasonably still. A little girl in her mother's arms next to me laughs. "That guy up there is acting dead!" she says. "Can you believe that?" One of the casualties props himself on one elbow to watch the action and the other just sits back up. It can't be much fun playing dead beneath the sun on a hot July afternoon.

Treating a Civil War battle as a spectator sport is a tradition as old as the Civil War. Charleston citizens lined the wharves to witness the bombardment of Fort Sumter. In July 1861, when Union and Confederate armies prepared to grapple with each other in the Virginia countryside in the first major battle of the war, civilians streamed out of Washington on horseback and in buggies to enjoy the spectacle. Then the battle—known as Bull Run in the North and Manassas in the South—turned into a rout for the Union army. Fleeing soldiers swept up many of the fun-seekers during the panicky dash back to the safety of Washington. New York congressman Alfred Ely experienced more adventure than he had reckoned when Confederates soldiers captured him and packed him back to Richmond to languish for a while in Libby Prison.

There's something both silly and noble about this reenacting. I understand and appreciate the desire to catch a glimpse of times long past. We'll never again see a Civil War army on the march, so even this little sample stirs the imagination. It's when the old rubs up against the new that strange frictions emerge, like the sight of a reenactor in period garb sitting on a cot in his tent, cell phone pressed to his ear. Or the gasoline generator humming behind a wall of hay bales. Or the Union general drowned out by the squealing feedback from his wireless microphone.

In between the fake battles the reenactment offers education. Beneath a large white tent, I join spectators sitting on bales of hay and listening to a reenactor explain about the life of a Confederate soldier and the way rifled weapons changed the face of war. The audience ranges from kids in kepis to a guy in a Tom Brady jersey. One youngster asks if it's possible to accidentally shoot out your own bayonet. No, the soldier replies, but people often shot out their ramrods. Another youngster asks the soldier if he ever would have tortured a Union prisoner. No, he says, he wouldn't have. A third kid asks if there was archery in the Civil War. "No, no archery in this one."

After the Confederate soldier has said his piece, Confederate generals assemble inside the big tent. They are members of a living history organization called Lee's Lieutenants. Gen. Robert E. Lee is here, and so are subordinates who were with him at Gettysburg. Jubal Early, Lee's "bad old man," is present. So are generals Richard Ewell, A. P. Hill, E. Porter Alexander, Isaac Trimble, James Kemper, and George Pickett, of Pickett's Charge fame. All of them more or less look like the people they're playing.

Al Stone plays Lee. In character, he explains to his audience about his career before the Civil War. "For thirty-two years I wore this," he says, and he takes off his coat of Confederate gray and dons one of Union blue. He explains how once war broke out he was offered command of the Union armies. Instead, he resigned his army commission and offered his services to his home state, Virginia. "On April 20 I tendered my resignation," this Lee says, and the audience applauds when he removes the Union coat and puts the gray one back on.

General Ewell turns to Lee. "We're missing somebody," he says.

"Sir, if you're thinking of General Stuart, we haven't heard from him," Lee replies. The audience laughs. This crowd knows a good Jeb Stuart joke when it hears one. Suddenly heads turn toward a disturbance in the back of the tent. "I'm here, sir!" a voice rings out, and a man in a Confederate officer's uniform, a big spade-shaped beard rippling down his chest and a broad-brimmed hat with a plume atop his head, runs down to the stage. He's a good facsimile of the real Jeb Stuart, who lost touch with Lee in the days leading up to Gettysburg, when he took his cavalry on an end run around the Union army.

"Why haven't I heard from you?" Lee demands of his cavalry commander.

"I tried calling you on my cell phone," Stuart replies. He holds up a tiny hand-cranked phone. The crowd roars.

Lee turns to the audience. "That's why we lost the war," he says.

Some historians do blame Stuart for the Confederate defeat at Gettysburg. By losing contact with Lee, Stuart deprived the Confederate army of his cavalry's eyes and ears in the important days before the battle. But Stuart needn't worry. People have been playing the blame game about Gettysburg from the moment the guns cooled. If it wasn't Stuart's fault, then you can blame James Longstreet. Or, as a question from the audience indicates, maybe it was "Old Baldhead" Ewell's fault.

"General Ewell, why didn't you take the high ground?" a man asks. The audience laughs and applauds.

People have been asking that question for a long time. On the battle's first day the Confederate army pushed the Union troops back, through the town of Gettysburg and up onto the high ground on Cemetery Hill to the south. Lee told Ewell to take the hill, "if practicable." Ewell, his men tired from a hot and bloody day of marching and fighting, decided it wasn't. So maybe it was all Ewell's fault that the Confederates lost the battle and, by extension, the entire Civil War.

Of course, all these explanations rest on the premise that the battle was entirely the Confederates' to win or lose. There was another factor at play here, though. Supposedly someone once asked the real George Pickett why the Confederate attack during the battle's third day failed. "I always thought the Yankees had something to do with it," he drawled in reply.

I find some Yankees beneath a tent at the other end of the reenactment grounds. They hail from another living history group, the Federal General Officer Corps, which often works events like this in conjunction with Lee's Lieutenants. There's an odd mix present in Union blue today, a grab bag of Civil War figures, including nurse Clara Barton and photographer Mathew Brady. Gen. William Tecumseh Sherman is present, even though he was in far-off Vicksburg, Mississippi, in July 1863. But Gen. John Buford, the tough-as-nails cavalry commander who held off the Confederates at Gettysburg on the morning of July 1, is here. So is Gen. John Reynolds, who arrived with his I Corps just in time to support Buford—and receive a fatal bullet in the head.

I notice one major absence among the Union generals. Where is Maj. Gen. George Gordon Meade? Meade commanded the Union army at Gettysburg. Certainly he should be here.

In one way his absence makes perfect sense. It seems as though Meade has largely disappeared from history books. Sure, Civil War buffs know about him, and no account of the Battle of Gettysburg is complete without some mention of Meade's name. Yet Meade has somehow missed being enshrined in the pantheon of Civil War greats occupied by Lee, Stonewall Jackson, Jeb Stuart, Sherman, and Ulysses S. Grant. Maybe Phil Sheridan has a seat in the hall, too, although that would surely make Meade grind his teeth. But history has shunted aside the general who won what is perhaps the Civil War's most important battle.

Meade is the Rodney Dangerfield of Civil War generals. He gets no respect. Grant became president and occupies the $50 bill. Civil War soldiers Rutherford B. Hayes, James A. Garfield, Benjamin Harrison, and William McKinley also reached the White House. As for Meade, after the Battle of Gettysburg, President Abraham Lincoln wrote him a letter chiding him about not destroying Lee's army. Adding insult to injury, later in the war, Meade had to testify about his generalship at Gettysburg before a congressional committee, mainly because the man who had almost cost him the battle—Maj. Gen. Daniel Sickles—was busy spreading rumors that Meade had intended to retreat from the battlefield. Even before the war ended Meade sensed that his reputation was in eclipse. "I suppose after awhile it will be discovered I was not at Gettysburg at all," he griped in a letter to his wife.[1]

There were other factors at work, too. In the last year or so of the war, Grant, by then the general in chief of the Union forces, was traveling with Meade and his army and looking over Meade's shoulder. Grant got credit for the victories. That situation was exacerbated when newspaper reporters, angered after the hot-tempered Meade kicked a reporter out of his army, began omitting Meade's name in their dispatches.

Meade seemed an unlikely general. He was balding and beaky and had big pouches under his eyes that gave him an air of melancholy. Maybe he was melancholy. Certainly he had plenty to worry about. He had not sought command of the Army of the Potomac, but it was thrust upon him, only three days before the battle at Gettysburg. But he was a fighter, badly wounded in one battle and with plenty of bullet-ridden horses and hats to testify to his courage. He took delight over a conversation an aide heard during a trip Meade made to Washington. "What major general is that?" a man asked a companion.

"Meade," replied the other.

"I never saw him before."

"No, that is very likely, for he is one of our fighting generals, is always on the field, and does not spend his time in Washington hotels." [2]

One reason why Meade's reputation declined lay in his own personality. He was not flamboyant. Like most of the generals around him he was very ambitious, but he rather naïvely expected that if he did his duty those in authority would recognize his virtues. He was wrong about that and it embittered him. Toward the end of the war Meade watched angrily as onetime subordinate Philip Sheridan grasped tenaciously for glory and found it, often to the detriment of the Army of the Potomac. Although Grant and Meade got along well enough during the war, once Grant became president he passed Meade over for advancement, preferring Sherman and Sheridan.

Meade also had a ferocious temper, "which under irritating circumstances became almost ungovernable," as another officer noted. [3] "He is a slasher, is the General, and cuts up people without much mercy," wrote Meade's aide-de-camp, Theodore Lyman. "His family is celebrated for fierceness of temper and a sardonic sort of way that makes them uncomfortable people; but the General is the best of them, and exhausts his temper in saying sharp things."[4] The temper sometimes created problems and enemies, as it did with the newspaperman, but Meade proved himself a capable warrior on the field of battle.

I wonder if another reason for Meade's relative eclipse lies in the way we remember the Civil War. A visit to the battlefield at Gettysburg provides a clue to what's going on. There is a statue of Meade here. It stands on Cemetery Ridge, the middle of the Union lines, not far from the little white house he used as headquarters. Another statue stands off in the distance, directly across the broad field, where the Confederate forces massed for the final assault we remember today as Pickett's Charge. This is the Virginia Memorial, which towers forty-one feet above the battlefield. Crowning it is an equestrian statue of Robert E. Lee. Compare this memorial to the more modest one of Meade and you might think that Lee won the battle.

During the war and in the years since, Lee has been lionized. Entire bookshelves groan beneath the weight of the volumes dedicated to him. He has come to symbolize a glorious "lost cause," a world of "cavaliers and cotton fields," as *Gone with the Wind* put it. In this view of the Civil War, the noble, freedom-loving South fought a valiant but doomed battle against the institutionalized and bureaucratic forces of the North. The Southern generals, men like Lee, Jackson, and Stuart, tend to be remembered as glamorous and noble warriors. The generals in the North come across more like CEOs of major corporations, faceless and colorless. Except perhaps for Ulysses S. Grant, who gained a reputation as a "butcher" willing to exchange his soldiers' lives for victory. Who wants to cheer for those guys, especially today, when public distrust of the federal government seems to have reached an all-time high? No, it's much cooler to cheer for the rebels.

Yet there's one thing that tarnishes this glamorous view of the rebellious South, an elephant in the room that many try to ignore. And that is slavery. The South fought to preserve a culture that rested on a foundation of human bondage. Don't take it from me—take it from the vice president of the Confederate States of America, Alexander Stephens. In a famous speech he made in March 1861, less than a month before the attack on Fort Sumter ignited the Civil War, Stephens declared that slavery "was the immediate cause of the late rupture and present revolution." Furthermore, he added, the foundation of the Confederate government—its very cornerstone, in fact—"rests upon the great truth that the negro is not equal to the white man; that slavery subordination to the superior race is his natural and normal condition." Claiming that slavery did not cause the Civil War is like clearing the iceberg of any responsibility for sinking the *Titanic*. That's why I find it galling to see the Sons of Confederate Veterans contend that the South's "motivating factor" for war was "the preservation of liberty and freedom." Except, of course, for the approximately four million people of African descent whom the slave-holding states kept in bondage. It's a stain that will forever sully the story of the Confederate States of America. There's no escaping it.

Not that people don't try. In 2010, the governor of Virginia, Bob McDonnell, waded into the matter when he issued his bland statement proclaiming April as Confederate History Month, but neglected to mention that slavery played any role in the conflict. The proclamation instead focused on "the sacrifices of the Confederate leaders, soldiers, and citizens during the period of the Civil War." McDonnell poured fuel on the flames in the uproar that followed by explaining that "there were any number of aspects to that conflict between the states." Once he removed his foot from his mouth McDonnell issued a revised statement that admitted, "It is important for all Virginians to understand that the institution of slavery led to this war." The problem is, once you allow slavery to enter the picture, it's tough to cast the story as the good and noble South against the remorseless Yankees. No longer is the picture black and white—slavery introduces, aptly enough, shades of gray.

Take slavery out of the picture, though, and the picture becomes much more romantic. As I wander through the sutlers' tents at the Gettysburg reenactment, I find plenty of books, postcards, posters, paintings, and items related to Lee and

Stonewall Jackson, but at first I see nothing related to Meade. Finally, I find a Meade postcard, and later I purchase a Meade coffee mug and a Meade bookmark, but Lee memorabilia outnumbers Meade by a huge factor at this commemoration of a battle the Confederates lost. This riles up my Yankee soul.

The next morning the Union generals gather in the main tent for a presentation about the Gettysburg battle. Gen. Winfield Scott Hancock steps forward. "General Meade was not able to be here this morning," he announces.

Meade finally arrives later that day. I find him sitting beneath a tent canopy with several other generals. It's not really Meade, of course. It's a fellow by the name of Bob Creed, who seems more pleasant-natured than the real Meade must have been. He talks to me about the tight-knit military fraternity of the Civil War years, which so often found friends, family, and acquaintances fighting on opposite sides. (Meade's sister Elizabeth married a Mississippi planter and her son, the general's nephew, died fighting for the Confederacy at Fredericksburg.) "While in Mexico I got to know an artillerist by the name of Thomas Jackson," this faux Meade says, keeping in character. "And also John Pope, whom General Buford didn't much care for." He acknowledges the cavalry commander, sitting nearby, with a nod of his head.

"Not after what he did," Buford growls. Pope, of course, was the general responsible for the Union rout at the Second Battle of Bull Run.

Meade talks about his trouble with the press. "When they asked me about Confederate spies, I said the best spy the Confederates had was the *New York Herald*," he says. He complains about how he was treated in the papers. He doesn't break character, and as I walk away I'm still wondering why admiring crowds flock around Al Stone's Lee but leave Meade alone. George Gordon Meade may have won the Battle of Gettysburg, but it seems he lost the war of reputation.

CHAPTER 1
The Early Years

Zachary Taylor, "Old Rough and Ready"
LIBRARY OF CONGRESS

• • •

The United States Military Academy at West Point sits on the site of a Revolutionary War fort high above the broad Hudson River. It is a beautiful location, with breathtaking views of a waterway that honestly can be called majestic. This is the place Benedict Arnold planned to betray to the British during the struggle for American independence. The river below played such an important strategic role in that war, the Americans stretched a huge chain across it to bar British warships. A portion of that mighty chain—each link weighing 114 pounds—is on display on the academy grounds today.

My wife and I have come to visit West Point to see the buildings, roads, and monuments named after George Gordon Meade, Class of 1835. When I get on the tour bus at the visitors center I ask the guide, an affable older gentleman named Joe, if he knows of anything at West Point bearing Meade's name. He stops to think. "He was the victor at Gettysburg?" I prompt. He thinks some more. "No, no, I don't think so," he says. He tells me I might find his name on the Battle Monument, the large memorial above the Hudson at Trophy Point. It's engraved with the names of Regular Army soldiers who died in the war.

"Meade survived the war," I point out.

"Oh. Well, you won't find him there," he says.

I do find references to Meade's contemporaries throughout West Point. Lee (Class of 1829) and Grant (1843) get name-checked in the visitors center, which even has a photo of Montgomery Meigs (1836), the Union's quartermaster, and something about Maj. Gen. Oliver O. Howard (1854), who commanded the Army of the Potomac's XI Corps under Meade at Gettysburg.

As the bus tours the grounds Joe points out the academy's baseball field, which was named after Abner Doubleday (1842), who is most famous for *not* inventing America's pastime. Meade did not think much of him. At Gettysburg he replaced Doubleday with John Newton (1842) as commander of the I Corps. Doubleday seethed over the perceived slight and earned a measure of revenge by providing negative testimony about Meade to the Joint Committee on the Conduct of the War.

West Point has a statue of John Sedgwick (1837) here, too. It faces the tall Battle Monument. Sedgwick, affectionately known to his men as "Uncle John," commanded the VI Corps under Meade. Joe the guide tells us that West Point cadets who suspect they need some luck on an exam will visit the Sedgwick statue in full dress uniform at midnight and spin its spurs. Sedgwick could have used a little luck himself. He died at Spotsylvania in May 1864, shot down by a Confederate sharpshooter.

Rain begins to fall from the heavy spring skies when my wife and I reach the small West Point cemetery. Many of Meade's contemporaries are buried here. I find Judson Kilpatrick (1861), the irresponsible cavalry general who earned himself the nickname "Kill Cavalry" for his reckless waste of his soldier's lives. A braggart and a glory seeker, Kilpatrick owed his general's rank to Meade, who promoted him shortly after receiving command of the Army of the Potomac. George Armstrong Custer (1861) is buried here too, brought back east after his fatal encounter at the Little Bighorn in 1876. Although most people remember Custer from his last battle, he fought well and bravely in the Army of the Potomac throughout the war.

Nearby I find the grave of a third cavalryman who served under Meade. John Buford (1848) provided invaluable service on the first day at Gettysburg and remained one of the Union's best cavalry commanders until his untimely death of typhoid in December 1863. George Sykes (1842), the general who succeeded Meade as commander of the V Corps, is buried here, too.

One of the most elaborate tombs at West Point is the ornate marble edifice that houses the remains of Daniel Butterfield. Unlike Meade, though, Butterfield never attended the military academy. He had to receive special dispensation from the secretary of war to be buried here. Butterfield was not well liked. "He is most thoroughly hated by all the officers at headquarters as a meddling, over-conceited fellow," wrote Charles Wainwright, the artillery chief for the V Corps.[1] When Meade took command of the Army of the Potomac he retained Butterfield as chief of staff, but only because he couldn't get anyone else to take the job. Butterfield later helped spread the story that Meade had intended to retreat from Gettysburg.

I find two mentions of Meade in West Point's museum, one on a label about the Battle of Gettysburg and another that mentions how Grant traveled with Meade's army as it fought its way through Virginia. But the museum also includes a little diorama depicting Robert E. Lee meeting George Pickett after the repulse of the Confederate attack on Gettysburg's third day. There are no dioramas about the general who won at Gettysburg. Joe tells me that West Point also has a barracks, a road, and a gate named after Lee. "But he was superintendent here," he points out. Still, it just doesn't seem fair.

Well, if life were fair, George Meade probably would not have attended West Point in the first place.

He had been born into wealth. His father was Richard Worsam Meade, a merchant, like his father before him. His father's father—the future general's great-grandfather—had come to Philadelphia from his native Ireland. He, too, had been a trader. As one of the city's prominent Catholics, he had supported construction of Philadelphia's first Catholic church.

Richard Worsam Meade, the general's father, was born in the Revolutionary War year of 1778 in Chester County, outside Philadelphia. He would have been born in the city but the family had fled during the British occupation. He became a trader in his father's firm and made voyages to the West Indies and Europe. In 1801, the same year that bad investments forced his father into bankruptcy, Richard married Margaret Coats Butler of Perth Amboy, New Jersey. Unlike her husband, Margaret was an Episcopalian. Her son the general would be, too.

Business called Richard to Spain and he decided to remain there. His wife and two children followed him in 1804. They settled in Cadiz and Richard began serving as an agent for the United States Navy. And that's why, on the last day of 1815, George Gordon Meade, the future hero of Gettysburg, was born in Spain, the Meades' eighth child (two more would follow). He entered the world to a life of opulence and a house filled with fine art and expensive trappings, including paintings by Titian, Van Dyck, and Gilbert Stuart.

Soon it all came tumbling down. Spain was then in the middle of the ruinously expensive Peninsular War against Napoleonic France, and Richard Meade had been loaning money to the Spanish government. He also became entangled in various business arrangements that went bad, and as a result ended up languishing in a Spanish prison for two years. After his release Meade decided to remain in Spain to recover his money, but his wife and children returned to the United States in 1817.

Two years later the United States and Spain ratified the Treaty of Florida. The treaty ceded Florida to the United States and obligated the American government to assume any Spanish obligations to American citizens. This seemed like a positive development to Richard Meade. He returned to Philadelphia and later moved to Washington so he could pursue the futile campaign to get the government to reimburse him the $375,879.75 he had lost to Spain. The U.S. government discovered loopholes that allowed it to dodge all responsibility to an increasingly bitter and disappointed Richard Meade. His grandson later wrote that "he had had to contemplate, year after year, the injustice through which the property which he as a private citizen of the United States had accumulated by honest industry, in a life of voluntary exile, had gone into the coffers of the state, never to be recovered, by means of a treaty of which his country had reaped the full benefit in the acquisition of territory." Worn down physically and mentally by his struggles, Richard Meade died in 1828 at the age of fifty. His widow took up the cause after his death, but with no better results.[2]

George was twelve when his father died and was attending a boarding school in Mount Airy, Pennsylvania, that modeled itself on West Point. "He was considered an amiable boy, full of life, but rather disposed to avoid the rough-and-tumble frolics of youths of his age; quick at his lessons, and popular with both teachers and scholars," said his son. George left his school at the end of the year and later became a pupil at a Washington institution run by Salmon P. Chase, the future treasury secretary under Lincoln. (Meade next encountered Chase in 1862. He did not mention their former acquaintance.)[3]

George was interested in law but his mother persuaded him to attend West Point. The free education would have been a very attractive prospect for a woman in Mrs. Meade's straitened circumstances. In 1831, President Andrew Jackson appointed young George Meade as a cadet. He was not quite sixteen years old.

West Point was a military school, but under Sylvanus Thayer, "Father of the Military Academy," its most prominent discipline was engineering. Cadets also studied French, mathematics, and natural philosophy (what we call physics). Meade learned French from Claudius Berard, a scholar who had fled his native France to avoid serving in Napoleon's army. He studied math under Charles Davis and Albert E. Church, the former an energetic writer of textbooks, the latter "an old mathematical cinder, bereft of all natural feeling," as one cadet recalled him.[4]

Meade's engineering professor was Dennis Hart Mahan, who assumed the post in 1832. "Over the next two decades most of the men who would lead the major units in the Civil War learned the art of war from Mahan," noted Stephen Ambrose in his history of West Point. One of Mahan's students described him as "a little slim skeleton of a man" who was "always nervous and cross."[5]

Meade did not embrace the military side of his education and didn't have to work very hard to maintain decent grades. If son George's testimony in *The Life and Letters of George Gordon Meade* can be relied on, Cadet Meade remained a paragon. "His bearing was dignified and manly, his manners affable, his opinions were of weight among the members of the corps, and he was universally liked and respected."[6]

He graduated in 1835, nineteenth out of fifty-six. Few of his classmates gained military distinction. Herman Haupt kept the trains running for the Union, Marsena Patrick became the notoriously cranky assistant adjutant general for the Army of the Potomac, Henry Prince commanded a division in the III Corps in Meade's army and helped mess up the Mine Run campaign, and Montgomery Blair became Abraham Lincoln's postmaster general. But aside from Meade no other big names emerged from the Class of 1835—no Grants, Lees, Longstreets, or Shermans.

Following graduation Meade worked for a time surveying railroads, then journeyed with his brother-in-law, a navy commodore, on an expedition to the West Indies aboard the USS *Constellation*. He was in Cuba when he learned of the outbreak of the Seminole War in Florida, so he sailed over and reported for duty at Fort Brooke near Tampa. Meade's initial stint in Florida was a short one, as he fell seriously ill, possibly with malaria. Pronounced unfit to continue serving in the tropics, Meade received orders to escort some Seminoles on a roundabout journey to Arkansas, after which he traveled to Washington and received a new assignment in the exotic locale of Watertown, Massachusetts.

Meade had little love for the military. In October 1836, having fulfilled his commitment to the army, he resigned his commission. He was certainly not the only West Point graduate to forgo the slow pace of advancement in the antebellum military for potentially more lucrative careers in the civilian world. Over the previous two years more than a hundred West Point graduates had left the army.[7]

Meade now traveled extensively around the country on various surveying missions. He did more railroad work, which brought him back to Florida. He conducted a survey of the mouth of the Mississippi and another one to chart the Sabine River, which formed the border between the United States and the newly born Republic of Texas. In 1840, Meade headed to Maine to survey the border between American and British territory there.

But his most pleasing visits were to Washington, D.C., where his mother still lived and where he could court Margaretta Sergeant. She was the daughter of Philadelphia congressman John Sergeant, a Whig politician who had run for vice president on the ticket with Henry Clay back in 1832. The congressman apparently felt some trepidation about his daughter marrying this engineer with an uncertain future but eventually warmed to the idea. The couple was married in Philadelphia on Meade's birthday in 1840.

When the government began using army engineers for its survey work, Meade decided his employment possibilities would improve if he were back in the military. He used the political clout of his brother-in-law, Governor Henry Wise of Virginia, to get a commission as a second lieutenant in the Corps of Topographical

Engineers. (He and Wise would meet years later under very different circumstances and with a lot of bloody water under the bridge, at Appomattox.) In late 1843 Lieutenant Meade began working out of Philadelphia, constructing lighthouses in Delaware Bay, reporting to yet another brother-in-law, Maj. Hartman Bache. It was a comfortable arrangement, but growing tensions with Mexico made war seem imminent.

On August 12, 1845, Lieutenant Meade received orders to report to Texas. He left Philadelphia two days later, leaving behind his wife and his children—John Sergeant, born in 1841; George, born in 1843; and daughter Margaret, born in February 1845. "No one can tell how my heart was rent at parting with you; but I believe it is for the best that we should be parted, if I am to go, for the terrible agony I endured at the very sight of you and my dear children, it would be impossible to describe," he wrote to his wife, whom he called Margaret, from Washington on August 15, 1845. "However, there is no use in fretting over what cannot be helped, and there only remains for us to pray God to protect us and bring us again together in his good pleasure."[8]

• • •

At the state information center in Harlingen, Texas, I tell the helpful woman behind the counter that I'd like to visit the town of Matamoros, just across the Rio Grande from Brownsville. I can tell by the look in her eye that she doesn't believe this is a good idea. "Too dangerous?" I ask.

"I hate to say it," she says, "but it's too dangerous. I grew up in Brownsville, and when I was young, Matamoros was our playground." Now, she says, you can sometimes hear gunshots, even during the day. Drug cartel violence has turned portions of Mexico into dangerous places, especially in the border towns. I've already given up my idea of following Meade's footsteps through Monterrey and then on to the Gulf Coast and down to Veracruz. I don't want to become the next Ambrose Bierce, another old gringo writer who vanished without a trace in Mexico. Instead, I settle with a plan to explore the places on this side of the border connected with the opening phases of the Mexican-American War. (The week after I return from my trip, Mexican police discover forty-nine mutilated corpses dumped outside Monterrey, apparent victims of a drug cartel. It is indeed a sad and troubling time for Mexico.[9])

People often refer to the Korean conflict as "the forgotten war," but the title is just as appropriate for the Mexican-American War, which began in 1846 and was officially ended by the Treaty of Guadalupe Hidalgo in 1848. It's safe to say the war is not something your typical American thinks about today, but it had a huge and long-lasting impact on both the United States and Mexico. When the ink dried on the treaty, the United States had doubled its territory, gaining land that would form all or part of seven of today's states, including California and New Mexico. Mexico's territory had been reduced by one half. Furthermore, something like twenty men who fought in Mexico later went on to become generals in the Civil War, among them Ulysses S. Grant, Robert E. Lee, George B. McClellan, and George Gordon Meade. To use a baseball analogy that would have gone over the head of Mexican War veteran Abner Doubleday, if the Civil

War was the major leagues, then the Mexican War was the minors, where the future stars honed their skills.

I can think of several reasons why the Mexican-American War might have had a limited impact on American consciousness. For the most part, the battles took place in another country, far from home. Out of sight, out of mind. Compared to the Civil War, it was a relatively small conflict, not a total war that impacted households throughout the nation. Finally, the United States couldn't claim to be the good guys in this one. Americans like to wear the white hats. They'd rather be the farmers fighting to keep their land, not the cattle barons plotting to steal it. (And that's why some people prefer to cast the Confederacy in a noble struggle for individual freedom and states' rights instead of a stand to preserve a society supported by slavery.) Like many others at the time, Meade was well aware of the inglorious aspects of the Mexican War. In a letter home to Margaret, he complained how the conflict was "brought on by our injustice to a neighbor, and uncalled-for aggression," while Mexico "in her stupidity and folly" gave the people in Washington "plausible excuses for their conduct."[10]

America waged war on Mexico because it wanted its territory, pure and simple.

◆ ◆ ◆

In the 1840s the United States was like a restless sleeper who stole the covers and eventually stretched over the entire bed. The term "Manifest Destiny" had entered public discourse and some Americans were greedily eyeing the lands west of their established borders and itching to expand into them. Texas, which had declared its independence from Mexico in 1836 and had become a republic, appeared open to annexation to the United States. Mexico's western territories of California and New Mexico were very tempting prizes to a nation eager to expand to the Pacific.

The issue of Texas annexation, initiated under President John Tyler and finished under the new administration of secretive, expansionist President James K. Polk, pushed the already tense situation with Mexico to the breaking point. In 1845, as annexation grew closer, Brig. Gen. Zachary Taylor received orders to move with two thousand men to Louisiana's Texas border. Hearty and unpretentious, with a "mahogany complexion, piercing eye, iron-grey hair, and stout frame," Taylor divided his time between his military career and his plantations in Louisiana and Mississippi.[11]

He was actually only a colonel but he had received a brevet (honorary) promotion to brigadier general for his services in Florida during the Seminole War. His men called him "Old Rough and Ready." He was a strong and steady warrior on the battlefield but so unassuming off it that a newly arrived lieutenant once offered the general a dollar to clean his sword, unaware that he was talking to his commanding officer and not an orderly.[12]

The Texas congress voted for annexation on July 4, 1845. Later that month, Taylor moved his force to the settlement of Corpus Christi, a dusty collection of no more than thirty buildings on the Gulf of Mexico that received an immediate population explosion when Taylor and his army arrived.

After a journey that took him to Wheeling, Virginia, and then to Cincinnati, Louisville (where he met his sister Elizabeth and her family), New Orleans (a "pestilential hole"), and Texas, Meade reached Corpus Christi on September 14. He met Taylor the next morning. Meade found the general to be "a plain, sensible old gentleman, who laughs very much at the excitement in the Northern States on account of his position, and thinks there is not the remotest probability of there being any war."[13]

Well, Taylor was a soldier, not a soothsayer.

Meade agreed with Taylor's assessment that war was unlikely, or at least that's what he told his wife. "Our duty is peaceful, will be peacefully accomplished, and there is no probability of hostilities on either side," he wrote on October 10.[14] As a topographical engineer—a "Topo," as they called themselves—Meade performed mapmaking and survey work. Life in camp was dully agreeable and Meade enjoyed running into old associates and making new acquaintances, some of whom would play important roles in his later life. One of those men was Capt. George McCall, who would later be Meade's commander in the Pennsylvania Reserves. Young lieutenant Sam Grant served in McCall's company. He would become better known in the Civil War as Ulysses S. Grant.

Overall, Meade was satisfied with the level of refinement he found among his fellow soldiers. "I have seen nothing like dissipation, except in some very few instances; but there will be black sheep in every flock, and I have been most gratified to find such a state of high-toned gentlemanly feeling, so much intelligence and refinement, among a body of men the larger proportion of whom have been in the western wilds for years." He would not feel that way about the volunteer soldiers who would soon make an appearance.[15]

Ironically, although he was born in Spain Meade could not speak Spanish, something he now regretted.

The impending war with Mexico was like a collision in slow motion. Fall made its way toward winter, and hostilities seemed no closer or farther away. The December winds made the weather disagreeable; in fact, Meade found it colder in Texas than it had been in Maine. A bout of jaundice turned him "yellow as an orange," but he refused a doctor's offer to use the illness as an excuse to go home. Taylor also invited Meade to join his mess, quite a sign of approval. "I believe the old man has taken something of a fancy to me, and I am considered as being in luck," he reported home.[16]

Then a change in the always volatile political situation in Mexico suddenly made war seem more imminent when General Mariano Paredes overthrew President Jose Joaquin de Herrara. "I hope for a war and a speedy battle, and I think one good fight will settle the business; and, really, after coming so far and staying so long, it would hardly be the thing to come back without some laurels," Meade wrote home on February 18, 1846. At that point he had already been in Texas for five months.[17]

In March, General Taylor began making preparations to advance to the Rio Grande opposite the Mexican town of Matamoros (which the Americans of the day spelled "Matamoras"). The small, sun-baked town was 180 miles away from Corpus Christi and on the far edge of the disputed territory that both Mexico and the United States claimed. Mexico said the Nueces River to the north formed the Texas border; the United States asserted that Texas extended to the Rio

Grande. Even though the Americans would be marching deep into the disputed territory, Meade still believed chances for war were slim. The Americans left camp on March 8. Traveling with the advance troops, Meade kept busy scouting routes, selecting campsites and mapping the flat and arid land.

The army reached the Rio Grande on March 23. Capt. Joseph Mansfield—who would later meet his death as a brigadier general at Antietam—laid out a fort. Built of dirt, it had nine-foot-high walls that were fifteen feet thick at the base. Fort Texas was nothing fancy but the Americans expected it to provide adequate protection from the Mexican artillery across the river at Matamoros. Then the Americans and the Mexicans waited, watching each other warily from across the brown and winding Rio Grande, to see if war would come.

There were incidents. The Mexicans captured two Americans, but gave them up when Taylor demanded their return. The captives' reports of their lenient treatment, however, encouraged other Americans to cross the river and desert. More seriously, Taylor's quartermaster, Col. Truman Cross, disappeared in April and was later found murdered. Around the same time Gen. Pedro Ampudia reached Matamoros and demanded that Taylor move back beyond the Nueces River. Taylor refused. Gen. Mariano Arista arrived to take over from Ampudia. And then on April 25, 1846, a Mexican cavalry force ambushed a party of U.S. Dragoons under Capt. Seth Thornton in the chaparral thickets of a place called Rancho de Carricitos, north of the Rio Grande. Eleven Americans died and forty-six were taken prisoner. When word of the attack reached Taylor at Fort Texas he sent a message to the president. "Hostilities may now be considered as commenced," he said.[18]

• • •

From Brownsville it's about a twenty-five-mile drive down Route 281, also known as the Military Highway, to the historical markers that commemorate the events at Rancho de Carricitos. The mirage puddles retreat down the road in front of me on the torrid afternoon when I make the drive. Off to my left, I occasionally spy the new and controversial border fence erected to thwart illegal immigrants and drug traffickers. At a dirt roadside pull off, I find three markers and a cannon near some scrubby trees alongside a cornfield. "The spot where American blood was shed on American soil, April 25, 1846," reads one stone marker. It appears that a plaque of some sort has been torn off, leaving holes in the stone. Bottles, cans, and even some sponges are scattered along the roadside, and the tattered remains of plastic shopping bags decorate the trees. A bedraggled brown dog emerges into the sun from the shade of the trees and wags her tail at the unexpected company. Somewhere across the fields on the other side of the road is the border fence and beyond that the Rio Grande. The inconstant river has changed its course and the area geography has changed so frequently that no one is really sure where Thornton and his party fought. These markers indicate only the approximate location.

There's some historical irony there, for opponents of the war with Mexico, questioning Polk's claims that the encounter happened on American soil, demanded to know the exact location of the fighting. One of them was a freshman congressman from Illinois named Abraham Lincoln. On December 22, 1847, Lincoln introduced measures that became known as the Spot Resolutions, insisting that the president provide information "to establish whether the particular spot of soil on which the blood of our *citizens* was so shed was, or was not, *our own soil*."[19] This may have been disputed territory, but the incident was good enough for the United States. Polk could say that Mexico had started the war.

Now that the embers had been fanned into flame, Taylor feared the Mexicans would attack his depot at Point Isabel on the coast, twenty-seven miles away, and cut off his supplies. He also sought to draw the Mexican forces across the Rio Grande. On May 1, he took part of his forces, including Lieutenant Meade, with him to Point Isabel, leaving Fort Texas defended by only about five hundred men under the command of Maj. Jacob Brown of the 7th Infantry. Once Taylor departed, the Mexicans in Matamoros launched the long-awaited attack against the American fortress by unleashing an artillery barrage at their foes across the river. Taylor and his men could hear the distant sound of the cannons from Point Isabel, which created great anxiety. However, a Texas ranger by the name of Walker—yes, Walker, Texas Ranger—made his way to the fort and returned with the news that Mansfield's earthen walls had proven stout enough to resist the Mexican artillery. In Point Isabel, Taylor made plans to return with his supplies to relieve the fort.

Today Point Isabel is Port Isabel, a small town just south of the tip of the spring break mecca called South Padre Island. As I drive into town, I'm surprised to spy a sports pub named Doubleday, named after Abner Doubleday, the world-famous non-inventor of baseball. Never in history, it seems, has anyone been better known for something he didn't do.

Port Isabel is a touristy little waterfront town at one end of the long, arched bridge that crosses over to the more exclusive South Padre Island. It's a little shabby on the outskirts, but has a number of small shops, restaurants, and museums near the water, and an apparent affinity for pirate culture. There's even a faux pirate ship that takes tourists on excursions from the long dock extending out from Pirate's Landing. The Port Isabel lighthouse overlooks it all from a rise just inland. Built here in 1853, the beacon is something that Meade would have appreciated. The waterfront also boasts the "World's Largest Fly Rod and Reel," a seventy-foot-long fishing pole. This is Texas, after all, where everything has to be the biggest and the best. According to the description at the rod's base, it could be handled only by two dozen strong men, "or one large Texan."

The Port Isabel Historical Museum, housed in an 1899 dry goods store, has a collection of Mexican-American War artifacts, so I pay my $3 to see them. I'm the only patron today in the small museum, which covers all aspects of local history. I look with varying degrees of interest at the exhibits, including one display case that houses a huge mammoth tooth dredged up by a shrimp boat in 1961. There's space devoted to the war on the first floor with some artifacts, paintings, drawings, and diagrams. Overhead the speakers play the song "Green Grow the Lilacs." I'm not sure why. Later I find out that the original folk song lays claim, apocryphally, to creating the word "gringo," which is what Spanish speakers allegedly heard in the title lyrics.

One wall in the museum bears the title "US-Mexican War: School for Legends" and has small black-and-white portraits of men who went on to achieve greater fame. I see Taylor, Davis, Lee, Grant . . . and George Meade. But I'm amused when I read the caption alongside Meade's photo, which is quite the collection of historical inaccuracies. It says he led an assault on Vicksburg—Vicksburg, Virginia, not Mississippi—and that "Gen. T. Sherman" placed him in command of the town once it had fallen to the Union forces. I assume that's supposed to be William T. Sherman. It's a bad sign when you can't even get your mistakes right!

Fortunately they get it correct upstairs in the long front room dedicated to the war. Glass cases in the room's center hold all kinds of artifacts, including shell, shot, swords, buckles, buttons, epaulettes, and the like. There's a bandanna from 1849 embroidered with Taylor's portrait and depictions of his victories, plus a flask with his picture surrounded by the words "A little more grape Captain Bragg." Bragg was Braxton Bragg, later a Confederate general, and the grape referred not to wine but grapeshot. The quote, a typically laconic utterance from Taylor, came from the Battle of Buena Vista.

As I'm leaving the museum, I see a map on the wall for something called the Walk of Generals. It seems that bronze medallions of officers who passed through here adorn the town's sidewalk corners. I head out into the sweltering heat to find Meade. I know I'm bad at map reading, but I have a lot of trouble finding him. He's not where the map says he is. As I wander from corner to corner, I locate generals Grant, Davis, Bragg, Wool, Worth, McClellan, and even Phil Sheridan, but I cannot locate the one I've come to find. Finally, I spot the Meade medallion on the corner of Tarnava and Queen Isabella Streets. He's across Tarnava from Zachary Taylor and right in front of the lighthouse. Perfectly fitting.

● ● ●

Taylor and his forces left Point Isabel on May 7. The next day, they reached a broad, somewhat swampy pond called El Palo Alto, where they found General Arista and his army arrayed in front of them. Taylor blithely allowed his men to get water and rest before advancing to meet his foe. This would be the first taste of combat for the vast majority of the American soldiers, and they gazed at the lines of enemy soldiers with some trepidation. "As I looked down that long line of about three thousand men, advancing towards a larger force also armed, I thought what a fearful responsibility General Taylor must feel, commanding such a host and so far away from friends," the former lieutenant Grant recalled years later, with some irony.[20]

Grant slightly overestimated the forces Taylor had. The Americans numbered about 2,300 men, facing Arista's 3,200. The Mexicans opened an ineffective artillery fire while their cavalry attempted attacks on the American flanks. Taylor's regulars formed their Napoleonic-era squares and repulsed them with the able support of Maj. Samuel Ringgold's "flying artillery." Ringgold had developed a tactic of rapidly moving his light six-inch guns where and when they were needed.

At one point, the artillery ignited the grass between the two armies, raising such great clouds of flame and smoke that the combatants could not see each other. "Soon this wild fire, beyond the control of man, darted forward, cleaving through the light-blue clouds that had sprung from the cannon's mouth and over-spread the plain, hissing and crashing like a mighty Demon of the Prairies roused from his slumber by the voice of battle," George McCall wrote in a letter to a friend. For the ninety minutes or so that the flames forced a pause in the fighting, Taylor rode along the American lines, calmly talking with his officers. Fighting resumed once the flames subsided. McCall noted some terrible sights—a captain whose jaw had been shot off and a soldier who had been decapitated by a can-nonball, spraying those around him with his blood and brains.[21]

The battle at Palo Alto was largely an artillery contest, not an infantry battle, which was perhaps for the best. "The infantry under General Taylor was armed with flint-lock muskets, and paper cartridges charged with powder, buck-shot and ball," Grant recalled years later, when he was in a position to look back on both wars. "At the distance of a few hundred yards a man might fire at you all day with-out your finding it out."[22]

Taylor felt he had to protect his wagons full of supplies and therefore did not fight offensively, but he still severely punished Arista's forces. More than one hun-dred Mexican soldiers died in the fighting, compared to nine Americans. One of the dead Americans was Samuel Ringgold, whose artillery tactics had proven so beneficial.

"I was in the action during the whole time, at the side of General Taylor, and communicating his orders, and I assure you I may justly say I have had my '*baptême de feu*,'" Meade wrote home to Margaret. "An officer of the General's staff had his horse shot under him, not two yards from me, and some five horses and men were killed at various times right close to me."[23]

• • •

My glasses steam up when I get out of the air-conditioned car at Palo Alto Bat-tlefield National Historic Park, north of Brownsville, Texas. It's only a little after 9:00 in the morning on May 4 and the day's already a scorcher. But the visitors center is cool and quiet, and I spend some time looking at the exhibits in the small display area before I brave the Texas heat again. It's like being at the beach—minus the beach.

I find ranger Doug Murphy sweating in the morning sun as he sets up canopies for the next day's event, a Saturday combination of a Junior Ranger pro-gram and National Park Day. The event will fall just three days short of the bat-tle's actual anniversary. Murphy tells me the park used to hold events on the real anniversary, but few people came. Now they aim for the weekends. "As you can see, you need to want to come here," he says. It's not like people passing by are apt to swing the wheel and drive in on an impulse. Development may be creeping closer to the battlefield, but it's still a ways outside Brownsville. And the Mexi-can-American War is not a subject that inspires a lot of passion today. Passion? It doesn't even inspire much interest.

Well, I'm interested. Despite the heat, I set out to follow the park's half-mile trail. It's a black asphalt ribbon that snakes across a flat and dry landscape dotted with cactus, yucca, and mesquite. I note signs warning of rattlesnakes, but figure no self-respecting serpent will be out in these temperatures. The dirt on each side

Mexican-American War

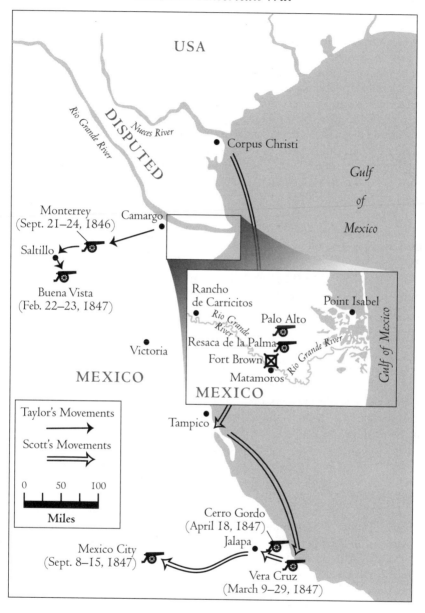

of the trail is pocked by holes that I guess were made by the lizards I see scurrying here and there, but I later find out they were dug by little land crabs.

The path branches off at the approximate position of the Mexican forces. Five Mexican flags posted in a long line indicate where the Mexican soldiers arrayed across the road to block the American advance. A couple replicas of Mexican eight-pound cannons sit in the sun, their carriages a vivid sky blue, just as the real ones had been. The Mexican guns were old and heavy with limited range, so Arista had hoped he could force the Americans into making a bayonet charge. Instead, Taylor held back and unleashed his superior artillery.

Farther down the path, beyond a shaded overlook that stands above a remaining trace of the Pointe Isabel/Matamoros Road, I approach the muzzle of an intimidating piece of artillery. This is an example of an American eighteen-pound gun. Taylor was bringing two of them with him for use at the fort but the heavy siege weapons provided deadly service at Palo Alto.

I return to the battlefield on the next day. It's Saturday and yesterday's quiet park has been transformed by dozens of schoolchildren bused in from schools all over the region to take part in Junior Ranger Day. There are activities for them in the visitors center's classroom, outside on the shaded rear courtyard, and beneath the tents that Murphy was setting up yesterday. Reenactors in uniform, volunteers from the park's living history unit, are on hand to demonstrate the era's weapons, including a replica six-inch gun.

Mark Spier, the park's superintendent, stands in the sun and watches the activity. "We are the only national park unit out of 397 national parks that deals with the American war with Mexico," he tells me. "We are the forgotten war and we've come to be the forgotten national park." Spier says that in its best years this relatively new park, dedicated as a national historic site in 1993, has drawn up to forty thousand visitors a year. (Compare that to Gettysburg, which pulls in at least a million visitors.) Last year, perhaps thanks to the economic slowdown, only twenty-six thousand people showed up, and that's too bad, because Palo Alto is a beautifully preserved battlefield from a war whose impact reverberates across the Southwest today. It had an important effect on Civil War history, too. "The Civil War has a lot of fans," Spier says. "We're sort of the bastard child of that conflict. We try to turn that to our advantage, but it isn't working, not as well as we'd like to see it work."

For the Junior Rangers, the park volunteers connect the two wars by posting photos of the men who fought here and then moved on to generalships in the Civil War. Meade, of course, is among them. Spier also takes particular pride in one of the artifacts on display in the visitors center—the sword that grateful Philadelphia citizens presented to native son John Pemberton in appreciation for his services in the Mexican-American War. Pemberton was one of those men who became a Civil War general, although he fought for the Confederates. In July 1863, Pemberton surrendered the city of Vicksburg, Mississippi, to Ulysses S. Grant. (Meade, I should point out again, had nothing to do with it, no matter what they say in Port Isabel.) Spier has a special interest in swords. "I'm a sword collector," he tells me. "It's my hobby, and the Mexican War was really and truly the genesis of sword art. The art of the presentation sword in America is owed to this war, because presentation swords were the gift of choice."

I ask Spier how Mexican visitors view the park. It strikes me that there could be parallels with how Americans view the Civil War, with the victors placing it on the shelf to gather dust with other history, and the losers clinging to the past with some bitterness. "People in Mexico do remember this battle and they do have a lot of preconceived notions here," says Spier. He tells me that park rangers worked extensively with Mexican scholars to tell the story of the fighting from both sides. Wealthier Mexican visitors, he says, who come to visit South Padre Island or have businesses in the area, tend to be pleasantly surprised by the park's presentation. "Conversely, here in Matamoros or here in Brownsville, not so much," Spier says. They tend to see the war as a black eye to Mexico's history. "I've had a lot of comments in my time here about, 'Why do we care, it's gringo history, it's wrong, it's bad,'" he says. "Whether or not that contributes to our lack of recognition in the community I don't know." Maybe the Mexican-American War is forgotten, but somehow its residual bitterness remains.

I approach three men who are talking in the sun, two of them dressed as American artillerymen from Samuel Ringgold's command and one as a Civil War soldier. Adrian Salazar and Michael Van Wagenen are the artillerymen and Bruce Johnstone is the Civil War guy. They attend these events every month as members of the park's reenacting group. Van Wagenen is an assistant professor at the University of Texas in Brownsville. He got into reenacting when he was writing his doctoral dissertation on how the United States remembers the Mexican War (published by the University of Massachusetts Press in August 2012 as *Remembering the Forgotten War: The Enduring Legacies of the Mexican War*). He wrote a chapter on reenactors and decided to become one himself. "I started by interviewing and then I got shanghaied in once that was all done," he says.

Salazar started out studying Texas history and then when he learned about this he "jumped in." "Being a multigeneration Texan," Salazar says, he was drawn into Texas history. "I studied my family history and sort of paralleled that with local history and Texas history." He hasn't found any ancestors who fought in the Mexican War, but he did learn that his great-great grandfather was registered as a Confederate citizen in the census rolls. "He raised cattle, so he may have supplied cattle to the Confederates."

Over by the shaded picnic tables Xavier Balderas wears the uniform of an American infantryman. He is explaining historical background to some children, who then take turns posing for photographs with his U.S. Model 1816 flintlock musket. "Four years ago I discovered this park," he says. "I actually came to the anniversary event myself. I asked if I could join and they said yes. Living history was always something I wanted to do. If I had the time and money I would do pretty much everything I could, from ancient to modern." One thing about living history, says Balderas, is you discover things you wouldn't necessarily get from books. For example, he now knows what it's like to wear a wool uniform in the hot Texas sun. "I'm dying here," he says, laughing. "As soon as you put this on you're sweating bullets."

Later in the day, children surround the artillery crew and their cannons while Van Wagenen, a teacher by profession, quickly sketches out the story of the battle here. "When the Americans came in one of the officers was a man named Samuel

Ringgold," he tells them. "Samuel Ringgold commanded a battery of cannons just like this. These are called six-pound cannons." Van Wagenen describes how Ringgold developed his mobile flying artillery and demonstrates how easy it is to raise the well-balanced gun carriage. "The Americans brought forward several of these cannons. They would move forward, close to the Mexican positions, open fire, take a few more shots, and then move their positions. The Mexican cannons that were on the other side were older, much older." The American cannons were made of light brass, while the Mexican cannons were cast iron and were heavy and hard to move. "What happened throughout the day was that the Mexican troops were just being pounded by the artillery."

Van Wagenen then asks a few questions. Kids who provide a correct answer get a Junior Ranger badge. "Does anybody know what day the battle took place?" A girl raises her hand. "May 8."

"May 8! You get a badge. Good for you. Does anybody remember Samuel Ringgold? He pioneered what kind of artillery?"

"Flying artillery," says a boy. He gets a badge and a round of applause. Van Wagenen hands out a few more badges and the crew prepares to fire the cannon. With all the noncombatants safely behind a rope barrier, the gun explodes with a satisfying boom, which makes a few kids squeal with surprise.

The cannons that were here in 1846 had more serious consequences. The Mexicans suffered the worst at Palo Alto, with 102 dead, 129 wounded, and 26 missing. The Americans lost nine killed (including Ringgold), 44 wounded, and 2 missing. During the night, Arista moved back about three miles and established a new defensive position in a dry portion of riverbed called Resaca de la Palma. He thought he had a better chance of facing the Americans among the thick chaparral that grew there. When the sun rose the next morning, the Americans found that the enemy had disappeared, leaving their dead and wounded behind. With his supply wagons secure in the rear, Taylor now felt more comfortable about going on the offensive.

The battle at Resaca de la Palma wasn't as one-sided as Palo Alto, but after some gallant charges by Taylor's dragoons—mounted infantry—and some fierce hand-to-hand fighting among the tangled undergrowth, the Americans once again drove the enemy from the field. Taylor exposed himself to fire so much that his officers pleaded with him to be more careful. "Well, we'll ride forward a little," he replied, "and the shot will drop behind us."[24]

Forty-five Americans had died and 97 were wounded, while the Mexicans had suffered 158 dead and 228 wounded. The Mexican army fled south and across the river. "We have whipped them in the open plain, and we done so in the bushes, and I now believe the war will soon be ended," wrote Meade.[25]

Palo Alto may have low visitation, but at least it has a visitors center. Resaca de la Palma, which became part of the Palo Alto park in 2009, doesn't have even that. When I reach the thirty-four acres of the battlefield that still remain, surrounded on all sides by bustling, modern Brownsville, I find that the gate to the site is closed and locked. I climb through the barrier and stand at the edge of a large, circular field, ringed by trees, with a brown-dirt track running around its perimeter, studded with benches and historical markers. "As you walk, imagine miles of thick, thorny underbrush instead of the streets and homes you see on all sides today," one of the historical markers advises. I try. At one point the trail veers away from the field and into the thick underbrush, which gives me a better idea of what it must have been like for the opposing forces to struggle here, in thickets so dense the Mexicans used picks to clear spaces to stand. But even with the terrain reducing the effectiveness of the American artillery, Taylor's forces gained another victory. "If I had with me $100,000 in silver I would have bet the whole of it that no 10,000 men could have driven us from our positions," said Mexican general Romulo Díaz de la Vega, who was captured here with his six cannons when he refused to abandon his post.[26]

After their victory at Resaca de la Palma, Taylor's men marched on to Fort Texas and found that its defenders had weathered the storm of iron from Matamoros almost with impunity. There were only two fatalities, one of them being Major Brown, who had been mortally wounded by an artillery shell. The fort was renamed in his honor and Brownsville, Texas, still bears his name today.

The only traces of the original Fort Brown's earthen embankments now lie on Fort Brown Memorial Golf Course. To get there, you have to drive through a gap in the border fence. Because of the Rio Grande's winding course around here, portions of the fence were erected up to a mile from the border, forcing some families—and one golf course—to reside between the fence and the river.

The remnants of the original Fort Brown are just earthen humps on golf course property. Few hackers know they're slicing their balls across historic ground, although the historical markers at the edge of the parking lot provide some clues. There's an even heftier reminder on the driving range, just beyond the 250-yard marker, where a huge artillery piece is embedded vertically in the soil. This is a cannon that once fired rounds across the Rio Grande into Matamoros on the other side.

I can't resist the idea of playing another kind of round on this unique course, so I go into the clubhouse to rent clubs and pay my greens fee. I get to talking with Joe Lucio, brother of the course's golf pro. "Did you see the border fence?" he asks me. "We're on the river, the border of the United States of America, and we're behind the fence. Where does that put us?"

"No man's land?" I venture.

He softly taps my arm. "Exactly!" he says. "No man's land!"

There's a sign in the clubhouse that warns, "Do Not Hit Golf Balls into Mexico." With my slice there are no guarantees, especially since a few of the fairways run parallel to the Rio Grande. I can see the buildings of Matamoros on the other side. I start on the tenth hole, which runs alongside the driving range and the remains of Fort Brown. From the green I can see the big artillery piece standing at permanent attention beyond some trees. After I finish the thirteenth hole, I climb up on the embankment that runs along the fairway and look over at Matamoros. I finally catch a glimpse of the Rio Grande, a narrow little river between high banks. I can hear the sound of trains from Mexico and see busses driving down the roads. I feel almost like a Cold War spy peering into East Berlin, although in this case I'm already on the opposite side of the wall that divides us.

After my round, I get rid of my golf balls at the driving range, in a futile attempt to hit the artillery piece. This must be a cannon's purgatory, forever stuck in the earth as a target for projectiles, with no opportunity to fire back.

◆ ◆ ◆

Meade was puffed up by his baptism of fire at Palo Alto. "It will make you happy I know to hear of so brilliant an affair, and of your good husband having had a share in it," he wrote to his wife. "I assure you it consoles me for all I have suffered during the last nine months, and I can now show my face with something to sustain me when I return to Philadelphia. I want to see Matamoras taken, our steamboats established on the river, and every preparation made for advancing into their country. Then we shall have done more than we came here for."[27]

Yet a few weeks later, after the adrenaline rush of battle had faded and the young lieutenant was feeling more thoughtful, he had second thoughts about "war and its terrible consequences." On May 28 he wrote to Margaret that he had "no stomach" for war. "I trust I shall always do my duty, from a stern sense of the propriety of assisting in the defense of my country, and giving my services to a Government by which I have been supported when there were no risks to run," he said. "But I candidly acknowledge I have no penchant for it; nothing but a sense of duty would keep me in it."[28]

But there were plenty of men who had a stomach for war—or at least an inclination to give it a try. Volunteers began streaming into camp, more volunteers than Taylor wanted or needed. Where his regular army soldiers were disciplined and trained, the new arrivals bristled at attempts to discipline them and ignored the restraints of military life. Meade quickly decided that this armed rabble was more trouble than it was worth. "Already are our guard-houses filled daily with drunken officers and men, who go to the town, get drunk and commit outrages on the citizens," he said. He also wrote home about another thing that irritated him, which would also affect him in the Civil War. "If there is anything I do dislike, it is newspaper notoriety," he said. "I think it is the curse of our country, and fear it is seriously injuring our little army, whose tone once was utterly opposed to making use of the public press to sustain their cause."[29]

The volunteers and the press left Meade cold, but he did admire the "grace and ease" of Mexican women. "It is even shown in the way they wear their clothes, always having them nicely made, clean, and gracefully worn," he wrote his wife (and I have to wonder at how she received this intelligence). "I have often stopped at what is here called a *Labor* (a farm of three or four acres) and asked for a glass of water, when some really pretty girl, with a *reboso* gracefully thrown over her shoulder to conceal her dress (which for comfort is ordinarily worn with the body unfastened and thrown off), with her pretty patterned French calico or printed muslin, the only article I have seen the lower orders wear, well made and fitting perfectly, will hand you a cup of water, in a graceful way that would put to blush many of our finely dressed ladies of the upper ten thousand."[30]

In the meantime, the war continued its slow, stately progress. Taylor decided to capture Monterrey (then spelled Monterey), some two hundred miles inland from Fort Brown. First he shifted his forces about one hundred miles up the Rio Grande to the settlement of Camargo, which would become his depot for the move into Mexico's interior. He began the movement on August 5, in temperatures so hot that the troops began getting up at midnight so they could march through the relative cool of night by the light of the moon. Camargo proved to be a bedraggled little town on the San Juan River about three miles from the Rio Grande, still suffering the ill-effects from a recent flood. As volunteers began streaming in to the American camp, disease started taking its toll on the invading forces.

Taylor's force of about thirty-two hundred regulars and three thousand volunteers began moving south from Camargo in late August. Meade reached the outskirts of Monterrey on September 19, riding with Taylor at the front of the army. Before them loomed a large fortress, which the Americans named the Black Fort. All appeared so quiet Taylor thought the town had been deserted. But then Texas cavalry began exchanging fire with Mexican troops and the guns in the Black Fort began spitting fire. No one was injured but one ball, Meade told Margaret, "came closer to me than I desire it to do again, just passing about two feet on one side of my knee." Taylor moved back and established camp.[31]

The next day he assigned Meade to accompany Gen. William Worth on a wide swing around Monterrey to approach the hills behind it. Meade was with Worth, the general's staff, and a guard of about fifty Texans when a Mexican force managed to swing around their flank, nearly catching them in an ambush. In the morning they resumed their march toward the hills, bloodily repulsing Mexican cavalry that awaited them on the Saltillo Road. Annoyed by artillery from Federación and Independencia Hills, Worth dispatched a force of 350 men under Capt. C. F. Smith to take the first of the two summits. "Men, you are to take that hill—and I know you will do it," ordered Worth, "a man of average height but noticeably strong, with a trim figure and a strikingly martial air." His men replied, "We will." They climbed up the steep, four-hundred-foot heights, chased away the defenders, and captured the three small forts on top.[32]

The action on the other side of town was supposed to be a diversion to support Worth, but it ended up being much bloodier. Fighting through Monterrey's eastern suburbs, Americans commanded by Col. John Garland came under brutal attack from defenders firing from the city's flat rooftops. Although they made some progress, capturing one fortress, "the slaughter here was terrific," Meade reported. "The two regiments constituting the brigade were literally cut to pieces, and they were obliged to return, leaving the dead and wounded on the ground." One of the attackers, leading the Mississippi Rifles, was a young officer and former congressman named Jefferson Davis.

Worth's soldiers, among them James Longstreet, continued their progress on September 22. At 3:00 a.m., in darkness made even more dismal by a steady rain, some five hundred men began silently climbing the even steeper heights of Independencia Hill. They had nearly reached the top before the defenders discovered them. The initial force secured a hold on the summit and Worth rushed forward reinforcements. They disassembled a heavy howitzer and hauled it up the steep hill to the summit, where it was reassembled. The Mexicans took shelter within the thick walls of a structure called the Obispado, or the Bishop's Palace, but the deadly fire from the howitzer turned the tide to the Americans' favor. The palace was theirs by 4:00 that afternoon.

On September 23, Worth sent Meade on a reconnaissance to the city below. He returned with word that the Mexicans had abandoned the western sections of town to take up a central defensive position in the city square. Worth moved into the city. Advancing down the long straight streets would have been an invitation for slaughter, so the Americans practiced a unique form of urban warfare. They moved from building to building, knocking holes in the walls of one structure and crossing over into the next attached building without exposing themselves on the streets. Soldiers on the roofs provided covering fire as the Americans approached the central square, house by house. The other part of Taylor's force resumed its advance from the opposite side of town. Ampudia and his men were stuck in the middle.

Ampudia knew his time was running out. On the morning of September 24, he dispatched a messenger with a white flag to open negotiations for his surrender. He told Taylor that not only did he still have a strong force, but he also had received word that Mexico and the United States were negotiating an end to the war. With his men exhausted by the strenuous campaign, Taylor offered a two-month armistice and allowed Ampudia to evacuate Monterrey and his soldiers to retain their weapons and six pieces of artillery. Many complained about Taylor's generous terms, but Meade supported his general, feeling that "we gained all we could, did away with any chance of failure, and made them believe they, as well as ourselves, were great people."[33]

The Mexicans did not look a great people, at least not to Sam Grant. "My pity was aroused by the sight of the Mexican garrison of Monterrey marching out of town as prisoners, and no doubt the same feeling was experienced by most of our army who witnessed it," he wrote. "Many of the prisoners were cavalry, armed with lances, and mounted on miserable little half-starved horses that did not look as if they could carry their riders out of town."[34]

On September 24, Meade sat down on a gun carriage and wrote Margaret a quick note about the capture of Monterrey. "Again return thanks to God for my providential escape from danger. Our little army appeared before this place on the 20th instant, finding it strongly fortified and garrisoned by about ten thousand men. We have been pretty much ever since engaged in fighting, and have suffered some terrible losses, but by skill and perseverance we brought the enemy to terms this afternoon, and a capitulation has been entered into by which a cessation of hostilities for two months is agreed upon, they guaranteeing peace, and they evacuate to-morrow, the town, leaving us masters of it, with all the public property."[35]

When word of Taylor's terms reached Washington on October 11, Polk was not pleased. He sent a message to Taylor ordering him to end the armistice. The message didn't reach Taylor until November 2.

• • •

All wars are political to some extent, but the Mexican-American War had an especially strong partisan component. "The Mexican war was a political war, and the administration conducting it desired to make party capital out of it," wrote Ulysses Grant years later. Polk was a partisan Democrat; Winfield Scott, the army's ranking officer and the man most people expected to take command in Mexico, was a Whig. People in Washington suspected Scott nursed his own political ambitions. Zachary Taylor was a Whig, too, but one with no apparent designs for office. Therefore the Polk administration sent Taylor to Mexico. Once Old Rough and Ready began winning, though, Whig newspapers began touting him as presidential timber. That would not do. Polk decided he would send Scott to Mexico after all, where he would take overall command. "It was no doubt supposed that Scott's ambition would lead him to slaughter Taylor or destroy his chances for the Presidency, and yet it was hoped that he would not make sufficient capital himself to secure the prize," noted Grant long after his own military successes had propelled him to the White House.[36]

It was a cynical approach to what was already a cynical war. Young lieutenant Meade was disgusted by the machinations going on behind the scenes in Washington. In a letter home he railed against "the mighty engine of political influence, that curse of our country, which forces party politics into everything."[37]

Gen. Winfield Scott was in many ways the direct opposite of Zachary Taylor. Where Taylor was approachable and unpretentious, Scott was imposing and zealously protective of his own pomp and dignity. He was a big man, standing 6 foot 4 and weighing in the neighborhood of 230 pounds, and he had been a military hero since the War of 1812, when President James Madison had promoted the twenty-seven-year-old soldier to brigadier general. He became general in chief in 1841. No green officer would ever mistake Winfield Scott for an orderly. "With his commanding figure, his quite colossal size and showy uniform, I thought him the finest specimen of manhood my eyes had ever beheld, and the most to be envied," recalled Grant of the first time he saw Scott, when the general came to review the cadets at West Point. Taylor was "Old Rough and Ready" and seldom wore his uniform; Scott was "Old Fuss and Feathers" and preferred to appear before his soldiers in full military regalia.[38]

Scott had never agreed with Taylor's northern approach through Mexico. He intended to land his army at the fortified city of Veracruz on the Gulf of Mexico and then march 260 miles inland and capture Mexico City. It was a bold and daring strategy, though one that relegated Taylor to a sideshow while Scott appropriated many of his regulars for his own needs.

One of those regulars was Meade. After the victory at Monterrey he had continued surveying the Mexican countryside for Taylor—"keeping up my reputation of always being among those who penetrate furthest into the country"—and began moving south with Taylor in December.[39]

In January, Meade received orders to report to Gen. Robert Patterson at the port of Tampico on the Gulf Coast. "I confess I regretted exceedingly parting with the old man," he wrote about leaving Taylor, who he felt had been betrayed by Washington. "He has been most outrageously treated by the Administration, which hopes to play off General Scott against him, and by depriving him of all his command, and leaving him in an exposed position, with one-third of the force which he had before, and which he deemed necessary, to break him down and destroy his popularity," Meade wrote to Margaret. "I trust that it will signally fail, and from having the plaudits of the people for bravery and skill, he will now have their sympathy for the injustice of the course pursued towards him."[40]

Scott arrived in mid-February and Meade had to abandon the very agreeable charms of Tampico and head south to Veracruz. On March 6, he boarded a steamship with Scott—as well as future Confederate generals Robert E. Lee, P. G. T. Beauregard, and Joseph E. Johnston—for a seaborne reconnaissance of Veracruz. Dominating the port town was the huge fortress of San Juan de Ulúa, on a reef about three-quarters of a mile out in the harbor. Scott directed the vessel to head that way. The little steamer cut through the waves as it chugged closer and closer to the fortress. The Mexican gunners opened fire. Shells splashed into the water around the ship, some falling short, others going too high. Finally, satisfied by what he had seen, Scott ordered the steamer to turn around. Meade felt the survey was "very foolish; for, having on board all the general officers of the army, one shot, hitting the vessel and disabling it, would have left us a floating target for the enemy, and might have been the means of breaking up the expedition."[41]

Meade remained anxious about the fate of Taylor's much-reduced force, which now faced a much larger army under Antonio López de Santa Anna, the man who had reduced the Alamo back in 1836. Santa Anna had lost a leg resisting the French in 1838 (and had the amputated limb enshrined in Mexico City), but had been forced into exile seven years later. Now Santa Anna had just returned from exile in Cuba—with the assistance of President Polk, who thought the wily general would help broker peace—and had regained power. Instead of ending the war, Santa Anna raised an army to throw the American interlopers out of Mexico. But Meade need not have worried about Taylor. On February 22 and 23, the general's forces defeated Santa Anna at the Battle of Buena Vista.

Scott achieved his own success on March 9, when he landed his army on the beaches near Veracruz and began bombarding the city. Meade found himself reduced to little more than a spectator as Scott's engineer corps took the lead. He regretted more than ever his separation from Taylor. On March 27, Meade wrote to Margaret and told her that Veracruz was on the point of surrendering. But when he wrote his next letter to her, on April 9, he was in New Orleans on his way home. The new chief topographical engineer had plenty of officers, so Scott gave Meade an honorable discharge and ordered him to Washington. He boarded the *Alabama* on March 31.

As a result he missed the surrender of Veracruz and Scott's march inland to Mexico City. He wasn't there when Scott's forces, aided by the daring scouting work of Capt. Robert E. Lee, sent Santa Anna's army reeling back into Mexico City after the battles of Padierna (Contreras) and Churubusco. And he missed the capture of Mexico City, the American occupation, and the signing of the Treaty of Guadalupe Hidalgo, which officially ended the war. As part of the settlement, the United States paid Mexico $15 million for the territories of California and New Mexico. Nestled within the settlement was a ticking time bomb—the loaded question of whether or not the United States would allow slavery in its new territories. The bomb wouldn't explode for years, but when it finally did it nearly tore the country apart.

• • •

Back in Philadelphia Meade resumed his lighthouse work under Major Bache on the Brandywine Shoal Lighthouse at the mouth of Delaware Bay, the first "screw-pile" lighthouse in the United States. Before he could complete the project, though, Meade received orders to report to Tampa and Maj. Gen. David Twiggs, who was dealing with an outbreak of violence by the Seminoles.

Twiggs had commanded one of Taylor's divisions in Mexico and "owing to some unpleasant passages occurring at that time no good feeling existed between them." Meade detected more than a fall chill in the air when he reported to Twiggs at Fort Brooke in October 1849.[42]

Twiggs asked Meade what he required to perform his topographical duties and select sites for a line of forts across Florida. Meade replied he needed only two men and a mule. Thus equipped, he set out into the Florida interior to create maps and find appropriate locations for a line of forts to run from Tampa's Fort Brooke to the east coast of Florida.

• • •

I've come to little Fort Meade, Florida, to see if the town remembers its name-sake. That fort is long gone now, but the town remains a quiet and very flat community about fifty miles east of Tampa. On the outskirts of town, I find a historical marker at Heritage Park, a spot where the trees are draped with Spanish moss. The marker says Meade "built" Fort Meade (he just chose the site) and states that he "later became commanding general of the Union forces during the Civil War." That would have come as quite a surprise to Meade, not to mention Ulysses S. Grant. Meade doesn't often receive *more* credit than he deserves, so maybe it's just the Polk County Historical Commission's way of balancing the historical scales.

However, another monument stands right next to the Fort Meade marker. The E. M. Law Camp of the Sons of Confederate Veterans placed it here in 1983. It memorializes Stonewall Jackson.

Young Thomas Jonathan Jackson—not yet Stonewall—arrived here several years after Meade selected the site. Jackson was an artillery lieutenant and he served here under Capt. William French. The relationship did not go well. French, who would later make a poor showing at the head of the III Corps under Meade, was a *bon vivant* who enjoyed the finer things in life. Jackson was straight-laced, puritanical, and uncompromising. Things came to a head when Jackson launched an investigation to determine if French was having an illicit affair with a servant girl. Jackson demanded a court of inquiry; French responded by insisting on Jackson's court-martial. Army officials just wanted the two men to drop the whole matter. In the end nothing came of the ugly situation, but it reflected poorly on both men. Jackson left Fort Meade behind forever on May 21, 1851, when he departed to take up a teaching post at the Virginia Military Academy in Lexington, Virginia.

That hardly seems like a good reason to erect a memorial to Jackson here at Fort Meade, but the Sons of Confederate Veterans obviously felt differently. They dedicated this monument on July 4, 1983, almost 120 years to the day after the Battle of Gettysburg.

The presence of Jackson's monument in a town named after the man who grappled with him during the Civil War is not the only historical irony associated with Meade and Florida. The treaty with Spain that ceded this territory to the United States—thus allowing Lt. Meade to come here and have a fort named after him—was also the treaty that should have required the United States to repay Richard Meade for the debts Spain owed him. Had the United States fulfilled its obligations Meade would not have required the free education that West Point offered. Did Meade ever muse about that irony and wonder about the strange fates that had directed him into the military?

Meade finished his work with Twiggs in February 1850 and returned to Philadelphia to help Bache finish the Brandywine Light. Then, in an example of typical army efficiency, he was sent back to Florida, this time for more lighthouse work. His assignment was to complete the screwpile beacon on Carysfort Reef off Key Largo. After he finished that in March 1852, Meade, now a first lieutenant, moved on to Sand Key Lighthouse near Key West, then Sombrero Key and Rebecca Shoal.

If not for the Civil War, Meade might be little more than a footnote in the history of American lighthouses. He might have been happy with that. When Meade was commander of the Army of the Potomac, a Philadelphia publisher issued a quickie biography to capitalize on his fame. It left Meade disappointed at how little space it devoted to the work he had done before the war. "I always thought my services in the construction of lighthouses, and subsequently on the Lake Survey, were of considerable importance," he said.[43]

One memorial to Meade's lighthouse work stands today on the New Jersey coastline. Barnegat Bay Light rises, tall and straight, from the water's edge at the tip of a narrow tongue of land that runs parallel to the ocean between Atlantic City and New York. Locals call the white and red lighthouse "Old Barney." Today I am laboring up the 217 steps of the yellow, spiral staircase to Old Barney's observation platform so I can gaze out over the magnificent ocean vista. No, I am not counting the steps. I take it on faith that the figure on the plaque at the lighthouse entrance is accurate. The plaque also warns away people with heart conditions, back problems, dizziness, medications, or a fear of heights.

It obviously does not warn away people with children. Youngsters by the score are summiting today. Mothers lug newborns strapped across their backs and chests, grandfathers assist toddlers, and fathers coax schoolchildren up the stairs. It's almost as though the adults are taking them up this great height to hurl them off as sacrifices to the gods. And if this lighthouse had a guardian deity it would have to be the man whose image sits atop a brick pedestal at the lighthouse entrance—none other than George Gordon Meade.

The bronze bust, by Philadelphia sculptor Boris Blai, was erected here in 1957 to commemorate the light's one hundredth birthday. At the pedestal's base is a bronze plaque, erected by the Civil War Roundtable of Northern New Jersey.

This one is better with the facts than the marker in Fort Meade. "Maj. Gen. George Gordon Meade built this lighthouse in 1856," it reads. "During the Civil War he commanded the Army of the Potomac from Gettysburg to Appomattox (1863–1865) under Lt. Gen. U. S. Grant." Well, it's almost right, anyway. Grant didn't enter the picture until after Gettysburg. But why quibble?

Hundreds of feet and 217 steps higher I reach the observation platform that rings the tower's summit. It's enclosed in a metal cage, just in case anyone feels tempted by the siren's call of the depths below.

The wind howls. The Atlantic Ocean stretches off to the horizon, the blue water dotted with whitecaps. Immediately below, people have used rocks to write messages and draw figures on the sand. I see a stick figure, a salute to the Philadelphia Eagles, and various initials. They remind me of the figures Peruvians cut into the desert for the gods to enjoy millennia ago, albeit on a much smaller scale. The view is stunning, for those with the nerves to enjoy it. A little blonde girl, no more than six years old, circles the platform with her family. "Don't look down! Don't look down! Don't look down!" she keeps repeating to herself.

Meade oversaw the construction of this 163-foot-tall seaside beacon after Congress budgeted $60,000 in 1856 for a new light to replace the inadequate one that stood here at the time. He decided to build the replacement lighthouse nine hundred feet inland from the old one so it would remain safe from the ever-encroaching sea. It officially entered service on January 1, 1859, and the sea has conducted siege operations against it ever since, eating away at the shoreline until it now almost laps at the tower's base. Until 1920, a huge, twenty-room keeper's house stood near the tower, but the sea crept too close and the house was sold to scrappers for $125 before it fell into the water.

The heart of the lighthouse—its very reason for existing—was a $15,000 Fresnel lens, named after the Frenchman who invented it. The light now resides in its retirement home at nearby Barnegat Light Schoolhouse Museum, where it looks less like a tool for maritime safety than some kind of modern art project. The light is a ten-foot tall glass beehive composed of more than one thousand separate glass prisms. The garrulous docent at the museum explains its workings to me. He says the lens sat on a platform atop a grandfather clock–like system of gears that rotated it. The light from the kerosene lamp inside, focused and amplified by the myriad glass shingles, flashed out from one of the twenty-four bull's-eye lenses around the beehive's perimeter every ten seconds. Mariners could see the light from nineteen nautical miles away, and they identified the lighthouse by the frequency of its flashes. During the day, the light's distinctive color pattern—white and red meant Barnegat Bay—served as another form of identification.

The lighthouse discharged its duties faithfully through the years and even survived an earthquake in 1886 that rattled the lens so badly the keeper thought the entire tower was going to come crashing down. Old Barney served until being decommissioned in 1927. New Jersey opened Barnegat Bay Lighthouse State Park on the beacon's one hundredth anniversary.

In 2008, the Friends of Barnegat Bay Lighthouse, a nonprofit organization founded to preserve the structure and its history, launched an effort to buy a new lens for the lighthouse. On January 1, 2009, 150 years after the light was first lit, a new Fresnel lens beamed out from atop old Barney.

Meade continued his work in the lighthouse service until April 24, 1856. Then he received orders to take charge of a survey of the Great Lakes. Promoted to captain, Meade worked on the survey from 1857 to 1861, about twice as long as his time spent commanding the Army of the Potomac and just about as long as the entire Civil War lasted. The survey was an immense task, begun in 1841 and not completed until 1881. It required surveying six thousand miles of shoreline along the American border and charting the lake bottoms, measuring currents, determining longitude and latitude, and building lighthouses and beacons. While in charge of the survey, Meade and his growing family settled in Detroit. However, the approaching war was about to bring Meade's scientific career to a close.

CHAPTER 2
War!

George B. McClellan with his wife, Ellen
LIBRARY OF CONGRESS

The statue of George Brinton McClellan in Washington, D.C., occupies a hilltop perch opposite the hotel where John Hinckley Jr. attempted to become a modern John Wilkes Booth in 1981 by shooting President Ronald Reagan. This bronze McClellan sits on his horse, one hand on his hip, and gazes out over the city. He appears determined to crush his enemies. The real McClellan cared deeply about crushing his enemies. His enemies were not necessarily Confederates, though—they were the men in Washington he believed were conspiring to destroy him and the army he loved.

You can't really understand Meade's story without knowing about McClellan. I say "knowing about," because quite frankly, I'm not sure that anyone can really *understand* the man they called the "Young Napoleon." He was vain, paranoid, self-righteous, and insubordinate in equal measures. He was also, by his own estimate, always outnumbered by "vastly superior numbers" of Confederates. He seemed incapable of admitting error. "It's not my fault" could have served as his personal motto. Throughout his stormy tenure in the Union army, he spared no one in the administration from his invective. President Lincoln was "nothing more than a well meaning baboon." Secretary of State William Henry Seward was "a meddling, officious, incompetent little puppy." Secretary of the Navy Gideon Welles was "weaker than the most garrulous old woman you were ever annoyed by."[1] Secretary of War Edwin Stanton was "without exception the vilest man I ever knew or heard of."[2] Surprisingly, McClellan once had good words to say about Postmaster General Montgomery Blair, Meade's old classmate. McClellan called him the "only man of courage & sense in the Cabinet." But then he added, "I do not altogether fancy him!"[3]

To McClellan's credit, he truly loved his army. He complained about his generals but never had a harsh word for his soldiers. He loved them and they loved him back. How he loved to write about how much they loved him! No, when things went wrong on the battlefield the fault never lay with McClellan or the ordinary soldiers. It was always somebody else's fault.

Like Meade, McClellan was a Philadelphian and his family was prominent in Philadelphia society. He began his schooling at West Point before he had even turned sixteen and graduated second in the Class of 1846. Among his classmates were Thomas Jackson, Ambrose Powell ("A. P.") Hill, and Truman Seymour, who would serve under Meade at South Mountain and Antietam. At the military academy, he gravitated toward men from the South. As he wrote, "I am sorry to say that the manners, feelings & opinions of the Southerners are far, far preferable to those of the majority of the Northerners at this place."[4]

McClellan served as a lieutenant in the engineering corps during the Mexican War, sometimes under Capt. Robert E. Lee. After the war, he was posted at Fort Smith in Arkansas, where he served under Capt. Randolph Marcy. He then went to Texas and performed some survey work for the future transcontinental railroad.

Captain Marcy had an attractive daughter back east and the young lieutenant became smitten when he met Mary Ellen Marcy during a visit to Washington. He proposed—and she rejected him. It was one of the few setbacks in McClellan's young life, but he took the blow and soldiered on. With support from Secretary of War Jefferson Davis, something of a mentor to the young soldier, McClellan received a promotion to captain in the newly formed 1st Cavalry. In 1855, the government sent him as one of three commissioners to the Crimea to observe the war there, an important responsibility for the up-and-coming officer.

Still, life in the antebellum service promised nothing if not low expectations, so in 1857, McClellan resigned his commission to test his fortunes in civilian life. He found a job working as chief engineer for the Illinois Central Railroad, where he rose to vice president. While there, he became good friends with fellow West Pointer Ambrose Burnside and found him a job. He also made the acquaintance of an Illinois lawyer who did some legal work for the railroad. McClellan decided that the lawyer was "destitute of refinement" and "not a man of very strong character."[5] He was neither the first nor the last person to underestimate Abraham Lincoln.

Throughout the years McClellan pined for Ellen Marcy, but Ellen had pinned her hopes on A. P. Hill, McClellan's former West Point roommate. Ellen accepted Hill's proposal, but her parents opposed the match, probably because they learned that Hill had once contracted a venereal disease. With Hill out of the picture, McClellan renewed his campaign. This time Ellen capitulated, and they wed on May 22, 1860.

McClellan made quite a success for himself as a railroad man, but when war broke out he decided to return to the military. New York wanted him to command its troops, while Pennsylvania's governor, Andrew Gregg Curtin, offered him command of the Pennsylvania Reserves. McClellan might have accepted Curtin's offer, but he did not receive the letter until he had already accepted an offer on April 23, 1861, from Ohio governor William Dennison to take charge of that state's troops as a major general of volunteers. He also received a commission as a major general in the regular army, meaning the only soldier who outranked him was Gen. Winfield Scott, the hero of the Mexican War and now the venerable general in chief of the American army. Scott had been in McClellan's wedding, and the young general called him "the General under whom I first learned the art of war."[6] Still, it wasn't long until the young general began maneuvering to replace the old one.

Now in command of the Department of the Ohio, which included Ohio, Illinois, Indiana, and later parts of Pennsylvania, Virginia, and Missouri, McClellan experienced some military success in western Virginia in July. Northerners eagerly grasped at the good news and turned him into a hero. The *New York Herald* proclaimed him "the Napoleon of the Present War."[7] Following Maj. Gen. Irvin McDowell's disaster at the Battle of Bull Run, McClellan received a summons to Washington to take command of the forces there. On July 27, he wrote to his wife that "by some strange operation of magic I seem to have become *the* power of the land." Three days later he wrote, "I learn that before I came on they said in Richmond, that there was only one man they feared & that was McClellan."[8] He was only thirty-four years old and he felt like God himself had placed him in a position to save his country. If that were true, then God does indeed work in mysterious ways.

McClellan was a skilled organizer and he immediately whipped Washington's defenses into shape and organized the force that would receive its official designation as the Army of the Potomac on August 20, 1861. He also began making persistent complaints to Lincoln and Scott about being outnumbered, when actually his forces always had the numerical advantage. In his letters to Ellen, he railed about his foes in Washington. On August 16, he wrote that he was in "a terrible place—the enemy have from 3 to 4 times my force—the Presdt is an idiot, the old General in his dotage—they cannot or will not see the true state of affairs." The "old General" was Scott, and McClellan's most pressing concern was how to get rid of him. "I do not know whether he is a *dotard* or a *traitor*!" he wrote Ellen, outraged that Scott did not share his fears about the "vastly superior numbers" of the enemy. "I am leaving nothing undone to increase our force," he complained, "but that confounded old Genl always comes in the way—he is a perfect imbecile. He understands nothing, appreciates noting & is ever in my way."[9]

Such was the state of affairs on August 31, 1861, when Meade received a commission as a brigadier general of volunteers in the Union army.

Meade had experienced some trouble getting a command but had no trouble stumbling into controversy. In the excitement following the attack on Fort Sumter, Detroit citizens organized a rally and asked the army officers there to publicly take an oath of loyalty to the United States. Meade and his other officers, save one, refused to do this on principle, although Meade said he would be happy to take the oath if the War Department requested it. Meade's stubborn, if principled, stand displeased Sen. Zachariah Chandler of Michigan. He would not forget the incident.

Captain Meade requested active duty. In June 1861, he traveled to Washington to plead his case. He returned to Detroit disappointed. In August, he began a survey of Lake Superior. When the governor of Michigan offered him command of a volunteer regiment, Meade prepared to accept. Then he received word that he had been appointed a brigadier general of volunteers with orders to report to General McClellan in Washington. There he received command of the 2nd Brigade of Maj. Gen. George A. McCall's division of the Pennsylvania Reserves.

The reserves came into being because Pennsylvania raised more than enough men to fill the original quota of troops the Federal government requested. Rather than send home all the extra men who volunteered, the commonwealth formed them into a "reserve" corps of thirteen infantry regiments, plus cavalry and artillery. Governor Curtin appointed McCall—the same McCall whom Meade had known in Mexico—to take command of the organization with the rank of major general of volunteers. Probably the most notorious reserve regiment was the 13th Pennsylvania Volunteers, a hard-bitten group of western outdoorsmen who became known as the Bucktails, because they wore deer tails attached to their caps.[10]

Civil War histories can become a bewildering mass of companies, regiments, brigades, and divisions, so it will probably help to provide a short sketch of army organization. The backbone of the army—its individual molecules, if you will—were the regiments. On paper a regiment was supposed to number about one thousand men and it possessed a strongly regional character. The states raised their own regiments and they were often composed of men from the same locality. A colonel commanded each regiment, which was subdivided into companies.

The regiments in turn were formed into brigades, with a brigadier general in charge. Two or more brigades combined into divisions. When McClellan took command, the division was the army's largest unit, but Lincoln insisted on organization by corps—two or more divisions. McClellan sullenly divided his army into four corps, under generals Samuel Heintzelman, Erasmus Keyes, Irvin McDowell, and Edwin Sumner. He later created two more corps—the V under Fitz John Porter and the VI under William Franklin. Franklin was another Pennsylvanian, born in York, and had come in first in his West Point Class of 1843 (Ulysses Grant had been a classmate). Like Meade, he was an engineer and had been in charge of constructing the new dome for the Capitol when war broke out.

Meade received command of one brigade in McCall's division. Stern-looking Edward Ord, his hair and mustache streaked with gray, commanded another and John Fulton Reynolds had the third.

Reynolds would play an important role in Meade's life over the next year and a half. He was a fellow Pennsylvanian, having been born in Lancaster in 1820, and a West Point graduate, from the Class of 1837. He had fought in Mexico, served in California and Oregon, and was an instructor at West Point when the Civil War broke out. One of his soldiers described him as "somewhat above the medium height, well-formed, but rather slight in build—had a stern face with black whiskers and mustaches, from which a set of beautiful white teeth now and then peeped forth—black hair, and dark, piercing, penetrating eyes. His look and manner denoted uncommon coolness, and he spoke not unpleasantly. His countenance was one not likely to encourage familiarity; his age, perhaps, thirty-eight."[11] One of Reynolds's aides described him as "somewhat rough and wanting polish," but thought him "brave, kind-hearted, modest," and "a type of the true soldier."[12]

Reynolds was a man of few words. Apparently, no one in his family or in the army knew that he was engaged to be married, which is why he wore a Catholic medal around his neck, with a gold ring shaped like clasped hands on its chain. He and Katherine Hewitt had met when Reynolds was returning east. They planned to marry and honeymoon in Europe if Reynolds survived the war. If he died, Kate pledged to enter a convent.[13]

Meade was forty-six when he took up his new responsibilities, determined to perform his duties as a soldier and avoid the entanglements of politics. "I have ever held it to be my duty to uphold and maintain the Constitution and resist the disruption of this Government," he wrote to a friend. "With this opinion, I hold the other side responsible for the existing condition of affairs. Besides, as a soldier, holding a commission, it has always been my judgment that duty required I should disregard all political questions, and obey orders. I go into the field with these principles, trusting to God to dispose of my life and actions in accordance with my daily prayer, that His will and not mine should be done."[14]

By September 22, Meade was settled into his camp in Tenallytown outside Washington. Margaret and his oldest son, John Sergeant, had just left him for Philadelphia and he was feeling a little down. "Sometimes I have a little sinking at the heart, when I reflect that perhaps I may fail at the grand scratch," he wrote home, "but I try to console myself with the belief that I shall probably do as well as most of my neighbors, and that your firm faith must be founded on some reasonable groundwork."[15] All in all, though, he found camp life agreeable and felt he was getting a feel for his duties, which consisted primarily of paperwork, punctuated by occasional alarms and rumors of war.

The Army of the Potomac received a baptism of blood on October 21 at the Battle of Ball's Bluff near Leesburg, Virginia. It was a disaster for Brig. Gen. Charles Stone and his soldiers. One of Stone's brigades, under former senator Col. Edward Baker, made an ill-advised crossing of the Potomac and received a bloody rebuff from the Confederate defenders on the other side. Baker died in the attack and Stone's military career died with him. "The whole affair was a bungle from the beginning," wrote Meade. McCall's division had been only ten miles away, but instead of sending it forward to help, McClellan ordered it back. Meade assumed that McClellan had been kept in ignorance of the true state of affairs.[16]

McClellan *had* been fighting, but his battles were taking place in Washington, where he was waging an all-or-nothing turf war against Winfield Scott. McClellan refused to hide his growing feelings of contempt from the older general. During a stormy late-September meeting at the White House with Lincoln and members of his cabinet, Scott told McClellan that when the younger man came to Washington he had possessed Scott's friendship and confidence. "You still have my confidence," the old man said acidly.[17]

Such a cold war at the top levels of the Union army could not last, and McClellan finally triumphed over his enemy. Old Fuss and Feathers retired on November 1, 1861, and McClellan became not only the commander of the Army of the Potomac but the general in chief of the Union forces as well. When Lincoln expressed concerns about McClellan taking on so much responsibility, the new general in chief replied, "I can do it all."[18]

And then the Army of the Potomac proceeded to do . . . nothing. Gen. Joseph E. Johnston's rebels occupied Centreville, only twenty-five miles from the nation's capital, and enemy batteries on the Potomac essentially closed the river to Washington. Government officials became increasingly restive over the lack of military action, but McClellan remained stubbornly close-mouthed about his plans. On one memorable occasion on the night of November 13, Lincoln, Seward, and Lincoln's personal secretary, John Hay, dropped by McClellan's headquarters at the Cutts-Madison house on Lafayette Square. The general was out at a wedding, so the president decided to wait for him. McClellan returned, spied his guests in the parlor, and went upstairs. A little later, a servant arrived to tell the president that the general had gone to bed. It was a provocative act—and in way a self-destructive one—but Lincoln shrugged it off.

Throughout the fall, the Army of the Potomac did little. The events of November 20 were typical. Meade rose from his bed at Camp Pierpont in Virginia at 3:30 on a very cold and frosty morning. At 6:00, his men began a nine-mile march to Bailey's Crossroads. They arrived around 10:00 and stood in six-inch-deep mud for four hours, and then they marched past McClellan and returned to camp. "I understand the object of the movement was to show the soldiers what a large and well disciplined army had been collected together, and thus give them confidence in themselves," Meade wrote. "I fear standing in the mud for four hours and marching nine miles there and back took away greatly from the intended effect."[19]

Such was the mundane life of the Army of the Potomac in late 1861. In addition, Meade had to sit through the drudgery of court-martial duty, which could take up an entire day and must have reinforced the negative feelings he had developed about volunteer soldiers back in Mexico. "The men are good material, and with good officers might readily be moulded into soldiers," Meade wrote to Margaret, "but the officers, as a rule, with but very few exceptions, are ignorant, inefficient and worthless. They have not control or command over the men, and if they had, they do not know what to do with them."[20]

On December 6, Meade took some men to the farm of a noted secessionist named Gunnell to confiscate whatever they could before the farmer handed his goods to the rebels. "I never had a more disagreeable duty in my life to perform," Meade wrote in disgust. "The men and officers got into their heads that the object of the expedition was the punishment of a rebel, and hence the more injury they inflicted, the more successful was the expedition, and it was with considerable trouble they could be prevented from burning everything. It made me sad to do such injury, and I really was ashamed of our cause, which thus required war to be made on individuals."[21]

Meade shared McClellan's views that the army should respect the private property of secessionists. He was more circumspect about his opinions on slavery. In the 1860 presidential election, he had voted for John Bell and Edward Everett of the Constitutional Union party and he determined to steer a moderate course.[22] "Let the ultras on both sides be repudiated, and the masses of conservative and moderate men may compromise and settle the difficulty," he noted. He believed the North needed to treat the South "like the afflicted parent who is compelled to chastise his erring child, and who performs the duty with a sad heart."[23] No wonder the Radical Republicans—the ultras—developed a dislike for Meade.

McCall's division finally got the opportunity to fight on December 20 in a small action at a Virginia hamlet called Dranesville. Fighting broke out when a foraging party under Ord's command stumbled onto a Confederate foraging party escorted by Jeb Stuart and his cavalry. The Confederates received the worst of the resulting action, and Stuart and his men withdrew. Meade's men never got a chance to get into the fight, having been left back at camp. Talking to Ord later, Meade learned that, with the exception of the Bucktails and the 9th Pennsylvania Reserves, the men had not behaved well under fire.

Limited skirmishes like Dranesville would not end the war. Lincoln could shrug off McClellan's deliberate rudeness back on November 13, but he could not ignore the army's continued inactivity, especially after McClellan fell ill with typhoid fever and everyone remained ignorant of his plans. Lincoln became despondent. Secretary of Treasury Salmon P. Chase told him the government was running out of money to finance the war and now the general in chief was out of commission. "The bottom is out of the tub," Lincoln moaned to quartermaster general Montgomery Meigs. "What shall I do?"[24] He decided to convene a meeting of cabinet members and generals Irvin McDowell and William Franklin to develop his own war strategy. McClellan learned of this attempt to trespass on his turf and managed to raise himself from his sickbed and visit the White House. Sullen and resentful, he told the president that he did, in fact, have a plan.

That was on January 13, the same day that Simon Cameron, a political fixer from Pennsylvania who had proven woefully inadequate as secretary of war, resigned. Edwin M. Stanton took his place. A short, pugnacious man with little, round spectacles and a graying thicket of a beard that spilled down his chest, Stanton had been a successful lawyer and had once worked with Lincoln on a railroad case in Illinois. Like McClellan, Stanton did not receive a good first impression of Lincoln. The new secretary of war was not overly blessed with social skills and his blunt talk often created enmity in Washington and the military. For a short time, McClellan considered Stanton to be his closest ally. Before long, however, he denounced him as his greatest enemy.

McClellan also had an antipathy for the Republicans in Congress who wanted to punish the South and destroy slavery. He believed in a "soft war" policy that would not interfere with slavery. He did not want a war of "servile insurrection," preferring a limited war that let the Southern states return to the fold with their dignity—and their slavery—intact. "Help me to dodge the nigger—we want nothing to do with him," McClellan wrote to a friend, Democratic lawyer Samuel Barlow. "*I* am fighting to preserve the integrity of the Union & the power of the Govt—on no other issue. To gain that end we cannot afford to raise up the negro question—it must be incidental & subsidiary."[25] Such opinions were anathema to the Radical Republicans in Congress.

Already battle lines were forming off the battlefield. The resulting struggles would buffet the Army of the Potomac.

After much prodding, McClellan finally unveiled his plan to defeat the Confederacy. He would move his army by boat from Annapolis to Urbanna on the Rappahannock River and proceed by land to Richmond.

Then the Confederates made the Urbanna Plan obsolete by retreating from Centreville to the south bank of the Rappahannock River. They left behind extensive fortifications and a number of logs painted black to look like cannons, which wags called "Quaker guns." As his army moved forward to occupy the vacant Confederate positions, McClellan went back to his drawing board and emerged with another operation. Now his army would board transports in Alexandria and sail to Fortress Monroe, at the very tip of the peninsula formed between the York and James Rivers, about seventy miles from Richmond. With some trepidation, Lincoln agreed to the plan, providing that McClellan left enough troops to "leave Washington entirely secure."[26] Done, said the general, who then began planning the huge logistical exercise necessary to transport his army and all its accoutrements to Virginia. Lincoln also stripped him of his role as general in chief, explaining that the campaign would be enough responsibility by itself.

Before McClellan departed from Alexandria on April 1, he left a report about Washington's defenses with the War Department. Lincoln crunched the numbers and discovered that the figures did not add up. The president believed that McClellan had violated his agreement to leave adequate protection for Washington. Lincoln, observed Senator Charles Sumner, was "justly indignant."[27] He wired McClellan that the thirty-five thousand men of Irwin McDowell's I Corps would have to remain behind to protect the capital.

McClellan was livid. Taking McDowell's corps was "the most infamous thing that history has recorded," he told his wife.[28] Perhaps somewhere deep in his subconscious he was relieved, because now McClellan had a ready-made excuse for any disasters that might befall him in Virginia. Although the army faced "greatly superior numbers," the politicians in Washington had deprived McClellan of the tools he needed to overcome the odds stacked against him. If he met defeat now, it would not be his fault.

That's why Meade and his brigade in McDowell's corps missed the initial stages of McClellan's grand Peninsula Campaign. They did not join the great flotilla that took the army to Fortress Monroe. They were not among the columns of men who marched up the peninsula toward Yorktown, the city where eighty years earlier the British under Lord Cornwallis had surrendered to George Washington. Nor were they in Virginia during the thirty-one-day siege of Yorktown, which began with McClellan and his one hundred thousand men facing a mere eleven thousand Confederates under Gen. "Prince John" Magruder. A master of stagecraft, Magruder ordered his meager forces to march back and forth behind his lines to create the illusion of a much larger army. McClellan, always willing to believe he was outnumbered, fell for the ruse. He settled in for a lengthy siege and General Johnston rushed reinforcements to Magruder.

McClellan's army spent weeks digging trenches and moving heavy artillery into position. On May 3, before everything was ready for the final onslaught, Johnston retreated from Yorktown, just as he had abandoned Centreville. It had been a relatively bloodless conquest to be sure, but one achieved at a great loss of time.

McClellan started cautious pursuit. There was bloody fighting outside Williamsburg on May 5, with Brig. Gen. Winfield Scott Hancock earning particular distinction. "Hancock was superb yesterday," noted McClellan, providing the general with the nickname by which he would become known: Hancock the Superb.[29]

Born in Pennsylvania in 1824 and named after Old Fuss and Feathers, Hancock had been an indifferent student at West Point, although he managed to graduate eighteenth in the Class of 1844. He was a conservative Democrat who would have preferred to see the Union reunited without any interference with slavery, but like Meade, he remained discreet about his political leanings. Brave and handsome, Hancock looked like a soldier and fought like one too. He was also a master of profanity, "one of the most colorful and sulphuric in the whole Union army," says biographer David M. Jordan.[30]

While McClellan made his slow progress up the peninsula, Meade and his men marched south to Manassas, passing through the old Confederate works in Centreville on the way and riding over the Bull Run battlefield. Things were progressing favorably, if a trifle deliberately, on the peninsula and Meade began to worry that he might miss the action. On May 14, he wrote, "I am afraid Richmond will be taken before we get there."[31]

Lincoln and Stanton came to call on May 23 and the president reviewed the troops. Earlier that month Maj. Gen. David Hunter had issued an order freeing the slaves under his control in the Department of South Carolina and Lincoln, always sensitive to the slaveholding border states that had remained in the Union, quickly rescinded it. Meade took the liberty of expressing his gratitude for Lincoln's action. "I am trying to do my duty," the president told Meade, "but no one can imagine what influences are brought to bear on me."[32]

• • •

By this time McDowell had received orders to march overland from Fredericksburg and link up with McClellan. To facilitate the linkage, McClellan placed Fitz John Porter's V Corps on the north bank of the swampy Chickahominy River, so that Porter could reach out to McDowell's forces as they moved south. The rest of McClellan's army remained on the other side of the river. That left the Army of the Potomac in a vulnerable position, like a man with one foot on a dock and the other on a canoe. If heavy rain flooded the fickle Chickahominy, crossing it would become difficult if not impossible.

Stonewall Jackson proceeded to "knock McDowell's plans into a cocked hat," as Meade put it.[33] Jackson went on the offensive in the Shenandoah Valley and drove Maj. Gen. Nathaniel Banks' forces north to the Potomac, throwing Washington into a panic and halting all plans for McDowell's move south. Then Johnston shattered the relative quiet on the peninsula on May 31 by attacking McClellan south of the Chickahominy at a battle later known as either Seven Pines or Fair Oaks. The fighting was brutal and the casualties high on both sides.

One of the wounded was Johnston himself. His removal from command had grave repercussions for the Union, because Robert E. Lee replaced him at the head of the newly christened Army of Northern Virginia. Whether he knew it or not, that change in command knocked McClellan's plans right into the cocked hat with McDowell's.

In a letter to Lincoln on April 20, 1862, McClellan wrote about potential adversaries Joseph Johnston and Robert E. Lee. "I prefer Lee to Johnston—the former is *too* cautious & weak under grave responsibility—personally brave & energetic to a fault, yet he is wanting in moral firmness when pressed by heavy responsibility & is likely to be timid & irresolute in action."[34] That's quite an amazing analysis coming from McClellan. Had he possessed a trace of introspection, he might have realized he was writing an excellent description of himself. But of course he didn't know himself any better than he knew his enemies.

To give McClellan some credit, others shared his poor opinion of Lee. Some called him "Granny Lee," and an unspectacular stint in West Virginia earned him the nickname "King of Spades." At this point in time he was not the Lee of legend any more than Lincoln was the president we revere today. He had to earn his reputation, and when he did, it came at the expense of the Army of the Potomac.

Lee's father was Henry "Light Horse Harry" Lee, who served under George Washington during the Revolutionary War and then as the governor of Virginia. Light Horse Harry's financial recklessness later brought shame and disgrace to the Lee name. Robert hardly knew his father, who spent his last years in the West Indies and died in 1818 on an island off the Georgia coast. Robert attended West Point, where he graduated second in the Class of 1829 and served with distinction under Winfield Scott in Mexico. But after the Mexican War, his career languished in the doldrums of the peacetime army. He served as the superintendent of West

Point from 1852 to 1855; when John Brown raided Harpers Ferry in October 1859, Lee led the soldiers who captured him (with some help from Jeb Stuart, one of his former West Point students). In general, though, Lee remained disappointed with the progress of his military career and he considered resigning from the army. And then the war came. Winfield Scott, who considered Lee a great soldier, offered him command of the Union armies, but Lee opted to fight for his home state of Virginia instead.

And the rest? Well, it wasn't quite history yet. Lee's efforts during the early days of the war proved lackluster. He was serving as Confederate president Jefferson Davis's military advisor when Johnston was wounded at Seven Pines. Even after Lee took over command from Johnston, few would have predicted his later veneration as a near Christ-like symbol of the Southern "Lost Cause."

Unlike McClellan, Lee demonstrated a superb ability to analyze his adversaries and factor their personalities into his strategic and tactical thinking. "A great commander must study the mental and moral characteristics of the opposing leader, and Lee was specially endowed with an aptitude in that direction," noted Confederate general D. H. Hill.[35] Lee gambled that he correctly read McClellan as a timid commander. He decided to bring Stonewall Jackson down from the Shenandoah Valley to attack the Union forces north of the Chickahominy on their flank and rear while he simultaneously hit them from the front. That would mean leaving Richmond dangerously vulnerable to an attack from the Union forces south of the Chickahominy, but Lee calculated that McClellan would not be gutsy enough to take such action. And he was right.

On June 9, McCall once again received orders to join McClellan on the peninsula. Meade's and Reynolds's brigades marched six miles below Fredericksburg and onto their transports, but before Meade could board, McCall and his staff took up the last available space. Meade had to remain behind and watch as the vessels with his men steamed down the Rappahannock. He worried that they would go into battle without him. He waited for three anxious days until another transport became available and he could follow his men down the Rappahannock, then up the York River to the Pamunkey and ashore at White House Landing. He arrived just after Confederate cavalry had seized and burned two Union vessels in the river, part of Jeb Stuart's famed ride around McClellan's entire army. Only a swift defense by members of Meade's command prevented the rebels from capturing the brigade's baggage train. Once the excitement subsided, Meade moved forward and rejoined his brigade near the Chickahominy. "I think in a day or two we shall go to the front, and then will commence the reality of war," he wrote home.[36]

McClellan sent McCall's men, including Meade's brigade, to support Porter's V Corps on the extreme right wing of the Union army. Porter was one of McClellan's favorites, a staunch loyalist whose devotion to his chief would lead to his downfall. Meade and his men established their camp near the Chickahominy at a crossing called New Bridge. They could see the rebels digging fortifications on the other side of the river so the Union gunners decided to interrupt the work by lobbing a few artillery shells their way. The Confederates suffered in silence for a day or two and then, on June 20, returned the favor. Meade told his men to remain in camp and out of sight of the enemy gunners, but some of them disobeyed orders and ran out from the trees into an open field "to stare about like idiots." The rebel artillerymen spotted the thrill seekers and opened up on them and the camp, fortunately without hurting anyone. Meade, however, was angry at the way his men had disregarded his orders. "I went in amongst them and remonstrated with them for their disobedience of orders, which had brought this on them, and after letting them stand the fire till they were pretty well subdued, I moved the camp to another position, and all has since been quiet."[37] The incident did not improve Meade's impressions of his volunteer soldiers, but it did demonstrate that their commander intended to enforce discipline.

On June 26, Meade wrote to his wife, "Everything is quiet on our part of the line."[38] He was a mere five miles from Richmond, so close to the enemy that the soldiers could hear the rebels' bugles and drums and see the city's church steeples from the high ground near their camp. So near and yet so far.

• • •

Unlike George McClellan, I have no trouble making my way directly to the center of Richmond. That's not the only thing that's changed in the years since the "Young Napoleon" stood poised outside the city. The differences are pretty obvious around the White House of the Confederacy, the square, three-story building that President Jefferson Davis and his family called home during the war. Modern structures tower over the eighteenth-century building. The hospital complex adjacent to it dwarfs the more modern building that houses the Museum of the Confederacy.

My wife and I have come here to get a glimpse at the Civil War from the other side of the mirror. My contact person at the museum is public relations specialist Sam Craghead. I am expecting to meet a young puppy in his twenties, but the Missouri-born Craghead turns out to be a retiree with a white beard and a deep knowledge of the Civil War. I also suspect he plans to toss a curveball or two my way to demonstrate that this is not the Museum of the Confederacy of old.

Like the city that has grown up around it, the museum has changed. It's no longer the bastion of Lost Cause sentiment it once was, although you can sense it percolating beneath the surface. Or maybe a Yankee like me is just a little more sensitive to it.

The Lost Cause was much more than subtext when a Richmond women's organization called the Confederate Memorial Literary Society originally founded this institution in 1891. Their immediate intent was to save the decaying White House from demolition. The society achieved that goal and opened the museum in the refurbished mansion five years later. It had separate rooms dedicated to and maintained by each of the eleven seceded states, as well as the border states Missouri, Kentucky, and Maryland. The "sacred items" on display were intended to enshrine the "glory, the hardships, the heroism of the war." The institution remained stubbornly unreconstructed and, as the years passed, became more and more overstuffed and dusty. Finally, the members of the controlling society decided an update was in order. They raised money for a new building that was finished in 1976, moved the exhibits there, and gave the White House a thorough, top-to-bottom restoration. In 1991, the society's board elected its first male and African American members. The museum will continue to change, too, starting with a new satellite museum at Appomattox Court House that opened in 2012.

Before taking us upstairs, Craghead shows us an artifact that could belong in either version of the museum. It's the sword that Lee wore when he surrendered to Grant at Appomattox Court House. Craghead says the shiny weapon has just returned to display after a restoration. Apparently the ladies who founded the museum had been a little overzealous with their polishing over the years and the weapon required regilding. It now resides in a glass case alongside the uniform coat that Lee wore at the surrender ceremony.

Those are just two items in a treasure trove of Confederate relics. I see Stonewall Jackson's forage cap and sword, as well as Jeb Stuart's famous plumed hat, cavalry boots, saddle, and saber. A reconstruction of Lee's headquarters tent includes his gray brimmed hat, gauntlets, boots, and various camp items. There's a bloodstained handkerchief that Capt. James Power Smith, who was riding with Jackson, used to staunch Stonewall's wounds when the general was mortally wounded at Chancellorsville. The still-visible bloodstains—reminiscent of a religious icon—are Jackson's. I also see Capt. James Keith Boswell's tattered notebook, torn by a bullet from the same fusillade that killed him and mortally wounded Stonewall.

Another case holds the sword that Gen. Lewis Armistead raised above his head, his hat atop its tip, as he led the men who briefly pierced the Union lines at Gettysburg's "high water mark" during Pickett's Charge. These are all relics that should be of import to anyone interested in the Civil War, Yankee or Reb.

I'm not surprised to find no mention of Meade here, not even in the Gettysburg section. This is the Museum of the Confederacy, after all. But in the display case dedicated to the Peninsula Campaign, I do find a Pennsylvania bucktail captured from a soldier of the 42nd Pennsylvania (13th Pennsylvania Reserves) at Harrisonburg and a sketch by Allen Redwood of the 55th Virginia attacking Randol's battery during the Battle of Frayser's Farm—an action that had some important consequences for General Meade.

Craghead takes us upstairs to the museum's library to meet with Teresa Roane, the library manager. Roane is the curveball I suspected Craghead wanted to toss my way, because not only is she female (which shouldn't be a big surprise from an institution that was founded by Richmond women) but she's also African American. I have to ask her the question I'm sure she gets all the time: What's it like for an African American woman to work at the Museum of the Confederacy? She laughs heartily and tells me it's "fabulous. The reactions I get are great, everyday." Roane, a Richmond native who has been working here for five years after logging fifteen at the nearby Valentine Museum, admits she did arrive with preconceived notions. People told her that blacks would think she was some kind of Uncle Tom and whites would be upset to see a black woman in her position. "And it all played out," she says. "It played out in the very first week I was here. I had two people come in to do research and when they saw who I was they were *furious*. Furious that I was here. But I just gave them what they wanted, smiled, and by the time they left they were like, 'She's okay.'"

Roane, who says she is "a staff of one," has to wear many hats. "My job is to make sure the information is available to the public, so that's what I work on all the time." She also participates in exhibitions, gives presentations, takes part in academic panels, prepares material for the Teachers Institute the museum offers each summer, and makes sure everything in the collection is catalogued properly, whether it's currency, stamps, lithographs, books, or letters. She does battlefield tours and says that people often assume that a woman like her will know nothing about military history.

I explain that I believe Meade has been overlooked by history while Lee's role has been overexposed. I ask her what she thinks about that. "My theory is," she says, "as soon as the war ended, on the Southern side, people began to publish memoirs, their opinions about the war, and in the process, Lee plays a big role."

It's often said that the winners write the history, but in this case the losers set out to make their side of the story known. "From the very beginning people started writing," Roane says. A new generation of Southerners was raised on the stories. "If you grew up in the South, most of the time, from the time you could breathe, you knew something about the war and about the leaders. It's ingrained in you," she says. "You can just name the Confederate generals. You just know them."

"It's not like that in the North," I say. In the North, the Civil War obligingly stepped aside and took its place in the history books. In the South, it seems less distant. I have to think that remembering the glory and forgetting the less savory aspects of the war helped the South endure the sting of defeat.

Roane takes us for a quick tour of some of the museum's holdings. She shows us a letter Jeb Stuart wrote at the start of the war to Samuel Cooper, the Confederacy's adjutant general, in which the self-confident horseman stated the positions he would prefer. Cavalry, light artillery, or light infantry were his first preferences, but he said he would take a position as assistant adjutant general or in the topographical corps, "if such a position will give me greater rank."

"I just love this letter," says Roane, who refers to Stuart as "Mr. Plumed Hat himself." "It cracks me up. Can you imagine telling the number-one-ranked Confederate general, 'This is what I want'?"

Next she pulls out a long box from a shelf. "This is my number-one favorite document," she says. "I get teased a lot about it." She unrolls a portion of a long, scrolled document on a table. "It's ten feet long and I can't show you the whole thing," Roane says apologetically. "This is the provisional Confederate Constitution, and it's the original." She points out the signatures of the men from the first states that seceded. I see Alexander Stevens, Howell Cobb, and Robert Barnwell Rhett. "So this starts the Confederate government."

She takes us through the library's other back rooms, which are full of newspaper collections, scrapbooks, archival boxes with letters and personal collections, and lots and lots of books. Roane chuckles when she points out a book about Ulysses S. Grant that's waiting to be shelved, letting us know that the other side is represented as well.

"It's been a really interesting journey for me," Roane says about her time at the Museum of the Confederacy. "Working here has given me exposure to a much more complex story that doesn't necessarily always get out." Slavery, she says, was of course very important for the "hot-headed men" from the South who started the war. But, she adds, the view from the Northern perspective had made slavery the one cause of the war, "which has caused lots of consternation for lots of people because people are passing this moral judgment over this war."

Our tour guide at the White House of the Confederacy is also African American. Now retired from the army, sixty-one-year-old Abdur Ali-Haymes tells our group how he used to visit the White House every weekend when he was a boy, when his guide was Robert E. Lee's granddaughter. "Perhaps you'll come back and work here one day," she told him. And he did. He conducts his tour with great knowledge and energy. But I am surprised to hear him praise Jefferson Davis as "a great American," while shushing us at the mention of Abraham Lincoln, even if he does seem to do it half in jest. Teresa Roane was right—things here are a little bit complicated.

• • •

Back in 1862, things were about to get a bit complicated for George B. McClellan and the Army of the Potomac. Following a defensive clash at Oak Grove on June 26, the Confederates under Robert E. Lee kicked off an offensive intended to drive the Union army away from Richmond. Gen. A. P. Hill crossed the Chickahominy, captured the hamlet of Mechanicsville, and then moved forward to challenge Fitz John Porter's men along a waterway called Beaver Dam Creek. The week of steady fighting that followed Oak Grove became known as the Seven Days Battles.

Beaver Dam Creek remains the very picture of creekiness. It's a swampy waterway of shallow, rust-colored water choked with mud and fallen trees. A small bridge arches across the water at the battlefield parking lot. On the opposite side a small trail follows the trace of the Old Cold Harbor Road away from the creek. Swampy and forested land stretches out on each side, a different vista from that of 1862, when this was largely open country, perfect for shooting at approaching Confederates. The rebels obliged by making an uncoordinated and bloody attack here against brigades of Pennsylvania Reserves commanded by Reynolds and Seymour, with Meade's brigade posted in the rear as a reserve. The Union troops held a strong position atop a bluff behind the creek's swampy approaches, but the Confederates, under generals D. H. Hill and A. P. Hill, decided to make a frontal attack anyway.

"We were lavish of blood in those days, and it was thought to be a great thing to charge a battery of artillery or an earth-work lined with infantry," D. H. Hill wrote years later, when he was older and wiser.[39] The Confederates never really had a chance against such a strong position, especially without Stonewall Jackson, who was supposed to bring his men in from the flank and the rear. By the time night fell, the rebels had received a bloody repulse, but McClellan worried that Jackson would arrive, so he ordered Porter to fall back.

The battle renewed the next day about a mile from a mill owned by Dr. William Gaines. Porter posted his Union troops in a semicircular line on a plateau above the swampy woodland along Boatswain Creek. He put the Pennsylvania Reserves in the rear as his reserve force.

The Gaines's Mill battlefield still looks like something out of the nineteenth century. The little white Watt farmhouse, a silent witness to the fighting, stands here like a sentinel from the past. A double line of snake-rail fences runs across the field away from the farmhouse in the direction of the Chickahominy, out of view to the south. The Watt House faces a wall of trees that line the edge of the field. They stand straight and tall and give me a disquieting feeling that something ominous must lurk beyond them. The trees provide a pretty good indicator of where Porter placed his line. Like Beaver Dam Creek, this was a great defensive position. The Confederates would have to advance across fields, descend to the creekbed, and then march back up the other side, all the while withstanding a tremendous Union artillery bombardment from the Watt Farm. I spot a historical marker that indicates the intensity of the struggle. "It was one continued roar of cannons & musketry you could not hear yourself think," said David Hyde of the 9th Pennsylvania Reserves. "Such desperate fighting never graced the pages of history."[40]

It's not like that today, of course. There's only one other car in the parking lot, so it appears that few others have braved the wilting June heat to wander the battlefield. When I emerge from my car's air-conditioned comfort, I hear only the peaceful sounds of buzzing insects and chirping birds. Off in the distance, though, I spot a line of people filing into the woods.

I follow a battlefield trail that enters the cool forest and descends to the creek, where I easily pick up the trail of this mysterious column. I decide to track them. Crossing the creek on a little wooden platform, I walk up the hill and through the trees that line the other side. I emerge into a clearing on the edge of a dirt road that runs alongside a wheatfield, where I find a few dozen people milling about or sitting on folding chairs near a small canopy erected by the road. Standing at a small lectern addressing the people is none other than Sam Craghead from the Museum of the Confederacy.

I've stumbled across the annual meeting of the Richmond Battlefields Association (RBA), a local nonprofit group that has just preserved this three-acre tract of the battlefield. The land we're standing on was the setting for an important part of the Confederate offensive, the spot where Brig. Gen. John Bell Hood's Texas Brigade advanced to break the Union line. Members of the Hood's Texas Brigade Association are also here for the meeting. "This is the most important property we've ever preserved," outgoing RBA president Julie Krick tells the assembled crowd.

I suspect that Krick is not originally from these parts, mainly because she's wearing a Minnesota Twins cap and T-shirt. Indeed, she was born in Minnesota, where she grew up with an intense interest in the past. "History has always been a family trait," she tells me.

Her great-uncle, a World War II veteran, sparked an interest in that conflict. When he died he left Julie a small sum of money, which she decided to use to take a weeklong tour of Stonewall Jackson sites. The tour was canceled at the last minute, so she took a Robert E. Lee tour instead. She and the tour guide were the two youngest people on the bus, and they began to bond after he teased her over the public address system. The tour guide was Robert Krick, now a

Peninsula Campaign

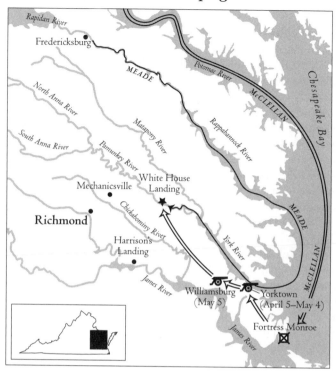

Seven Days Battles

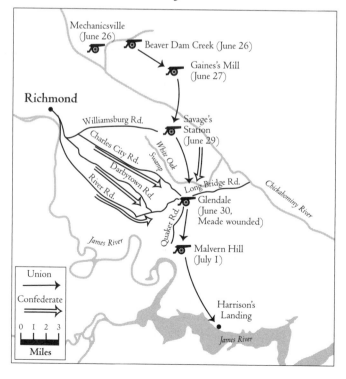

ranger with the National Park Service and a frequent writer about the Civil War. The two later married. "It was really kind of fate," Julie Krick says.

The preservation impulse came later, after a key property of the Gaines's Mill battlefield sold at auction before anyone in the local Civil War community knew about it. "A key property lost," Krick says. She says it acted as a wake-up call for a lot of people. Despite the amount of battlefields in the region, she says, "Richmond was the only area that didn't have a preservation group or a friends group."

She was taking a tour of Gettysburg with a couple other future members of the RBA when they decided to start their own preservation organization. "It just took—and it's too late to take it back." That was more than eleven years ago, and Krick has been president ever since—until today, when she's stepping aside to give someone else a chance to run things. The new president of the RBA is Sam Craghead.

The RBA has had a number of successes during Krick's years at the helm. It started by saving eleven acres at Fort Harrison. The Civil War Preservation Trust (now simply the Civil War Trust) loaned them the money to buy the property and the brand-new membership raised $55,000 to cover it. Next came the purchase of forty acres at Glendale, a joint project with the Civil War Trust. The next parcel, a piece at West Point, was a donation, but the RBA had to bear the cost of surveys and lawyers. Then came eleven acres at Cold Harbor, thirty acres at Fussell's Mill, nearly two acres at Weir Bottom Church, four acres at Malvern Hill, and now this piece of Gaines's Mill.

One thing Krick has learned from her experience is that it's important for people to volunteer to help prevent historically important lands from being lost. "Anybody can be helpful, can be a pivotal member of an organization or a member of the board," she says. "You don't have to have any real special skills. You just have to have a willingness and it will go from there."

Before I plunge back into the woods and head back to the official battlefield, I stop and talk to Ben Brockenbrough, the RBA's property manager. He's tall, wears glasses, and has a gray-streaked beard. He laughs when I tell him he looks a little like Meade. "I'm not sure that's a compliment," he says. He tells me he thinks Meade doesn't get enough credit for Gettysburg. I agree. He also says that Lee doesn't get enough blame. For example, although Lee knew that Richard Ewell—Jackson's replacement after Chancellorsville—did not have the same aggressive streak that his predecessor did, Lee still issued vague, discretionary orders instead of taking matters in hand himself.

Despite all this pro-Yankee talk, Brockenbrough is a Richmond native, where you don't so much learn about the Civil War growing up as you become "indoctrinated," he says. When I mention that Sam Craghead had shown me around the Museum of the Confederacy the day before, he tells me that the museum used to be much more "strident in its advocacy" and that its unreconstructed approach to the war ended up costing it financial support. The exhibits I saw, he assured me, had been toned down in comparison to years past. He says that attitudes in Richmond overall have been changing and that the opening of a slave jail exhibit in the city had helped draw African Americans into the topic. He also tells me that it was one of his ancestors, John W. Brockenbrough, who constructed the building that later became the future White House of the Confederacy. Sometimes the Civil War in Richmond feels like a cozy community.

• • •

The battle at Gaines's Mill began around 12:30 on the afternoon of June 27, when A. P. Hill's Confederates attacked Porter's strong position. The battle raged on throughout the afternoon, with Hill now joined by Stonewall Jackson, who was hitting the Union right, while D. H. Hill's and Longstreet's troops struck farther down the line. Porter soon had to throw McCall's division into the fray on the Union left, where the fighting devolved into primitive savagery. An 1865 history of the Pennsylvania Reserves observed, "Several regiments had already been driven from the swamp; the ground was strewn with the mangled bodies of the dead and wounded; the waters of the swamp were red with gore; the trees, torn and riddled with shot and shell, were spattered with brain and blood, and the bursting shells filled the air with hideous noises and sulphurous vapors."[41]

The Confederates made charge after charge, and some of Meade's men rushed to support an artillery battery commanded by Capt. Mark Kerns that became the focus of rebel attention. The cannons fired canister that ripped great bloody holes in the oncoming lines, but the enemy soldiers closed ranks and pushed on, an officer in front waving a regimental flag. The rebels came within twenty paces when the cannons fired again, killing the entire front rank and burying the officer and his flag beneath the dead. Kerns and his men limbered up their cannons and carried them safely back to a new line.[42]

Fighting was equally intense up and down the line as the Confederates attacked all along the front. "For nearly two hours the battle raged, extending more or less along the whole line to our extreme right," wrote Porter. "The fierce firing of artillery and infantry, the crash of the shot, the bursting of shells, and the whizzing of bullets, heard above the roar of artillery and the volleys of musketry, all combined was something fearful."[43] Men fired their guns until the barrels became so hot they blistered their fingers on them or so clogged with burnt powder they couldn't be reloaded.

Archibald F. Hill, who was in Company D of the 8th Pennsylvania Reserves under Reynolds, waited to go into battle with his regiment when an enemy shell exploded into the line near him. Through the dust and smoke he saw one bloodsoaked man fall to the ground and quiver in his death convulsions. Another, an Irish soldier, had his arm torn off. He retrieved the severed limb and brandished it above his head as he ran to the rear crying for a doctor.[44]

Finally it was Hill's turn to go into battle. "Now, Company D, remember that you are just as good as any rebel company we may meet," their captain shouted. "Don't be afraid, boys! Never let them call us cowards!"

"Up, boys, up!" shouted the regiment's colonel. "Forward!" The soldiers leapt to their feet and advanced into what seemed like a perfect storm of lead. Men dropped left and right. Rebels emerged from the woods in front of them. Hill and his company advanced to within twenty or thirty paces of them, firing into smoke so dense they could see nothing but the flashes of the enemy's guns. Bullets hissed by Hill's ears as he concentrated on keeping his aim low. Finally, the regiment received the order to fall back to where the 5th Pennsylvania Reserves waited to take their place.[45]

The battle continued until nightfall, and then the Confederates finally forced a breakthrough and the Union line began to come apart. The collapse accelerated after Gen. Philip St. George Cooke led an ill-advised cavalry charge through the Union lines. The onrushing Confederates bloodily repulsed Cooke's horsemen and they fell back, sowing chaos and confusion and precipitating a final and total breakdown of the Union position. The soldiers streamed backward toward the Chickahominy, exultant rebels in pursuit and Union cannons left behind to be captured.

The end came so quickly and amid such smoke, darkness, and confusion that one of Meade's regiments, the 11th Pennsylvania Reserves, became surrounded by the enemy and was forced to surrender. Only two companies, which had been ordered to the rear to add handles to ax heads so they could chop down trees for fortifications, managed to escape.[46]

Later that night Reynolds found himself surrounded, too. The exhausted general had lain down in some woods and fallen asleep. When he woke up his men had gone. He was now behind enemy lines. Confederate general D. H. Hill, a friend from West Point, recalled when the Union general was brought in as a prisoner. Reynolds sat down, with his face buried in his hands, looking "confused and mortified." "We ought not to be enemies," he told Hill, who tried to console him with words about the fortunes of war. Reynolds was sent to Richmond as a prisoner.[47]

If the victory at Beaver Dam Creek had unnerved McClellan, how would he respond to the defeat at Gaines's Mill? It didn't matter. He was already making plans to fall back. It seems Beaver Dam Creek had taken a psychological toll. By the time Porter's broken corps was streaming back across the Chickahominy, McClellan was already planning to cut his losses and move all the way across the peninsula to the James River, where his army could find shelter under the protection of navy gunboats. He decided to shift his line of supply from White House Landing on the Pamunkey River to Harrison's Landing on the James. McClellan called it a "change of base," but to most eyes it looked suspiciously like a retreat.

Sitting by a blazing fire at his headquarters that night, the commanding general wrote a telegram to Secretary of War Stanton. He pointed out that the army's setbacks had not been his fault. "I again repeat that I am not responsible for this," he declared. And then he concluded with statements so inflammatory that the officer in Washington who received the telegram did not include them when he recopied the message to pass on to Stanton. "If I save this Army now I tell you plainly that I owe no thanks to you or any other person in Washington—you have done your best to sacrifice this army," McClellan wrote.[48]

To reach the James River, McClellan's army had to cross a tangled and boggy mire called White Oak Swamp, which had only one major road that led in the right direction. Passage promised to be slow and tortuous. Lee would do his best to make it even more difficult. McCall's division received responsibility for escorting the army's reserve artillery, a column of guns, ammunition wagons, and other baggage that stretched seven miles.[49] In addition, they had to drive twenty-five hundred cattle, "beef on the hoof," to feed the army.

The roads the Confederates would use to intercept the Army of the Potomac converged near the crossroads of Glendale. It was an ideal spot for Lee to cut McClellan's retreating army in half.

During the night, McCall's guide led the soldiers down the wrong road, toward Richmond instead of the James. Even in the darkness, Meade's topographical instincts told him something was amiss. He told McCall they had gotten off track. The division was still attached to the V Corps, so Porter rode over to determine the reason for the delay. Meade insisted they were on the wrong road. Porter disagreed, but he told McCall to stop where he was for the night. Later, believing that the reserves were no longer attached to his command, Porter had the V Corps reverse course and find the right road. He left McCall's division behind. For all intents and purposes, the Pennsylvania Reserves was on its own.

They spent a tense and uncomfortable night in the swamp. At one point, musket fire broke out in the rear, jangling everyone's nerves, but it was only men mistakenly firing on Porter's corps as it found its way to the right road in the darkness. The jittery soldiers got another jolt in the middle of the night when horses from an artillery battery broke loose and stampeded down the lines. Shots rang out as soldiers tried to bring down the panicked animals. One of the wounded horses lay moaning in the darkness, "the most distressing sound possible to imagine." Farm dogs near and far kept barking though the night, probably indicating the presence of the enemy.[50]

The next morning, June 30, R. Biddle Roberts, a regimental commander in the 3rd Brigade, shared a quick breakfast with Meade served on the tailboard of a wagon. They ate bacon with their fingers and drank black coffee from tin cups. Meade was in "unusually good spirits," Roberts recalled.[51]

It was a beautiful day, warm and sunny. The reserves did not expect a battle that day, after all their fighting and hard marching. Furthermore, it was the last day of the month, so what they really expected was their pay. The paymasters dutifully mustered in the men and doled out the money.

McCall positioned his men just to the west of the hamlet of Glendale, along the Long Bridge Road. A man named Nelson owned the land and before that it was the property of the Frayser family, which is why the encounter here is sometimes called the Battle of Nelson's Farm or Frayser's Farm. Unlike today, with thick woods covering the site, the terrain was largely open farmland with some woods to the right and more than a thousand yards in front. "It was a beautiful battle-field," McCall noted, "but too large for my force, the lands on either flank being open."[52]

McCall placed Meade's brigade nearly astride the road, with Seymour's to his left. Joseph Hooker's division of the III Corps was off to Seymour's left and a little to the rear. Behind them the army's long train of wagons was slowly bouncing and creaking down the Quaker City Road, on its way to Malvern Hill and the safety of the James River beyond. Longstreet and A. P. Hill would be moving down the Darbytown Road toward the Union forces, hoping to smash through the reserves to reach the Quaker City Road and cut the Army of the Potomac in half. Once he had placed his men, McCall waited.

Sometime around two o'clock, the opposing sides began an artillery duel. Then rebels from James Kemper's brigade of Longstreet's division quickly broke through

Seymour's men and sent them scampering to the rear and through Hooker's command. Union counterattacks kept the assault from turning into a rout.

In front of Meade's position, a battery commanded by Lt. Alanson Randol became the focus of violent fighting. Randol's cannons wreaked havoc on the enemy, but the Confederates kept advancing until they reached the artillery. The two sides lay into each other with bayonets and hand to hand. The 7th Pennsylvania Reserves moved forward and collided with Cadmus Wilcox's Alabamians. The rebels pushed them back to Randol's guns, which couldn't fire without killing their own men. As the Confederates swarmed over the batteries, the crews resisted with hand-spikes and sponge-staffs. Meade's men made a desperate charge and pushed the Confederates back, but a fresh rebel onslaught reversed the tide once again. It was savage, desperate combat, "one of the fiercest bayonet fights that perhaps ever occurred on this continent," according to McCall. "Bayonets were crossed and locked in the struggle; bayonet wounds were freely given and received. I saw skulls crushed by the heavy blow of the butt of the musket, and in, short, the desperate thrusts and parries of a life and death encounter."[53]

At some point during the fighting Meade's aide, Lt. Hamilton Kuhn, was killed and his other aide, Lt. William Watmough, was wounded. Meade, too, was in the thick of the fighting for Randol's battery, riding his horse Blacky and exhorting the men to greater efforts, when two Confederate bullets struck him.

One bullet hit him in the arm and another in the side. Meade winced slightly but remained in his saddle. The arm wound was the more painful and he thought it was the worse of the two. He rode up to the battery commander. "Randol, I am badly wounded in the arm, and must leave the field," he said. "Fight your guns to the last, but save them if possible."[54] Meade rode back a ways—Blacky had been wounded, too—and continued to give orders until he began to feel weak from loss of blood. Darkness was bringing the battle to a halt, anyway. Col. Horatio Sickel of the 3rd Pennsylvania Reserves took over command of the brigade and Meade set out with an orderly to find a hospital.

Hundreds of wounded men were searching for the same thing amid the chaos of battle. To Meade's great fortune, though, one of the wounded men he encountered happened to be a doctor. He took Meade under his care and examined his wounds. The arm wound was not serious, but it appeared as though the other bullet had hit Meade in the back. Being shot with your face to the enemy was one thing; being shot in the back implied that you had been running away. "Just think, doctor, of my being shot in the back!" Meade groaned in despair.[55] Closer examination, however, cleared his conscience. The ball had actually struck him in the side near his hip and exited from his back, missing his spine by mere inches.

The wounded general, now in great pain, was wondering if he would be able to remount his horse when he spotted, amongst the flotsam and jetsam carried along by retreating army, the little wagon that carried his mess supplies and tent. He had it halted and emptied and he lay down in the back for a bumping, grueling journey to Haxall's Landing on the James River. He arrived there sometime after midnight.

There he wrote a short note to his wife. "After four days' fighting, last evening, about 7 p.m., I received a wound in the arm and back," he said. "Fortunately I met Dr. Stocker, and got hold of a little cart I had, in which I was brought here. Dr. Stocker says my wounds are not dangerous, though they require immediate and constant medical attendance. I am to leave in the first boat for Old Point, and from thence home. Kuhn, I fear, is killed. Willie Watmough was not hurt, the last I saw of him.

"Good-by!"[56]

After Meade left the field, the fighting quieted as darkness fell. McCall rode forward to reconnoiter, but he went too far and straight into the arms of rebel infantry, who took him prisoner. At 11:00 that night, the shattered, exhausted remainder of the Pennsylvania Reserves received orders to withdraw and march south to Malvern Hill, where Porter had posted the V Corps.

Malvern Hill provided the setting for the bloody climax of the Seven Days Battles. Despite the name, Malvern Hill seems like less of a hill and more of a slightly sloped field. On July 1, 1862, it must have seemed hilly enough to the Confederate soldiers who advanced across these open expanses, only to be repulsed by deadly sheets of Union fire. The rebel attack was poorly planned and poorly coordinated. "Lee never before nor since that action delivered a battle so ill-judged in conception, or so faulty in its details of execution," wrote an early historian of the Army of the Potomac.[57] Confederate major general D. H. Hill was more succinct. "It was not war," he said, "it was murder."[58] At dawn the next day a Union officer reported that the wounded soldiers writhing on the ground in front of the Union position gave "the field a singular crawling effect."[59] The Confederates lost this battle—in fact, they never scored a decisive victory during the Seven Days—but they still managed to drive McClellan's army away from Richmond.

● ● ●

The official reports written after a battle often elicited heated correspondence, both by those who felt they were unfairly criticized or those who felt unfairly overlooked. The official reports of the fighting at Glendale were no exception. McClellan and Hooker were both harshly critical of the Pennsylvania Reserves' performance. McClellan reported that McCall's division "broke and lost most of its artillery" but that Hooker cleaned up the mess.[60] Hooker was even more scathing. He said that "the whole of McCall's division was completely routed," and that some of the panicked men "actually fired on and killed some of my men as they passed."[61]

McCall sent Meade a copy of Hooker's report in November. Meade was inclined to ignore it, figuring that the reserves had more than established their reputation in the fighting since then. As the divisional commander at the time, it was McCall's responsibility to respond, anyway. Meade wrote, "It was only the stubborn resistance offered by our division (the Pennsylvania Reserves), prolonging the contest till after dark, and checking till that time the advance of the enemy, that enabled the concentration during the night of the whole army on the James river, which saved it."[62] Fitz John Porter agreed. "Had not McCall held his place on New Market Road, that line of march of the army would have been cut by the enemy," he wrote.[63]

From the Confederate perspective the Seven Days Battles had been a series of missed opportunities. Time and again Lee appeared to have the perfect chance to crush McClellan's retreating army, and time and again his plans went awry. Stonewall Jackson, in particular, failed to move with his usual vigor. "Jackson was a very skillful man against such men as Shields, Banks, and Frémont," noted James Longstreet, "but when pitted against the best of the Federal commanders he did not appear so well."[64]

Fitz John Porter tried to put things in a more favorable light for the Union when he later declared that *both* sides had won the Peninsula Campaign, because both had achieved their goals—the Confederates by driving the Union army back from Richmond and McClellan by "gaining security on the north bank of the James."[65] In that case, then, McClellan's greatest failure may have been underachievement.

Union general Alexander Webb had a more downbeat assessment. "The history of the campaign, in short, is the history of a lamentable failure—nothing less," he wrote in 1881.[66]

CHAPTER 3

Civil War Redux

An artillery crew from the North-South Skirmish Association
PHOTO BY TOM HUNTINGTON

The gunfire comes from somewhere beyond the woods to my left. It is not just a hunter after a deer—this is sustained and heavy firing. It sounds as if I'm heading into a war zone.

I'm driving down a bumpy and muddy access road just north of Winchester, Virginia, on a sunny October afternoon following a couple days of torrential rain. The gunfire doesn't come as any surprise. In fact, I've been listening for it. I'm heading to the North-South Skirmish Association's fall nationals, a huge shooting competition conducted with Civil War–era weapons. The event brings thousands of black-powder enthusiasts and their families to a location the organization calls Fort Shenandoah. Founded in 1950, the N-SSA has around four thousand members, all of whom belong to various units based on real companies from the Civil War. Not only do these skirmishers shoot Civil War weapons—originals and reproductions—but they use real ammunition and wear period uniforms. I figure this skirmish will be the closest experience to Civil War combat that I'm likely to get.

War has obviously changed a great deal since the Civil War, and it continues to evolve. Today America fights with airplanes, airborne drones, and computers. The technology of war was also in a state of flux during the Civil War. It witnessed many firsts—the first time railroads were used to transport armies to the battlefield, the first time ironclad vessels battled each other, the first time a submarine sank a warship. The trench warfare we associate with World War I became a major factor in the Civil War.

The weapons the soldier used and the tactics they followed reflected a mixture of the old and the new. Old-fashioned smoothbore weapons were being replaced by more accurate and murderous rifled guns. These new weapons forced changes in the old close formations of the Napoleonic era of fighting. Soldiers could kill more effectively and from a greater range, especially if they had rapid-firing breech-loading weapons.

Now I'm about to get a taste of the weapons that Meade and his men would have known. Fort Shenandoah sprawls across some five hundred acres at the north end of the Shenandoah Valley, which was hotly contested territory throughout the real Civil War. Once I drive through the main entrance, I find myself in the middle of something like a heavily armed scout camp. Campers, RVs, and tents jam the camping areas. There are some sutlers here, too. They occupy a complex of little wooden storefronts like the stands on a carnival boardwalk. Unlike the merchants at Civil War reenactments, these sutlers are much more oriented toward shooting equipment. You'll find not just guns but also powder, caps, balls, and all the equipment you need to keep them firing.

A creek runs through the property, with one wooden auto bridge and several pedestrian bridges spanning it. The reason for it all lies on the far side of the creek. The shooting range is huge, a long field that stretches for more than a quarter mile, with a separate pistol range at one end. The main observation tower stands near the line's center, with two smaller towers covering the flanks. The shooters on the firing line face a wooded rise more than one hundred yards in front of them. The bottom portion, the backstop, has been denuded of vegetation. It will absorb thousands more bullets over five days of shooting at the nationals.

Hundreds of skirmishers have gathered at the range, all dressed in appropriate Civil War garb. Union soldiers mix with Confederates, while civilian men and women mill about and provide variety. Most of the competitors have little two-wheeled pull carts they tug along behind them to transport their arms and equipment. Unlike their Civil War counterparts, many of them also use protective earphones and glasses. The competitors in the individual matches carry rolled-up paper targets that you could mistake for maps, which makes them look like well-armed topographers. For the team shooting events, though, the targets are clay, either clay pigeons wired to big pieces of cardboard and hung from wooden frames or square clay tiles dangling from wires on the frames. For other competitions the skirmishers hang the pigeons directly from the frames.

The guns here are the same kinds of weapons that Civil War soldiers would have known. There are two basic kinds: smoothbore and rifled. Smoothbores are the older guns, weapons like the 1842 Springfield. The insides of their barrels are smooth, which limits their accuracy and range. Rifled guns have spiral grooves inside their barrels, which apply a spin to their projectiles. The spin allows the bullet to travel farther and with greater accuracy, like a spiraling football. The 1861 Springfield and 1853 Enfield were common rifled guns on Civil War battlefields. Both of them were muzzleloaders, so the soldiers equipped with them used a ramrod to stuff powder and balls down the barrel before each shot. According to the drill manual, it took seventeen separate movements to load and fire a single round in a rifled musket, eighteen for an 1836 smoothbore.[1] That obviously wasn't an easy task to master when you were facing hundreds of people trying deliberately to kill you, and perhaps screaming the unnerving rebel yell as they did so. No wonder people often found weapons on battlefields with the barrels stuffed with multiple rounds, one pounded in after another in the heat of combat until the gun became useless. For well-trained soldiers in better command of their emotions, three shots a minute was considered a good firing frequency with a muzzleloader.

Breech-loading weapons, such as the 1859 Sharps, were easier to load. The shooter simply snapped open the breech and inserted the bullet. It took only six movements to load and fire a breechloader—eleven less than a rifled musket.[2] Soldiers with breechloaders could fire up to nine shots a minute and could load and fire while lying down or hiding in a tree, which made them ideal for skirmishers and sharpshooters. Cavalrymen often used shorter breech-loading carbines, which were easier to handle on horseback. Muzzleloaders, breechloaders, smoothbores, and rifled guns are all here in profusion at Fort Shenandoah.

After I set up my tent I wander down to the line to watch the team smoothbore competition, in which teams of four shoot at clay targets, first from twenty-five yards and then fifty. As I watch I get to talking with Al Otash, who hails from North Attleboro, Massachusetts, but belongs to the 4th Virginia Infantry, Company F, known as Grayson's Daredevils. Otash tells me that he has long had an interest in the Civil War, but even while growing up in New England he thought the South had a certain "mystique." It seems that sectional divisions in the

North-South Skirmish Association are somewhat blurred. (Except on a bathroom stall, where some Yankee has written, "Rebels: do not eat the large pink mints in the urinals.")

The original 4th Virginia belonged to the famed Stonewall Brigade, but the modern version has only two Virginians. As we talk about the war Otash motions to one of them, a man sitting behind the firing line in a sling chair. "He knows everything about the Civil War," Otash says.

The man turns around. "I thought I knew everything," he says in a slight drawl, "until I saw the politically correct movie they show at Gettysburg. Then I realized I didn't know anything." He gets up and introduces himself as David Wright. We immediately get into a discussion about the causes of the Civil War. Wright doesn't blame slavery. "It was the economic squeezing of the South," he says. He admits that slavery was part of the overall economic picture but stresses the importance of import taxes passed by Congress, which he tells me forced Southerners to buy products from the North instead of European products that would have been cheaper.

I ask him about Alexander Stephens's statement in his famed "Cornerstone" speech from March 21, 1861, that slavery was, in fact, "the immediate cause of the late rupture."

"That's his opinion," Wright replies.

"But he was the vice president of the Confederacy!" I protest. Wright shrugs. "The bottom line is that slavery was evil," he says. "Evil, evil, evil." But Wright insists that the ordinary Southern soldier was not fighting for slavery. He tells me that he has researched ninety-eight of the men who served in the real 4th Virginia and that at least ninety-six of them did not own slaves. "They fought for Virginia," he says, but admits, "I'm sure the big boys who had the money had their eyes on something different."

I disagree with him about slavery's impact on the outbreak of war, but there's no doubt that Wright knows his history. He informs me that his great-grandfather fought in the Civil War and that he's related to Robert E. Lee, Lewis Armistead, Meriwether Lewis, and Thomas Jefferson. "If you can trace your line back to colonial days you're related to everyone," Wright says. He tells me about the time his allergist introduced him to another doctor in the building who was the grandson of John McCausland, the Confederate general who burned Chambersburg, Pennsylvania, in 1864. The grandson was in his nineties at the time, still practiced medicine, and remembered riding side-by-side with his grandfather, their horses so close the riders' legs touched, cavalry style.

Despite our differences I like talking to Wright. He's full of information and is willing to listen to this unapologetic Yankee. Before I leave he talks a little bit about the N-SSA. "We're honoring those that fought on both sides, blue and gray," he says. "And we mix that honor with a love of shooting."

There is plenty for shooters to love. The competition takes place over five days. While this is largely a white male event—and, if bumper stickers are a reliable indicator, a politically conservative one at that—some women do participate. (In fact, later in the day the 1st Maryland Cavalry will field the first all-woman mortar team.)

A horn over the public address system signals the start of the next round of the smoothbore competition. The guns begin firing, and the clay pigeons up and down the line start exploding into orange powder. The bullets create little puffs of dirt on the backstop. The spectators sitting behind the line cheer their teams. The crackling waves of gunfire and the smoke rising into the air make it seem as if a real war has broken out. The echoes rebounding from the backstop sound as though an enemy force hidden in the woods is returning the fire.

It may sound like war, but everything here is done with a strict attention to safety—the exact opposite of the real thing, where the intention was to kill as many of the enemy as you could.

Al Bumford of Southampton, Pennsylvania, and his son, Adam, are two of the nineteen members of the 149th Pennsylvania Volunteer Infantry, Company C. They wear deer tails on their hats, which identify them as members of the Bucktails. The 13th Pennsylvania Reserves were the original Bucktails. The 149th came later, organized in August 1862 in response to the battlefield exploits of the originals. The Bumfords have just finished shooting in the smoothbore competition, and their hands are dark with powder. Al shows me his weapon, an 1816 Springfield .69-caliber smoothbore. In 1861 the gun was converted to fire with percussion caps in place of the old-style flintlock mechanism. Adam hands me one of the balls they use. It's covered with wax and lies heavily in the palm of my hand. During the war the real Bucktails might have loaded their smoothbores with "buck and ball," a paper cartridge filled with a combination of three pieces of buckshot and a single .69-caliber lead ball. At the short ranges required for smoothbore firing, such a charge would prove devastating against human flesh.

Even though the weapons are period Al tells me that the modern shooters are much more accurate than their Civil War counterparts. Today's competitors, he says, weigh their powder with digital scales to get the exact loads they need to shoot with consistency. Their powder comes from Switzerland. He tells me that modern-day musket shooters lubricate their weapons with a combination of yellow beeswax and Mobil One oil. "Back then they used tallow and lard," Al says. But "this is very competitive," he adds.

Later in the day teams begin setting up for the mortar competition. As Allen Torday of the 4th Virginia's mortar team awaits the signal to fire, he tells me he got interested in black-powder weapons after he helped his wife's uncle, a Louisianan, fix a tractor and received a Civil War pistol in exchange. Intrigued, he bought a magazine about black-powder shooting and saw an ad for the N-SSA. "Now my wife is happy because I wear a Confederate uniform and she's from the South," he says. His crew is firing a 12-pounder, but it looks tiny next to the armament of the Confederate group next to them. That group has an a 8-inch mortar, a squat, wide-mouthed weapon so heavy the crew uses a huge wooden tripod with a pulley to haul it into position.

When the mortars fire, the heavy cannonballs arc gracefully through the air and land with a splash of wet soil near their targets, poles stuck into the ground one hundred yards away. Some of the crews are so good they hit the pole, prompting applause from the spectators.

Saturday morning's carbine competition promises even more of a spectacle. As the morning sun casts long shadows down the range, more than 250 shooters line up in teams of four. The line stretches so long that from where I'm standing at the right of the line, I can't even see the teams at the far end.

These guns are breech-loading weapons. After firing percussion caps only, as a precaution to ensure that the weapons have not been loaded, the team members load the first bullet and wait for the horn to sound. Once the horn blows, the line explodes with a roar. The first loud volley leads into an unorganized cacophony that ebbs and flows in intensity during the five-minute match. After each shot the skirmishers snap open their weapons, reach inside the cartridge pouches on their belts for another shell, reload, snap their weapons shut, aim, and fire. More clay pigeons shatter. A thick cloud of smoke begins to rise above the line and block the morning sun; the acrid smell of black powder fills the air. Once a team hits all its targets, an official records its elapsed time. The shooters snap open the weapons and hold them up so a safety officer can peer into the breeches and see that they are empty.

I wander up and down the line watching the shooting. During the hundred-meter carbine competition I run into David Wright again. "You know, at Second Manassas the Stonewall Brigade was eighty yards from the Yankees," he says. "They were firing at the Iron Brigade, the Black Hats, who were just as intimidating. They just stood there eighty yards apart and shot at each other." He gestures out at the range as the little tiles hanging from the wooden frames up and down the line shatter and dirt flies on the backstop beyond. "That's one hundred yards," he says.

One of Jackson's officers, Brig. Gen. William B. Taliaferro, later described that contest between the Stonewall and Iron Brigades. "It was a sanguinary field; none was better contested during the war," he wrote. "A farm-house, an orchard, a few stacks of hay, and a rotten 'worm' fence were the only cover afforded to the opposing lines of infantry; it was a stand-up combat, dogged and unflinching, in a field almost bare. There were no wounds from spent balls; the confronting lines looked into each other's faces at deadly range, less than one hundred yards apart, and they stood as immovable as the painted heroes in a battle-piece."[3]

Later that day it's time for the big guns—the field artillery. Cannons, like mortars, are measured in two ways: by the diameter of the bore and by the weight of their projectiles. For example, a 3-inch Parrott gun, named after its inventor, Robert Parker Parrott, had a 3-inch-diameter bore. The largest Parrott was a 300-pounder. The smaller guns were a familiar presence on Civil War battlefields and were recognizable by the iron band wrapped around the breech to provide more strength. Parrotts did have an unfortunate tendency to burst near the bore, though. During the Battle of Fredericksburg in December 1862, a Confederate Parrott exploded and the shrapnel could have killed or seriously wounded generals Robert E. Lee and James Longstreet, who were standing nearby.

Like the smaller guns, there are also smoothbore and rifled cannons. In the Civil War, artillery crews usually used the more accurate rifled guns to knock out the enemy's cannons. When trying to kill enemy soldiers they loaded smoothbores with canister shot, a tin can that contained many iron balls, like a shotgun shell on steroids. Case shot was similar, but with musket balls in an iron container. Canister at close range would decimate the ranks of advancing soldiers. Gen. Alpheus Williams, who fought with the Union XII Corps at Antietam, wrote about the devastating effects he witnessed when one of his batteries fired canister at a charging line of Confederates. "Each canister contains several hundred balls," he wrote. "They fell in the very front of the line all along it apparently, stirring up dust like a thick cloud. When the dust blew away no regiment and not a living man was to be seen."[4]

Archibald Hill of the 8th Pennsylvania Reserves described what it was like to endure an artillery barrage at Gaines's Mill. "There was not a second that the air above our heads was free from either shot or shell," he recalled. "They were sent one after another so rapidly, that a constant, prolonged, and connected whizzing, shrieking, and screaming was maintained. Shell were exploding every second— now in front of us, now in our rear, and frequently over our heads. Grape-and-canister came whistling shrilly about us; while solid shot came rushing madly along, now flying a few feet above our heads, now striking the hillside with a dull crash, and ricocheting a hundred feet into the air, and falling far in our rear."[5]

The firing won't be quite so intense today.

Before the shooting starts the artillery crews wait to enter the range and set up at the far end of the line, their cannons lashed down on trailers attached to an assortment of pickup trucks. I get into conversation with Scott Lynch, a high school history teacher from nearby Berkeley Springs, West Virginia. I mention that I'm working on a book about Meade. "The unsung hero of Gettysburg," he says. "He had to work in Grant's shadow." We agree that Meade never got his due.

Lynch belongs to the 27th Virginia Volunteer Infantry. He got involved with the N-SSA in 1973, after his brother took him to a gun show in Baltimore and he saw some vintage weapons. Even after thirty-seven years of experience he claims to be a "newbie, still wet behind the ears." He tells me he also does some reenacting, and I ask him what the difference is between the skirmishers here and reenactors. "They look down on us because our uniforms aren't right," he replies. "We look at them and say, 'You don't know how to shoot your gun.'"

Lynch and his crew know how to shoot their gun, a 10-pound Parrott. They also have a mascot, a windsock of a parrot wearing a Hawaiian shirt that hangs on the front of their trailer. "This is our party parrot," Lynch says. He reaches into a box on the trailer and hands me some "Parrott food." It's one of the projectiles he'll be shooting, a hollowed-out piece of pointed, polished lead that weighs a little less than six pounds. Lynch casts them at home himself and has carefully noted the exact weight on each one. The charge he will use is $5\frac{1}{3}$ ounces of cannon-grade powder.

During the competition I'll observe Charlie Smithgall and his crew of the 3rd U.S. Artillery. They seem to be the team to beat. Charlie, a portly, white-haired former mayor of Lancaster, Pennsylvania, has been a member of the N-SSA for fifty years now. It's safe to say that few people know more about Civil War artillery than Charlie Smithgall. He has a personal collection of more than seventy cannons, and he served as the artillery consultant for the 1993 movie *Gettysburg* and various television shows.

The artillery bug first bit Smithgall back in the early 1960s, when he watched the artillery competition at a national N-SSA event. "I was right behind the guns, standing as a spectator," he recalls. The target was a 1938 Plymouth. The announcer asked the gunners not to shoot out the rear axle so that the hulk could be towed to the junkyard afterward. Smithgall remembers watching a member of the crew in front of him smile and look over at the announcer. "He adjusted the gun and took the rear axle right out," he says. "I was hooked." Smithgall went out and bought a mortar. Then he bought a cannon. Then another cannon. And another. Now he keeps his collection in a warehouse near his home in Lancaster. He also owns almost every one of the small arms the U.S. military has used from the Revolutionary War through World War II.

For the first round Smithgall and his crew are shooting a 3-inch ordnance rifle, one of four he owns. Designed by John Griffen, this rifled piece was a very durable, dependable, and accurate weapon that had an effective range of two thousand yards but could reach four thousand in a pinch.[6] (That's about two and a quarter miles.) Today's competitors will be firing at targets two hundred yards away. They will have twelve shots, with the best ten counting toward the score. They have two targets, mounted on big rectangles of wallboard in front of the backstop. One is a standard bull's-eye target. The rifled guns have a 24-inch bull's-eye with a 12-inch V-ring in the center. (Smoothbores, which are less accurate, get a larger target.) The second target is a "counter battery," which bears the front silhouette of a cannon.

Smithgall spends a long time lining up the cannon's sights. When he's satisfied he yells, "Load!" Crewmember Ned Friedenthal trudges forward from the cannon's limber, the box on wheels that holds the charges and projectiles. Inside the leather satchel over his shoulder he carries a 6-ounce charge in a plastic bag wrapped inside aluminum foil. At the cannon he takes the charge from the satchel and hands it to crewmember James Murray. Murray rams the charge down the barrel. He follows the charge with a projectile that Friedenthal hands him. It's a copy of a Hotchkiss shell from the Civil War but made of aluminum instead of iron. Donald Brubaker next takes a metal vent pick and sticks it though the vent hole near the breech to pierce the charge. He inserts a fuse into the vent. Once it's ready, Smithgall hollers, "Fire!" Mark Gehron, Smithgall's son-in-law, touches the fuse with a bit of smoldering rope wrapped around a wooden pole. The fuse sputters into flame. A few seconds later the cannon explodes with a thunderous roar and jerks back a foot or two. Amid the smoke that belches out of the barrel, pieces of aluminum foil scatter like confetti.

The first shot is just to the left of the center of the V-ring. Smithgall peers into the sight and makes tiny adjustments with the elevating screw at the barrel's base. Frank Potts pounds lightly on the right side of the cannon's stock—the wooden base that extends behind the carriage—with a fluorescent orange mallet to adjust the side-to-side position. They go though the loading routine again. The next shot is just a hair above the first. The rest are equally impressive.

At the end of the contest Smithgall and his team get the highest score, meaning they win the Pelham, an award named after a Confederate cavalryman who bedeviled Meade at Fredericksburg with his artillery. Smithgall also takes first in howitzers. Not a bad day's shooting.

Between events I sit down and read a book I found in a box of old volumes for sale by one of the sutlers. It's called *Abraham Lincoln and Men of War-Times*, written by Alexander McClure and published in 1892. McClure was an interesting man. He was born in Chambersburg, Pennsylvania, became a newspaper publisher, and by the time war broke out in 1861, he was a mover and a shaker in the state's Republican circles. Late one night in October 1862 he received a surprise visit by some of Jeb Stuart's cavalrymen when the rebels raided southern Pennsylvania. McClure and the Southern horsemen sat up until the wee hours talking about the causes of the war. He wasn't so lucky in 1864, though, when John McCausland's men burned his house to the ground.

McClure had personal acquaintances with everyone from President Lincoln on down, including George Gordon Meade. In fact, in the book I bought he wrote, "The country has never done justice to General Meade as a military commander, and our varied histories, as a rule, have grudgingly conceded to him only what could not be withheld from him. The man who fought and won the Battle of Gettysburg should have been the commander-in-chief of the armies of the Union and held that position during life. It was the great battle of the war; it was the Waterloo of the Confederacy, and the victory there achieved was won by the skill of the commanding general and the heroism of his army."[7] I sit in the warm October sun and read those words as the sounds of Civil War weaponry split the air. I'd like to think seeing these weapons at work has given me a sense of what it must have been like for Meade and his men to face them for real, but I realize there's no way I can really know. For that I'm thankful.

CHAPTER 4

Back to Bull Run

John Fulton Reynolds, Meade's division commander at Second Manassas
SPECIAL COLLECTIONS, FRANKLIN AND MARSHALL COLLEGE, LANCASTER, PA

◆ ◆ ◆

I discover bones on the Second Bull Run battlefield during a nasty, rainy afternoon. I'm the only person dumb enough to be out exploring in such weather, but I have come equipped, with a raincoat, gum rubber boots, and a big new umbrella. I can easily imagine that the steady drumming of raindrops on the umbrella is the distant sound of musketry.

The bones are no figment of my imagination. I spot the first one, a piece maybe seven inches long, on the far side of the slight rise behind the Brawner farmhouse, the Civil War–era structure that serves as the Park Service's interpretive headquarters for the second battle that bloodied these grounds. There's another, smaller fragment farther down the trail. I pick this one up to make sure it is bone and not just a piece of weathered wood. A little farther down the trail, in a swampy depression, I find two more pieces. I'm no forensics expert, but I think the bones are too big for a deer and could possibly be human. I take some pictures with my phone's camera, using my baseball cap for scale.

There probably are some soldiers buried and forgotten beneath the fields around me. Here on August 28, 1862, men under Stonewall Jackson and John Gibbon—his black-hatted soldiers not yet calling themselves the Iron Brigade—blazed away at each other for more than two hours at distances under a hundred yards. This was the encounter David Wright described to me when I talked to him at the North-South Skirmish Association event. Frank Haskell, who later wrote a famous account of the Battle of Gettysburg, described the fight here as "a roaring hell of fire."[1]

I splash through the mud and rain back to the Brawner House and tell the two people on duty there—a volunteer and a ranger—about my find. They seem curiously unconcerned. "I guess with the rain there's been a lot of erosion," the volunteer says. "It's possible that it uncovered a grave."

"We could call law enforcement," the ranger says to the volunteer. "That's what we usually do in situations like this." She makes a call—to park headquarters, I think—and leaves a message. I give them my number in case anyone wants to contact me, and then I head back out into the rain. Most likely they are just animal bones—but you never know.

I've come here to try to make sense of Second Bull Run. The battle confuses me—maybe because most everyone in the Union chain of command seemed to be just as confused at the time. Robert E. Lee had planned a fairly complicated, wide-ranging campaign, and the Union's blundering attempts to counter him led to a bewildering series of marches and countermarches. Adding to the confusion, the Union had two armies here: portions of McClellan's Army of the Potomac and a new entity, the Army of Virginia under Maj. Gen. John Pope, which had about forty-five thousand men cobbled together from three separate commands.

No wonder I'm confused.

Political currents always roiled the Army of the Potomac, but John Pope's arrival on the scene intensified them in new ways. Pope, a moon-faced man with a King Tut beard and an overabundance of self-esteem, had fought with some success in the West as the commander of the Army of the Mississippi. Lincoln thought he would offer an antidote to McClellan's cautious ways, so he summoned Pope east to take command of the Army of Virginia, newly formed from the forces of Franz Sigel (replacing John Frémont, who resigned his commission in a huff rather than serve under Pope), Nathaniel Banks (whom Stonewall Jackson had already manhandled in the Shenandoah Valley), and Irvin McDowell (the commander at the first—and at that point the only—Battle of Bull Run).

Pope made a bad first impression on his eastern troops by issuing a blustery proclamation. "I have come to you from the West," he announced, "where we have always seen the backs of our enemies; from an army whose business it has been to seek the adversary and to beat him when he was found; whose policy has been attack and not defense." The implied rebuke, of course, was that the Army of the Potomac shared none of those qualities. A story began making the rounds that Pope proclaimed that his "headquarters would be in the saddle," prompting many inevitable jokes about his hindquarters. Decades later Pope still fumed about the "fanciful story," one he said "furnished General Lee with the basis for the only joke of his life."[2]

Pope aroused Confederate anger by issuing proclamations warning Virginians that he would tolerate no civilian support for the rebel cause. This hard war policy stood in stark contrast to the soft war that McClellan and other conservatives, including Meade, preferred.

McClellan, still with his army at Harrison's Landing alongside the James River, seethed about this arrogant interloper. As early as July 22 he wrote to his wife, "I see that the Pope bubble is likely to be suddenly collapsed—Stonewall Jackson is after him, & the paltry young man who wanted to teach me the art of war will in less than a week either be in full retreat or badly whipped."[3]

Other officers in the Army of the Potomac grumbled, too, none more than Fitz John Porter, McClellan's most loyal subordinate. Pope, he wrote to a confidant, "has now written himself down . . . as an ass."[4] He included scathing commentary about the new arrival in military communications he sent to fellow general Ambrose Burnside, who dutifully forwarded the communications to Washington. Porter would regret his comments later.

Brig. Gen. Samuel Sturgis, a Pennsylvania native who had fought out west before heading east to help defend Washington, had little regard for Pope as well. When Herman Haupt, the Union's capable railroad supervisor, ordered Sturgis and his men off trains intended for Pope's use, Sturgis responded with one of my favorite quotes from the Civil War: "I don't care for John Pope one pinch of owl dung."[5]

Pope wasn't the only new and divisive personality on the scene. The Union also gained a new general in chief after Lincoln took those duties from McClellan. In July the president appointed Maj. Gen. Henry Halleck to the position. Halleck had graduated from West Point's Class of 1839 but missed out on the Mexican War while posted in California. He did not miss out on California's financial opportunities, however, and amassed a substantial nest egg through a successful law practice and interests in a bank, railroads, and mining. Halleck had retired from the army in 1854 but rejoined after the outbreak of war. Back in the 1840s the then-young soldier's theories on the art of war had impressed Gen. Winfield

Scott, so Scott had recommended Halleck for a major generalship. As commander of the Department of the Missouri and later the Mississippi, Halleck enjoyed some military success, much of it thanks to a subordinate named Ulysses S. Grant. When on the field during the siege of Corinth, Mississippi, though, Halleck demonstrated the same kind of caution that characterized McClellan's operations.

Halleck had a large forehead and bulging eyes that gave him an intellectual air. People nicknamed him "Old Brains." "Old Bureaucrat" may have been more suitable. Halleck proved less of a military spark plug for the Union and more of a cautious administrative type who became skilled at dodging risk and responsibility. Gideon Welles, Lincoln's navy secretary and a close observer of events in the capital, later said of the general in chief: "I have been unable to see, hear, or obtain evidence of power, or will, or talent, or originality on the part of General Halleck. He has suggested nothing, decided nothing, done nothing but scold and smoke and scratch his elbows."[6] (The elbow scratching was one of Halleck's peculiar nervous tics.) Halleck was a good administrator, but if Lincoln had expected Old Brains to guide Union war strategy with a firm hand, the president was sorely disappointed.

While all this turmoil was going on, Meade was in Philadelphia recovering from the wounds he had received on the peninsula. A hospital transport had taken him to Fortress Monroe, where he was transferred to a steamer bound for Baltimore. Margaret had met him there and accompanied him on another steamer to Philadelphia. A doctor was waiting for him on July 4 when he arrived at 2037 Pine Street, the brick rowhouse the Meades called home during the war. Margaret tenderly nursed her husband back to health. (Afterward the general wrote to his wife, in a touching passage that his son George left out of *The Life and Letters of George Gordon Meade*, "You were so kind and loving to me when I lay wounded and helpless that tho' I thought I loved you as much as it was possible for man to love woman I think now I love you more than ever.")[7]

Meade didn't remain home for long. News from Virginia indicated that McClellan's army might lurch into motion again, and Meade began fretting that his brigade would fight without him. On August 11, only forty-two days after being wounded, he said good-bye to his wife and family and boarded a steamer for Baltimore. "I cannot tell you how miserable and sad I was and am at parting from you and the dear children, and as the boat pushed off and I saw those three fine boys standing on the dock, I thought my heart would break," he wrote home. "But it cannot be helped and must be endured, and we must try and bear our trials as cheerfully as we possibly can."[8]

In Baltimore Meade found himself among a large crowd of soldiers returning to the front. He soon heard rumors that McClellan was preparing to evacuate the peninsula. The rumors were correct, although the "Young Napoleon" was making the move under protest and not nearly as rapidly as he could have. When Lincoln visited Harrison's Landing on July 7, McClellan had also had the effrontery to hand the president a letter offering him advice on "a civil and military policy" that covered "the whole ground of our national trouble." Lincoln read the letter, placed it in his pocket, and never said anything about it.[9]

When Meade finally reached Harrison's Landing, he learned that his division had already departed. McCall had been paroled by the Confederates but returned with his health broken and had gone to Washington. Reynolds, also paroled after his capture, now commanded the Pennsylvania Reserves. He greeted Meade warmly and told him he would receive command of the 1st Brigade, consisting of the 3rd, 4th, 7th, 8th, and 13th Pennsylvania Reserves. Truman Seymour had the 2nd brigade and Conrad F. Jackson the 3rd.

Meade doubtless was somewhat jealous of Reynolds's promotion, and in his letters to Margaret (passages also excluded from *Life and Letters*) he expressed his burning ambition to get his own division as well as his distrust of Seymour, whom he felt was sucking up to Reynolds. "I am sad to say that Reynolds appears to be greatly under Seymour's influence and I hear my position in the Reserves will not be as agreeable as it has been," he told Margaret, adding that he would be "greatly mortified" if Seymour were promoted above him. It was office politics, military style.[10]

Reynolds suggested that Meade rejoin his brigade at the Aquia Creek railhead on the Potomac River. So Meade had to return to Baltimore, find passage to Washington, and from there travel down the Potomac to Aquia Landing. It must have seemed like an incredibly inefficient and uncomfortable circuit for a man still recovering from bullet wounds. Perhaps irritation over being shuffled back and forth like this added to his growing disillusion with McClellan. The more he saw, he wrote Margaret, "the more I am satisfied that McClellan is irretrievably gone, and has lost the greatest chance any man ever had on this continent."

From Aquia Landing Meade traveled by rail to a camp in Falmouth opposite Fredericksburg, where he finally found his regiments. He rode among his men, stopping to say a few words at each camp and receiving their cheers. "I really believe the whole command, officers and men, were sincerely glad to see me back," he reported with some satisfaction.[11] He also met with the hearty and gregarious Ambrose Burnside and was struck by the general's affability and devotion to McClellan.

Like other members of the Army of the Potomac, Meade felt little affection for John Pope. He had known him back in Mexico—they had been messmates at one point—and Meade had considered Pope a braggart even then. He had scoffed when newspapers printed some of Pope's Mexican letters in which the young lieutenant had reported how the entire army admired his gallantry. In a letter home to Margaret, Meade had written that if such were the case, "the army never knew it till after the letter so stating the fact came back in the papers. Lieutenant Pope behaved very well, and did his duty, but nothing more than the rest of the army did."[12]

Now Pope had to deal with Robert E. Lee, even as Lee was deciding how to deal with Pope. Lee's analysis of McClellan's character told him the Army of the Potomac offered little threat to Richmond, so he turned his attention farther north and searched for an opportunity to attack the new arrival. Stonewall Jackson drew blood on August 9 when he defeated outnumbered forces under Banks at the Battle of Cedar Mountain. Under this threat Pope felt compelled to withdraw from his position along the Rapidan River and move back behind the Rappahannock. Meade was one general who experienced a little schadenfreude at Pope's discomfort. "It appears that General Pope has been obliged to show *his back* to the enemy and to select a *line of retreat*," he noted on August 21. "I expect that in a few days we will have exciting times, and expect hourly orders for us either to hurry up to Pope's rescue or to fall back upon Washington."[13]

As the armies glowered at each other from opposite sides of the Rappahannock, Lee probed for a weakness in the Federal position. He knew he must move before McClellan could evacuate his army from the peninsula and combine forces with Pope. For his part, Pope felt a need to maintain contact with Fredericksburg so he could link up with elements of McClellan's army as they arrived from Aquia Landing. At the same time he needed to stretch his limited forces along the Rappahannock to prevent Lee from crossing.

Lee finally decided on a typically bold strategy. He sent Stonewall Jackson and his "foot cavalry" on one of its trademark rapid marches, a long, roundabout journey north around Pope's flank and then east through Thoroughfare Gap in the Bull Run Mountains. That put him behind Pope and in a position to sever the Union army's line of communications and supply. Longstreet remained along the Rappahannock to keep Pope pinned in place.

Jackson and his men broke camp and set out early on the morning of August 25. The next night they captured Bristoe Station on the Orange and Alexandria Railroad, and then on August 27 they moved north up to Manassas Junction, destroying Union stores and cutting the vital rail link. Pope quickly swung into action in an attempt to get Jackson, determined, he said, "to bag the whole crowd."[14] But to do that he expected to receive plenty of reinforcements from the Army of the Potomac.

While it may be saying too much to claim that McClellan contrived to see Pope beaten and embarrassed, it's fair to say that he did not support Pope as readily as he could have. "I have a strong idea that Pope will be thrashed during the coming week—& very badly whipped he will be & ought to be—such a villain as he is ought to bring defeat upon any cause that employs him," McClellan peevishly wrote to his wife.[15] Pope waited and waited to receive reinforcements from the Army of the Potomac, but they were slow in coming. Porter's V Corps and Samuel Heintzelman's III Corps reached Aquia Landing on August 22, but McClellan delayed the movement of the corps under Franklin and Sumner until it was too late for them to help Pope. At the very least, McClellan demonstrated a lack of initiative. "But to suggest that McClellan actively schemed to see Pope destroyed requires evidence that McClellan's performance in moving his troops was slower, more deliberate than usual," wrote John J. Hennessy in *Return to Bull Run*, his detailed account of the campaign. "It was not. He was always slow, always cautious and usually grumbly and insolent."[16] In short, McClellan was behaving exactly in character.

Reynolds's division reached Pope first. Meade's brigade began to move from its camp near Falmouth on the night of August 21. It had been provided with only two wagons for transportation, so anything the men couldn't carry had to be left behind, including all the hospital tents and supplies. Making things worse, the march began in a night of drenching rain. The next day brought wet, tropical heat, with temperatures reaching 100 degrees Fahrenheit. Reynolds called it a "severe and arduous march."[17] Members of the Bucktails, some of them recovering from wounds and others recently exchanged after suffering in Confederate prisons, slipped from the ranks to drink from scum-covered puddles along the route. Finally, the brigade halted and refused to move. Meade rode back in person to handle the men. It was the first real test of his leadership. "Considerate as ever, he realized the calibre of the men with whom he had to deal," read a division history. "Briefly he told them that he recognized their sufferings; but explained that upon their reaching a certain point, on a certain day, depended the safety of a portion of General Pope's army and the lives of thousands of soldiers. Then he asked them what they wished him to do; and ringing down the line came the answer: 'Go ahead.'"[18]

During the grueling march, Sgt. Archibald Hill of the 8th Pennsylvania Reserves had a less pleasant encounter with Meade. The sergeant had just broken ranks to see if he could get some water at a nearby farmhouse when he heard someone shouting at him. "I turned toward the road and saw General Meade, who was riding at the head of the column, beckoning to me in a decidedly savage manner," Hill recounted. "'Come back here!' he cried.

"There was nothing left for me but to obey; for I knew that the old general carried a brace of strong-shooting revolvers; and how was I to know that he wouldn't blaze away at me if I didn't return?" Hill wrote. "I, therefore, retraced my steps, wishing General Meade's spectacles at the bottom of the well at that house, and three pints of water in my canteen in exchange for them." In a footnote Hill explained, "General Meade usually wore a pair of spectacles, and it was through them that he saw me; his powers of perception were astonishing."[19]

On August 23 Reynolds's division reached Pope at Rappahannock Station, where his division was attached to McDowell's corps. Four days later Pope sent the army on its hunting expedition to bag Jackson. However, Jackson refused to wait for Pope to come and get him. Once his men had feasted on the Union stores at Manassas Junction, Jackson had the remaining supplies destroyed and then slipped away to the north. He found a perfect place to lie in wait near a crossroads hamlet called Groveton, by the old Bull Run battlefield. Jackson hid his command in the woods behind an abandoned railroad cut just north of the Warrenton Turnpike. Then he waited—for Longstreet to come through Thoroughfare Gap and join him, and for a chance to attack the Union army.

Sergeant Hill, for one, shared Pope's conviction that the army was about to "bag" Jackson. He and his regiment marched through Virginia with high expectations. "We began to think that General Pope was a very great man, and that, after this mighty achievement, the great warlike deeds of Alexander the Great, of Julius Caesar, and Napoleon Bonaparte would be cast entirely into the shade—would sink into gloomy oblivion."[20]

But it didn't take long for his great expectations to tumble back to earth. Hill's regiment was marching down the Warrenton Turnpike the next day, and as the Union formations passed Groveton a pair of Confederate cannons opened fire. Hill saw one shell explode near him, killing and mangling several soldiers, including a close friend "who was torn in a shocking manner."[21] Reynolds ordered Meade's brigade forward. Union artillery began returning the rebel fire, and

Meade sent some of the Bucktails ahead to skirmish. More men followed in an attempt to flank the enemy position. The rebels pulled back. Reynolds had no idea that Jackson's entire force lay hidden in the trees beyond the turnpike and assumed the Confederates were just a small band protecting a wagon train he had seen in the distance. McDowell agreed with Reynolds's assessment; the Federals resumed their march up the Warrenton Turnpike.

Late that afternoon Reynolds heard the sounds of battle to the rear. He turned the division around and rode back to survey the situation. What he had heard was the standoff between Jackson's and Gibbon's men near the Brawner Farm. By the time Meade and his brigade reached the field, darkness had ended the fighting.

Hill's hopeful feelings about Pope had deflated by the time he fell into an exhausted sleep that night. Accounts circulated among the soldiers of Jackson's raid on Manassas Junction and another attack Jeb Stuart had made on Catlett Station, where he captured Pope's formal uniform coat, among other things. It sounded as though "the rebels had been 'taking pleasure-rides in their carriages all around us,'" Hill recalled. "I felt sure that the morrow would be a terrible day, and I just wondered, by the way, whether I would be living at that time of night one day later."[22] No doubt hundreds of men shared his gloomy sentiments.

◆ ◆ ◆

Meade had missed the First Battle of Bull Run, but he had ridden over this ground before, back in April when he and the rest of McDowell's corps were being held back from the peninsula to protect Washington. Had he suspected he might fight here one day? "A more beautiful ground for a battle never existed," he wrote then; "country open, with rolling ground of gentle slopes, offering equal advantages to the attacking and attacked."[23]

The immediate landscape hasn't changed since then, but its surroundings certainly have. The modern world now laps at the battlefield's boundaries. Drive south down the Sudley Road from the National Park Service visitors center on Henry House Hill and you'll run smack dab into the twenty-first century and its highways, gas stations, fast-food restaurants, and businesses that stretch all the way down to the former site of Manassas Junction.

Yet the battlefield's overall geography remains reasonably untouched. Two major roads divide the Bull Run battlefield neatly into four quadrants, like the x- and y-axes on a graph that's been tilted just a bit to one side. The x-axis, running almost west to east, is today's Route 29, also known as the Lee Highway. During the war this was the Warrenton Turnpike, a modern macadam road that ran from Warrenton, through Gainesville just west of the battlefield, and then crossed Bull Run on a narrow stone bridge in the direction of Centreville. The y-axis, running roughly north and south, is the Sudley Road, which crosses the Bull Run to the north at Sudley Ford.

Then, as now, a large stone house stood where the two roads intersected. The Stone House was a prominent landmark that served as a hospital during both battles. Two wounded Union soldiers from the second battle scratched their names on the floor upstairs, and you can still see their names.

Second Battle of Bull Run: August 30

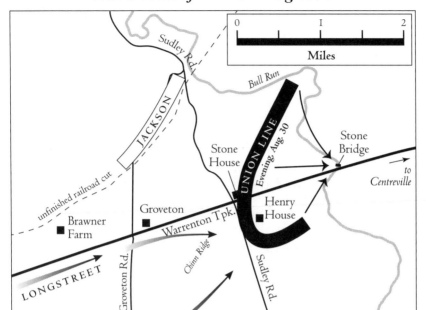

The Stone House faces across the highway in the direction of Henry House Hill, the center of the first battle and the place where Thomas Jonathan Jackson became "Stonewall." Fellow Confederate general Barnard Bee provided the christening when he yelled to his soldiers, "Look men! There is Jackson standing like a stone wall!"[24] Jackson won immortality; Bee fell mortally wounded and died the next day. A somewhat modernistic statue of Jackson dominates the field here today, not far from the colonnaded visitors center.

For two days much of the fighting at the second battle raged along the unfinished railroad cut in front of Jackson's position. The cut runs at an angle from the Sudley Road down toward the Lee Highway. After Jackson announced his presence here with the fighting at the Brawner Farm, Pope planned to destroy him by attacking the Confederate left along the railroad cut while Fitz John Porter and his V Corps, recently arrived from the peninsula, moved up and crushed Jackson's right. The fighting was hot and furious along the cut on August 29, but much to Pope's rage and frustration, Porter never attacked. Pope refused to believe that a major obstacle stood in Porter's way—James Longstreet and his men. Accompanied by Lee, Longstreet had detached his corps from the Rappahannock and followed Jackson's footsteps through Thoroughfare Gap. Longstreet's twenty-five thousand men reached the field sometime on the morning of August 29 (the exact time would become the subject of great debate) and linked up with Jackson's right. The Confederate lines now extended in a great curve that looked something like the jaws of a bear trap—with John Pope playing the unlucky bear.

Pope wanted Reynolds to attack Jackson's right and rear. Like Porter, though, Reynolds realized Pope apparently did not know that another Confederate force had arrived on this part of the battlefield. He ordered Seymour and Conrad Jackson to move their brigades forward, but stiff resistance sent them falling back again. Reynolds sent word to Pope that a considerable force threatened the Union left. Pope refused to believe it.

◆ ◆ ◆

If not for the fighting here, the railroad cut would have vanished long ago, with the land taken over by development. Even during the war the cut was little more than a reminder of a failed capitalistic endeavor, an attempt by one railroad company to bypass its rival's exorbitant fees. Today it's a fading scar across the landscape that passes through woods and forest. Two trails, dotted with historical markers outlining the vicious fighting that took place here, follow its course. After discovering the bones by the Brawner Farm, I follow the Unfinished Railroad Trail through the cold and rain, all by myself in this somewhat eerie landscape. I scare up a wild turkey that races like a cartoon character down the trail ahead of me. It dashes around a curve in the trail, looking as though it should be accompanied by skidding sound effects, and disappears from view. A little farther on I spy white flags flashing in the woods. They're the tails of two deer that bound across fallen tree trunks and disappear into the tangled undergrowth.

Union troops came closest to breaking through the lines near here when Brig. Gen. Cuvier Grover's brigade made a desperate bayonet charge. Over the course of twenty bloody minutes Grover lost 407 men, a third of his command, before he had to withdraw. A marker along the trail tells me part of the story: "Without artillery and without supports, our men advanced," recalled Chaplain Warren Cudworth of the 1st Massachusetts. "We reached a railroad bank when from the rear of the embankment arose the enemy. They poured a tremendous volley into our lines. The effect was terrible. Men dropped in scores, writhing and trying to crawl back, or lying stone-dead where they fell. The Union line began to waver and sullenly fell back into the forest again."

The rain has stopped by the time I hike the second trail that follows the track of the unfinished railroad. This is the Deep Cut Trail, and the markers here focus on the events of August 30. The trail passes through cleared fields that look like a blasted heath or a setting from Tolkien. A few solitary trees stand in the clearing, and patches of woods look silent and ominous here and there. Crowning the rise in the middle of the field is the Second Bull Run Monument, dedicated on June 10, 1865. Made of large bricks and tapering to a flat top, it's been weathered, battered, and pocked by time. I've seen etchings of this monument in *Battles and Leaders of the Civil War*, so it's like encountering a familiar face.

On August 30 the fighting was hot and furious all along here. Porter had finally moved forward to take part in one final assault on Jackson's position. Pope was convinced, despite all evidence to the contrary, that the Confederates were retreating. He continued to ignore the obvious fact of Longstreet's presence on his left. But the Union's attacks on the railroad cut here were as fruitless as they had been the day before. "The Rebel infantry poured in their volleys, and we were scarcely a dozen feet from the muzzles of their muskets," said Cpl. John Slater of the 13th New York. "Oh, it was terrible! For twenty minutes the shattered regiments held the slope swept by a hurricane of death, and each minute the bullets hummed like swarming bees, and then those yet alive and able to do so received orders to fall back. We who fell—the dead, dying, and the disabled—held the field."[25] At one point the Confederate defenders ran so low on ammunition that they started hurling stones at their assailants. The Union soldiers replied in kind.

For a time the desperate Union assault threatened to break Jackson's line, and the proud Stonewall had to send a message to Longstreet asking for reinforcements. Finally, the Union soldiers had to fall back, retreating across a field raked by shells fired from cannons on a rise to the Confederate right. The final assault on the railroad cut had been a slaughter—beginning, middle, and end. It was terrible and it was hopeless, especially after Longstreet finally put his men into motion and began pushing forward to close the bear trap on Pope's army.

● ● ●

As part of Reynolds's division, Meade's brigade had participated in an attack on Jackson's right behind the railroad cut late on August 29, but without success. Once again darkness ended the fighting.

August 30 dawned quietly, under dull, oppressive cloud cover. Pope wanted Reynolds to push his men forward across the Warrenton Turnpike and attack. The enemy's resistance was so fierce Reynolds found it hard to share Pope's belief that the rebels were retreating. He rode forward to see things for himself and was startled to encounter a line of enemy cavalry that was obviously screening masses of infantry. Enemy skirmishers thought Reynolds offered a terrific target, and he made a mad dash back to his own lines as bullets hissed past him and killed his orderly. What he had seen, though, convinced him that the Confederates were certainly not in retreat.

Reynolds's men held a rise called Chinn Ridge. After Jackson repulsed Porter's attack on the railroad cut, McDowell ordered Reynolds to leave the ridge and move north of the turnpike to support Porter's retreating troops. That meant the Union left was only thinly defended against Longstreet's impending onslaught. John J. Hennessy called McDowell's move "the single most important tactical error of the battle,"[26] but like Pope, McDowell remained in denial about Longstreet's presence and unaware that the Confederates were now in a position to crush Pope's army and prevent it from retreating up the Warrenton Turnpike to the relative safety of Centreville.

Pope finally realized the gravity of his situation and prepared to retreat. Extricating himself from the trap would require Union forces to hold Henry House Hill long enough to allow the army to fall back safely along the Warrenton Turnpike. Seymour and Meade formed their men on top of the hill near the ruins of the house. (The widow Henry, too much of an invalid to evacuate her home, had been killed there during the first battle.) They received help from George Sykes's regulars and Brig. Gen. Robert Milroy's brigade. Their defensive line stretched along the same grounds that the Confederates had held at the First Battle of Bull Run.

As the day advanced into the late afternoon, the dimming sun obscured by dense clouds of dust and smoke, the victorious Confederates advanced from Chinn Ridge in the direction of the Stone House. Reynolds saw an opportunity to hit them on the flank. He ordered his men to attack down the slope of the hill toward the Sudley Road. When Sergeant Hill saw Reynolds, Seymour, and Meade on horseback observing the charge, he thought "they appeared to be enjoying themselves prodigiously." Perhaps they were. More than likely they anxiously realized that the fate of Pope's army was in their hands. Reynolds rode up to lead the division and jumped off his horse to grab up a fallen regimental flag. Remounting, he waved the banner. "On, my brave fellows—on!" he shouted.[27]

"The scene at this moment was the most magnificently grand man ever beheld," wrote a soldier in the 2nd Pennsylvania Reserves. "In the van, towering above the masses, rode the gallant Reynolds, waving aloft a standard shot from its staff. Near him was the cool-headed Meade, who in the heat of battle almost became excited as he urged the men forward, and next followed Seymour with his brigade, who by the gentle waving of his hand restrained the ardor of his men and preserved the distinctness of the lines.

"Onward we pressed, pushing the enemy into the woods, when their reserve of five or six lines deep opened upon us a withering fire, while several batteries of artillery that had obtained our exact range, poured into us their flaming missiles, which bursting in our midst, produced fearful havoc."[28]

Hill described the havoc the projectiles created among the Union lines. One exploded so close to him he thought it would tear off the top of his head. "A moment after, another shell went screaming over our heads, struck a wounded man who was limping from the field leaning on the arm of a comrade, and, exploding, tore him to fragments—almost to nothing—while his comrade was uninjured." The survivor dropped his gun and ran, blind with panic, until he collided with a tree. The blow seemed to restore his senses. He picked up another gun from the ground and rejoined the Union lines.[29]

The Confederates pushed Reynolds's division back, and McDowell feared that the Federals would lose the vitally important hill. An encounter with General Milroy, brought to a state of crazed incoherence, didn't lessen his anxiety. Then he received a message from "that intelligent as well as gallant officer Brigadier-General Meade," which said that if he could get some reinforcements, he could not only hold the position but drive out the enemy. "Meade shall have reinforcements!" McDowell declared[30], and he rushed in more men.

The fighting lasted until dark. Sergeant Hill, for one, thought they had gained a victory—but then the men received orders to fall back to the turnpike and retreat to Centreville. For the Union, the Second Battle of Bull Run had been no more glorious than the first one. But it had not turned into a rout, and Pope managed to extricate his army and move it in reasonably good order to Centreville.

Lee made one more attempt to outflank Pope, and in fighting near Chantilly during a ferocious thunderstorm, Union generals Philip Kearny and Isaac Stevens were killed. But Washington remained safe.

Meade wrote home from Centreville on August 31: "I write to advise you that after three days' continuous fighting I am all safe and well."[31] Meade picked up his narrative a few days later, praising the work of the reserves but not the Union effort as a whole. "In a few words, we have been, as usual, *out-maneuvered* and *out-numbered*, and though not actually defeated, yet compelled to fall back on Washington for its defense and our own safety. On these recent battle-fields I claim, as before, to have done my duty. My services, then, should, I think, add to those previously performed, and that I may now fairly claim the command of a division."[32]

Second Bull Run was the Civil War's bloodiest battle to date, but that record would be topped soon enough. Some thirty-three hundred men from both sides had been killed. Maybe the bones I discovered on the trail by the Brawner Farm belonged to one of them.

CHAPTER 5
The Maryland Campaign

Dead soldiers lie in front of the Dunker Church after the Battle of Antietam
LIBRARY OF CONGRESS

♦ ♦ ♦

The Federals didn't have much time to lick their wounds before word reached Washington that Lee had aimed the Army of Northern Virginia north toward Maryland. General Pope, however, would not get a rematch. Despite the heated arguments of his cabinet and his own grave misgivings, Lincoln decided to put McClellan back in command of a unified Army of the Potomac. "It is something of a triumph that my enemies have been put down so completely," McClellan gloated to his wife on September 9—but he was not talking about the Confederates. He was talking about Generals Pope and McDowell. Pope returned to the west, but not before he lashed out at one of his own enemies, Fitz John Porter. He had Porter tried by court-martial on various charges related to his conduct at Second Bull Run, including not attacking Jackson on August 29.

To his credit, once Pope was out of the picture, McClellan launched into a blur of activity as he reorganized and reequipped his demoralized army. Whatever his other faults, he was a great organizer. Morale began climbing when the army learned that Little Mac was back in the saddle. "From extreme sadness we passed in a twinkling to a delirium of delight," wrote George Kimball of the 12th Massachusetts. "A Deliverer had come. A real 'rainbow of promise' had appeared suddenly in the dark political sky. The feeling in our division upon the return of General McClellan had its counterpart in all the others, for the Army of the Potomac loved him as it never loved any other leader."[1]

McClellan's reorganization made an immediate impact on Meade. His corps commander, the unfortunate Irvin McDowell, had lost one Bull Run too many and with it any remaining confidence of his men. So McDowell headed out and Maj. Gen. Joseph Hooker received his command, now called I Corps of the Army of the Potomac. Hooker had received the nickname "Fighting Joe" because of a proofreading error—a newspaper article was supposed to have read, "Fighting—Joe Hooker," but the omitted dash gave him a nickname that stuck. It was an apt label, too, because Hooker was a clearly a fighter—and he had dash. "General Hooker's was a face which lighted up when the battle began," wrote New York Tribune correspondent George Smalley, who observed him closely during the Maryland campaign. "The man seemed transformed. He rode carelessly on the march, but sat straight up in his saddle as the martial music of the bullets whistled past him."[2]

The face that lit up in battle was clean-shaven and florid, and Hooker was a "tall, fine-looking soldier, one of the finest looking in the Army," as one of his subordinates described him, with "skin as clear and a hand as small as many a lady" and "clear blue eyes."[3] He also had a somewhat raffish reputation, with a taste for the ladies and the bottle. Although there's no truth to the oft-told story that prostitutes became known as "hookers" because of Fighting Joe's proclivities, he did enjoy a drink and a good time. He was also quite adept at undermining his superiors, a talent he put to good use in the following months.

McClellan organized his army into three sections: a center and two wings. The left wing, under Maj. Gen. William B. Franklin, included a division of the IV Corps under Darius Couch and Franklin's own XI Corps. Old Edwin Sumner commanded the center, which had his II Corps and the XII under venerable Joseph Mansfield, the man who had supervised construction of Fort Brown on the Rio Grande sixteen years earlier. He was now almost sixty and had the white hair and beard to prove it. The right wing became the responsibility of Maj. Gen. Ambrose Burnside. It consisted of Hooker's I Corps and Burnside's own IX Corps, now under the direct command of Brig. Gen. Jesse L. Reno.

Burnside was a big and gregarious man who had limited confidence in his own military abilities. Unlike Hooker's hookers, it appears there is truth to the story that sideburns got their name from the garlands that decorated Burnside's face. He was personally close to McClellan, and after the failure on the peninsula he had turned down Lincoln's offer to take command of the Army of the Potomac out of loyalty (and perhaps a clear sense of his own limitations). He turned down another offer following Pope's debacle.

Meade liked Burnside. "He is quite different from McClellan in his manners, having great affability and a winning way with him that attracts instead of re-pelling strangers," he noted.[4] Like the rest of the army, however, Meade eventually recognized that for all of Burnside's outward heartiness, he lacked internal stiffening. As one officer noted, "Burnside represented a well-recognized type in all armies, the California-peach class of men, handsome, ingratiating manners, and noted for a soldierly bearing,—that is, square shoulders, full breast, and the capacity on duty to wear a grim countenance, while off duty all smiles and a keen eye to please,— who, in times of peace, not only in our country but everywhere, invariably land in high places, and who almost as invariably make utter failures when they are given commands on the breaking out of war."[5]

McClellan started a slow and cautious move north. During the march Archibald F. Hill of the 8th Pennsylvania Reserves witnessed an example of Meade's furious temper. He watched as Meade posted a cavalryman to guard a peach tree to make sure the passing soldiers did not steal any of the fruit. Meade then left to make some inquiries at the owner's farmhouse. He returned just in time to see the cavalryman succumb to temptation and steal peaches from the very tree he was supposed to be guarding. Meade's temper flared. "You mercenary villain," Hill reported him exclaiming, "I set you to guard that tree, and—and—you—" Speechless with rage, he drew his sword and rode at the terrified sentinel. "I'll cut your head off!" he cried and struck the man on his neck—but with the flat of his sword. The terrified man nearly fell from his horse.

Meade sheathed his sword. "Don't you think I ought to kill you?" he de-manded. "Yes, sir," the man managed to reply. With that the general rode away and, as Hill related, "I imagined I saw a slight smile play about his firm lips."[6] He had made his point. It would not be the last time that Meade drew his sword against his own men.

Hooker's corps reached the outskirts of Frederick, Maryland, on September 12, the day Meade learned that he had received command of the division. This was a position he had coveted in his letters home, yet its acquisition left a bitter taste in Meade's mouth. The promotion happened because Lee's move north had thrown Pennsylvania governor Andrew Gregg Curtin into a panic. Curtin de-manded that Washington do something to protect the commonwealth, so Halleck dispatched Reynolds to Harrisburg to raise militia. Meade took Reynolds's place at the head of the Pennsylvania Reserves.

Hooker did not have a high opinion of the division, feeling they had broken and run at Glendale, and he protested the decision to send Reynolds to Pennsylvania. His reaction made the proud Meade bristle. He had finally received the division he felt he deserved, but now it seemed his superiors felt he wasn't up to it. When he ran into Brig. Gen. Seth Williams, the army's assistant adjutant general, Meade told him that he felt Hooker's response to Reynolds's removal reflected on his ability to command.[7] In his letters home to Margaret he complained bitterly of his "humiliation and sorrow" over the way he had been treated.[8]

Lee's Frederick sojourn had some real consequences for the Confederate general's immediate future, though. Following the rebels' departure a Union corporal spied an object in the field where his regiment was camping. It was a paper wrapped around three cigars. The corporal's eyes must have popped out of his head when he began reading the handwritten document. The paper quickly made its way up the chain of command until it reached McClellan (the cigars were apparently smoked somewhere en route). McClellan read the paper with increasing excitement. "Now I know what to do!" he exclaimed.

The paper was a copy of Lee's General Order 191, in which the general outlined his plans for the Maryland campaign. This copy was intended for Gen. D. H. Hill, but the courier must have dropped it by accident. Hill, who had received a separate copy from Stonewall Jackson's headquarters, never knew that this copy from Lee had gone missing. No one else did, either. If the nameless courier ever realized his blunder, he kept it to himself.

Lee's order outlined another audacious plan. He had sent more than half of his army to capture Harpers Ferry and its garrison, which presented a potential threat to his rear. A division under Maj. Gen. Lafayette McLaws targeted Maryland Heights, the peak that dominated Harpers Ferry from across the Potomac, while Brig. Gen. John Walker aimed at Loudoun Heights, an equally imposing position that reared above Harpers Ferry from across the Shenandoah River. At the same time, Stonewall Jackson was taking fourteen thousand men on a roundabout journey from Frederick, across South Mountain, through Boonsboro, across the Potomac River, and on to Martinsburg, where he would eliminate a Union garrison and then approach Harpers Ferry from the west. Once all these Confederate forces, numbering about twenty-three thousand men, were in place, the twelve thousand Federals in Harpers Ferry, under Col. Dixon Miles, would have no option but surrender. Lee gambled that his men could take Harpers Ferry and reunite with him before McClellan attacked. It was a risky undertaking, but Lee wagered on his opponent's timid character. He expected McClellan to move slowly and with great caution.

He did not expect McClellan to discover his plans, however. Now McClellan realized he had a heaven-sent opportunity to attack the separate elements of Lee's army and defeat them piecemeal—"in detail," as the terminology puts it. Later that night McClellan showed Lee's order to Gen. John Gibbon. "Here is a paper with which if I cannot whip Bobbie Lee, I will be willing to go home," he gloated.[9] Yet rather than grab the opportunity fate had dropped into his lap, McClellan dithered. Not until eighteen hours after he had received his unexpected intelligence coup did the first units of the Army of the Potomac begin sluggishly stirring.

Meade and his division left their camp near the Monocacy River east of Frederick on the morning of September 14. They marched through town and along the Hagerstown Turnpike, over the ridge of the Catoctin Mountains and down the other side into Middletown, today a pretty little town nestled between the Catoctins and South Mountain to the west. Squint a little bit and you can almost believe the place hasn't changed a bit since artist Alfred Waud sketched the army passing down its main street in September 1862. When I stop on a splendid but breezy September afternoon, I pause to read a roadside marker on Main Street across from the blindingly white Zion Lutheran Church, which served as a Union observation post. The marker describes the reaction Stonewall Jackson received here. "In Middletown two very pretty girls with ribbons of red, white and blue in their hair and small Union flags in their hands, came out of their house as we passed, ran to the curb-stone, and laughingly waved their colors defiantly in the face of the General," wrote Henry Kyd Douglas in his memoir, *I Rode with Stonewall*. "He bowed and lifted his cap and with a quiet smile said to his staff, 'We evidently have no friends in this town.'"[10]

The reception wasn't all sweetness and light for the Union forces, either. Capt. Francis Adams Donaldson of the 118th Pennsylvania recorded that townspeople removed the handles from their pumps so the soldiers could not get water. The men took their revenge by filling the pumps with rocks and dirt. "This was the first time I ever heard threats of vengeance against a town," Donaldson wrote, "and I feel satisfied should the army have occasion to again pass this way they will destroy it."[11]

By 1:00 p.m. the Pennsylvania Reserves were outside town and facing the long green hump of South Mountain, which rises about thirteen hundred feet at its highest point here. The wooded ridgeline is punctuated by a series of gaps that provide slightly easier routes over the hump. Frosttown and Turner's Gaps lie to the north. Fox's Gap is about a mile south of Turner's, and Crampton's Gap lies even farther south. McClellan directed Franklin and his left wing to take Crampton's Gap and push on over the mountain, down into Pleasant Valley beyond, and then on to relieve Harpers Ferry. Burnside's right wing would tackle the gaps to the north, with Reno and the IX Corps taking Fox's Gap and Hooker's I Corps, including Meade's division, swinging farther north to attack the Confederates' left flank around Frosttown Gap.

George Kimball of the 12th Massachusetts recalled seeing McClellan on the road outside Middletown as his unit marched toward South Mountain. The general sat on horseback like an equestrian statue made flesh. "As each organization passed the general, the men became apparently forgetful of everything but their love for him," noted Kimball. "They cheered and cheered again, until they became so hoarse they could cheer no longer. It seemed as if an intermission had been declared in order that a reception might be tendered to the general-in-chief." McClellan remained impassive, surrounded by cheering men, many of whom stopped to stroke his horse's legs and mane. McClellan pointed dramatically toward South Mountain, smoke already rising from the fighting as Reno

Maryland Campaign

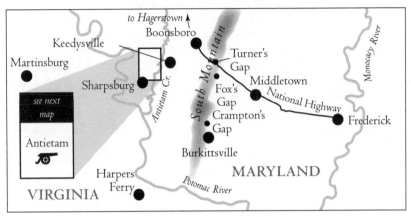

and the IX Corps went into action. "It was like a great scene in a play, with the roar of the guns for an accompaniment," Kimball recalled.[12]

Based on his close reading of Lee's order, McClellan expected that James Longstreet's men were lying in wait just on the other side of South Mountain in Boonsboro. In fact, Lee had altered his plans so that Longstreet and most of his men were actually another twelve miles away in Hagerstown. For a time, only the cavalry under Jeb Stuart defended South Mountain, until D. H. Hill, whose division *was* at Boonsboro, arrived. Hill established a headquarters at an old stone inn the locals knew as the Mountain House. (The inn still stands on Alternate Route 40 today and does business as the South Mountain Inn.) Hill must have looked east with a sinking heart. "The marching columns extended back far as eye could see in the distance," he later recalled, "but many of the troops had already arrived and were in double lines of battle, and those advancing were taking up positions as fast as they arrived. It was a grand and glorious spectacle, and it was impossible to look at it without admiration. I had never seen so tremendous an army before, and I did not see one like it afterward."[13] When writing about this battle for *Century* magazine, Hill also complimented his adversary: "Meade was one of our most dreaded foes; he was always in deadly earnest, and he eschewed all trifling."

Meade moved his men to the right of the turnpike (today's Alternate Route 40) and formed his three brigades to the army's right, at the north end of South Mountain. He planned to swing around and outflank the Confederate left. He placed the 1st Brigade, under Seymour, on the right; the 3rd, commanded by Col. Thomas Gallagher, in the center; and Col. Albert Magilton's 2nd Brigade on the left. The Bucktails moved in front as skirmishers. Some locals thought this all looked like great entertainment and came out to watch the battle. Like the ill-fated folk who went to see the fighting at First Bull Run, they received more excitement than they had bargained for when rebel cannons opened up from high on the hill. "The children lay down upon the ground, the women shrieked and the men displayed wondrous agility in leaping the fences, which caused considerable amusement among us," noted one soldier.[14]

The task ahead of them was anything but amusing. The men of the Pennsylvania Reserves had to climb up rough and broken terrain that would make it difficult for different regiments to see each other as they advanced. Back with McClellan, staff officer David Strother watched their progress. "Slowly trailing across the open ground," he wrote, "now entering a piece of wood, and again emerging on the upper side, winding over spurs and up ravines, the march resembled the course of a black serpent with glittering scales stealing upon its prey."[15]

The Bucktails were the serpent's head. Behind them the 11th Pennsylvania Reserves pushed forward against stubborn resistance. They received unexpected encouragement from one of their corporals "who was possessed of great powers of mimickry." The soldier "crowed lustily, like a cock uttering the note of triumph. The familiar sound, heard amid the pauses of the battle, so inspired the men that they went forward with renewed zeal to assured victory."[16]

Archibald Hill of the 8th Pennsylvania Reserves recalled moving forward at about 4:00 in the afternoon and toiling up a steep slope, only to discover at the top that it was just a ridge that descended into a little valley before ascending the mountain's main body. A stone wall stood at the mountain's base. "When within fifty yards of the stone-fence, a murderous fire of musketry was opened upon us by the rebels, who lay concealed behind it, and swarms of bullets whistled about our ears," Hill recalled. "With a wild shout, we dashed forward—almost upward—while volley after volley was poured upon us; but we heeded it not; we rushed madly on. The rebels, intimidated by our voices, and taken aback by our recklessness and disregard of their bullets, began to give way. We reached the stone-fence, and sprang over. The rebels reformed among the rocks, and fought with remarkable obstinacy."[17]

The 5th Pennsylvania Reserves also fought at the stone wall. "Colonel, put your regiment into that corn-field and hurt somebody!" Seymour told the regiment's colonel. "I will, general, and I'll catch one alive for you," he replied. He was as good as his word. His regiment charged over the wall and captured eleven prisoners. As Josiah Sypher described it in his history of the Pennsylvania Reserves, "From behind every rock, tree, and log, they forced the enemy with ball and bayonet; the color bearers struggled up the mountain side, and the men rallied round the flag, cheer after cheer responded to the rebel volleys from the summit; onward and upward the fiery line rolled and surged; the bewildered rebels saw in astonishment the smoke and flame rising from rock to rock."[18]

"Steadily the line advanced up the mountain side," Meade wrote in his official report, "where the enemy was posted behind trees and rocks, from whence he was slowly, but gradually, dislodged, Seymour first gaining the crest of the hill, and driving the enemy to the left along the ridge, where he was met with the fire of the other two brigades." Worried about being outflanked, Meade requested reinforcements, but the fighting was just about over by the time they arrived.[19] By then darkness was approaching, and the Union troops bedded down for a tense night on the mountaintop. When dawn broke the next day the victorious Federals discovered that their foes had slipped down the other side, as though they had vanished in the heavy mist that cloaked South Mountain on September 15, 1862.

As I explore South Mountain almost a century and a half later, I suspect the soldiers who fought here in 1862 would still recognize the landscape. It is still rugged and steep, and some of the roads are very narrow and curvy. I can't imagine what it must have been like to move uphill while other people on these slopes are trying to kill you.

People seeking a battlefield with lots of monuments might want to visit someplace else. Much of South Mountain remains private property, as copious No Trespassing signs indicate. That's not to say that everything here is private or that monuments are entirely missing. South of Fox's Gap, in the woods just off an access road on the ridgeline, I am surprised to find a beautiful monument to the North Carolina troops who fought and died here. Atop it is a statue of a dying soldier lying on his back, one hand clutching his wounded side and the other grasping a flag. The monument sits all by itself in a little clearing, near a stone wall that looks out onto some open land. It would have been a good place to fight a battle. Maybe that's what Confederate general Samuel Garland thought as he stood just a few yards from here, when a Union bullet struck him. Garland bled to death at the Mountain House.

The capture of Fox's Gap had been the responsibility of Reno and the IX Corps. Reno died here that day, hit by a Confederate sharpshooter. A monument marks the spot where he fell, along the side of the aptly named Reno Monument Road, just north of the North Carolina monument. The fields across the road once belonged to a farmer named Daniel Wise. He returned to his war-ravaged home after the fighting and found that fifty-eight dead Confederates had been thrown down his well. A roadside marker down the hill indicates the spot where Reno died, lying beneath an oak tree that outlived him by 117 years, until a thunderstorm blew it down in 1979.

South Mountain is also the site of the first monument erected to commemorate the nation's first president. Originally constructed in 1827, the Washington Monument was little more than a pile of rubble by the time of the battle. Now nicely reconstructed, it looks like a big stone vase. You can climb up the rough-hewn stone stairs to an observation platform at the top for some breathtaking views across Maryland, Pennsylvania, and West Virginia. The Antietam battlefield is visible off in the distance. When my wife and I visit, we find two bird-watchers on the platform, peering at hawks and kestrels through their binoculars. It's long been a great observation post. During the South Mountain battle Confederate artilleryman E. Porter Alexander almost unleashed some artillery at the monument's ruins when he spotted some figures moving about up here, but a reconnaissance showed him that the people were local citizens who wanted to get a good view of the fighting. Some people never learn.

There are more personal reminders of the battle in a small museum that occupies a windowless log building near the parking lot. It includes a collection of Civil War firearms, most of them connected to the battle. One of them is an 1860 Colt army revolver that belonged to Cpl. Charles C. Goodwin of the 1st Maine Cavalry. The corporal was delivering a message to Reno when the general received his mortal wound. Goodwin grabbed the reins of the general's horse and led the dying man through the gathering darkness to the oak tree where he died.

The museum also has a Model 1841 Harpers Ferry rifled musket that belonged to Pvt. Samuel Slaton of the 12th Alabama Infantry's Company 5. The 12th belonged to the brigade commanded by Brig. Gen. Robert Emmett Rodes, which faced Meade's division during the battle. Slaton, who survived the war, had engraved his name on a brass plate on the musket's stock. A local man found it after the battle.

Late in the afternoon we drive through the little town of Burkittsville, which nestles against the mountain's southeastern flank and looks as though it hasn't changed a great deal in the past century and a half. During the battle its buildings served as hospitals. Crampton's Gap lies farther on. This was the objective for William Franklin and his twelve thousand men, who faced only about twelve hundred Confederates. Franklin took his time making his dispositions before he attacked, but he then moved quickly and pushed the defenders off the mountain. Still, the small Confederate force delayed the slow-moving Franklin long enough to give Stonewall Jackson time to bag the Union forces at Harpers Ferry. Jackson then hurried to rejoin Lee, leaving a division under A. P. Hill to mop things up.

Today woodsy Crampton's Gap is the site of Gathland State Park, on land that once belonged to George Alfred Townsend, the Civil War's youngest war correspondent. He was also a prolific writer and reporter who wrote under the pen name Gath, derived by adding an "h" to his initials and inspired by a biblical passage in 2 Samuel 1:20 that reads, "Tell it not in Gath, publish it not in the streets of Ashkelon." That's surely an odd motto for a journalist. After the war Townsend built a grand estate here. He called it Gathland and designed its many stone buildings, including a mausoleum he never used. When Townsend died in 1914 he was buried in Philadelphia's Laurel Hill Cemetery—the same cemetery where Meade lies.

Most of his buildings are gone now, but there's a little museum about the man and his legacy in one that remains. Townsend's strangest legacy, though, is the huge stone War Correspondents Arch he built here in 1896. It's an odd object, a classic Victorian-era "folly" designed to look like the ruins of castle battlements and decorated with unusual ornamentation. A statue of what looks like Pan crouches in a niche. Two terra cotta horse heads stare out from near the top. A bas-relief bust of Mercury appears just above a placard the reads, "Speed," balanced by the head of Apollo over the word "Heed." It's all very strange, its meaning lying beyond sober understanding.

On the other side of the arch Townsend had a sandstone tablet engraved with the names of his fellow Civil War correspondents. One name on the worn tablet jumps out at me: E. Crapsey. I know that Meade had an encounter with Mr. Crapsey, one that had some far-ranging consequences for the general's reputation. But all that would come later.

Meade emerged from South Mountain with his reputation enhanced. "I desire to make special mention of Brigadier General Meade for the great intelligence and gallantry displayed by him," Hooker noted in his official report. "Meade moved forward with great vigor and soon became engaged, driving everything before him."[20] It appears that Meade had earned the Pennsylvania Reserves a measure of vindication in the eyes of Joe Hooker. Bigger things—much bigger and far bloodier—lay just ahead across Antietam Creek near the town of Sharpsburg, Maryland.

◆ ◆ ◆

Ranger Keith Snyder strides across the field in front of the visitors center at Antietam National Battlefield with about twenty-five visitors trailing behind him. It's a gorgeous September day, sunny and warm, much like the weather here 148 years ago when bloody combat raged back and forth across the peaceful rolling fields in front of us. It's the kind of day that makes you fill your lungs with air and feel glad to be alive. That's sadly ironic, since we are here to remember the events of September 17, 1862, which still holds the unenviable record as the bloodiest single day in America's history. By the time the fighting ended here, around twenty-three thousand men were dead, wounded, or missing.

Snyder carries a clear plastic container with a green top. He tells us it's his "battlefield in a box." He places the container on the grass at his feet and has us stop and face east. We can see the blue line of South Mountain off in the distance. He points south toward the gap in the ridgeline that indicates the location of Harpers Ferry. He explains how Robert E. Lee sent part of his army, including Stonewall Jackson, off to capture the Federal garrison there. Another portion of Lee's army delayed the Army of the Potomac at South Mountain and then fell back across Antietam Creek, hidden behind trees in front of us, to take up a position where we are now.

Snyder opens up the box and removes a long blue-and-white rope. With the help of a volunteer he stretches it out on the ground in front of us. "This is Antietam Creek," he says. He rummages around in the box again and removes a brown rope. He stretches this out on the ground between us and the blue rope. "This is the Hagerstown Turnpike." The path of the real turnpike lies behind us, beyond the visitors center.

Out comes another brown rope. Snyder places it on the ground at a right angle to the Hagerstown rope so that it crosses the creek rope. This indicates the route of the Boonsboro Turnpike (today's Route 34), which passes through the little town of Sharpsburg to our south. He next removes a little white wooden block with tiny painted windows. This represents the Dunker Church, an important battlefield landmark. We can turn around and see the real Dunker Church—actually a re-creation of the real building, which collapsed back in 1921—across the old Hagerstown Turnpike. Snyder places the little church alongside the rope turnpike. He removes another piece of brown rope and lays it down like an L with its ends crossing the two turnpike ropes to make a crude rectangle. This indicates the course of a farm lane that connected the two pikes, a road that long use had sunk into the landscape. After the battle it became known as "Bloody Lane."

Snyder takes another blue-and-white rope and places it in a line behind us. This indicates the location of the Potomac River, which lay a few miles at Lee's back. Finally, Snyder removes three little wooden bridges and plops them down in their proper places across the Antietam rope. These represent the upper, middle, and lower bridges that spanned the creek. The Union army crossed the creek on the upper bridge. On the day of the battle Maj. Gen. Ambrose Burnside permanently affixed his name to the lower bridge when the men of his IX Corps forced a costly passage across it.

His battlefield map complete, Snyder sketches out the fighting that took place here, and as he talks the day's events take on a measure of coherence. He tells us to keep in mind a key characteristic for each commander. Robert E. Lee's is "movement." During the fighting he shifted his troops around the battlefield to place them where he needed them most to blunt the Union attacks. For McClellan the word is "piecemeal." Rather than launch coordinated attacks on each of Lee's flanks, the Union army went into the fighting division by division, giving Lee the opportunity to make the movements necessary to counter the Federal assaults.

The center of Lee's line was just about where we are standing in front of the visitors center. When Stonewall Jackson's men arrived from Harpers Ferry after making one of Jackson's characteristic forced marches, they formed the Confederate left. James Longstreet—his headquarters in the Piper farmhouse, just visible in a small hollow to the south—formed Lee's right. The Potomac River was behind the Confederates, with a gap of about four miles from the army's right and the river. Lee had only about 40,000 men to defend this position. McClellan and the Army of the Potomac numbered about 80,000. McClellan, of course, did not see things that way. He figured he faced at least 120,000 Confederates.

Meade was still in command of the 3rd Division in Hooker's I Corps, but Hooker was no longer under the control of Ambrose Burnside. For some reason McClellan had taken the I Corps away from the right wing, leaving only his own IX Corps under Burnside's direct command. Some historians speculate this led to a deliberate sulkiness on Burnside's part and a determination to do only exactly what McClellan told him to. Relations between the two generals, once fast friends, did appear to cool after South Mountain. Burnside also seemed to nurse resentment toward Hooker, whom he suspected had been advocating for his own independent command.[21]

After determining that the enemy had left South Mountain on the misty morning of September 15, Hooker moved the I Corps down the other side, through the little town of Keedysville and to the banks of the Antietam, where it camped for the night. Once again Hooker's corps was on the army's right, aiming for the enemy's left flank. And once again the Bucktails acted as skirmishers, probing ahead of the army to find out where the Confederates were. On the afternoon of September 16 they found out. Near a farm owned by J. Miller, the Bucktails encountered the enemy in a patch of forest that became known as the East Woods. The fighting intensified. One early casualty was Col. Hugh Watson McNeil, the Bucktails' commander, killed by a bullet to the head as the regiment approached a fence at the edge of the woods. "A mad fury seized his men," said a regimental history. "Raging to revenge the death of the man to whom they were devoted, they cleared the fence in an instant. Outnumbered, they cared nothing."[22] Meade ordered Truman Seymour's brigade forward to support the Bucktails. The rebels were shelling the advancing Federals from a cornfield, so Meade ordered up his other two brigades, supported by artillery. The Union cannons made things too hot for the rebel artillery, which pulled back. Before the fighting could intensify further, the sun set and darkness brought a tense truce to the battlefield. The enemy combatants slept on the ground, weapons handy, in some cases just a few yards from each other. The pickets remained anxious and watchful, keeping a close eye in the darkness and no doubt wondering whether they would still be alive to see the sun set again.

Before my group heads out to explore the battlefield, Ranger Snyder warns us of the greatest danger we will face: groundhog holes.

Groundhogs do more than trip up today's visitors. In October 2008 people on the northern part of the battlefield saw a groundhog hole and, looking closer, noticed what appeared to be human remains inside it. Park authorities immediately called in the coroner, and the site was declared a crime scene, just in case. For three days archeologists carefully excavated until they uncovered some New York buttons and then a buckle from a dead soldier. They determined that he had been seventeen to nineteen years old and from a New York regiment. Beyond that his identity will remain a mystery. On September 17, 2009, the unknown soldier was buried with full honors at the Saratoga National Cemetery in New York. "So when you walk this ground we must always remember how sacred it is," Snyder tells us. "And finding a soldier who was lost for 147 years is a good reminder." It's a little eerie, too, as I explore the Antietam battlefield, to think that other soldiers might lie just a few feet below my feet, dead and forgotten by all but the groundhogs.

We head out under the insistent September sun and head north toward a piece of ground whose history earned it the right of capitalization. Today we know it as simply the Cornfield. As we move across the fields toward it, Snyder gives us a little lesson in the important role that terrain plays in battle. He tells us to keep an eye on a van driving down the road in front of us. When we walk up and down the rolling swells of this pastureland, the van and the road appear and disappear as we rise and descend. Enemy soldiers, too, could appear to vanish in the little valleys of this deceptively not-flat landscape—only to seemingly spring up from the soil itself to unleash a volley right into your ranks. The situation was even more deadly in the West Woods to our left, where Confederate soldiers could shelter behind rocky ledges in a deadly game of hide-and-seek.

Meade and his men were up before dawn on September 17. It had rained during the night, and the morning was damp and foggy. As the sun began to pierce the fog, Hooker ordered two of his divisions, under Brigadier Generals Abner Doubleday and James Ricketts, to advance south toward the Dunker Church. For the time being most of Meade's men remained in reserve, with orders from Hooker "to spring to the assistance of either, as circumstances might require."[23] Between the advancing Federals and the church lay the not-yet-capitalized cornfield, with head-high stalks ripe for harvest. The field belonged to a farmer named Miller, whose house still stands nearby, its log exterior shorn of the stucco that once covered it, now partially obscured by scaffolding and tarps that flap in the breeze as the Park Service works on its restoration.

Hooker noted that Miller's cornfield was full of enemy soldiers, and as the morning sun fought its way through the fog, it glistened off the points of bayonets

Battle of Antietam

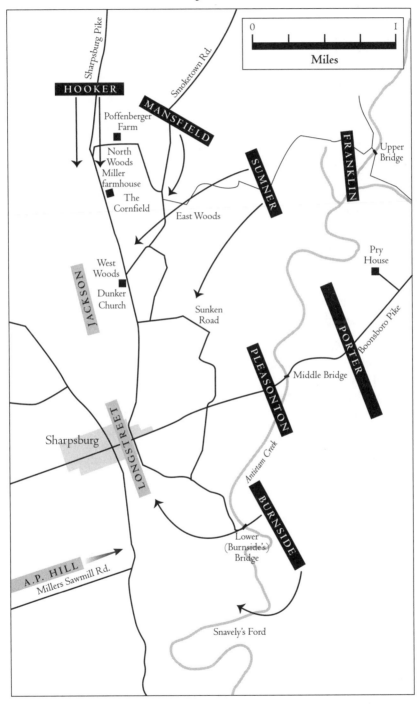

projecting above the stalks. "Instructions were immediately given for the assemblage of all of my spare batteries near at hand, of which I think there were five or six, to spring into battery on the right of this field, and to open with canister at once," Hooker reported. "In the time I am writing every stalk of corn in the northern and greater part of the field was cut as closely as could have been done with a knife, and the slain lay in rows precisely as they had stood in their ranks a few moments before."[24]

The Union forces made their way past the dead and through the cornfield to chase the rebels into the West Woods lying beyond. "But out of those gloomy woods came, suddenly and heavily, terrible volleys; volleys which smote, and bent, and broke in a moment that eager front, and hurled them swiftly back for half the distance they had won," wrote Josiah Sypher in his history of the Pennsylvania Reserves.[25] Stonewall Jackson had ordered Hood's Texas division, which had been allowed to go behind the lines to make a long-overdue breakfast, back to the front. The men pitched in with a fury. It was now time for Meade to "spring to assistance." He ordered Col. Albert Magilton's brigade forward into the bloody cornfield. Archibald F. Hill, the soldier from the 8th Pennsylvania Reserves who had watched Meade chastise the terrified peach-stealing cavalryman, was with them. "I saw General Meade sitting quietly upon his horse by the battery; he was calmly surveying the prospect in front through his spectacles, while the rebel bullets were spattering the ground at his horse's feet, and many, no doubt, singing about his ears," Hill recalled.[26] At some point during the battle a piece of spent grapeshot struck Meade in the thigh, giving him a nasty bruise. His horse, Old Baldy, received a bullet through the neck.

Hill and his regiment received orders to clear the Confederates from the East Woods. They were advancing in that direction when rebels hidden in the cornfield rose and poured a withering fire into their ranks. "The slaughter was fearful; I never saw men fall so fast; I was obliged to step over them at every step," Hill recalled. The carnage elevated Hill to command of his company. He didn't have the position long before a Confederate bullet hit him the thigh and shattered his leg. Two of his men carried him to the rear, where a surgeon amputated the broken limb. Hill's war was over.[27]

What could motivate a normal human being to move forward in the face of such deadly fire? Years after the war Frank Holsinger, who had been with Hill in the 8th Pennsylvania Reserves at Antietam, presented a paper on the subject. Holsinger recalled the scene as he prepared to move out of the North Woods toward the cornfield, with artillery shells ripping through the branches above him and minié balls zipping by and smacking into the tree trunks. He felt that "the shock to the nerves were indefinable—one stands, as it were, on the brink of eternity before he goes into action." It proved too much for one man near him, who hid behind a tree. "Get that man in the ranks!" Meade ordered a sergeant. Still the man refused. Holsinger watched as Meade pulled out his sword. "I'll move him!" he cried and struck at the cowering soldier, who fell to the ground. "[W]ho he was I do not know," Holsinger wrote. "The general has no time to tarry or make inquiries. A lesson to those witnessing the scene. . . . I felt at the time the action was cruel and needless on the part of the general. I changed my mind when

I became an officer, when with sword and pistol drawn to enforce discipline by keeping my men in place when going into the conflict."

For many men the worst part was the agonizing period of waiting before going into combat. Once they were in the thick of things the fear disappeared, replaced by an adrenaline rush of exhilaration. Holsinger found that a funny comment could relieve the tension during the anxious wait. Before plunging into the fray at Antietam, as the bullets and shells flew by, he recalled hearing one of his company's men remark off-handedly, in a nasal drawl, "Damned sharp skirmishing in front." "There is a laugh, it is infectious, and we are once more called back to life," Holsinger said. He also felt that a great comfort in battle was the presence of a friend, "one in whom you had confidence, one you felt assured would stand by you until the last." In combat most men weren't fighting to preserve the Union, end slavery, or win Southern independence. They were fighting to keep from looking like cowards in the eyes of their comrades.

Holsinger's regiment approached the cornfield, unaware that the 6th Georgia was taking advantage of the little dips in the terrain that Snyder had told us about. The Pennsylvania soldiers approached within thirty feet before the Georgians rose up and poured a volley into them. Holsinger admitted that he was "stampeded" and fled to the rear. "I did not expect to stop this side of the Pennsylvania line," he said. But then he encountered a tall, thin, boyish soldier. "Rally, boys, rally!" the young man shouted, swinging his hat in the air. "Die like men; don't run like dogs!" Holsinger felt his panic subside. "Why can I not stand and take what this boy can?" he thought. "I commenced loading and firing, and from this on I was as comfortable as I had been in more pleasant places."[28]

The cornfield was anything but a pleasant place. Again and again it changed hands as the toll of dead and dying rose and rose. "The line swayed forward and back like a rope exposed to rushing currents," noted Confederate general James Longstreet. "A force too heavy to be withstood would strike and drive in a weak point till we could collect a few fragments, and in turn force back the advance till our lost ground was recovered."[29] The current finally turned in the Union's favor, and the Federals pushed the rebels out of the Cornfield.

Hooker himself became a casualty. Around 9:00 he had ridden forward to survey the ground, his white horse making a conspicuous target, and a rebel bullet struck his foot. Weakened by loss of blood, Hooker left the field. He turned over command of the entire corps to Meade, even though the 2nd Division's James Ricketts outranked him. (Strangely enough, Ricketts was the brother of the woman who had married Meade's brother Robert. It was a small world.) Meade thought it must have been a mistake. He rode over to Ricketts and turned command over to him until he received a note from McClellan. "The Commanding Gen'l directs that you at once take command of the Army Corps, which was under the command of Genl. Hooker this morning," it read. "This order is given without regard to rank and all officers of the Corps will obey your orders."[30]

By this point, though, the I Corps was a spent force, exhausted, decimated, and running low on ammunition. When the XII Corps under Mansfield arrived— an example of the piecemeal tactics that characterized the Union fighting— Meade pulled his men back. Poor Mansfield didn't retain command of his corps for long. As the old general arrived on the field he noticed his men firing into the East Woods. He rode over and told them they were shooting at their own men. The soldiers argued fiercely that the general was mistaken. Mansfield peered through the smoke. "Yes, yes, you are right," he said, and then a volley of Confederate bullets underscored the point. Mansfield fell, mortally wounded, in his first action as a corps commander.

Edwin Sumner's II Corps arrived after the XII Corps. Sumner, known as "Old Bull," was even older than Mansfield and, while brave, took a somewhat limited approach to fighting, one that presumed vigorous action by itself would lead to positive results. As an early historian of the army put it, "General Sumner was the ideal of a *soldier*; but he had few of the qualities that make a *general*."[31] Sumner found Hooker as Fighting Joe was being removed from the field, and as Maj. Gen. Jacob Cox later tactfully put it, "the few words he could exchange with the wounded general were enough to make him feel the need of haste, but not sufficient to give him any clear idea of the position."[32] Sumner had two divisions with him, and he accompanied the one under Brig. Gen. John Sedgwick, which marched at right angles to the I Corps' movements and directly into the West Woods. There Confederates under McLaws and Walker, just arrived from Harpers Ferry and sheltered behind rocky ledges and hollows, cut them to pieces.

Sumner's other division, under Brig. Gen. William French—Stonewall Jackson's nemesis in the prewar days at Fort Meade—became separated from Sedgwick. While Sedgwick marched to disaster in the West Woods, French moved off to the southwest in the direction of the sunken road that passed through the battlefield. His men would help baptize it as Bloody Lane.

George W. Smalley, a reporter for the *New York Tribune* who had attached himself to Hooker's side and wrote an eyewitness account of the battle, summed up the first phase of the fighting. "At one o'clock affairs on the right had a gloomy appearance," he wrote. "Hooker's troops were greatly exhausted, and their general away from the field. Mansfield's were no better. Sumner's command had lost heavily, but two of his divisions were still comparatively fresh. Artillery was yet playing vigorously in front, though the ammunition of many of the batteries was entirely exhausted, and they had been compelled to retire." Around this point Franklin reached the field, and his troops, "cheering as they went, swept like an avalanche through the corn-fields, fell upon the woods, cleared them in ten minutes, and held them till darkness had ended the battle.

"The field and its ghastly harvest which the reaper had gathered in those fatal hours remained finally with us," Smalley wrote. "Four times it had been lost and won. The dead are strewn so thickly that as you ride over it you cannot guide your horse's steps too carefully. Pale and bloody faces are everywhere upturned. They are sad and terrible, but there is nothing which makes one's heart beat so quickly as the imploring look of sorely wounded men who beckon wearily for help which you cannot stay to give."[33]

As fighting quieted on the northern part of the battlefield, it intensified in the center, where the two sides battled for control of the sunken road. For a time the Confederates managed to hold off the soldiers of the II Corps under French and Israel Richardson, but the Union's superiority in numbers eventually forced the

Confederates back, leaving Bloody Lane so packed with the dead and dying that it appeared you could walk down it without touching the ground. Costly as it had been for both sides, the loss of this strongpoint left Lee's center nearly defenseless. Things looked so desperate that James Longstreet found it necessary to pitch in and help a gun crew that was desperately working to check the enemy advance. Once again McClellan had a chance to exploit an opportunity to beat Lee's army—and once again he failed to take it. Convinced that he faced superior numbers and worried that Lee was preparing to attack him with reserve forces that he didn't realize did not exist, McClellan held back. Franklin was on the field with fresh troops, but Sumner, shaken by the ferocity of the attack on Sedgwick, advised McClellan against using them to make another attempt. McClellan concurred.

Except for one brief episode, Meade and the I Corps didn't participate in the afternoon's fighting. Later in the day Jeb Stuart contemplated making a counterattack against the Union's right flank in an attempt to get into the army's rear. As Stuart prepared to make his move, his forces received a terrific barrage from thirty-four cannons that Meade had arrayed near the Joseph Poffenberger Farm. It was probably just before Stuart's attack fizzled that Capt. George F. Noyes, a member of Abner Doubleday's staff, reached this part of the battlefield. "General Meade, who succeeded to the command of our corps after General Hooker was wounded, rode up to the crest where we were stationed, and reconnoitered the position of the enemy's batteries as coolly as if at a review," Noyes wrote. "Already decorated with a bullet-hole in his cap as a trophy of today's battle, his almost nonchalant manner, and the quiet way in which, amid the tornado of rebel wrath, he gave his orders to make ready for the storm, greatly impressed me."[34]

That ended Meade's role in the Battle of Antietam. I'm eager to see more of the battlefield so I join the afternoon walk, a four-mile tour of Antietam's southern portion. Rangers Keith Snyder, John Hoptak, and Brian Baracz will be guiding us, and it looks as if pretty much everyone from the morning hike has returned for round two. We've received warnings that the terrain here is more difficult, but no one seems to mind. These are hardcore Civil War folk. One of them, Jeff Evans, is a former ranger from Gettysburg who teaches sixth grade at a private school near Cleveland. He's brought one of his students along to tour the battlefield. Dave Zwolak of Middletown, Maryland—the town near South Mountain that gave Stonewall Jackson the nice Union welcome—is busily taking notes in a notebook. He's a recent convert to Civil War buffdom and wants to make sure he understands everything. Dennis Sullivan is a retired history teacher from New Jersey who belongs to the Friends of Gettysburg. He tells me he's already booked a room in Charleston for April 12, 2011, the 150th anniversary of the attack on Fort Sumter. "I don't know what they'll be doing, but I knew I had to be there," he says. Talking to Sullivan I mention how intimidating it can be to write a book about the Civil War when it seems that everyone I meet knows more about it than I do. A man walking in front of us turns around. "Civil War people are all know-it-alls," he says with a smile.

The centerpiece of the struggle on Antietam's southern portion is a modest stone bridge that arches across the creek in a small valley formed by steep bluffs on each side. The attackers, soldiers of Ambrose Burnside's IX Corps, approached from the east side. A tiny force of defending Confederates—Georgia troops under Brig. Gen. Robert Toombs, a fire-eating politician-turned-soldier—waited on the west side, ready to rain deadly fire on any Union forces who tried to take the bridge. The span has been known as Burnside Bridge ever since.

In his original report on the battle McClellan said, "The design was to make the main attack upon the enemy's left—at least to create a diversion in favor of the main attack, with the hope of something more, by assailing the enemy's right—and, as soon as one or both of the flank movements were fully successful, to attack their center with any reserve I might then have in hand."[35] That was a sound plan, but McClellan executed it poorly. As Snyder told us early in the morning, the attack on the Confederates' left had been piecemeal, with first the I Corps, then the XII, and finally the II going in one by one instead of working together. On the other side of the battlefield the IX Corps never launched its attack until things quieted on the right. The poor coordination allowed Lee to detach troops from this end of the battlefield and rush them into the fighting to the north. When Burnside did get his troops moving here, though, the Confederates stalled their attack at the bridge's bottleneck.

And it was a classic bottleneck. Maj. Gen. Jacob Cox, in nominal command of the IX Corps while Burnside technically remained in command of the no-longer-existent right wing, recalled, "Our advance upon the bridge could only be made by a narrow column, showing a front of eight men at most." Cox determined that the Confederates' position was "virtually impregnable to a direct attack over the bridge."[36]

Ranger Hoptak defends Burnside. He points out that the IX Corps had marched and fought more than any other corps. He dismisses the notion that Burnside was sulking over the removal of Hooker's corps from his command. There's also the question of when, exactly, Burnside received the orders to attack the bridge. In his report Burnside said he did not receive the order until 10:00 in the morning, after the fighting on the left flank was pretty much over.

Did some five hundred Confederates really hold off twelve thousand Federals here? "Well, technically," Hoptak tells us. But when we look at the bridge we all realize that twelve thousand men weren't going to charge across the narrow span all at once. Like McClellan's overall strategy here, they would have to cross piecemeal, regiment by regiment. In the meantime, Burnside waited for a report from Brig. Gen. Isaac Rodman, whom he had sent downstream to find a ford below the bridge. Poor scouting by the Union engineers, though, meant Rodman had to move farther down the creek than anyone had planned, to a place called Snavely's Ford. There were other fords closer to the bridge but McClellan's scouts had overlooked them.

Our group approaches the bridge from the eastern side—the way the Union forces came. It does give me a different perspective. What would it have been like to make this approach with bullets raining down from the bluffs above? A huge sycamore tree, a living veteran of the battle, towers above the bridge on the east side. A stone wall runs alongside the creek north and south of the bridge. Bodies were buried at the wall's base after the fighting. Today this is a beautiful spot—white puffy clouds punctuating the blue sky, insects quietly chirping, and wind rustling the leaves of the trees. It's hard to believe that exactly 148 years ago this pleasant creek was absolute hell on earth, with soldiers in blue stumbling down the steep approaches on the east side and racing to cross the bridge.

Two of those regiments, the 51st New York and the 51st Pennsylvania, finally managed to force a passage and obtain a foothold for the Union on the opposite bank. It was around noon or maybe 1:00 by that point. Once across the bridge the IX Corps formed a line about a mile long and proceeded to move north to roll up the Confederate line, pushing their way toward Sharpsburg. In the meantime, Rodman found his place to cross downstream and began moving his forces north. Once again the fate of Lee's army hung in the balance. By the time the IX Corps was ready to move it was around 3:00. Time was running out.

We toil up the same hill the men of the IX Corps scaled 148 years earlier and pause to rest at the base of my favorite monument on the battlefield. This one commemorates the actions of William McKinley, who served here with the commissary of the 23rd Ohio, carrying buckets of hot coffee instead of a gun. It's a safe bet the monument would not be here if McKinley had not become president of the United States and then the victim of an assassin's bullet. (Another future president, Rutherford B. Hayes, also of Ohio, fell wounded on South Mountain.) I'm not disparaging young McKinley's courage, but it does seem a little strange that this field where so many people died should have a monument to commemorate a man who brought hot coffee to the soldiers. Perhaps the soldiers who received the coffee would have felt differently. McKinley did perform his duty at some risk to his life, but I've always felt that an appropriate title to his monument would be "They Also Serve."

Throughout the walk the rangers have been reading us accounts of the battle written by David Thompson, who fought here with Company G of the 9th New York. Thompson and his company had crossed the creek at a waist-high ford just below the bridge—one of the fords that McClellan's engineers had missed—and formed up in the mile-long line as the IX Corps began its final push against the Army of Northern Virginia's right flank. Writing years later Thompson displayed a somewhat jaundiced eye about the combat experience. "We heard all through the war that the army 'was eager to be led against the enemy,'" he wrote. "It must have been so, for truthful correspondents said so, and editors confirmed it. But when you came to hunt for this particular itch, it was always the next regiment that had it. The truth is, when bullets are whacking against tree-trunks and solid shot are cracking skulls like egg-shells, the consuming passion in the breast of the average man is to get out of the way. Between the physical fear of going forward and the moral fear of turning back, there is a predicament of exceptional awkwardness from which a hidden hole in the ground would be a wonderfully welcome outlet."[37]

The monument to Thompson's regiment, the 9th New York, is a large granite obelisk atop a hill overlooking the battlefield. It's a beautiful spot, with views stretching to South Mountain. The town of Sharpsburg lies just to the north. This marks the farthest advance of the Union army on September 17. Moving forward against fierce resistance, the men of Thompson's regiment reached here as McClellan's great opportunity to defeat Lee's divided army slipped out of his fingers. For the 9th New York had gone this far when flags appeared off to the south. They were banners carried by the men of A. P. Hill's division, the last part of Lee's scattered army, which had made a brutal seventeen-mile forced march from Harpers Ferry. Although badly disorganized by straggling, with men falling out of the ranks from sheer exhaustion, Hill's men had enough fight left to slam into the Union soldiers and force them back into a defensive position above the creek. Then the day and the battle ended.

The total casualties were staggering. The Union had lost 2,100 dead, 9,550 wounded, and 750 missing, for a total of 12,400. Confederate losses were 1,550 dead, 7,750 wounded, and 1,020 missing, for a total of 10,320. The field of battle looked like a landscape from hell, with shattered guns, abandoned equipment, severed limbs, and dead bodies scattered about in heaps. One soldier recalled passing a spot where a soldier had lost a leg. "It was laying there with shoe and stocking on the foot, the bloody and ragged end of the thigh showing the terrible force of the missile," he wrote.[38]

● ● ●

I can't pretend to be an expert on Civil War combat. My battlefield experience ended with G.I. Joes sometime around first or second grade. But the consensus among those who do know about such things is that McClellan threw away opportunity after opportunity to destroy Lee's army. Convinced as always that he was facing "vastly superior" numbers, the "Young Napoleon" refused to send in his reserves to crush the Confederates when he had the chance. He could have sent in Franklin's men in the morning when he had Lee's men on the Confederate left hanging on the ropes. He could have swept through Lee's center once the Union soldiers had finally pushed the Confederates back from the Sunken Road. He could have made sure that Burnside and the IX Corps made a determined attack on Lee's right and prevented the rebel commander from detaching troops from that end of the battle to reinforce his beleaguered left. Or he could have just moved faster as soon as he found the Lost Order and caught Lee before the Confederate general reunited his entire army. He could have done many things, but he did not.

McClellan spent most of the battle at the Pry House, a handsome brick building about two miles away from the battlefield. Near the end of the day on the battle's anniversary I drive out to see the Pry House for myself. I get there in late afternoon to find that the building has closed for the day. The only other person here is a reenactor setting up a tent in the backyard. Behind the house I walk out onto a raised wooden platform that faces in the battlefield's direction. McClellan and his staff posted themselves near here, with comfortable chairs and binoculars hanging from racks within easy reach. Capt. George F. Noyes of Abner Doubleday's staff arrived here in the afternoon and could make no sense of the fighting from such a distance. "It was only the usual battle panorama, and I could not distinguish a single battery, nor discern the movements of a single brigade, nor see a single battalion of the men in gray," he wrote.[39]

McClellan staff member David Strother was also here. He saw Fitz John Porter—whose court-martial had been put on hold at McClellan's request—intently watching the fighting through a telescope and quietly communicating what he saw to McClellan. The "Young Napoleon" stood calmly smoking and "giving his orders in the most quiet under-tones." His chief of staff (and father-in-law) Raymond B. Marcy passed the orders to couriers who sped off to the commanders on the field. "Every thing was as quiet and punctilious as a drawing-room ceremony," Strother wrote.[40]

Things were not so calm elsewhere on the battlefield. Late in the afternoon reporter Smalley of the *New York Tribune* met Lt. James Harrison Wilson of Hooker's staff, who expressed his dissatisfaction with what McClellan had accomplished. "Most of us think this battle is only half fought and half won," Wilson told Smalley. "There is still time to finish it. But McClellan will do no more." He pressed Smalley to see if Hooker was in any condition to take command of the army.

Officers such as Wilson thought McClellan had lost a great opportunity. The "Young Napoleon" felt quite differently. Once again he exercised his great talent at seeing things that others could not. "Those in whose judgment I rely tell me that I fought the battle splendidly & that it was a masterpiece of art," he wrote his wife on September 18.[41]

Meade also wrote home that day. "When General Hooker was wounded, General McClellan placed me in command of the army corps, over General Ricketts's head, who ranked me," he told his wife. "This selection is a great compliment, and answers all my wishes in regard to my desire to have my services appreciated. I cannot ask for more, and am truly grateful for the merciful manner I have been protected, and for the good fortune that has attended me. I go into the action to-day as the commander of an army corps. If I survive, my *two* stars are secure, and if I fall, you will have my reputation to live on. God bless you all! I cannot write more. I am well and in fine spirits."[42]

CHAPTER 6

Fredericksburg

Ambrose Burnside
LIBRARY OF CONGRESS

I'm standing by the side of Lee Drive at Fredericksburg National Military Park on a gray December afternoon. As I peer into the woods before me I try to get an idea of what it must have been like here on December 13, 1862. The day is quiet now, with just a few dried leaves rattling against the branches and the faint murmur of traffic in the distance. Back in 1862 the din would have been terrific—muskets crackling, artillery roaring, officers shouting commands, and the wounded screaming in agony. Men from Meade's division would have emerged from the woods in front of me, with Jubal Early's Confederates swarming out of the trees to my rear, screaming the rebel yell as they fought to stem the Union penetration of their lines. Someplace around here Brig. Gen. Maxcy Gregg— "fiery and uncompromising on the issue of slavery and states' rights," according to the roadside marker—tried to stop his men from shooting at the approaching soldiers. He thought they were fellow Confederates. Gregg received a Union bullet through his spine as the price for his mistake.

But there's little to see here now besides woods, so I drive on. Just down the road the terrain opens up to reveal the railroad that proved such an important feature during the fighting. Just beyond the rails I see something better suited to the Egyptian deserts than a Civil War battlefield. It's a large stone pyramid, twenty-three feet tall, rising from a clearing on the opposite side of the train tracks. I stop the car to look at it as the sound of an approaching train increases to a roar. A long freight train thunders by, heading toward Fredericksburg.

This structure marks the approximate place where the soldiers of Meade's division crossed the railroad during the Battle of Fredericksburg. People call this strange monument the Meade Pyramid, but its creators had no intention of honoring a Union general. The Confederate Memorial Literary Society, the ladies' group that founded the Museum of the Confederacy, came up with the idea for the pyramid, and the Richmond, Fredericksburg and Potomac Railroad did the actual construction work for the society in 1903. The idea was that it would alert train passengers to when they were passing through the battlefield. The granite pyramid was modeled on a larger memorial to Confederate dead that stands in Richmond's Hollywood Cemetery.

Meade's story at Fredericksburg, like Meade himself, is often overlooked. The part of the battle here that people tend to remember happened to the north, where the Federals made futile and bloody attacks against a near-impregnable Confederate position behind a stone wall at the base of Marye's Heights. On that part of the battlefield the Union never stood a chance.

At this southern portion, though, Meade's division pushed its way through the center of Stonewall Jackson's corps and gave the Union its best shot at beating Robert E. Lee. Lack of support from the other divisions on the field ultimately snatched the opportunity from the North's grasp. What if Meade had received the support he needed to exploit the breach his men made? It's just one more "what if?" to add to the growing pile.

By the time the Army of the Potomac reached here, its situation had changed dramatically since Antietam. In a sense the entire war had changed. McClellan's ambiguous result in Maryland back in September wasn't a clear victory, but it was good enough for Lincoln. It gave the president the chance he had been waiting for since the summer. In July he had drafted a preliminary emancipation act to free all the slaves in territory held by the Confederacy. Secretary of State William Seward advised him to hold it back until the Union army won a significant victory. Otherwise, Seward counseled, the world might look on it as "our last shriek on the retreat." Antietam was the best victory Lincoln had. The president announced his preliminary Emancipation Proclamation on September 22 and once and for all transformed the conflict into a war to end slavery.

The irony, of course, is that George McClellan did not want the war to become a struggle of "servile insurrection." Now his work at Antietam had handed Lincoln the victory he needed. In fact, emancipation and the administration's suspension of habeas corpus angered McClellan so much that he toyed with the idea of resigning his commission.

John Reynolds returned to the army on September 29, after a frustrating experience dealing with Pennsylvania militia, and took command of the I Corps. Meade, who enjoyed being in command of a corps, had mixed feelings about his return. "I do wish Reynolds had stayed away, and that I could have had a chance to command a corps in action," he wrote to his wife. "Perhaps it may yet occur. At any rate, it would be great ingratitude in me to complain, after all my recent good fortune."[1] The two generals rode over to meet with McClellan, who eased Meade's disappointment by telling both men that he had requested they receive promotions to major general.

Meade's doubts about McClellan were beginning to gnaw at him. "I don't wish you to mention it," he wrote Margaret, "but I think myself he errs on the side of prudence and caution, and that a little more rashness on his part would improve his generalship."[2] Ironically, this would be the same thing some people later said about him.

Lincoln shared Meade's concerns as days and then weeks passed and the Army of the Potomac remained motionless near Sharpsburg. The president decided it was time to prod McClellan into action and traveled to Sharpsburg to apply pressure. Meade accompanied McClellan when he took the president on the tour of the battlefield and was quite gratified when McClellan made a point of telling Lincoln, "here it was that Meade did this and there Meade did that."[3] He also noted that Lincoln seemed particularly interested in what Hooker had done that day.

Meade had doubts about McClellan, but he also shared Little Mac's concerns about the army's preparedness for battle. He even had to pay for the shoeing of twelve hundred horses out of his own pocket. In his letters home he hinted darkly that perhaps Washington was holding back supplies for reasons of its own—reasons that didn't bode well for McClellan's future.

As the army remained motionless behind Antietam in October, Col. Charles Wainwright, who handled the artillery for the I Corps, witnessed the fury that scavenging could rouse in Meade. One day in October Meade saw a private from his division walk by with a load of pillaged corn. "What are you doing with that corn!" he demanded. As he berated the soldier, Meade grew angrier. He swore at him and then struck the soldier a blow on the side of the head, nearly knocking him down. Unabashed, the private, a big, strong man, turned to Meade and said, "If it warn't for them shoulder straps of your'n, I'd give you the darn'dst thrashing you ever had in your life." With that Meade, "very much ashamed of himself, cleared out," Wainwright wrote in his journal.[4] "Meade does not mean to be ugly," the colonel observed, "but he cannot control his infernal temper."[5]

The army finally lurched into motion on October 26, making a cautious crossing of the Potomac at Berlin and moving slowly toward Robert E. Lee and the Army of Northern Virginia. "If I can crush him I will—relentlessly & without remorse," McClellan told his wife in a letter dated October 31.[6] The man he intended to crush, however, was not Lee. It was Secretary of War Edwin Stanton, the man he now considered his archnemesis. Stanton's "magnificent treachery & rascality," McClellan wrote to his wife, "would have caused Judas to have raised his arms in holy horror & unaffected wonder."[7] I wonder if he realized that by comparing Stanton to Judas, McClellan was comparing himself to Jesus.

McClellan never got the chance to crush any of his enemies. Lincoln's patience finally ran out, and with midterm elections over (they had gone badly for Lincoln's Republican Party), he decided he could finally rid himself of the general. Many suspected that Lincoln would select Hooker to replace McClellan—why else was he so interested in what Fighting Joe had done at Antietam?—but the president once again offered the army to Burnside. This time Burnside felt unable to refuse. Despite his own well-justified doubts about his military abilities, Ambrose E. Burnside took command of the Army of the Potomac.

The celebration was not just muted, it was nonexistent. "The army is filled with gloom and greatly depressed," Meade noted. "Burnside, it is said, wept like a child, and is the most distressed man in the army, openly says he is not fit for the position, and that McClellan is the only man we have who can handle the large army collected together, one hundred and twenty thousand men."[8]

Burnside wasn't alone in his depression over McClellan's departure. "The news fell on us like a thunderclap," recalled a captain from a Pennsylvania regiment who actually sat down and cried when he heard. "How can I describe it, how can I tell the utter despondency of the soldiers, at the loss of their idolized commander?"[9] Another Pennsylvania soldier noted, "His departure from the army was a scene never to be forgotten; the deafening shouts of the columns he had so often led to honor; the caps tossed high in the air; the tears, those true tests of affection, stealing their courses down the weather-beaten cheeks of the veterans of the Peninsula, truly told the deep hold he had upon the hearts of the men. The officers of some of the regiments sent in their resignations in a body, but their generals returned them, with a gentle admonition."[10]

Once he dried his tears, though, Burnside moved with commendable alacrity. He decided to make an attack on Richmond—"the great object of the campaign," he said—by first capturing Fredericksburg, which sat on a direct line to the Confederate capital. Lincoln and Halleck preferred that he make a direct attack on Lee's army in the neighborhood of Culpeper, but Burnside argued that it would be more realistic to supply his army via the Richmond, Frederick and Potomac Railway, which traveled from Aquia Landing on the Potomac down to Fredericksburg, instead of using the Orange and Alexandria Railroad, which would support a thrust at Culpeper.

Meade, a mere division commander, was not consulted. If he had been, he could have stated that both approaches were wrong and that McClellan's approach to Richmond via the James River had been the best course. He also believed that Richmond itself should not be the target, "that the proper mode to reduce it is to take possession of the great lines of railroad leading to it from the South and Southwest, cut these and stop any supplies going there, and their army will be compelled to evacuate it and meet us on the ground we can select ourselves."[11] This is pretty much what Ulysses S. Grant ended up doing when he aimed at the railroad hub of Petersburg, south of Richmond, in 1865. But that still lay in the future, separated by a great gulf of suffering and death.

In order to simplify the chain of command, Burnside reorganized his army into three "grand divisions." Old Edwin Sumner received command of the Left Grand Division, consisting of the II and IX Corps and cavalry under Brig. Gen. Alfred Pleasonton. Hooker, recovered from his Antietam wound, took command of the Center Grand Division, which included the III and V Corps and Brig. Gen. William Averell's cavalry. Hooker didn't bother to hide his ambition to command the entire army or his disdain for Burnside. Meade's division, still part of Reynolds's I Corps, belonged to the Left Grand Division, commanded by William Franklin. In addition to the I Corps, Franklin controlled the VI Corps and the cavalry of Brig. Gen. George D. Bayard. Abner Doubleday and John Gibbon commanded Reynolds's other two divisions.

Burnside made one change that rankled Meade. He put Daniel Butterfield in command of the V Corps after Fitz John Porter departed to answer the charges Pope had brought against him after Second Bull Run. Meade outranked Butterfield, yet he was still stuck commanding a division when by rights he should have received the corps. Meade was an ambitious man but he felt that honors should come naturally to those who earned them. He remained unsure about how to act in this "delicate matter."

In the meantime, even more important matters were afoot. Winter approached and the weather was turning nasty, subjecting the Union soldiers to miserable periods of cold, ice, and snow. The administration obviously wanted the army to move before winter weather ended the campaigning season. Burnside knew this and began his campaign by repairing his supply lines, starting at Aquia Landing.

● ● ●

Aquia Landing is one of those names that pops up time and again in accounts of the Civil War. I'm curious to see the place for myself. On a cold December morning I detour from busy Interstate 95 on my way to Fredericksburg and head down winding country roads through the Virginia countryside. When I reach the access road to Aquia Landing, where a historical marker tells me I've found the right place, a deer jumps across the road just ahead of me. I drive past a narrow sandy beach and down to a wide parking area that looks out on the junction of Aquia Creek and the broad Potomac River. The weak December sun casts pale light through the clouds. Duck hunters offshore are retrieving their decoys on the flat water. Real ducks, oblivious to the men who plot their death, paddle just offshore.

Sometimes ghosts make themselves felt most strongly by their absence. There are some historical markers here with photographs of Aquia Landing during the war, and looking at them I get an almost palpable sense of the bustle and chaos and noise of steamships landing, locomotives hissing and puffing, and soldiers laughing and shouting and calling out orders. Newspaperman Noah Brooks described it as "a village of hastily constructed warehouses, and its water-front was lined with transports and government steamers; enormous freight-trains were continually running from it to the army encamped among the hills of Virginia lying between the Rappahannock and the Potomac."[12] That's all vanished, replaced by empty picnic tables in a deserted waterside park. Before the war travelers came here by boat from Washington and boarded a train for a journey to Fredericksburg, about 15 miles away, and farther on into Virginia. (The old rail bed is now the road I drove down to get here.) Then war came and started a cycle of destruction and rebuilding. Confederates destroyed everything here in April 1862 and tore up the tracks. The Union rebuilt the landing but destroyed it in September 1862, only to rebuild it again before Burnside's Fredericksburg campaign. The Confederates tore everything down once more in June 1863 when the Union army abandoned Aquia Landing before pursuing Robert E. Lee north into Pennsylvania. Grant had everything rebuilt once more before the Confederates destroyed it one final time after the Army of the Potomac had moved south on Grant's Overland Campaign.

As I leave the park I stop the car on the side of the road so I can follow a trail, littered for some reason with oyster shells, into the woods and up a hill to the site of a Confederate battery that threatened Union shipping on the Potomac. From May 29 through June 1, 1861, Union vessels steamed down here to give the rebels a good pounding, but the naval attack did little damage. One Confederate said the only loss on this shore was a chicken, but "a stray ball killed a horse on the opposite side of the creek." Such are the fortunes of war.

As his engineers rebuilt Aquia Landing, Burnside made a feint toward Culpeper to keep Lee guessing about his intentions. Then he left Warrenton on November 16 to begin his move toward Fredericksburg. Three days later he reached Falmouth, on the opposite side of the Rappahannock River from his target. It had been a swift march by an army that, unlike Lee's, had no reputation for rapid movement. Burnside was in Falmouth before Lee knew what he was up to. Unfortunately, Burnside also arrived long before his pontoon bridges did— and the bridges were the key to the entire attack. Without the bridges, the army remained immobile and impotent on the wrong side of the Rappahannock.

Pontoon bridges required a great deal of material and manpower. Engineers constructed the temporary spans on top of a chain of boats, each thirty-one feet long and almost six feet wide. Assembling it all required a prodigious array of cable, timber, oars, rope, anchors, boat hooks, tools, and other supplies, all of which had to be transported by road in long wagon trains, and the wagon trains were still on their way. There was much finger-pointing and blame shifting over who should take responsibility for the pontoons' delay. Halleck certainly bore some blame but in characteristic fashion dodged responsibility. It wasn't Burnside's fault, although he could have double-checked to make sure the pontoons were coming. In any event, it seems that no one along the entire chain of command up to Washington had placed transporting the pontoons at the top of the priority list. The ponderous pontoon wagon trains finally reached the army on November 25, but by then Robert E. Lee's army had begun filing into their defenses behind Fredericksburg. Once again the Army of the Potomac could have adopted "opportunity lost" as its motto.

In the meantime the Butterfield situation was eating away at Meade. On Sunday, November 23, he paid a visit to Burnside. "I have come to pick a crow with you," he said as playfully as he could. Then he explained his feelings about Butterfield getting command of the V Corps. Burnside acted surprised. He said that he had no idea Meade ranked Butterfield and certainly had meant no disrespect. His intention was for Butterfield to command the corps only temporarily, perhaps until someone senior to both men—John Sedgwick, perhaps—could take over. Meade pronounced himself satisfied and rode back to his tent.[13]

Meade received some happier news when he learned that his son George was nearby. Born on November 2, 1843, George had followed his father to West Point, although with less happy results: he flunked out of the military academy in 1862 after receiving too many demerits. He accepted a commission as a lieutenant in the 6th Pennsylvania Cavalry, an elite Philadelphia regiment known as Rush's Lancers. The regiment received its name from its commander, Col. Richard Rush, and the long spears they carried, an archaic bit of cavalry gear that Meade called a "turkey-driving implement."[14] Meade reassured Margaret that their son would have "a comparatively pleasant time" in the cavalry as "we have not lost over a dozen cavalry officers since the war began."[15] Brig. Gen. George Bayard, who commanded the cavalry for Burnside's Left Grand Division, offered to add George to his staff, but Meade declined the offer. "I certainly believe it is better for a young officer to serve with his regiment before accepting a staff appointment," he said.[16] Nonetheless, he found it comforting to know his son was nearby.

• • •

Early on the morning of December 11 the engineers with Franklin's wing moved to the banks of the foggy Rappahannock downstream from Fredericksburg and began assembling their pontoon bridges. The Confederates on the opposite bank provided only token resistance. The Union soldiers marched across on December 12, and Meade moved his men to a position farther downstream.

As the sun rose on December 13, 1862, a dense fog shrouded the flat ground by the river. Meade and Reynolds reported to Franklin at his headquarters, a large and handsome house owned by a man named Bernard, who told Franklin he was a good Union man. Reynolds, who had served as military governor in Fredericksburg the previous summer, knew otherwise and had Bernard arrested. Franklin told Meade that his division would lead the attack.[17] Franklin had met with Burnside the night before and believed he had talked him into making his main attack at this point. The vague orders he received in the early-morning hours made it appear that Burnside intended Franklin's attack to be more of a diversion, with the main assault aimed at Marye's Heights behind the town. Burnside ordered Franklin to "send out a division, at least," and "seize if possible the heights occupied by the enemy."[18] The heights in question were a wooded rise set back from the river. In front of them was a wide plain, with the tracks of the Richmond railroad running through it. The land was flat and clear, which meant that once the fog lifted Meade's men would advance in plain view of the enemy, who were hidden in the woods.

Perhaps feeling a bit sulky that Burnside had disregarded his advice, Franklin decided to follow his orders to the letter. He would send a single division, Meade's, with John Gibbon's division in support. With about four thousand men, Meade's division was also the smallest one Franklin had. Meade protested. If forces were sent piecemeal, he said, it would be Antietam all over again. He told Franklin that although his men could take the heights, they would not be able to hold them.

Those are your orders, replied Franklin.[19]

Meade returned to his division and had it move downstream, parallel to the river, for about seven hundred or eight hundred yards. He then swung right and crossed the Bowling Green Road (today's Route 2). His men had to spend some time removing fence rails, so it wasn't until sometime between 9:00 and 10:00 that the division was ready to advance. Col. William Sinclair's 1st Brigade took the lead, with the 6th Pennsylvania Reserves acting as skirmishers. Magilton's 2nd Brigade was about three hundred paces behind the 1st, and the 3rd, under C. Feger Jackson, was on the flank.

An enemy battery opened fire from the left. Meade ordered his artillery forward to reply. After about twenty minutes the Confederate guns retired, but not before drawing blood. Lt. John Simpson of Battery A, 1st Pennsylvania Light Artillery, lost eleven men and sixteen horses under a fire so galling that the men had to move their cannons by hand to get them to safety.[20] The infantry could do little more than lie in the cold mud and endure "a terrific fire of round shot and shell . . . which plowed up the earth in deep furrows, or went howling and bursting over our heads, filling the air with iron hail and sulphur," as a member of the 2nd Pennsylvania Reserves described it. The only casualty in the 2nd was the regiment's flagstaff. When a Confederate shell cut it in two the men of the regiment jumped to their feet, gave a defiant three cheers, and then settled back down into the mud.[21]

The 121st Pennsylvania was not so fortunate. An untested regiment, newly attached to the 1st Brigade, it received its first fatality at Fredericksburg during the initial Confederate shelling when a cannonball cut Pvt. John B. Manson cleanly in half. "The annoying and appalling noise of the flying shells was altogether new and unexpected, differing according to the kind or size, and the elevation from and at which they came," wrote William B. Strong in a regimental history. "One gun sent shells whose noise resembled the sudden flight of a great flock of pigeons. A solid shot would land with a heavy thud and rebound to the rear, or come right at the line with the sound of a huge circular saw ripping a log, or pass shrieking through the air in quest of a victim." Despite the nerve-racking bombardment, some of the men took advantage of the halt to nap. "Nature demanded her measure of rest even under such novel circumstances."[22]

Battles of Fredericksburg and Chancellorsville

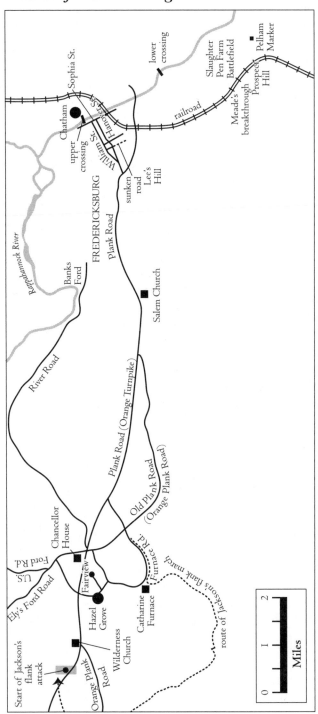

The Union soldiers did not know that the guns wreaking such havoc were just a pair under Maj. John Pelham, the baby-faced, twenty-four-year-old Alabamian who commanded Jeb Stuart's horse artillery. The spot where he set up his guns is now called Pelham's Corner, on the corner of Routes 2 and 608, right next to the parking lot of an abandoned drugstore. Pelham and his gun crew bedeviled Meade's men and earned a bit of Lost Cause immortality from this spot until the Union artillery finally silenced the Confederate cannons. It took some time, though, because Pelham kept moving his guns around to make them a difficult target. He managed not only to delay the Union attack but also to freeze Abner Doubleday's division in a defensive posture on the Federal left, removing it as a factor in the upcoming battle. "It is glorious to see such courage in one so young!" Lee said about the young artilleryman, who became known as "the gallant Pelham" after a description in Jeb Stuart's report of the battle.

Jackson's 3rd Brigade also had to deal with the problem of Confederate sharpshooters on their front, further delaying progress. Finally, the 1st and 3rd Brigades formed into a line of battle and prepared to move forward. Then more Confederate batteries began shelling them from the extreme left. Meade ordered his artillery back into action, and they drove the rebel guns back after a half hour of shelling, loudly punctuated by the explosions of two enemy limbers.

The 1st Brigade began its advance. The ground had been frozen in the cold morning but had since thawed and the soldiers churned it into mud. The morning fog had long since burnt away and Meade's men marched across the wide field with the lowering late-season sun shining on their faces. The enemy soldiers on the wooded rise ahead of them watched and waited. "They saw Meade's light field batteries rushed to their positions at full speed; his mounted officers riding with sabres drawn; his flags flying in the breeze, and the rifle barrels of those long lines of infantry, that had been well drilled by some of the best officers of the Union army and were now advancing with the precision of a parade, shining like silver in the brilliant winter sunlight," wrote biographer Pennypacker, based on testimony from one of Stonewall Jackson's officers.[23]

Meade's men pushed forward across the railroad and toward a swampy, woody area that projected like an upside-down triangle toward them. The Confederates had wrongly assumed the swamp provided a natural defensive barrier and left it unprotected. Instead, the Union troops pierced the rebel lines in the boggy woodland and surprised the enemy beyond. Somehow they found Brig. Gen. Maxcy Gregg's South Carolinians completely unprepared for the Union attack. The rebels' arms were still stacked when the Federals suddenly emerged from the woods. Like Mansfield at Antietam, Gregg received his mortal wound in a case of mistaken identity, when he thought the approaching Union troops were on his side.

Lt. Evan M. Woodward was with the 2nd Pennsylvania Reserves as they passed over the railroad through a galling fire from a Confederate rifle pit behind it and to their left. Wheeling in the direction of the enemy, they attacked the position and poured a murderous fire into it from the rear. The 7th Pennsylvania Reserves fired from the pit's opposite side and the two regiments unwittingly shot each other in their excitement. Woodward said they also slaughtered the Confederates "like sheep. Many of them attempted to escape by running the gauntlet in front of our regiment, they becoming perfectly wild with fright, not heeding our calls to halt, but with their arms up to shield their heads, some of them staggered to and fro up the hill, within a few yards of us, meeting certain death." Woodward waded between the lines to end the slaughter and give the Confederates a chance to give up. "We will surrender if you will allow us," a rebel said. Woodward received thirteen bullet holes through his clothing but he captured the 19th Georgia's flag and later received the Medal of Honor for his actions—but so did a soldier from the 7th Pennsylvania Reserves who took the flag behind Union lines and concocted an elaborate tale of his own brave work in obtaining it.[24]

The 2nd Brigade followed the 1st. After reaching the railroad it began receiving severe fire from its right. The 4th Pennsylvania Reserves stopped to deal with this while the rest of the brigade moved forward almost as far as the First Brigade had gone. The 7th Pennsylvania Reserves captured prisoners and flags, but enemy reinforcements began pouring into the breach and started driving them back. The Confederate artillery on the left resumed its fire, pouring death and destruction into the 3rd Brigade. Meade sent his aide-de-camp, young Lt. Arthur Dehon, to Jackson with orders for him to move to the left and capture the battery, but enemy fire killed both Dehon and Jackson. "The loss of their commander, and the severity of the fire from both artillery and infantry to which they were subjected, compelled them to withdraw, when those on their right withdrew," Meade wrote in his report.[25]

Meade's official language is bland and objective, but his language on the field was not. At some point Meade confronted an officer who refused to move forward. Mad with panic, the soldier pointed his gun at the general. Meade broke his sword over the soldier's head and knocked him to the ground. "Meade is a rough customer when under fire," another soldier noted.[26]

The Union attack began to disintegrate in confusion in the woods, as a wave that crashes on a beach ultimately falls back to the sea. The Union soldiers, running low on ammunition and assaulted ferociously by the fresh Confederate troops of Jubal Early's division, had no choice but to retreat. "Never did I look back for support with more anxiety than on that fatal day; for seeing but a single line of advance I had anticipated the result," remembered Lt. Daniel Coder of the 11th Pennsylvania Reserves. "We lost color bearer after color bearer, I know not how many. I picked up the colors three different times myself. The flag staff was shot off and the flag perforated in nineteen different places by the rebel bullets. I took thirty-one men into the engagement, only one of whom came back safely." Seven men of Coder's company either died then or later of their wounds, twenty-two others were wounded, and one was captured.[27]

Meade knew he would lose everything he had gained if he did not receive support. He dispatched officers to both Gibbon and Brig. Gen. David Birney to urge them to send support. Gibbon was bogged down in a severe fight on the right, one that included the desperate use of bayonets and muskets as clubs.

Birney did not belong to Franklin's Grand Division. His brigade was part of the III Corps in Hooker's Center Grand Division, but Burnside had sent him to provide support for Reynolds and the I Corps. As one of Meade's aides later described him, Birney "was a pale, Puritanical figure, with a demeanor of unmovable coldness; only he would smile politely when you spoke to him. He was spare in person, with a thin face, light-blue eye, and sandy hair."[28] He had been born in the South, but a hatred of slavery motivated his father to pack up the family and move north. Birney took up the law and was practicing in Philadelphia when war broke out.

When Birney received Meade's request for support, he replied that he could not move forward until he received word from Reynolds to do so. This outraged Meade. He sent another officer to Birney with another demand for reinforcements. Birney again refused. Now Meade galloped over himself. He had his recent commission as a major general in his pocket, and that meant he outranked Birney. "General, I assume the authority of ordering you up to the support of my men," he said, according to one account.[29] According to another, Meade said much more, in language strong enough to "almost make the stones creep."[30]

Birney later testified before Congress that he received only one message from Meade and in his official report he said he responded "immediately." However, in a letter to a friend that Birney wrote shortly after the battle, he said that when a reporter from the *New York Herald* urged him to send some of his artillery to help Meade, "I told him the Reserves might run and be damned, that not a gun should leave my Division."[31] Whatever the truth, by the time Birney got his men moving forward, they could do nothing but support Meade's retreating division, which had begun stumbling back over the railroad. Attempts to stop them proved futile "as they sullenly and resolutely marched to the rear," Birney reported. Meade and Reynolds tried to stop the flood by positioning themselves on the railroad, with Meade waving the 2nd Pennsylvania Reserve's regimental flag as a rallying point. It proved hopeless.

"Meade's division fared as Pickett's division fared at Gettysburg," Francis Winthrop Palfrey wrote in a 1912 account of the battle. "Having made a most brilliant advance, and penetrated the hostile line more deeply than Pickett's did, it was enveloped by fire closing in upon it from every direction, and compelled to withdraw."[32]

Meade rode back to Franklin's headquarters to report. He took off his slouch hat and showed Franklin he had two bullet holes in. With deliberate understatement he said that things had been hot enough for him on the battlefield.[33] His horse had suffered, too, receiving a bullet through the neck.

As Meade had predicted, his men had taken the Confederate position but they could not hold it. Lt. Col. Robert Anderson, who took command of the 3rd Brigade following Jackson's death, made his disappointment over the outcome apparent even in the stilted language of an official account: "I cannot close this portion of my report without expressing the conviction that had we been properly supported, that portion of the field gained by the valor of our troops could have and would have been held against any force that the enemy could have been able to have thrown against us."[34]

Meade also turned his anger on Reynolds, who, as corps commander, should have taken some action to support the 3rd Division. "My God, General Reynolds, did they think my division could whip Lee's whole army?" he asked in frustration, gesturing toward the battlefield. "There is all that is left of my Reserves."[35]

Later Meade wrote to his wife about Reynolds. "*He* knows *I* think *he* was in some measure responsible for my not being supported on the 13th as he was commanding the corps & had the authority to order up other troops—and it was his business to have seen that I was properly supported, and the advantage that I had gained, secured by promptly advancing reinforcements."[36] Yet Meade retained his affection for his corps commander. "He is a very good fellow, and I have had much pleasant intercourse with him during the past eighteen months, and considering how closely we have been together and the natural rivalry that might be expected, I think it is saying a good deal for both that we have continued good friends."[37]

• • •

Earlier in the day I drove down Lee Drive to see the ground over which Meade's men had advanced from the Confederate side. Now I want to see it from the Union perspective. I can do that thanks to the Civil War Trust, the preservation organization that saved this portion of the battlefield, known as the Slaughter Pen Farm, from development. The large parcel of land, a field where five Americans won the Medal of Honor, went on the market in 2005 and was zoned for industrial development. The Civil War Trust managed to raise enough money to purchase the site and save it. Today deteriorating farm buildings stand here, but nothing more. There are industrial buildings to the left and a small airport to the right. Ahead of me the flat landscape stretches out to a line of trees that marks the railroad. Beyond that lies Prospect Hill, the heights that Meade attacked and the spot where Stonewall Jackson had his headquarters. From the deserted farm a one-and-three-quarter-mile trail connects several historical markers that stand out in the field, most of them describing the fighting done here on Meade's right by Gibbon's division.

The land looks much as it did on December 13, 1863, when a Maine lieutenant, his words preserved on a marker here, described it as "a plowed field, now trampled into mud, the winter stubble crushed into it by hoofs of straining horses and heavy wheels of cannon and the slogging feet of hundreds of men." I see the winter stubble, but the tracks in the dried mud tell me modern farm equipment did the crushing, not cannons, horses, or soldiers. The only hoof marks here are from deer that have emerged from the woods to feed on the corn the harvesters left behind.

I am the only person present on this huge field. As small airplanes take off from the adjacent airfield I think about Cary Grant being chased by a crop duster in *North by Northwest*. The airplanes leave me alone, but I do get a strong sense of vulnerability out here on this flat, featureless surface. Imagine how the Union soldiers felt as Pelham's shells—fired from an unseen hand off to the left—went tearing through their ranks or the minié balls from Confederate sharpshooters picked off comrades to the left and right. It's a long walk to the railroad tracks from this direction, and I'm sure it would have seemed even longer with grim death lying in wait on the other side.

• • •

Meade's soldiers could at least console themselves with the knowledge they had pierced the enemy line. The Union forces to the north didn't even have that.

Nothing had gone smoothly upstream, not even the bridge building. A Mississippi division under Brig. Gen. William Barksdale holed up in town and picked off the engineers as they tried to construct the bridges. A Union artillery barrage shattered Fredericksburg in response but couldn't dislodge the rebels. Finally, Burnside ordered soldiers to cross the river by boat to repel the Confederates. After some fierce fighting in the streets the Federals pushed the rebels out of town, the engineers finished the bridges, and Sumner's Right Grand Division began marching across the spans to take up positions for their early-morning assault.

Behind Fredericksburg the Confederates under James Longstreet had an even better defensive position than Jackson did farther south. The Confederates established a line behind a stone wall along a sunken road at the base of Marye's Heights, while the artillerists above them carefully presighted their guns in preparation for the Union attack. "A chicken could not live on that field when we open on it," artillery head E. Porter Alexander told Longstreet.[38] The men of William French's division were the first to learn the truth of Alexander's observation. The Union attackers didn't stand a chance as they moved out from the town and advanced across the bare ground that separated it from the heights. A hail of shot and shell ripped through their ranks, tearing off arms, heads, and legs and leaving heaps of dead and wounded. "It was a much harder battle than Antietam," remembered one soldier. "I don't see how a worse place could by any means have been made," said another.[39] Maj. Gen. Darius Couch, watching the battle from the steeple of the courthouse in town, was horrified. "Oh, great God!" he exclaimed to Brig. Gen. Oliver Otis Howard. "See how our men, our poor fellows, are falling!"[40]

After French's division was driven back, Brig. Gen. Winfield Scott Hancock's division made its attempt. One of Hancock's units was the famed Irish Brigade. Today, on the battle's anniversary weekend, I've come to Fredericksburg to walk in their footsteps. Around noon on a rainy day people begin gathering in a parking lot alongside the Rappahannock, along with a small group of Union reenactors. Our guide will be Frank O'Reilly, a park ranger and author of *The Fredericksburg Campaign: Winter War on the Rappahannock*. He does this walk every year, rain or shine. Today it's going to be rain. "Better rain than bullets," he says cheerfully after I introduce myself and complain about the weather. I tell him that I'm working on a book about Meade but I realize this was not his part of the battlefield. "Everything that happened here was predicated on what Meade did," O'Reilly says.

About forty-eight of us are willing to brave the cold December rain to take O'Reilly's tour. There's a tall, silent woman in a Union greatcoat whom I remember from my Antietam walks. There's a man with a long, scraggly gray beard who will tell anyone who listens—and some who don't—that he's been researching the Irish Brigade for the past twenty-six years. There are men and women and even some children. One woman hands out green sprigs of boxwood, which the men of the real Irish Brigade wore during the battle—in such profusion, O'Reilly tells us, that one sergeant major said the combat line looked like "a living, breathing shrub."

The Irish Brigade was the 2nd Brigade of the 1st Division of the II Corps. Its commander was the flamboyant Brig. Gen. Thomas Francis Meagher, an

Irish revolutionary whom the British had sent into exile in Tasmania for his sedi-
tious activities. Meagher managed to escape and travel to New York, where he
became an American citizen and a lawyer. When war broke out he raised a company and later a brigade. By the time of Fredericksburg his command had already
seen plenty of action in the Peninsula Campaign and at Antietam, where it took
part in the vicious struggle for the sunken road. Meagher had both a gift for or-
atory and a weakness for the bottle. The latter habit would lead to his death after
the war, when he tumbled drunk off the deck of a steamer and drowned in the
Missouri River.

The reenactors here today are portraying men from Company B of the 28th
Massachusetts, a late addition to the Irish Brigade. They will accompany us on
the entire walk. Two of them carry flags—a green Irish flag and the Stars and
Stripes—while a third plays a fife. After O'Reilly gives us an overview of the Irish
Brigade and the battle, the regiment lays a wreath at a commemorative marker
and we step off on our soggy way through town.

Our route will follow exactly the course taken by the brigade on December
13, 1863. We start up Sophia Street, which runs parallel to the river, and stop in
a parking lot. O'Reilly, the rain dripping off his plastic-covered ranger hat, tells
us how the 116th Pennsylvania stood here, subject to shelling from the Confederate batteries on Marye's Heights, and contemplated what was to come. They
saw wounded men being brought back from French's first catastrophic attack.
Two men were toting a wounded soldier on a shutter, the wounded man's leg
dangling off the edge and attached by a single tendon. The soldiers waiting here
screamed at the bearers to put the wounded man down. Finally, a soldier stepped
from the ranks and severed the tendon with a knife. The leg plopped to the
ground. One of the new soldiers of the 116th Pennsylvania tumbled down in a
dead faint.

At another stop at the base of George Street, O'Reilly tells us about a sergeant
named Marley who was standing here with his regiment when shrapnel from an
exploding shell neatly decapitated him. It happened so quickly that the headless
body remained standing for a moment. Then it slumped to its knees and remained
in that position, propped up by Marley's gun.

We continue our march up George Street and past the Presbyterian church,
which still has two cannonballs embedded in a pillar. By Kenmore Street we stop
in a bank parking lot, and I press myself against the building to get some shelter
from the rain. Kenmore Street didn't exist in 1862; instead there was a water-
course or millrace that presented a difficult obstacle for the Union soldiers. The
Confederates had removed the planks from a bridge that crossed it, so the soldiers
of the Irish Brigade had to step carefully on the remaining stringers or wade
through three feet of frigid water to get to the other side, all the time withstanding
a blizzard of lead. One man's head was cut in two, exposing his brains. A sergeant
pointed at him and said with grim, dark humor, "Look at the watermelon." After
O'Reilly tells us this story his voice softens and he shifts down from the almost
military cadence he's been using for his narration. "We'll forgive him that," he
says. Such gallows humor sometimes provided a grim shield from the death and
destruction all around.

The Irish Brigade fixed bayonets and continued on. Our brigade members do the same. Throughout the walk O'Reilly has been reading from an account written by Pvt. William McCarter, who was crippled during the battle. McCarter described the sound of the bayonets and said that "the clink, clink, clink of the cold steel sounding above the din made one's blood run cold."[41] Across from a brick building called the Stratton House O'Reilly tells us of the final, brutal portion of the brigade's futile attempt to reach Marye's Heights. It was nothing more than slaughter, "a living hell from which escape seemed scarcely possible."[42] The Union soldiers fought their way forward against "a blizzard of shot, shell, and fire,"[43] bending low as though walking into a strong wind. Some of its members approached to maybe thirty yards from the stone wall, but no more. That was about as far as any Union soldier advanced that day. When the fighting was over the Irish Brigade had suffered 545 casualties out of 1,200 men.[44]

More Union attacks followed that day, none of them any more successful. Hooker, ordered in after Sumner's wing had failed, oversaw the last part of the battle. "Finding that I had lost as many men as my orders required me to lose, I suspended the attack," he reported.[45]

The battle was over. Now there only remained the terrible coda that followed every Civil War battle—the screams and moans of the wounded. As the unseasonably warm day turned to a cold December night, those still alive between the lines used the frozen bodies of their dead comrades as barricades against the bullets that flew their way.

When it came time to count the costs, the Army of the Potomac had lost 12,653 dead, wounded, and missing. The Army of Northern Virginia's casualties numbered 5,309. One of the Union dead was George Bayard, the cavalry general who had offered to place young George Meade on his staff. He had been sitting against a tree at Mansfield when an artillery shell exploded nearby, mortally wounding him.

Burnside planned to resume the fighting the next day—he even said he wanted to lead his old IX Corps personally—but his other generals talked him out of such a rash plan. Instead, both armies remained warily facing each other until the Union soldiers crossed back over the river under the cover of darkness. When day dawned on December 15 they were on the other side of the Rappahannock.

Meade wrote to his wife the next day: "I cannot give you all the details of the fight, but will simply say my men went in *beautifully*, carried everything before them, and drove the enemy for nearly half a mile, but finding themselves unsupported on either right or left, and encountering an overwhelming force of the enemy, they were checked and finally driven back. As an evidence of the work they had to do, it is only necessary to state that out of four thousand five hundred men taken into action, we know the names of eighteen hundred killed and wounded. There are besides some four hundred missing, many of whom are wounded. All the men agree it was the warmest work the Reserves had ever encountered."[46]

One loss struck Meade personally, and that was Arthur Dehon, hit in the heart by a bullet while delivering Meade's orders to C. Feger Jackson. Meade had his body recovered under a flag of truce and sent to Washington. The general had liked the young man—Dehon's father had even paid a visit to Margaret back in

Philadelphia—and four months later Meade was still brooding about his loss and the death of another aide, Hamilton Kuhn, who died at Glendale. "To be cut off in the way they were, is truly mournful," he wrote to Margaret the next April, "and I feel sometimes as if I was individually responsible, and in some measure the cause of the misfortune of their friends."[47]

Meade also complained about the reporting in the *New York Herald*, which said the Pennsylvania Reserves immediately fled when faced with enemy fire. Meade had seen the reporter on the field—the same reporter who had urged Birney to use his artillery to support the Reserves—and said he should have known better. "What his object in this falsifying the facts was I cannot imagine, but I would advise him not to show himself in our camp if he values his skin, for the men could not be restrained from tarring and feathering him."[48]

Newspaper reports notwithstanding, Meade continued his climb within the Army of the Potomac. Shortly before the Fredericksburg battle he learned of his promotion to major general; on December 23 Burnside told him he was giving him command of the V Corps. That left him with some tricky diplomatic work not only with Butterfield but also with Joe Hooker. Butterfield was a Hooker crony, and the V Corps belonged to Hooker's Grand Division. Meade heard rumors that Hooker was not happy with the change of commanders. Nonetheless, the news called for a celebration. Meade obtained some champagne and invited his fellow generals, including Franklin, Reynolds, and William F. "Baldy" Smith, to share it with him. "Whereupon it was unanimously agreed that Congress ought to establish the grade of lieutenant general, and that they would all unite in having me made one, provided I would treat with such good wine," Meade reported.[49]

On the day before Christmas Meade rode to Hooker's tent to officially report for duty. He found Hooker with Butterfield. After what must have been an awkward few minutes, Butterfield excused himself.

"I told Burnside, when he informed me of his intention, that there was no officer in the army I would prefer to you, were the corps without a commander and the question of selection open," Hooker told Meade, "but Butterfield having been placed there and having discharged the duties to my satisfaction, particularly through the late battle, I deemed myself authorized to ask that he might be retained."[50] Hooker said it was nothing personal, and then he signed the order relieving Butterfield and giving Meade command.

Butterfield invited his successor to a Christmas dinner the next day, a handsome entertainment shared by all the brigade and division commanders. After everyone else had left, Meade remained behind to talk with Butterfield. He understood his feelings, Meade told him. "Poor Butterfield then opened his heart," said Meade. Burnside had promised him that command of the V Corps was permanent, Butterfield complained. Meade sympathized but pointed out that the original injustice had been done when Butterfield was promoted over him. When he said good night to Butterfield, Meade felt that the situation was "definitely and satisfactorily settled."[51] He would have further unpleasant dealings with Butterfield in the future.

The new year began with more turmoil within the army. Lincoln had summoned Burnside to Washington on December 31 and told him that he had lost the confidence of his generals. Burnside demanded to know which of his subordinates had been telling tales to the president. Lincoln refused to say, but the main ringleaders were Franklin and "Baldy" Smith, who commanded the VI Corps. He asked Burnside to meet with him the next day.

That was January 1, the day on which Lincoln signed the Emancipation Proclamation into law. At the New Year's meeting Burnside offered his resignation. Lincoln wouldn't accept it. Burnside then handed Lincoln a written protest against Halleck and Stanton, who were present. Lincoln read it and handed it back. Burnside repeated the letter's charges that Halleck and Stanton also had lost the army's confidence. The whole situation was, in short, a mess.

"I am tired of this playing war without risks," Meade wrote to Margaret. "We must encounter risks if we fight, and we cannot carry on war without fighting. That was McClellan's vice. He was always waiting to have everything just as he wanted before he would attack, and before he could get things arranged as he wanted them, the enemy pounced on him and thwarted all his plans. There is now no doubt he allowed three distinct occasions to take Richmond slip through his hands, for want of nerve to run what he considered risks. Such a general will never command success, though he may avoid disaster."[52]

Burnside had already suffered one disaster, but the fates weren't quite through with him yet. He decided to make another attempt to dislodge the Army of Northern Virginia from Fredericksburg, this time by moving up the Rappahannock, crossing the river there, and thus outflanking Lee's army. The army began moving on January 19. All proceeded well until the next night, when Mother Nature, not Robert E. Lee, provided a knockout punch. It began to rain—not just normal rainfall, but a torrential, drenching downpour that turned the roads to rivers of mud. It rained all night, then the next day, and the day after that. Pontoons, cannons, horses, mules—all became trapped in the muck and mire. Meade had his men cut trees into logs and build eight miles of corduroy road, but even that monumental effort proved useless. Burnside finally ordered his wet and weary army back to the camps they had so recently abandoned. The Mud March was over.

Soldiers began singing a bit of doggerel about this latest debacle to strike the Army of the Potomac:

> Now I lay me down to sleep
> In mud that's many fathoms deep;
> If I'm not here when you awake,
> Just hunt me up with an oyster rake.[53]

Perhaps it was for the best. Burnside had lost the confidence of his officers and of the administration, hardly good portents for a renewal of battle. On January 23 he issued an order relieving those generals he felt had been undermining him. One of them was Joe Hooker, who Burnside said had "endeavored to create mistrust in the minds of his officers." Lincoln refused to approve the order. Two days later Burnside returned to the army from a visit to Washington with news that Hooker was replacing him as commander of the Army of the Potomac.

"With all my respect, and I may almost say affection, for Burnside—for he has been most kind and considerate towards me—I cannot shut my eyes to the fact that he was not equal to the command of so large an army," Meade wrote to his wife. "He had some very positive qualifications, such as determination and nerve, but he wanted knowledge and judgment, and was deficient in that enlarged mental capacity which is essential in a commander." It did not help that Burnside was so willing to share his poor opinion of his own abilities with the officers serving under him. "I believe Hooker is a good soldier," Meade continued; "the danger he runs is of subjecting himself to bad influences, such as Dan Butterfield and Dan Sickles, who, being intellectually more clever than Hooker, and leading him to believe they are very influential, will obtain an injurious ascendancy over him and insensibly affect his conduct. I may, however, in this be wrong; time will prove."[54]

CHAPTER 7

Chancellorsville

Joseph Hooker
LIBRARY OF CONGRESS

$\bullet \quad \bullet \quad \bullet$

Since I'm visiting the Chancellorsville battlefield, I figure I should pay my respects to the arm. The limb, or whatever remains of it, lies buried in a family cemetery at a house called Ellwood, a few miles from the Chancellorsville visitors center. I follow Route 3 for a few miles and then turn left on Route 20. A sign points me down a narrow dirt road, along a line of trees and past some fields. Ellwood looms up at the end of the little parking lot. It's a reddish wooden building that looks out over open fields. A man named William Jones built the house around 1790; supposedly Robert E. Lee's father, "Light-Horse Harry," wrote his memoirs in a room upstairs. During the war this was one of the homes of wealthy Virginian J. Horace Lacy. He also owned Chatham, the brick mansion outside Falmouth that overlooks Fredericksburg and served as a Union headquarters during the battle there.

The National Park Service acquired the house and property in 1977 and has been restoring it. Volunteers from the Friends of the Wilderness Battlefield, a nonprofit group that works with the Park Service, staff the house when it's open on weekends from spring through October. It's still a respectable-looking farmhouse, in a bucolic spot surrounded by towering trees—hackberry, Kentucky coffee tree, sugar maple. A huge catalpa "witness tree" stood here for at least 170 years until it plunged to earth in September 2006.[1] In a back room there's a large photograph of J. Horace Lacy, the so-called "Lion of the Wilderness." Lacy looks young and confident, one hand on a large book, with bristling chin whiskers and a determined look in his eyes. He seems very much like a young man who knows he is a young man of promise. Of course, it helped that he married into money.

On the other side of the social spectrum, one of the hundred or so slaves who toiled for Lacy here, a Charles Sprow or Sprout, fled to the Union army and served in the cavalry. He is one of only twenty African Americans buried in Fredericksburg National Cemetery.[2]

The family cemetery lies in a field off to one side of the house. I follow a narrow pathway that takes me between some high hedges, down a little flight of wooden stairs, and across a rising field. On this May afternoon stubs of old cornstalks poke in neat rows through tall grass and yellow flourishes of buttercups. The smell of cut grass sweetens the air. Near the brow of the rise a copse of trees rears above the cemetery, which is ringed by a single-railed wooden fence. There is only one stone here, a simple granite marker that tilts a bit to one side. The words engraved on it read:

Arm of
Stonewall Jackson
May 3, 1863

I suppose that when the sun is right, Jackson's arm rests in the shade of the trees.

I was here years ago, before Ellwood opened to the public. That had been late on a fall afternoon. I parked out by the road, stepped over the rope intended to bar my entrance, and walked by myself down the dirt lane. Ellwood looked like a haunted house then, derelict and deserted, and I half expected to see spectral faces peering from the upper windows. It provided a suitably atmospheric place to find a severed arm.

Things are a little more upbeat on this bright May afternoon. The sun is shining and birds sing. The weather is probably a lot like it was on May 2, 1863, when Stonewall Jackson made a seventeen-mile roundabout march during the Battle of Chancellorsville and brought thirty thousand men into the tangled woods on the Army of the Potomac's unprotected right flank. Jackson received a mortal wound and died, minus one arm, in an outbuilding of a farmhouse twenty-seven miles away. Chancellorsville ended up being another debacle for the Union, but Jackson's death dealt a great blow to the Confederates as well.

For his part Meade didn't get an opportunity to do much at all during the Chancellorsville fighting, despite his vehement insistence that he be allowed to. Nonetheless, the battle helped set the stage for his ascension to command of the Army of the Potomac.

But I'm getting ahead of myself.

On January 28, 1863, "Fighting Joe" Hooker returned from meetings in Washington to take up his new command. Meade saddled up his horse and rode three miles through blowing snow to meet with him. He found Hooker in fine spirits. Hooker told Meade that administration officials had treated him like a prince and said he could have whatever he wanted. Hooker did not disclose any plans—he tended to remain secretive about his intentions, a characteristic that Meade would find irritating—but he hinted that he would spring into action as soon as the weather permitted.

Back in October, while McClellan's army remained inert near Sharpsburg and speculation favored Hooker as his most likely replacement, Meade had mused about Fighting Joe in a letter to his wife. "Hooker and I are old acquaintances," he wrote. "We were at West Point together, served in Mexico together, and have met from time to time since. He is a very good soldier, capital general for an army corps, but I am not prepared to say as to his abilities for carrying on a campaign and commanding a large army. I should fear his judgment and prudence, as he is apt to think the only thing to be done is to pitch in and fight." Meade knew that Hooker was a Democrat and an antiabolitionist. Those weren't qualities Lincoln necessarily sought in an army commander, but Meade suspected Hooker would shape himself to fit circumstances. "What he will be, when the command of the army is held out to him, is more than any one can tell, because I fear he is open to temptation and liable to be seduced by flattery." He also distrusted the company Hooker kept. "Such gentlemen as Dan Sickles and Dan Butterfield are not the persons I should select as my intimates, however worthy and superior they may be," he wrote home.[3]

Margaret fretted that her husband might end up as commander of the army. Meade assured her that such a thing was neither likely nor to be desired. Meade felt no envy for Hooker and predicted his eventual fate: "undue and exaggerated praise before he does anything, and a total absence of reason and intelligence in the discussion of his acts when he does attempt anything, and a denial of even ordinary military qualifications unless he achieves impossibilities."[4] He could have been describing his own future.

The Army of the Potomac underwent other changes following Hooker's ascension. Ambrose Burnside left to command the Department of the Ohio. Old "Bull" Sumner left, too, after asking to be relieved because of his health. He died of pneumonia before he could report to a new assignment in the Department of the Missouri. Meade's former corps commander, William Franklin, also left the army for a post out west. "Baldy" Smith, who had gone to the president with Franklin to complain about Burnside, was sent packing as well. Maj. Gen. John Sedgwick took Smith's place as commander of the VI Corps. He was a Connecticut native who had graduated from West Point two years after Meade. A lifelong bachelor, he was "married" to the army and enjoyed passing the time playing long games of solitaire. War correspondent Smalley called him "one of the best generals we had: a man of utterly transparent honesty, simplicity, and truth of character; trusted, beloved, ardently followed by his men; a commander who had done great things and was capable of greater."[5] His men loved him and called him "Uncle John."

Hooker immediately began whipping his army back into shape. He raised morale by establishing a furlough system and improving food and living conditions. He picked Daniel Butterfield as his chief of staff, and Butterfield designed unique emblems for each of the army's corps to aid in recognition. The V Corps received a Maltese cross. For a short time Meade commanded the army's Center Grand Division, but Hooker reverted to a regular corps organization and Meade returned to lead just the V Corps. He had three divisions under him. Brig. Gen. Charles Griffin commanded the 1st Division; Maj. Gen. George Sykes, whose grave I saw at West Point, had the 2nd; and Brig. Gen. Andrew A. Humphreys, who later served as Meade's chief of staff, commanded the 3rd.

Hooker also reorganized the cavalry, combining the units that had been scattered among individual brigades and divisions into a separate corps. Hooker placed this new cavalry corps under the overall command of Maj. Gen. George Stoneman. Meade's son George remained with the 6th Pennsylvania Cavalry. He had been assigned to headquarters, "a lazy, loafing sort of duty," his father said, and the senior Meade thought the changes would allow him to perform more useful service.[6]

Meade spent more time in Washington in the months before the weather allowed the armies to stir from their winter camps. Congress's Joint Committee on the Conduct of the War had launched an investigation of the Fredericksburg affair and called Meade to testify in March. Meade made his way to the Capitol one morning and met with Sen. Ben Wade, who asked what Meade thought would have happened had Franklin supported him with his whole force. "I said I believed such a movement would have resulted in the driving back of the enemy's right wing," Meade reported; "though it would, without doubt, have produced a desperate and hard-contested fight." It seemed the committee had Franklin in its sights, and Meade, who liked Franklin, felt bad for him. "I sometimes feel very nervous about my position," he told Margaret, "they are knocking over generals at such a rate."[7]

Spring approached and the warfare being conducted in the halls of Washington was about to be replaced by the real thing. On Sunday, April 5, President

Lincoln reached the army in the middle of a driving snowstorm. He looked "care-worn and exhausted," noted Meade, who had dinner with the president and his wife, Hooker, the rest of the corps commanders, and other dignitaries on Monday night. Meade knew that there was a vacant brigadier general position open in the Regular Army so, always ambitious, he attempted to curry favor with the president by telling him some ribald stories. As he told Margaret, "I think I have made decided progress in his affections."[8] For a brief moment it appeared he had made a good impression on the first lady, too. A few days after the dinner a messenger delivered a bouquet of flowers to Meade's tent, along with a card that read, "With the compliments of Mrs. A. Lincoln." "At first I was very much tickled, and my vanity insinuated that my *fine appearance* had taken Mrs. L's eye and that my fortune was made," Meade informed Margaret. "This delusion, however, was speedily dissolved by the orderly who brought the bouquet inquiring the road to General Griffin's and Sykes's quarters, when I ascertained that all the principal generals had been similarly honored."[9]

The season of such frivolity was drawing to an end. Hooker had made his plans. Unlike Burnside he would not make a frontal attack on Lee's strong position behind Fredericksburg—although he wanted the rebels to think he would. Instead, Hooker would attempt to move around Lee, much as Burnside had wanted to do on his Mud March. Sedgwick and the VI Corps, supported by the I Corps under Reynolds and the III Corps under Sickles, would distract Lee by crossing the Potomac below Fredericksburg, with Sedgwick crossing where Franklin had made his ill-fated passage the previous December. But the real attack would take place to the north. The II, V, XI, and XII Corps would march up the Rappahannock. Darius Couch and the II Corps would halt behind United States Ford and wait. The other three corps would continue on and cross the Rappahannock at Kelly's Ford and then separate. Meade's V Corps would cross the Rapidan River at Ely's Ford, and the other two corps would use Germanna Ford. They would converge at a crossroads known as Chancellorsville, about ten miles west of Fredericksburg. Lee, already weakened because Longstreet was in southern Virginia with two divisions, would have to either retreat or come out from behind his fortified position to give battle. Hooker felt confident. "I have the finest army the sun ever shone on," he boasted. "I can march this army to New Orleans. My plans are perfect, and when I start to carry them out, may God have mercy on General Lee, for I will have none."[10]

• • •

Deciding to follow in Meade's footsteps as closely as possible, I set out to find Kelly's Ford. I start in Fredericksburg, which feels a lot different on a bright May morning than it did on that cold and rainy December afternoon when I followed in the footsteps of the Irish Brigade. The Union soldiers camped on the opposite side of the Rappahannock around Falmouth must have similarly welcomed their spring in 1863, although they still had rain to deal with—lots and lots of rain. "It seems as though it were never to stop raining; the longer it rains the harder it seems to come down," noted one of Hooker's aides on April 24 as the army waited to move. "Could you come into Headquarters at any time during the day you would see that something was wrong; every one is moving around in an aimless, nervous way, looking at the clouds and then at the ground, and in knots trying to convince themselves that it is going to clear off and they will be able to move day after to-morrow."[11]

The rain did interfere with Hooker's plans. He wanted Stoneman and his cavalry to cross the Rappahannock on April 15 and ride into Lee's rear to cut his lines of communication and supply and perhaps even force the Confederates to retreat toward Richmond. The high waters, however, kept Stoneman from crossing until April 29, seriously interfering with the cavalry's mission and Hooker's strategy. It was a bad beginning to the campaign.

Meade's corps broke camp on April 27 to begin the twenty-five-mile march to Kelly's Ford. As they tramped along some of the Union troops sang a song:

Joe Hooker is our leader, he takes his whisky strong,
So our knapsacks we will sling, and go marching along.
Marching along, marching along.
With eight days' rations we'll go marching along.[12]

It takes me some time and not a little cursing before I finally find Kelly's Ford, which isn't indicated on any of my road maps. I park my car in a small dirt parking lot by the bridge that Route 620 uses to cross the Rappahannock. A little dirt path leads down to the riverside. A brochure I picked up at park headquarters informs me that the Civil War ford was actually some three hundred yards downstream. The Rappahannock has narrowed this far above Fredericksburg, but I can still see how the river would have created quite an obstacle for an army encumbered with wagons, cannons, pack mules, and all the accoutrements of war.

Kelly's Ford is another one of those names that pop up frequently in Civil War histories. Like the gaps in the mountains, the fords across rivers provided natural routes for armies and became the focal points for military activity. Armies needed to use them for their movements, so they became the settings for conflict. Throughout the war armies splashed their way in both directions back and forth across the Rappahannock here and sometimes came to blows.

My park brochure details one clash here that served as a prelude to the Battle of Chancellorsville, when Union cavalry under Brig. Gen. William Averell battled Fitzhugh Lee's Confederate horsemen on March 17, 1863. Averell had a score to settle with his old friend Fitzhugh Lee, Robert E. Lee's nephew. After an earlier cavalry skirmish had gone badly for the Union, Lee left behind a taunting note for Averell: "I wish you would put up your sword, leave my state, and go home. You ride a good horse, I ride a better. If you won't go home, return my visit, and bring me a sack of coffee."

Averell brought about three thousand men with him to answer Lee's taunt. He made a difficult crossing of the swiftly flowing river at Kelly's Ford and launched a spirited cavalry battle on the other side. Averell's ingrained caution prevented him from routing Lee's forces, but he made a surprisingly good showing for the until then toothless Union cavalry. He also left behind some coffee and a note. "Dear Fitz," it read. "Here's your coffee. Here's your visit. How do you like it?"

One of the Confederates mortally wounded during the fighting was the "Gallant" John Pelham, the young man who had caused Meade so much trouble at Fredericksburg with Stuart's horse artillery. A National Park Service driving tour I've printed out indicates there's a monument to Pelham near the spot where he was wounded, so I decide to find it. The directions tell me to park in a little parking lot off Route 674, in the C. F. Phelps Wildlife Management Area. Accompanied by the incessant chatter of insects I follow a trail toward the Rappahannock that passes through the woods, lined by pine trees and dotted with goldenrod. I see no trace of a monument until the path turns to the right, and there, off in the bushes, stands a small tombstonelike marker. "Major John Pelham, C.S.A., commanding the Stuart Horse Artillery, was mortally wounded at this site in the battle of Kelly's Ford, March 17, 1863," it reads. The marker was erected in 1981 by "the admirers of the Gallant Pelham." At lunchtime I find more reminders of Pelham at the nearby Kelly's Ford Inn, which offers food and drink at Pelham's Pub, as well as a life-size painting of him just outside the rear entrance.

I push on toward Ely's Ford and the Rapidan. The river today is quiet and subdued. When Meade's men reached here they found it swollen with rain, up to four feet deep and with a swift current. To save time Meade ordered his men to cross without undressing. Some soldiers raised their haversacks and cartridge boxes on their bayonets to keep them dry; others hung their personal items around their necks. A few men lost their footing and were swept away, eventually rescued by cavalry posted just downstream. The sun set during the long crossing but the wet and shivering men found large bonfires waiting on the opposite shore. By then it was lightly raining again, a guarantee that the members of the V Corps would have an uncomfortable and relatively sleepless night.[13]

The corps resumed its march from Ely's Ford on April 30, and Meade reached Chancellorsville sometime around 11:00. The name was misleading—there was no "ville" here, just a large house owned by the prominent Chancellor family, set in the midst of the tangled area of second-growth forest and small clearings called the Wilderness. "It was a large, commodious, two-story brick building, with peaked roof and a wing, and pillared porches on both stories in the centre of the main building," wrote a member of the 118th Pennsylvania, part of Charles Griffin's division. "Upon the upper porch was quite a bevy of ladies in light, dressy, attractive spring costumes. They were not at all abashed or intimidated, scolded audibly and reviled bitterly."[14]

Today there is neither ville nor house here. The only remaining traces of the building are portions of brick foundation that mark the outlines, plus a chunk of the front steps, looking so old and weathered it could be a remnant of the Parthenon.

Chancellorsville was important because it stood at an intersection of several roads. One was the Ely's Ford Road, which the V Corps had followed from the Rapidan. The Orange Turnpike, today's Route 3, was another. It led directly into Fredericksburg, with a small house of worship called Old Salem Church on the road about seven miles away. The Orange Plank Road headed south from Chancellorsville and then curved back to reconnect with the turnpike about a mile before Salem Church. The River Road followed a looping course in the direction of another Rappahannock crossing, Banks Ford. The United States Ford Road came in from United States Ford. All these roads gave Chancellorsville an importance that belied the fact that little was actually there.

XII Corps commander Maj. Gen. Henry Slocum, a sharp-faced West Point graduate with a devilishly pointed beard and high forehead, arrived some three hours after Meade. He had command of this wing of the army until Hooker could arrive and take over. Meade greeted Slocum with excitement. "This is splendid, Slocum; hurrah for old Joe," he exclaimed. "We are on Lee's flank, and he does not know it. You take the Plank Road toward Fredericksburg, and I'll take the Pike, or *vice versa*, as you prefer, and we will get out of this Wilderness."

Slocum quickly punctured Meade's enthusiasm. "My orders are to assume command on arriving at this point, and to take up a line of battle here, and not to move forward without further orders," he said.[15] It was the first hint of things to come. Hooker was determined to remain on the defensive and force Lee to fight him on ground of his own choosing.

The army continued to grow as it awaited its commander. Maj. Gen. Oliver Otis Howard and the XI Corps reached Chancellorsville around 4:00. Born in Maine and a graduate of Bowdoin College and West Point, Howard was an exceedingly pious man who became known as the Christian General (or, less favorably, as "Old Prayer Book" by his men). He had lost an arm at Seven Pines and had been in command of the XI Corps since only March 1, replacing the popular German-born Maj. Gen. Franz Sigel. So far it had not been an easy transition. The XI Corps had a high proportion of Germans and they had been fiercely loyal to Sigel but not necessarily to Howard. Following Hooker's orders, Slocum posted the XI Corps on the army's right flank.

Hooker finally reached Chancellorsville around 6:00. As though to demonstrate that John Pope wasn't the only general with a fondness for windy proclamations, Hooker issued General Orders No. 47, which read, "It is with heartfelt satisfaction the commanding general announces to the army that the operations of the last three days have determined that our enemy must either ingloriously fly or come out from behind his intrenchments and give us battle on our own ground, where certain destruction awaits him."[16]

Once Hooker's army had moved forward enough to "uncover" the approaches to United States Ford, Maj. Gen. Darius Couch and the II Corps crossed over and added their numbers to the growing ranks of Union soldiers. Couch found the army in very high spirits: "As I rode into Chancellorsville that night the general hilarity pervading the camps was particularly noticeable; the soldiers, while chopping wood and lighting fires, were singing merry songs and indulging in peppery camp jokes."[17]

Still, doubts began to gnaw at parts of the army. Brig. Gen. James Barnes's brigade of Griffin's division had pushed on a couple miles down the old turnpike. The men halted at the base of some high ground when they unexpectedly stumbled upon a rebel force at the top of the hill. Both sides seemed equally surprised by the encounter. The opposing pickets were close enough to carry on a conversation, yet not a shot was fired. "What magic spell came upon these brave men and prevented an instant death grapple I can never know," noted a member of the 118th Pennsylvania, "but after a pause which seemed minutes to me, but which, in reality, was but a few moments, the enemy, still facing us, drew back gradually and disappeared into the depth of the thicket without a shot being fired on either side."[18] The Union soldiers advanced and took the high ground. Griffin arrived and fell into an earnest conversation with Barnes as they waited for orders from Meade. Finally, word came to fall back to the flat land around Chancellorsville. "Call that a position?" the excitable Griffin exclaimed. "Here I can defy any force the enemy can bring against me."[19]

The men of his command were equally bothered by the orders to fall back from such a fine spot. "The soldiers were as discomfited as if they had been checked by a serious repulse," read a history of the 118th Pennsylvania. "All enthusiasm vanished, all the bright hopes of success disappeared. The belief that had grown to conviction that the campaign would culminate in the utter rout of the enemy was changed to sullen disappointment."[20]

● ● ●

One of the stops on the driving tour of the Chancellorsville battlefield is a small field with a walking tour around its perimeter. The path is called the McLaws Trail after Confederate general Lafayette McLaws, who attacked through here on May 3, but also has connections with George Sykes of Meade's corps. Sykes was yet another West Point graduate, a Delaware native who had been fighting since First Bull Run. He looked like a cartoon general, with a big beard that jutted out in front of his chin and a firm, determined nose like the prow of a ship. Sykes's men had camped at this forward position on April 30. On May 1 they began moving down the turnpike toward Fredericksburg until Confederate resistance brought them to a halt. Sykes felt increasingly isolated and vulnerable amid the tangled Wilderness and feared the Confederates would outflank him. "Griffin was far to my left, Slocum far to my right, the enemy in front and between me and both those officers," he reported. Still, like Griffin, he had a good position on some high ground and wanted to hold it as long as possible. Brig. Gen. Gouverneur K. Warren, then serving as an engineer on Hooker's staff, rode out to find Sykes and determine his situation. He reported back to Hooker and returned with orders for Sykes to retreat toward Chancellorsville.[21] Pulling back, Sykes found a another good position on some high ground where he could expect some support from Winfield Scott Hancock's II Corps, but once again he received orders to move closer to Chancellorsville. As the men fell back Meade joined Couch, Sykes, and Slocum. Meade watched the withdrawal in disgust. "My God," he grumbled, "if we can't hold the top of a hill, we certainly can't hold the bottom of it."[22]

Couch rode back to the Chancellorsville house. The once quiet rural crossroads was humming with activity. Hundreds of horses were tied up outside the house and officers crowded inside. But Couch sensed that the high spirits he had witnessed the night before were already starting to deflate, and he worried that fighting a defensive battle amid the thickets and forests of the Wilderness would be a doomed effort. Hooker told him not to worry: "It is all right, Couch, I have got Lee just where I want him; he must fight me on my own ground." Couch did

not feel reassured. "I retired from his presence with the belief that my commanding officer was a whipped man," he said later.[23]

Brig. Gen. Alpheus Williams, a division commander in the XII Corps, also
sensed a mood of unease that morning. "It was known that Hooker had boastingly
declared the night before that 'God Almighty could not prevent his destroying
the Rebel army,'" said Williams. "The blasphemy did not please the most irreli-
gious as appropriate to any, and least of all to an, occasion so momentous, but al-
lowance was made for excitement. Still, there was an uneasiness in the best
military minds. There was too much boasting and too little planning; swagger
without preparation."[24]

Lee and Jackson intended to end the Union swaggering, and the battlefield's
driving tour takes me to the Lee-Jackson Bivouac, the place where they determined how they would do it. This quiet spot in the woods at the intersection of
the Old Plank and Furnace Roads is holy ground in Southern Civil War lore. On
the night of May 1 Lee and Jackson met here to plot the destruction of Joe
Hooker's army. As they consulted their maps and talked with their scouts, they
realized the Federals appeared vulnerable on their right, where Howard's XI
Corps rested with its flank "in the air," meaning it had no solid anchor. All
Howard had shielding the right of the Union line was the thick, tangled forest of
the Wilderness. Howard thought this was protection enough, but Lee and Jackson, sitting on cracker boxes as they talked into the night, believed otherwise.

Lee never lacked audacity, and the plan he hatched on the night of May 1 may
have been his most audacious move yet. Although badly outnumbered, and with
part of his army still confronting Sedgwick behind Fredericksburg, he decided to
divide his army even more by sending Jackson and thirty thousand men on a wide
swing against the Union right while he remained in place with only about fifteen
thousand men to distract the rest of the Federals.

Jackson set out the next morning, his long column of men marching four abreast
down narrow trails through the forest. The line stretched for almost ten miles—
two hours after the head of the column began marching the tail end had yet to move.
It was a huge, gray-clad, and tattered serpent snaking through the Virginia woods,
making slow but steady progress to pounce on unsuspecting prey. At the ironworks
of Catharine Furnace, of which only a single chimney remains today, the column
veered south on its roundabout course. Once it reached the Brock Road it turned
north, heading for the Plank Road and the unsuspecting men of the XI Corps.

Jackson's movement did not remain a secret from Hooker's army, though. The
marching troops were clearly visible off in the distance as they passed a clearing.
Union artillery took the opportunity to fire some shells their way. Hooker sent
a message to Howard and Slocum. "We have good reason to suppose that the
enemy is moving to our right," it warned. "Please advance your pickets for purposes of observation as far as may be safe, in order to obtain timely information
of their approach." He warned Howard that he was not in position to withstand
a flank attack.[25] In response Howard did pretty much nothing.

Daniel Sickles, ordered up from Sedgwick's diversionary movement below
Fredericksburg, had reached Chancellorsville at 9:00 that morning. Sickles was a
politician, not a professional soldier, but his connections had helped propel him

to command of the III Corps. Hooker gave him permission to attack Jackson's marching men but by the time Sickles moved forward most of the Confederates had made the swing south from Catharine Furnace. The Federals managed to snap up most of the 23rd Georgia, which served as the Confederate rear guard. Sickles interpreted the rebel movement as a retreat. Hooker seemed pleased to accept Sickles's view that Lee had decided to "ingloriously fly." Pope had thought that at Second Bull Run, too.

The hours passed. Jackson's men continued their tramp through the woods. Late in the day they finally reached the Plank Road, and Jackson began positioning his men north and south of the road. It was about 5:00 before all was ready. On the far side of a screen of tangled undergrowth, Howard's troops remained serenely unsuspecting, their weapons stacked, fires burning to cook supper, men lying on blankets and resting or playing cards. Jackson's men began pushing forward. For the Federals, the first sign that something was amiss came when terrified deer, birds, and rabbits, fleeing in front of the Confederate advance, burst out of the woods and scampered through the Union campsites. And then Jackson's men, screaming the rebel yell, fell on the XI Corps.

It was a rout. Some regiments stood and fought but most of the XI Corps broke under the unexpected onslaught and began streaming, confused and frightened, toward the Chancellorsville house. "The Eleventh Corps men, in wild disorder, a perfect mob, without the slightest semblance of organization, were rushing back upon us in an incontrollable torrent," wrote Capt. Porter Farley of the 140th New York. "It was useless to halt and detain the straggling crowds, for their demoralization was so great that they were an element of weakness rather than strength." Around the Chancellorsville house military bands energetically struck up national airs—"Yankee Doodle," "The Star-Spangled Banner," "The Red, White, and Blue"—in an attempt to instill some spirit in the stampeded troops. "In front, the fight was raging furiously," Farley recalled. "A perfect storm of artillery lighted up, with fitful flashes, the forest opening. The rattle of musketry was incessant. The shouts of the officers and the shrieks of the wounded filled the air."[26]

As the sun set, Hooker and his generals struggled to regain control over their men and stem the flood, even as the Confederate attack fell victim to its own overwhelming success. The pursuing columns became disorganized, and the soldiers, exhausted after their long march, lost their momentum as night fell. Jackson, however, wasn't satisfied with merely rolling up the Union right. He wanted to get behind the enemy army and cut off its retreat to the Rappahannock. He encountered Gen. A. P. Hill, one of his division commanders, on the Plank Road beneath the light of a full moon. "General Hill, when you reach Chancellorsville, allow nothing to stop you!" Jackson commanded. "Press on to the United States Ford!" Then he took some staff officers forward with him to make a personal reconnaissance. As the group rode back toward its own lines in the woods, it neared some nervous North Carolina troops who heard horsemen approaching them in the night. Shots rang out in the darkness.

"Cease firing!" a member of Jackson's escort shouted. "You are firing into your own men!"

"Who gave that order?" came a voice from in front of them. "It's a lie! Pour it to them, boys!" The crackle of musketry ripped the air. Three bullets hit Jackson—one in the right hand, another in the left forearm, and a third near the left shoulder. [27]

• • •

Stonewall Jackson is a fascinating person, but I confess to having mixed feelings about him. I must admit that, as Lee's "right arm," he carried out some superb tactical maneuvers. He became a legend after his campaigns in the Shenandoah Valley, and we've already seen how he wreaked havoc behind Pope's lines at Second Bull Run and captured Harpers Ferry prior to Antietam. But the insistent Stonewall hagiography gets on my nerves after a while. I grow tired of the omnipresent Lee-Jackson iconography I find at Civil War sites and reenactments, as well as the paintings I see of Lee and Jackson on their cracker boxes at Chancellorsville. I resent the Sons of Confederate Veterans marker that steals Meade's thunder at Fort Meade in Florida. From where I stand Stonewall Jackson may have fought well, but he fought on the wrong side.

Jackson was wounded on a spot of land right behind the Chancellorsville visitors center, where I find not one but two monuments that memorialize the event. The original monument is a rough-hewn boulder that's nearly hidden in the bushes. Admirers lugged it here sometime after 1876. Nearby is a large granite memorial that was dedicated on June 13, 1888, before a crowd of five thousand. Resting in its figurative if not literal shadow is a little stone set flat into the ground that memorializes an unknown Union soldier.

A good part of the reason Jackson is so fascinating is that he was so damned *weird*. He had strange dietary habits, often restricting himself to stale bread and salted meat. (There's also a story that he loved to suck on lemons, but it seems to be a myth. That doesn't keep people from tossing lemons on his grave in Lexington, Virginia.) He was also something of a religious fanatic, guided by a stern, inflexible Presbyterianism that granted God credit for all his victories. He would not even post a letter if he thought it would still be in transit on the Sabbath. On the other hand, he found it nearly impossible to remain awake during church sermons, much to his mortification. His antics at Fort Meade, where he nearly derailed his career by pursuing an obsessive morals case against William French, show what could happen when the didactic and self-righteous side of his personality took charge. Like his religion, he was stern and inflexible in wartime, with his secretiveness and apparent unwillingness to admit of human frailty often creating friction with his subordinates.

Of course, those traits also helped make him the kind of officer who could drive his men to perform great feats of marching and fighting. Those traits hadn't served him so well in peacetime, though. Before the war he had been a figure of fun when he taught at the Virginia Military Institute, where the cadets called him "Tom Fool" and even "Square Box," a jab at his overly large feet. As a teacher he lacked passion and the ability to inspire his students. "There was so little animation, no grace, no enthusiasm," one cadet wrote. "All was stiffness and awkwardness." It took war to rescue Thomas Jackson from mediocrity—the same favor that war did for Ulysses S. Grant.

Yet there are some other sides to Jackson. Off the battlefield there was something touchingly damaged about him. He liked children and displayed great tenderness toward his infant daughter, who was born only a few months before Chancellorsville. In his hometown of Lexington, Virginia, he violated Virginia law by starting a Sunday school for slaves. Still, I find it hard to reconcile the all-encompassing Christian faith that drove him with his avowed purpose of killing the enemy. There's a story that when one of Jackson's officers said he regretted killing some courageous Union soldiers, Jackson replied, "No, shoot them all. I do not wish them to be brave." I think he strayed from Jesus's teachings there. I appreciate Jackson's skills in war, but I grow tired of seeing the business of killing wrapped in a package of such inflexible Christian piety.

Of course, it was a religious age and Jackson certainly wasn't unique in feeling that God was on his side. Meade, too, peppered his letters with references to God and his hope that the Almighty would side with the Union cause. Yet Meade didn't seem to share Jackson's unshakeable self-righteous certainty about which side God was backing. Later in the war Theodore Lyman overheard a conversation that Meade had with a Southern bishop who was crossing through Union lines under a flag of truce on his way to Richmond. The bishop told Meade he felt certain that Providence would not desert the South in its righteous cause. "Yes," said Meade, "but then *we* feel that Providence will not desert *our* cause; now how are you going to settle that question." Both men laughed.[28]

◆ ◆ ◆

When Jackson's men fell on the unlucky XI Corps, Meade was on the other end of the Union line, behind a stout defensive position. As the panicked remnants of the XI Corps flowed past their lines, Meade quickly dispatched Sykes to cover the Ely's Ford and United States Ford Roads and keep the rebels from getting in the army's rear. "This was done in an incredibly short period of time," wrote James Biddle, who was serving on Meade's staff, "and I have always thought that *if* the *advance* the rebels always claimed would have been made if Jackson had lived had been made, they would have been quickly driven back."[29]

Once darkness fell, the ever aggressive Sickles decided to try a risky nighttime attack to recapture some of the artillery that Jackson's men had seized and then fight his way back to a more secure position. Led by David Birney's division, the assault achieved little except for the almost inevitable confusion created by fighting in the dark. Brig. Gen. Alpheus Williams of the XII Corps described the "tremendous roll of infantry fire, mingled with yellings and shoutings, almost diabolical and infernal. Human language can give no idea of such a scene—such an infernal and yet sublime combination of sound and flame and smoke, and dreadful yells of rage, of pain, of triumph, or of defiance."[30]

When May 3 dawned, though, Hooker still held the advantage, with his army positioned between the two sections of Lee's divided force. Sickles and his men occupied a dominating position called Hazel Grove, which offered an ideal artillery platform. Hooker, however, ordered Sickles to abandon Hazel Grove and move closer to Chancellorsville. Confederate artilleryman E. Porter Alexander called this "a fatal mistake," saying, "There has rarely been a more gratuitous gift of a battle-field."[31] Once Sickles pulled back, the Confederates hurried more than thirty of their own guns up here and began a spirited artillery duel with Union cannons at a Chancellor farm called Fairview. Sickles would remember the loss of Hazel Grove a month later at Gettysburg, while Hooker would have good cause to rue his decision later that day.

The fighting on May 3 was some of the bloodiest of the war, with something like 17,500 casualties during the day—not quite as bloody as Antietam but impressively sanguinary nonetheless. Joe Hooker was one casualty. A messenger from Sickles had reached the Chancellorsville house, and Hooker was leaning over the porch railing to speak with him when a Confederate cannonball fired from Hazel Grove crashed into one of the house's columns. A fractured portion smashed into Hooker and sent him sprawling. For a moment his men thought he had been killed. It might have been better for the Union cause if he had been. Although he received a serious concussion and was incapable of commanding for a time, Hooker would not relinquish control of the army.

Meade, in the meantime, had remained largely on the sidelines. When William French, Jackson's old adversary in Florida and now a division commander in the II Corps, requested help, Meade told Humphreys to send him a brigade. He also dispatched Alexander Webb of his staff to scout the left of Jackson's line, now under command of Jeb Stuart. When Webb returned the two men rode over to Hooker's headquarters. They found the general lying down in his tent. Meade requested permission to go on the offensive. "I have never known any one so vehemently to advise an attack upon the field of battle," Webb later recalled.[32] Not only did the general refuse to let Meade attack, but Hooker also rebuked him for sending men to support French.

The fighting intensified around the Chancellorsville house. Confederate artillery fire from Hazel Grove continued to wreak havoc. Shells exploded in rooms, knocked down chimneys, and set the building ablaze. Nineteen civilians, including the young ladies in the summer dresses who had taunted the Union soldiers, cowered in the basement, unaware that the house was burning down around them. Lt. Col. Joseph Dickinson, Hooker's chief of staff, entered the burning building to guide the terrified civilians to safety—or relative safety, anyway. They emerged into what must have seemed like hell. "The sight that met our eyes as we came out of the dim light of that basement beggars description," recalled Sue Chancellor, who was only eleven at the time. "The woods around the house were a sheet of fire, the air was filled with shot and shell, horses were running, rearing, and screaming, the men, a mass of confusion, moaning, cursing, and praying."[33] One riderless horse galloped around in panic, blood spraying from a chest wound. A mounted officer tried to put it out of its misery with his pistol. But after he rode off, the horse, only further wounded, staggered back to its feet and wandered off into the chaos.[34]

At some places on the battlefield the undergrowth in the forest caught fire, burning the dead and wounded indiscriminately. "It was pitiful to see the charred bodies hugging the trees, or with hands outstretched, as if to ward off the flames," recalled one officer. Around some of the dead were signs of their last frantic attempts to ward off the flames, little areas of scraped earth where they tried to rake away flammable debris.[35]

Hooker, still feeling the effects of the blow, remained in his tent. He called now for Couch, who later remembered the scene: "Raising himself a little as I entered, he said: 'Couch, I turn the command of the army over to you. You will withdraw it and place it in the position designated on this map.'"[36] When Couch emerged from the tent he found Meade waiting outside, looking as though he expected to finally receive orders to attack. Once again he was disappointed. Hooker wanted the army to retreat to a point even farther north of the smoking ruins of Chancellorsville.

In the meantime "Uncle John" Sedgwick was attempting, in a tentative way, to reach the other side of Lee's army. His earlier demonstration below Fredericksburg hadn't been aggressive enough to fool Lee, who had headed west to deal with Hooker. On May 3 Sedgwick attacked in earnest, crossing the Rappahannock at Fredericksburg, marching through town, and assaulting Marye's Heights. Once again Union soldiers weathered a hail of fire from the stone wall, but this time the Confederate defenses were stretched too thin. Triumphant Yankees swarmed over the barrier and captured the hill beyond. One of the Confederate fatalities was Frank Ingraham of the 1st Mississippi, the son of Meade's sister Elizabeth.[37]

Sedgwick could now move his command up the Plank Road toward Chancellorsville, giving Hooker a chance to crush Lee between Sedgwick's hammer and his own anvil. But instead of launching an active attack on Lee, Hooker remained hunkered down behind his lines at Chancellorsville. As Abner Doubleday colorfully put it in his history of the battle, "Hooker did not hold up his end of the log, and the whole weight fell upon Sedgwick."[38] This gave Lee the opportunity to detach some of his men from one front and reverse direction to attack Sedgwick. The forces collided at Salem Church, a little brick house of worship on the Plank Road whose name comes from a biblical word for "peace."

There's no peace for Salem Church today. It's a little oasis of the nineteenth century stranded amid Northern Virginia's modern world of strip malls, gas stations, and heavy traffic. The building sits on a small patch of land, the grass overgrown and unkempt. Its exterior walls still display pockmarks from bullets and shells. This is as far as Sedgwick got. Hooker sent him orders to withdraw across the Rappahannock at Banks Ford. By the time he received another order from Hooker, countermanding his instructions to retreat, Sedgwick had already begun his withdrawal.

Around midnight on May 4 Hooker gathered his corps commanders together in his tent for a council of war. Sedgwick and Slocum were not there but Meade, Sickles, Howard, Reynolds, and Couch were. Brig. Gen. Gouverneur Warren—Hooker's chief engineer—was there, too, and so was Butterfield. Hooker started out by stating that his orders were to protect Washington, not jeopardize his army, making it clear that he inclined toward retreat. Then he excused himself and left the tent with Butterfield so his corps commanders could discuss the matter freely.

Reynolds, who had arrived with his men at 1:00 that morning and now was lying exhausted on the floor, said that since his corps had not been fighting, he didn't think it should be entitled to a vote. He would agree with whatever Meade decided. Meade said he was in favor of attacking, seeing that retreat was probably impossible anyway. Howard also wanted to attack, perhaps to restore some honor to his humiliated XI Corps. Couch was undecided but eventually voted for retreat. Sickles made a little speech. As the only nonprofessional there, he said, perhaps his opinion wasn't worth considering, but he thought a defeat would be worse for the country than a withdrawal. When Sickles began criticizing Hooker for placing the burden of the decision on their shoulders, Warren excused himself. He had already told Hooker that he was in favor of an attack but felt he should not be present if the assembled generals were going to criticize his commander.

Once he believed he had given his generals enough time to discuss the matter, Hooker returned and announced that he was going to retreat. Reynolds left the tent grumbling. "What was the use of calling us together at this time of night when he intended to retreat anyhow?" the normally taciturn I Corps commander complained.[39]

Hooker assigned Meade's relatively fresh V Corps to serve as the rear guard while the army recrossed the river at United States Ford. The weather, which had been pleasant for the work of fighting and dying, turned nasty once again for the retreat, with rain falling in torrents, "a wide opening of the sluice-gates of Heaven," as Porter Farley described it. "Every effort was made to keep the guns and ammunition dry, but it is hardly likely that an hour after the storm broke on us half the muskets in the army could have been discharged."[40] The river began to rise. An engineer rode up to Meade and told him that the high waters were sweeping across the pontoon bridges and the men could not cross. Why tell this to me? Meade demanded, directing the engineer to find General Hooker. The engineer told him he had been trying. It turned out that Hooker was already on the opposite bank. Couch was in nominal command on this side of the river.

Meade dispatched James Biddle to find Hooker and tell him what was going on. Biddle rode through driving rain to the river, over a road covered with six inches of mud and water. He found one bridge still in service, and the artillery was crossing it. Realizing it was impossible to ride a horse across the unstable span, Biddle walked over to the other shore and then continued more than a mile to the house Hooker was using as headquarters. Hooker was asleep on the floor. Biddle talked to Butterfield, who told him the second bridge would be back in service soon.

Back on the other shore, Meade hoped that the rising water would stop the retreat and force the army to turn and fight. "What an act of Providence!" he exclaimed. "Perhaps the salvation of the country will be brought about by this."[41] Couch met with Meade and decided to suspend the withdrawal. He would "fight it out," he said. At 2:00 in the morning Couch received a "sharp message" from Hooker to resume the withdrawal. Reynolds rode up to Meade, and the generals talked together in the rain. "General," said Reynolds, "I will remain with you and if there is any battle to be fought we will fight it together."[42]

It was probably fortunate that there wasn't a further battle. For Captain Farley, waiting in the cold rain as part of the rear guard, unsure if his ammunition was dry enough to fight, the crossing seemed to drag on forever. He thought the XI Corps was making its way across the bridge at a snail's pace. Finally, it was the V Corps' turn to cross. "We breathed easier when our feet at last struck the planking of the bridge," Farley recalled.[43]

Meade was back in camp near Falmouth on the evening of May 6, "fatigued and exhausted with a ten day's campaign, pained and humiliated at its unsatisfactory result, but grateful to our heavenly Father that, in His infinite goodness, He permitted me to escape all the dangers I had to pass through."[44]

He was not happy with Hooker. "General Hooker has disappointed all his friends by failing to show his fighting qualities at the pinch," he wrote to Margaret. "He was more cautious and took to digging quicker even than McClellan, thus proving that a man may talk very big when he has no responsibility, but that it is quite a different thing, acting when you are responsible and talking when others are. Who would have believed a few days ago that Hooker would withdraw his army, in opposition to the opinion of a majority of his corps commanders? yet such is absolutely and actually the case."

Other generals shared his disappointment. Rumors of Hooker's removal from command swept through camp. Couch, Slocum, and Sedgwick all sent word to Meade that they would be happy to serve under him. Col. Charles Wainwright, artillery chief of the I Corps, was talking with some fellow officers on May 6; they decided Meade would be the best replacement for Hooker, with Gouverneur Warren as his chief of staff. "From what I had seen of Meade during the three days I was at Chancellorsville, and from my previous knowledge of him, I had given him the preference, and was glad to find there were others, good judges, who agreed with me," Wainwright noted in his journal.[45]

Shortly after the battle Alexander S. Webb wrote a letter home. "I wish you would tell *all*, that General Meade was head and shoulders above *all out in the field*," he said. "He advised the attacks *which were not* made, and which would have gained the day. He asked to be allowed to attack with his corps, supported by Reynolds; it was refused. He advised *not to fall back*. And since this battle he has received messages from three senior generals stating that they would willingly serve under him."[46]

The butcher's bill for the Chancellorsville campaign had been predictably horrific—something in the neighborhood of thirty thousand dead, wounded, and missing from both sides.

Hands down, the most famous casualty here was Stonewall Jackson. Following the general's wounding on the night of May 2, some of his soldiers hoisted him onto a stretcher and lugged him through the moonlight-drenched woods. Sporadic gunfire erupted in the night, and cannonballs crashed through the trees above them. After being hit, one of the bearers dropped the stretcher, which fell to the ground. Jackson landed on his wounded arm with a loud groan. Before they could get the general to an ambulance, the stretcher bearers dropped him a second time. He must have been in excruciating pain. He made a bumpy ride in an ambulance west down the Plank Road to a field hospital where, in the early hours of May 3, Dr. Hunter McGuire removed his left arm. After visiting the wounded general, Chaplain Beverly Lacy noticed the severed limb lying outside the hospital tent. He wrapped it up and brought the arm to the home of his brother, J. Horace Lacy, about two miles away. That's how Jackson's arm came to be buried in Ellwood's family cemetery.

The rest of Stonewall Jackson took a twenty-seven-mile ambulance ride to a farmhouse at Guinea Station. (The National Park Service brochure of the Fredericksburg-area battlefields even includes the route that the ambulance followed, for those who might wish to retrace the journey.) For a time he seemed to rally, but then the general contracted pneumonia, perhaps brought on by his rough treatment while on the stretcher. In the delirious state leading to his death he shouted out battlefield commands to unseen subordinates, but then he seemed to find some inner peace. "Let us cross over the river and rest under the shade of the trees," he said, and then Stonewall Jackson died on May 10, 1863.

The only farm building remaining is the little white structure where Jackson spent his final days. The deathbed and a clock that ticked away the last minutes of his life are still there. For years the site has been known as the Stonewall Jackson Shrine, which makes the late general sound like some kind of saint.

CHAPTER 8

Gettysburg

*The Widow Leister's house, which served
as Meade's headquarters at Gettysburg*
LIBRARY OF CONGRESS

‿ ‿ ‿

George Meade's papers are in the collections of the Historical Society of Pennsylvania. Founded in 1824, the society has its headquarters on Locust Street in Philadelphia, just a few blocks from Broad Street in one direction and Rittenhouse Square in the other and not far from where the Meades lived on De-lancey Place. When I arrive at the society one Thursday afternoon, the young man behind the counter in the lobby hands me a clipboard with a sheet to fill out to register. Then I pay my $8 fee, clip on a blue "Researcher" button, and proceed into the old-fashioned reading room. Its walls are lined with books, and the big windows behind the tall librarian station look out on the sunny street. The young woman behind the counter takes my call slips and eventually drops the first gray cardboard container at my desk.

The boxes I've requested today include Meade's Civil War correspondence. I feel my pulse quicken as I begin to look through the papers stored inside neatly la-beled manila folders within the box. One of the first pieces of paper I pick up reads:

Genl,

The Commanding General directs that you temporarily assume command of Hooker's Corps, and use every effort to re-organize it and make it serviceable. It is <u>absolutely</u> <u>necessary</u> that the right should be held, and the troops must be got together into positions for that purpose as rapidly as possible.

I realize that this is the note Meade received at Antietam ordering him take over the I Corps following Hooker's wounding. It's a little piece of history.

I dig out Meade's reports on South Mountain and Antietam and Fredericks-burg. In the Fredericksburg report he wrote that under the conditions his men faced, "the best troops would be justified in withdrawing without loss of honor." Then there's a sentence that he scratched out and does not appear in the official report: "This is my calm judgment after reviewing all the circumstances, that the Division did all that it was possible under the peculiar"—and then did he write "curious" or was he starting to write "circumstances"?—"conditions in which it was placed." This isn't even the first draft of history—it's a draft that's still being roughed out.

Over the course of my first afternoon here I have time to look through only three boxes of the kind of history normally kept at a distance behind glass in a museum or available as images in history books. I find a handwritten list of fords across the Rappahannock, written out prior to Chancellorsville, and an organi-zational chart of the Army of Northern Virginia that Daniel Butterfield sent to Meade on April 30, 1863. One folder holds Meade's various army commissions—big sheets of heavy paper that have been carefully folded. It says something about the pace of promotion within the pre–Civil War army that each of these five com-missions bears the signature of a different president: Andrew Jackson, John Tyler, James Polk, Millard Fillmore, and Franklin Pierce. The last commission, his 1856 promotion to captain in the Corps of Topographical Engineers, also has the sig-nature of Secretary of War Jefferson Davis.

I've read the texts of many of the papers I find here in one book or another, but I still get excited when I come across correspondence I recognize—especially when I start reading a letter from Henry Halleck. The handwritten note bears the date of June 27, 1863. My feeling of excitement, though, can't come close to matching what Meade must have felt when he first read this letter early the next morning. "General," it began, "You will receive with this the order of the President placing you in command of the Army of the Potomac."

• • •

The relationship between Meade and Hooker went steadily downhill after the disappointing results at Chancellorsville. "I am sorry to tell you I am at open war with Hooker," Meade wrote to his wife on May 19. Things came to a boil after Hooker read an article in the *New York Herald* that said four of his corps commanders had opposed retreating from Chancellorsville. That wasn't true, Hooker told Meade during a heated conversation. In fact, Reynolds and Meade had helped *persuade* him to retreat.

The statement stunned Meade. Hooker outlined his reasoning: Meade had said that since the army wasn't able to retreat, he preferred to attack. Hooker knew very well that the army could retreat, he now explained, so he interpreted this to mean that Meade preferred to retreat as well. "I replied to him that this was a very ingenious way of stating what I had said," Meade recounted.[1] The meeting became so heated that Alexander Webb, who also was there, left Hooker's tent and took Meade's staff with him because he worried that Meade's intemperate language might lead to a court-martial.[2] Meade told Hooker that he had been emphatically in favor of advancing and would poll the generals who were present that night to see how they recalled the conversation. In his papers I find a copy of the circular he sent, as well as the handwritten replies from Reynolds, Sickles, and Howard. There's also a letter that Gouverneur Warren sent in 1888 to Meade's son George, with a page from Warren's own Chancellorsville report. "There is no doubt in my mind that Genl Meade was opposed to retiring across the river," Warren wrote.

The relations between the two generals had become strained even before this conversation. A week earlier Pennsylvania governor Andrew Gregg Curtin had visited the army. In conversation with Curtin, Meade had unguardedly expressed his opinion of Hooker's actions at Chancellorsville. Curtin repeated Meade's private conversation in Washington. When word of this got back to Hooker, the great intriguer felt certain that he was now the target of others' intrigue.

He was, but Meade wasn't one of the guilty parties. Darius Couch had tried to get Meade to join him in a meeting with Lincoln, but Meade had refused. Couch went anyway and resigned from the Army of the Potomac rather than serve under Hooker. He ended up in Harrisburg as commander of the Department of the Susquehanna and Winfield Scott Hancock received command of the II Corps on June 9. Slocum had also asked for Meade's support in getting Hooker removed. Meade said he wouldn't initiate such talk but would be happy to speak with Lincoln if the president summoned him. All this swirling distrust and unhappiness strained the relationship between Hooker and Meade. "Still, I should be sorry to see him removed, unless a decidedly better man is substituted," Meade wrote.[3]

People were wondering about Hooker outside the army, too. After Chancellorsville the *New York Tribune* sent George W. Smalley to Virginia to determine
what had gone wrong. "If I am to be investigated, it might as well be by you as
anybody," Hooker told him. Smalley liked Hooker, but he put his personal feelings aside. During the course of his investigation he decided that the general had
lost his army's confidence. Several staff officers even urged Smalley to tell Meade
he was their choice to command. Smalley agreed to speak to him and found
Meade just as the general was getting on his horse. The general invited the reporter to ride along with him.

As Smalley began to explain his mission, Meade turned and looked sharply at
him. "I don't know that I ought to listen to you," he said. Smalley told the general
that he was not acting in any official capacity; he intended only to explain what
he had heard. Meade allowed him to continue. "I said my say," Smalley related.
"From beginning to end, General Meade listened with an impassive face. He did
not interrupt. He never asked a question. He never made a comment. When I
had finished I had not the least notion what impression my narrative had made
on him; nor whether it had made any impression. He was a model of military discretion. Then we talked a little about other things. I said good-bye, rode away,
and never again saw General Meade."[4]

There was at least one welcome development during these days of turmoil.
On May 26 Capt. George Meade became his father's aide-de-camp. As part of
Rush's Lancers, the young Meade had taken part in Stoneman's lackadaisical attempt to break Lee's lines of communications during the Chancellorsville campaign, but he had come down with a serious case of the measles and had to be
sent back to Philadelphia to recover. Now that he had served with the regiment
his father felt comfortable with appointing him to a staff position.

◆ ◆ ◆

Robert E. Lee had not been idle in Chancellorsville's aftermath. After Jackson's
death he reorganized his army from two corps into three plus a cavalry division
under Jeb Stuart. James Longstreet, Lee's "old warhorse," remained in command
of the I Corps, with three divisions under Major Generals Lafayette McLaws,
George E. Pickett, and John Bell Hood. The II Corps, previously Jackson's, was
now commanded by Lt. Gen. Richard S. Ewell, who had lost a leg at Second Bull
Run. Like his predecessor, the high-strung Ewell had a reputation for strangeness.
Brig. Gen. John B. Gordon described him as "the oddest, most eccentric genius
in the Confederate army."[5] Ewell, too, had three divisions, under Major Generals
Jubal A. Early, Edward "Allegheny" Johnson, and Robert E. Rodes.

Lee selected A. P. Hill—McClellan's old rival in love—to command the newly
created III Corps. Hill had three divisions under Major Generals Richard H. Anderson, Henry Heth, and William D. Pender.

Lee began moving his army of about seventy-five thousand men north in early
June. On June 9 Union cavalry under Brig. Gen. Alfred Pleasonton, Stoneman's
replacement, surprised Jeb Stuart at Brandy Station and nearly won the day. The
Federals ended up withdrawing, but the spirited fighting demonstrated that the
much-maligned Union horsemen were finally coming into their own.

With Stuart's cavalry screening the army's movements, Lee's troops began moving north down the Shenandoah Valley. Their first target was Winchester, Virginia, where Maj. Gen. Robert Milroy refused to withdraw his forces until it was too late. Early's men routed the Union defenders, capturing thirty-four hundred and killing or wounding another thousand. Those who could escape fled north, and soon the remnants of Winchester's defenders were streaming across the Maryland border into Pennsylvania.

Hooker began moving his army north to shadow Lee, always keeping it between the Confederates and Washington, D.C. Even as "Fighting Joe" prepared to grapple with Lee again, his days at the helm of the Army of the Potomac were drawing to a close. On June 12 Reynolds dropped in to visit Meade. Rumor had it that Reynolds was being talked about as Hooker's replacement; he told Meade he had traveled to Washington to tell Lincoln he did not want the job.

Back in Philadelphia, Margaret fretted that her husband would be thrust into the thankless position. On June 25 he wrote and told her not to worry. Despite his fine military record, he lacked the political connections necessary to reach such heights. Furthermore, there were other men who were equally competent. "For these reasons I have never indulged in any dreams of ambition, contented to await events, and do my duty in the sphere it pleases God to place me in," he wrote, "and I really think it would be as well for you to take the same philosophical view; but do you know, I think your ambition is being roused and that you are beginning to be bitten with the dazzling prospect of having for a husband a commanding general of an army. How is this?"[6]

• • •

Few drivers on Route 85 just south of Frederick, Maryland, at the point where the road descends into a little depression and crosses Ballenger Creek, realize they have just passed a historically significant site. There are no historical markers to tell them so, just a large home and farm called Arcadia standing at the crest of the hill, just as it did during the war when a man named Robert McGill owned it. On June 27, 1863, Meade established the headquarters for the V Corps here on McGill's land, unaware that the relationship between Hooker on one side and Halleck and Lincoln on the other had suffered its final rupture.

Hooker had never gotten along with Halleck. The clash of personalities dated to at least the prewar days, when both men served in California and Hooker never paid back money he had borrowed from Halleck. Whatever the cause, whenever possible Hooker bypassed Halleck and communicated directly with Lincoln. As the president's doubts about Hooker grew, Lincoln felt increasingly unwilling to have him fight Lee again. Matters finally came to a head when Hooker requested that Harpers Ferry, once again in Union hands, be abandoned and its garrison, under Gen. William French, be given to him. Halleck refused. Hooker tendered his resignation. Perhaps he was bluffing. If so, Halleck called his bluff and accepted.

Back in Washington on June 27 Col. James A. Hardie of Halleck's staff received orders to travel to Frederick and find Meade. Hardie looked more like an accountant than a soldier, with straggly side whiskers, hair slicked down and combed back, and pince-nez clamped to his nose. Wearing civilian clothes in case he encountered Confederate raiders, Hardie took a train from Washington to Frederick, where he found the streets thronged with boisterous and drunken soldiers from the Army of the Potomac. He rented a horse and buggy and made his way through the dark night to Meade's headquarters at Robert McGill's farm.

Meade was asleep in his tent, unaware of the agent of fate making his inexorable way toward him. Hardie arrived around 3:00 in the morning. He pushed open the tent flaps and rapped on the flagpole to wake the sleeping general. I've come to bring you trouble, he told Meade. Meade's first thought was that he was being either relieved or placed under arrest, which says something about the state of dysfunction, paranoia, and suspicion that plagued the Army of the Potomac. The groggy general told Hardie he had a clear conscience.

Hardie explained the trouble he had brought. He had orders for Meade to take command of the Army of the Potomac. Meade protested. He wasn't the right man, he said. Reynolds was. Hardie explained that the decision had been made—Meade had no choice but to obey his orders.

"Well, I've been tried and condemned without a hearing, and I suppose I shall have to go to execution," said Meade.[7]

Hardie handed the general the letter from Halleck that I saw in the Meade papers. "Considering the circumstances," Halleck wrote, "no one ever received a more important command; and I cannot doubt that you will fully justify the confidence which the Government has reposed in you.

"You will not be hampered by any minute instructions from these headquarters," Halleck continued, and then went on for an entire sentence before providing instructions. "Your army is free to act as you may deem proper under the circumstances as they arise," he said. "You will, however, keep in view the important fact that the Army of the Potomac is the covering army of Washington, as well as the army of operation against the invading forces of the rebels. You will therefore manoeuvre and fight in such a manner as to cover the Capital and also Baltimore, as far as circumstances will admit. Should General Lee move upon either of these places, it is expected that you will either anticipate him or arrive with him, so as to give him battle.

"All forces within the sphere of your operations will be held subject to your orders.

"Harper's Ferry and its garrison are under your direct orders." (This would have come as no surprise to Hooker, who later said, "It was often remarked that it was no use for me to make a request, as that of itself would be sufficient cause for General Halleck to refuse it.")[8]

Halleck continued, "You are authorized to remove from command and send from your army any officer or other person you may deem proper; and to appoint to command as you may deem expedient." This is a power Meade would indeed use—and one that would earn him future enmity from a few officers.

"In fine, General, you are intrusted with all the power and authority which the President, the Secretary of War, or the General-in-Chief can confer on you, and you may rely on our full support," Halleck wrote.

"You will keep me fully informed of all your movements and the positions of your own troops and those of the enemy, so far as known.

"I shall always be ready to advise and assist you to the utmost of my ability."[9]

• • •

Accompanied by Hardie and son George, Meade rode on horseback to Hooker's headquarters, on the grounds of a building called Prospect Hall. There are some historical markers here today. Prospect Hall is a stately, columned building that stands atop a rise along Butterfly Lane. Since 1958 it has housed a Catholic prep school. The building was already sixty years old in 1863; the Marquis de Lafayette had visited here in 1824 when the French hero of the Revolutionary War made a triumphant return to the United States. Two Maryland Civil War Trails markers at the bottom of the drive leading from the mansion explain the site's significance. Nearby, a large stone monument, crafted from boulders taken from near Devil's Den on the Gettysburg battlefield, bears a metal plaque dating from 1930. Another was placed on the rock in 1963, on the hundredth anniversary of Meade's assumption of command. The big rock has lost some of its dignity over the years, flanked on one side by a leaning Do Not Enter sign and on the other by a modern apartment complex. Its base is caked with dried grass tossed there by lawn mowers.

As Meade made his way in the predawn hours to Hooker's headquarters, did he wonder if he would ever be so memorialized? He remained largely silent, apparently lost in thought. He had a great deal to think about. He had just been named the commander of an army whose disposition remained largely a mystery to him, since he had not seen Hooker in almost two weeks. As he had complained to his wife a few days earlier, "I hear nothing whatever from headquarters, and am as much in the dark as to proposed plans here on the ground as you are in Philadelphia. This is what Joe Hooker thinks profound sagacity—keeping his corps commanders, who are to execute his plans, in total ignorance of them until they are developed in the execution of orders."[10]

Rumors fly quickly in camp—as Daniel Butterfield once put it, "If it be true that village gossip runs an express train, it may be said that camp gossip goes by telegraph"[11]—and Hooker had already heard about the visitor from Washington. He could guess what it meant. When he emerged from his tent to greet Meade's party, Hooker was wearing his dress uniform. Meade and Hardie entered the tent. It was an uncomfortable meeting. When Meade learned how scattered the army was, he "unguardedly expressed himself." Hooker "retorted with feeling."[12]

Capt. George Meade waited outside, officially in the dark about the unfolding events. Eventually his father emerged. Although the general looked grave, his son thought he detected a slight twinkle in the eye, "denoting the anticipation of surprise at the information to be imparted." After a time Meade finally spoke. "Well, George, I am in command of the Army of the Potomac," he said.[13]

Reynolds arrived to pay his respects later that morning. Meade grabbed him by the arm and earnestly told him he wished Reynolds had received the assignment. Reynolds replied that Meade was the right choice and he would do whatever was necessary to support him.[14]

That evening Hardie and Hooker climbed aboard a wagon for the ride to the train station. Hardie was going back to Washington, and Hooker had been ordered to report to Baltimore. Officers crowded around the wagon to say their good-byes but drew back respectfully when Meade approached. Meade shook Hooker's hand, and the two men exchanged some quiet words. War correspondent Charles Carleton Coffin of the *Boston Journal* observed Meade as Hooker made his farewells: "He was standing with bowed head and downcast eyes, his slouched hat drawn down, shading his features. He seemed lost in thought. His uniform was the worse for wear from hard service; there was dust upon his boots."[15]

Then the wagon clattered off, and Meade turned and walked quietly back to what was now his headquarters tent.

One important item of business was getting a new chief of staff. Meade and Butterfield, who had held that position under Hooker, did not get along. The new commander first asked Seth Williams, the assistant adjutant general, if he would do it, but Williams declined. So did Maj. Gen. Andrew A. Humphreys, who commanded a division of the III Corps. Chief engineer Gouverneur Warren declined as well. It would have to be Butterfield then. This was a decision that would come back to haunt Meade. When James Biddle told General Sedgwick that Meade had retained Butterfield, Biddle said that the VI Corps commander "looked solemn and said he regretted it, that he knew Butterfield well, that he was a bold bad man and that Meade would live to regret it."[16]

Meade then issued General Orders No. 67. "By direction of the President of the United States, I hereby assume command of the Army of the Potomac," he began. "As a soldier, in obeying this order—an order totally unexpected and unsolicited—I have no promises or pledges to make.

"The country looks to this army to relieve it from the devastation and disgrace of a foreign invasion. Whatever fatigues and sacrifices we may be called upon to undergo, let us have in view, constantly, the magnitude of the interests involved, and let each man determine to do his duty, leaving to an all-controlling Providence the decision of the contest.

"It is with great diffidence that I relieve in the command of this army an eminent and accomplished soldier, whose name must ever appear conspicuous in the history of its achievements; but I rely upon the hearty support of my companions in arms to assist me in the discharge of the duties of the important trust which has been confided to me."[17]

Overall, the reaction from the army appeared positive. Brig. Gen. John Gibbon greeted the change with a "sigh of relief."[18] The I Corps artillery chief, Charles Wainwright, who knew that Reynolds had been offered command, wrote in his journal, "For my part, I think we have got the best man of the two, much as I think of Reynolds." He thought Reynolds would "do better at carrying out plans than at devising them." He also noted that many men believed that Meade's appointment was only temporary and McClellan would eventually take command.[19]

When he heard the news, wrote Lt. Frank A. Haskell of Gibbon's staff, he "breathed a full breath of joy, and of hope. The Providence of God had been with us—we ought not to have doubted it—General Meade commanded the Army of the Potomac." The eve of a major battle may not have been the best time to change commanders, Haskell realized, but the change was worth the risk. "I now felt that we had a clear-headed, honest soldier, to command the army, who would do his best always— that there would be no repetition of Chancellorsville."[20]

The change of command felt more personal in the Pennsylvania Reserves. The men in the 11th Pennsylvania Reserves "shouted themselves hoarse over the welcome news," the division's colonel later recalled.[21] "We were proud to know that one of our own generals, one for whom we felt that we had won the 'stars,' should be placed in this very highest position in the army in the very crisis of the nation's fate," said Sgt. A. P. Morrison of the 9th Pennsylvania Reserves. "We had confidence in him for we knew him to be an energetic, brave, cool and determined leader."[22]

Meade appeared determined to battle Robert E. Lee and the Army of Northern Virginia. "I am going straight at them, and will settle this thing one way or the other," he wrote to his wife the day after he assumed command. "The men are in good spirits; we have been reinforced so as to have equal numbers with the enemy, and with God's blessing I hope to be successful. Good-by!"[23]

• • •

Meade didn't tarry long near Frederick. The next day he headed north to Middleburg and on the thirtieth he relocated again near Taneytown (pronounced "Tawneytown"). I follow his tracks, watching the scenery change as I leave Frederick behind and the landscape slowly shakes off the modern world. Cornfields gradually replace shopping malls, and farmhouses take the place of housing developments.

Taneytown strikes me as a somewhat dusty little place, probably because when I stop here the main street is being torn up. I step inside the building that houses a little historical society museum to see if it has anything about Meade. A woman working in the office inside the entrance tells me the museum will be closed for most of the year because of the construction outside. I ask her if she knows of any Meade items in the collection.

She looks at me quizzically. "William Meade?" she asks.

"No, George Gordon Meade," I reply. "He was the commanding general at Gettysburg. I know he had his headquarters outside Taneytown during the buildup to the battle."

"I'm sorry," she says, "that name doesn't mean anything to me." I thank her and say I'll try to return when the museum reopens. North of town on Route 94 I find a historical marker. "Meade's Headquarters," it reads. "Major General George G. Meade, commander of the Army of the Potomac, maintained headquarters on the nearby Shunk Farm from June 30 until the night of July 1, 1863."

It was there on June 30 that officers from the 11th Pennsylvania Reserves arrived to congratulate him on his new position. "We found him in close conference with Generals Reynolds, Hancock, Sedgwick and others," recalled Samuel Jackson. "He seemed delighted in welcoming us back to the army. Thanked us for our congratulations, but said that he did not know whether he was a subject of congratulation or commiseration. He appeared anxious and showed that he fully realized the responsibility of his position. He said however that he had all confidence in the bravery of the officers and men of the army and felt assured that we would achieve a glorious victory in the coming conflict."[24]

Whitelaw Reid, a correspondent for the *Cincinnati Gazette*, passed through this "pleasant Maryland hamlet" on July 1 and noted the confused activity of an army on the move. "Army trains blocked up the streets," he wrote; "a group of quartermasters and commissaries were bustling about the principal corner; across on the hills and along the road to the left, as far as the eye could reach, rose the glitter from the swaying points of bayonets as with steady tramp the columns of our Second and Third corps were marching northward." He found Meade's headquarters at the Shunk Farm. "In a plain little wall tent, just like the rest, pen in hand, seated on a camp-stool and bending over a map, is the new 'General Commanding' for the Army of the Potomac." Reid went on to describe Meade: "Tall, slender, not ungainly, but certainly not handsome or graceful, thin-faced, with grizzled beard and moustache, a broad and high but retreating forehead, from each corner of which the slightly-curling hair recedes, as if giving premonition of baldness—apparently between forty-five and fifty years of age—altogether a man who impresses you rather as a thoughtful student than a dashing soldier—so General Meade looks in his tent."[25]

It was in that "plain little wall tent" on the Shunk Farm that Meade tried to figure out how to concentrate his scattered army and determine his strategy. According to Gettysburg historian Edwin Coddington, Meade's work to pull his army together in his first twenty-four hours of command "was no mean achievement." General Humphreys wrote, "I don't know that anyone has an idea of the vast labor connected with the movement of a great Army, unless it is those few that have had experience in moving such an Army. I take it too that this Army has never been moved so skillfully before as it has been during Meade's command."[26]

Lee had been deprived of the eyes and ears of Stuart's cavalry, which had lost contact with the army during a wide swing around the Union forces, so he didn't learn until June 28, the day that Meade assumed command, that the enemy army had crossed the Potomac. Lee reacted by summoning the scattered portions of his forces from their positions throughout south-central Pennsylvania and directing them to concentrate near the town of Gettysburg.

Meade continued to wait and watch. It was becoming clear that Gettysburg was growing in importance. The town was like the hub of a wheel with roads radiating out in all directions. Armies passing through the region would almost inevitably pass through. On June 30 Meade issued two circulars to his commanders. "The Commanding General has received information that the enemy are advancing, probably in strong force, on Gettysburg," one read. "It is the intention to hold this army pretty nearly in the position it now occupies, until the plans of the enemy shall have been more fully developed." Corps commanders were told to be prepared to march "at a moment's notice." The second circular outlined the importance of the impending engagement and ended with a chilling note: "Corps and other commanders are authorized to order the instant death of any soldier who fails in his duty at this hour."[27] This was serious business.

Meade hoped he could fight a defensive battle against Lee, so he had his engineers examine the area and find a favorable position. A line behind a little waterway called Pipe Creek offered a good spot. On June 30 he put together a document he called the Pipe Creek Circular.

Big Pipe Creek still makes its meandering way through this stretch of northern Maryland. It's a small but pretty little waterway that runs in a generally east-to-west direction until it joins the Monocacy River east of Middleburg. It passes north of modern Route 77, which undulates like an asphalt ribbon across rolling fields, past farms, and through little towns. There should be a historical marker someplace along Pipe Creek, and it could read, "On this spot, July 1–3, 1863, nothing happened."

To be sure, this portion of Maryland saw plenty of military activity during the Gettysburg campaign as soldiers marched this way and that and established camps and headquarters here and there. There were some skirmishes. But this region generally witnessed only portents of the coming storm, not the storm itself. Had things unfolded differently, though, today the little towns of Middleburg and Uniontown might be crammed with souvenir shops and restaurants that bear the names of Civil War soldiers. The landscape here could be dotted with monuments and memorials, while Gettysburg would be a quiet town people passed on their way to the big battlefield just south of the Mason-Dixon Line. Had things fallen out differently, we might talk today of the Battle of Middleburg or the Battle of Westminster.

As Meade envisioned it, the army's Pipe Creek line would have run from the town of Manchester, which is where Sedgwick would have extended the right of his VI Corps, all the way west to Middleburg, to be held by Reynolds and the I Corps. The position would have been strong defensively, with good lines of supply, and it would have placed the army squarely between Lee and Washington and Baltimore. However, in the circular Meade issued early on July 1 he made it clear that events could force a change of thinking. "Developments may cause the commanding general to assume the offensive from his present position," it read.

"They were, under any circumstances, wise and proper orders," said the army's artillery chief, Henry Hunt, "and it would probably have been better had he concentrated his army behind Pipe Creek rather than at Gettysburg; but events finally controlled the actions of both leaders."[28]

Reynolds apparently never received a copy of the Pipe Creek Circular. The two generals parted for the last time after Meade put Reynolds in command of the army's left wing, consisting of the I, III, and XI Corps, and sent him north toward Gettysburg.

● ● ●

Around 11 a.m. on July 1 Hancock arrived at Meade's Taneytown headquarters. The two generals had a long conversation about the growing situation to the north. About a half hour later Capt. Stephen M. Weld, one of Reynolds's aides, came galloping in with a report. He found Meade cursing Butterfield for his slowness in getting orders out. "Good God!" he exclaimed when Weld told him fighting had broken out to the north. "If the enemy get Gettysburg, we are lost!" Then Weld delivered Reynolds's message. "Tell him the enemy are advancing in strong force," Reynolds had ordered Weld, "and that I fear they will get to the heights beyond the town before I can. I will fight them inch by inch, and if driven back into the town, I will barricade the streets and hold them back as long as possible."

"Good!" Meade exclaimed. "That is just like Reynolds; he will hold on to the bitter end."[29]

Around that same time Meade also received a message from Brig. Gen. John Buford, the no-nonsense commander of the 1st Cavalry Division of Pleasonton's cavalry corps. Buford had reached Gettysburg on June 30 and encountered a force of Confederates on the town's outskirts. On July 1 he had begun fighting a stubborn defense against Confederate troops approaching down the Chambersburg Pike from the west. These were the men of Henry Heth's division of A. P. Hill's corps. Lee had issued orders to his men not to start a general engagement until he had concentrated his entire army, but Heth rashly pushed forward toward Gettysburg despite growing evidence that the men resisting him were from the Army of the Potomac, not a local militia.

Buford hurriedly wrote a message to Meade at 10:10 a.m. "The enemy's force (A. P. Hill's) are advancing on me at this point and driving my pickets and skirmishers very rapidly. There is also a large force at Heidlersburg, that is driving my pickets at that point from that direction. General Reynolds is advancing, and is within three miles of this point, with his leading division. I am positive that the whole of A. P. Hill's force is advancing."[30]

Events were gaining momentum as the two armies began a slow-motion collision on Gettysburg's outskirts. Then, around 1:00 that afternoon, Meade received grim news: Reynolds had been wounded, perhaps mortally, shot in the head by a Confederate sharpshooter.

Reynolds had reached the battlefield, conferred with Buford, and was in the process of positioning the I Corps on McPherson's Ridge when the fatal bullet hit home. He died almost instantly. A simple memorial at the edge of the woods marks the spot where he met his death, with the words "Here Gen. Reynolds Fell" engraved on the back. His statue stands nearby on Route 30, the old Chambersburg Pike. The general is mounted on a horse with two hooves raised off the ground, an unofficial code that the rider died in battle. A statue of Buford stands in front of Reynolds. The cavalryman is not mounted. He stands, field glasses in hand, peering westward down the highway. Four cannons are set in concrete blocks around the pedestal. One of them is supposed to be the gun that fired the first artillery shot of the Gettysburg battle.

There's another Reynolds relic a short distance down Route 30 toward Gettysburg, at the General Lee Headquarters Museum, a little stone building at what today is the Quality Inn. Lee set up his headquarters near here when he reached the battlefield on July 1, and now it's a privately owned museum with a small collection of artifacts. It has some furniture that Lee used when he was here, as well as the requisite Civil War weaponry. It even has a wooden leg that once belonged to Col. Alexander Piper of the 10th New York Heavy Artillery. The museum also has what it says are the saddle and reins Reynolds was using when he fell—although another museum, now closed, in Philadelphia claimed to have the saddle, and I've heard that a private collector owns a third such saddle. Unless some miraculous cloning process happened after Reynolds died, at best one of them is the real thing.

Whatever saddle Reynolds was using, his death was the start "of a series of disasters that but for the skillful generalship of the army commander and the fighting qualities of the troops would probably have given to Lee the victory which he sought and to the South a separate republic," as one of Meade's early biographers put it.[31] Oliver O. Howard took over the command of the Union forces at Gettysburg and posted his own XI Corps to the right of the I Corps. When elements of Ewell's corps, summoned by Lee from their positions in York and Carlisle, began arriving from the north, they started to overlap the flanks of the XI Corps, sending it reeling back through the streets of Gettysburg. The collapsing XI Corps took the I Corps down with it, and those soldiers also began retreating. The town became a battlefield as Federals and rebels skirmished on the streets and even in the houses. Walk down Baltimore Street today and you can peer into the backyard of the private home where Brig. Gen. Alexander Schimmelfennig, one of the German officers from the XI Corps, scrambled to safety and hid for the rest of the battle. The surviving Federals continued their retreat until they finally came to a halt on the heights of Cemetery Hill just south of town.

Reynolds had been one of the rocks that Meade could depend on, and the news of his death must have come as a shock. Despite occasional tensions, the two men had been through much together. Meade later referred to Reynolds as "a friend and a brother."[32] Winfield Scott Hancock was another general whom Meade trusted implicitly. Once he heard the news about Reynolds, Meade ordered Hancock to move immediately to Gettysburg, take charge of the situation there, and report back to him. "If you think the ground and position there are a better one to fight a battle under existing circumstances, you will so advise the General, and he will order his troops up," read Hancock's orders.[33] Hancock began his trip north riding in the back of an ambulance so he could have time to consult maps and familiarize himself with the terrain. John Gibbon took over the II Corps.

Meade realized that events had already overtaken his plan to fight a defensive battle behind Pipe Creek. Before he even heard back from Hancock, he started moving his army toward the fighting. He sent a messenger to Sedgwick to get the VI Corps moving up to Taneytown and sent the V and XII Corps in the direction of the spreading conflict.

Things were looking grim for the Army of the Potomac when Hancock reached Gettysburg. Despite some initial Union successes, including the capture of Confederate general James Archer, the rebels had clearly won the day. It was fortunate indeed that Howard had posted a reserve on Cemetery Hill, the site of the town's Evergreen Cemetery and a good place to defend. This was the new keystone of the Union defenses. Culp's Hill lay just to the east. It was another important position destined to witness fierce combat over the next three days. Stretching south from Cemetery Hill was a low ridge known as Cemetery Ridge, which petered out in a low swampy area before rising again as it approached two hills, the Round Tops.

Looking west from the Union position, the terrain ran in a broad, undulating field, perhaps a mile across, to a wooded rise running parallel to Cemetery Ridge. This was Seminary Ridge, named for the Lutheran seminary that stood on the end near town. Beyond that was McPherson Ridge, where the morning's fighting

Gettysburg Campaign and Lee's Retreat

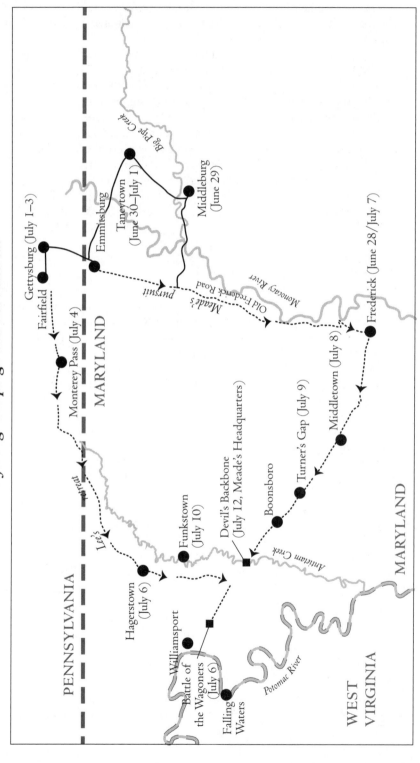

Gettysburg: July 2, 4 p.m.

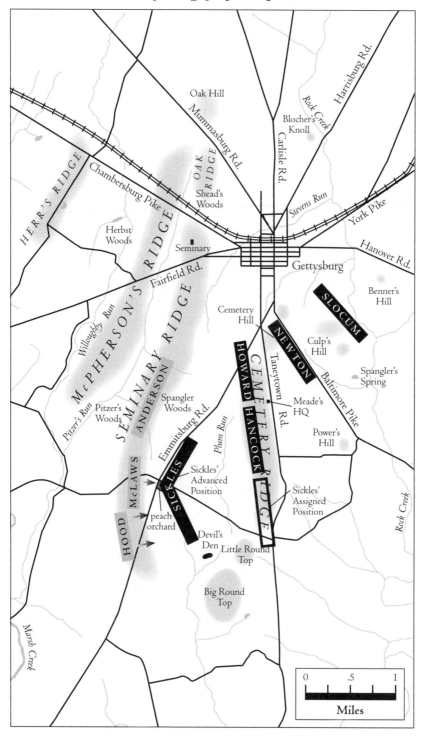

Harrisburg Rd.

Oak Hill

Mummasburg Rd.

Rock Creek

Blocher's Knoll

Carlisle Rd.

HERR'S RIDGE

Chambersburg Pike

OAK RIDGE

Shead's Woods

Stevens Run

York Pike

Herbst Woods

Seminary

McPHERSON'S RIDGE

Fairfield Rd.

Gettysburg

Hanover Rd.

Willoughby Run

Cemetery Hill

SLOCUM

Benner's Hill

SEMINARY RIDGE

ANDERSON

Pitzer's Run

Pitzer's Woods

Spangler Woods

Emmitsburg Rd.

NEWTON

Taneytown Rd.

Culp's Hill

CEMETERY RIDGE

Baltimore Pike

Spangler's Spring

HOWARD

Meade's HQ

Plum Run

HANCOCK

Power's Hill

HOOD

McLAWS

SICKLES

Sickles' Advanced Position

peach orchard

Devil's Den

Sickles' Assigned Position

Rock Creek

Little Round Top

Big Round Top

Marsh Creek

0   .5   1

Miles

had started. Dotting the landscape were several farms with their houses and out-buildings. The Emmitsburg Road passed at an angle through the farmland in front of the Union position. Behind the Federal lines ran the Baltimore Pike and Taneytown Road. This was the terrain that Hancock and Howard had to work with as they faced the daunting task of whipping their confused forces back into sufficient shape to stop the advancing Confederates.

One soldier from the I Corps recalled seeing Hancock on his horse on Ceme-tery Hill, "superb and calm as on review; imperturbable, self-reliant, as if the fate of the battle and of the nation were not his to decide. It almost led us to doubt whether there had been cause for retreat at all."[34] Meade knew his man. He had sent Hancock to take charge even though Howard was the senior officer. Halleck's orders gave Meade the power to do that, but Howard still bristled at the implied rebuke. According to E. P. Halstead, an aide to Brig. Gen. Abner Doubleday, when Hancock told Howard that Meade had sent him to take charge, Howard dug in his heels and stated that he was the senior officer. "I am aware of that, General," Hancock replied, "but I have written orders in my pocket from General Meade, which I will show you if you wish to see them."

"No; I do not doubt your word, General Hancock," replied Howard, "but you can give no orders here while I am here." Rather than force the issue, Han-cock turned diplomat. "Very well, General Howard, I will second any order that you have to give," he said. The two generals then agreed that Cemetery Hill was indeed a good defensive position. According to Howard, they decided that Han-cock would handle the placements to the left of the Baltimore Pike and Howard those to the right.[35]

At 5:25, about an hour after he arrived, Hancock wrote a message to summa-rize the situation for Meade. Slocum's XII Corps was approaching and could pro-tect the army's right once it arrived, and Hancock assumed that Sickles and the III Corps were on their way and could take the left. The II Corps, now under Gibbon, could help out wherever necessary. "I think we will be all right until night," Hancock reported. "When night comes it can be told better what had best be done. I think we can retire; if not, we can fight here, as the ground appears not unfavorable with good troops." At the end of his message Hancock added a sentence that would lead to trouble for Meade down the road: "Howard says that Doubleday's command gave way."[36]

Brig. Gen. Abner Doubleday had taken over the I Corps after Reynolds's death. A native of Ballston Spa, New York, Doubleday had been in the war from the very start, having served as captain at Fort Sumter when the Confederates attacked back in April 1861. He may have even fired the first Union shot of the war. Doubleday had a reputation for being slow, but he had actually handled the I Corps capably during the battle's first day. Howard's XI Corps—the same corps that Jackson had routed at Chancellorsville—had broken first, starting a domino effect that rippled through the I Corps. Howard's claim that the I Corps had broken may have been an attempt to deflect blame for another embarrassing collapse.

But Meade had no love for Doubleday anyway. When he had learned that Dou-bleday would succeed him as the commander of the Pennsylvania Reserves he wrote to Margaret that the move was "a good thing for me, for now they will think a great deal more of me than before."[37] Charles Wainwright, who handled the I Corps' artillery, shared Meade's opinion. "I have no confidence in Doubleday," he wrote in his journal, "and felt he would be a weak reed to lean upon; that it would not do for me to wait for orders from him, but that I must judge and act for myself."[38] Now Meade once again used the freedom Halleck's orders gave him to promote a junior officer, Brig. Gen. John Newton, to take command of the I Corps over the senior Doubleday. Newton, a Virginian who had elected to fight for the Union, was commanding a brigade in the VI Corps when Meade promoted him. Doubleday returned to command of his division; he would never forget the apparent slight or miss an opportunity to chip away at Meade's reputation.

Meade kept his headquarters at Taneytown, about fourteen miles from the battlefield, so that he could remain in a central position as his scattered army began its concentration on Gettysburg. From there he sent a flurry of orders to his corps commanders to get them moving as fast as possible toward the fighting. Then, sometime around 10:00 p.m. on July 1, he saddled up and left Taneytown behind. Coming with him were Gouverneur Warren, the army's chief engineer, and Brig. Gen. Henry Hunt, its chief of artillery. With Capt. William Paine of the engineering staff serving as guide up the dark road, choked with soldiers, wagons, horses, and artillery, Meade and his party made their way north. Within an hour he reached II Corps headquarters and spent fifteen minutes in consultation with Gibbon before riding on. He finally reached Gettysburg sometime around midnight.

Howard and Slocum were waiting when Meade rode up to the gatehouse on Cemetery Hill. Slocum, as the senior officer present, had taken over from Hancock when he arrived with the XII Corps. Howard waited anxiously. The XI Corps' behavior at Chancellorsville and now at Gettysburg had dealt severe blows to Howard's self-esteem, and he worried about Meade's reaction to the day's events. Meade told him he wasn't assigning any blame.

"I am confident we can hold this position," Howard declared.

"It is good for defense," said Slocum.

"It is a good place to fight from," added Sickles, who had ridden up to join the discussion.

"I am glad to hear you say so, gentlemen," said Meade, "for it is too late to leave it."[39]

It was also too late to observe any details of the landscape, although Meade could see the many twinkling campfires of the enemy soldiers off to the north and west. As dawn began lighting the eastern sky, Meade, Howard, Hunt, and Paine set off to examine the Union position. The line the army had established is often described as a fishhook, starting with the barb at Culp's Hill, then curving around Cemetery Hill and following the line of Cemetery Ridge down to the Round Tops. Paine made a sketch of the ground, and Meade used it to indicate where he wanted to post his troops. The corps commanders received tracings from Paine's map to show them where to go. Slocum and the XII Corps went to the far right of the Union line, from Culp's Hill around to Cemetery Hill. There it connected with a division of the I Corps. Farther to the left was the XI Corps. The II Corps, now under Gibbon, followed the line of Cemetery Ridge down the straight shank of the fishhook. Meade intended for Gibbon's men to link up with Sickles and the III Corps, which should have continued the line down to Little Round Top. But more about that later.

Gen. Carl Schurz, one of the German divisional commanders in Howard's German-dominated XI Corps, saw Meade on Cemetery Hill that morning. He thought Meade looked careworn and tired, as though he hadn't slept the night before—probably because he hadn't. "There was nothing in his appearance or his bearing—not a smile nor a sympathetic word addressed to those around him—that might have made the hearts of the soldiers warm up to him, or that called forth a cheer," recalled Schurz. Meade was no McClellan, leading through the force of personality. "There was nothing of pose, nothing stagey, about him," continued Schurz. "His mind was evidently absorbed by a hard problem. But this simple, cold, serious soldier with his business-like air did inspire confidence. The officers and men, as much as was permitted, crowded around and looked up to him with curious eyes, and then turned away, not enthusiastic, but clearly satisfied."

Schurz watched as Meade studied the Union defenses. He asked Meade how many men he had. "In the course of the day I expect to have about 95,000—enough, I guess, for this business," Meade replied. He looked over the landscape one more time. "Well, we may fight it out here just as well as anywhere else," he said quietly to himself, and then he rode off.[40]

• • •

Portions of Meade's army continued to arrive throughout the day. The last corps to reach the field was Sedgwick's VI Corps, which had made a thirty-six-mile forced march from Manchester and arrived around 4:00 in the afternoon. "All night long we marched, stopping only for a few minutes' rest at intervals, and once after midnight long enough for the men to make coffee," recalled one of its officers; "then on we toiled, the load of musket, knapsack, haversack, three days' rations and sixty rounds of ammunition made more burdensome by the shadows of the night rendering our footsteps more uncertain."[41] It was a march that even Stonewall Jackson's "foot cavalry" could have admired and "one of the most extraordinary marches of the civil war."[42]

The V Corps, formerly under Meade and now commanded by George Sykes, had made an almost equally impressive march, having covered some twenty-six miles since 7:00 p.m. on July 1, for a total of sixty since June 29. It arrived around 5:00 a.m. on July 2 and went into reserve.[43]

As his army gradually came together, Meade considered his options. According to Meade's son in *Life and Letters*, "He then gave certain directions to his chief of staff, with respect to obtaining knowledge of the roads and country to the rear—information that might be needed as the basis for instructions under specified contingencies."[44] This might seem like a fairly innocuous passage, but it hints at an issue that arose after the battle, an accusation that Butterfield would soon sling at his chief—that Meade intended from the start to retreat from Gettysburg.

In fact, Meade's first impulse was to launch an attack from his army's right at Culp's Hill. On the morning of July 2 he asked Slocum and Warren to examine the ground there and determine whether it provided an opportunity for an offensive. Both generals recommended against making the attack over the hill's rough, boulder-strewn slope. Meade decided to wait and see what Lee would do.

Lee had decided to send Longstreet on a movement to turn the Federals' left by swinging around the Union army and then pushing up along the Emmitsburg Road. Lee wasn't exactly sure where the enemy's left was, though. A faulty reconnaissance misled him about the Union lines, which extended much farther south than he had thought. It turns out that Meade didn't know where his left lay, either, and that was thanks to Daniel Sickles.

The subject of what Dan Sickles did at Gettysburg and why he did it has been covered so much over the years that when Richard Sauers wrote a book on the subject, he titled it *A Caspian Sea of Ink*. Indeed, ink by the barrelful has been spilled over the topic. Some people—most notably Dan Sickles—have claimed that Sickles's actions saved the battle for the Union; others have said he almost gave it to the Confederates.

Meade had intended for Sickles to take up a position to the left of the II Corps and extend down Cemetery Ridge to the low rise we now call Little Round Top. The troops of Brig. Gen. John Geary of the XII Corps had occupied this position the night before, but Meade had ordered them rejoin the rest of the XII Corps on the army's right and defend Culp's Hill. He expected Sickles and the III Corps to take their place.

Meade had already chastised Sickles for letting his supply wagons block the road during the movement toward Gettysburg, and he held no love for the notorious political general. Perhaps that's why he sent his son George to visit the III Corps around 9:00 on the morning of July 2 to check up on things. The only officer the young Meade found at the corps headquarters was Capt. George E. Randolph, Sickles's head of artillery. Randolph told George Meade that Sickles was resting. Meade delivered his father's message, and Randolph retired to Sickles's tent. When he returned he said that General Sickles was not sure where his corps should go.

George Meade galloped back to army headquarters. His report did not please his father, who instructed him to tell General Sickles "that his instructions were to go into position on the left of the Second Corps; that his right was to connect with the left of the Second Corps; that he was to prolong with his line the line of that corps, occupying the position that General Geary had held the night before." Back again to Sickles galloped the young Meade. This time he found the general on horseback, his tent struck and his troops ready to move. Meade delivered the instructions. Sickles replied that his men were about to start moving but said something about Geary not having had a position the night before, stating that he had merely been "massed in the vicinity."

Before George Meade could ride off again, Captain Randolph asked him if Brig. Gen. Henry Hunt, the army's efficient artillery head, could come over and provide guidance about the placement of his guns. Hunt, a thickly bearded man with a long, saturnine face made more solemn looking by the bags under his eyes, arrived and rode out with Sickles to examine his lines. Sickles said he wanted to move forward, out of the general depression along the Union line where Cemetery Ridge ceased being a ridge, and take a position on the higher ground alongside the Emmitsburg Road. He was especially concerned about a peach orchard that would offer Confederate artillery an excellent position to wreak havoc on the Union line, not unlike Hazel Grove at Chancellorsville. Hunt agreed that the forward line had some advantages but felt it also had some serious drawbacks. Then Hunt heard firing from the direction of Cemetery Hill and prepared to ride off and investigate. Before he left Sickles asked him if he should move his troops forward.

"Not on my authority; I will report to General Meade for instructions," replied Hunt. He found Meade and told him that Sickles's proposed line had favorable offensive possibilities but that he would not recommend it.[45]

Sometime around 2:00 Sickles decided to move his troops forward without authorization from Meade. To his right, Hancock and John Gibbon with the II Corps were shocked to see the long line of men that was supposed to connect with their left march forward about three-quarters of a mile in front of the Union line. "We could not conceive what it meant, as we had heard of no orders for an advance and did not understand the meaning of making this break in our line," Gibbon recalled.[46] At the peach orchard Sickles bent his line sharply so it would connect with Devil's Den, a jumble of huge boulders at the base of Little Round Top. This bend in his line, a "salient," created a particularly vulnerable point. Furthermore, the line Sickles had chosen was much longer than the one Meade wanted him to take. He did not have enough men to defend it adequately.

Except for some fighting on the Union right, July 2 remained remarkably quiet, considering that two enemy armies faced each other with nothing more than the fields outside Gettysburg between them. Meade had requested a meeting of his corps commanders for around 3:00. As they waited for the generals to gather, Warren told Meade that something odd was taking place on Sickles's front. When Sickles arrived Meade told him not to dismount; he wanted to examine his position. The notorious Meade temper was rising—Captain Paine said, "I never saw General Meade so angry if I may so call it."[47] Meade's temper did not improve when he examined Sickles's line in person. He turned and pointed behind him. That was the line he had ordered Sickles to take, he said. He could not be supported in this forward position.

Sickles appeared chastised. He offered to move his men back. "Yes, you may as well, at once," Meade replied. "The enemy will not let you withdraw without taking advantage of your position, but you have to come back, and you may as well do it at once as at any other time." This, at least, is how his son George reported his words. We can assume that his actual phrasing was somewhat more colorful. He likely used the kind of language that he had hurled at David Birney during the Battle of Fredericksburg—the same David Birney who now commanded the III Corps division that held the most vulnerable part of Sickles's exposed line, from the peach orchard to Devil's Den.

But the time for words had passed. Even as Meade told Sickles he probably wouldn't have time to correct his position, Confederate artillery opened up from the front and left. Longstreet was finally launching his much-delayed attack.

Meade told Sickles that it was too late to retire now; he would have to hold on as best he could. Meade promised to send what support he could.

That's exactly what Meade did throughout the rest of the day, as the Confederate divisions of Lafayette McLaws and John Bell Hood ferociously attacked the III Corps and came perilously close to breaking through to the main Union line on Cemetery Ridge. Meade sent Sykes's V Corps forward to help Sickles and ordered Hancock to support the army's beleaguered left. He had Slocum on the far right of the Union line send what troops he could spare to help. Slocum later said that Meade had ordered him to send his entire corps, but on his own authority he retained a brigade under Brig. Gen. George Greene, the army's oldest general, at Culp's Hill. The division he did send, John Geary's, got lost along the way and never reached the fighting. "Meade was in the saddle most of this long afternoon and evening, taking many of these decisions based on what he saw personally, at one point riding close enough to the fighting that his horse was wounded," Stephen Sears wrote in his book about Gettysburg.[48]

Longstreet's divisions unleashed a furious assault on Sickles's corps. There was vicious fighting in the Peach Orchard and Wheatfield, two places, like Antietam's Cornfield, that earned the right of capitalization that day. Slowly and bloodily, the Confederates forced back the men of the III Corps until they eventually reached the position that Meade had intended for them in the first place, at great cost. One of the wounded was Sickles himself. As he sat on his horse near the large brick barn on the Trostle farm, a cannonball smashed into his leg, nearly severing it. The story is that as stretcher bearers carted Sickles off the battlefield, the wounded general insisted on sitting up and smoking a cigar to keep from dispiriting his men. David Birney took over command of the corps.

◆ ◆ ◆

One of the keys to the battlefield on July 2 was the rocky prominence that we now call Little Round Top. It didn't bear that name back then. People sometimes called it Sugar Loaf Hill, High Knob, Rock Hill, Granite Spur, or Broad Top Summit but more often than not just considered it a continuation of the other Round Top just to its south, which we now call Big Round Top.[49] Today Little Round Top is one of the most popular sites on the battlefield. On a hot July 2 afternoon I creep in slow motion up the blacktopped road to get there, part of a long line of cars and RVs that have come here on the battle's anniversary. Parking is at a premium here.

Meade realized the importance of this position, which is why he told Sickles to extend his line to this point. Even when the only Union soldiers here were a handful of signalmen, waving their flags to communicate with other portions of the army, Little Round Top played a role in the battle's outcome. When James Longstreet began his movement to turn the Union left, he realized the signalmen would see his columns and spoil the surprise. Longstreet had to reverse course—"countermarch" is the term—and find another, less exposed route. The result was a good hour-and-a-half delay in the Confederate attack. That extra time proved a blessing for Meade and the Army of the Potomac.

But there is little obvious glory in the story of men waving flags and peering through field glasses. The people who endure battlefield gridlock to visit Little

Round Top on hot summer weekends come to hear other, bloodier stories, where the stakes are more obvious. They come for the stories of defenders who arrived just in the nick of time and laid down their lives to save the Union left.

It's also the story of Gouverneur Warren's finest hour. At this point in the war Meade was learning he could rely on Warren even though the army's chief engineer didn't look or act the part of a great fighter. "General Warren is a small man, about thirty-five years old, dark complexioned, with black eyes, and long, straight black hair; he has a little of the look of an Indian, and evidently is of a nervous temperament," Charles Wainwright of the I Corps described him.[50] Warren was a finicky micromanager who too often proved willing to let his own sense of what should be done trump the orders of his superiors. He was serious and scholarly but also displayed a great love for limericks and would often sit in his tent laughing over a book of them or bore others with recitations at meals.[51] Born in New York State, Warren had graduated second in the West Point Class of 1850 and had commanded a regiment and a brigade as a fighting general before becoming the army's engineer. Today his likeness stands on a rocky outcrop on Little Round Top, field glasses in hand, as he appeared on July 2 when he realized that the signalmen were the only Union defense against the advancing Confederate forces, bayonet points glistening in the sunlight.

There's another statue below the south crest of Little Round Top. This is the likeness of Col. Strong Vincent, the elaborately sideburned commander of a brigade in the V Corps. When Warren dispatched an aide to find defenders for Little Round Top, the aide found Vincent. On his own responsibility Vincent took his four regiments—the 16th Michigan, 44th New York, 83rd Pennsylvania, and 20th Maine—and headed up the slope. He set up a defensive line on the hill's southwestern shoulder, with the 20th Maine, under Col. Joshua Lawrence Chamberlain, at the far left of the Union line.

These days it's become somewhat fashionable to disparage Chamberlain. On July 2 I attend a presentation about the fighting for Little Round Top, and the ranger describes Chamberlain as "Hollywood's favorite colonel," a reference to *Gettysburg*, the movie based on Michael Shaara's Pulitzer Prize–winning novel, *The Killer Angels*. Some historians say that the fighting on Little Round Top wasn't all that important anyway. Based on the stones visitors have left on the small 20th Maine memorial in the woods on Round Top's shoulder and the written testimonials left by school groups that have come here today, I suspect that the general public disagrees. "Thanks 20th Maine!" reads one note. "Thank you for being brave enough to point the way for our GREAT country," says another, placed atop a small American flag. "From one soldier to another I will forever be thankful for your sacrifice."

The 20th Maine did not fight alone. Other units played equally important roles here. Farther north along Little Round Top's crest is a monument to the 140th New York, commanded by Col. Patrick O'Rorke. When Warren set out to find more men to defend Round Top, he encountered O'Rorke. "Paddy, give me a regiment," Warren demanded. O'Rorke told him that they had orders to support the III Corps and his brigade commander, Brig. Gen. Stephen Weed, had gone to choose a position. "Is that the 140th?" asked Warren. The regiment had been part of his brigade at Fredericksburg.[52] "If so, take your regiment immediately up the hill and form a junction with Vincent on the left. There is a gap there that must be filled without delay, or the position is gone."

O'Rorke ordered his men to move at double-quick up the rocks. At the top of the hill he started to align his men but Warren arrived and stopped him. There was no time for alignments, Warren told him. "Take your men immediately into action."

"Face to the rear, forward, follow me," O'Rorke ordered, and down he went through the rocks ahead of his men and straight to his death. There's a bronze likeness of O'Rorke on his regiment's monument, the nose rubbed bright by the touch of thousands of hands.[53]

"The struggle for Round Top was about the hardest fighting I was witness to," wrote one of the defenders. "The assault was most ferocious and the resistance extremely obstinate and I pray God I may never again witness such scenes as were enacted upon that bloody field that terrible July afternoon."[54] O'Rorke, Vincent, and Weed were just three of the soldiers killed or mortally wounded here that day, but they and their comrades saved Little Round Top for the Union.

● ● ◆

Throughout this July weekend I've been listening to the real-time ranger presentations, short talks that describe the events that happened at that time and on the specific portion of the battlefield where they occurred. I've heard about Longstreet's delayed attack on July 2, the fight on Round Top, and the struggles in Devil's Den, the Wheatfield, and the Peach Orchard as the rebel onslaught decimated Sickles's exposed III Corps and pushed toward the Union defenses on Cemetery Ridge. But the talk I most want to hear takes place late in the day. It's titled "Meade Defeats Longstreet." The group, by now a gaggle of familiar faces from the previous programs, meets near the 1st Minnesota statue.

The memorial commemorates a charge by that regiment to stem the Confederate attack. Hancock, who more than lived up to his nickname of "the Superb" on this bloody day, had seen rebel soldiers pushing their way forward toward a gap in the Union line. He galloped up to Col. William Colville, commander of the 1st Minnesota. "My God! Are these all the men we have here?" Hancock asked. But he had no options. "Advance, Colonel, and take those colors," he ordered, pointing to an enemy flag in the distance.[55] Colville and his regiment advanced at double-quick—just as the figure on their memorial is doing—and delayed the Confederate advance long enough for other Union soldiers to arrive. The 1st Minnesota suffered 68 percent casualties, Colville among them.

But Ranger Bill Hewitt is here to tell us about Meade. "A lot of people believe General Meade didn't have much to do with the battle," he says; "that he was an innocent bystander." That was not the case, says Hewitt, and he describes for us how Meade was right in the thick of things as he dispatched troops one way and another to plug holes in the lines. The ranger tells us a story of an incident that happened here around 7:00 p.m. on July 2. The III Corps had been broken and things appeared "a little blue," as Meade later described it to his wife.[56] He had sent orders to Newton and the I Corps to move up and fill a gap that had opened between the III and II Corps. Sitting atop his horse, here on Cemetery Ridge, Meade peered anxiously at an approaching line of enemy soldiers. No Union defenders stood between him and the rebels. "The general realizes the situation but too well," his son, George, later described the scene. "He straightens himself in his stirrups, as do also the aides who now ride closer to him, bracing themselves up to meet the crisis. It is in the minds of those who follow him that he is going to throw himself into the breach—anything to gain a few moments' time."[57] Meade drew his sword. His aides nervously followed suit. It appeared that the commander of the Army of the Potomac was about to lead a charge against the approaching enemy.

"There they come, general!" someone shouted. John Newton came galloping up ahead of Doubleday's division, and the Union troops behind him began forming into lines of battle. Yelling with excitement, they advanced toward the enemy. Meade rode with the skirmish line, shouting encouragement. "Come on, gentlemen!" he cried and waved them onward with his hat. The crisis had passed, but Meade's horse paid the price, receiving a bullet through the neck.

Lt. Paul A. Oliver of Meade's staff recalled watching Meade and Newton conversing on horseback. Newton offered Meade his flask. Just then a shell landed in front of them, showering both generals with dirt. "It did not seem to interfere in anyway with the important duty then under consideration," wrote Oliver. "I have always looked on this act of pluck and dareing [sic] on the part of General Meade as of considerable importance at the time, as it restored the courage and morale of the troops, and helped to inspire the men with confidence."[58]

Later someone mentioned that things had looked pretty desperate. "Yes, but it is all right now," said Meade, "it is all right now."

• • •

Darkness descended on the battlefield. The Union line had bent but it hadn't broken. Sickles's corps had suffered greatly. With a casualty rate of 40 percent, the III Corps "was wrecked beyond further use on this field," wrote Sears,[59] but Meade and Hancock had rushed in reinforcements at timely intervals and kept the line from crumbling. The Army of the Potomac had lived to fight another day—but so had the Army of Northern Virginia.

As the firing died down Meade sent out couriers to all his corps commanders to call them together at his headquarters. The little white building was the home of a widow named Lydia Leister, but she had wisely fled when the fighting erupted on July 1. Lt. Frank Haskell of Gibbon's staff described the structure as "a shabby little farmhouse."[60] For Meade, though, its location just behind Cemetery Ridge near the center of the Union line was ideal.

The little structure had only two tiny rooms, and on the night of July 2 the close confines became even more claustrophobic as the generals arrived to confer in the back room. In his short account of the Gettysburg battle Haskell described the only furniture as "a large, wide bed in one corner, a small pine table in the center, upon which was a wooden pail of water, with a tin cup for drinking, and a candle, stuck to the table by putting the end in tallow melted down from the wick, and five or six straight-backed rush-bottomed chairs."

Haskell also sketched out brief cameo portraits of most of the generals present. He described Meade as "a tall spare man, with full beard, which with his hair, originally brown, is quite thickly sprinkled with gray—has a Romanish face, very large nose, and a white, large forehead, prominent and wide over the eyes, which are full and large, and quick in their movements, and he wears spectacles. His fibres are all of the long and sinewy kind. His habitual personal appearance is quite careless, and it would be rather difficult to make him look well dressed."

Newton, the new I Corps commander, "was a well-sized, shapely, muscular, well-dressed man" who had "somewhat of that smart sort of swagger, that people are apt to suppose characterizes soldiers." Hancock, in charge of the II Corps, "always dresses remarkably well, and his manner is dignified, gentlemanly, and commanding. I think if he were in citizen's clothes and should give commands in the army to those who did not know him, he would likely to be obeyed at once, and without any question as to his right to command." Gibbon was clean shaven except for a red mustache and possessed "an air of calm firmness in his manner." The V Corps' George Sykes was "a small, rather thin man" who had "the general air of one who is weary and a little ill-natured." Sedgwick of the VI Corps had "a magnificent profile" and eyes that "have plenty of animation when he is aroused," wrote Haskell. "Like Meade, he looks and is honest and modest." Oliver O. Howard of the XI Corps, the youngest general present, struck Haskell as having "nothing marked about him," despite his missing arm. The XII Corps' cautious Henry Slocum moved in a "quick and angular" fashion and dressed "with a sufficient degree of elegance," while the cavalry's Pleasonton was "quite a nice looking dandy," wearing a straw hat cocked to one side.[61]

David Birney, with whom Meade had clashed at Fredericksburg, was also present as Sickles's replacement with the III Corps, and Alpheus Williams was a second representative of the XII Corps. Chief of staff Butterfield was there, too, as was Warren. Having been struck on the neck and slightly wounded, Warren promptly rolled up in a corner and fell fast asleep.

By the flickering candlelight the gathered generals carried on an informal conversation as they discussed the day's events. Then Newton spoke, saying he felt that "this is no place to fight a battle in." Gibbon, knowing that Newton was an engineer by training, asked him why he believed that. Newton expressed some minor complaints about the line but said no more. "General Meade said little," Gibbon recalled, "except now and then to make some comment, but I cannot recall that he expressed any decided opinion upon any point, preferring apparently to listen to the conversation."

Finally, Butterfield suggested that the group put the relevant issues to a vote. The first question: Should the army stay where it was or move? Gibbon, as the junior officer present, went first. He voted to stay but make any necessary corrections in the army's position. The other generals voted to remain, too, with Hancock and Newton also recommending making any needed corrections in position. The second question: Should the army attack or remain on the defensive? All voted for defense. The final question: How long should the army wait for Lee to attack? The answers varied from "until Lee moves" to Hancock's "can't wait long; can't be idle."

Once the voting was done Meade quietly said, "Such then is the decision."[62] Gibbon said he saw nothing in Meade's demeanor to suggest he disagreed with the vote. Others who were not present later portrayed Meade as having been unwilling to remain on the field. In a version of the meeting he published in 1882, Abner Doubleday had Meade snap, "Have it your own way, gentlemen, but Gettysburg is no place to fight a battle in."[63] Doubleday, however, did not attend the meeting, and when he wrote his account of Gettysburg he was still smarting over being relieved of command of the I Corps. Apparently there are some wounds that time does not heal.

After the meeting ended and Gibbon was preparing to leave the little house, Meade turned to him. "If Lee attacks tomorrow, it will be *in your front*," he said.

Gibbon asked why he thought that. "Because he has made attacks on both our flanks and failed and if he concludes to try it again, it will be on our centre," Meade replied.

"Well, general, I hope he does," Gibbon replied, "and if he does, we shall whip him."[64] The meeting broke up around midnight. Gibbon joined Hancock and Newton in the back of a nearby ambulance and fell asleep.[65]

◆ ◆ ◆

The little Leister House still stands on the battlefield, and I'm waiting outside it one warm spring day when a bus pulls into the parking lot on the other side of the Taneytown Road. The passengers emerge into the sunshine and cross the street to gather in front of the building. They all wear name tags around their necks from the Gettysburg Foundation, the nonprofit that works in partnership with the National Park Service here. I ask one man what's going on. He tells me it's a business seminar about leadership lessons one can learn from the Civil War. "Like 'Don't get killed,'" he says, laughing. "Or 'Don't be a Sickles.'"

The two women leading the tour take turns talking about what happened here. One of them discusses Meade's leadership. "Meade seemed to be everywhere," she says. "He was a very hands-on kind of guy." She says that he had done very well for himself at Gettysburg even though he had been in command for mere days. "Not a bad showing for a new guy." Then she gives an account of the "council of war" that took place in this building late in the night of July 2. "What are the dynamics of what's going on in the meeting here?" she asks. "Meade was the authority figure here but he actually took a vote. It took courage to risk that the vote might come out contrary to what you wanted to do." She praises Meade for making sure that "everyone was on the same page." As the commander of a division, she says, Gibbon would have been equivalent to "middle management," and she reads from his account of the meeting, in which he tells how Meade took him aside and said that Lee would attack on his front in the morning.

Then the other woman holds up charts and graphs measuring both Meade's and Lee's leadership abilities. Lee apparently was a "developer," whereas Meade was "better at collaboration."

I have absolutely no idea what the charts and graphs mean, but I do find it interesting to hear this appraisal of Meade from a business perspective. However, that's not why I'm here. I've come to meet Greg Goodell, Gettysburg's chief of museum services. He is going to let me inside the little house, which is normally closed to the public. In fact, when I peek around the side of the building I see that Goodell is already here, an affable young man with close-cropped red whiskers. As the tour group heads off to its next stop, Goodell wrestles with the padlocks and then opens the door. I step across the threshold. The place smells of mothballs. Goodell reaches behind the door and pulls out a mousetrap, complete with mouse.

The place is tiny—just two little rooms. It hardly seems like an apt setting for important historical events. It has a low, beamed ceiling and worn wooden floors. The front room has a fireplace, table, and corner cupboard. The other room, where Meade held his council of war, contains a bed, bureau, and even a chamber pot. "It's outfitted to represent what kind of materiel would have been here in 1863," Goodell tells me. Some of the original furniture is on display in the museum at the visitors center. He also tells me that the building underwent a pretty thorough restoration in the 1960s. "Most likely the outside panels are from the 1960s," he says, but the interior should be largely original materials.

It's still a "mean little room" in a "shabby little farm house." Normally a building like this probably would have been torn down years ago and forgotten. History, though, has given it special stature.

◆ ◆ ◆

Meade was on horseback early the next morning, examining the enemy lines through his field glasses. "His manner was calm and serious, but earnest," Haskell related. "There was no arrogance of hope, or timidity of fear discernible in his face; but you would have supposed he would do his duty conscientiously and well, and would be willing to abide the result. You would have seen this in his face."[66] Fighting already had broken out on the Union right, on the rocky and wooded Culp's Hill. When the XII Corps troops Meade had dispatched from there the previous day to support the III Corps returned to the breastworks they had left behind, they found them occupied by Confederate troops. They launched an attack early on the morning of July 3, and after some intense fighting they drove the rebels out.

William Wheeler of the 13th New York Independent Battery had an encounter with Meade on July 3. The young lieutenant was waiting with his guns at Cemetery Hill when "an elderly Major General with spectacles, looking a good deal like a Yale Professor," rode up and asked him if he had enough ammunition. Wheeler replied he had as much as he could get without an order from Maj. Thomas Osborne, the XI Corps' artillery chief. With some excitement the general replied, "You must have ammunition; the country can't wait for Major Osborne or any other man." He told Wheeler to go to the artillery reserve and have a wagonload of ammunition sent up immediately.

Wheeler had just been at the artillery reserve and knew they didn't have any ammunition to give him, but something in the general's face warned him about answering back. Instead, Wheeler spurred his horse and rode behind some trees, where he stayed until the general departed. When he returned he found out the "Yale professor" was General Meade himself.[67]

• • •

Whitelaw Reid dropped by the Leister House in the morning and found it to be a hub of activity as messengers arrived with reports and departed with instructions. Meade came to the door occasionally to ask something of his staff, who were sitting in the shade of a tree. "Quick and nervous in his movements, but calm, and as it seemed to me, lit up with the glow of the occasion, he looked more the General, less the student," Reid observed.[68] Despite Meade's words to Gibbon the night before, he also remained concerned about his left. There had been severe and bloody fighting on the Union right at Culp's Hill, but after the Confederate repulse there the battlefield remained strangely quiet as the morning stretched into a hot, sultry, and silent afternoon. Some of Gibbon's staff managed to scrounge up a loaf of bread, some potatoes, and a chicken. The meal, supplemented by toast, tea, and coffee, proved more than satisfactory. Meade and some of his staff rode up as the food cooked, and Gibbon invited them to share. Somebody found Meade a cracker box to sit on. Newton and Pleasonton arrived next, but there was enough food for all. After eating, the generals retired under a tree, lit cigars, and discussed the previous day's events. Sometime around 12:30, the generals began to disperse until only Gibbon and Hancock remained. Even with an enemy army threatening, some of the men managed to nap, with just the buzzing flies to disturb them.

General Schurz remembered the long quiet of July 3 as "a tranquility like the peaceful and languid repose of a warm midsummer morning in which one might expect to hear the ringing of the village church-bells." Yet Schurz also felt there was something ominous about the silence.[69] He was right. It was merely the calm before a storm unlike anyone had ever witnessed.

The storm broke sometime around 1:00, announced by first one cannon shot and then another. And then all hell broke loose. The Confederates artillery, more than 160 guns, opened fire and unleashed a rain of shot and shell upon the Union lines. The Federal artillery responded in kind. It was the largest cannon barrage ever seen on the North American continent. "For two hours the roar was continuous and loud as that from the falls of Niagara," said Charles Wainwright, the artillery chief for the I Corps.[70]

"Every size and form of shell known to British and to American gunnery shrieked, whirled, moaned, and whistled, and wrathfully fluttered over our ground," wrote a reporter for the *New York Tribune*. The blizzard of metal killed horses tied up around Meade's headquarters. An ambulance went clattering by through the chaos and destruction, pulled by a horse that had lost one of its hind legs.[71]

As shells began to crash to earth all around, soldiers dashed about in confusion. Gibbon's groom was mounting his horse when a shell struck him in the chest, tearing him to pieces. Shells killed more soldiers milling about on the Taneytown Road. "A soldier was lying on the ground a few rods distant from where I was sitting," wrote *Boston Journal* reporter Charles Carleton Coffin. "There was a shriek, such as I hope never again to hear, and his body was whirling in the air, a mangled mass of flesh, blood, and bones!"[72]

In fact, the area behind the lines was the most dangerous, for the rebel guns tended to fire too high and were lofting their shells over the Union front lines and into the rear. "General Meade's headquarters were for a time in the hottest place," recalled General Howard; "the house was riddled with shot, the chimney knocked in pieces, the dooryard plowed with them, officers and men wounded, and the many patient horses killed, and, what seemed worse, others dreadfully wounded."[73]

Meade appeared unconcerned. He even used the occasion to tell a mildly humorous story. As he paced up and down between the Leister House and the Taneytown Road, he noticed some of his staff trying to find shelter behind the little farmhouse. "Gentlemen, are you trying to find a safe place?" he asked pleasantly. "You remind me of the man who drove the ox-team which took ammunition for the heavy guns on to the field of Palo Alto. Finding himself within range, he tilted up his cart and got behind it. Just then General Taylor came along, and seeing this attempt at shelter, shouted, 'You damned fool, don't you know you are no safer there than anywhere else?' The driver replied, 'I don't suppose I am, general, but it kind o' feels so.'"[74]

There's no record of whether any of his staff laughed. They did suggest that Meade move to a safer place. Worried that messengers would not know where to find him, he refused. Finally, he agreed to move to a barn on the other side of the Taneytown Road. It proved to be no safer than the widow's house. A shell fragment struck Butterfield there, wounding him slightly. He left for the rear.[75] Meade's staff suggested moving to Slocum's headquarters on Powers Hill, telling him he could communicate effectively from there with the signalmen at the Leister House. Once he reached Slocum's headquarters, though, Meade discovered that the signalmen had left their position at the Leister House. He decided to return there.

Across the fields, facing the Union army from Seminary Ridge, Robert E. Lee prepared to make Meade's prediction to Gibbon come true. The powerful artillery assault had been merely a prelude to the main attack, a movement against the Union center led by Maj. Gen. George Pickett's fresh division and supported by divisions commanded by Brig. Gen. James Pettigrew, who had taken over from the wounded Henry Heth, and Brig. Gen. Isaac Trimble, the replacement for the mortally wounded William Pender. After two hours of earsplitting bombardment, the Confederate guns gradually fell silent. Henry Hunt, on his own authority, had cannily ordered his guns to slow their firing as well. He wanted the Confederates to believe their artillery fire had been more effective than it actually had been, and he also wanted to save ammunition for the inevitable attack. Hunt was pleased when he received orders from Meade to do exactly that. Hancock, however, became angry when he saw Union artillery units cease firing and he ordered them to resume—an action that later sparked a bitter war of words between him and Hunt.

As silence descended over the battlefield, the Confederates began emerging from the woods in front of Seminary Ridge. There were at least thirteen thousand men in all, fifteen thousand by some counts, long gray lines that stretched for a mile across the broad fields. It was a sight that veterans on both sides would remember until they died—which for many of them would be very soon.

This was the start of Pickett's Charge, the march to the "high-water mark of the Confederacy." Longstreet had earlier told Lee he though the assault was doomed to failure. "I have been a soldier, I may say, from the ranks up to the position I now hold," Longstreet had argued. "I have been in pretty much all kinds of skirmishes, from those of two or three soldiers up to those of an army corps, and I think I can safely say there never was a body of fifteen thousand men who could make that attack successfully."[76] Lee remained adamant. He would make the kind of frontal assault that had already proven disastrous for him at Malvern Hill and for the Union at Fredericksburg. It was also the kind of frontal assault that Meade later avoided at Williamsport and Mine Run—attacks that he had the wisdom to call off before thousands of men lost their lives in proving their futility. Lee lacked that wisdom on July 3, 1863. His men had beaten the Army of the Potomac before. He believed they would do it again.

Pvt. E. M. Hays was with a Union battery atop Little Round Top when the Confederates moved forward. He had a wonderful vantage point from which to watch the advance—and also a great artillery platform from which to kill the men making it. "There was no faltering there, and how my heart leaped and fluttered and my blood rushed and boiled as I gazed in awe upon the steady advance, the grand courage and fortitude of those heroes as they marched into the very jaws of death," Hays wrote. "As I stood there, a breathless spectator, I almost wished them success as a reward for such matchless bravery."[77]

Alexander Webb, the soldier who had touted Meade's virtues at Chancellorsville and witnessed his anger at Hooker afterward, was now a brigadier general, waiting with his brigade at a stone wall on Cemetery Ridge. He was at the spot where the wall turned at a sharp angle near a prominent clump of trees. The men here were ready to punish the oncoming rebels. Many of them had been busy scavenging the battlefield to gather as many weapons as they could find. Some had as many as twelve loaded muskets at hand to pour death into the neat Southern lines.

The rebels marched inexorably toward Webb's position even as Hunt's artillery, silent no more, began taking an awful toll. When the rebels came close enough musket fire added to the destruction. "As they steadily advanced I ordered my few guns to fire and we opened great gaps on them," Webb wrote in a letter to his wife.

Even as their ranks became more and more depleted by the hell of shot and shell, the soldiers ripped apart by artillery or shot to death by muskets, the Confederates advanced across the field. Union soldiers began pouring destructive fire into the enemy's flanks and their ranks continued to thin. Still, the survivors moved forward until a remnant reached the stone wall. With Gen. Lewis Armistead in advance, lifting his hat high atop his sword—the same sword I had seen at the Museum of the Confederacy—the rebels fought their way over the wall. Attackers and defenders engaged in a fierce melee, shooting, stabbing, and clubbing each other with their muskets. "When they were over the fence the Army of the Potomac was nearer being whipped than it was at any time of the battle," Webb wrote.[78] Some of his men did break and dash toward the rear. The fate of the battle appeared to hang in the balance. More Union soldiers rushed in to join the fighting and steady the line.

"Many things cannot be described by pen or pencil; such a fight is one," Frank Haskell wrote. Nevertheless, he tried. "The line springs," he wrote; "the crest of the solid ground, with a great roar, heaves forward its maddened load,—men, arms, smoke, fire, a fighting mass; it rolls to the wall; flash meets flash; the wall is crossed; a moment ensues of thrusts, yells, blows, shots, an undistinguished conflict, followed by a shout universal, that makes the welkin ring again; and the last and bloodiest fight of the great battle of Gettysburg is ended and won."[79]

On the way back from Powers Hill, Meade encountered some of his staff and his son George, whose horse had been killed. "Hello, George," his father said. "Is that you? I am glad you are here. You must stick by me now, you are the only officer left."[80] He remarked that it was "a pretty lively place" and told his son to take one of his orderly's horses. Continuing on, he came across a large body of prisoners being taken to the rear. Recognizing him as an authority figure, the Confederates asked him where they should go. He laughed. "Go along that way and you'll be well taken care of," he said, pointing. Just then Confederate shells began raining down. The prisoners scattered and ran away, some of them cheering the show of force from their side. Meade asked one of the Union officers escorting them, Lt. John Egan of the 1st Regiment of U.S. Artillery, if the attack had been repulsed. Egan replied that it had and that Gen. Alexander Hays had one of their flags. "I don't care for their flag," Meade replied crossly. "Have they turned?" Egan repeated that they had. Meade and his son then rode on.[81]

Hancock had been one of the battle's casualties, wounded in the thigh by a Confederate bullet that tore through his saddle and carried a nail into the wound. As he lay bleeding on the ground Hancock dictated a message for an aide, Maj. William Mitchell, to bring to Meade. "Tell General Meade that the troops under my command have repulsed the enemy's assault and that we have gained a great victory," Hancock said. "The enemy is now flying in all directions from my front." Mitchell delivered the message as Meade was riding up to the crest of Cemetery Hill. The news that Hancock had been wounded seemed to affect Meade. "Say to General Hancock that I regret exceedingly that he is wounded and that I thank him for the Country and myself for the service he has rendered today," he told Mitchell.[82]

Frank Haskell also encountered Meade at this time. "How is it going here?" Meade demanded.

"I believe, General, the enemy's attack is repulsed," replied the young lieutenant.

"What? Is the attack already repulsed?" Meade asked, apparently still unwilling to believe the good news.

"It is, sir."

Meade finally reached the crest of Cemetery Ridge—somewhere around the spot where his statue stands today—and saw for himself that the enemy had retreated. His face lit up. "Thank God," he said. Haskell thought Meade began to reach for his hat as though he were going to sweep it off his head, but then he caught himself. He simply waved his hand and shouted, "Hurrah!" Young George felt less restrained. He waved his hat over his head and gave out three loud cheers.[83] Under its new commander the Army of the Potomac had finally defeated Robert E. Lee and the Army of Northern Virginia.

• • •

The easily recognizable figure on the speaker's platform at the National Cemetery at Gettysburg steps forward to address the crowd. He wears a stovepipe hat, black frock coat and vest. His craggy features are set off by a scruffy beard. He removes his hat and looks out at the faces assembled before him. He begins to speak. "Four score and seven years ago," he says, "our forefathers brought forth on this continent a new nation, conceived in liberty and dedicated to the proposition that all men are created equal."

No, it is not 1863 and this is not Abraham Lincoln making his Gettysburg Address. It's 2010 and the speaker is Jim Getty, who has established himself as Gettysburg's official Lincoln since moving here in 1977. Each year he appears as Lincoln to recite the Gettysburg Address on November 19, the anniversary of the president's speech at the dedication of the new National Cemetery here. I am not the first and certainly won't be the last person to point out the irony of these words from Lincoln's short speech: "The world will little note nor long remember what we say here." The Gettysburg address—all 272 words of it—has since become regarded as one of the greatest speeches in American history. It's safe to say that Lincoln's speech is now more famous than the man who commanded the army that made the speech possible. "It is a commentary on the power of words that what Lincoln said at Gettysburg has eclipsed what Meade did there," wrote a reviewer for *The Dial* magazine way back in 1913. "To be bowled over by an [*sic*] eulogy celebrating your own performance is a hard fate."[84]

Indeed it is. But Meade wasn't the only man Lincoln bowled over. The headliner here on November 19, 1863, was noted orator Edwin Everett, a former president of Harvard and once Lincoln's political opponent, having run for vice president on the Union platform with John Bell, the ticket for which Meade voted in the 1860 election. Everett's speech ran for more than two hours—about sixty times longer than the president's—but who today remembers what he said? The situation reminds me of the scene in *Raiders of the Lost Ark* where Indiana Jones encounters a scimitar-wielding assassin who dazzles him with an elaborate display of swordsmanship. Indy then draws his gun and shoots him dead with a single shot.

A lot of myths have become attached to Lincoln's speech. The president did not hastily write it down on the back on an envelope on his way to Gettysburg, nor did people receive it with universal condemnation. Depending on their political orientation, some newspapers did deride the speech, but others offered praise, although few thought the president's brief remarks would become such a cornerstone of the American legacy.

Newsman Sam Donaldson, today's keynote speaker, would undoubtedly like to avoid Everett's fate. A former White House correspondent, Donaldson has his own firsthand knowledge of presidential politics, and he tells the assembled crowd a little bit about how Lincoln might have fared on television in today's fractious political climate.

Lincoln did Gettysburg's tourism industry a good turn when he decided to attend the ceremony here. The annual Dedication Day ceremonies now lead into a Remembrance Weekend, and Gettysburg is hopping this year as visitors provide one last infusion of cash before winter comes and shuts things down. The town is filled with men and women in nineteenth-century clothing. The parking lots by the site of the old visitors center fill up, and hordes of people stream into the cemetery across the street. They are mostly older and white, but there are also school groups and even a high school band in Civil War attire. It's another beautiful autumn day, but there's a chill breeze that cuts through your outerwear. This is one of the few Civil War events I've attended where I wouldn't mind wearing wool.

A naturalization ceremony follows the speeches. Sixteen people are here today to take the oath of citizenship. They hail from Canada, Egypt, Great Britain, Hungary, India, China, and the Philippines. In a time when immigration has become a hot-button political topic, it's refreshing to attend a ceremony that welcomes people from other countries to U.S. citizenship. A representative of the nation's Citizenship and Immigration Services makes a few remarks and points out that many people who fought and died here had not been born in this country. Immigrants formed a large proportion of the Union army, whether they hailed from Ireland, Germany, or even Hawaii. Later in the war thousands of men of African descent fought in the Union armies.

The parade kicks off at 1:00. This is a big event for Gettysburg. People have set up folding chairs all along Baltimore Street, and crowds fill the sidewalks. For almost an hour more Civil War units follow them down Baltimore Street. Bands march by with period instruments, and there's even a funeral wagon complete with casket, trailed by sorrowful women in mourning dresses. Union marchers make up the first part of the parade and the Confederates bring up the rear, marching once again through the streets of Gettysburg as they had in 1863. I see at least three Robert E. Lees as well as a Jeb Stuart, who rides by with a bouquet of yellow roses tucked into the top of his cavalry boots. Flags wave, drums pound, fifes play, and the sound of marching feet fills the air. There must be thousands of participants, and the front of the parade has long since disappeared over the rise in Baltimore Street before the last units turn the corner from East Middle Street.

Lincoln came to Gettysburg to dedicate the National Cemetery, so it's altogether fitting and proper that the day's events end there. Since 2003 the Gettysburg Foundation has held a Remembrance Illumination in the cemetery. Volunteers place a single luminary—a candle in a bag—atop each of the 3,512 Civil War graves in the seventeen-acre grounds. Other volunteers take turns reading the names of the soldiers buried here. This year I've volunteered to take a slot in the recital. My wife and I arrive around 6:30 in the evening. It's already dark, but a bright full moon casts a quicksilver light over the landscape. We have to park a ways down Baltimore Street, and we carefully make our way through the darkness, past the Evergreen Cemetery gatehouse, which stood here during the battle, and down to the National Cemetery entrance. Once inside the cemetery I get a quick whispered briefing from a volunteer.

It's a surreal experience. Up the hill we can see the orange glow from the thousands of luminaries on the graves and along the cemetery pathways. Other than the candles and the light from the moon and a dim light at the podium, the cemetery is dark. The podium is near the entrance, below a statue of John Reynolds illuminated by moonlight. I wait in line for my turn to begin reading. When my time comes, I stand at the podium and read my assigned pages, all names from Massachusetts regiments. Many of them are listed as simply "Unknown." Halfway through my list I hear the sound of taps coming faintly through the night from farther within the cemetery. Per my briefing I stop reading until the last note dies away. A red "Stop" at the end of a column tells me when I've reached the end of my section, and I hand the list to the next reader in line.

My wife and I make our way through the night to the graves. We can hear the faint sounds of a fife and drum coming from a Civil War encampment on Steinwehr Avenue. A lone sentry holding an American flag stands in front of the tall Soldiers National Monument. Now and then someone takes a flash photo and the scene lights up as though by lightning. Otherwise all is hushed and silent. As we walk down the pathways people suddenly emerge from the darkness like ghosts. The fact that some of them are in nineteenth-century costumes heightens the sense of eeriness and the feeling that here in Gettysburg it's still 1863 and the war still hangs in the balance.

CHAPTER 9
The Old Brute

Old Baldy, back when his head was still attached to his body
LIBRARY OF CONGRESS

◆ ◆ ◆

My wife and I are driving in Northeast Philadelphia through a warren of narrow streets and alleys on a route that a MapQuest printout promises is the best way to reach our goal. I don't know this part of Philadelphia at all, and the neighborhood is starting to look a little dicey, with small and somewhat shabby attached homes mixed with parking lots ringed by chain-link fences. I'm beginning to think that MapQuest has played a cruel prank—and then I spot two men in Civil War uniforms walking down the sidewalk.

This must be the place.

We have come to the Grand Army of the Republic Museum and Library in Gen. George Meade's hometown to visit a horse's head. Not just any horse's head, mind you. This head was once attached to the body of Old Baldy, the faithful steed that carried Meade through several Civil War battles.

If they awarded Purple Hearts to horses, Baldy would have earned a chest full. He suffered his first wound during First Bull Run, when Gen. David Hunter owned him. Meade bought Baldy from the quartermaster for $150 in 1861. He wasn't much to write home about. In fact, Meade was always worrying about finding a good horse. "I am never fortunate with them," he told his wife. "I should like much to have a really fine horse, but it costs so much I must try to get along with my old hacks."[1] His aides learned to dislike Baldy because the horse moved at an awkward pace somewhere between a walk and a run, making it difficult to keep pace, but Meade thought him a loyal and steadfast mount.

Baldy received a second wound at Second Bull Run; at Antietam he was so badly injured that Meade gave him up for dead.

Baldy suffered his final wound during the second day at Gettysburg. He carried the Confederate bullet he received there inside him for the rest of his life. "I did not think he could live, but the old fellow has such a wonderful tenacity of life that I am in hopes he will," Meade wrote to his wife back in Philadelphia.[2] In April 1864, on the eve of the Overland Campaign, Meade decided to send the horse to a well-earned retirement at a farm outside Philadelphia. "He will never be fit again for hard service, and I thought he was entitled to better care than could be given to him on the march," the general said. When his wife later sent him a positive update about Old Baldy in retirement Meade wrote back, "I am glad to hear the good news about Baldy, as I am very much attached to the old brute."[3]

Meade continued to ride Baldy in Philadelphia after the war. They were two old veterans, both wounded in the line of duty. Meade's wounds helped take him to an early grave and the horse ended up outliving the rider. On November 11, 1872, Baldy marched, riderless, in Meade's funeral procession. The horse lived for another ten years, until the ailing steed was put down at the ripe old age of thirty on December 16, 1882. That Christmas Day two Union veterans received permission to remove his head and have it mounted. They attached the relic to a wooden plaque outlining Baldy's war record and presented it to the George Meade Post of the Grand Army of the Republic (GAR) in Philadelphia. (The Old York Road Historical Society in Jenkintown, near the Old Brute's final resting place, has one of the horse's hooves.)

Founded in 1866, the GAR once wielded considerable political clout, with five hundred thousand members at posts around the country. But membership was restricted to honorably discharged Union veterans, so the organization had a built-in shelf life. In 1949 the final six surviving members officially closed the GAR's books. The last member standing, 109-year-old Alfred Woolson, died in 1956. Baldy's head went into the GAR Museum and Library, the institution founded to care for the old Meade post's collections. In 1979 the museum decided it couldn't afford refurbishment work on the head, so it loaned Old Baldy to the Civil War Museum on Philadelphia's Pine Street. He remained a mainstay there, a centerpiece in the General Meade Room, until the institution closed in 2008.

Suddenly Old Baldy was in equine limbo. The Pine Street museum decided it would lend out its collections to other institutions, but the GAR Museum and Library sued to get Baldy back. Lawyers worked out the case in Philadelphia's Orphan Court and agreed that Old Baldy could return to his former home. And today, on a gray and drizzly Sunday, my wife and I have arrived at the museum for the gala unveiling.

A crowd of about sixty-five people have gathered for the big event. We meet for a short ceremony on folding chairs under a canvas covering in the parking lot behind the museum. Sounds of heavy machinery from somewhere behind us and occasional blasting music from the street add a certain charm to the proceedings. Reenactors representing the 98th Pennsylvania Volunteer Infantry serve as a color guard and present the flags for the Pledge of Allegiance. Then Dr. Anthony Waskie, the museum's vice president and the founder and president of the General Meade Society of Philadelphia, starts the proceedings. "We're very, very happy to have this icon back here on display where he originally came from," he tells the gathering. The Reverend Richard Partington gives a short invocation. "Help us remember the past so we can be better guided in the future," he closes.

Waskie is the other personage I've come to see today. He is the center of the Meade universe, if such a thing exists. "Have you met Andy Waskie?" is almost inevitably the first question I get when I tell Civil War people that I'm working on a book about Meade. A history professor at Temple University, Waskie also makes appearances as Meade at Civil War events throughout the area, including an annual appearance at Barnegat Bay Lighthouse.

Once the ceremony ends we all troop inside the museum for the ribbon cutting, past the bust of Alfred Woolson, which sits inside the back entrance with, for some reason, a plastic lei around his neck. Bud Atkinson, the museum's president emeritus, and his wife, Margaret, a board member, do the honors, and then people file through the room to pay respects to Old Baldy in his new home on the museum's ground floor. The old brute, enshrined in a brand new mahogany-and-glass cabinet, shares the small space with a number of Meade artifacts. A chair from the Leister House, Meade's headquarters at Gettysburg, sits against the opposite wall, beneath photographs of Meade and his wife that come from Waskie's personal collection. A glass case holds other Meade relics—his Bible, cufflinks that contain locks of his hair, his calling card, Baldy's bridle.

Baldy himself . . . well, let's be honest. He's a horse's head on a plaque. I can't even say he looks particularly lifelike. He shows his age and has a somewhat glassy-eyed stare—probably because he has glass eyes. I note the white markings on his nose that gave him his name (they reminded Meade of an equine characteristic called "bald face"), but I search in vain for visible signs of wounds. Still, there's something weird and wonderful about visiting the business end of this equine warrior at his new home and sensing the excitement here about getting him back where he belongs.

He's certainly not the first Civil War horse to become the object of veneration. I've seen Stonewall Jackson's horse, Little Sorrel, at the Virginia Military Institute in Lexington, where he's stuffed and mounted. A five-minute walk away I visited Robert E. Lee's horse, Traveller, who has his own grave just outside the Lee Chapel where his master is enshrined. Phil Sheridan's horse Winchester, also known as Rienzi, is in a glass case at the Smithsonian Institution's National Museum of American History in Washington. During the war flocks of admirers were almost as eager to see George McClellan's horse, Dan Webster, as they were to spot the "Young Napoleon" himself. So Civil War horse veneration is neither new nor surprising. What does surprise me, though, is that throughout the entire afternoon I don't hear a single reference to *The Godfather*.

Once I pay my respects to Baldy, I look around the other rooms in the little museum. It occupies the Ruan House, a stately brick presence that rears up above its neighbors like an elderly dowager determined to keep up appearances even as the family fortunes decline. It was built in 1796 by a physician named John Ruan, and the museum bought the building in 1958. Now it's a house-size cabinet of curiosities, with display cases in the four small rooms on the ground floor filled with a somewhat eccentric collection of Civil War curios, including bloody strips taken from the pillow that cradled the dying Abraham Lincoln's head and the handcuffs that John Wilkes Booth intended to use on the president when he hatched his original plan to kidnap him.

Baldy isn't the only severed head on display here, either. Looking out over the adjoining room is the head of a mule, a tribute to all the army mules that labored for the Union during the war. Mules, like horses, played an important role in the conflict. As a regimental history of the 118th Pennsylvania said of the army mule, "It bore hard usage and scoffs and sneers with uncomplaining heroism, and was found dead on all the battlefields of the war. It was of inestimable value to the army, and it is doubtful if the varied operations could have been conducted without it."[4]

In one display I find the medical case of Mary Edwards Walker, a Civil War doctor who won the Medal of Honor for her actions—the only woman to do so. The government, in its wisdom, revoked her medal in 1917 but reversed its reverse in 1977. That was far too late to do any good for Walker, who died two years after learning about the revocation. Theodore Lyman, who served as Meade's aide-de-camp starting in 1863, once wrote to his wife about running into this "female doctor" on a train. "She was attired in a small straw hat with a cockade in front, a pair of blue pantaloons and a long frock coat, or sack," he noted. "Over all she had a linen 'duster'; and this, coupled with the fact that she had rips in her boots, gave her a trig appearance. She was liberal in her advice to all comers and especially exhorted two newspaper boys to immediately wash their faces, in which remark she was clearly correct."[5] I have to assume that Lyman uses "trig," which means "smart and trim," sarcastically.

A post from the stockade of the infamous POW camp at Andersonville sits near another display case that hold relics from various battlefields, including a piece of wood embedded with bullets from Spotsylvania's Bloody Angle. These are relics in the old sense of the word, as in "an object esteemed and venerated because of association with a saint or martyr." As crusaders returned with pieces of the true cross from the Holy Land, Civil War veterans brought home these little pieces of the fields where they had fought and where their comrades had died. So that's not just an ordinary stone I see in one case—it's a piece from the wall at Fredericksburg. The chunk of wood came from the church that gave the Shiloh battlefield its name. These relics, sanctified by blood and death, have been elevated from the realm of the ordinary, just as the hills and fields where they originated have become something more than simple pastures and woodlands.

I have a great affection for these little museums, which keep history alive through the love and dedication of their volunteers. People here have donated items from their own collections and made handwritten cards to identify the artifacts on display. They use their enthusiasm to keep the past alive.

After people have had a chance to view the museum's latest relic in his glass case, we head upstairs to the big back room for a champagne toast and refreshments. Men—and women—in Civil War uniforms mix with civilians. I take the opportunity to find a quiet corner and ask Waskie some questions about his fascination with Meade. We talk beneath a row of portraits of generals that line one wall—Joe Hooker, George McClellan, Winfield Scott Hancock, and cavalryman David McMurtrie Gregg. A portrait of President Abraham Lincoln stares down the long room from the other side, looking over at a full-length portrait of Ulysses S. Grant that hangs above a glass case containing books and items for sale.

Waskie doesn't look all that much like Meade, and he's gregarious and enthusiastic, not sardonic and irritable. He has a deep, booming voice that seems perfectly attuned for the lecture hall. Like Meade, he does have a beard, and when I see him in profile I get a quick flash of the general. But he lacks Meade's pouchy eyes and prodigious nose. "I've always been a history buff," Waskie says, and he tells me he long nursed a fascination with Gettysburg. "I always knew Meade but I really didn't know anything about him. It was like saying Don Carlos Buell. What do you know about Don Carlos Buell? So I started to read as much as I could about him. I just got more and more fascinated. Why is he not better known? This man is unbelievable. Three days before the battle, he's named to command . . . all the good things he did . . . the humble unpretentious background . . . he rose in competence, was promoted, and on and on and on."

Waskie learned that Meade was buried in Philadelphia's Laurel Hill Cemetery and he fell in love with the place when he visited. He now serves on the cemetery board, conducts tours there, and has written a history of Laurel Hill. In 1990 he cajoled people into coming to the cemetery on December 31 for a ceremony on Meade's birthday. That became an annual tradition. After the ceremony in 1996 a bunch of attendees sat around drinking and talking and decided to form the General Meade Society, its mission "to promote and preserve the life and service of Maj.-Gen. George G. Meade (USA), commander of the Army of the Potomac."

In 1985 Waskie did his first talk as Meade, with the general's own great-grandson in attendance. "I did my talk and he was smiling, a very generous, genteel gentleman, and I'd look over at him, looking for affirmation, and he'd smile. After the talk was over he came up to me and he said, you know, you know a hell of a lot more about my granddad than I do." Waskie's been Meade ever since, doing his part to keep the general's memory alive—something Old Baldy and the GAR Museum also do.

• • •

A few weeks later I drive down to Gettysburg to meet up with members of the General Meade Society of Philadelphia. In contrast to the bleak and rainy weather that greeted me in Philadelphia, it is a crisp and windy October morning with a sky so blue it almost hurts my eyes. The members of the Meade Society are meeting at the Widow Leister's tiny white house. They come here every fall to clean up the grounds. About a dozen people have shown up today. The main topic of conversation isn't the Civil War, though—it's the Philadelphia Phillies, who lost the first game of the National League Championship Series to the San Francisco Giants the night before.

Everyone pitches in. Some begin weeding the garden. I trim a large bush that sits in front of the house. Ken Garson, a retired librarian, helps me collect the clippings. When I'm done with the bush I start painting the weather-beaten garden fence, and then I do a little touch-up work on the house. I wonder if battlefield guides will tell people, "Disregard the painting here. It's obviously twenty-first-century work. And not very good, at that." After a couple hours of reasonably productive activity the house looks a little bit better, and we all retire to the Farnsworth House on Baltimore Street for pizza and beer.

The restaurant building was here during the battle, and if you look closely you can see the bullet marks that pock its brick walls. Inside it's small and cozy, decorated with a Civil War motif. One very large glass case holds second-generation Gettysburg relics—costumes from the 1993 movie *Gettysburg*, including the hat Richard Anderson wore as Meade. There's also a framed movie poster signed by many members of the cast.

As I wait at the bar for a beer I start talking with Jerry McCormick, the society's treasurer. He tells me the group has about 250 members, some of them from as far away as the West Coast. McCormick became involved after he met Waskie at Antietam during the battle's 135th anniversary. They started talked about doing living history. "I told him, 'Well, I'm not going to grow a beard,'" McCormick says, so Waskie suggested he could portray Gen. Andrew Atkinson Humphreys, who sported only a mustache and served as Meade's chief of staff after the Battle of Gettysburg. "I didn't know who he was, but I began to research him," says McCormick. Now he does living history events as Humphreys for an organization of living historians called the Confederation of Union Generals (COUG). Waskie is the organization's Meade.

Ken Garson, who helped me trim the bush at the Leister House, was always aware of Meade because he attended George Gordon Meade Elementary School in Philadelphia, where he says he was the only white kid. He saw something about the society in the paper and eventually attended one of the birthday ceremonies at Laurel Hill. "It seemed like a cool thing," he says. Later he became even more enthused when he found out that Meade had served as a commissioner and a vice president for the city's Fairmount Park, one of Garson's favorite places in Philadelphia. "He's really the father of Fairmount Park," he says.

After lunch, which includes a toast to Meade, I head back to the battlefield to walk around. It's an absolutely stunning autumn day, brisk and windy, with the leaves on the trees beginning to turn. I walk from the Leister House up to the Meade statue that stands on the crest of Cemetery Ridge. Meade is mounted on Old Baldy and stares across the wide fields toward the statue of his old adversary, Robert E. Lee, on top of the Virginia Memorial. I walk on down Cemetery Ridge, roughly following the Union line, until I reach the huge, domed Pennsylvania Memorial.

This monument to the Commonwealth's native sons is the largest one on the battlefield. Pennsylvania has the home-field advantage here, but it also owns a good claim to bragging rights. As one Union general noted, "It is remarkable that, in the one Pennsylvania battle of the war, the men of that State should have borne so prominent a part. It was a Pennsylvanian [Meade] who directed the movement on Gettysburg and commanded there in chief. It was a Pennsylvanian [John Reynolds] who hurried the left wing into action and lost his life in determining that the battle should be fought at Gettysburg, and not at any line more remote. It was a Pennsylvanian [Winfield Scott Hancock] who came up to check the rout and hold Cemetery Hill for the Union arms, who commanded the left center in the great battle of the second day, and on the third received and repelled the attack of Pettigrew and Pickett."[6]

The monument to these Pennsylvanians and the men they commanded weighs in at a hefty 3,840 tons and stands 110 feet high. Perched atop the dome is the Goddess of Victory and Peace who bears aloft a sword and a palm branch. Statues of Pennsylvania generals stand at attention around the monument's perimeter. Meade poses with a hand on a hip and one leg thrust out, which unfortunately makes him look like a model at the end of the runway, poised to spin around and flounce backstage. Reynolds stands next to him, clutching his chest with one hand and wearing an expression that speaks more of heartburn than combat. Cavalry chief Alfred Pleasonton rears back as though affronted by something he's just heard. The heavily bearded David McMurtrie Gregg, first cousin to Pennsylvania's wartime governor, leans on his sword and looks suitably general-like. Next to Gregg, Winfield Scott Hancock has binoculars in one hand and rests the other on his sheathed sword. Sharing the front of the structure are Gov. Andrew Gregg Curtin, holding one lapel in a classic politician's pose, and Abraham Lincoln, who also holds a lapel with one hand. He extends his other as though he intends to pat an invisible pony on the nose. Around the base of the memorial are ninety bronze tablets that list the names of all 34,530 soldiers from Pennsylvania who served during the war.

Walking back to my car, I spy a small blue flag fluttering from an overgrown stone wall in the middle of the field, so I detour cross-country to investigate. It's a small Minnesota flag flapping in the breeze next to a tiny empty staff. I assume it's a tribute to the 1st Minnesota, sent by Hancock from a position near here on its desperate holding action during the fighting on July 2. It's interesting to see the tributes that people leave on the battlefield. Earlier I saw a glittery owl pendant sitting on top of the small stone that marks the right flank of the 93rd New York near Meade's headquarters. The monument to the 20th Maine on Little Round Top also receives tributes throughout the years, and people often place flags—Union or Confederate—on memorials here. People complain that Americans are terrible when it comes to remembering their own history. That may be true in general, but when you visit Gettysburg—or any other Civil War battlefield—you find a stubborn core of people who refuse to forget. Just ask the members of the General Meade Society of Philadelphia.

CHAPTER 10

The Pursuit

*Andrew Atkinson Humphreys, who served
as Meade's chief of staff after Gettysburg*
LIBRARY OF CONGRESS

• • •

Inside the huge white Springfield Barn and Museum in Williamsport, Maryland, historian Eric J. Wittenberg is talking to a small audience of Civil War buffs. Wittenberg's presentation is just one event of a "Retreat through Williamsport" weekend, a series of talks, demonstrations, walks, and music that commemorates what happened around here in July 1863. The town swelters in the summer heat but large fans keep everyone comfortable inside the historic barn.

Wittenberg's subject today is Meade's pursuit of the Army of Northern Virginia to Williamsport following the Battle of Gettysburg. Lee's Confederates ended up in and around this town on the Potomac, their backs to the rain-swollen river, on their retreat to Virginia. Williamsport became a stinking, muddy, fly-infested, overcrowded mass of wagons, livestock, and Confederate soldiers. Dead horses rotted in the streets; live ones filled the town with their waste. Houses and churches were crowded with Confederate wounded, while some of the dead lay beneath piles of fresh earth in pretty Riverview Cemetery.

Wittenberg is the author or editor of seventeen books about the Civil War.[1] Today he's talking about one of them, *One Continuous Fight: The Retreat from Gettysburg and the Pursuit of Lee's Army of Northern Virginia, July 4–14, 1863*. He's here to demolish some myths that have risen over the years—the ideas that fighting between the two armies essentially stopped after July 3 and that Meade's pursuit of his defeated adversaries was dilatory and lackluster. It's undeniably true that Lee and the Army of Northern Virginia crossed the Potomac River into Virginia before Meade launched an all-out attack. But the idea that Meade did not move energetically after the Southern army "is simply not true," Wittenberg says. He points out that Meade worked under the handicap of losing several corps commanders—Hancock, Reynolds, and Sickles—and that their replacements were not exactly aggressive, fighting generals. He also explains that Meade had specific orders from Halleck to keep his army between Lee and Washington, which required him to conduct the pursuit as he did, along a much longer line than Lee followed. And Wittenberg says that once Meade confronted Lee here around Williamsport, he found the Southern army holed up behind "nearly impregnable defensive positions."

After Wittenberg finishes speaking, he and his wife pack up the books they have brought with them, and he sits down for a short talk with me about Meade. Wittenberg, now a lawyer in Ohio, is a native of Reading, Pennsylvania, and can trace his fascination with the Civil War—as so many can—to his first visit to Gettysburg as a kid. "There were three things about that first trip to Gettysburg that I remember," he tells me. "One, of course, was Devil's Den. That's every kid. But the other two things that really stuck with me were the story of John Buford's stand and the death of John Fulton Reynolds. So I had an interest in Civil War cavalry actions literally since my first time at the battlefield of Gettysburg."

There's plenty of cavalry action in *One Continuous Fight*, but Wittenberg says the book has the strongest infantry component of any he has written. He also tells me that despite his cavalry orientation, he has long had an appreciation for Meade. "I've always been a fan of the old goggle-eyed snapping turtle," he says.

"I've always believed that he did an extraordinary job at Gettysburg under the worst imaginable circumstances. He's never gotten the proper credit that he deserves for it. I think that when you look at the cards he was handed, he played it as well as he possibly could have. When you really study the retreat, when you really understand what happened, you realize and you understand that Meade could not move definitely until he knew for sure what Lee's intentions were. Once he realized and was made aware that Lee's army was moving to Williamsport, Meade moved hyperaggressively. How else can you ask an entire army that's marching to cover fifty-five miles in two days like the XI Corps did? And then to fight? To say he wasn't aggressive and didn't pursue aggressively is not true, and it surely doesn't do the man justice."

That's nice to hear but it's something of a minority opinion, not only now but also back in 1863. "My dear General," Lincoln wrote him in a letter he decided not to send, "I do not believe you appreciate the magnitude of the misfortune involved in Lee's escape. . . . Your golden opportunity is gone, and I am distressed immeasurably because of it."[2] The Confederates had reached their "high-water mark" in the last minutes of Pickett's Charge, and it seems that Meade's reputation did, too. From that point it suffered a gradual descent as people began to wonder why he didn't order an immediate counterattack at Gettysburg or criticized him for being too slow and cautious in his pursuit of Lee's defeated army. Had Meade crushed the Army of Northern Virginia in July 1863 his reputation would have been assured. It might have been Ulysses S. Grant who slipped away into relative obscurity, a western general whose greatest victory, the capture of Vicksburg, was overshadowed when Meade sealed the victory in the East. The inhabitants of that alternate timeline might even remember President George G. Meade.

But not in this one. Here the picture is a thicket of "what ifs" and "why nots." It's possible, I suppose, that a more aggressive general could have launched a counterattack and destroyed Lee's army at Gettysburg. It's equally possible that a rash offensive might have reversed all the Union success and placed the country in an even worse position. A more vigorous pursuit might have bagged the entire Army of Northern Virginia—or it may have left a weakened, stretched-out Army of the Potomac vulnerable to a Confederate counterattack. Then again, it may have made no difference at all. As Kent Masterson Brown notes in *Retreat from Gettysburg: Lee, Logistics and the Pennsylvania Campaign*, his masterful study of Lee's movements after the battle, "Although he was being severely criticized in Washington and by some in the army for his failure to attack Lee at Williamsport, there was nothing Meade could have done to prevent Lee from winning the race to the Williamsport defense line or holding it."[3]

We do know that once Meade realized his army had repulsed the enemy's attack on July 3, he rode to Cemetery Hill to check on things there. Then he rode back along Cemetery Ridge as his soldiers began to cheer him. He continued riding down to Little Round Top, accompanied by cheers. Even the Confederates across the fields on Seminary Ridge noticed the commotion. "We thought it might mean an advance upon us, but it proved to be only a greeting to some general officer riding along the lines," wrote Longstreet's artillery chief, E. Porter Alexander.[4]

Meade wanted to determine whether he could launch a counterattack from his left, but he found his army was much too disorganized for a sudden change to the offensive. Various units had been ordered this way and that to plug gaps in the lines during the fighting, and the result was a hodgepodge instead of an army. Such a disorganized collection of soldiers would have suffered from a lack of unified control had they attempted an immediate counterattack against the Confederate lines. Meade did throw pickets and skirmishers forward to test the enemy defenses. They encountered stiff resistance, indicating that though Lee's army had been beaten, it was still able to fight. Still, Meade ordered preparations made for an assault, but before the army could restore sufficient order from the chaos of battle, it was late in the evening. Meade decided not to attack.[5]

Should he have? That's a scenario that we can add to the bulging file of Civil War "what ifs." Henry Hunt, for one, disputed the notion that the Union army could have made a swift change from defense to offense, writing that the idea of a prompt advance was "a delusion."[6] Maj. Charles Wainwright of the I Corps also believed Meade made the right decision. "Meade was too wise to try the attack and so Lee cleared off," he wrote in his journal. "A number of our generals I know think that we ought to have attacked. I for one am glad that we did not. Lee had doubtless lost very heavily, but we had suffered almost as much, and our men were quite as exhausted as his. In every respect the two armies are so well balanced that the assaulting party is sure to fail if the other has time to post itself and do anything at entrenching."[7]

Even some Confederates believed that Meade was smart not to counterattack. "Genl Meade never brought his 'rascally virtue' of caution to a better market than when he left us alone," said one of Gen. Ewell's staff officers, "for we should probably have given a good account of him."[8] Longstreet agreed. "I had Hood and McLaws, who had not been engaged," he said; "I had a heavy force of artillery; I should have liked nothing better than to have been attacked, and have no doubt I should have given those who tried as bad a reception as Pickett received."[9]

The Leister House was now being used as a hospital, as was practically every available building and barn. As a result, that night the victorious commander at Gettysburg found a place in a field near the Taneytown Road for some long-awaited sleep.

July 4 turned into a wet and miserable Independence Day. Rain started falling in the afternoon and developed into a downpour of biblical proportions, one in which "the very flood gates of heaven seemed to open upon us," as an officer in the 118th Pennsylvania described it. "Each moment it increased in fury until every man was drenched by the cold rain."[10] The army remained poised for action, waiting to see what the Confederates across the fields planned to do.

The first indication of what that might be came when a father and his two sons from Gettysburg brought Meade the news that the Confederates had moved out of town. Union troops moved in to take their place. No doubt one of the most relieved people they found was General Schimmelfennig, who had been hiding in a backyard since the XI Corps retreated through Gettysburg on the battle's first day. As General Schurz rode into town he was pleasantly surprised to see his fellow German standing in a doorway, waving his hat and shouting a greeting. "I knew you would come," said Schimmelfennig, who also offered the welcome news that he had found some eggs. "Get off your horse and let us take breakfast together."[11]

Around noon Meade wired Halleck. "The enemy apparently has thrown back his left, and placed guns and troops in position in rear of Gettysburg, which we now hold," he reported. "The enemy has abandoned large numbers of his killed and wounded on the field. I shall require some time to get up supplies, ammunition, &c., rest the army, worn out by long marches and three days' hard fighting. I shall probably be able to give you a return of our captures and losses before night, and return of the enemy's killed and wounded in our hands."[12] Meade wasn't going to risk becoming another John Pope. He wanted to be sure he knew what Lee was doing—if Lee were really retreating—before he went on the offensive. The Army of Northern Virginia remained a dangerous foe, even in defeat. "All in all, on July 4 Lee's army, instead of being ripe for the plucking, still had the determination and capacity to punish severely, if not wreck any incautious or unskillful foe who might pursue it," wrote Edwin Coddington in his landmark study of Gettysburg.[13]

Unlike Pope, though, Meade had scored an unquestioned victory over the Army of Northern Virginia, and on July 4 he issued an order thanking his army for its actions at Gettysburg. It included one line that especially angered President Lincoln when he read it. "Our task is not yet accomplished," Meade said, "and the Commanding General looks to the Army for greater efforts to drive from our soil every vestige of the presence of the invader." "Drive the invaders from our soil!" exclaimed the president. "Great God! Is that all?" To another listener the president complained, "Will our Generals never get that idea out of their heads? The whole country is *our* soil."[14]

Back in Gettysburg Meade held another council with his corps commanders. It was still pouring rain, and the Leister House remained uninhabitable, so they met at the headquarters of Gen. Thomas H. Neill, who commanded a brigade in the VI Corps. Meade began by telling his generals that his orders were to cover Washington and Baltimore. Then he asked for their advice. The gathered generals voted on three main questions: Should the army remain at Gettysburg? If so, should it assume the offensive? And would it be best to move toward Lee's Potomac crossing at Williamsport by passing through Emmitsburg, essentially a flanking maneuver, or should the army attack on Lee's direct line of retreat? The answers were strongly in favor of staying at Gettysburg until they could determine what the Confederates were doing and strongly against taking the offensive. Opinions on how to pursue were mixed.[15]

As July 5 dawned it became apparent that the Confederates were not going to attack. Meade sent Sedgwick and the VI Corps toward Fairfield, a little town at the base of South Mountain, in cautious pursuit. "The battle-field was horrible," recalled a soldier in the VI Corps of the march over the scenes of the fighting. "Dead men were thickly strewed over the fields with their faces blackened, and eyes starting from their sockets; and upturned, swollen horses lay, sometimes in groups of six or eight, showing where some battery had suffered fearfully."[16] Near Fairfield, Sedgwick's men encountered the rebel rear guard. After a little skirmishing Sedgwick determined that the Southerners were retreating through the mountain passes beyond. He warned Meade that a direct pursuit through those easily defended passes would prove bloody and difficult. Meade also knew that it would risk leaving Washington and Baltimore unprotected and make it difficult if not impossible to get supplies to his army.

On July 5 he found time to write to his wife. "It was a grand battle, and is in my judgment a most decided victory, though I did not annihilate or bag the Confederate Army," he said. "This morning they retired in great haste into the mountains, leaving their dead unburied and their wounded on the field. They awaited one day, expecting that, flushed with success, I would attack them when they would play their old game of shooting us from behind breastworks—a game we played this time to their entire satisfaction. The men behaved splendidly; I really think they are becoming soldiers. They endured long marches, short rations, and stood one of the most terrific cannonadings I ever witnessed. Baldy was shot again, and I fear will not get over it. Two horses that George rode were killed, his own and the black mare. I had no time to think of either George or myself, for at one time things looked a little blue; but I managed to get up reinforcements in time to save the day. The army are in the highest spirits, and of course I am a great man. The most difficult part of my work is acting without correct information on which to predicate action."[17]

July 5 was also a day of arrivals and departures. The departure was that of Daniel Butterfield, who was relieved of duty as Meade's chief of staff. He had been wounded by a piece of shell on July 3, although apparently it had not broken the skin. He left the army but later resurfaced as a thorn in Meade's side. Warren and Pleasonton together took over his duties as chief of staff until Maj. Gen. Andrew Humphreys assumed the position on July 8.

Humphreys was from Philadelphia. An engineer like Meade, he had graduated from West Point four years before him. He had served on McClellan's staff and later commanded a division at Antietam and during the bloody battle for Marye's Heights at Fredericksburg. As a division commander in the III Corps at Gettysburg he had held the right of Sickles's advanced position. "He was a small, bowlegged man, with chopped-off, iron gray moustache; and when he lifted his army hat you saw a rather low forehead, and a shock of iron-gray hair," a staff member recalled. "His blue-gray dauntless eyes threw into his stern face the coldness of hammered steel."[18] Assistant Secretary of War Charles Dana, who would get to know Humphreys during the Virginia Campaign of 1864, considered him to be "the great soldier of the Army of the Potomac." "He was a very interesting figure," Dana wrote. "He used to ride about in a black felt hat, the brim of which was turned down all around, making him look like a Quaker. He was very pleasant to deal with, unless you were fighting against him, and then he was not so pleasant. He was one of the loudest swearers that I ever knew." Although Humphreys desired a corps command, he consented to become Meade's chief of staff, Dana believed, out of pure patriotism.[19] Later in the war he would get the corps command he wanted so badly.

The arrival was Brig. Gen. Herman Haupt, the remarkably efficient man responsible for the Union's railroads. The stern and bristly bearded Haupt was a

Philadelphian who had graduated with Meade from West Point's Class of 1835. He had once taught at Gettysburg's Pennsylvania College, so he knew the area well. On July 4 he was in Hanover, Pennsylvania, and telegraphed Halleck of his intentions to make his way to Gettysburg and oversee the repair of rails and telegraph wires as he went. "I fear that while Meade rests to refresh his men and collect supplies, Lee will be off so far that he cannot intercept him," Haupt fretted to Halleck.[20]

In Gettysburg he found a friend with a buggy who drove him to Meade's headquarters. Meade and Pleasonton greeted him there. They filled him in on the battle, as aides brought in various relics recovered from the field, including Confederate general William Barksdale's sword. Haupt asked Meade what his next moves would be. Meade said he would not move immediately because his men required rest. Haupt bristled at that. They men had plenty of rations, he protested, and had been fighting from behind stone walls so they could not be footsore. If the Army of the Potomac did not chase after Lee immediately, said Haupt, the Confederates would cross the Potomac to safety. Meade replied that Lee had no pontoons and the river was too high to ford. "Do not place confidence in that. I have men in my Construction Corps who could construct bridges in forty-eight hours sufficient to pass that army," Haupt retorted. Meade insisted that his army required rest. Haupt, "much discouraged," left to report his misgivings to Halleck, who passed them on to the president.[21]

There was plenty of fighting during Meade's pursuit of Lee, which is why Wittenberg titled his book *One Continuous Fight*. Meade quickly put his cavalry units into motion to harass the Confederates. Col. J. Irvin Gregg rode off to attack the long Southern wagon trains that were heading toward South Mountain through Frederick. John Buford's men, who had been guarding the supply base in Westminster, received orders to move to Frederick and then on to Turner's Gap on South Mountain so they could attack the Confederates as they made their way down the Cumberland Valley toward Williamsport.[22]

On July 4 Brig. Gen. Judson Kilpatrick set out from Emmitsburg to nip at Lee's heels. Kilpatrick commanded a division in Pleasonton's cavalry. He was short and pugnacious, with a big nose and long, scraggly sideburns that made him look like a disreputable leprechaun. He was, at least, disreputable. Like Daniel Sickles, Kilpatrick was a rogue. A recent biographer conceded that a case could be made that Kilpatrick was "a coward—an egotistical, lying, sadistic, philandering, thieving miscreant whose lofty reputation had been gained by words, not deeds."[23] On July 3 Kilpatrick had goaded one of his brigade commanders, Brig. Gen. Elon Farnsworth, into making a futile charge near Little Round Top. When Farnsworth protested that the mission was suicidal, Kilpatrick suggested that he was a coward. Seething, Farnsworth made the charge. The Confederates cut his command to pieces and shot him down. Such reckless disregard for his men's lives (though not necessarily his own) earned Kilpatrick the nickname "Kill-Cavalry."

Kilpatrick and his men headed south to Emmitsburg and then swung to the west to reach the ridge of South Mountain. There a seventeen-mile-long wagon train carrying wounded soldiers and captured supplies, under the protection of Confederate brigadier general John Imboden, was making a slow and difficult passage over Monterey Pass through the rain and mud. Kilpatrick and his forty-five hundred men were on a collision course, but as they made the steep ascent in the black night and pouring rain, a single artillery piece and less than one hundred men stymied their progress. The Union cavalry finally pushed their way to the top and sometime around midnight Kilpatrick ordered George Armstrong Custer to charge the wagon train as it struggled across the ridge. Custer initiated a confused struggle in the rain and wet, punctuated by claps of thunder and bolts of lightning. Kilpatrick's men captured three hundred wagons and some thirteen hundred men, but the rest of the Confederate train continue its retreat toward the Potomac and, it hoped, safety.

• • •

Using a driving tour in Wittenberg's book I set out one day to follow in the footsteps of Lee's retreating army and Kilpatrick's pursuing cavalry. From Gettysburg I take Route 116 toward Fairfield. I pass the Black Horse Tavern, a landmark that stood here by the road as the long Confederate trains splashed by on their way to Virginia. Fairfield is a little town near the base of Jack's Mountain and the long ridge of South Mountain. Its main street contains a lot of small, brick, Civil War–era buildings, some of which served as hospitals. Today its sidewalks are lined with vendors for the town's annual Pippinfest, a celebration of all things apple. People are selling—and consuming—apple fritters, apple butter, apple cider, and apple pies, as well as other foods guaranteed to increase the waistline and cholesterol level. Other vendors peddle arts and crafts. An Uncle Sam on stilts makes his way down the sidewalk past someone in a costume that looks like a mutant amphibian of some sort.

Down a side street in the crafts section I find Bill Hewitt standing under a canopy with a banner that says "Gettysburg Sentinels." He's selling all sorts of Civil War–related wooden knickknacks—everything from oversized minié balls to a reproduction of Lee's field desk. He also has a George Meade refrigerator magnet. What makes Hewitt's pieces special is their wood, which comes from trees that stood on the Gettysburg battlefield. Some of them are "witness trees," which were standing back in July 1863 (and make for more expensive items), and some are from postbattle trees. Hewitt buys the wood from the service that removes the trees when they fall or have to be taken down. He has also purchased the wood from the Gettysburg Foundation—and he keeps the invoice in a scrapbook on his counter to prove it. To get the wood, he tells me, "You have to be alert" and make your offer before anyone else does.

Hewitt, who retired in 2001 after thirty-one years in the army, tells me he's a big fan of Meade's. He says he got into the battlefield tree business three or four years ago when he went to a local lumberyard to get wood for a wainscoting project. The owner asked him if he was interested in a battlefield tree. A man from Georgia had expressed interest but never showed up to make the purchase. Hewitt bought as much as he could afford. Now his company crafts walking sticks, business card holders, clock cases, pens, and other items from trees that might have once sheltered Union and Confederate soldiers—maybe even soldiers who passed through Fairfield after the battle.

Back on the road, I leave Fairfield behind and take a right onto Iron Springs Road. The big mass of Jack's Mountain is to my left as the road begins to climb up South Mountain on the road to narrow Fairfield Pass. I can see how this steep approach would have given the Confederates some fine defensive possibilities. Even on a modern paved surface the road is narrow and winding. It gets even more so once I turn onto Old Waynesboro Road and follow the course that Kilpatrick and his troopers took on that dark and stormy night when they pushed their way up toward the Confederate wagon train at the top of the mountain.

There aren't many traces of the battle at Monterey Pass today. There are a couple of new Civil War Trails markers, but the Monterey Springs Hotel, where Kilpatrick made his headquarters, is long gone. There are reportedly some traces of the old Maria Furnace Road, over which the Confederate trains traveled, but they are on private property. Beyond busy Route 16, I continue on the Waynesboro Road, which drops precipitously off to my right. I'm glad there's a guardrail. The Confederate wagons had no such protection, though, and when the Union cavalry attacked, some of the Confederates' animals panicked and plunged, wagons and all, over the edge.

My ultimate goal today is Hagerstown, Maryland, a town that saw more action than its citizens probably wanted over the course of Lee's retreat. The city's historic core is dotted with Civil War–era buildings that witnessed the battles that raged back and forth in the streets here on July 6, when Kilpatrick's men tangled with the rebels again. This time things did not go as well for Kill-Cavalry. As the Union forces swept into town from the south, Confederate cavalry under Alfred Iverson, John Chambliss, and Beverly Robertson approached from the north. After a short artillery duel that terrorized the townspeople, the Union cavalry charged down Potomac Street. "The cutting and slashing were beyond description," reported Hagerstown resident W. W. Jacobs, who had found a ringside seat on the roof of the Eagle Hotel. Jacobs watched, rapt, as the enemy cavalrymen attacked each other with pistols, carbines, and sabers. It was, he said, "a scene such as words cannot fully portray."[24]

The timely arrival of Confederate infantry forced Kilpatrick's men to retreat from Hagerstown in great confusion, which proved to be a severe setback for the Army of the Potomac. Had Union forces captured Hagerstown they would have stood right between Lee and the fords he needed at Williamsport.

One of the Union wounded in the melee was Capt. Ulric Dahlgren. The son of Rear Adm. John Dahlgren, twenty-one-year-old Ulric had served ably on the staffs of Generals Franz Sigel and Joe Hooker and then with Meade. He had participated in the great cavalry battle at Brandy Station on June 8, which prompted Alfred Pleasonton to say, "His dashing bravery and cool intelligence are only equaled by his varied accomplishments."[25] In a fight in Greencastle, Pennsylvania, on July 2 Dahlgren had captured rebel dispatches that let Meade know Lee could expect no reinforcements from Virginia, a key piece of intelligence. After the battle Dahlgren had been harassing Lee's retreating trains. When he reached Hagerstown he fell in with a regiment of Kilpatrick's cavalry and led them in a charge down Potomac Street. During the fighting a Confederate bullet struck Dahlgren in the right foot. The wounded foot and part of his right leg later had to be amputated—and were buried with full honors in the foundation of a government building in Washington that was since torn down.[26] The loss of a limb did not end the war for young Dahlgren. A future exploit of his—once again in a partnership with Kilpatrick—would later create difficulties for Meade.

Hagerstown still remembers Ulric Dahlgren. On July 9, 2011, the town's minor league baseball team, the Suns, presented a lucky one thousand fans with bobbleheads of the heroic cavalryman. "This is the first time that a bobblehead of Civil War Union Officer Captain Ulric Dahlgren has ever been given out at a professional baseball game," said a press release from the Hagerstown-Washington County Convention and Visitors Bureau. Dahlgren descendants threw out the first pitches at the night's game. Dahlgren joined a select and somewhat eclectic roster of previous Hagerstown bobbleheads, which included a romance author; George Washington; the director of the Maryland symphony orchestra; Little Heiskell, the weathervane that serves as Hagerstown's symbol (a Confederate sharpshooter fired a bullet through the original when it was swinging atop City Hall during the war); and, of course, Abner Doubleday.

While Dahlgren and Kilpatrick were fighting in Hagerstown, Union cavalry under John Buford made an ineffectual attack later on July 6 against rebels who had already reached Williamsport. Confederate brigadier general John Imboden put up a spirited and desperate resistance against the Federals, pulling defenders from the ranks of the wounded and from the teamsters driving the wagons. The "Battle of the Wagoners" is remembered today with a Civil War Trails marker in the parking lot of the Red Men Lodge outside Williamsport.

While the cavalry did what it could, Sedgwick's report from Fairfield convinced Meade that a flank pursuit was the proper course for his infantry to take. He ordered Brig. Gen. Thomas Neill's brigade of the VI Corps to shadow the retreating Confederates though the passes and across South Mountain but had the rest of the VI Corps pull back and join the flanking movement. If he moved his army to Frederick and—in a repeat of the Maryland campaign of the previous year—westward to concentrate at Middletown, he could move over South Mountain and down through Boonsboro to hit Lee's retreating army in the flank. Such a move would let him obey his orders to protect Washington and Baltimore and allow him to move the army along the macadamized National Road over South Mountain—no small factor to consider when the rains were turning dirt roads into rivers of mud.

On July 7 Meade left Gettysburg and traveled all the way to Frederick, not far from the spot where Colonel Hardie had arrived to bring him trouble just nine days earlier. For Meade it must have seemed like a lifetime. He had been living in "a great state of mental anxiety," he wrote Margaret. "Indeed, I think I have lived as much in this time as in the last thirty years."[27] Since taking command he had not changed his clothes, had a full night's sleep, eaten a regular meal, or even had much chance to wash his face and hands.

Meade found the streets of Frederick crowded with people eager to get a glimpse of him. The citizens treated him "like a lion," but he did not allow it to go to his head. After the botched opportunities of Antietam, George McClellan had written to his wife that he had fought a "masterpiece of war." Meade was cut from a different cloth. The papers, he said, were making too much of him. "I claim no extraordinary merit for this last battle, and would prefer waiting a little while to see what my career is to be before making any pretensions," he said. "I did and shall continue to do my duty to the best of my abilities, but knowing as I do that battles are often decided by accidents, and that no man of sense will say in advance what their result will be, I wish to be careful in not bragging before the right time."[28]

Meade also received a telegram from Halleck, which offered him some bragging rights. "It gives me great pleasure to inform you that you have been appointed a brigadier-general in the Regular Army, to rank from July 3, the date of your brilliant victory at Gettysburg," it read. Halleck also forwarded a message from Lincoln with some good news about the war effort. "We have certain information that Vicksburg surrendered to General Grant on the 4th of July," Lincoln wrote. "Now, if General Meade can complete his work, so gloriously prosecuted thus far, by the literal or substantial destruction of Lee's army, the rebellion will be over."[29]

Meade had every intention of completing his work. "I think we shall have another battle before Lee can cross the river, though from all accounts he is making great efforts to do so," he wrote to Margaret. "For my part, as I have to follow and fight him, I would rather do it at once and in Maryland than to follow into Virginia."[30]

As the cavalry did what it could to harass the retreating Confederates, the infantry made its tortuous way though driving rain and cloying mud on a roundabout flank march. The torrential rains transformed roads into quagmires that sucked the shoes off the feet of the soldiers still lucky enough to wear them. Even traveling on the National Road proved difficult. "Napoleon crossing the Alps will no longer be mentioned as the climax of heroic achievements. Sedgwick marching over the Catoctin Mountains has entirely eclipsed that," one soldier noted.[31]

On July 8 Meade made his headquarters in Middletown, the village whose residents had given Stonewall Jackson a cold reception the previous September but also had removed their pump handles so the Union troops couldn't get water. Captain Donaldson of the 118th Pennsylvania, who had been so outraged by this, had apparently forgotten about his threats of vengeance. He merely noted that Middletown "looked just the same as it did Sept. last, when on the march to Antietam we passed through it."[32]

With both Mother Nature and his supply situation taking a toll on his army, Meade began to worry about his ability to catch Lee before the rebels crossed the river. He knew that on July 4 Union cavalry had destroyed the Confederates' pontoon bridge below Williamsport and the continual rain had kept the Potomac too high to ford, yet he was concerned about Lee escaping. On July 8 he wired Halleck. "Be assured I most earnestly desire to try the fortunes of war with the enemy on this side of the river, hoping through Providence and the bravery of my men to settle the question, but I should do wrong not to frankly tell you of the difficulties encountered," he warned. "I expect to find the enemy in a strong position, well covered with artillery, and I do not desire to imitate his example at Gettysburg, and assault a position where the chances were so greatly against success. I wish in advance to moderate the expectations of those who, in ignorance of the difficulties to be encountered, may expect too much. All that I can do under the circumstances I pledge this army to do."

In Washington this no doubt conjured up memories of McClellan and his constant excuses and requests for resupply and reinforcements. Yet the comparison is not fair to Meade. McClellan waited for more than a month after the Battle of Antietam before he initiated a full pursuit of the enemy. Meade allowed only a day to elapse before he began his pursuit, after a three-day battle that had left his army seriously bloodied and his officer corps sadly diminished. Still, the telegraph wires between Halleck and Meade hummed with messages from Washington. "There is reliable information that the enemy is crossing at Williamsport," Halleck wired on July 8. "The opportunity to attack his divided forces should not be lost. The President is urgent and anxious that your army should move against him by forced marches."

Meade began to bristle. "My information as to the crossing of the enemy does not agree with that just received in your dispatch," he replied. "His whole force is in position between Funkstown and Williamsport. I have just received information that he has driven my cavalry force in front of Boonsborough. My army is and has been making forced marches, short of rations, and barefooted. One corps marched yesterday and last night over 30 miles. I take occasion to repeat that I will use my utmost efforts to push forward this army."

"Do not understand me as expressing any dissatisfaction," Halleck replied; "on the contrary, your army has done most nobly. I only wish to give you opinions formed from information received here."

On July 9 Meade made his headquarters at the Mountain House at Turner's Gap, today's South Mountain Inn. It was another landmark from the Maryland campaign. The little town of Boonsboro sat at the base of South Mountain on the west side. If the Confederates held Boonsboro they could keep the Federals from streaming down South Mountain. Meade ordered Howard and the XI Corps and Sedgwick and the VI to hurry to Boonsboro, where John Buford's cavalry was opposed by Jeb Stuart's horsemen. On July 8 Buford's cavalry managed to force their opponents back toward the little town of Funkstown, but Stuart had accomplished his goal of standing between the Union and Lee's retreating army.

Halleck continued to telegraph jittery messages to Meade. "Do not be influenced by any dispatch from here against your own judgment," he wired on July 9. "Regard them as suggestions only. Our information here is not always correct." The next day Halleck seemed to be sharing Meade's caution. "I think it will be best for you to postpone a general battle till you can concentrate all your forces and get up your reserves and re-enforcements," he wired. "Beware of partial combats. Bring up and hurl upon the enemy all your forces, good and bad." The arriving troops, though, were not all that Meade could have desired. Back in Harrisburg, Darius Couch sent a force under cantankerous Brig. Gen. William "Baldy" Smith south to reinforce Meade. But these men were untested militia, and Meade had no intention of using them in situations where they could do more harm than good.

On July 12 Meade established his headquarters on Antietam Creek at a spot called the Devil's Backbone, the site of a pretty creekside park today. It would be much lovelier without the construction, which has blocked access and left several big steam shovels, looking like slumbering robotic dinosaurs, waiting by the side of the road. Meade was here when his pursuit of Lee approached its climax. On July 12 he sent another wire to Halleck. He planned to attack the next day "unless something intervenes to prevent it."[33]

When the chaplain of the 118th Pennsylvania approached him and asked if he could avoid fighting on the Sabbath, Meade responded with surprising good humor. He said he "was like a man who had a contract to make a box—he had the four sides and bottom made & was abt. to put on the lid, hence the fight would take place," recalled one of the regiment's officers.[34] The chaplain protested that God would not allow it to happen. Shortly afterward, it began to rain and then pour.

If God was telling Meade not to attack, he picked an odd way of showing it. Rain was actually a good thing for the Army of the Potomac—it would keep the river too high for the Confederates to cross. In the end, though, it was not God but another council of war that stayed Meade's hand.

The council took place in Meade's small and crowded tent at Devil's Backbone. Howard and Maj. Gen. James Wadsworth, who had taken over the I Corps from an ill Newton, voted to attack. The rest of the corps commanders voted to hold off until the army could better investigate Lee's defenses. Perhaps remembering what had happened at Chancellorsville when Hooker overruled his corps commanders, Meade decided to defer to his generals' advice. He postponed his attack for a day.

Meade wired Halleck the next day. It was a lengthy message with a slightly defensive tone. "In my dispatch of yesterday I stated that it was my intention to attack the enemy to-day, unless something intervened to prevent it," he said. "Upon calling my corps commanders together and submitting the question to them, five out of six were unqualifiedly opposed to it. Under these circumstances, in view of the momentous consequences attendant upon a failure to succeed, I did not feel myself authorized to attack until after I had made more careful examination of the enemy's position, strength, and defensive works. These examinations are now being made. So far as completed, they show the enemy to be strongly intrenched on a ridge running from the rear of Hagerstown past Downsville to the Potomac. I shall continue these reconnaissances with the expectation of finding some weak point, upon which, if I succeed, I shall hazard an attack."

He received a terse message from Halleck in reply. "You are strong enough to attack and defeat the enemy before he can effect a crossing," said the general in chief. "Act upon your own judgment and make your generals execute your orders. Call no council of war. It is proverbial that councils of war never fight. Reenforcements are pushed on as rapidly as possible. Do not let the enemy escape."[35]

On the morning of July 13 war correspondent Charles Carleton Coffin of the *Boston Journal* rode over to Meade's headquarters at Devil's Backbone. There he found Seth Williams, the army's assistant adjutant general, in Meade's tent. Williams told Coffin that Meade was out reconnoitering the rebel lines.

"Do you think that Lee can get across the Potomac?" Coffin asked.

"Impossible!" replied Williams. "The people resident here say that it cannot be forded at this stage of the water. He has no pontoons. We have got him in a tight place. We shall have reinforcements to-morrow, and a great battle will be fought. Lee is encumbered with his teams, and he is short of ammunition."

As Coffin talked with Williams, Meade entered the tent, dripping wet from the rain. "His countenance was unusually animated," Coffin wrote. "He had ever been courteous to me, and while usually very reticent of all his intentions or of what was going on, as an officer should be, yet in this instance he broke over his habitual silence, and said, 'We shall have a great battle to-morrow.' The reinforcements are coming up, and as soon as they come we shall pitch in.'"[36]

Meade had based his thinking on the idea that Lee's army would not be able to cross the river. He knew that the 14th Pennsylvania Cavalry, acting under William French's orders, had destroyed the pontoon bridge the rebels had used to cross the river when they headed north. Because of a major blunder by the rebels, the bridge had been only lightly guarded, and the Federals had routed the defenders on the West Virginia side of the river, floated the bridge to the Maryland side, and then set it ablaze. The *New York Times* declared it "one of the most daring exploits of the war."[37] What Meade didn't know was that the Confederates had been busily constructing a replacement bridge. Engineering teams had been tearing apart Williamsport warehouses and other structures for raw materials and using borrowed teapots to heat the tar they needed to seal the sixteen boats they built to support the bridge. This did not go down well with Williamsport residents, but Confederate quartermaster John Harman responded to their complaints by saying, "Just charge it to Jeff Davis. Our army is worth more than all your lumber in gold."[38]

• • •

Following Wittenberg's driving tour, my wife and I set out from Williamsport to find the site of the pontoon bridge. We drive down the pretty Falling Waters Road, which makes its way along a landscape that rises and falls like huge ocean swells. The terrain must have offered great opportunities for the Southern defenders. We pull off the road where it stops at the gate to the privately owned Potomac Fish and Game Club. Another gate to the right blocks vehicle access to an undeveloped dirt road that snakes down into the woods. It's been raining off and on over the past few days and the road is wet and muddy—just as it would have been in 1863. Crows caw and cicadas provide their omnipresent buzzing as we descend into the damp landscape, through woods and past large cornfields. The oddest thing we encounter is a set of two large wooden panels standing on the side of the road, each decorated with a metal skull against what looks like a gate. "Trail of Screams" is written across the tops of the panels. I hope they have something to do with Halloween.

As we approach the river we reach the remnants of the C&O Canal, including crumbling stonework from a bridge that once spanned it. The remains of the canal are muddy and filled with trees. The towpath stretches off into the woods in both directions. There are a couple historical markers down here in the shade, the older metal one standing by the crumbling stonework beneath a huge, spreading tree. We continue on and reach the river, a quiet and serene setting today. I can see a boat ramp, railroad bridge, and trailer campground on the opposite bank, about 250 yards away.

In *Retreat from Gettysburg* Kent Masterson Brown included a photo of this site, taken sometime after the war. The photographer must have been on the hill behind us looking down at the river, for the picture was taken from a high angle. Two figures that look like little boys are holding hands at the near end of the canal bridge. I can imagine them standing there, the gravel crunching under their shoes as they shift impatiently, waiting for the photographer to take the picture. What really strikes me, though, is the absence of trees in the photographs back then. The landscape was flat and featureless except for a strip of trees atop the ridgeline over on the West Virginia shore and a few straggly specimens here and there. There's something eerie about the image, with the two anonymous figures standing amid the desolation like ghostly twins.

Starting late at night on July 13 Longstreet's and A. P. Hill's corps crossed the Potomac here, while Ewell's men forded the river just above Williamsport. In contrast to the languid and peaceful atmosphere on the banks of the Potomac when I visit, on July 14, 1863, all was bustle and confusion in the dark, rain, and mud. "At the river was a dense mass of wagons, and brigade upon brigade, with stacked arms, the division resting and waiting for its turn to cross; for there was but one bridge, over which a stream of men was yet passing, and it would take hours for all to cross," recalled one Southerner.[39]

Most of the army was across by 11:00 a.m. on July 14, with only a rear guard remaining to greet Judson Kilpatrick when he arrived with his cavalry, eager to wound the enemy. Too eager, in fact. Rather than coordinate his movements with Buford, who was coming in from the north, Kilpatrick made a disorganized and understrength attack on the Confederates. The defenders were under the command of Maj. Gen. Harry Heth, the same man who had inadvertently started the Battle of Gettysburg when he advanced down the Chambersburg Pike thirteen days earlier. The fighting was wild and chaotic, with Southern defenders even using fence rails to club Union horsemen off their mounts. One victim was Confederate general Pettigrew, who had survived Pickett's Charge only to suffer a mortal wound about a mile away from the crossing. His men took him across the river, where he died on July 17.

Once the last of the Southern soldiers who could make it across the bridge reached the Virginia side, the commander of the final regiment cut the ropes behind him, and the current pushed the bridge over to the far side. Meade had lost his chance to bag the Army of Northern Virginia.

Halleck sent a wire to Meade as soon as he received the bad news. "I need hardly say to you that the escape of Lee's army without another battle has created great dissatisfaction in the mind of the President," he said, "and it will require an active and energetic pursuit on your part to remove the impression that it has not been sufficiently active heretofore."

Quartermaster Rufus Ingalls entered the tent as Meade was reading the telegram. "Ingalls, don't you want to take command of this army?" Meade asked.

"No, I think it's too big an elephant for me," replied Ingalls.

"Well, it's too big for me, too," said Meade. "Read that." He handed him the telegram.[40]

Meade then sent a reply to Halleck. "Having performed my duty conscientiously and to the best of my ability," he replied, "the censure of the President conveyed in your dispatch of 1 p.m. this day, is, in my judgment, so undeserved that I feel compelled most respectfully to ask to be immediately relieved from the command of this army."

Halleck backpedaled. "My telegram, stating the disappointment of the President at the escape of Lee's army, was not intended as a censure, but as a stimulus to an active pursuit. It is not deemed a sufficient cause for your application to be relieved." Meade was not mollified. He found the idea that he had to be spurred, he wrote to Margaret, "more offensive than the original message."[41]

Meade did receive a telegram that he welcomed more than the censures from Washington. It came from his former commander, George McClellan. "I wish to offer you my sincere and heartfelt congratulations upon the glorious victory you have achieved, and the splendid way in which you assumed control of our noble old army under such trying circumstances," McClellan said. "You have done all that could be done and the Army of the Potomac has supported you nobly. I don't know that, situated as I am, my opinion is worth much to any of you—but I can trust saying that I feel very proud of you and my old Army. I don't flatter myself that your work is over—I believe that you have another severe battle to fight, but I am confident that you will win."[42]

Meade replied on the ill-fated July 14. He told McClellan he was "perfectly prepared for a loss of all my rapidly acquired honors the first time the fortune of war fails to smile on me. Already I am beginning to feel the reaction, Lee having crossed the river last night without waiting for me to attack him in one of the strongest positions he has ever occupied."[43]

● ● ●

There was disgruntlement within the army over Lee's escape, too. "Why General Lee and his army were allowed to cross the Potomac unmolested, we do not attempt to explain; nor do we condemn the determination of General Meade not to give battle," noted a soldier in the VI Corps. "When men of such well-known military ability and bravery as General Sedgwick advise against a movement, it may be well to hesitate; yet it will doubtless be the verdict of history, that the hesitancy of General Meade at this time was his great mistake."[44]

Others, though, felt the Army of the Potomac had escaped disaster by not attacking the Army of Northern Virginia's strongly defended position. After examining the Confederate entrenchments Maj. Charles Wainwright said they "were by far the strongest I have seen yet; evidently laid out by engineers and built as if they meant to stand a month's siege."[45]

Maj. Gen. Andrew Humphreys later testified to Congress, "Subsequent information showed that the enemy had a very strong position, and indicated that had we made an attack we should have suffered very severely." But he still felt the army should have moved by making a "reconnaissance in force." Nevertheless, he counseled the inquiring congressmen, "You may take field-works, in which there are small garrisons, by assault; but when you have to attack a whole army, well intrenched, you will suffer terribly in getting up to them."[46]

Henry Hunt said that an attack on Lee's entrenched position at Williamsport "would have been disastrous to us," and he criticized the "meddling and hectoring" from Washington following Lee's escape. "It was promptly manifested, too, and in a manner which indicates how harshly and unjustly the Army of the Potomac and its commanders were usually judged and treated," Hunt wrote.[47]

Col. Rufus Dawes of the 6th Wisconsin, part of the famed Iron Brigade, examined the rebel defenses and found them to be "strong and well-constructed." "I think General Meade would have certainly failed to carry them by direct assault," he said. "I take no stock in the stuff printed in the newspapers about the demoralization of the rebel army after Gettysburg. They were worn out and tired as we were, but their cartridge boxes had plenty of ammunition, and they would have quietly lain in their rifle pits and shot us down with the same coolness and desperation they showed at Gettysburg."[48]

The war would not end in Pennsylvania, or in Maryland, either. "I start tomorrow on another race with Lee," Meade wrote Margaret on July 14.[49] It was back to the killing grounds of Virginia.

One officer noted that his regiment "crossed the Potomac amid the curses and groans of the men who detest the soil of Virginia, and declair [sic] that 'Old Meade, the four eyed loafer' is again leading them to the graveyard of the Army of the Potomac (Fredericksburg). My own feelings at again entering the state can be imagined better than described. Even the name Virginia is hateful to me."[50]

CHAPTER 11

Back to Virginia

From left, Gouverneur K. Warren, William French, Meade,
Henry Hunt, Andrew Humphreys, and George Sykes in Culpeper,
Virginia, September 1863

I've come to think that an effective way to map the Civil War campaigns that ranged back and forth across Northern Virginia—First Bull Run, Fredericksburg, Second Bull Run, Chancellorsville, Mine Run, and the Overland Campaign among them—would be to follow the example from anatomy books. I'm thinking about the ones that depict the body's various systems on overlapping plastic transparencies. One shows the skin, the next the muscles, then the circulatory system, organs, and skeleton. This is what a Civil War map of Virginia would resemble—layer after overlapping layer of campaigns and battles, bloodshed and devastation.

In November 1863 Alexander Morrison Stewart, the chaplain for the 102nd Pennsylvania, noted that war had turned Virginia into "a great charnel-house, a vast Golgotha, a wide-spread Aceldama, a literal field of blood."[1] Like swarms of locusts, the contending armies had also picked Northern Virginia clean of food for soldiers and forage for animals. That had been a factor in Lee's decision to move north into Pennsylvania, where he could employ his army on one huge re-supply mission.

Now Meade had driven Lee back to Virginia and was poised to follow. On July 17 and 18 his army recrossed the Potomac and moved south through the Loudoun Valley. The Confederates were moving up the Shenandoah Valley, and Meade chose to move along a parallel course on the opposite side of the Blue Ridge Mountains. Various passes provided access across the ridgeline that separated the armies—the same passes that had witnessed spirited cavalry actions the month before when the rebels had moved north.

On July 22 Meade sensed an opportunity and sent a force, with William French and the III Corps in advance, through Manassas Gap with the design of slicing the long serpent of Lee's army in half. Unfortunately, French made only a halfhearted push through the gap and didn't reach the vicinity of Front Royal until near evening, much too late to surprise the rebels. It must have been with a heavy heart that Meade telegraphed Halleck the next day: "I regret to inform you that, on advancing this morning at daylight, the enemy had again disappeared, declining battle, and though an immediate advance was made and Front Royal occupied, nothing was seen of him but a rear guard of cavalry with a battery of artillery."[2] Meade withdrew his army from the valley and moved south to Warrenton, while Lee moved his army back behind the Rappahannock. Essentially things had reverted to the way they had been back in June.

Both armies had become considerably weakened—and not just from the fighting. Meade received orders to send some of his men north to help quell riots that had broken out in New York City over the enforcement of the draft. On July 30 Halleck wired him that he could expect no reinforcements. "Every place has been stripped to the bare poles. Keep up a threatening attitude, but do not advance," directed the general in chief.[3] Including those whose terms of enlistment had expired, the nine-month and three-year men, Meade lost about fifteen thousand troops.[4]

As Meade commenced his pursuit through Virginia, General Howard took it upon himself to write a letter to the president and defend the army's commander.

Lincoln replied on July 21. His mood had seemingly improved in the week since the rebels had abandoned Williamsport. "I was deeply mortified by the escape of Lee across the Potomac, because the substantial destruction of his army would have ended the war, and because I believed such destruction was perfectly easy—believed that General Meade and his noble army had expended all the skill and toil and blood up to the ripe harvest, and then let the crop go to waste," Lincoln wrote Howard. "A few days having passed I am now profoundly grateful for what was done, without criticism for what was not done. General Meade has my confidence as a brave and skillful officer and a true man."[5]

Meade also received a letter from Halleck, which the general in chief hoped would ease the army commander's bruised feelings. "Your fight at Gettysburg met with universal approbation of all military men here," said Halleck. "You handled your troops in that battle as well, if not better, than any general has handled his army during the war. You brought all your forces into action at the right time and place, which no commander of the Army of the Potomac has done before. You may well be proud of that battle." So far, so good. "And now a few words in regard to subsequent events," Halleck continued. "You should not have been surprised or vexed at the President's disappointment at the escape of Lee's army. He had examined into all the details of sending you reinforcements to satisfy himself that every man who could possibly be spared from other places had been sent to your army. He thought that Lee's defeat was so certain that he felt no little impatience at his unexpected escape. I have no doubt, General, that you felt the disappointment as keenly as any one else. Such things sometimes occur to us without any fault of our own. Take it all together, your short campaign has proved your superior generalship, and you merit, as you will receive, the confidence of the Government and the gratitude of the country. I need not assure you, General, that I have lost none of the confidence which I felt in you when I recommended you for the command."[6]

Meade replied in kind, a lengthy missive in which he explained the differences between the president feeling "disappointment" versus "dissatisfaction." He also said that if the administration believed someone else could do a better job, then he would like to be relieved, "not on my own account, but on account of the country and the cause."[7] That he meant it appears obvious.

Back in April the Pennsylvania Reserves had raised $1,500 to purchase a sword they wished to present to their former commander. Such presentations were a common way for units to show pride in the officers and in themselves. Other, more pressing, matters had postponed the ceremony, but Meade could no longer avoid it. He would have to give a speech, even though he had "a great horror of being made a lion, and having to roar for the benefit of outsiders."[8] On August 27, the morning of the ceremony, he wrote to Margaret, "I have not made the slightest preparation in the way of a speech, and have not the slightest idea what I shall say."[9]

Maybe he should have prepared more. Charles Wainwright of the I Corps, for one, thought that Meade "replied lamely" when it came time for him to talk. Wainwright also reported that the dinner turned into a drunken rout. A bald-headed friend of Governor Curtin's stood on a table and sang bawdy songs, while people shoved and pushed to get food and drink and privates hobnobbed with captains.[10] The presentation ceremony also led Meade into the kind of political controversies he wished to avoid. One newspaper reported that Meade had advocated Curtin's reelection in November. He had said no such thing, Meade protested. He did like the sword, though. It had a blade of Damascus steel and a scabbard of gold. His initials were engraved near the hilt and inlaid with enamel, gold, and diamonds. Precious stones circled the handle. Engraved on the blade were the battles that Meade and the Reserves had shared.[11] "The more I examine my sword the more I am delighted with its beauty," he wrote home. "It is really most chaste and artistic. It seems a pity, though, to waste so much money on an article that from its great value is actually rendered useless."[12]

There was much more serious business to attend to the next day—the execution of five deserters. The men were "bounty jumpers," meaning they had signed up to obtain the government bonus for enlisting, and then deserted once they received it. It's questionable whether the men—all immigrants, and only one of whom spoke English—realized the penalty they would pay if caught. On the afternoon of Saturday, August 29, the V Corps assembled on a slight rise looking down on the spot where the execution would take place. The funeral procession started at 3:00. The five condemned men appeared in manacles, accompanied by other soldiers lugging the coffins. They marched slowly to their freshly dug graves. Four of the men walked steadily, but one needed support to stay on his feet. The soldiers placed the coffins on the ground next to the graves, and the prisoners sat on them. By then it was nearly 4:00, and the orders stated the executions had to be carried out by that time. "Shoot these men, or after 10 minutes it will be murder!" shouted Brig. Gen. Charles Griffin. "Shoot them at once!"

A sergeant of the guard covered the condemned men's faces with white cloth and the artists from *Harper's* and *Frank Leslie's* magazines who had been sketching the scene packed up their easels and supplies. The clergy—a rabbi, a priest, and a chaplain—withdrew. The executioners, twelve riflemen for each prisoner, marched into position. "Ready. Aim. Fire!" shouted the captain in charge. Sixty rifles roared and flashed. Four of the men fell with dull thumps onto their coffins and rolled onto the ground, dead. The fifth remained in a seated position until the examining surgeon laid the body back on the coffin.[13]

Desertions had been a plague on the army, and Meade hoped this sanguinary example would provide a remedy. "Not a murmur against the justice or the propriety of the act was heard," he told Margaret. "Indeed, the men are the most anxious to see this great evil cured, as they know their own security will be advanced thereby."[14]

• • •

In September Lee sent Longstreet and most of his corps south to support Gen. Braxton Bragg in Tennessee. When Meade learned of Lee's weakened position he moved forward, and the Confederates retreated behind the Rapidan River. Meade established a new headquarters at Culpeper Court House. He had started planning a new offensive when he received a summons to Washington. At a meeting with Stanton, Halleck, and Lincoln, Meade said that if they thought he was too slow or prudent, then they should feel free to replace him. Halleck smiled.

No doubt Meade would rejoice at that, Halleck said, but he wasn't going to have such good luck. Then Lincoln spoke. He said he thought the army was too large for a purely defensive role, so he proposed taking some troops away from it. Meade protested at the idea of reducing his forces. He thought he had won his case, but on his return to headquarters he received word to send the XI and XII Corps—some sixteen thousand men—to Tennessee to aid in the fighting around Chattanooga.[15] With such a weakened army, Meade had little choice but to acquiesce in the stalemate in Virginia.

It was around this time that Theodore Lyman joined Meade's staff. Lyman was a Boston patrician and Harvard graduate who traveled among the best families and married well. He had first met Meade in Florida in 1856, when he was studying starfish and Meade was overseeing lighthouse construction. While in Europe during the war, a conflict that had already killed many in his circle, Lyman wrote to the general and asked about a staff position. "My military accomplishments are most scanty," he admitted. "I can ride, shoot and fence tolerably, speak French fluently and German a little, have seen many thousands of troops of most nations of Central Europe, and have read two or three elementary books."[16]

Meade wrote back and warned him that it would not be an "easy berth." Two of his aides had already been killed, he warned. "If you join my staff, which I would be most delighted were you to, you must make up your mind to see the elephant in his most formidable proportions."[17] "Seeing the elephant" was army slang for experiencing combat. Lyman was willing, and once he returned to the United States, he used his Boston connections to get a commission as a lieutenant colonel. He reached Meade's side on September 3, 1863, and served under him until Lee surrendered.

Tall, bearded, and balding, Lyman was trained as a scientist and brought a scientist's skill at observation to the journal and letters he wrote while with the Army of the Potomac. Although Lyman certainly viewed the war through the lens of a staff officer, he spent his share of time on or near the front lines, dodging shells and bullets and seeing the dead and wounded. His accounts offer incisive and often humorous portraits of the personalities he encountered and the petty grievances and unpredictable human interactions that sometimes gummed up the army's works.

His portrayals can be sympathetic or cutting. Of Judson Kilpatrick, Lyman noted, "His colorless eye, big nose, and narrow forehead, with an indescribable air between a vulgarian & a crack-brain, combine to render him almost laughable. He is pushing & managing in the extreme, but I don't believe he is worth a fig as a general."[18] Lyman was a little more favorable about George Armstrong Custer, at one time the Union's youngest general and still years away from the disaster at the Little Bighorn. "This officer is one of the funniest looking beings you ever saw, and looks like a circus rider gone mad!" Lyman wrote. "He wears a huzzar jacket and tight trousers, of faded black velvet trimmed with tarnished gold lace. His head is decked with a little, gray felt hat; high boots and gilt spurs complete the costume, which is enhanced by the General's coiffure, consisting in short, dry, flaxen ringlets! His aspect, though highly amusing, is also pleasing, as he has a very merry blue eye, and a devil-may-care style."[19]

Lyman described John Buford as "a compactly built man of middle height, with a tawny moustache and a little, triangular gray eye, whose expression is determined, not to say sinister. His ancient corduroys are tucked into a pair of ordinary cowhide boots, and his blue blouse is ornamented with holes; from one pocket thereof peeps a huge pipe, while the other is fat with a tobacco pouch. Notwithstanding this get-up he is a very soldierly looking man. He is of a good-natured disposition, but not to be trifled with."[20]

The III Corps commander, William French, had a taste for drink and fine living and had a nervous tic that earned him the nickname of "Blinky." "He looks precisely like one of those plethoric French colonels, who are so stout, and who look so red in the face, that one would suppose some one had tied a cord tightly round their necks," Lyman said. "Mounted on a large and fine horse, his whole aspect was martial, not to say fierce."[21] French may have looked fierce, but he was a poor general, "unquestionably the army's worst corps commander," according to historian Jeffry D. Wert.[22]

Gouverneur Warren, now commanding the II Corps while Hancock recovered from his Gettysburg wound, struck Lyman as a much less martial personage than French. "Fancy a small, slender man, with a sun-burnt face, two piercing black eyes, and withal bearing a most ludicrous resemblance to cousin Mary Pratt!" he wrote. "He was dressed in a double-breasted blouse, buttoned awry, a pair of soldier's pantaloons, rather too short, and a very old little straw hat, of the kind called 'chip.' Such is the *personnel* of one of the very best generals in the Army of the Potomac! He is a most kind man, and always taking care of hysterical old Secesh ladies and giving them coffee and sugar. As to Secesh *males*, in the army, he is a standing terror to them."[23]

Lyman's notebooks contain more nuts-and-bolts details about which corps moved where and when, but both his letters and his journals remain fascinating reading today, not least because of the rich lode of anecdotal detail he provides about Meade. Although generally positive, he was not blind to the general's faults, especially that ungovernable temper. He called him "the Great Peppery." "General Meade is of a perverse nature," Lyman said; "when he gets in a disagreeable place, he is apt to stay there. I think he likes to have officers who are prone to comfort feel decidedly *un*comfortable."[24]

◆ ◆ ◆

Things remained relatively quiet along the Rapidan until early October, when the Army of Northern Virginia began stirring once again, starting what has been called "a campaign of maneuver." As Chaplain Stewart described it, "This new science, play, or pastime may be designated '*Chasing and being chased—running after and being run after.*'"[25]

Lee moved on October 9, starting a sweep around Meade's right that threatened to turn into the kind of flanking maneuver that had undone John Pope at Second Bull Run. Meade quickly determined to move his army out of the jaws of the trap and pull back across the Rappahannock. The movement started in the wee hours of the morning on October 11 as wagons, artillery, ambulances, and soldiers splashed across fords and marched over pontoon bridges. The entire army had crossed by evening.[26]

All of this had the air of novelty to new arrival Lyman, who captured the activity in a letter to his sister: "Down comes General Meade," he wrote; "I clap the pencil in my pocket, and in two minutes we are off, escort, orderlies, Staff and all, winding our way midst miles of baggage and ammunition waggons and slow columns of moving infantry. Ha, ha, ha! They don't look much like the 'Cadets,' these old sojers on the march." He then proceeds to give a colorful description: "There is their well-stuffed knapsack, surmounted by a rolled gray blanket, the worse for wear; from their belt is slung a big cartridge-box, with forty rounds, and at their side hangs a haversack (satchel you would call it) quite bursting with three days' rations. Hullo! what has that man, dangling at the end of his musket? A coffee-pot! an immense tin coffee-pot! and there is another with a small frying-pan—more precious to them than gold. And there goes a squad of cavalry, the riders almost obscured by the bags of oats and the blankets and coats piled on pommel and crupper; their carbine hangs on one side and their sabre clatters from the other. And then behold a train of artillery (the best-looking arm of the service), each gun drawn by six or eight horses, and the caissons covered with bags of forage," he continued. "And so the face of the country is covered, when an army is on the march, the waggons keeping the road, the infantry winding through the open land. It is singular, in regard to the latter, that, however dirty or slovenly the men may be, their muskets always shine like silver; they know it is an important member."[27]

Meade's quick movement stymied Lee's attempt to flank him. Then Meade received reports from his cavalry that Lee had halted at Culpeper—right in the middle of the triangle of land between the Rapidan and Rappahannock. He reversed course to see if he could perhaps coax the Confederate army into battle. "If Bob Lee will go into these fields there and fight me, man for man, I will do it this afternoon," he told Lyman.[28] So the army put on the brakes, shifted gears, and moved back. Chaplain Stewart said, "We had now been chased far enough, and must, in consequence, chase awhile."[29]

Meade's information, however, was wrong. Lee had continued north on his flanking attempt. When Meade learned of the new danger he shifted gears once again. "It was now our turn to run, and be chased," wrote Stewart.[30] Meade resumed his movement back to the strong defensive positions outside Centreville.

During the marching back and forth through the Virginia countryside, Francis Adams Donaldson and the 118th Pennsylvania crossed the old Bull Run battlefields, where the shocked soldiers saw the bodies of those who had died there almost a year earlier. Donaldson heard one story about soldiers who identified a dead comrade by his unusual teeth, and he saw the skeletal remains of a cavalryman, still clad in his uniform, who apparently had died while trying to crawl to a stream to slake his thirst. One officer even recovered the small album with pictures of his family that he had dropped in June on the way north to Gettysburg.[31]

Halleck wasn't happy about Meade's "retrograde" movements or his complaints about his inability to obtain accurate information about the enemy's where-

Bristoe and Mine Run Campaigns

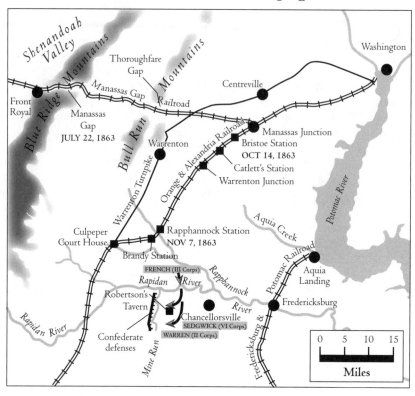

abouts. "Lee is unquestionably bullying you," he telegraphed Meade on October 18. "If you cannot ascertain his movements, I certainly cannot. If you pursue and fight him, I think you will find out where he is. I know of no other way."

"If you have any orders to give me, I am prepared to receive and obey them," Meade snapped back, "but I must insist on being spared the infliction of such truisms in the guise of opinions as you have recently honored me with, particularly as they were not asked for."[32] When drafting this message Meade had initially used the words "bunsby opinions," a reference to a character in Charles Dickens's *Dombey and Son* who was noted for his baffling advice. Before sending it he asked Lyman if he thought that was the best choice of words. Lyman didn't. He advised "that the joke was capital, but not in accordance with the etiquette of a commander-in-chief." They decided to use "truisms" instead.[33]

During all the movements to and fro, it was Lee's army that suffered the only serious punishment. The encounter took place near Bristoe Station along the Orange and Alexandria Railroad. It happened on October 14 when Gen. A. P. Hill's forces made a rash attack on what they thought was the Army of the Potomac's rear guard as the Union forces moved north. Had Hill taken the time to adequately reconnoiter, he would have discovered that Warren's II Corps was still nearby.

Today Bristoe Station Heritage Park sits right on the edge of a somewhat soul-less upper-scale housing development called New Bristow Village. Its streets bear such names as Brevet Court, Iron Brigade Unit Avenue, 10th Alabama Avenue, Rifle Road, Poagues Battery Drive, and Battalion Square. The development laps right on the edge of Heritage Park. But I suppose we must give the developers their due—they did donate most of the park's 133 acres to the Civil War Preservation Trust. In return they got permission to build more houses on the remaining land than they would have been able to do otherwise. Battlefield conservation often depends on such compromises.

Two battles were fought here—the Battle of Kettle Run to the south, part of the Second Bull Run campaign back on August 27, 1862, and the Battle of Bristoe Station. The park's A. P. Hill's Folly Trail follows the events of the latter battle. There's also a Tragedy in Camp Trail, which leads down through the woods to gravesites of Confederate soldiers who died of disease at Camp Jones here in 1861.

I pull into the parking lot on a bright and blustery Saturday afternoon in October, just a day after the battle's actual anniversary. Rob Orrison of the Prince William County Preservation Division waits under a canopy in the parking lot. He has a table with some books, Bristoe Station baseball caps, and brochures and waits for people to show up for the morning's tour. He tells me about how the developers donated the bulk of the land, while the county bought another six acres down by the railroad track across the field. Orrison's office is in a 1960s-style house on top of a rise by the parking lot. The house used to belong to the people who owned this farmland. He says it might become the visitors center, it might be torn down, or it might be rehabbed at some point. This winter he plans to work on some historical markers for the battlefield, and he has some Boy Scouts coming in to clean up the cemetery. This is not a big-budget operation.

Today a couple volunteers, John DePue and John Pierson, will conduct a tour of the battlefield and explain what happened here on October 14, 1863. DePue is a New Jersey native and, if his baseball cap is any indicator, a Vietnam veteran. He has had a longtime interest in the Civil War. "I've been interested in it ever since I could read," he says. Pierson grew up around here. DePue is the more verbose of the two; Pierson tries to keep the tour moving on schedule, with limited success. By the time the one-hour tour is over about two hours have passed. I get the sense that the two Johns would be happy to spend the entire day talking about the battle. In fact, as soon as our tour returns to the parking lot they head out with two late arrivals to start another presentation.

There wasn't much here in 1863. "The village, big or little, which had once given name to the place had disappeared; only a few 'burnt chimneys' remained to show where once it stood," wrote a historian of the II Corps.[34] The sole dwelling was a little shanty that belonged to someone named Dobbs. When the II Corps, taking up the rear of the northward-moving Army of the Potomac, reached here, Warren expected to find George Sykes and the V Corps waiting on the opposite side of Broad Run. Instead, Sykes had moved on, intent on reaching Centreville, and left Warren's small corps alone and isolated as A. P. Hill and the Confederate III Corps approached from the south. DePue tells us that Hill spotted a portion of the V Corps as it departed and thought it was the tail end of the Union army. Without making a proper reconnaissance he sent his men after it.

Warren heard the sounds of battle and galloped to the front. "His quick intelligence, his falcon eye, his trained engineering sense, instantly took in the whole field; and hardly could he turn in his saddle, before he shouted to his adjutant-general, 'Tell General Hays to move by the left flank, at the double-quick, to the railroad cut!'"[35]

That was Alexander Hays, who had performed so admirably at Gettysburg and delighted his soldiers by dragging a captured flag through the dirt behind his horse. His division and the rest of the corps won the race to the railroad cut, and from this strong defensive line they successfully beat back the Confederate attacks. As the two Johns explain the fighting, I can picture the Union troops behind the railroad, which still runs across the bottom of the field, while Hill's Confederates moved down the slope of the field we have just crossed. The Union had artillery on a hill on the far side of the railroad, while Confederate batteries fired from behind us, where a shopping mall stands today across from modern Route 28. "Except for the momentary wavering of a company or two, the troops have kept up their fire with regularity and coolness, even the very conscripts fighting like men," Francis Walker wrote in his history of the II Corps. The Confederates managed to pierce the Union line at the point where Route 619 now crosses the railroad tracks, but they were soon beaten back. "Quick as thought, amid loud cheers, the men of half a dozen regiments spring across the railroad, and dash forward to gather the trophies of the fight."[36]

The fighting slowed as the October darkness fell. With Ewell's entire corps threatening to come up in support of Hill, Warren and the II Corps withdrew under the cover of night. The Union suffered around 350 casualties and the Confederates about four times that.[37]

If Gettysburg had been Warren's finest hour, Bristoe Station must count as his second finest. John Pierson tells me his theory about Warren. The general had been called away from his honeymoon on the eve of the Gettysburg battle, he points out. Warren had gone home to visit his bride just before the Bristoe campaign and had been summoned back once again, only to have another excellent day on the battlefield. "Maybe Meade should have allowed him to go home more often," Pierson says, half seriously.

For A. P. Hill the defeat had a personal dimension. Like McClellan, Warren had married a woman who had once been the object of Hill's attentions. "I have not only whipped you, but married your old sweetheart," Warren wrote in a note he had delivered to his old romantic rival after the battle here.[38]

Warren was something of a rising star in the Army of the Potomac, and Meade appreciated his abilities. "The skill and promptitude of Major-General Warren, and the gallantry and bearing of the officers and soldiers of the Second Corps, are entitled to high commendation," he noted.[39] It was perhaps the high point of a relationship that soon started to unravel.

The army continued its march until it reached Centreville. "We had now run far enough—made a long run, and did it well; here halted, and soon had strong earthen breast-works thrown up between us and the rebels," reported Stewart.

"So soon, however, as a little rested, it was fairly the rebels' turn to run, and we to chase." Now the Army of the Potomac pushed the Army of Northern Virginia south, with Lee's men tearing up the railroad as they passed. Soon the rebels were back behind the Rappahannock, and Meade's forces had returned to the Warrenton area, "on the precise ground we occupied when arriving here the latter part of July," said Stewart. "We await another race; yet whose turn next to be chased deponent saith not."[40]

In his letters home Meade appeared a little defensive about his recent operations. His movements had not been a retreat, he asserted; they had been "a withdrawal of the army—maneuvering to get into a proper position to offer battle, and made to prevent Lee from compelling me to fight at a disadvantage." The men in the army understood what he had done, he said, which is why they had cheerfully put up with all the hardships of the forced marches. He knew the administration wasn't happy with the results, but he felt they should remove him from command if they thought someone could do better. Yet when he did propose a plan of action—an attempt to flank Lee's army by crossing the Rappahannock at Banks Ford and Fredericksburg—Lincoln had refused permission. Perhaps Meade's projected strategy aroused bad memories of Burnside's disastrous campaign, but almost certainly the president worried that the movement risked leaving Washington exposed. "Now I have clearly indicated what I thought feasible and practicable and my plan is *disapproved*," Meade complained.[41]

Within the army rumor had it that Meade was going to be replaced. "Candidly, we feel every confidence in Meade, and if anyone succeeds him but McClellan, the dissatisfaction will be intense," noted one officer.[42]

Meade knew he had to take action, and soon. When he did put his army into motion he had a small but unexpected triumph at a spot called Rappahannock Station. Today the small village alongside the river is called Remington, but it's been a place of many names. First a riverside gristmill gave it the name of Millview. In 1850 it became Bowenville, after a prominent resident. Three years later the arrival of the Orange and Alexandria Railroad rechristened it Rappahannock Station. In 1890 the post office requested a change because of confusion with a town called Tappahannock. A Captain Remington was supposedly a popular conductor on the railroad, so the residents decided to name it after him.

To learn more about the Battle of Rappahannock Station, I drive down to Brandy Station, Virginia, to meet Mike Block at the Graffiti House, the headquarters of the Brandy Station Foundation. From the outside, the building, built in 1858, is a fairly bland-looking place—a square little structure of two stories with a front porch and a little side extension that throws off its symmetry. While the downstairs holds some exhibits on Civil War history, with artifacts inside glass cases and informational panels on the walls, it's the upstairs that sets the place apart. During the war soldiers from both sides took shelter in the building, and many of them took charcoal from the fireplace and scrawled on the walls. Many just signed their names, among them Jeb Stuart. Other soldiers drew cartoons. In one of them a soldier holds his nose uncomfortably close to a horse's hindquarters. "He smells a rebel," the caption says. The walls were covered after the war, and the graffiti was forgotten until 1993, when the building underwent renovation. In 2002 the nonprofit Brandy Station Foundation bought the house and now operates it as a museum.

I had met Mike Block when I was touring Bristoe Station. He lives in nearby Bealeton now, but he's originally from Atlantic City, New Jersey. He moved to Arizona when he was fourteen, joined the air force there, and became an intelligence analyst. He tells me he can't remember exactly what sparked his interest in the Civil War, but it wasn't his first visit to Gettysburg. "I remember absolutely nothing about that trip," he says, "except that my dad killed a bee on the bus. I was seven years old." As he got older he started reading about the war—first about the battles, then about the leaders, and then regimental histories. "Now I'm into the people," he says. After a while he decided he wanted to give something back, so when he moved to this area he began volunteering for the Brandy Station Foundation. As in so many cases the Civil War began to consume him. He became more involved with local history and especially preservation issues. He tells me he realizes that his increasing commitment to the Civil War will probably come at the expense of promotions within his company. He says he can accept that. "I've only got about ten years of work left in my life, anyway, that I *want* to do."

He's now working on a project to compile the names of all the Union soldiers who died around here during the winter encampment of 1863–64. He'd also like to do a tactical study of the fighting here. He says he doesn't know anyone who has a better understanding of the Battle of Rappahannock Station than he has.

Today is a bright November day with an autumnal bite in the air, not unlike what the men experienced here on November 7, 1863. I've joined a small group that Block is taking on a tour of the Rappahannock battlefield. One of them is Mark Allen, who was born in Portland, Maine, and now lives in Warrenton. Allen has been researching Otis Roberts, a Civil War soldier from Dexter, Maine, who won the Medal of Honor here for capturing the flag of the 8th Louisiana in a hand-to-hand struggle.[43]

Before taking us out to the battlefield Block gives us some background on some of the people involved. He tells us about twenty-four-year-old Col. Emory Upton, young, ambitious and newly in command of a brigade in the VI Corps. There's Peter Ellmaker, colonel of the 119th Pennsylvania and a man who Block says did not leave much of a historical trail. About all Block can determine is that his men did not like him. Archibald Godwin was the colonel of the 57th North Carolina and in temporary command of a brigade in Jubal Early's division. A former forty-niner, Godwin had sought his fortune in California and almost became the Democratic nominee for governor there in 1860. Brig. Gen. Harry Hays commanded the Louisiana Brigade in Early's division.

Block hands us maps and shows us photos and sketches of the area during the war. Today we'll be crossing some private land—Block has permission from the owner—and then head over to the forty acres of public land that Fauquier County plans to turn into a park.

We climb into cars and drive down Route 29 toward Remington, make an exit, cross the Rappahannock, and drive into the little town. Busy Route 15/29 sends traffic zipping past Remington without a sideways glance, heading toward

Warrenton to the north or Culpeper to the south. Remington is like the Bates Hotel in *Psycho* after they took away the road, a quiet and easily overlooked backwater with a tiny main street, a few halfhearted little shops, and the usual assortment of gas stations and convenience stores. A railroad bridge crosses the river today, but there was no bridge here in the fall of 1863, the span having become a casualty of war.

We park in a dirt parking lot across from a gas station that doubles as a market and deli. Block points out the Civil War Trails marker in the parking lot, the only reference to the battle in town. It wasn't a big battle, certainly not "one of the most brilliant achievements of this fiercely contested war," as Chaplain Stewart described it.[44] It was more of an anomaly, one of the few occasions when attacking soldiers managed to storm and capture strong entrenchments with relatively little loss of life.

From the parking lot Block leads us down a short dirt track into a small field surrounded on three sides by belts of trees. The fourth side of the field leads up a rise crested by some derelict farm buildings. The Confederates had fortifications where the buildings stand. The Union troops marched past where we are standing and up the hill to storm the works.

Meade's plan called for William French and the III Corps to cross the river downstream at ever-busy Kelly's Ford. At the same time Sedgwick, in overall command of the V and VI Corps (with Brig. Gen. Horatio Wright taking immediate command of Sedgwick's corps), would attack the rebel breastworks here. Most of the Confederate army lay in wait on the other side of the river, but the rebels had constructed a strong advance position here on the north bank, using entrenchments that Union soldiers had constructed earlier in the war. Meade thought he had the chance to fight "a great and decisive battle," he wrote. "My army is in excellent condition and in high spirits, and confident of success, if they can get anything of a fair chance, and so far as mortals can anticipate such doubtful matters as battles, I have a right to be hopeful."[45]

For once, not only did everything go according to plan, but everything went better than anyone dared hope. On the morning of November 7 French successfully crossed the river at Kelly's Ford ("Blinky French's only good day, that I could find, in the army," Block says). Farther upstream Sedgwick prepared to attack. He observed the formidable position, then rode over to Gen. Horatio Wright. "Wright, what do you think are the chances of an assault with infantry on that position?" he asked.

"Just as you say, General," Wright replied.

"What does Russell think about it?" Sedgwick asked. Brig. Gen. David Russell had command of Wright's division while Wright led the VI Corps.

"Here comes Russell; he can speak for himself," Wright replied. Up rode Russell, who had graduated fourth from the bottom of West Point's Class of 1841 but had gradually been demonstrating his ability during the war.

"Russell, do you think you can carry those works with your division?" asked Sedgwick.

"I think I can, sir," replied Russell.

"Go ahead and do it," Sedgwick said.[46]

Ellmaker's and Upton's brigades bore the brunt of the attack. Capt. Francis Adams Donaldson of the 118th Pennsylvania Regiment of the V Corps was able to enjoy the show as his corps advanced through open country on the VI Corps' left. "It was an indescribable spectacle, grand, stirring, impressive, and from my position in the centre of two corps, I gazed upon a pageant such as was never before seen by me, and a sight never to be forgotten by any one who beheld it," he wrote in a letter to his brother.[47] The November sun was setting, painting the scene in an orange glow. Donaldson admired this "golden glory" but was brought back to earth when he turned to look behind him and saw the stretcher bearers waiting in the rear.

As the long lines of men in Union blue advanced across the fields, the VI Corps to the right of the railroad, the V Corps to the left, the Confederate artillery began to fire. The blue lines continued on. Then the men of the VI Corps began charging the rebel lines at double-quick and rushed over the works like a tsunami. The first man over the Confederate breastworks was supposedly a sergeant from the 6th Maine, who looked around, realized he was surrounded by rebel troops, and shouted that he surrendered. Then he saw other men from his regiment jumping over the works behind him. "I take it back!" he cried and snatched up an enemy flag.[48] The fighting was fierce and concentrated until elements of the V Corps attacked from the flank and rear, shattering the rebel defenses. Night fell and the battle was over. It was a sudden and unexpected victory, with the Federals having killed, wounded, or captured more than sixteen hundred Confederates.

Union losses were much lighter. "Only about one hundred were killed, and three hundred wounded," reported Chaplain Stewart. "Yet how strange this language, 'only one hundred killed!'" he mused. "Cruel war does greatly transform both our language and our sensibilities. 'Only one hundred killed!' Only one hundred noble young men in the flower of manhood swept together into eternity. Only a hundred homes and home circles thus quickly thrown into inconsolable sadness and irreparable grief."[49]

Throughout our tour Block has been reading us excerpts from letters and reports. We advance up the hill and around the farm buildings, then tromp across the county's holdings below. On the other side of the field a head pops up from the grass, and then a fox goes scurrying across the field toward the Rappahannock, the sunlight glinting off the water through the trees. On the opposite side of the field, beyond another narrow band of trees, we can see cars zipping by on Route 29.

To the left, also behind trees, are the houses of a modern development. Block points that way. "Upton's men punched through there," he says, "and then pushed forward to the top of the hill." He reads us an account by a soldier who saw a man from the 6th Maine, who happened to be named Jeff Davis, club a Confederate with such ferocity that he shattered both his musket's stock and the rebel's skull.

Harry Hays, one of the Confederates Block had told us about, estimated that the attacking force numbered somewhere between twenty thousand and twenty-five thousand men. "He was only off by eighteen thousand to twenty-three thousand," says Block, who puts the attackers at around two thousand. Mark Allen laughs at that. "He's from the McClellan school of accounting," he says of Hays.

After the fighting ended Chaplain Stewart walked over the battlefield and observed the burial of the dead. He noted thirty fatalities from the 6th Maine and observed that most of them had died from wounds to the face or upper part of the body, killed as they advanced right up to the Confederate gun barrels. "All noble-looking young men; still, calm, bloody, dead," said Stewart. "They came from that far off northeast, to sleep their last long sleep on the quiet banks of this lonely river."[50]

His position along the Rappahannock no longer tenable, Lee retreated across the Rapidan. "I must say I was greatly disappointed when I found Lee refused my offer of battle," Meade wrote home, "because I was most desirous of effecting something decisive, and I know his refusal was only a postponement of a question that had to be met and decided." He did get the gratification of receiving a telegram from Lincoln, in which the president expressed his satisfaction with Meade's operations.[51]

He also received accolades from his men. "The effect of this Rappahannock Station success seemed to have worked some little enthusiasm into the now non-demonstrative army," reads a history of the 118th Pennsylvania. "Within a few days General Meade, or 'Old Four-eyes,' as he was still familiarly called in his absence, appearing in the vicinity of one of the divisions of the 5th Corps, was received with rousing, approving and appreciative cheers."[52]

Summer had turned into fall, and fall was giving way to winter, when the unpredictable weather would end the active campaigning season. The two armies continued to glower at each other while the entire Virginia theater remained in stalemate. "Of course, we lived in tents and as the autumn came on our huge headquarter camp fire became a point of reunion for all headquarter officers, especially after nightfall," remembered Lt. Col. James F. Rusling of the army's quartermaster corps. "Here every evening you would find Meade, with his hands clasped behind him and his head bent forward, with his fatigue cap or old slouch hat well down over his eyes, chatting gravely with Humphrey[s], his chief of staff, or Seth Williams, his adjutant general, or Ingalls, his chief quartermaster, or Hunt, his chief of artillery, or Warren, his chief engineer, or other general officers that happened along, and midnight often found his solitary candle still burning in his tent and the commander in chief hard at work there.

"As a rule," Rusling continued, "he was a better listener than talker. Ingalls and Hunt were the great talkers there, and they both talked exceedingly well, and Warren, too, was keen and bright. What campaigns they planned and unplanned! How they outwitted Lee and ended the rebellion again and again! What camp stories they told! What old soldier 'yarns' they spun! But no space for them here. Meade's sense of humor was not large, but he was keen and intelligent, his mind worked broadly and comprehensively, his patriotism was perfect, his sense of duty intense; and he would willingly have laid down his life at any time had our cause required it. In manner he was often sharp and peremptory, but this was because of his utter absorption in great affairs."[53]

Those "great affairs" revolved around defeating the Army of Northern Virginia, something Meade would have to do quickly if he wanted to accomplish it in what little remained of 1863. He decided to take one last crack at Lee, this time an attempt to make the kind of flanking attack that had served the Confederates so well. Unfortunately for Meade, this time things did not go as smoothly as they had gone at Rappahannock Station, and he ended up facing what was probably the most difficult decision of his life: should he attack Lee's entrenched position behind the creek called Mine Run, almost certainly leading to wholesale slaughter of his men, or should he call off the attack and probably lose command of the army as a result?

• • •

My wife and I drive through the Virginia countryside, looking for evidence of Meade's Mine Run campaign. On this August afternoon the weather displays an alarming split personality as it alternates between periods of cheery sunshine and torrential downpours. We're following a short driving tour I printed out from the National Park Service's Fredericksburg website. The twisting route takes us down one narrow side road after another; at one point we're driving through the rain down a washboard-rough gravel road. For the most part there are no roadside markers or anything to indicate that Civil War action ranged over this region. Only when we reach Zoar Baptist Church on Route 611 do we find some Civil War Trails markers that tell the story of the Battle of Payne's Farm. The Civil War Trust has preserved 685 acres of land here and established a one-and-a-half-mile trail through the woods. But with the heavens opening up on my umbrella, I decide I will walk the trail another day.

Meade planned to cross his army at various fords along the Rapidan below Lee's right and make a flanking attack instead of risking a frontal assault against his strong entrenchments. The III Corps would cross at Jacob's Ford, with the VI Corps following, and then make its way through various woods roads to a place called Robertson's Tavern. The roads the army had to follow were narrow and winding, as they still are today. The II Corps would cross at Germanna Ford, while the I and V Corps would use Culpeper Mine Ford. Cavalry would guard the flanks. "The plan promised brilliant success," said chief of staff Andrew Humphreys; "to insure it required prompt, vigorous action, and intelligent compliance with the programme on the part of the corps and other commanders."[54]

Therein lay the proverbial rub. Meade wanted his army to rumble into motion on November 24, but heavy rainfall delayed the movement until the twenty-sixth. Then French and the III Corps were two hours late in reaching their ford. Two pontoon bridges turned out to be too short, forcing the engineers to do some time-consuming improvisation, and the banks on the opposite side of the river were steep and difficult to climb. Like many best-laid plans, Meade's attempt to flank Lee began to unravel. Things slipped further and further behind schedule, giving the Confederates time to react to the Federals' threatening move.

Warren and the II Corps reached Robertson's Tavern on November 27 and began "a brisk little contest" with the rebels there.[55] But French's III Corps was nowhere to be found. That's because once the commander of French's lead division, Brig. Gen. Henry Prince, managed to cross the river, he sat at a crossroads for a couple hours while he tried to determine which road to take; a historical marker stands at this crossroads now.

After driving around here I can understand how the generals became confused. I spend a lot of time stopped at crossroads myself as I peer at my directions and try to figure out which way to go. The stakes, though, were considerably higher for French and Prince. Around 11:30 headquarters finally received a message from French. He said he was waiting for Warren—who was already at Robertson's Tavern skirmishing with the enemy. Steam must have been shooting out of Meade's ears at this point. But before French could join Warren, he stumbled into battle on the land of a man named Payne.

The Battle of Payne's Farm was the only serious fighting of the Mine Run Campaign—although I'm sure the skirmishers and other soldiers who had been killed and wounded in other actions would have said their fights had been serious enough. The Confederates here were commanded by Maj. Gen. Edward "Allegheny" Johnson, also known as "Clubby." The eighteen thousand men of the III Corps greatly outnumbered Johnson and his fifty-three hundred troops, but the Confederates fought stubbornly enough to delay French even longer.

Humphreys later complained that French's tardiness and the holdup at Payne's Farm essentially paralyzed the entire operation. By the time the army was in a position to attack on the twenty-eighth, Lee had moved his army to a strong position behind Mine Run, a line "crowned with intrenchments for infantry and artillery, strengthened by abates," said Humphreys.[56] Any frontal assault appeared doomed, but Warren thought he could shift his forces and, reinforced by a division of the VI Corps, attack Lee's weak right flank. Meade later gave him two additional divisions from the III Corps. While the V and VI Corps made a diversionary attack on the enemy's left, Warren would make the main attack on its right.

Warren shifted his position on November 29. He planned to launch his offensive the next morning, with an artillery barrage signaling the start of the attack. Warren would go in at 8:00, and then Sedgwick, on the opposite end of Lee's line, would begin his movement. The guns began roaring on time at 8:00, but at 8:50 Capt. Washington Roebling (of later Brooklyn Bridge fame) came galloping up to Meade's headquarters with a message from Warren. Meade read it. "My God!" he exclaimed. "General Warren has half my army at his disposition!"[57]

Warren had carefully surveyed the enemy position opposite his and decided, on his own authority, that the Confederates had strengthened it so much during the night that it was now much too strong to attack. Lyman, observing the developments, thought Meade and Humphreys took the news fairly well.[58] Meade jumped on his horse and, along with Lyman, Humphreys, and two other aides, rode over to consult with Warren. It was a bitterly cold day, and the generals stood by a fire to keep warm as they consulted.

The Mine Run defenses did appear strong indeed. Chaplain Stewart of the 102nd Pennsylvania felt certain an attack on them would lead to a great loss of life. The men in his regiment agreed, and as the day passed they came to him and filled his pockets with all the mementos of the lives they expected would soon end—money, photographs, rings, watches. Some soldiers began pinning their names to their coats so their bodies could be identified. What impressed Stewart, though, was that despite the terrible odds, these soldiers were still willing to go into battle.[59]

Lt. Col. Charles H. Morgan of the II Corps staff suspected that many officers shared their soldiers' misgivings but kept their doubts to themselves. One picket from the 1st Minnesota, not realizing that Morgan was an officer, didn't hide anything. He told Morgan the enemy position was "a damned sight worse than Fredericksburg" and added, "I am going as far as I can travel; but we can't get more than two-thirds of the way up the hill."[60]

Pvt. Wilbur Fisk of the 2nd Vermont, at the other end of the Union line with Sedgwick's VI Corps, studied the Confederate defenses with great interest because there seemed a pretty fair chance that he would soon be testing them personally. "There was a deep creek between us and the enemy, and the rebels had been busy digging rifle-pits and strengthening their position ever since we came up to them," he wrote. "Both banks were abrupt and steep and difficult to get over, while on the rebel side they had added to these disadvantages by placing every conceivable obstacle in the way of our advance. Trees were felled, abattis made, breastworks were thrown up until they occupied a position that if *we* had occupied we should have considered impregnable against all the rebels in the universe."[61]

After consulting with Warren and examining the defenses for himself, Meade reluctantly agreed with his subordinate's opinion—but Warren's decision to call off his attack on his own initiative hinted at a troubling aspect of his personality, at least for an army officer. If Warren felt he were right, he would stubbornly follow his own course of action, regardless of his orders. That personality quirk would gradually erode Meade's confidence in him and lead to problems down the road.

But at Mine Run in the frigid late November 1863, Meade decided that attacking Lee's position here would be nothing more than a useless slaughter, another Fredericksburg. Meade suspected someone else would have to take the responsibility for renewing the war against the Army of Northern Virginia, because he expected to be removed from command for canceling his attack. On December 2 he wrote a long letter home to Margaret, which reads more like a statement for posterity than a letter from a husband to his wife. "I expect your wishes will now soon be gratified, and that I shall be relieved from the Army of the Potomac," he began. He considered his fate to be settled, he said, "but as I have told you before, I would rather be ignominiously dismissed, and suffer anything, than knowingly and wilfully have thousands of brave men slaughtered for nothing."[62]

"Wherever the fault lies, I shall always be astonished at the extraordinary moral courage of General Meade, which enabled him to order a retreat, when his knowledge, as an engineer and a soldier, showed that an attack would be a blunder," said Lyman. "The men and guns stood ready: he had only to snap his fingers, and that night would probably have seen ten thousand wretched, mangled creatures, lying on those long slopes, exposed to the bitter cold, and out of reach of all help! Then people would have said: 'He was unsuccessful; but then he tried hard, and did not get out.'"[63]

Instead, Meade withdrew back across the Rapidan, and the army began preparing its winter quarters in the area around Brandy Station. "But for the restrictions imposed on General Meade from Washington, he would have fallen back toward Fredericksburg, taking up a position in front of that town," noted

Humphreys. "Had he done so, the first battle with Lee, in May, 1864, would not have been fought in the Wilderness, but in a more open country."[64] Add that one to the growing pile of "what ifs."

Winter had arrived with a vengeance. Following the rain that had delayed the Mine Run campaign the weather had turned cold—so frigid, in fact, that some army pickets were found frozen to death at their posts. The campaigning season was over. It had been a long and trying season indeed, one filled with blood and death, triumph and disappointment. It had started with high hopes in the spring, hopes that tumbled down to earth with the disaster at Chancellorsville. It had climaxed with the triumph at Gettysburg, and then sputtered to a close with inconclusive maneuvering punctuated by occasional outbursts of killing. Spring would bring more fighting and a new general in chief. First, though, Meade had to wage some battles in Washington.

CHAPTER 12
Troubles in Washington

Daniel Butterfield, who testified against Meade before
the Joint Committee to Investigate the Conduct of War
LIBRARY OF CONGRESS

• • •

When we last saw Dan Sickles's right leg it was still attached, albeit only slightly, to the general's body, and he was being carried off the Gettysburg battlefield after a cannonball struck him. At a field hospital Dr. Thomas Sim severed the remaining connections between limb and general, who made a quick recovery. Then one day the new Army Medical Museum in Washington, D.C., received a package. Inside, the story goes, was a miniature wooden coffin, and inside that rested Sickles's leg. There was also a card from the general. "Courtesy D.E.S." it read. For the rest of his life Sickles went to the museum on the Gettysburg anniversary to visit his limb—and according to legend he was very angry to learn that the museum hadn't saved his foot as well.

Sickles's leg bone is still on display at the National Museum of Health and Medicine, which, until it moved to Silver Spring, Maryland, at the end of 2011, was on the grounds of Walter Reed Army Medical Center in Washington. You can see where the cannonball shattered the leg bone, for a series of pins and rods holds it together. Next to it is a cannonball like the one that robbed the general of his limb. The leg shares a glass case with other examples of skulls, ribs, vertebrae, knees, and other body parts that suffered from enemy fire during the Civil War.

I've come to the medical museum on a damp December morning to visit this portion of Dan Sickles but also to see the other interesting artifacts in this unique institution. Its collections include more than twenty-five million items, among them documents, photographs, medical illustrations, weapons, equipment, prosthetic devices, and anatomical samples. It has pieces of several presidents—fragments of Lincoln's skull, samples of Grant's tumor (Grover Cleveland's, too), and a section of James Garfield's vertebrae. Of course, all twenty-five million items won't fit into the museum's modest confines, but there is still plenty of "holy crap" stuff to gross out those with weak stomachs. Some people might blanch when they come face-to-face with the embryonic fetal twins in a jar or the swollen, severed elephantiasis-infected leg. But I also find an extensive display of artwork about the subject of medical trauma, much of it done by wounded veterans, and a temporary exhibit that includes part of Trauma Bay II from Balal, Iraq, a frontline medical facility that can take grim credit as being "the place where the most American blood spilled since the Vietnam War." Microscope buffs will find a bit of heaven in the numerous historic examples of that instrument. There's also a fascinating exhibit about the forensic identification of war dead. From it I learn that only 359,000 of the 620,000 who died in the Civil War were ever identified. That's only 58 percent.

The army's surgeon general, William Hammond, founded the museum in 1862 so he could research ways to improve care for wounded soldiers. Hammond sent out an order to Union generals asking for specimens of "morbid anatomy," which is why Sickles thought it would make a good home for his leg. Using such contributions from the dead and wounded, the staff put together the huge, six-volume *Medical and Surgical History of the War of the Rebellion*, which was completed in 1888.

Gwen Nelmes, the museum's young tour program manager, shows me around. She tells me that the examples of shattered limbs from a century and a half ago still have relevance. "Today with IEDs [improvised explosive devices] in Iraq and Afghanistan we see a lot of similar wounds," she says. "Here at Walter Reed you'll probably see a lot of people who are amputees or with prosthetics, because that's what IEDs do—they rip apart the flesh and the bone. The minié ball did similar damage, and cannonballs, so we do have a lot of doctors who come here and do research with our collection, comparing what they see today to what happened in the Civil War."

Civil War doctors tend to get a bad rap. The popular image is of well-meaning but ignorant butchers, chopping off limbs willy-nilly as their tortured patients bit down on bullets or pieces of rope. In fact, the doctors of the 1860s were well-educated and knowledgeable men—and they were almost all men—whose work led to advances in triage techniques, plastic surgery, modern nursing, occupational therapy, and hospital sanitation. Furthermore, doctors performed something like 95 percent of their battlefield operations with general anesthesia. On display in the museum is an image of a small pile of severed limbs at Washington's Harewood Hospital, but such amputations were usually a matter of necessity. The relatively slow-moving projectiles of the Civil War took a terrible toll on the human body, fragmenting bones and often carrying pieces of uniform into the wounds. Without X-ray technology doctors had no way to find all the pieces, and they had no antibiotics to fight the infections that would occur. So give the Civil War doctors some credit. "They were very advanced for the time," Nelmes tells me. "The only thing they didn't know was germ theory, which is what hindered them." Admittedly, that was a pretty big gap in their medical knowledge, but you can't blame the doctors. They did what they could with what they had.

One compelling element of the doctors' handiwork on display here is how personal much of it is. These body parts are not just anonymous medical specimens; they come with names attached. The portion of vertebrae with shattered ribs attached was once part of Pvt. Christian Britch of Company B, 11th Pennsylvania. He was shot at Hatcher's Run near Petersburg on April 2, 1865, and died twenty-six days later. I see a knee that once belonged to Pvt. Charles Maddocks of Company F, 1st Maine Heavy Artillery, who was mortally wounded at Petersburg. The skull that looks like it came from a Cyclops belonged instead to Pvt. J. Lumson of Company A, 122nd Ohio. A minié ball created the huge hole when it struck him in the face at Mine Run on November 27, 1863. Lumson lingered for more than two weeks despite the horrific wound.

Even more personal are the pieces of humanity inside a glass case devoted to poet Walt Whitman, physician Mary Walker, and hospital reformer Dorothea Dix. Whitman, the author of *Leaves of Grass*, had traveled to Fredericksburg to find his wounded brother, and the sights he saw shocked him to the depths of his soul. Back in Washington he began visiting wounded soldiers and offering what comfort he could. Sometimes he wrote about the men he encountered. For example, in this exhibit case there is an excerpt of something Whitman wrote about Pvt. Oscar F. Wilber of Company G, 154th New York. "He talk'd of death, and said he did not fear it. I said, 'Why Oscar, don't you think you will get well?' He said, 'I may, but it is not probable.'" Wilber died a few days later. And now, in the case next to the Whitman excerpt, sits Private Wilber's upper thigh bone.

There's also a thigh bone that came from Cpl. Frank H. Irwin of Company E, 93rd Pennsylvania, who was wounded at Fort Fisher, Virginia, on March 25, 1865. After Irwin died on May 1 Whitman wrote a letter to the dead soldier's mother. "He seem'd quite willing to die—he had become very weak and had suffer'd a good deal, and was perfectly resign'd, poor boy," said Whitman. "I do not know his past life, but I feel as if it must have been good. At any rate what I saw of him here, under the most trying circumstances, with a painful wound, and among strangers, I can say that he behaved so brave, so composed, and so sweet and affectionate, it could not be surpass'd. And now like many other noble and good men, after serving his country as a soldier, he has yielded up his young life at the very outset in her service." That kind of thing certainly adds something personal that lifts the war beyond the history books.

Of course, Dan Sickles made the war personal, too. He was very much an individual, a "picturesque and interesting character," as the *New York Times* diplomatically described him in an obituary after the former general died in 1914 at the ripe old age of ninety. Or was it ninety-four? "Even his age can be debated," wrote James A. Hessler in his book on Sickles.[1] As I stand and gaze at his leg bone it strikes me that if you can judge a man by his enemies, then George Meade must rate pretty highly. You can't find a much better enemy than Daniel Sickles. He looked something like a vaudeville villain, with a large mustache and a simmering gaze, lacking only the top hat and cape. According to legend—and those are three words that you can often use to preface statements about Sickles—while serving as an aide to future president James Buchanan when Buchanan served as minister to Great Britain, Sickles traveled to England with his favorite prostitute. In 1859, while a U.S. congressman from New York, Sickles shot and killed his wife's lover in Lafayette Square, just across the street from Buchanan's White House. The victim was none other than the son of Francis Scott Key of "Star-Spangled Banner" fame. Then Sickles hired Edwin Stanton, later Lincoln's secretary of war, as part of his legal team and became the first person to successfully use the "temporary insanity" defense. If that weren't enough to scandalize society, he took his wife back—and continued, as before, to neglect her while carrying on his own affairs. Like the best villains, though, Sickles was more than just a bad guy. He may have been a rogue, but he was a fascinating rogue.

Once the war started Sickles raised a brigade back in New York City, where he had been a lawyer and a mover and shaker within the powerful and powerfully corrupt Tammany political machine. He became a brigadier general of volunteers, one of the "political generals" who rose through political influence instead of military experience. As a brigadier general he saw some action on the peninsula in Hooker's division, and at Fredericksburg and Chancellorsville he commanded the III Corps, demonstrating personal bravery and a somewhat erratic ability as a commander. At Gettysburg he moved his command forward from Cemetery Ridge to the area around the Peach Orchard. Sickles's critics said that this foolhardy action could have cost the Union the battle; no one can argue that

Longstreet's men severely manhandled the III Corps and that Meade's line eventually ended up where he had wanted it in the first place.

Sickles refused to admit that his unauthorized advance had in any way jeopardized the Union forces. In fact, he insisted that his actions had saved the army at Gettysburg. According to the Sickles version, by moving forward—to a better position than the one Meade had assigned him, he said—he helped instigate the fighting on the second day just in time to prevent Meade from retreating back to Pipe Creek. As Edwin Coddington put it, "General Sickles apparently preferred to be guilty of willful insubordination than of stupidity—and he got away with it because even the most stiff-necked military man would hesitate to court-martial a general who had incurred a severe wound while fighting valiantly for the cause. As a cynic might explain it, when Sickles lost his leg at Gettysburg, he saved his reputation."[2]

Meade's critics quickly latched on to the Sickles version—the story that Meade had intended to retreat from Gettysburg. That charge would haunt Meade to the end of his days—and beyond. We can lay a good share of the blame for the eclipse of Meade's reputation at the foot of Dan Sickles.

Sickles returned to Washington, and President Lincoln visited the wounded general on July 5, accompanied by his son Tad. It may have been at this meeting that Sickles began laying some foundations for Lincoln's doubts about Meade's generalship. Later Sickles found the ideal platform from which to sketch his version of history when he joined forces with the Joint Committee on the Conduct of the War when that congressional agency cast its baleful eye on Gettysburg.

Michigan's Republican senator Zachariah Chandler had spearheaded the committee's creation to investigate war-related matters following the Union disasters of Bull Run and Ball's Bluff. Three senators and four congressmen served on the committee. Chandler and another Republican senator, Ben Wade of Ohio, were the committee's driving force, but Democrats served on it as well, including Andrew Johnson, later Lincoln's vice president and successor. In the years since the Civil War historians have gone back and forth on the question of the committee's impact on the war. Some think it had a negative effect, others a positive, and still others little cumulative effect at all. Yet writing in 1881 Alexander S. Webb, who won the Medal of Honor for his actions at Gettysburg and even served as Meade's chief of staff, wrote, "That body must be counted among the President's most influential advisors. It was a power during the war."[3]

In that case, Chandler and Wade were the powers behind the power. You could describe both men as combative. To their credit they were staunch opponents of slavery at a time when many people classified abolitionists as rabble-rousers and firebrands who just stirred up trouble. Both men originally hailed from New England—Wade from Massachusetts and Chandler from New Hampshire—which might account for their strong puritanical streaks and Yankee stubbornness. Both men also appeared willful and seemingly blind to anything but their own righteousness. Like other Radical Republicans they demanded an aggressive pursuit of war, the eradication of slavery, and serious repercussions for the seceded states once the Union was restored. They had little patience for generals who did not share their goals. Chandler had become suspicious of Meade's commitment to the cause back in 1861, when the general had refused to have the men in his command swear an oath to the United States, believing it was not proper for them to do so under pressure from civilian authorities. Meade was perfectly aware of Chandler's hostility. Writing to his wife following a lunch he had shared with Chandler and other Washington notables shortly after Fredericksburg, he noted sardonically, "Old Chandler inquired very affectionately after *you*, but did not refer to your loyalty."[4]

Neither Wade nor Chandler had military experience and remained stubbornly ignorant about the realities of maneuvering and wielding armies in the field, yet they eyed West Pointers with suspicion. Because so many graduates had sided with the South, the politicians considered the place little more than a breeding ground for secession, "the hot-bed from which rebellion was hatched," as Wade put it. And they despised General McClellan. "McClellan is an imbecile if not a traitor," Chandler said following the Peninsula Campaign. "He has virtually lost the army of the Potomac." He denounced the general on the Senate floor, with Wade seconding the attacks.[5]

The committee had bite as well as bark. It had received an early taste of blood when it zeroed in on Brig. Gen. Charles P. Stone, who had commanded the division that met with disaster at Ball's Bluff in October 1861. Stone was everything the committee disliked—a conservative West Pointer, a friend of McClellan's, and a man with no antislavery feelings at all. By later standards Ball's Bluff wasn't a big battle at all, but it turned into a huge embarrassment for the Union army. It gained further prominence because one of the dead was Col. Edward Baker, a former senator and a longtime friend of the president's. Baker's bumbling performance in the field was the real reason for the Union debacle, but Stone paid the price. The committee launched an investigation and, armed with testimony from a colonel whom Stone had previously accused of cowardice and fraud, decided that Stone was not only incompetent but probably traitorous as well. Committee members informed Secretary of War Edwin Stanton of their conclusions, and Stanton eventually ordered Stone's arrest. The disgraced general was sent to Fort Lafayette in New York. In his account of the case, Stephen Sears notes that the disgraced general even had to pay for his own train ticket to prison.[6] Stone remained behind bars for six months but no charges were ever filed against him.

Meade believed that Stone had been "the victim of political malice."[7] The committee had targeted Stone because of a Union defeat, but it aimed at Meade because of a great Union victory—Gettysburg. The committee members, Wade and Chandler in particular, had become quite disenchanted with Meade's leadership. They felt he hadn't been aggressive enough after Gettysburg or during the maneuverings in Virginia in the fall. They suspected him to be a McClellanite, with all that meant—an ingrained caution and an unwillingness to wage the total war necessary to eradicate the Old South and slavery.

Starting in February 1864 and continuing through April, seventeen generals from the Army of the Potomac trooped through the Capitol's corridors so they could testify in the basement room where members of the Joint Committee on the Conduct of the War examined its witnesses. They brought with them a collection of bruised egos, simmering resentments, and unrestrained ambition—leavened here and there by a dash of true patriotism and a desire to see more progress in the war.

Chandler and Wade wanted Joe Hooker returned to command, even though he was another West Pointer who had once resisted the idea of emancipation. Later, though, he apparently had seen which way the wind was blowing and shifted his position on that subject. His aggressive talk about fighting also made committee members think he was the aggressive, offensive-minded general they needed, Chancellorsville notwithstanding. Perhaps most important, Hooker showed no signs of political ambition; any military success he achieved would not create a potential rival at the ballot box.

Sickles was an equally unlikely ally for a committee dominated by Radical Republicans, for he was a partisan Democrat who had emerged from the highly politicized party machinery in New York City. Yet "the enemy of my enemy is my friend." Sickles was out to get Meade and so was the committee.

Sickles testified on February 26. Wade asked all the questions. When he did not outright lie—for example, by saying the III Corps had occupied Little Round Top when it clearly had not—Sickles used his lawyer skills to carefully skirt the truth. For example, when he read into the record Meade's Pipe Creek Circular, which he said demonstrated that Meade had intended to retreat from Gettysburg, he did not read this line: "Developments may cause the commanding general to assume the offensive from his present position." In other words, it was a contingency plan, not a plan to retreat.

Abner Doubleday testified on March 1. Like Sickles, he was still nursing grievances against Meade because Meade had replaced him at the head of the I Corps with John Newton following Reynolds's death. The aggrieved Doubleday told the committee that Meade's plan was to make him and General Howard scapegoats in case the battle turned out badly. Meade, he said, liked to place his personal friends in power. "There has always been a great deal of favoritism in the army of the Potomac," he claimed. "No man who is an anti-slavery man or an anti-McClellan man can expect decent treatment in that army as at present constituted."[8]

Brig. Gen. Albion Howe, "a zealot who despised anyone he thought to be an admirer of General McClellan,"[9] had commanded a division of the VI Corps at Gettysburg. He continued Doubleday's line of reasoning when he testified on March 3 and 4. Responding to some leading questioning by Wade, Howe explained that Meade and other generals in the Army of the Potomac had been tainted by the connection with McClellan, that there were "certain sympathies, feelings, and considerations of action which seem to govern now as they did then." In fact, Howe decided, the problem within the Army of the Potomac was an epidemic of "copperheadism."[10]

After hearing all this Wade and Chandler went to see Stanton and Lincoln and urged them to replace Meade with Hooker.

Meade remained blissfully unaware of what had been transpiring when he traveled to Washington three days later, on March 4, 1864, for meetings about reorganizing the army. However, he had received one indication about his standing in

Washington the previous month when Congress passed a resolution of thanks for the victory at Gettysburg. The first name on the list of those Congress thanked was Joseph Hooker. Meade's was second, followed by Howard.[11]

While in Washington Meade heard that Sen. Morton S. Wilkinson, a Republican from Minnesota and a Chandler ally, had attacked him on the Senate floor the previous day. Wilkinson told the Senate he had learned that before the Battle of Gettysburg, "the order went forth from the commander of that army to retreat; and but for the single fact that one of the corps commanders had got into a fight before the dispatch reached him, the whole army would undoubtedly have been retreating."[12] If that weren't bad enough, Meade discovered "the whole town talking" about the serious charges that Sickles and Doubleday had been making on Capitol Hill.

Meade received a summons on Saturday, March 5. He went that day to the Capitol, its proud new dome standing as a symbol of Union continuity, to find Wade waiting for him in the Senate's Committee on Territories Room. It was a grand setting for an inquisition, with a high vaulted ceiling and a huge bronze chandelier decorated with such Western symbols as Indian heads and buffalo. Wade, who had earned the nickname "Bluff Ben" after he once faced down a challenge to a duel by selecting squirrel rifles as his weapons, acted very civil. He assured Meade that the committee was not making a case against him. It was merely putting together a history of the war.

Meade probably knew better. He spent three hours explaining his viewpoint of the battle. Perhaps unaware of the depth of Sickles's perfidy, he was restrained in his criticisms of the general's movements on July 2. "It is not my intention in these remarks to cast any censure upon General Sickles," he said. "I am of the opinion that General Sickles did what he thought was for the best; but I differed with him in judgment." And, Meade said, subsequent events proved him right and Sickles wrong.[13]

Meade did realize he was in dangerous waters. After testifying before Wade he sought out Stanton, who assured him that his position was secure even though "a certain party" was trying to replace him with Hooker. Meade found it all very dispiriting, but in a letter home to his wife he told her it would all work out in the end. "It is a melancholy state of affairs, however, when persons like Sickles and Doubleday can, by distorting and twisting facts, and giving a false coloring, induce the press and public for a time, and almost immediately, to take away the character of a man who up to that time had stood high in their estimation. However, I suppose we cannot change human nature; we must be patient, await the period when the truth will slowly and surely make itself be known."[14]

Col. Charles Wainwright of the I Corps put it more succinctly when he wrote in his journal about the testimony of Sickles and Doubleday. "A pretty team!—Rascality and Stupidity. I wonder which hatches the most monstrous chicken."[15]

Meade returned to his army in Virginia, but the parade of witnesses continued in Washington. On March 7 Alfred Pleasonton arrived at the basement room in the Capitol. As the head of the Army of the Potomac's cavalry corps, Pleasonton had embarrassed Jeb Stuart at Brandy Station just before Lee's push north into Pennsylvania, but he had a less-than-sterling reputation. One cavalry officer said

Pleasonton owed his position to "systematic lying," and another called him "the greatest humbug of the war."[16] According to Pleasonton's testimony he was with Meade following the repulse of Pickett's Charge on July 3 and "urged him to order a general advance of his whole army in pursuit of the enemy." Instead, Meade sent him to determine whether the enemy was retreating.[17] A year later Pleasonton remembered even more about his dealings with Meade. This time he recollected that on the afternoon of July 2, Meade had ordered him to prepare his cavalry to cover the army's retreat, and he had spent the entire remainder of July 2, until around midnight, doing just that. Apparently this had all slipped his memory when he first testified.[18]

David Birney testified the same day as Pleasonton. He had his own ax to grind with Meade following the unpleasant encounter at Fredericksburg. "Meade is a fraud," he had written to a friend in March. To help speed Meade's departure from the army, Birney decided to cast his lot with Hooker and Sickles. "We must have Hooker back to this army and I believe he will be sent to us!" he wrote. He also had great hopes for the future of Dan Sickles. "Sickles will I think command this army and in time will be President," he had predicted back in October. So when Birney testified before the committee, he claimed that on July 5 he had wanted to attack the retreating Confederates but received an order not to do so. That was just the kind of example of timidity the congressmen were seeking. No matter that such an order never appeared in any official record, nor had Birney mentioned this incident in his official report.[19]

Following these unfriendly witnesses, the committee called a few who were better disposed toward Meade. Gouverneur Warren explained that Meade had in fact intended a counterattack on July 3 after the repulse of Pickett's Charge, but that the V Corps had moved too slowly to move forward before dark. Humphreys testified about Lee's defenses at Williamsport. "Subsequent information showed that the enemy had a very strong position, and indicated that had we made an attack we should have suffered very severely," he said.[20] Hancock testified on March 22. He said he had never heard anything about an order from Meade to retreat from Gettysburg.[21]

After these largely friendly witnesses, the committee called a decidedly unfriendly one. This was Daniel Butterfield, who had even left his new post out west without orders so he could travel to Washington and testify against Meade, no doubt at Sickles's urging. Like Sickles, Butterfield clearly had some scores to settle. "There is something strange, if not uncanny, about the way Meade got into difficulty with those two cronies of Hooker, Generals Butterfield and Sickles," Edwin B. Coddington noted archly in his book on Gettysburg. Humphreys had once described Butterfield as "false, treacherous, and cowardly."[22] Now Butterfield took his opportunity before the committee to portray Meade as a befuddled man who was out of his depth and consistently sought and received the wisdom of his chief of staff—Daniel Butterfield. Confused and uncertain, the Meade of Butterfield's testimony relied on plans that Hooker had already made, so therefore Hooker was the true architect of the victory at Gettysburg. Butterfield also told the committee that on July 2 Meade had asked him to prepare an order to withdraw from Gettysburg. "He may have desired it prepared for an emergency, without any view of executing it then, or he may have had it prepared with a full view of its execution," Butterfield said, carefully covering his own behind.[23] His testimony, though, indicated well enough what he thought Meade wanted to do, which was retreat.

The plot had thickened somewhat by the time Meade returned to Washington on April 4 to resume his defense. On March 12, a week after Meade's original testimony, a letter signed "Historicus" appeared in the *New York Herald*. It purported to tell the *real* story of what had happened at Gettysburg. The anonymous author had only one motive, he wrote: "to vindicate history, do honor to the fallen and justice to the survivors when unfairly impeached." Readers might suspect other motives, such as burnishing the reputation of General Sickles and tearing down that of General Meade. "It has since been stated, upon unquestionable authority, that General Meade had decided upon a retreat, and that an order to withdraw from the position held by our enemy was penned by his chief of staff, General Butterfield, though happily its promulgation never took place," Historicus related. "Without meaning to do injustice to General Meade, it must be admitted that his report of this great battle is at such variance with all the statements which have appeared in the press, that it is due not only to history, but to the indomitable prowess of our heroic army, that every fact sustained by concurrent testimony should be given in order to fully establish the truth. I reserve for any suitable occasion, abundant documentary evidence to support the facts furnished."[24]

The article enraged Meade. On March 15 he wrote to the army's assistant adjutant general, Col. E. D. Townsend. "I cannot resist the belief that this letter was either written or dictated by Major General D. E. Sickles," he said, and requested a court of inquiry to get to the bottom of the matter. Both Halleck and the president counseled Meade to avoid getting involved a public dispute with Sickles. "The country knows that, at all events, you have done good services; and I believe it agrees with me that it is much better for you to be engaged in trying to do more, than to be diverted, as you necessarily would be, by a Court of Inquiry," the president wrote on March 29.[25]

Historicus returned to the fray on April 4, not only defending his previous account but also intensifying the attack on Meade. "The evidence of General Butterfield, Chief of Staff to General Meade, is known to be so ruinous to the reputation of the Commander of the Army of the Potomac that it will be a singular indifference to public opinion on the part of the government if he is allowed to remain longer in that important post," the pseudonymous scribe wrote.[26]

Meade's blood was boiling when he returned to Washington on April 4. He vehemently refuted Butterfield's implications that he had planned to retreat from Gettysburg. "I utterly deny, under the full solemnity and sanctity of my oath, and in the firm conviction that the day will come when the secrets of all men shall be made known—I utterly deny ever having intended or thought, for one instant, to withdraw that army, unless the military contingencies which the future should develop during the course of the day might render it a matter of necessity that the army should be withdrawn," he said.[27]

Other generals testified in his support. Henry Hunt asserted that, as head of artillery, he certainly would have known about any move to retreat because he would have had to move his ammunition trains. Sedgwick said that, as second in command at Gettysburg, he certainly would have known if Meade intended to retreat—and if Meade did intend that, then why did he have the VI Corps make its forced march to Gettysburg in the first place? He also explained why he did not recommend an attack at Williamsport.

The committee didn't publish its report on the Meade investigation until May 22, 1865. It criticized Meade for not attacking Lee after Gettysburg and for letting him escape from Williamsport. In the book he edited on the Meade hearings, Bill Hyde characterized the report as "filled with innuendo, half-truths, and outright lies."[28] With the war over, the country gave a collective shrug at the time but the persistent attacks have echoed down through the years. "Although the attacks against him did not succeed in driving him out of the army in disgrace, they greatly contributed to an unfavorable opinion of him, which has persisted to this day," Edwin B. Coddington wrote in 1961.[29]

Sickles never commanded a corps again, nor did he get Meade removed from command. Still, he did damage enough. For the rest of his life—and it was a long life indeed, crammed to the brim with scandal and chicanery—Sickles reinforced his version of what happened at Gettysburg. In speeches, articles, and letters he repeated again and again that Meade had intended to retreat on July 2 and that only Longstreet's attack on Sickles's extended position prevented the Union army from withdrawing to Pipe Creek. His attacks on Meade's abilities and his own revisionist history of the Gettysburg battle permanently sullied Meade's reputation.

That could be one reason why Meade was one of the last Civil War generals to get a monument in Washington, D.C. Winfield Scott has two, one erected in 1873 and another a year later. Hancock's statue, just down the street from Meade's, went up in 1896. One was built for McClellan in 1907 and Phil Sheridan the following year. Meade didn't get a monument in the nation's capital until 1927, more than sixty years after the Civil War ended.

Today the Meade memorial stands on Pennsylvania Avenue between Third and Fourth Streets across from the National Gallery of Art. This is not the original site. The marble Meade first stood almost literally in the shadow of the huge memorial to Grant that dominates the reflecting pool in front of the U.S. Capitol. Construction of a highway tunnel forced the Meade statue into storage for fourteen years, until it finally reemerged at its current location in 1983. It's lucky the statue exists at all. Pennsylvania authorized $200,000 for its creation in 1915, but bureaucratic wrangling between the Meade Memorial Commission in Philadelphia and the Commission of Fine Arts in Washington brought everything to a standstill for three years. The head of the Meade commission was one John W. Frazier, a Union veteran who had fought at Gettysburg. Frazier could have learned a thing or two about diplomacy from Meade, and that's really saying something. He was notoriously truculent in his dealings with art commission members and stubborn about his own vision for the monument, which he insisted should include, among other things, corn and cotton production statistics for the years 1860 to 1912.

Things remained deadlocked until Frazier died in 1918 and more amenable Pennsylvanians found common ground with the Fine Arts Commission. They hired sculptor Charles Grafly of Philadelphia to design the memorial, even though Grafly's other sculptures "had drawn criticism, indeed scorn, for being incomprehensible."[30] The Fine Arts Commission must have thought Grafly's design for Meade was comprehensible enough, although it may seem a little odd to modern viewers. The marble statue depicts Meade standing back-to-back with a winged figure representing war. Loyalty and Chivalry helpfully remove his coat ("the mantle of war") while the naked figures of Fame, Energy, Progress, and Military Courage also share the pedestal. It's such a crowded scene that I can't imagine where Loyalty and Chivalry are going to find a place to put down that mantle.

The statue was dedicated on October 19, 1927, with President Calvin Coolidge and Pennsylvania governor John S. Fisher speaking. I'm not sure what Meade would have thought of the whole thing, but I suspect the statue wouldn't be his cup of tea. Nor would its current location. Although it stands in front of a federal courthouse now, in Meade's day the site was the headquarters of the publication now known as the *Congressional Record*. And his relationship with Congress was, shall we say, strained.

Meade could take solace in one thing, though—there is no statue of Daniel Sickles at either Gettysburg or Washington, D.C.

CHAPTER 13
Know-It-Alls

Daniel Sickles, Meade's archenemy
LIBRARY OF CONGRESS

• • •

When Jim Hessler meets me at the Gettysburg visitors center he sees my sweatshirt and lets out an audible sigh. "So you're a Red Sox fan?" he asks. Hessler is a native of Buffalo, New York, and he supports the New York Yankees. As the author of *Sickles at Gettysburg: The Controversial Civil War General Who Committed Murder, Abandoned Little Round Top, and Declared Himself the Hero of Gettysburg*, Hessler is an authority on the man some might call Meade's archenemy, and as we have seen, the Meade-Sickles rivalry makes the relationship between the Red Sox and the Yankees look positively friendly. Hessler is also a Licensed Battlefield Guide here at Gettysburg, and I've arranged to take a battlefield tour with him so that I can not only get his perspective on Meade and Sickles, but also find out what he tells his tour groups—and what they tell him.

Hessler is in his early forties. He's wearing a battlefield guide cap. He has blue eyes and a trim goatee and looks a little like—and I don't have the heart to tell him this—former Red Sox knuckleballer Tim Wakefield.

It wasn't a visit to Gettysburg that initially sparked Hessler's interest in the Civil War, at least not directly. It was a Christmas gift. He was already something of a history enthusiast when, sometime in the early 1990s, his future mother-in-law gave him a copy of Michael Shaara's Gettysburg novel *The Killer Angels*. The novel and its movie adaption, *Gettysburg*, pulled him into the topic. "A lot of hardcore people like to criticize that stuff, but it is a good way to get you hooked on the story," says Hessler. As he read more and more about the Civil War, he and his wife started talking about the possibilities of moving to Gettysburg. When they finally did, Hessler decided to become a licensed battlefield guide.

Some Civil War buffs can come across as know-it-alls, but that's a job requirement for battlefield guides. If you want to get a guide license you must be prepared to spend a *lot* of time reading about Gettysburg and the war. Hessler says he went "super hardcore" for about two years as he focused his reading exclusively on the Civil War and the battle here. "Every day and every night," he says. "For that period I was thinking of nothing but Gettysburg."

The first hurdle is a written exam, normally administered to candidates in January every other year. Those who make the cut on the written test next take an oral exam in the guise of a mock two-hour tour with a park ranger and a licensed guide assuming the roles of visitors. "To say the least it is a nerve wracking experience that once endured, you do not wish to do again," say the guidelines for the Association of Licensed Battlefield Guides. Hessler tells me a lot of people freak out over the oral exam; some even pass the written test but quit the process before they have to take the oral part. Hessler says he was more worried about the written portion. "I don't think the oral exam is quite as excruciating as some people let themselves make it out to be," he says, though it's not necessarily something he'd want to go through again.

The Park Service determines how many licensed guides it needs—currently there are about 150 at Gettysburg, give or take—and considers them self-employed contractors. On a day when they are available, the guides sign in at the visitors center and wait in a guide room until it's their turn to give a tour. It sounds to me a little bit like being a caddie. Some guides might give two hundred tours a year, but Hessler, who has to balance his full-time job in banking and a young family, averages about sixty.

Most of the people who take his tours are average folks who are not that well versed in the Civil War. The hardcore buffs may sometimes scoff at them, Hessler says, "but at least they've taken the effort to come here," and maybe the tour will spark an interest that turns someone into an enthusiast. Hessler has heard the old jokes that visitors ask why the soldiers didn't just hide behind the monuments or why the armies always fought at national parks, but he's never received such questions. "I think the average person is just a little smarter than that," he says.

There's also the other side of the spectrum—the beyond hardcore Civil War people who sometimes challenge him on his knowledge. "I had a couple instances where I'd get into the car and some old-timer would say, 'I'm going to put you through your paces, boy, 'cause I know the Civil War,'" he tells me. Sometimes one person in a group will derail a tour by asking extremely specific questions that the others don't care about, such as the position of a single regiment on a map. "Heaven forbid that you provide a guy with a map that he doesn't quite agree with," Hessler says. "Then you're arguing with someone about a map, and the other twenty-eight people aren't getting their money's worth." He calls that kind of person an "intellectual bully." Then there was the man on one tour who accused Hessler of glorifying war and told him to get a real job. "So, yeah, you get the challenges," Hessler says, but he says the vast amount of his encounters are positive and enjoyable. When he first started, he received a bit of valuable advice from an experienced guide: "People are here to see the battlefield, not you."

Hessler's book arose from his experiences on the battlefield. "When I became a guide I found I really liked telling Sickles stories," he says. "You can get off the battlefield and get into murder, adultery and prostitution, and political underhandedness. You can't talk about that stuff with Robert E. Lee." Or with George Meade, I might add. He says that Sickles still excites passion from more knowledgeable people who see him as a classic villain and automatically assume that because he wrote a book about him Hessler takes Sickles's side. "A lot of people couldn't get this notion out of their heads that you can talk about a guy like Dan Sickles and not be a 'Sickles guy' or an 'anti-Meade guy,'" he says. "I never had a desire to get into one of those camps. I wanted to get rid of the nonsense on both sides of the house." *Sickles at Gettysburg*, which won the Bachelder-Coddington and the Gettysburg Round Table Literary Award for the best book on Gettysburg in 2009, is a very evenhanded work that avoids painting things in black and white. "Do I think Sickles was an interesting guy?" asks Hessler. "Hell yeah. Do I think he was right? Do I think he was wrong? I didn't really want to say in writing; I wanted to let people decide for themselves." He says the idea that he's a "Sickles guy" out to demolish Meade has subsided now that people have had a chance to read the book, but he can't go to any Civil War–related event without having a few Sickles jokes lobbed his way. That comes with the territory.

We walk out into the visitors center parking lot on this brisk but sunny morning and climb into my car. Hessler takes the wheel. The guides always drive—to keep from having to shout out directions all the time, he says.

From the visitors center we pull out onto Taneytown Road, drive past the Leister House, and head into town. This is when Hessler provides his groups with some basic battlefield orientation—Cemetery Ridge is here, Seminary Ridge is over there—and he points out Meade's headquarters as we pass by. "At this point most people know little or nothing about Meade," he says. We drive past the National Cemetery, where Lincoln gave the Gettysburg Address—something else that many visitors don't know a lot about, says Hessler. Most have heard of the Gettysburg Address but usually don't know any specifics about why or when Lincoln made it. "They seem to know that it was a short piece, and someone might ask, 'Didn't they hire someone else to talk?' But the actual occasion is a mystery to a lot of people." I ask him whether people bring up the legend that Lincoln wrote his speech on the back of an envelope. Occasionally, Hessler says, "but if someone even has that much of a background, that's usually the exception than the rule."

We head down Washington Street through the town. Another thing that many people don't know, Hessler says, is the history of Gettysburg. Sometimes they don't even know there is a town, much less that there was plenty of fighting in the streets. "By 1800s standards Gettysburg was a pretty good-size town," Hessler tells me, with a population of about twenty-four hundred people. He pulls to the curb for a moment to point out a gray brick building that is pocked and pitted with holes from bullets and shells. "I show them that and people are surprised that private residences have damage."

He pulls the car over again when we reach Buford Avenue opposite the Lutheran Seminary so he can show me the Carrie Sheads House, a three-story brick building, painted gray, with some gingerbread trim around the eaves. Something black protrudes from the bricks near the top of the building. "That's an artillery shell," Hessler tells me. "That blows people's minds." Carrie Sheads was the headmistress of a girls' school in this house when the fighting erupted. On July 1 the Confederates captured some Union officers here; Carrie hid the sword of a New York officer so the Confederates couldn't get it. Guides try to weave such human-interest stories into their battlefield narratives.

We continue over to Reynolds Avenue. Hessler pulls over again. This is where he takes time to give his visitors an overview of the Gettysburg Campaign and explain how the two armies got here. "Lee is definitely a focal point of my tours," he tells me, a little apologetically. He explains his reasoning. "Ultimately the Confederates are on the offense at Gettysburg, and it's a little more direct and compelling to talk about the offensive strategy than the defense." But this is also a good place to bring Meade into the story, Hessler says, for it was on June 28, the same day a spy informed Lee that the Army of the Potomac was farther north than he realized, that Meade received command. Hessler shows his groups a photograph of Meade—long gray beard, big nose, bags under his eyes. "Do you know who this guy is?" he asks them, and more often than not, he says, the answer is "no."

"Yes, there is a notion among the general public that Grant is in command of the army here at Gettysburg, or they really don't know who's commanding the Union army," he tells me. "I always get a little chuckle when I say, 'Ladies, even though he doesn't look it, he's actually younger than Lee, fifty-six to forty-seven. People will always look at the bags and the wrinkles and say, 'Wow, there's some hard living.'" He also points out that Meade had been in command for only three days when the fighting started here. "Put yourself in Meade's shoes," he tells them. "What would you do?" He mentions that Meade had orders to keep Washington and Baltimore covered. "And after that Meade disappears from the tour for a little while."

We resume our drive up Oak Hill and get out at the Eternal Light Peace Memorial, which President Franklin Roosevelt dedicated in 1938 on the battle's seventy-fifth anniversary. Hessler shows me a photograph of the event and mentions that a few veterans of the fighting were present in the audience. Since he became a guide eleven years ago Hessler has met people, some of them fellow guides, who were in that crowd as kids. "What I like to tell people is that I don't consider myself that old of a guy, but I knew people who knew people who fought in the Battle of Gettysburg. That gives you a sense that it's not that long ago."

Oak Hill is a fine place from which to look out over the battlefield and get an idea of the fighting on the first day. A. P. Hill's corps had approached from the west. Ewell's corps, in the meantime, was coming onto the battlefield around where we stand, moving in from the north in response to Lee's orders to concentrate the army. The Union I and XI Corps were down in the fields below us, stretched too thin in an unfavorable position to face enemy soldiers coming from two directions. Outflanked, the Union forces had to retreat through the town and up to the heights of Cemetery Hill, its position indicated by trees we can see off in the distance.

As we drive back toward Seminary Ridge we pass several houses right on the battlefield, something that almost always surprises Hessler's visitors. This provides him with a good opportunity to explain that Congressman Daniel Sickles was the driving force behind the battlefield's preservation. In December 1894 Sickles introduced a bill to have some eight hundred acres of land preserved as a national military park. When the bill passed, the boundaries it established for the park came from a map Sickles had drawn up. "I find it interesting that many people today who hate Sickles with as much enthusiasm as anyone that I know make their living off the battlefield," Hessler tells me. "A friend of mine says, 'Well, it's not such a big deal, someone else would have created the battlefield.' Well, it doesn't matter if somebody else would have—he did." According to legend, when someone asked the aged Dan Sickles why he didn't have a monument at Gettysburg, he replied, "The whole damn battlefield is my monument."

We pass over a little bridge across some railroad tracks. On July 1, 1863, this railroad cut was the site of fierce fighting. Hessler tells me that in the 1990s a man was walking his dog by here when he came across a soldier's skeletal remains. We pass by the Lutheran Seminary—Buford climbed up into the cupola atop its main building to scout the terrain when he arrived here—and Hessler shows me another artillery shell embedded in the south side of the building where the seminary president lived.

Now we're driving down Seminary Ridge, where the Confederates formed after the fighting of July 2. Lines of cannons aim their muzzles over a stone wall toward Cemetery Ridge, where Meade formed his army. We stop the car and walk beyond the cannons, looking across the fields toward the abandoned hulk of the old Cyclorama building on Cemetery Ridge. This is where Hessler explains to his groups the significance of the two armies' positions. Meade had the advantage of interior lines with his fishhook-shaped line, while Lee had to cover more ground by wrapping his army along the outside of Meade's fishhook. The interior lines gave Meade a great advantage. Not only did he have less ground to cover, but he also could shift men from one side of the line to the other much more easily. "I absolutely do believe that the fishhook is ultimately why the Union army won here at Gettysburg," says Hessler.

"I think what Meade ultimately does well here at Gettysburg is that he takes command quickly, gets the army in such a position that they can get up quickly, helps ensure that they stay in a good position, and ultimately will resist what's got to be a temptation, with pressure from Lincoln—and I'll often focus on the pressure that Lincoln's putting on Meade—but Meade resists the temptation to come out of that position and attack. And he really, at Gettysburg, lets Lee make mistakes."

He talks about Lee's plan on the battle's second day to have Longstreet make an attack on Meade's left flank. Ewell was poised on the Confederate army's other end, opposite Cemetery and Culp's Hills, to press the Union lines there, as either a diversion or, if he saw an advantage, a full-fledged attack. Hessler also tells me about the "backlash" against the perceived importance of Little Round Top, its rocky slopes visible across the battlefield and to the south. Some people today disparage the importance of Little Round Top and say that Culp's Hill, on the opposite side of the Union line, was much more vital. "I'm not going to battle what I could call the Culp's Hill people," he says. "A lot of them make some good points, and I definitely agree that Culp's Hill is important." He agrees that had the Confederates captured Little Round Top, it would have offered only a limited advantage as an artillery position. But the fighting there did slow Longstreet's flank attack on July 2, and that helped the Union.

We get back in the car and continue on down Seminary Ridge and circle the Virginia Monument, with Robert E. Lee's statue high atop it. I mention my opinion that if people without knowledge of the battle compared the statues, they might surmise that Lee won. "And historically, he probably did win," says Hessler.

When we stop to take a look at the Longstreet statue farther down Seminary Ridge, Hessler tells me that some people on his tours are more familiar with Longstreet than they are with Meade. He shows me a photo taken at the Gettysburg anniversary in 1888 with the aged figures of Joshua Chamberlain, James Longstreet, and Dan Sickles posing for the camera. "I'm not a big fan of the brother against brother, shaking hands over the wall kind of stuff," he says. "Some of it is hokey and overplayed. But I do love the stories of these guys being drinking buddies into the night, and Sickles saying things to Longstreet like, 'You should apologize for shooting my leg off,' and Longstreet saying, 'Apologize? You should thank me for leaving you one leg to stand on.'"

We turn left down the Wheatfield Road and pull off the road at the Peach Orchard. Now we are in Sickles country, on the high ground that he wanted to control when he moved the III Corps forward on July 2. Down below toward Cemetery Ridge I can see the Trostle barn, a spot of black in the red brick indicating where a cannonball hit it, and near the barn I can see the monument that marks the spot where Sickles was wounded. Farther below that is the line where Meade wanted Sickles to form his corps. Instead, Sickles moved his men way out here. We're standing near the spot where Meade rode out to talk personally to Sickles on July 2, just before Longstreet started his attack.

Hessler talks about Longstreet's flank attack and how the Confederates remained unclear about exactly where the Union left flank was. And he talks about the reasons Sickles gave for moving forward as he did. "His story over the next fifty years remains relatively consistent. What he basically says was that he was given verbal orders to replace the XII Corps in the morning, but the XII Corps left and he wasn't sure where they had been." More importantly, he didn't like the low ground north of Little Round Top. As the day advanced Sickles became more concerned about this high ground in front of him, and he did make efforts to communicate his worries to Meade. "Do I think Sickles moved into a weak position?" Hessler asks. "Absolutely. The results show that. The III, V, XII, VI Corps, artillery reserve—all these guys help him and he still can't hold the position." But he believes that Sickles was doing what he thought was best at the time and that he had tried to explain his thinking to Meade. "It's the classic example of a failure to communicate," he says. "Two guys new to their roles—God only knows how tired and worn out they are and how much that's affecting their abilities—two guys who don't like each other, who just don't know how to play nice together.

"Love Sickles or not, he is a hugely important guy at Gettysburg," Hessler says. "He is now influencing the whole flow of fighting here on July 2. Everything that is now happening is happening the way it happens because he moved forward." While you can criticize the way Sickles attacked Meade throughout the years, Hessler says, you have to admire his tenacity in the public relations war he fought until his death. Because Meade didn't pull him back from here—it was too late to withdraw safely—Sickles claimed that was proof that Meade had in fact approved his position. "That's where you do have to feel empathy for Meade," Hessler says.

After stopping to admire the view from Little Round Top we continue our tour, driving up along Cemetery Ridge toward the "high-water mark." Hessler points off to our right. "Somewhere up in here you've got Meade actually leading troops into action during those late hours of July 2," he says. "That's an interesting contrast with Lee," he continues. "At Gettysburg you don't see Lee getting hands-on like that. Meade does get hands-on on the afternoon of July 2."

We park across the road from the Meade statue and walk down to a spot to the right of the Copse of Trees, near the spot where Lewis Armistead, hat on his sword, passed through the Union lines. At this point in the tour, Hessler will talk about Pickett and how the name Pickett's Charge is a myth—it should be called Longstreet's Assault or the Pickett-Pettigrew-Trimble Charge. He talks about the Pennsylvania troops who defended this position, the cannonade that preceded the attack, and then the charge itself. "The infantry part of the attack really lasted only about an hour," he says, and once it was over, Lee had lost the ability to fight on the offensive here. At that point in a tour Hessler has everyone turn around to face Meade's statue. "There's the winner at Gettysburg," he tells them.

But while Hessler believes that Lincoln was being unrealistic when he wrote that Meade had only to "stretch forth [his] hand" to capture Lee, he does feel that Meade's actions at Williamsport, when he bowed to the advice of his corps commanders and delayed the attack on Lee's lines for an extra day, are open to challenge. "To me there was a little bit of leadership lacking there," he says. "I'm not saying it would have been a Union victory, but I think Grant would have said, 'Gentlemen, we're going in,' and if Grant would have suffered heavy losses, he would have said, 'Okay, we suffered heavy losses but we're going to keep going.' That's the difference between a Grant and a Meade."

◆ ◆ ◆

There are many other ways to explore the Gettysburg battlefield. You can drive around with a Licensed Battlefield Guide. You can walk or ride a bike. You can rent a Segway. Or you can ride a horse.

Today I'm going to ride a horse. It's not something I do often—in fact, it's something I tried to do only once, and then I couldn't get the horse to move. I hope I will have better luck today or I'll be wasting the $75 fee for the two-hour historical tour offered by Artillery Ridge, a combination campground and stables on Taneytown Road. After paying my fee and filling out the waiver form in the campground store (which, strangely enough, has a large selection of *Star Wars* collectibles inside glass cases), I head down to the stables. The rest of my group waits there in a little open-faced shelter.

We are a varied group. There's a family of four from Watkins Glen, New York. The two boys have never ridden horses before, although one of them offers the fact that he's ridden ATVs. A young woman has taken this ride before. A couple others have been on horses but not recently.

Diane, one of the wranglers who will be accompanying us, arrives to explain the riding rules and regulations to us. She tells us that if she or the other wranglers need to get our attention, they will call us by our horse's name. So when I'm assigned to ride a horse called Stony, I'm a little relieved—it's certainly better than getting Ariel or Sadie. I have to admit I had a hankering to get the horse called Rio, but he belongs to wrangler Paul, who reminds me a little bit of the late character actor Richard Farnsworth.

We set out on this bright October afternoon, a long line of thirteen riders plus three wranglers. We cross the Taneytown Road—Meade rode past here on the dark night of July 1 on his way to Cemetery Hill—and head onto the battlefield. Way off in the distance to the right I can see the statue of Meade atop Old Baldy on Cemetery Ridge.

I am a little disappointed that we don't have a live guide, but Diane explains that only a few guides are qualified to do the trail ride and none of them are available today. Instead, we all have on headphones, with little radio receivers clipped to our saddles, and we listen to a taped tour.

We ride into the battlefield and cross the line that Sickles was supposed to hold. It is a low portion of the field, and I can understand the attraction Sickles felt for the higher ground in his front. As we approach the higher ground up by the Emmitsburg Road, I swivel around and look over the broad expanse of the battlefield. The big dome of the Pennsylvania Monument is to my right. The boulder-strewn face of Little Round Top is to my left, with the tree-shrouded hump of Big Round Top right next to it. We pass the handsome brick Trostle barn, with its cannonball wound in the side. Next to it is the small monument that marks the spot where Sickles got hit by a similar cannonball. He was on horseback at the time, and I have to marvel that his horse didn't spook. Stony, who seems remarkably placid, probably wouldn't have either. In fact, Paul sometimes has to get behind me so Rio can coax Stony into putting a little more pepper into her amble and keep too large of a gap from opening between me and the rider ahead.

Before we swing right to go past the Trostle barn, a man stops his car on the road and gets out to take our photograph. I guess a long line of horses on the Gettysburg battlefield makes a picturesque sight.

We cross Emmitsburg Road near the statue of Andrew Humphreys, leaning as though frozen in the act of lunging forward. Humphreys's division held this position on July 2, forming the right of the III Corps. We continue on to the Spangler Farm, where we turn around and retrace our steps. By the time we return to the stables I'm feeling a mite sore.

The price for the riding includes free admission to the Gettysburg Diorama, a tabletop version of the great struggle. The diorama recently moved from its old home at the stables to a building on Steinwehr Avenue at the edge of tourist Gettysburg. This is where you can go to buy T-shirts, get your faux-Victorian portrait taken, eat ice cream and french fries, sign up for a ghost tour, or dine at a restaurant named for someone who died during the battle. Actually, you can do all that stuff pretty much anywhere in the Gettysburg town center, but there's a special concentration of it here. The strip remains a throwback to the time when families visited Gettysburg in wood-paneled station wagons, their legs sticking to the seats in the un-air-conditioned cars, and the kids wearing coonskin caps.

The diorama fills a large room at the aptly named Gettysburg Diorama and History Center. About twenty thousand miniature soldiers remain frozen in combat on a 1:72 scale battlefield that covers some eight hundred square feet. It's wonderfully detailed, with little puffs of cotton smoke coming out of the cannons and dead and wounded soldiers and horses littering the battlefield. After I study the diorama and the other artifacts in the room, I stay for the thirty-minute narration. I'm joined by the family from Watkins Glen. The dad is very impressed by the diorama, the kids less so. They're audibly squirming by the end of the half hour—especially since much of the narration is the same as what we heard on the tour—but we're all impressed when the diorama reverts to a night-time scene. The little houses light up from within, and tiny campfires dot the miniature landscape.

Then the lights snap back on, and before I head out toward the sunshine, I stop beneath a figure high up in one corner who overlooks this miniature Gettysburg. This lifesize figure sits in a wheelchair and has only one leg. It is Dan Sickles. I guess the whole damned diorama is his monument.

CHAPTER 14

The New Boss

Ulysses S. Grant
LIBRARY OF CONGRESS

◆ ◆ ◆

There was a time when Grant's tomb might have ranked with the Seven Wonders of the Ancient World. Even in today's more jaded modern one it remains pretty impressive. The huge domed building of granite, with columns and pediments, stands upon a bluff above the Hudson River in Manhattan's uptown Riverside neighborhood. Two large stone eagles stand alert, wings spread, at the base of the broad steps in front. They lead up toward six Doric columns that guard the entrance. Even higher, two classical figures lean against a stone plaque that bears the words "Let us have peace." Above that the dome rests on a ring of more elaborate Ionic columns.

When it comes to tombs, they just don't make 'em like this anymore. Ulysses S. Grant's tomb is more than just a punch line to an old joke, it remains North America's largest mausoleum, erected through the efforts of what was then the nation's biggest public fund-raising effort (even if the $600,000 it raised seems like small change today). Construction took twelve years.

When completed in 1897 the tomb appeared even more impressive than it does today, for this part of New York was largely undeveloped and Grant's final resting place dominated the landscape. Now other buildings, including the grandiose Riverside Church, diminish Grant's monument, much as Grant's reputation has shrunk over the years. People now consider him one of the nation's worst presidents, a man whose administration was plagued by corruption and scandal. There's even talk of taking Grant off the $50 bill and replacing him with Ronald Reagan.

Except for the park ranger on duty just inside the entrance, the huge building is empty when I visit the tomb one weekday afternoon. I detect a faint smell of mildew when I enter. The main level is largely empty, a vast, echoing chamber of solemnity. The 150-foot dome towers above me. On the walls below the dome are three large mosaic images—Grant at Vicksburg with Sherman, Grant at Chattanooga with George Thomas, and Grant at Appomattox with Lee.

Directly below it, visible through a large circular opening at the main level, lie the twin red-marble sarcophagi that house the remains of Grant and his wife, Julia. When I peer down and see the name "Ulysses S Grant" engraved on the lid, I feel a strange emotion—almost shock—to find myself nearly face-to-face with this man about whom I've read so much. Unfortunately the mood is broken when I suddenly realize what those twin sarcophagi remind me of—the side-by-side bathtubs in the omnipresent erectile dysfunction commercials on television.

Descending to the lower level I see that the huge coffins are partially ringed by niches that hold busts of five Union generals. Surely Meade will be one of them, I think. But, no—they are George "The Rock of Chickamauga" Thomas, Edward Ord, William Tecumseh Sherman, James McPherson, and Philip Sheridan. Meade, who served loyally under General Grant until the end of the war, is not here.

At the visitors center I ask a park ranger about the busts. He tells me that gas candelabra originally stood in the five niches. They were removed in 1928 when Thomas Edison wired the tomb for electricity. The monument commission later decided to fill the empty spaces with the busts of generals who had served under Grant in the Western Theater. Still, it doesn't seem right that the commander of the Army of the Potomac does not get a slot here.

Adding insult to injury, I discover another statue in the little park on the other side of Riverside Drive that depicts none other than Daniel Butterfield, the man who "has never lost the occasion to stab General Meade's reputation under the fifth rib," in the words of early Gettysburg historian John Bachelder.[1] The statue, by Mount Rushmore sculptor Gutzon Borglum, was erected here in 1918 under the terms of the will of Butterfield's widow. I resist the temptation to shake my fist at it and shout, "Butterfield!" First he gets his own grandiose tomb erected at Meade's alma mater, and then he gets a spot in the shadow of Ulysses S. Grant's last resting place. There is no justice.

• • •

In many respects the Army of the Potomac that Grant found in the spring of 1864 was a new organization. Meade had requested that the army be consolidated from five corps to three, and the War Department issued the official orders on March 23. The I and III Corps, both terribly battered at Gettysburg, were broken up, their units distributed to the II, V, and VI Corps. That meant the departures of John Newton and William French, moves that created little regret. George Sykes was also removed from command of the V Corps; prickly, perfectionistic Gouverneur Warren now filled that post.

Alfred Pleasonton, the dapper self-promoter who commanded the cavalry, had departed, too. His replacement was the short, pugnacious, and eager-for-glory Philip Sheridan. "Little Phil" had commanded cavalry for a grand total of only about three months during his military career, but he had served under Grant in the West and the new general in chief liked his aggressive nature. When Lyman met him he described him as a "small, broad-shouldered, squat man, with black hair and a square head. He is of Irish parents, but looks very like a Piedmontese."[2]

"He was brusque, demanding, profane, and unforgiving," wrote biographer Roy Morris Jr. "He was also hardworking, patriotic, uncomplaining, and brave."[3] Sheridan would become one of the crosses that Meade had to bear during the war and afterward. He was a hard fighter on the battlefield and was equally aggressive at furthering his own reputation.

Unfortunately for the Army of the Potomac, Sheridan would not have a chance to command John Buford. The tough and dependable cavalry general, worn down by his grueling campaigning, had died in December of typhoid fever. The Army of the Potomac had also seen the last of Judson Kilpatrick, banished to Sherman in the West following an inglorious grab for glory. In February Kill-Cavalry had gone directly to Lincoln to suggest a raid on Richmond to free Union prisoners. Lincoln approved the scheme. Ulric Dahlgren, the one-legged hero of Hagerstown, volunteered to take part. Kilpatrick planned to take 3,600 men and approach Richmond from the north while Dahlgren, with 460 men, came from the south. Infantry and Custer's cavalry division would make diversionary attacks. Meade recognized that the undertaking was "a desperate one" but gambled that, if successful, it would be "the greatest feat of the war."[4]

It was anything but. Thwarted outside Richmond, Kilpatrick retreated down the peninsula to find safety behind Union lines at Yorktown. Dahlgren was killed in an ambush. When the Confederates searched his body they found papers outlining a plan to burn Richmond and assassinate Jefferson Davis and his cabinet. Lee sent photographs of the papers to Meade with a letter asking him if the U.S. government had authorized such actions. Meade replied that he doubted the papers were genuine, although he told Margaret that "Kilpatrick's reputation, and collateral evidence in my possession, rather go against this theory. However, I was determined my skirts should be clear, so I promptly disavowed having ever authorized, sanctioned or approved of any act not required by military necessity, and in accordance with the usages of war." It was, Meade admitted, "a pretty ugly piece of business."[5]

Some familiar faces had returned. Winfield Scott Hancock was back in command of the II Corps, although his Gettysburg wound continued to trouble him. Meade had not seen Hancock since Gettysburg and rushed out from his headquarters to greet him with obvious joy when he returned two days after Christmas. A staff member recalled, "I can hear his rich-toned voice as he said, 'I'm glad to see you again, Hancock,' and grasped the latter's outstretched hand with both of his."[6]

Lyman was meeting Hancock for the first time. "He is a tall, soldierly man, with light-brown hair and a military heavy jaw; and has the massive features and the heavy folds round the eyes that often mark a man of ability," he judged.[7]

Following the elimination of the III Corps, David Birney received a division under Hancock. He realized he had backed the wrong horse. "Grant killed the demonstration for Hooker, that was assuming shape, and would have ended in the decapitation of Meade," he noted in a letter on April 5.[8] Two weeks later he appeared, hat in hand, to mend fences. He told Meade he had never entertained unfriendly feelings toward him and hoped to serve under him again. Meade listened with an icy silence, saying only that he had never heard that Birney had unfriendly feelings toward him.[9] ("I am again on very pleasant terms with Gen. Meade," Birney wrote to a friend. "He assured me of his high regard, and desire for me to remain.")[10]

Perhaps the most surprising return of all was that of Ambrose Burnside. Following his disastrous stint at the head of the Army of the Potomac, Burnside had commanded the Department of the Ohio and fought in Tennessee, where he captured Knoxville. Now he had returned east to resume his position at the head of the IX Corps. It created a somewhat ticklish situation, though. Not only had he once commanded Meade's army, but he also outranked Meade. To prevent friction, Grant kept the IX Corps as a separate command directly under him instead of assigning it to the Army of the Potomac. This made an already difficult command structure a little more complex.

Burnside's corps added something else new to the Federal armies. One of his divisions consisted of African American soldiers. When he issued the Emancipation Proclamation Lincoln also opened the door for black men to fight for the Union, but many white soldiers did not accept the new arrivals with open arms. "As I looked at them, my soul was troubled and I would gladly have seen them marched back to Washington," Lyman wrote. "Can we not fight our own battles, without calling on these humble hewers of wood and drawers of water, to be bay-onetted by the unsparing Southerners?" Lyman either was unaware of the irony in his words or refused to acknowledge that Lincoln had transformed the war into more than a crusade to restore the Union. It was now a war to end slavery as well. Like many in the army, Lyman had little faith in the black soldiers' fighting abilities. "We do not dare trust them in the line of battle," he wrote in a letter. "Ah, you may make speeches at home, but here, where it is life or death, we dare not risk it." By the end of the war Lyman had gained a grudging respect for the African American soldiers, but he never abandoned his conservative views on race.[11]

The most important new arrival was undoubtedly Lt. Gen. Ulysses S. Grant, the new general in chief of the Union armies, as Halleck remained in Washington to advise the president as the army's chief of staff. Hiram Ulysses Grant was born on April 27, 1822, in a little house in Port Pleasant, Ohio, the son of a successful tanner. Grant's father wanted his son to get a West Point education, but after the Ohio congressman who nominated him to the U.S. Military Academy mistakenly called the future cadet Ulysses Simpson Grant (his mother's maiden name was Simpson), the incorrect name stuck. At West Point Grant's new initials earned him the nickname "Sam," after Uncle Sam. He was an unremarkable cadet, graduating twenty-first out of the thirty-nine members of the Class of 1843, and he fought bravely in Mexico without earning any particular distinction. Unlike Meade, he remained with Gen. Winfield Scott's army all the way to Mexico City.

After the war Grant married Julia Dent, the sister of a West Point roommate. It was a very happy marriage. Grant was posted to several dreary locations on the West Coast, where, bored, homesick, and lonely, he drank too much. The extent of Grant's drinking, especially during the Civil War, remains a much-discussed topic even today, but there is no doubt he seriously overindulged when he was at California's isolated Fort Humboldt. He was there in 1854 when he resigned his commission, supposedly over his drinking. Civilian life was not good to him. Although happy to be back with his growing family, Grant struggled to make a living by farming and by selling firewood on the streets of St. Louis. He was plagued by bad luck and poor business skills and ended up in Galena, Illinois, working with his younger brothers as a clerk in his father's leather goods store.

As it had for Stonewall Jackson, war rescued Grant from mediocrity, but it took a little time. When war broke out Grant offered his services to the War Department, saying he felt competent enough to command a regiment. He never heard anything back. A visit to George McClellan's headquarters in Cincinnati proved just as fruitless, as the "Young Napoleon" wouldn't even grant him an audience. Finally Illinois governor Richard Yates, aware of Grant's work mustering in local volunteers, appointed him the new colonel of the 21st Illinois. Before long he was promoted to brigadier general, thanks largely to the patronage of Illinois congressman Eli Washburne, who had taken a liking to the quietly competent officer.

In Missouri General Grant fell under the command of Henry Halleck, who was already honing his skills at criticizing and infuriating his subordinates. With Halleck's grudging approval, Grant planned campaigns against Forts Henry and

Donelson on the Tennessee and Cumberland Rivers. Both forts fell to the Union forces in February 1862, and Grant's demand for Donelson's unconditional surrender led to a new nickname that played off his incorrect initials. Halleck, though, remained distrustful of "Unconditional Surrender" Grant. Whether motivated by envy over Grant's success or concern that Grant didn't share his innate sense of caution, Halleck even took steps to remove him from command. For a brief time his military career hung in the balance.

But Halleck backed off, and Grant, now a major general, resumed his operations. At the Battle of Shiloh on April 6, 1862, Confederates under Albert Sidney Johnston pushed Grant's Army of the Tennessee back to Pittsburg Landing on the Tennessee River. Reinforced by an army under Don Carlos Buell, Grant reversed fortune's course on the battle's second day. Once again, though, he had incurred Halleck's displeasure. Bothered by stories that Johnston had surprised an unprepared Grant and perhaps by new rumors of Grant's drinking, Halleck insisted on taking command in the field. Halleck led such a slow, cautious advance on Corinth, Mississippi, that the Confederate army under P. G. T. Beauregard (replacing Johnston, who had been mortally wounded on Shiloh's first day) was able to escape. Embarrassed and depressed by the way Halleck had shunted him aside, Grant once again contemplated resigning. Gen. William T. Sherman, his most trusted division commander, helped talk him out of it.

Grant's greatest victory was his capture of the Mississippi River city of Vicksburg, "the Gibraltar of the Confederacy." Following a lengthy campaign in which Grant had cut loose from his supplies to live off the land and then placed the city under siege, Vicksburg surrendered on July 4, 1863, the day after Meade's victory at Gettysburg. The capture of Port Hudson shortly afterward gave the Union control of the entire Mississippi. Grant added to his laurels later that year by lifting the siege of Chattanooga and defeating Braxton Bragg's Confederate Army of Tennessee. In March he became the army's highest-ranked officer when he received promotion to lieutenant general after his congressional patron, Eli Washburne, had introduced the bill reinstating the rank. Grant traveled to Washington to receive his new commission and assume the post of general in chief of the Union armies.

The new lieutenant general often confounded people's expectations. Horace Porter, who met Grant during the Chattanooga campaign and became his aide-de-camp, said, "Many of us were not a little surprised to find in him a man of slim figure, slightly stooped, five feet eight inches in height, weighing only a hundred and thirty-five pounds, and of a modesty of mien and gentleness of manner which seemed to fit him more for the court than for the camp."[12]

Grant received his commission as lieutenant general on March 9. He was the first American to hold that rank since George Washington. The next day Grant took a train down to Brandy Station to visit the headquarters of the Army of the Potomac. Meade, who was almost seven years older than his new superior, had known Grant slightly during the Mexican War and considered him "a clever young officer, but nothing extraordinary."[13] They had not met since.

Grant made the fifty-mile trip from Washington to Brandy Station on the Orange and Alexandria Railroad, arriving in a pouring rain. His reception, however, was anything but stormy. Meade suspected that Grant might want his own man at the head of the army, so when the two generals met, Meade told Grant not to hesitate if he wanted to put somebody else in command. The work to be done was more important than the feelings of any individual, he said. Grant replied that he had no intention of replacing him. "This incident gave me even a more favorable opinion of Meade than did his great victory at Gettysburg the July before," Grant wrote.[14]

Meade also left the meeting with a good first impression. "In the views he expressed to me he showed much more capacity and character than I had expected," he wrote Margaret. "You may rest assured that he is not an ordinary man." In fact, Grant began to remind Meade of Zachary Taylor, which was high praise indeed. But he also warned his wife that instead of remaining in Washington, Grant intended to make his headquarters in the field with Meade's army. "[Y]ou may look now for the Army of the Potomac putting laurels on the brows of another rather than your husband," he said.[15]

It was a potentially uncomfortable position for both generals. Meade's relationship with Halleck, far away in Washington, had been testy enough. Now his immediate superior would be looking directly over his shoulder and perhaps interfere with how he handled the army. Meade might have seen this as yet another no-confidence vote from officials in Washington, but if he had any deeply wounded feelings he determined to keep them in check. "My duty is plain, to continue quietly to discharge my duties, heartily co-operating with him and under him," he said.[16]

Grant, who had suffered his own humiliation when Halleck took command on the field after Shiloh, was well aware of the situation's pitfalls. "I tried to make General Meade's position as nearly as possible what it would have been if I had been in Washington or any other place away from his command," he wrote. "I therefore gave all orders for the movements of the Army of the Potomac to Meade to have them executed. To avoid the necessity of having to give orders direct, I established my headquarters near his, unless there were reasons for locating them elsewhere. This sometimes happened, and I had on occasions to give orders direct to the troops affected."[17]

For many people, Grant remained an enigma. Morris Schaff, who served as Meade's chief of ordnance and later wrote a book about his experiences in the Wilderness, felt that he could never solve "the fascinating mystery in his greatness." Schaff had expected to encounter a dominating warrior. Instead, he discovered that the new general in chief was a "medium-sized, mild, unobtrusive, inconspicuously dressed, modest and naturally silent man. He had a low, gently vibrant voice and steady, thoughtful, softly blue eyes. Not a hint of self-consciousness, impatience, or restlessness, either of mind or body; on the contrary, the centre of a pervasive quiet which seemed to be conveyed to every one around him—even the orderlies all through the campaign were obviously at their ease."[18] Where Meade wore his nerves on the outside, Grant possessed an almost Zen-like sense of calm.

Like everyone else, Lyman tried to size up the new general in chief. "Grant is a man of a good deal of rough dignity; rather taciturn; quick and decided in speech," he noted. "He habitually wears an expression as if he had determined to drive his head through a brick wall, and was about to do it. I have much confidence in him."[19]

• • •

The Wilderness battlefield does not have a fancy visitors center. Instead, there's just an "exhibit shelter" on Route 3 near the intersection with Route 20. The shelter is a roofed structure, open at the front, that has a number of informational placards on the inside walls. One of them is titled "The Forgotten Commander." It is, naturally, about Meade. "Respected but little applauded, possessed of an acerbic temper, and overshadowed by Ulysses S. Grant, Major General George Gordon Meade commanded the Army of the Potomac during the Battle of the Wilderness," it says. There's an often reproduced photo of Meade standing in front of his tent near Cold Harbor, with a caption. "He has none of the dash and brilliance which is necessary to popularity," reads a quote from one of his officers.

I find more disparaging comments about Meade down the road at the site of Grant's headquarters, in a small clearing in the woods just off busy Route 20. This is approximately the spot where both Grant and Meade waited during the battle. The marker here is titled "An Uneasy Partnership." It has pictures of Grant and Meade and includes Grant's order to Meade: "Lee's army will be your objective point. Wherever Lee goes, there you will go also." It goes on to say that Grant had to fight not only against Lee, "but also against the conservative, sometimes timid, methods of the Union Army of the Potomac," adding that Meade was "a cautious leader" and that Grant "increasingly found it necessary to impose his will upon his subordinate."

It seems to me there's a lot more to the story, but it would be hard to fit it all onto a historical marker. The full story is one about how Grant gradually woke to the realities of fighting against the Army of Northern Virginia. Robert E. Lee was no John Pemberton, the general Grant had faced at Vicksburg, or Braxton Bragg, the general he had chased out of Chattanooga. Over the course of the Overland Campaign Grant learned some tough lessons about fighting in the East.

At the start of the campaign Grant warned Meade that he did not intend to fight by "maneuvering for position." Meade must have seen that as a critique of the army's campaigns from the previous fall. He replied, "General Grant, you are opposed by a general of consummate ability, and you will find that you will have to maneuver for position."[20] Meade was right. Throughout the Overland Campaign Grant attempted to overwhelm the Confederates with direct assaults, and then ordered Meade's army on wide, sweeping maneuvers in attempts to outflank Lee.

In fact, Grant and Meade wanted to begin the spring campaign by maneuvering to take the army through the Wilderness to terrain more suitable for fighting the rebels. The Wilderness was no place to fight a battle. Because its poor, acid-rich soil was bad for crops, there were few farms and clearings. The region's original forests had been largely cut down to feed local iron furnaces, and the second-growth woods were thick and in places nearly impenetrable, with innumerable little streams, or runs, snaking here and there, making maneuvering even more difficult. Commanders could not see their entire lines as they disappeared into the thick forests, and advancing units quickly lost all cohesion in the tangled undergrowth. Years later Francis Walker, Hancock's adjutant, still sounded frustrated by the difficult terrain. "How can a battle be fitly ordered in such a tangle of wood and brush, where troops can neither be sent straight to their destination nor seen and watched over, when, after repeatedly losing direction and becoming broken into fragments in their advance through thickets and jungles, they at last make their way up to the line of battle, perhaps at the point they were designed to reinforce, perhaps far from it?"[21]

On May 3 Meade wrote a letter home. "To-morrow we move," he wrote. "I hope and trust we will be successful, and so decidedly successful as to bring about a termination of this war. If hard fighting will do it, I am sure I can rely on my men. They are in fine condition and in most excellent spirits, and will do all that men can do to accomplish the object." In this letter Meade enclosed the note Lee had sent him about Kilpatrick so his son Spencer could have the Confederate general's autograph.[22]

The army began moving at midnight. "There is a kind of weird excitement in this starting at midnight," noted Col. Charles Wainwright, now handling artillery for the V Corps. "The senses seemed doubly awake to every impression—the batteries gathering around my quarters in the darkness; the moving of lanterns, and the hailing of the men; then the distant sound of the hoofs of the aid's horse who brings the final order to start. Sleepy as I always am at such times, I have a certain amount of enjoyment in it all."[23]

The plan for the campaign had the II Corps crossing the Rapidan at Ely's Ford and the V and VI Corps farther upstream at Germanna Ford. Meade and his staff left their winter camp at 5:25 a.m. on their way to Germanna Ford. The sun rose at the start of a beautiful spring day and illuminated a mighty host on the move. "As far as the eye could reach the troops were wending their way to the front," wrote Horace Porter. "Their war banners, bullet-riddled and battle-stained, floated proudly in the morning breeze. The roads resounded to the measured tread of the advancing columns, and the deep forests were lighted by the glitter of their steel."[24]

Meade soon found an occasion for an outburst of temper. At 7:00 he encountered a cavalry wagon train blocking the road, one of his pet peeves. The general gave the quartermaster a tongue-lashing and ordered him to move his wagons out of the way. An hour later he reached the ford, the same spot where his men had camped during the withdrawal from Mine Run. It had been bitter cold then and the army had been disheartened; now spring was bursting out in all its glory and the Union soldiers felt confident. "The troops were very light-hearted, almost as joyous as schoolboys; and over and over again as we rode by them, it was observed by members of the staff that they had never seen them so happy and buoyant," recalled a staff member.[25]

Meade and his staff crossed the river at 9:30. Grant and his staff, accompanied by Congressman Eli Washburne, joined them shortly afterward. Lyman noted that some of Grant's staff talked "flippantly" about Lee and his army and regarded the war as nearly won.[26] Grant established his headquarters at an old

Overland Campaign

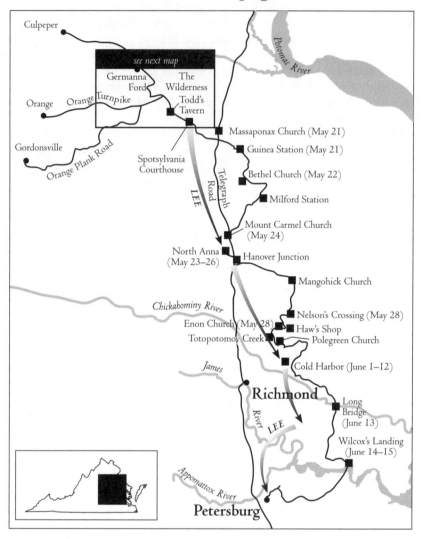

farmhouse overlooking the Rapidan. Meade dropped by that evening and took a camp chair by a blazing fire of fence rails. Grant offered him a cigar and helped him light it. The two generals sat by the cheery fire, smoking their cigars and talking over their plans for the next day. The move across the Rapidan had gone off without a hitch. "This I regarded as a great success," said Grant, "and it removed from my mind the most serious apprehensions I had entertained: that of crossing the river in the face of an active, large, well-appointed, and ably commanded army, and how so large a train was to be carried through a hostile country and protected."[27]

Battles of the Wilderness and Spotsylvania

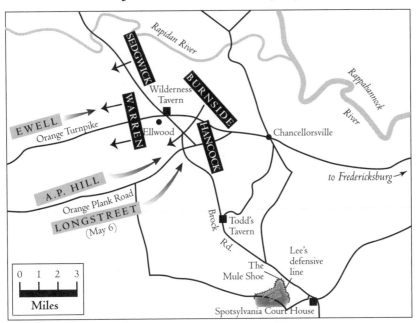

As Grant and Meade talked, messengers brought telegrams informing Grant that the other armies under his command—Ben Butler's on the James River, Franz Sigel's in the Shenandoah Valley, and Sherman's in Georgia—were advancing according to his plan to apply pressure all over the Confederacy. The Army of the Potomac appeared to be playing its own part in Grant's grand design. So far, so good. But the army had yet to emerge from the Wilderness.

Two major roads cut across the Wilderness, the Orange Turnpike (today's Route 20) and the Orange Plank Road (now Route 3). They ran roughly parallel to each other, about three miles apart. The turnpike lay to the north. Each route angled slightly southwest to northeast, until they bent toward each other and converged beyond Wilderness Church (west of today's Chancellorsville visitors center). Determined to strike the Federals while they remained in the Wilderness, Lee sent portions of his army down each road. Richard Ewell's II Corps took the turnpike, while A. P. Hill's III Corps advanced along the Plank Road. Lee instructed his generals to avoid a major engagement until Longstreet's I Corps had time to reach the field. But as it had at Gettysburg, fighting broke out despite Lee's intentions.

The Army of the Potomac resumed its movements early the next morning, May 5. Sometime around 6:00 a.m. Warren sent word to Meade that Charles Griffin's division of the V Corps had encountered the enemy along the Orange Turnpike. Meade and his staff hurried up to meet Warren. "If there is to be any fighting this side of Mine Run, let us do it right off," Meade said. He sent word to Grant, who was waiting for Burnside and the IX Corps back by the river.

"If any opportunity presents itself for pitching into a part of Lee's army, do so without giving time for disposition," Grant replied.[28]

At this point neither Grant nor Meade believed that Lee was moving his entire army to attack beyond the strong entrenchments at Mine Run. "They have left a division to fool us here, while they concentrate and prepare a position towards the North Anna," Meade surmised; "and what I want is to prevent those fellows from getting back to Mine Run."[29] Meade established his headquarters on a knoll near the turnpike, identified by a new standard he had adopted, an eagle surrounded by a wreath. The grandiose flag amused Grant. "What's this?" he asked when he first saw it. "Is Imperial Caesar anywhere about here?" Perhaps the pennant was a little gaudy, but it was important that couriers and commanders be able to quickly determine where headquarters lay.[30]

Warren established his own headquarters at Ellwood, the J. Horace Lacy house where Stonewall Jackson's arm lay moldering in the family cemetery. The house's front room now has a re-creation of Warren's headquarters; in another room is a large painting of Warren greeting Grant and Meade on May 5 at Ellwood, the two arriving generals on horseback. "The Forgotten Commander," a placard reads. "Grant never commanded the Army of the Potomac," adding that while Meade "thought highly of Grant . . . he resented Grant's presence—recognizing that Grant would get credit for success, while he would suffer blame for failure."

Warren dispatched a message to Griffin from here on the morning of May 5: "Have your whole division prepared to move forward and attack the enemy, and await further instructions while the other troops are forming." Then, wearing the yellow sash that marked him as a corps commander, Warren rode forward with his staff. When one aide ventured to point out a knoll he thought would be a good spot for artillery, Warren checked him. If he wanted advice from his staff, the general said, he would ask for it.[31]

The VI Corps' John Sedgwick found Meade at army headquarters shortly afterward. "Sedgwick, I am short of staff officers," said Meade. "Will you lend me one?" Sedgwick beckoned to Maj. Thomas Hyde. Meade directed the young major to ride back to Grant and tell him Lee was advancing and that Meade had sent the V and VI Corps forward to meet him. Hyde found Grant about four miles back and returned to Meade's headquarters with his party. Meade briefed Grant on the situation. "That is all right," Hyde heard Grant say. Then the general in chief sat down by a tree, lit a cigar, and started to whittle.[32]

Meade next dispatched Hyde with a message to Burnside. When the major returned, Meade sent him with orders to Brig. Gen. James Ricketts, the man Meade had leapfrogged over to take command of the I Corps at Antietam. Ricketts now commanded a division of the VI Corps. When Hyde reached Ricketts he found that an aide from Grant was already there with contradictory instructions. Hyde suggested that Ricketts follow Meade's orders, and then galloped back to explain the situation to the army's commander. "You did right, sir, but go back as soon as possible and tell General Ricketts to obey General Grant's order," Meade told him. "These words made an indelible impression in my memory, and show that Grant, while leaving the command practically in Meade's hands during this campaign, did sometimes interfere in details," Hyde wrote.[33] It also provided a good demonstration of the command structure's inherent awkwardness, as well as how Meade appeared determined to discharge his duties and cooperate with Grant.

Hyde rode some thirty miles and wore out two horses before Meade released him from his duties as a staff officer. The major returned to the VI Corps, which had been forming on Warren's right near the Orange Turnpike in the face of an unseen enemy someplace off in the thick woods. The forest was too thick for the Union artillery to do any good, but the rebels had managed to unlimber a gun or two someplace, for a cannonball suddenly came ripping through the trees and tore the head off a New Jersey soldier. The head struck Hyde, knocking him off his horse and leaving him covered in brains and gore. "Even my mouth, probably gaping in wonder where that shell would strike, was filled, and everybody thought it was all over with me," Hyde recalled. It took him a good fifteen minutes to pull himself together.[34]

The fighting intensified around the Orange Turnpike. "The rebels fought like demons, and under cover of the dense underbrush poured deadly volleys upon us," remembered Theodore Gerrish, a private in the 20th Maine, part of Griffin's division of the V Corps. "The air was filled with lead. Minie bullets went snapping and tearing through the pine limbs; splinters flew in every direction; trees were completely riddled with bullets in a moment's time; blood ran in torrents; death lost its terror; and men for a time seemed transformed to beings that had no fear." As the regiment prepared to charge across a clearing called Saunders Field, Gerrish saw rebel bullets kick up little clouds of dust and it reminded him of the first heavy raindrops striking the ground before a deluge.

With Brig. Gen. Joseph Bartlett at the head of his brigade, the Union soldiers pushed forward through a storm of bullets toward the trees on the opposite side, where the rebels waited to kill them. "A red volcano yawned before us and vomited forth fire, and lead, and death," Gerrish recalled. The Union lines staggered, but then lunged again against the rebel line. "North and South arrayed against each other, man against man," wrote Gerrish. "The sons of the Pine Tree State crossed bayonets with those who were reared under the orange groves of the far South. The rifle barrels touched, as from their muzzles they poured death into each others faces; the ground shook with the roar of musketry; the forest trees were flaming with fire, and the air was loaded with death." Amid a cacophony of gunfire, screams, cheers, shouts, prayers, and curses, the Union soldiers slowly pushed the rebels back.[35]

Horatio Wright's division of the VI Corps was supposed to be protecting Warren's right flank, but the dense undergrowth had delayed his progress. Warren had wanted to delay his attack until Wright secured his flank, but insistent orders from Meade finally spurred him forward before he felt ready. Warren's caution proved justified. The rebels outflanked him on the right and forced his men back to their starting positions. "We lost heavily in this attack, and the thick woods caused much confusion in our lines," Warren reported.[36]

The situation became even more horrific for the wounded still lying on the tangled and overgrown battlefield when fire broke out in the woods and, feeding on dead leaves and branches, raced swiftly across the ground. Wounded men desperately pulled themselves toward the turnpike to avoid being burned to death.

"Some were overtaken by the flames when they had crawled but a few feet, and some when they had almost reached the road," recalled a survivor of the 7th Indiana. "The ground, which had been strewn with dead and wounded, was in a few hours blackened, with no distinguishable figure upon it."[37]

Enraged by the lack of support from both Warren and Wright, Griffin rode up to Meade's headquarters at around 2:45, his face "stern and flushed." Griffin, who had started the war as an artillery commander, was a "tall slim man" with a "stalking walk, drooping mustache and sunken cheeks" who had an "air of decision," observed Schaff.[38] Like Meade, he had a volcanic temper. Griffin dismounted and launched into a tirade about his lack of support. He cast aspersions on Wright and Warren. Then he stormed off.

Grant had been observing Griffin's outburst. He turned to Meade. "Who is this General Gregg?" he asked. You ought to arrest him!"

"It's Griffin, not Gregg," Meade replied; "and it's only his way of talking."[39] Meade was no doubt aware of his own temper; he was hardly going to condemn a hard-fighting subordinate for his display of gunpowder.

It was becoming apparent that Lee had sent out more than a division. Meade needed Hancock now. The II Corps had been threading its way south from Chancellorsville toward Todd's Tavern, on the Brock Road about four miles south from the point where it intersected the Orange Plank Road. Meade sent Hancock orders to move north toward the fighting. He also dispatched Brig. Gen. George Getty's division of the VI Corps south in Hancock's direction to hold the vital intersection of the Plank and Brock Roads before A. P. Hill's division could get there first and drive a wedge between Hancock and the rest of the Union army. Getty—"a determined spare-faced man with a brown moustache and hazel eye," according to Schaff, "who never got all the praise he deserved for what he did at critical times on so many fields"—won the race just in time. He held the intersection until Hancock reached it around 2:00.[40]

Meade had Lyman galloping back and forth delivering orders and messages, which took him right into the middle of the action. "It's all very well for novels," Lyman later wrote in a letter home, "but *I* don't like such places and go there only when ordered." Around 4:15 Meade sent Lyman south to get a report on Hancock's situation. Lyman found Hancock in the tangled Wilderness on the Union left, musket balls zipping past through the trees. "Report to General Meade that it is very hard to bring up troops in this wood, and that only a part of my Corps is up, but I will do as well as I can," said Hancock. The situation appeared to be spiraling out of control. Lyman watched an officer ride up to tell Hancock that Getty was nearly out of ammunition. Another officer arrived to say that Gen. Gershom Mott's division had broken and was retreating.

"Tell him to stop them, sir!" Hancock roared, even as Mott's men came streaming back out of the woods. Hancock spurred his horse among the retreating soldiers. "Halt there! Halt there!" he cried. He dispatched his ubiquitous aide, Maj. William Mitchell, to find Gibbon and order him forward on the double-quick. Reinforcements began arriving. Among them was Alexander Hays's division, which entered the thick undergrowth and vanished. A few minutes later Lyman saw soldiers bring back Hays's blood-drenched body, a bullet through the head. Hays had been one of the heroes of Gettysburg when his division helped hurl back the Confederate charge on the third day. "He was a strong-built, rough sort of man, with red hair, and a tawny, full beard," wrote Lyman; "a braver man never went into action, and the wonder only is that he was not killed before, as he always rode at the very head of his men, shouting to them and waving his sword."[41]

When darkness brought the fighting to a halt, the two sides remained in a state of bloody stalemate on both the Orange Plank Road and the turnpike. In his history of the Wilderness battle, Gordon Rhea blames Meade for "failing to organize a concerted attack," yet he also acknowledges that Grant kept insisting that the Army of the Potomac attack "without waiting for disposition." Grant's inclination was to slug things out, whereas Meade's was to make sure everything was ready first. "The two schools of fighting were incompatible," Rhea writes, "at least as practiced by these strong-willed men. Mixing their styles produced ambivalent results that satisfied neither general and failed to achieve what either, acting alone, might have accomplished."[42]

At least one soldier disagreed with that assessment. Maj. Henry Abbott of the 20th Massachusetts believed that Meade and Grant together were "the next thing to having a man of real genius at the head." Meade was "a good combiner and maneuverer" and "unquestionably a clever man intellectually," while Grant had "force" and "character" and wasn't "afraid to take the responsibility to the utmost."[43] Together Abbott believed they made a good combination.

• • •

Fighting resumed bright and early on May 6. Grant had wanted the army to move at 4:30 a.m., but Meade, thinking that was too early for the exhausted and disorganized men—and perhaps because he suspected Burnside and the IX Corps would be late as usual—suggested 6:00. Grant said he would delay things by half an hour. Near dawn Meade and Lyman rode out to the Germanna Plank Road to find Burnside, who was supposed to move his men into the gap between the forces on the plank road and the turnpike. Burnside was late, however, delayed in part because the roads were clogged with artillery. One of his aides arrived and told Meade that if the general authorized the clearing of the roads, he would go back and hurry Burnside along. "No, Sir, I have no command over General Burnside," Meade replied. The IX Corps was not under his control—that was Grant's responsibility.

Back at headquarters the general ordered Lyman to report on Hancock's progress down by the Brock Road intersection. Lyman mounted his horse at around 5:00 in the morning. Already he could hear musket fire from skirmishers, followed by the loud, crashing volleys that meant major fighting had erupted.

He found Hancock in a good mood. "We are driving them, sir; tell General Meade we are driving them most beautifully," he said. But Hancock's mood darkened when Lyman informed him of Burnside's delay. "Just what I expected," Hancock snapped. "If we could attack now, we would smash A. P. Hill all to pieces!"[44]

The Union forces were doing a pretty good job of it even without Burnside's help. The situation was looking increasingly desperate for Lee's army. But then, as a blood-red sun rose higher in the sky, its light diffused by the smoke of battle, James Longstreet and the I Corps arrived, moving east down the Orange Plank Road toward the fighting.

A historical marker on the Wilderness battlefield driving tour details an incident that occurred as Longstreet's men came up and prepared to counterattack. It took place near the Widow Tapp farm, where Lee had his headquarters. As the Texas Brigade, under the command of Brig. Gen. John Gregg, began to advance, Lee rode along with it, swept up in the excitement of battle. But Gregg's men refused to let him risk his life with them. "Lee to the rear! Lee to the rear!" they yelled, some of them tugging on his bridle, until the general reluctantly turned back.

"Lee to the rear!" is a stirring story, even to a dyed-in-the-wool Yankee like me. It has entered the treasury of great Civil War tales. But as I read the story on the marker I think about Meade at Gettysburg on day two, sitting atop his horse on Cemetery Ridge, sword unsheathed, aides nervously arrayed behind him, with nothing between him and the advancing enemy. No markers recount that moment. No one after the war sought to add the patina of glory that would elevate the incident into legend. True, Meade lacked Lee's charisma. He had been in command of his army for mere days at that point. His men hardly knew him. Yet it is also a great story and one that deserves to be told.

But perhaps Union soldiers felt less need to repeat such tales of glory. After all, Meade's army had won the war. Lee's veterans had to find solace in something other than victory.

In any event, Longstreet's arrival gave Lee the chance to pluck success from a rapidly deteriorating situation along the plank road. The fresh Texans, Georgians, and Alabamians of his corps crashed into the men from Pennsylvania, New York, Wisconsin, and Massachusetts and forced them back.

The ghost of Stonewall Jackson haunted the Union army in the tangled Wilderness where the general had fallen almost exactly a year earlier. Hancock worried that Longstreet would attempt another flank attack up the Brock Road on his left. When he heard the cacophony from a cavalry clash taking place to the south, Hancock became even more certain that some of Longstreet's men were approaching from that direction. When he received orders to send troops down the plank road to support Burnside's arriving forces, Hancock also felt he had to send men to protect his left. Hancock's fear of a flank attack "paralyzed a large number" of his best soldiers whom he could have sent into battle instead of leaving them guarding his left.[45]

In fact, Longstreet had not sent men up the Brock Road. Instead, he had exploited yet another of those unfinished railroad cuts that so often played roles during the Civil War. This one ran through the woods off to Hancock's left and provided an excellent right-of-way by which Longstreet could spring a surprise attack on the Union flank. Hancock believed that John Gibbon was covering that general area, but Gibbon later swore he never received the orders. In any event, four brigades of charging Confederates under Lt. Col. Moxley Sorrel made their way through the woods along the railroad cut and then swung north to hit the Federals on the flank. The attack sent them reeling. "I well remember the route as the men streamed by in panic, some of them breaking their guns to render them useless in the hands of the rebels," said the chaplain of the 57th Massachusetts. "Nothing could stop them until they came to the cross-roads."[46]

The crossroads was the intersection of the Brock and Orange Plank Roads, where Lyman and Hancock watched the developing situation with increasing alarm. "The streams of wounded came faster and faster back; here a field officer, reeling in the saddle; and there another, hastily carried past on a stretcher," Lyman noted. Then a retreating mass of men emerged from the tangle of woods. Lyman noticed that they didn't appear panicked nor had they thrown away their guns. They had simply decided they had fought enough. "If there is anything that will make your heart sink and take all the backbone out of you, it is to see men in this condition!" Lyman wrote despairingly.[47]

Simultaneously with the flank attack, the rest of Longstreet's command, on Hancock's front, pushed forward. "When Longstreet's attack upon us began, it first struck the right flank of General Wadsworth's division," said Rufus Dawes, who commanded the division's 6th Wisconsin, part of the Iron Brigade. "General Wadsworth seeing his lines broken and scattered by the rebel onset on his flank, rode at once forward through his lines and I saw him pass through the ranks of the one hundred and forty-ninth Pennsylvania in the front line on our left, and ride in front of that regiment. He was instantly killed." Actually, Wadsworth, a wealthy New Yorker who had run for governor in 1862, lingered in Confederate captivity until May 8. When Dawes later asked why Wadsworth was allowed to ride to almost certain death, a lieutenant told him, "My God, Colonel, nobody could stop him!"[48]

Burnside was supposed to be coming to Hancock's support but had not yet arrived. Things were suddenly looking very bad for the Army of the Potomac. Then, in a near repeat of what had happened at Chancellorsville a year earlier, Confederate soldiers stole the momentum from their own successful flank attack. Longstreet had been riding between two units of his attacking force when shots from his confused troops rang out through the trees. One of the generals riding with him was killed instantly, and Longstreet was seriously injured. His wounds would not prove mortal, but he was removed from the battle and the army. His loss drained the energy from the attack. When the movement eventually resumed, the rebels encountered stiffening resistance from Hancock's men, who had retreated to the Brock Road intersection and entrenched behind a formidable log barricade.

You can still see traces of the trenches Hancock's men dug here, faint ghosts of the fierce struggle that took place on those beautiful spring days in 1863. A relatively new loop walk winds through the woods near the Brock and Orange Plank Road intersection to a new monument standing alone among the trees. The Vermont Brigade monument was erected in 2006 to commemorate the men from the Green Mountain State who fought and died here during the Wilderness battle. It's a seventeen-ton block of Vermont granite, with the shape of the state's Camelback Mountain crowning the top. On one side it reads, "In these woods, during the Battle of the Wilderness on May 5 and 6, 1864, Vermont's 'Old Brigade' suffered 1,234 casualties while defending the Brock Road and Orange

Plank Road intersection." On the other side is a quote from the brigade's commander, Brig. Gen. Lewis A. Grant—the battle's other General Grant: "The flag of each regiment, though pierced and tattered, still flaunts in the face of the foe, and noble bands of veterans with thinned ranks, and but a few officers to command, still stand by them, and they seem determined to stand so long as there is a man to bear their flag aloft or an enemy in the field."

The five regiments of the Vermont Brigade belonged to Getty's division of the VI Corps. They had been part of the force Getty brought with him to secure the intersection of the Brock and Orange Plank Roads on May 5. The next day they were involved in the furious combat when the Federals drove Hill's command back down the Orange Plank Road, only to be driven back in turn by the arrival of Longstreet's corps. Still later they fought off Confederate attacks in the entrenchments at the Brock Road intersection following Longstreet's flank attack. Their memorial stands here today thanks to the efforts of the Vermont for the Wilderness Committee, which lobbied for it and for the preservation of this portion of the battlefield. The purchase of 425 acres here in 2002 ensured preservation of the land, and $40,000 from the state of Vermont paid for the memorial. There's something about it that reminds me of the North Carolina monument on South Mountain. It, too, stands all alone off in the woods, as if it wants to have a quiet moment by itself.[49]

My wife and I, however, are not alone in the woods here. As we continue along the loop trail we catch up to a large, somewhat hulking man in a Washington Redskins T-shirt and calf-length jeans shorts. He has a wispy mustache and wears glasses. Like a modern Pied Piper without the music, he's leading a number of children of varying ages along the trail. It's an odd little group to encounter in the woods. "I used to hate the Civil War," the man tells us. "Then I moved here." He says his yard borders on park property and his proximity to the battlefield sparked an interest in the conflict. "But only about this battle," he says. "I'm not interested in the rest of the war."

● ● ●

After reporting back to Meade around 1:30 p.m., Lyman returned to the Brock Road. He found Hancock sitting under a tree, exhausted yet "very pleasant and talkative." Hancock told Lyman that his troops had rallied but they were disorganized and tired and in no shape to go on the offensive. When sounds to the right indicated that Burnside was finally making a spirited attack (which, in the end, accomplished little), Lyman encouraged Hancock to go on the offensive too, but Hancock said regretfully that it would be too hazardous. Hancock was, however, in a fine position for defense. The rebels learned this for themselves when they made one last charge around 4:00. The sound of the firing was "something fearful," said an officer in the 57th New York. "The horses plunged and reared; the balls whistled around our ears, and the noise was simply too terrible to describe."[50]

The Union forces, behind their barricades on a line that ran north and south of the plank road, held them off until flames swept through the forest and set a portion of the barricade ablaze. The scene had been hellish enough already; now the heat and the smoke drove the Union defenders back. Attacking rebels managed to capture a portion of the works. "I saw a rebel officer mount the rampart with a flag in his hand, waving it over the heads of his men," wrote one officer. But then a brigade under Col. Samuel Carroll, who had been wounded in the arm but insisted on retaining command, came to the rescue. "As the rebel flag was flaunting over the burning ramparts, Carroll's brigade came sweeping up at the double quick, and with a wild hurrah drove the rebels back into the mass of flames and smoke and recovered everything that had been temporarily lost."[51]

Meade had wanted Hancock to begin an offensive down the Orange Plank Road at 6:00, but he called it off after Hancock reported he was low on ammunition. Fighting around the Brock Road intersection was essentially over.

Compared with the intense work of killing along the Orange Plank Road, things to the north on the Union right had been relatively quiet. Fighting there commenced at 4:45 a.m., when Ewell's Southerners took the initiative and struck first by attacking the VI Corps. Farther south, Warren hesitated to sacrifice his men against the strengthened rebel positions on the far side of Saunders Field. Despite receiving increasingly testy orders from Meade, the cautious V Corps commander did not attack. For the rest of the day the contending forces around the turnpike remained in a stalemate, the rebels behind strong earthworks and the Federals unable to dislodge them.

The uneasy face-off continued until evening began to pull its curtain of darkness down on the battlefield for a second day. Then the Confederates launched a flank attack on the VI Corps on the Union right. The attackers were under Brig. Gen. John Gordon, a hard-fighting Georgian. The first troops the screaming rebels hit were brigades under the command of Brigadier Generals Alexander Shaler and Truman Seymour. It was the continuation of a string of bad luck for Seymour, the general Meade had suspected of sucking up to Reynolds back in 1862. Since then Seymour had been disastrously defeated at the Battle of Olustree in Florida and seriously injured leading an attack on Battery Wagner outside Charleston, South Carolina. Now his bad luck continued. His troops broke for the rear. The Confederates captured both Seymour and Shaler.

The men of the VI Corps fell back against Warren's V Corps to their right. "Suddenly there was a wild, fearful yell, a terrific crash, and the tide of battle rolled backward," remembered Pvt. Theodore Gerrish of the 20th Maine. "A portion of the Sixth corps had given way, and the enemy followed up the advantage thus gained, until they had completely turned our flank, and the firing was almost in our rear. Some of the regiments in our brigade showed signs of alarm at this situation, but the sons of Maine were determined to hold their position, even if they were surrounded and destroyed in so doing. The enemy's advance on our right was finally checked, and our line was re-established."[52]

When Meade received reports that another Confederate flank attack had routed a portion of the Army of the Potomac in the Wilderness, he appeared less concerned about it than Grant did. Fixing a cold eye on the panicked courier who had reported the VI Corps' destruction, he demanded sarcastically, "Do you mean to tell me that the Sixth Corps is to do no more fighting this campaign?"[53] In fact, Sedgwick had ridden to the front to help rally his demoralized men and soon had things under control.

Things did look bad for a time. Horace Porter reported an incident in which a general whom he did not identify reached Grant's headquarters and expressed his fears that Lee would seek to get between the Union army and the Rapidan, cutting off the line of communications. "I know Lee's methods well by past experience," the officer declared with some self-importance. The normally unflappable general in chief reacted with uncharacteristic temper. He stood up and yanked the cigar from his mouth. "Oh, I am heartily tired of hearing about what Lee is going to do," Grant barked. "Some of you always seem to think he is suddenly going to turn a double somersault, and land in our rear and on both of our flanks at the same time. Go back to your command, and try to think what we are going to do ourselves, instead of what Lee is going to do."[54]

Meade and Grant were right not to worry. Gordon's flank attack was the last major action of the Battle of the Wilderness. It had been two days of bloody and confused conflict, "a battle fought with the ear, and not with the eye," according to Horace Porter. "All circumstances seemed to combine to make the scene one of unutterable horror. At times the wind howled through the tree-tops, mingling its moans with the groans of the dying, and heavy branches were cut off by the fire of the artillery, and fell crashing upon the heads of the men, adding a new terror to battle. Forest fires raged; ammunition-trains exploded; the dead were roasted in the conflagration; the wounded, roused by its hot breath, dragged themselves along, with their torn and mangled limbs, in the mad energy of despair, to escape the ravages of the flames; and every bush seemed hung with shreds of blood-stained clothing. It was as though Christian men had turned to fiends, and hell itself had usurped the place of earth."[55]

It had also been something of an eye-opener for the new general in chief. Grant told Meade that Gen. Joseph Johnston, who had returned to command armies out west following his wounding at Seven Pines, would have retreated after two days of such punishment.[56] According to his aide John Rawlins, following two days of unrelieved tension, much whittling, and a great deal of cigar smoking, Grant retired to his tent, threw himself on his cot, and was wracked by sobs. On the other hand, Horace Porter said he looked into Grant's tent that night and saw the general sleeping as peacefully as a baby.[57]

When he awoke the next morning Grant knew what he would do next. Rather than renew the futile fighting against the enemy's entrenched positions, he decided to maneuver around Lee's right and toward Spotsylvania Court House. If he could capture this important crossroads, he could cut off the Confederates' line of communications with Richmond. Orders went out in the morning for the army to move that night and leave the Wilderness behind.

•　•　•

The Battle of the Wilderness had been a draw, a bloody stalemate. That, however, is not the verdict of a bronze plaque the Daughters of the Confederacy placed in 1927 on a boulder on the edge of Saunders Field, at the corner of Route 20 and Hill-Ewell Drive. This marker says the Confederates defeated the Union army at the Battle of the Wilderness. Historians might question that judgment, but the Wilderness did witness one clear victory recently: In January 2011 the retail giant Walmart abandoned its plans to build one of its supercolossal stores on part of the battlefield.

In August 2009 the company had received a special-use permit to build a supercenter on a plot of land near the intersection of Routes 3 and 20, about a quarter mile from the battlefield's exhibit shelter. Walmart claimed the property it wanted had little historical importance, an assertion historians challenged. "We're now pretty certain that the Union army command was on the Walmart property," says Jim Campi, the director of policy and media for the Civil War Trust, which spearheaded the battle to preserve the land. "Certainly, it was where the provost marshal was, where the artillery park was, hospitals, there was a signal station. We've got at least one drawing of Grant and Meade that we're pretty certain was drawn on the hilltop."

Those protesting the announcement included more than 250 historians and even actor Robert Duvall, who not only is descended from Robert E. Lee but also portrayed him in the movie *Gods and Generals*. To its credit, Walmart recognized the wisdom of a strategic retreat. Campi says that's "probably one of our biggest victories, certainly against our toughest adversary ever." In November 2011 the trust also announced that it had arranged the purchase of a 1.4-acre piece of land where Grant had his headquarters. The total cost was more than $200,000, about half of which came from the state of Virginia.

I've come to Washington to talk with Campi at Civil War Trust headquarters. He's decorated his office with several images of Meade, including a shot of the general wearing his characteristic slouch hat and standing in front of his tent at Cold Harbor. Campi, it turns out, is a longtime Meade enthusiast. Back in the 1990s he started a website he called the Meade Archives, in part because of his intense interest in Meade and also because he wanted to teach himself website design. A native of Lancaster, Pennsylvania, Campi was working for Congress at the time, so he had excellent access to the historical records in the Library of Congress. He collected as much Meade material as he could find, scanned it, and posted it in the Meade Archive. "I think I had almost every photo known of Meade on the site at one time," he tells me.

Campi thinks that history has given Meade a bad rap. "An objective study of Meade would demonstrate that the guy did a pretty good job, given what he had," he says. "The Army of the Potomac was never smaller than when he was in command of it up until Grant took over, and then he was, for all intents and purposes, no longer in command." As someone involved with politics, Campi was especially interested in the Joint Committee on the Conduct of the War and Meade's relationship with the press, which took a steep downward turn during the Overland Campaign. "He almost strikes me as a Patton-like character in a lot of ways: his temper, his fire, his no-nonsense approach," Campi says of Meade. "He was clearly a little more cautious than Patton was, but as a corps commander he was exceptional. It's hard to find fault with anything he did as a corps or a division commander."

While Campi defends Meade's reputation, the Civil War Trust fights to save many of the battlefields where he and others on both sides of the conflict fought. Started in 1987 as the Association for the Preservation of Civil War Sites, the organization later morphed into the Civil War Preservation Trust and in 2011 became simply the Civil War Trust. The name has changed but the goal remains consistent—to preserve the Civil War battlefields. "It's a race against time," says Campi. So far the trust has saved thirty-two thousand acres of land in twenty states, including land around Glendale, where Meade received his wounds on the peninsula. "Glendale is one of the great private sector success stories," says Campi. "Before the Civil War Trust became involved in Glendale, there was about an acre around the National Cemetery. Today, combined with Malvern Hill, there's over a thousand acres of land protected." Campi won't characterize those battlefields as intact, but he says they are in great shape "thanks to the preservation efforts over the last ten years." He says about a thousand acres around another of Meade's battlefields, South Mountain, still need to be protected. Maryland just provided money to save some of it.

Gettysburg continues to be a battle zone, as preservationists have twice beaten back efforts to build a casino nearby. On his door Campi keeps a photo of the local developer who served as the spearhead for the casino effort—just as some generals like to keep photos of their greatest adversaries. "He got his butt handed to him the first time," says Campi of the casino push. "He came back better organized; theoretically he had greased more wheels. I was frankly worried about it, but he got his butt handed to him again. Hopefully he's learned his lesson, but I don't know. The vision of riches probably does not go away quickly."

Nor will the threat development poses to Civil War battlefields. At least we know that Walmart shoppers won't be finding bargains on the land where doctors treated Union casualties from the Wilderness. Still, the pressure to develop in Northern Virginia remains intense. The fight to preserve the region's battlegrounds likely will continue for a long time.

CHAPTER 15

On to Richmond

Union generals at Massaponax Church, May 21, 1864, with Meade consulting a map at the end of the pew on the left, Theodore Lyman at his right, and Grant sitting with his back to the trees
LIBRARY OF CONGRESS

• • •

John Cummings and I crunch our way across the dry leaves that carpet the forest floor on our way to Myer's Hill, a place where Confederate soldiers almost captured Meade on May 14, 1864, near Spotsylvania. We are trudging up a slope through the trees on this crisp fall afternoon when we see them: five men moving slowly in a line off to our right. They're sweeping metal detectors back and forth across the ground, and Cummings immediately knows what's going on: these men are relic hunters, searching for bullets, belt buckles, buttons, and other items from the Civil War. That's a problem, though, because we are on private property. Cummings has permission to bring me here today, but as far as he knows, the landowner has never allowed relic hunters on the site.

Cummings, a heavy-set, trimly bearded man with a black baseball cap that bears the logo of the National Prisoner of War Museum at Andersonville, veers off and approaches the closest man. "Do you have permission to be up here?" he asks him.

"Those guys up there brought me here," the man replies in a Southern drawl, pointing up the hill. "They said they did."

As Cummings walks determinedly up the hill to the lead hunter, the man puts his metal detector down in the leaves at his feet. His cap says "Rebel" across the front, and his big plastic headphones are emblazoned with a picture of the Confederate guerrilla John Mosby and the words "Gray Ghost." There's little doubt where his loyalties lie. He wears a light camouflage jacket and has a belt that holds a foldable shovel, a bottle of soda, and a spade.

The relic hunter's name is Jim. It turns out that he and Cummings have met before, when Cummings was doing salvage archeology at the site of a new firehouse in town. Jim tells Cummings that someone told him this property had been condemned and that they were free to search it. "That's very interesting," says Cummings. "I'll have to call the owner and see what the hell happened." He makes a call on his cell phone and leaves a message. For the time being it appears we've reached an impasse. Neither party shows any inclination to budge. "We're all ex-military and ex–law enforcement," Jim says. "We don't want to break any laws." He tells Cummings they plan to donate anything they find to the county museum. Then Cummings's cell phone rings. It's the property owner calling him back. After a short conversation Cummings hangs up and tells Jim the owner doesn't want relic hunting on his property.

"Damn," Jim says softly. "We definitely don't want to break the law."

Cummings is diplomatic but firm. "I know that *you're* not telling me a fib, but someone gave you wrong information," he says. Reluctantly, Jim picks up his metal detector and slings it over his shoulder. Then he and the other four men trudge off through the woods. Cummings and I head in the other direction. As we head back up Myer's Hill, Cummings tells me he's not against relic hunting, provided "it's controlled, it's documented, and it's done with the owner's permission. Looters, no."

Cummings, born in Fairfax in Northern Virginia, is not only the guardian of this property, but since he moved here about twelve years ago, he's become a guardian of Spotsylvania's Civil War memories, too. "I was born with the centennial, in March of '61," he says. "I'm a mixed breed. My father's from New York and my mother's from southwestern Virginia." Cummings was only four months old when his father, a Lincoln buff, attended the events commemorating the one hundredth anniversary of the First Battle of Bull Run—Manassas, as they call it here. His father shot a roll of color slides of the reenactment, and as a boy Cummings grew fascinated by those little color photos and by his father's collection of history books, especially the illustrated ones. "That's all she wrote," he says. "By 1969 I had taken my first trip to Gettysburg." Now he spends all his available time on historical writing, research, and preservation issues. He has his work cut out for him. Just a few years ago, he tells me, the Civil War Trust declared all of Spotsylvania County one of the nation's ten most endangered areas.

◆ ◆ ◆

Flash back a few months earlier to a damp and dreary Sunday morning, when I arrive at the Spotsylvania Battlefield National Military Park to get a sense of what happened to Meade and the Army of the Potomac after the brutal fighting in the Wilderness. Like that battlefield, Spotsylvania has only an open-faced exhibit shelter, and it's the meeting place for a ninety-minute driving tour of the battlefield. The only other people here are an older couple from New York State. That means a healthy two-to-three ratio of guides to guided, for two rangers, Kyle Windahl and Jake Struhelka, will be showing us around this morning.

Today's tour will cover the events of May 8, 1863. The night before, the Army of the Potomac had disengaged from the Wilderness to begin a movement to skirt Lee's army by heading south toward Spotsylvania Court House. As at Gettysburg the town's network of roads provided strategic importance. If the army could capture this little hamlet, it would stand astride Lee's lines of supply and communications with Richmond.

Meade and his staff didn't get moving until nearly 9:00 p.m. on May 7. They began heading south through darkness made even more impenetrable by the clouds of dust the marching army sent into the air and the smoke from the fires that blazed and flickered throughout the Wilderness. Around the Brock Road intersection, where Meade stopped to talk with Hancock, exhausted soldiers slept by the side of the road where they had dropped, still clutching their weapons. Their officers paced back and forth and peered into the night.

The men who remained awake recognized Grant as he passed, and word of his presence spread through the ranks. They realized that despite the battering they had suffered, the army was moving on toward Richmond. "Soldiers weary and sleepy after their long battle, with stiffened limbs and smarting wounds, now sprang to their feet, forgetful of their pains, and rushed forward to the roadside," wrote Horace Porter. "Wild cheers echoed through the forest, and glad shouts of triumph rent the air." The fires still burning in the forest cast the scene in an eerie, flickering light. Grant worried that the cheering would reveal the army's movement, so he had his staff ride forward and quiet the soldiers. Then Meade and Grant resumed their course down the Brock Road toward a landmark called Todd's Tavern.[1]

Even generals, accompanied by their staffs, can get lost. The retinue took the wrong fork in the road and started heading toward the enemy, who were also moving south down a road off to the west. R. S. Robertson, an aide to Col. Nelson Miles in the II Corps' 1st Brigade, was surprised by the sound of horses heading toward him in the darkness. "Halt!" he cried. When the party stopped, Robertson recognized Meade at the head of the procession.

"Who halts me?" Meade demanded. "Do you know who I am?"

"Yes, you are General Meade," replied Robertson, who hastily identified himself. Then he politely pointed out that not only were Meade and his men about to trample over the sleeping soldiers of Miles's brigade, but they were also about to ride beyond the Union lines.

"How can that be—is this not the Brock Road?" asked Meade. No, it was not, Robertson said. He explained where they had gone wrong.[2]

Grant, who abhorred the idea of retracing his steps at any time, wanted to find an overland route that would get them on the right track without reversing course. His staff persuaded him that in this case a "retrograde movement" was necessary.[3]

The group finally reached Todd's Tavern around midnight, and soon afterward the friction between Meade and Phil Sheridan became combustible. Meade had ordered the cavalry to clear the road all the way to Spotsylvania Court House, but the Confederates still blocked the road to the south, and the cavalry division under David McMurtrie Gregg was sleeping at the tavern. Meade had no choice but to issue orders to the cavalry directly, bypassing Sheridan. He was, to put it mildly, not in a good mood when Sheridan arrived at his headquarters near Piney Branch Church.

"Meade was possessed of an excitable temper which under irritating circumstances became almost ungovernable," wrote Horace Porter. "He had worked himself into a towering passion regarding the delays encountered in the forward movement, and when Sheridan appeared went at him hammer and tongs, accusing him of blunders, and charging him with not making a proper disposition of his troops, and letting the cavalry block the advance of the infantry. Sheridan was equally fiery, and, smarting under the belief that he was unjustly treated, all the hotspur in his nature was aroused." Sheridan insisted that the problem lay with Meade's orders. He had already begun bridling under Meade's command, especially his orders that the cavalry should guard the army's trains and scout the enemy's position. Sheridan told Meade he wanted to be unleashed. "His language throughout was highly spiced and conspicuously italicized with expletives," said Porter. Meade, it appears, was the first to cool off, even putting his hand soothingly on Sheridan's shoulder. "No, I don't mean that," he said in response to Sheridan's remark that perhaps Meade should direct the cavalry himself. Sheridan angrily turned aside. "If I am permitted to cut loose from this army I'll draw Stuart after me and whip him too," the cavalryman insisted.

Meade then went over to Grant's tent and reported the encounter. He repeated Sheridan's boast that he could ride out and whip Stuart. "Did Sheridan say that?" asked Grant. "Well, he generally knows what he is talking about. Let him start right out and do it."

Meade must have been taken aback by Grant's reaction. Sheridan had been insubordinate to a superior officer, but instead of punishing him, Grant rewarded Little Phil with an independent command. Nonetheless, Meade returned to his tent and wrote out the orders giving Sheridan permission to move out on the offensive. The next day Little Phil embarked with ten thousand men. Riding four abreast, they moved down the Telegraph Road (today's Route 1) toward Richmond with a sound "like the rush of a mighty torrent" as they passed.[4]

Now I'm about to find out what happened to the Army of the Potomac on May 8. From the Spotsylvania shelter the members of our little group climb into our cars and make a short drive until we're on the other side of a low rise called Laurel Hill. We are now behind the Confederate lines. We walk through a narrow patch of woods and into a field. Looking back at where we came from, we can see the entrance to the battlefield park off in the distance.

Windahl tells us about the fighting at Laurel Hill. At first only a thin line of Confederate cavalry under Jeb Stuart held the ridge here, with Spotsylvania Court House to their backs and Union forces off in the distance marching down the Brock Road. But Maj. Gen. Richard Anderson, who had received command of the I Corps after Longstreet fell, had wanted to put some distance between himself and the suffocating smoke and the stench of death in the Wilderness. He had pulled his men out on the night of May 7 instead of waiting for morning and marched them south parallel to the Brock Road. These were the troops that Meade and Grant almost joined on their confusing night march. Anderson reached Laurel Hill just in time to throw his weight behind the cavalry.

The Union troops the rebels saw assembling before them belonged to Warren's V Corps. Windahl tells us that maybe things would have worked out better for the Federals had Warren taken the time to form up his men and make a concentrated attack. But both Meade and Grant had chastised Warren for his slowness in the Wilderness, and this time he launched his men piecemeal at the rebel line. The enemy forces, now being reinforced by Anderson's timely arrival, drove them back. The Confederates had won the race to Spotsylvania Court House.

From where we're standing we can see the heavy stone memorial at the park entrance. This marks the spot where John Sedgwick died, killed by a Confederate sharpshooter who fired from someplace around here. If there were a Famous Last Words Hall of Fame, Sedgwick would hold a place of honor. On the morning of May 9 he was near the Union front lines when he noticed some of his artillerymen dodging sharpshooters' bullets. He chastised them for their fear. "Why, what are you dodging about?" he asked. "They couldn't hit an elephant at that distance." Just then a bullet struck him below his left eye. His chief of staff, Col. Martin McMahon, was standing next to him when the bullet hit. Sedgwick turned toward him, and McMahon saw blood spurting from the wound like a fountain. Then the general fell, knocking McMahon to the ground, too. Sedgwick died almost instantly, a smile still on his lips.[5]

Poor Sedgwick! "We bore him tenderly to an ambulance, and followed it to army headquarters where an evergreen bower had been prepared, and there he lay in simple state with the stars and stripes around him," remembered Maj. Thomas Hyde, whom the general had been good-naturedly teasing just before he died. "All who came remained to weep; old grizzled generals, his comrades for many years; young staff officers, and private soldiers: all paid this tribute to his modest greatness."[6]

Meade was bothered by the fact that he had been sharp with Sedgwick at their last meeting the night before. Meade thought Sedgwick had been relying too much on Warren's judgment, so he snapped at him, saying he wished "he would take command of his own corps." It was the last time they spoke. "I feel more grieved at his death because we had not parted entirely in good feeling," he told Lyman.[7] Maj. Gen. Horatio Wright took over the VI Corps.

Lee's men immediately began strengthening their line with breastworks and repulsed Warren and Hancock's attempts to break them. Warren remained eager to prove he could be aggressive. On May 10, reinforced by John Gibbon's division from the II Corps, Warren hurled his men at the Confederates' now nearly impregnable line. The result was as bad as his soldiers had feared. As in the Wilderness, fires sparked by the shooting raged along the front, devouring the dead and wounded.

Bloodied but unbowed, Grant sought another means to break the rebel lines. This time he turned to Col. Emory Upton.

Lee's defensive position here above Spotsylvania had one very distinctive characteristic: there was a large bulge in his line. Because of its shape, this protrusion, or salient, became known as the Mule Shoe. Such salients were usually weak spots in a defensive line because attackers could strike them from multiple angles. On the west side of the big Mule Shoe salient was a smaller bulge, called Doles's Salient after the Confederate general whose brigade defended it. This is the spot where Upton intended to make his attack.

Doles's Salient is the next stop on the driving tour. When we get here the rain has stopped and the sun makes its first feeble appearance through the clouds. We get out of our cars at the side of the park road. There are still traces of earthworks here, shallow ditches that run alongside the road, but they are little more than hints of the strong positions the Confederates built.

The war had entered a new phase. Early in the war, when Lee had resorted to defensive measures, people had derided him as the "King of Spades." No more. By the time of Mine Run, the Army of the Potomac had come to understand the futility of attacking a well-dug-in position. "With the formidable rifles now in use, a single line of veteran soldiers, behind a three-foot breastwork of earth and rails or a stone fence, can drive back and almost destroy three similar lines approaching to attack them," noted one Union captain. "Give either our army or the rebels twenty-four hours' notice of an approaching attack, and they will select a good position, and throw up intrenchments, which it is folly for any but overwhelmingly superior numbers to attempt to carry."[8]

The defensive works here had proven equally resistant to attack, but Upton thought he could breach them. Ranger Jake Struhelka, who takes over the narrative at this point in the tour, tells our little group—now augmented by a father and son from Rochester, New York—that Upton was a young man with a burning ambition. He was determined to leave the field either "a live brigadier general or a dead colonel." Upton planned to make a rapid and concentrated assault at a single spot, and Doles's Salient seemed to offer the perfect opportunity.

From the road Struhelka leads us down the slightly sloping field to the tall trees at the forest edge opposite. We stop where a narrow trail emerges from the trees. This is the path that Upton and his men took when they silently approached the enemy lines late in the day on May 10. A monument to Upton and his men, erected in 1994, stands just inside the trees. At its base someone has left two little American flags and a postcard portrait of Upton, a severe-looking young man with roundish face, high cheekbones, a mustache, and a trim beard. He looks fierce and resolute. Born in New York, Upton attended Ohio's Oberlin College before he entered West Point. In 1859 he fought a duel with a fellow cadet Wade Hampton Gibbes, a South Carolinian who had declared that Upton, an ardent abolitionist, had slept with black students at integrated (and co-educational) Oberlin. The two cadets fought with swords one evening in an upstairs room at the barracks. Upton received a cut on the face but emerged with his honor intact. He graduated from West Point in May 1861; just over two months later he fired the first gun at the First Battle of Bull Run.

Upton's brigade had participated in the successful charge at Rappahannock Station the previous fall, so that may have influenced his thinking here. His plan was to have his men rush the enemy in a narrow column without stopping to fire. Once they broke through the enemy's works, they would swing left and right to widen the breach and wait for reinforcements. He had twelve hand-picked regiments, about five thousand men. The regiments are listed on the monument here. They came from Maine, Pennsylvania, Wisconsin, Vermont, and New York.

Struhelka assigns each of us in the group to represent a regiment. When I tell him my native state, he gives me the 5th Maine. He becomes the 5th Wisconsin, while the New Yorkers among us take on regiments from the Empire State.

Now we follow in the soldiers' footsteps from the edge of the woods, back up the slight slope to the road. I try to imagine what that fast, desperate charge must have been like for the Maine men I represent, knowing that at the end I would have to kill or be killed, that I might feel minié balls rip through my body or experience the sensation of thrusting my bayonet into another man. My imagination isn't up to the task. It's too pretty a day for the idea of sudden, bloody death to make any impact.

The soldiers didn't have to rely on imagination. On hearing the command "Forward," one man with the 121st New York remembered, "I felt my gorge rise, and my stomach and intestines shrink together in a knot, and a thousand things rushed through my mind." He knew the terrible odds against him. So did all the others. "I looked about in the faces of the boys around me, and they told the tale of expected death." The men charged across the two hundred yards or so that separated them from the enemy. They saw puffs of smoke appear from behind the log breastworks—each one an announcement of potential death or dismemberment. Men began to fall. The orders, though, prohibited stopping for any reason—not even to fire and certainly not to help a wounded comrade.[9]

Upton's men dashed through the hail of Confederate lead until they reached the enemy's line. They tore down the abatis—tangled tree limbs and branches thrown down as a barrier—and clambered over the log breastworks. The rebels on the other side waited, guns cocked, to fire bullets through the first heads that appeared over the works. Union attackers tumbled down dead. "Others seeing the fate of their comrades, held their pieces at arm's length and fired downwards, while others, poising theirs vertically, hurled them down upon the enemy, pinning them to the ground," Upton reported. His men poured over the enemy breastworks. "The enemy's lines were completely broken," said Upton, "and an opening had been made for the division that was to have supported, but it did not arrive."[10]

That supporting division belonged to the II Corps' Gershom Mott, but because of confusing orders and limited manpower (and, rumor had it, because Mott was drunk), his attack proved ineffectual. Down to the right, Warren, eager to show his fighting spirit, had already made his attack. Even farther down the line a brigade of Hancock's II Corps under Brig. Gen. J. Hobart Ward made another temporary break in the Confederate line before being driven back. On the far Union left Burnside made a feeble advance that accomplished nothing. Upton's men killed and captured more than a thousand enemy soldiers, but they lost nearly as many. Lacking support, they were finally forced to withdraw, past the spot where their monument stands today, and into the sheltering woods.

Grant gave Upton his promotion to brigadier general, and Upton's attack gave Grant an idea. If something like that could almost work with five thousand men, what would happen if he tried it with four times that number? Why not attack the Mule Shoe with the entire II Corps?

Ranger Beth Parnicza leads an afternoon tour, which answers Grant's question. We've gathered behind the rebel lines on a portion of the Mule Shoe, a broad, sloping field in front of us. She points out how peaceful the landscape is today, in stark contrast to what it was like here on May 12, 1864, when soldiers stood up to their knees in water, blood, and gore, fighting, killing, and dying for twenty-two hours in the pouring rain. Just behind the shallow remains of the entrenchments she shows us a relatively new memorial, erected to honor soldiers from South Carolina who defended the Confederate lines here. Parnicza tells us she likes this monument because when it rains, a little trench in the polished red sandstone around the base seems to fill with crimson liquid—just as the entrenchments here turned red with the blood of the men who fought and died in some of the most savage fighting of the war.

◆ ◆ ◆

Hancock's attack was ordered to begin at 4:00 a.m. That morning Meade rode over to Grant's headquarters to monitor news of the attack via the telegraph wires that had been strung between the various corps commands and headquarters. Around 5:00 the army's assistant adjutant general, Seth Williams, emerged from the telegraph tent with a glad smile. Hancock, he reported, had carried Lee's first line. A half hour later came even more good news: Hancock had captured guns and prisoners, including two generals. "Great rejoicings now burst forth," Lyman wrote. "Some of Grant's Staff were absurdly confident and were sure Lee was entirely beaten. My own experiences taught me a little more scepticism."

Shortly afterward a "strongly built man of a stern and rather bad face" wearing a shabby blue-gray coat and battered felt hat rode up to the group gathered around headquarters. Meade peered at the man and recognized him as Gen. Edward "Allegheny" Johnson, who commanded a division in Richard Ewell's II Corps. Hancock's men had captured him and sent him to the rear. The Confederate general dismounted and Meade grasped his hand. "Why, how do you do, general?" he asked. He then introduced Johnson to Grant.

"It is a long time since we last met," said Grant.

"Yes, it is a great many years, and I had not expected to meet you under such circumstances," said Johnson, who Lyman said appeared to be "horribly mortified" by his capture.

"It is one of the sad misfortunes of war," said Grant. He gave Johnson a cigar and had him sit by the fire.[11]

The other general captured that day was Brig. Gen. George Steuart, called "Maryland" to distinguish him from Jeb Stuart. "Maryland" Steuart was much less gracious in captivity and refused to shake Hancock's hand when the two generals met. Instead of getting a horse, a cigar, and a place by the fire, Steuart was sent to the rear on foot with the other wet and cold prisoners. His lack of grace appalled Union officers. "One of the pleasant features of our fighting is that none of us consider it a personal affair and individually are as friendly to any of our captured antagonists as though no state of war existed," noted one II Corps officer. "There is no personal animosity whatever, so far as I have seen." In other words, this was supposed to be a civil war.[12]

The realities at the Mule Shoe on May 12, 1864, were anything but civil. At first Hancock's men had indeed experienced success. They had massed opposite the Confederate lines in the pitch blackness and at 4:30 in the morning began their charge, moving silently through the darkness and then rushing forward with a cheer, the divisions under David Birney and Francis Barlow leading. They stormed the Confederate works in a rush, stabbing with their bayonets and clubbing with their muskets. They captured some four thousand prisoners, including the two generals, and forced the enemy back to a second line of defense. And there the wave crested. "Crazed with excitement Birney's and Barlow's men could not be restrained, but followed the flying enemy until their second line of works, half a mile in the rear, was reached," wrote Gen. Francis Walker. "Here the disorganized masses were brought to a stand by the resolute front presented by the Confederate reserves, true to those traditions which made the men of that army even more dangerous in defeat than in victory." Rebel reinforcements pushed the Federals back to the first line of entrenchments, where the fighting became even more brutal. By now it was raining hard. "For the distance of nearly a mile, amid a cold, drenching rain, the combatants were literally struggling across the breastworks," recounted Walker. "They fired directly into each other's faces, bayonet thrusts were given over the intrenchments; men even grappled their antagonists across the piles of logs and pulled them over, to be stabbed or carried to the rear as prisoners." Hancock ordered artillery brought up and the cannons fired over the heads of the Union soldiers into the mass of defenders.[13]

Meade now sent Lyman to Horatio Wright with the VI Corps to see how preparations were going for his attack, intended to support Hancock on the right. Lyman found the VI Corps already under fire and reported back to Meade. "Well, now you can take some orderlies and go to General Wright and send me back intelligence from time to time," the general told him. "There are some duties that are more honorable than pleasant!" wrote Lyman. He found Wright in a slight depression that provided some shelter from the enemy bullets and artillery, nursing bruises from a spent shell that had struck his leg. Lyman remained there for five harrowing hours as the Confederates, tipped off by the presence of horses, realized that officers must be present and tried to lob shells their way.[14]

Col. Rufus Dawes of the 6th Wisconsin called May 12 "the most terrible twenty-four hours of our service in the war." In the early morning his regiment had made one futile attempt to breach the enemy's lines on Laurel Hill. In the afternoon it received orders to move to the left and support the fighting at the salient. Dawes and his men moved through the pouring rain and thick mud choked with dead bodies. About one hundred feet from the enemy lines, the 6th Wisconsin stopped and opened fire. The Confederates remained hidden behind their entrenchments, but whenever the Federals attempted to move closer they stood and unleashed deadly volleys. Like many other participants, Dawes marveled at the huge trees behind the enemy lines that became too riddled with bullets to remain standing. "We had not only shot down an army, but also a forest," said Horace Porter.[15] (The stump of one tree ended up in the collections of the Smithsonian Institution in Washington, where it still remains.)

While Hancock and Wright attacked the salient, Warren was hesitant to move against the Confederate left, despite increasing pressure from Grant and Meade. Grant had just about reached the end of his patience with the V Corps' commander. He told Meade to relieve Warren if he did not attack immediately. Meade, who had also grown tired of Warren's stubbornness, concurred. Warren did finally launch an attack, but it failed to accomplish anything except kill soldiers who already knew any attempt to take Laurel Hill was doomed.

On the far left, Burnside launched an attack on the western side of the salient, but it soon sputtered out.

Fighting for the western corner of the Mule Shoe salient was so brutal the spot became known as the "Bloody Angle." The Confederates had elaborate defenses here, made of logs and earth piled up to four feet high. At the top of the embankment the defenders placed a "head log," elevated on sticks so the soldiers could insert their guns through the gap at the bottom without exposing their heads. Inside the works the rebels had shelves on which they could place their ammunition so it was always within easy reach.[16] Tangled abatis, fronted by a ditch, stood in front of the works.

Horace Porter thought the fighting at the Angle was "the most desperate engagement in the history of modern warfare, and presented features which were absolutely appalling." The fighting was savage, sometimes hand to hand, sometimes fought with bayonets and muskets fired nearly muzzle to muzzle or wielded as clubs. "Skulls were crushed with clubbed muskets, and men stabbed to death with swords and bayonets thrust between the logs in the parapet which separated the combatants. Wild cheers, savage yells, and frantic shrieks rose above the sighing of the wind and the pattering of the rain, and formed a demoniacal accompaniment to the booming of the guns as they hurled their missiles of death into the contending ranks." The fighting lasted through the day and on into night.[17]

After nearly a full day of such horrors, Lee abandoned the salient and moved back to a new defensive line his men had been preparing. After the rebels retreated, Rufus Dawes and his men from the 6th Wisconsin moved forward to occupy their entrenchments. They found a scene from hell. Dead and wounded men lay everywhere in the mud and filth. Dawes saw one corpse propped up in the corner, the head missing and the neck and shoulders badly burned. Dawes presumed it was the work of a Union mortar.[18]

Porter surveyed the result of the fighting the next day and found it "harrowing in the extreme. Our own killed were scattered over a large space near the 'angle,' while in front of the captured breastworks the enemy's dead, vastly more numerous than our own, were piled upon each other in some places four layers deep, exhibiting every ghastly phase of mutilation. Below the mass of fast-decaying corpses, the convulsive twitching of limbs and the writhing of bodies showed that there were wounded men still alive and struggling to extricate themselves from their horrid entombment." Another soldier who viewed the devastation called it "the most horrible sight I had ever witnessed."[19]

• • •

On May 13 Meade found time to scribble a quick note to his wife, in which he presented an overly optimistic account of the fighting for the Mule Shoe. "By the blessing of God I am able to announce not only the safety of George and myself, but a decided victory over the enemy, he having abandoned last night the position he so tenaciously held yesterday. Eight days of continuous fighting have thus resulted with the loss to the enemy of over thirty guns and eight thousand prisoners. Our losses have been frightful; I do not like to estimate them. Those of the enemy fully as great. Our work is not over, but we have the prestige of success, which is everything, and I trust our final success will be assured. I have not time to write much. God's blessing be with you and the dear children! Pray earnestly for our success."[20]

That same day Grant wrote to Stanton: "General Meade has more than met my most sanguine expectations. He and Sherman are the fittest officers for large commands I have come in contact with. If their services can be rewarded by promotion to the ranks of major-generals in the regular army the honor would be worthily bestowed, and I would feel personally gratified. I would not like to see one of these promotions at this time without seeing both."[21]

While the general in chief expressed his satisfaction with the Army of the Potomac's commander, his staff had reservations. Horace Porter recounts an incident on May 14 when Grant's staff had "an animated discussion" about Meade and his role in the campaign. They complained about the need to transmit orders through the army's commander. They said that Meade had little real responsibility yet stood to reap the rewards of any success. Furthermore, there was that temper. Grant's staff complained that Meade's prickly demeanor often irritated the officers who had to deal with him.

Grant listened to the sometimes "heated" debate and then expressed his views. He had other armies to deal with, he said, so he could not devote all his attention to just this one. "Besides, Meade has served a long time with the Army of the Potomac, knows its subordinate officers thoroughly, and led it to a memorable victory at Gettysburg," said Grant, according to Porter. "I have just come from the West, and if I removed a deserving Eastern man from the position of army commander, my motives might be misunderstood, and the effect be bad upon the spirits of the troops. General Meade and I are in close contact on the field; he is capable and perfectly subordinate, and by attending to the details he relieves me of much unnecessary work, and gives me more time to think and to mature my general plans. I will always see that he gets full credit for what he does."[22] By praising Meade and requesting his promotion, perhaps Grant was merely being politic, but there's no reason to doubt his sincerity.

In Porter's view Meade displayed "an excellent spirit" despite his sometimes awkward position. Since the two generals usually set up their headquarters near each other, Meade ordinarily showed Grant his orders before he sent them and sometimes handed Grant the communications he received before he even read them himself. Wrote Porter, "As Grant's combativeness displayed itself only against the enemy, and he was a man with whom an associate could not quarrel without furnishing all the provocation himself, he and Meade continued on the best of terms officially and personally throughout this long and eventful campaign."[23]

While the armies still faced each other outside Spotsylvania, Meade received a delegation from Washington. Sen. John Sherman of Ohio, who was General Sherman's brother, and Sen. William Sprague, who was also the former governor of Rhode Island, stopped by his headquarters. Lyman described them thus: "The Governor is a brisk, sparrowy little man with perky black eyes, which were shaded by an enormous straw hat. He is very courageous, and went riding about in various exposed spots. Sherman is the tallest and flattest of mortals—I mean physically. He is so flat you wonder where his lungs and other vitals may be placed. He seems a very moderate and sensible man."[24] Meade reported that both were very complimentary and said they understood that the fighting in Virginia had been his battles. Meade corrected them: "I told them such was not the case; that at first I had manoeuvered the army, but that gradually, and from the very nature of things, Grant had taken the control; and that it would be injurious to the army to have two heads."[25]

Meade, too, was wrestling with the exact definition of his role in the campaign. He told Margaret that one newspaper account said Grant handled the grand strategy and Meade handled the grand tactics, and another account described the army as "directed by Grant, commanded by Meade, and led by Hancock, Sedgwick and Warren." Meade considered that a "quite good distinction," saying it "about hits the nail on the head." Yet Meade was proud and ambitious and he did chafe under Grant's supervision. He complained to Margaret about how the papers overlooked his part in the campaign while praising the "rising sun" that was Ulysses S. Grant, but he did his duty.[26]

In his book about the Spotsylvania campaign, Gordon Rhea writes that by this point "Grant and Meade's military partnership had failed."[27] Yet I'm not so sure that the partnership was responsible for the failures in the Wilderness or outside Spotsylvania. After all, Grant had direct control over the IX Corps, but

Burnside's efforts throughout the first week's campaigning had been even slower and more ineffectual than those of the Army of the Potomac. It seems to me the real problem lay with Grant, not Meade. Grant had underestimated Lee and the Army of Northern Virginia—something Meade never did—and believed that brute force would be enough to achieve victory. Instead, it had achieved appalling losses—the army had suffered about thirty thousand casualties since the start of the campaign—and had little to show for it.

Of course, the rebels had also suffered terribly during the first week of Grant's Overland Campaign. In the long run that played to the Union's advantage, something of which President Lincoln was perfectly aware. After the Battle of Fredericksburg Lincoln had talked of the "awful arithmetic" of war. The Union had lost more men than the Confederates, Lincoln said, but if the armies fought the same battle day after day over several weeks with the same results, "the army under Lee would be wiped out to its last man, the Army of the Potomac would still be a mighty host, the war would be over, the Confederacy gone. No general yet found can face the arithmetic, but the end of the war will be at hand when he shall be discovered."[28]

While Grant could face the arithmetic, Meade certainly weighed the Union's side of the equation. He told Maj. Henry Abbott of the 20th Massachusetts that "Uncle Abe was very tender hearted about shooting a deserter, but that he was perfectly willing to sacrifice a thousand brave men in a useless fight."[29] Less than a month after that conversation with Meade, Henry Abbott fell victim to the "awful arithmetic." On May 6 Theodore Lyman had watched Abbott, one of his Harvard classmates, ride into battle near the Brock Road. Abbott caught his former schoolmate's eye, grinned, and waved his sword. Minutes later a Confederate bullet struck him down. Lyman went to Abbott's bedside at the field hospital and watched him die. Many more men would follow Abbott into the grave before the war was over.

• • •

After the terrible bloodshed of May 12 the two armies continued skirmishing for the next few days, without much to show for it except more dead and wounded. Grant decided to attempt an attack on Lee's relatively weak right flank. On the night of May 13 Warren moved out of his earthworks before Laurel Hill, leaving behind a token force to lull enemy suspicions, and made a wide swing from one side of the army to the other. Wright and the VI Corps were supposed to follow once Warren passed. Unfortunately for the Union forces, though, unremitting rain, dense mud, and pitch-black darkness stymied their efforts to reach the new position in time. Grant and Meade called off the attack.

On May 14 Meade almost fell into enemy hands when he rode forward to observe the Union position on Myer's Hill, the spot where John Cummings and I encounter the relic hunters. The landowner sold the timber rights a few years ago, and the site has become so thickly overgrown since the logging that we have to swing around the hill and take a less direct route—sort of a flank attack. A few trees still stand around the site of the Myer House at the top of the hill, and we push our way through bushes and brambles to get there. At the edge of the trees Cummings points out the hole in the ground that marks the farm's icehouse; a much bigger hole just beyond indicates where the main house stood.

Upton's brigade was holding this forward position on May 14 when Meade and Horatio Wright rode forward to examine the ground. The generals were conferring inside the house when the rattle of muskets and the thud of bullets striking the building delivered unwelcome news: the Confederates were attacking. Meade had to move fast. He jumped on his horse and, guided by Capt. Nathaniel Michler, a topographical engineer with some knowledge of the terrain, hastily made his way back toward the Ni River. A Confederate major galloped over to intercept him and even grabbed Meade's bridle before his headquarters guard intervened and captured the rebel. The only thing Meade lost, other than his dignity, was his glasses.[30]

The farm's owner, John Henry Myer, was a draftee in Lee's army. He was inside the Confederate lines nearby when Union soldiers set his house ablaze on May 15. Myer must have seen the smoke and realized his home was on fire. A week later he became a prisoner at the North Anna River—Cummings suspects he probably let himself be captured. Myer took an oath of allegiance to the United States in December.[31]

On May 18 the Union forces launched an attack from the north against Lee's new line. The men advanced past the old Mule Shoe salient, in some cases walking over the bloated corpses left from the fighting six days earlier. This attack proved just as futile. Burnside, attacking from the east, had equally dismal results. The next day Union troops, many of them green artillerymen pulled from Washington's defenses and converted into infantry, fended off an attack by Ewell's II Corps around the Harris Farm on the Union's northern flank.

The Army of Northern Virginia forced Grant to review his own arithmetic. "General Grant, who is one of the most candid men I ever saw, has repeatedly said that this fighting throws in the shade everything he ever saw, and that he looked for no such resistance," wrote Lyman.[32] Before the campaign Grant had told Meade that he did not maneuver for position, yet he had pulled out of the Wilderness to maneuver around Lee's army. At Spotsylvania on May 11 he had sent a letter to Halleck back in Washington. "I intend to fight it out on this line if it takes all summer," he had written. If by "this line" he meant the position in front of Spotsylvania, he would leave it before the summer even began. Within a week he started making plans to send Meade's army on another maneuver around Lee's right. The army began to move on the night of May 20.

Before I leave Spotsylvania I drive around with Cummings so he can point out the various sites where Meade established his headquarters when he was here. Some are now just fields or patches of woods; one of them, the Anderson House, has been swallowed up by a quarry. The Armstrong House still stands, but a plan to turn it into a bed-and-breakfast recently fell through and the large white house appears deserted. Mr. Armstrong had fled to the North, and his wife remained loyal to the Union. She was pleased to host Grant and Meade for lunch on May 12, the day of the savage fighting at the Mule Shoe. Meade enjoyed her fresh butter, "though it was intolerably garlicky to my mind!" noted Lyman.[33]

We also drive by the old Harris House, where the green Union heavy artillery units fought off Ewell's attack on May 19. It now stands in the middle of a modern "McMansion" development, with a For Sale sign posted at the driveway entrance. Nearby, Cummings points out a monument to the Massachusetts Heavy Infantry regiments that fought here. It looks out of place in the middle of a housing development.

Cummings is a font of local history. He's the kind of guy who, when his wife told him the address of the house they eventually wound up buying, said, "Do you realize it sits right on the path of Ayres's brigade?" He offers his services as a guide around the area. He has published a couple books on regional history and is working on another one about the medical photographs of a Union surgeon. He also has a book in the works about First Bull Run, maintains a blog about local history, and has organized a reenactment group that commemorates the United States Colored Troops. The unit so far has three soldiers and two white officers, so it has a ways to go. "By 2014 I think it's vitally important to do something to commemorate the first time that black troops actually fired on the Army of Northern Virginia," he says. That happened when members of Brig. Gen. Edward Ferrero's brigade—the soldiers who so distressed Lyman when he saw them—fended off an attack by Confederate cavalry north of here on May 15.

As we head back to Cummings's house, he points out another site. Late on May 17, 1864, he says, his great-great-grandfather, a soldier in the 7th New York Heavy Artillery, reached this intersection in the dark of night. "Most of the regiment turned to the right and went that way," Cummings tells me. "The rear four companies, which included his, turned left." By the time they managed to rejoin the regiment the next morning, they had just missed the bloody and futile assault on the Confederates' second line. However, they did not miss the battle at the Harris Farm the next day. During the fighting there, Cummings's ancestor received a bullet through his arm. "He was clearly in the position of shooting his rifle, as the bullet entered below the wrist and exited above the elbow," Cummings says. If things had gone just a little differently—— the company hadn't made the wrong turn or if that Confederate bullet had been just a few inches to the left— John Cummings might not be here today to tell me all this.

◆ ◆ ◆

I set out from Spotsylvania to follow the army's movements on my own driving tour, following the "Lee vs. Grant" map issued by Virginia Civil War Trails and using David Lowe's book of Lyman's journals to provide local color. My first stop is Massaponax Church, on Route 1. During the war Route 1 was called the Telegraph Road; today, with no sense of irony, it's Jefferson Davis Way. Lyman mentioned stopping at "the plain brick building" on May 21. He was here when Timothy O'Sullivan took a famous series of images from the church's second floor while Meade, Grant, and their staffs sat in church pews set up outside. In one of the three photographs, Grant is leaning over Meade's shoulder to consult a map. Lyman sits next to Meade.

Another man in the photos is Charles Dana, the assistant secretary of war. Lyman described him as "a combination of scholar and newspaper editor, with a dab of amiability, a large dab of conceit, and another large dab of ultraism."[34] Dana had accompanied Grant during the Vicksburg Campaign, and Lincoln dispatched him from Washington to report from Virginia. In a memoir Dana recounted his rather critical impressions of Meade. "He was a tall, thin man, rather dyspeptic, I should suppose from the fits of nervous irritation to which he was subject," Dana said. "He was totally lacking in cordiality toward those with whom he had business, and in consequence was generally disliked by his subordinates. With General Grant Meade got along always perfectly, because he had the first virtue of a soldier—that is, obedience to orders. He was an intellectual man, and agreeable to talk with when his mind was free, but silent and indifferent to everybody when he was occupied with that which interested him."[35]

From the church I follow Lyman's directions exactly. As soon as the V Corps' artillery passed, he said, "we remounted, went down the Telegraph Road a few hundred yards and turned sharp to the left towards Guinea Station." I do the same. Not only am I following in Meade's footsteps, I'm also tracing the route that Stonewall Jackson's ambulance took back in May 1863 as it bumped and clattered its way to Guinea Station. After a short drive through the Virginia countryside I cross railroad tracks and follow a sign to the Stonewall Jackson Shrine, the little white outbuilding where the general died.

On May 21 Meade and Grant established their two headquarters near here at the Motley House, where Grant caused a stir when one of his cigars ignited a chair on the porch. Perhaps to escape the recriminations of Mrs. Motley, Grant went over to the Chandler Farm, where Jackson had died, and met Mrs. Chandler. "She was ladylike and polite in her behavior, and she and the general soon became engaged in a pleasant talk," recounted Porter, who accompanied Grant. When Mrs. Chandler mentioned that Jackson had died at her farm, Grant told her that he had been in West Point with Jackson for a year and had served with him in Mexico. "He was a gallant soldier and a Christian gentleman, and I can understand fully the admiration your people have for him," Grant said.[36]

I get crossed up on the backroads on my way to the next stop—the Civil War Trails maps can be frustratingly minimalist—but eventually I find Bethel Church. Grant, Meade, and their entourage reached the church on the afternoon of Sunday, May 22. Like Massaponax, Bethel Church is a simple brick building with no steeple, but its rural setting has kept it relatively free from modern influences. If I ignore the plastic playground equipment out back by the neat cemetery, I can almost think it's 1864. When Meade and Grant arrived here they found Burnside waiting at the church, "sitting, like a comfortable abbot, in one of the pews, surrounded by his buckish Staff whose appearance is the reverse of clerical," wrote Lyman.[37]

Meade and Grant had their headquarters nearby, on the grounds of a house where a Mrs. Tyler and her mother-in-law lived. The younger Mrs. Tyler's husband was serving with the Confederate army in the west under Joseph Johnston; the older woman had just returned from Richmond, where, she told the Union officers, she enjoyed seeing Yankees imprisoned on Belle Island. Then Burnside rode up. Ever gallant, he raised his hat to the ladies and remarked pleasantly to the older woman, "I don't suppose, madam, that you ever saw so many Yankee soldiers before."

"Not at liberty, sir," she snapped, causing the other generals to roar with laughter.[38]

The Army of Northern Virginia had not been idle as the Union army made its way south. Grant had sent Hancock and the II Corps ahead of the army to the railroad terminal of Milford Station, hoping they would serve as bait to lure the Confederates from their positions at Spotsylvania Court House. Lee did not bite, but once he determined that the rest of the Federals had indeed abandoned their positions around Spotsylvania he sent his army marching south down the Telegraph Road toward the North Anna River. Grant and Meade, still without Sheridan's cavalry to inform them of the enemy movements, remained uncertain of Lee's whereabouts.

Sheridan had not been idle either. On May 12 he and his troopers had fought the Battle of Yellow Tavern, where they mortally wounded Jeb Stuart. The Confederate cavalryman—the "plumed cavalier" who had plagued the Union forces for so long—would fight no more. "Deep in the hearts of all true cavalrymen, North and South, will ever burn a sentiment of admiration mingled with regret for this knightly soldier and generous man," wrote one of his adversaries.[39]

But while Sheridan had deprived Lee of Stuart, he had also deprived Grant and Meade of his cavalry at a time when they needed it. Until Sheridan returned to the army on May 24, Meade and Grant had to make their moves against Lee's army blindly—much as Stuart's absence had hampered Lee before Gettysburg. To his critics, this was typical of Sheridan, who they said valued his own personal glory over the needs of the Army of the Potomac. Indeed, Meade and Grant remained uncertain of the Confederate army's movements until it had won the race to the North Anna River and crossed over to the southern bank. From this position Lee could cover the important railroad supply stop of Hanover Junction.

Meade wrote home the next morning: "We expected yesterday to have another battle, but the enemy refuses to fight unless attacked in strong entrenchments; hence, when we moved on his flank, instead of coming out of his works and attacking us, he has fallen back from Spottsylvania [sic] Court House, and taken up a new position behind the North Anna River; in other words, performed the same operation which I did last fall, when I fell back from Culpeper, and for which I was ridiculed; that is to say, refusing to fight on my adversary's terms. I suppose now we will have to repeat this turning operation, and continue to do so, till Lee gets into Richmond."[40]

The generals pushed on the next day. Grant, who was a very good rider, was mounted on a spirited black horse and soon rode ahead of Meade. His competitive spirit aroused, Meade spurred his horse forward in a cloud of dust and rode ahead of Grant. George Jr. and Meade's aides scrambled to keep up. The two generals set up their headquarters near the Moncure House on Polecat Creek, where Mrs. Moncure, "a perfect old railer," taunted the Yankees that they would soon be "coming back on the double-quick."[41]

On May 24 the generals reached another neat little brick church, this one called Mount Carmel. "If you want a horrible hole for a halt, just pick out a Virginia church, at a Virginia cross-roads, after the bulk of an army has passed, on a hot, dusty Virginia day!" Lyman complained. Meade, Grant, and Seth Williams used boards laid across the church aisle to write out their orders. "It looked precisely like a town-hall, where people are coming to vote, only the people had unaccountably put on very dusty uniforms," Lyman said.[42]

They were here at the church when a telegram arrived from William Sherman, who was moving through Georgia on his way toward Atlanta. Dana made a point of reading it out loud to Grant. Sherman grandly announced that "success would crown our efforts" if Grant could inspire the Army of the Potomac to do its share. As Meade listened, his "grey eyes grew like a rattlesnakes," reported Lyman. Then, "in a voice like cutting an iron bar with a handsaw," he growled, "Sir! I consider that despatch an insult to the army I command and to me personally. The Army of the Potomac does not require General Grant's inspiration or anybody else's inspiration to make it fight!" Lyman said that Meade fumed about the insult for the rest of the day and called the western armies "an armed rabble."[43] David W. Lowe, who edited Lyman's journals for publication, points out, "Having witnessed more than 30,000 of his soldiers rendered *hors de combat*, Meade's outrage seems justifiable. If one compares casualties alone, Sherman's men were having an easy time of it."[44]

As if to put the lie to the idea that Grant felt he could not rely on Meade, Grant issued orders that same day placing Burnside and the IX Corps under Meade's command. The old system obviously had not worked, but it remained to be seen whether the new one would be an improvement. Burnside apparently accepted it with good grace. He outranked Meade, the reason why Grant initially had the IX Corps report directly to him, but Burnside was also well aware of his own shortcomings.

Just south of Mount Carmel Church, Warren and Hancock began testing the Confederate defenses at the North Anna River. On May 23 Warren crossed upstream at a ford called Jericho Mills. The men of his lead brigade waded through the swift current in cold water up to their armpits while engineers began assembling a pontoon bridge. Wright and the VI Corps prepared to follow. Jubal Early's men launched an attack, but the V Corps drove them back. Downstream Hancock threw back defenders on the north side of the river and crossed at Chesterfield Bridge the next morning. Burnside was poised to attack in the middle, at Ox Ford. Now that Lee realized the Union forces intended to attack him here instead of making another swing around his army, his soldiers began working hard with picks, shovels, spades, and even spoons and bayonets. Once again the Army of Northern Virginia began digging in.

◆ ◆ ◆

A little brown sign marks the turnoff for the North Anna battlefield. It's a state park, not a national one, and this portion of the ground, where the fighting around Ox Ford occurred, lies behind a large quarry. I spot the little sign just before I speed by. I have to jam on my brakes and make a sharp right turn, much to the consternation of the motorcyclist right behind me. Then I drive through a gate that lies between two quarry entrances and down a long dirt road into the woods. The road ends at a dirt parking lot surrounded by tall pines. I am the only person here.

It's late on a fall afternoon. I look at the large painting by D. J. Neary that stands at the entrance to the park trail. It depicts the attack made here by Lt. Col. Charles Chandler and the 57th Massachusetts, part of Brig. Gen. James Ledlie's brigade of the IX Corps. When I was with John Cummings, who was involved with the park's creation, he told me about the painting. "About four of us did all the modeling for Donna Neary," he said. "That's me as Chandler; that's me as a dead guy."

I start walking through the park on a well-maintained gravel path that winds through the silent woods. I was expecting more fields and certainly more river. The autumn sun angles through the trees and tints everything with a greenish cast. It's like being underwater. The soft green moss carpeting the path in several places adds to the enchanted forest feeling.

The most amazing thing about North Anna, though, is the trenches that remain here. They are the best-preserved earthworks I've seen, at least chest high in places. The traverses, ninety-degree breaks across the trenches that would operate almost like watertight doors on a ship if the enemy ever made a breach, are clearly visible, and the earthworks stretch on and on by the trail. Along the way are 10 waypoints with informational panels that explain the fighting here.

With Warren on one side of his army, Hancock on the other, and Burnside threatening the center from the river's opposite side, Lee and his engineers devised a great defensive position. They placed their men in a wedge-shaped line, with the point resting on the river near Ox Ford. It proved a tough nut for the Army of the Potomac to crack. The Union troops could attack one side of the V or the other, but the attacking forces would not be able to support each other without first crossing to the north side of the river and then back over to the south side. Lee, in his well-entrenched defensive positions, could attack the Union forces on one side of the V while holding the other in place with only a small force.

Brig. Gen. James H. Ledlie, whose brigade fought here, was a New Yorker and one of the Union's worst generals, with a shaky grasp of his new command and an unfortunate appetite for drink. "The General was inspired with that artificial courage known throughout the army as 'Dutch courage,'" recalled one of his soldiers. In short, Ledlie was plastered when he sent his men forward on an ill-advised attack. The enemy in the entrenchments here beat back his attacks with ease. Chandler fell mortally wounded and was cared for by the soldiers within the Confederate trenches. "Such noble characters do honor even to a bad cause," said the historian of his regiment.[45]

Hancock and Warren, on opposite sides of the V, fared equally poorly. In fact, if it weren't for the fact that Lee was too ill to command in person, Grant might have suffered an unfortunate reversal here on the North Anna. Instead, he had time enough to realize that Lee had checked him again, and on May 26 he ordered Meade's army on another flanking maneuver.

I hurry down the trail at the North Anna park as the late-afternoon light dims around me. I have a hankering to see the river, which isn't visible through the trees. I don't get my wish until stop number nine, a raised wooden platform that straddles the trenches atop a steep bluff that plunges to the fast-flowing water. The Confederates placed an artillery battery here to fire upstream at the Union troops who had crossed. The glimpse I get of the river below me matches Lyman's description. "The North Anna is a pretty stream, running between high banks, so steep that they form almost a ravine, and, for the most part, heavily wooded with oak and tulip trees, very luxuriant," he wrote. "It is perhaps 125 feet wide and runs with a tolerably swift and deep stream, in most places over one's head. The approaches are by steep roads cut down the banks, and how our waggons and artillery got across, I don't know!"[46]

I hate the thought that I have to hurry through such a beautiful and evocative place, but the park closes at dusk and I don't want to be locked in for an entire night. I don't believe in ghosts—at least not the physical spirits of dead people—but being stuck here alone in the darkness might test my skepticism.

◆ ◆ ◆

The army pulled back from its positions on May 27 and returned to the river's north bank. Meade and his staff moved on ahead of the infantry, with the cavalry taking the lead to make sure no rebels were lying in wait. The road was strewn with dead horses, and the smell of their rotting flesh tainted the air. The entourage stopped at the home of "a thin ill dressed common-looking woman," who said the cavalry had scavenged everything she had. "We shall starve!" she cried. Meade gave her his lunch and $5, "for he is a very tender-hearted man," Lyman said.[47]

The army moved south to cross the Pamunkey River, formed by the junction of the North and South Anna Rivers. Once again using my Virginia Civil War Trails map, I follow narrow, winding Route 615 toward Nelson's Crossing, the place where Meade would have crossed the river. At the bottom of a small decline in the road, I pull off to the side and get out. Other than the Civil War Trails marker here, it seems that little has changed since Grant and Meade passed by on May 28, 1863. The Widow Nelson's house stood here then as it stands here now, a big white house on a bluff overlooking the fields leading to the river.

As a passing soldier crossed the pontoon bridge over the swampy Pamunkey, he noticed the generals—Meade thoughtfully rubbing his face, Hancock talking and gesturing, and Grant watching the soldiers marching past "as though trying to read their thoughts." The men stared back at Grant. "He had the power to send us to our deaths, and we were curious to see him," the soldier said. "But the men did not evince the slightest enthusiasm. None cheered him, none saluted him."[48]

Once I cross the river I make a left turn on Route 605, a narrow country road that roughly parallels the river's course. I'm looking for the Newton House, where Lyman found Grant and Meade on May 28 after they crossed the river. But the road is closed and I have to make a long detour to approach from the opposite direction. I finally get a glimpse of the building, called Summer Hill today. The white house is nearly hidden among trees down a fence- and shrub-lined drive. It's private property and I don't intrude, unlike Charles Carleton Coffin, the correspondent for the *Boston Journal*. When Lyman reached here he found the newspaperman in the garden stealing onions. James Biddle, one of Meade's aides, tried to convince the Newton women that they should rejoin the Union, but he met his match when an aunt, a Mrs. Brockenbrough, arrived and laid into Grant. He accepted her abuse with his usual calm, much to her surprise.[49]

As the army crossed the Pamunkey and moved south, the soldiers could hear the sound of gunfire from a fierce cavalry battle being waged at Haw's Shop, now the crossroads of Routes 615 and 606. David Gregg's Union cavalry drove Wade Hampton's Confederates back from the crossroads to nearby Enon Church, another little house of peace that became a landmark for war. When Lyman passed there, he called it "a dreary, sandy clearing, with scrub pines about it." Dead Confederates still lay on the ground, and all the trees were riddled with bullets.[50] There's a Civil War marker there today, along with an obelisk commemorating the Confederate soldiers who died here and were buried in the cemetery across the road.

"We began to derive one satisfaction from the situation," wrote a soldier from the 20th Maine about the fighting south of the Pamunkey, "and that was from the fact that we were now so near to Richmond that the sounds would be borne from the battle-field to that city, and each booming cannon would be a solemn reminder to the people of the rebel capital that justice was thundering at its gates, and demanding its dues."[51]

Farther to the south lies Totopotomoy Creek. Lee placed his army behind the creek to block the Union advance. A marker in a school parking lot at a place once known as Polly Hundley's Corner describes the skirmishing that took place up and down the line from May 28 to 30. One of the victims was the nearby Pole Green Church, "the birthplace of religious freedom in Virginia," down Route 643. Confederate artillery set it ablaze, and the church burned to the ground. Today it's represented by a white-frame skeleton of the building in a little park by the side of the road.

At Totopotomoy Creek, Grant once again declined the option of hurling the entire army against entrenched Confederates. Instead, he had the army sidle over to the east and aim at a crossroads called Cold Harbor.

No one seemed to know why the place had that name. Some called it Coal Harbor, and Lyman chose to use "Cool Arbor," "because it is prettiest, and because it is so hideously inappropriate."[52] This was territory that Meade and the Army of the Potomac knew well. Meade had fought the Battle of Gaines's Mill two years earlier near this same ground. This time, though, the army's positions were reversed, and now the rebels had their backs toward the swampy Chickahominy.

Sheridan and his cavalry had rejoined the army by this point, and they occupied the strategic crossroads. Meade ordered Sheridan to hold it "at all hazards." He did, despite determined Confederate attacks, until Wright and the VI Corps arrived on June 1. Once they had come up, Sheridan and the cavalry moved back.

There was a new arrival on the scene—or, rather, the return of a once-familiar face. Maj. Gen. William F. "Baldy" Smith had been sent west after intriguing against Burnside in the wake of the Fredericksburg debacle. He had redeemed himself, in Grant's eyes, at least, by performing capably in the campaign to break the siege of Chattanooga. He then accompanied Grant back east, amid rumors that Smith would replace Meade at the head of the Army of the Potomac. However, Grant assigned him to the Army of the James under Maj. Gen. Benjamin Butler, the most political of political generals. The cockeyed Butler and his army were supposed to form one of the prongs in Grant's multipronged campaign against the

Confederacy. Instead, Butler had gotten his army bottled up at Bermuda Hundred with his back against the James River, where they remained, impotent and useless.

Grant had ordered Butler to dispatch Smith and the seventeen thousand men of the XVIII Corps to help fight against Lee. Delayed by orders that had sent him to the wrong location, Smith arrived just in time to take up a position at the right of the Union line at Cold Harbor. Lyman described him as "a short, quite portly man, with a light-brown imperial and shaggy mustache, a round, military head, and the look of a German officer, altogether."[53] He was not really bald, although his hair was thinning. He possessed "unusual powers of caustic criticism" and quarreled incessantly with his superior officers.[54]

Meade and Smith got off on the wrong foot when Smith sent a messenger to report his arrival on June 1. Meade was already in one of his irritable moods, angry at Warren for advancing without orders and at Wright for moving too slowly. When Smith's messenger, Capt. Francis Farquhar, arrived, he reported that Smith had arrived with little ammunition and no transportation, and that "he considered his position precarious." "Then, why in Hell did he come at all for?" Meade roared, surprising Lyman with the rare oath. Smith was so angry when Farquhar told him this that he included the incident when he wrote his official report two months later.[55]

Smith lined up his men on Wright's right, and the two corps launched themselves against the rapidly entrenching enemy. "The whole line thundered with the incessant volleys of musketry, and the host and shell of the artillery shrieked and howled like spirits of evil," one VI Corps veteran recalled. "The sun was sinking, red, in the west, and the clouds of dust and smoke almost obscured the terrible scene. Hundreds of our brave fellows were falling on every side, and stretcher bearers were actively engaged in removing the wounded from the field."[56] Union soldiers advanced up a ravine that the Confederates had neglected to defend and pierced the enemy lines before rebel reinforcements stopped the Union movement. Night ended the fighting.

• • •

I reach Cold Harbor after sunset, and even though the park closes at dark, I decide to make a quick drive on the road that runs through it. As I round a curve in the dark, the soft hummocks of earthworks that remain from the war appear and disappear in my headlights.

I return early in the morning, a couple hours before the little visitors center opens. I'm the only car in the parking lot. It's gray and chilly. I can hear a rooster crowing from across Route 156, where several small houses stand on what would have been part of the battlefield. Quite likely dead and dying soldiers once lay on the land where they were built. There's much more battlefield on private property than on park land, anyway. The visitors center stands near what was the center of the Confederate lines, which stretched about three miles in each direction. On one side of the compact building are words that Grant wrote in his memoirs: "I always regret that the last assault on Cold Harbor was ever made."

I start walking through the gray morning on the park trail, which passes through the field that parallels Route 156 for a bit and then enters the woods.

Gravel crunches under my feet. I stop at the remains of a zigzag trench that Union soldiers dug here to provide some protection as they carried ammunition and supplies from earthwork to earthwork. The soldiers at Cold Harbor had learned their lessons about entrenchments well during Grant's Overland Campaign. The war here looked less and less like the early battles of 1861 and more like the trench warfare that later zigzagged across Europe in World War I.

Farther down the trail a little footbridge spans some more earthworks. As I cross it, I notice movement off in the woods. A deer emerges cautiously from the trees to look me over. Two others join it, and then all three dash off into the trees, waving their white flags of surrender as they go.

The little platform crosses a trench the Confederates dug on June 1. That evening Emory Upton's VI Corps soldiers attacked here and captured the fruit of the rebels' labor. Upton called the fighting that day murderous. "I say *murderous*, because we were recklessly ordered to assault the enemy's intrenchments, knowing neither their strength nor position," he wrote his sister. "Our loss was very heavy, and to no purpose. Our men are brave, but can not accomplish impossibilities."[57]

Beyond the trench the trail turns sandy, almost as though I'm approaching a beach. The trail emerges from the woods into a more open space by the auto road, where tall, skinny pines reach high into the sky. There's a monument here to the 2nd Connecticut Heavy Artillery, one of the units that had been in the Washington defenses when Grant's call for reinforcements got them posted to the front lines, where the veterans taunted them as a "bandbox regiment." A marker nearby tells the regiment's story. The 2nd Connecticut, under Col. Elisha Strong Kellogg, advanced past this point on June 1 to kick off the fighting here. "It was the work of almost a single minute," recalled one officer of the charge. "The air was filled with sulphurous smoke, and the shrieks and howls of more than two hundred and fifty mangled men rose above the yells of triumphant rebels and the roar of their musketry." Kellogg fell dead, and the regiment's survivors re-formed under Upton and continued on to capture the trenches I saw a few minutes ago.

June 2, Lyman noted, was "occupied with strategy; but our strategy is of a bloody kind," enlivened by constant firing up and down the line.[58] The Federal soldiers were exhausted after their long marches and seemingly endless skirmishing, especially Hancock's II Corps, which had shifted during the night from the right to the left of the line. Grant decided to postpone his attack until 4:30 the next morning. This gave the Confederates more than enough time to make their lines impregnable.

As Horace Porter made his way along the front on the evening of June 2, he noticed that many soldiers appeared to be busy sewing. "This exhibition of tailoring seemed rather peculiar at such a moment," Porter wrote, "but upon closer examination it was found that the men were calmly writing their names and home addresses on slips of paper, and pinning them on the backs of their coats, so that their dead bodies might be recognized upon the field, and their fate made known to their families at home. They were veterans who knew well from terrible experience the danger which awaited them, but their minds were occupied not with thoughts of shirking their duty, but with preparation for the desperate work of the coming morning. Such courage is more than heroic—it is sublime."[59]

It probably appeared more sublime to an officer at headquarters than it did to the soldiers on the front lines.

The June 3 attack at Cold Harbor was a relatively simple one. The Confederate line ran approximately north and south, facing east. The Union line ran parallel, facing west. Hancock and the II Corps held the left, and then, running south to north, came Wright and the VI, Baldy Smith's XVIII, Warren's V, and finally Burnside's IX, whose line swung around in a curve to the east. The resulting line was shaped a bit like a question mark. At 4:30 the Union soldiers moved forward all along the line. Within the hour some seven thousand of them were dead, wounded, or missing. "The time of actual advance was not over eight minutes," wrote Gen. Martin T. McMahon, Horatio Wright's adjutant. "In that little period of time more men fell bleeding as they advanced than in any other like period of time throughout the war."[60] One of the men who fell was McMahon's brother, the colonel of the 164th New York in Gibbon's division of the II Corps, who leaped atop the rebel fortifications before the enemy riddled him with bullets. His brother could later identify the body only from the buttons on the sleeves.

Francis Barlow's division of the II Corps captured a portion of the rebel entrenchments but couldn't hold them. Col. Frank Haskell, who had written the fine account of Gettysburg when he was Gibbon's aide-de-camp, died at Cold Harbor at the head of the 36th Wisconsin. He had taken over his brigade when its commander was killed and took his men across an open field toward the enemy works. Protected by a slight rise, the men halted until Haskell ordered them forward once again. They didn't stand a chance. Facing a storm of bullets, Haskell ordered his men to lie down. "For an instant it seemed that he was the only man standing," recalled Capt. Clement E. Warner of the 36th Wisconsin, "and for only an instant, for as he stood surveying the havoc around him, and glanced toward the enemy's line, he was seen to throw up his arms and sink to the earth, his forehead pierced by a rebel ball. And this was the last of Frank Haskell's consciousness."[61]

Upton, who had demonstrated his willingness to attack at Spotsylvania, stayed put. Those who had attacked and were lucky enough to survive now fell back and began digging. "In some cases our men lay within thirty yards of the enemy; at other places, according to the configuration of the ground, the line ran away to fifty, seventy, a hundred, or more," Francis Walker noted. "Here the troops intrenched themselves, by bayonet and tin-plate, until a beginning had been made, and waited for night to go to work on a larger scale with better tools."[62]

The assault had ended almost before it had begun. Meade, at Wright's headquarters, sent out a flurry of messages to his corps commanders urging that they press the attack. The replies were not encouraging. "I shall await your orders, but express the opinion that if the first dash in an assault fails, other attempts are not apt to succeed better," Hancock reported at 6:15 that morning.[63]

"I should be glad to have your views as to the continuance of these attacks, if unsuccessful," Meade wrote to Grant. It appeared he felt very much between a rock and an extremely hard place. He understood the futility of storming entrenched works, yet he also understood his superior officer's demands that the

Army of the Potomac think offensively at all times. Grant's reply was not exactly illuminating. "The moment it becomes certain that an assault cannot succeed, suspend the offensive, but when one does succeed push it vigorously, and if necessary pile in troops at the successful point from wherever they can be taken," he wrote.[64] Faced with apparently impregnable positions and commanders unwilling to renew the fighting, Grant finally called off the attack, and Meade ordered the army to entrench where it lay.

"And there the two armies slept, almost within an easy stone-throw of each other; and the separating space ploughed by cannon-shot and clotted with the dead bodies that neither side dared to bury!" wrote Lyman. "I think nothing can give a greater idea of deathless tenacity of purpose, than the picture of these two hosts, after a bloody and nearly continuous struggle of thirty days, thus lying down to sleep, with their heads almost on each other's throats! Possibly it has no parallel in history. So ended the great attack at Cool Arbor."[65]

For the next few days hundreds of wounded soldiers lay between the lines while Grant and Lee dickered over the terms that would allow their recovery. Anyone venturing outside the trenches faced almost certain death from sharpshooters. Grant balked at the idea of requesting a truce, which would make it look as if he had lost the contest (which he had). He suggested that Meade should make the request. Meade replied that the Confederates would not recognize him as commander while Grant was present with the army. For his part, Lee had few wounded outside his lines to recover and was hardly prepared to accommodate Grant. While the delicate dance took place between the two commanders, the wounded lay suffering between the lines.

It actually fell to Lyman to open negotiations once Grant decided to request a truce. On the afternoon of June 5 Meade called for his aide. Lyman found the general lying on his cot, his feet on the headboard. "Lyman, I want you to take this letter from General Grant and take it by a flag of truce, to the enemy's lines," he said. "General Hancock will tell you where you can carry it out."

Lyman put on his best uniform, including a sash and white gloves, and rode with a cavalry sergeant over to Hancock's headquarters. He found that general also lying on his cot. "Well, Colonel," Hancock told him, "now you can't carry it out on my front, it's too hot there." He advised that Lyman ride farther to the left. Hancock called for his aide, Major Mitchell, and asked him to get some whiskey for the Confederates and a white flag. The flag created a problem, for the only white thing around was Hancock's always-pristine shirt. Finally, Hancock's servant found a pillowcase and attached it to a staff. Thus equipped, Lyman and Mitchell set off. They found an efficient guide in the person of Col. Charles Hapgood, "a thorough New Hampshire man—tall, sinewy, with a keen black eye, and a driving way about him." They rode to the end of the Union line and then entered a pine woods. Skirting a field where they would be easy targets for enemy sharpshooters, the men rode on until they found the army's pickets on the outskirts of the Union position. The pickets shouted across to their rebel counterparts to let them know an emissary was approaching.

The Union officers rode cautiously forward. "The sun was near setting, and, in the heavy oak woods, the light already began to fade," Lyman wrote. "On the road stood a couple of rebel officers, each in his grey overcoat, and, just behind, were grouped some twenty soldiers—the most gipsy-looking fellows imaginable; in their blue-grey jackets and slouched hats; each with his rusty musket and well-filled cartridge-box." Slightly embarrassed by his own spiffy white gloves, Lyman explained his mission to Maj. Thomas Wooten of a regiment in A. P. Hill's corps. Wooten sent a man off with the letter, and the officers sat down to wait, uncomfortably aware that a gunshot from either side could spark a deadly crossfire. At one point guns did begin blazing. Officers jumped up and ran down the line, ordering the men to stop firing. They all listened nervously as muskets rattled and cannons boomed farther up to the north.

The hours stretched by as the officers sat in the dark woods, the smell of dead horses filling the air. At 10:00 Wooten left to see what the delay was. Finally, around 11:00, a lieutenant arrived and said that Lyman needn't wait any longer. Lee would have a reply delivered in the morning.

On his way back to headquarters Lyman stopped by Francis Barlow's division. Like Lyman, Barlow was a Harvard man. He had practiced law before the war and looked more like a newsboy than a general, but Barlow had been wounded at Antietam and left for dead at Gettysburg. He carried an especially large sword—so that when he hit stragglers with it, he would hurt them, he told Lyman. Lyman called him "an eccentric officer." Lyman found Barlow in a good mood. He had placed some stragglers—his *bêtes noires*—in a field during the shelling, and two of them had been killed.

When Lyman finally made it back to headquarters, Meade simply said, "Hullo, Lyman, I thought perhaps the Rebs had gobbled you during that last attack."[66]

It wasn't until June 7 that the two sides agreed on truce arrangements. By then most of the wounded were dead. "Better the consuming fires of the Wilderness and the Po than the lingering, agonizing death of these poor men, whose vain calls for relief smote upon the ears of their comrades at every lull in the firing," wrote Francis Walker.[67]

● ● ●

It was obvious that the assault had been a disaster. In Grant's initial message to Halleck, sent at 2:15 in the afternoon on June 3—when he must have known better—he wrote that the army's loss was "not severe." Later, he would come to regret having ordered the attack at Cold Harbor, as the quote on the visitors center wall attests. According to Horace Porter, Grant's officers soon learned not to bring up the battle in conversation.[68]

"Our men have, in many instances, been foolishly and wantonly sacrificed," Upton wrote bitterly to his sister. "Thousands of lives might have been spared by the exercise of a little skill; but, as it is, the courage of the poor men is expected to obviate all difficulties."[69]

Years later, Baldy Smith recounted a conversation he had with Meade on June 5. Smith asked Meade why he had given such orders for the assault. "He replied that he had worked out every plan for every move from the crossing of the Rapidan onward, that the papers were full of the doings of *Grant's* army, and that he was tired of it, and was determined to let General Grant plan his own battles,"

Smith recalled.[70] Smith was a cantankerous man and adept at sowing discord. By the time he wrote those words, he had developed deeply rancorous relationships with both Meade and Grant. I find it hard to believe that Meade—the general who was willing to throw away his career rather than kill his men in a fruitless attack at Mine Run—would willingly see those same soldiers sacrificed at Cold Harbor in a fit of pique. Charles Wainwright, Warren's head of artillery, believed the attack at Cold Harbor must have been Grant's idea. "The orders came to us from Meade, but I cannot think it is his, having the opinion I have of his ability as a general."[71]

The reasons for the disaster at Cold Harbor seem to lie less in the command structure and more in the general in chief, who had once again underestimated the Army of Northern Virginia. "Lee's army is really whipped," Grant had written to Halleck back on May 26. "The prisoners we now take show it, and the action of his army shows it unmistakably. A battle with them outside of intrenchments cannot be had. Our men feel that they have gained the morale over the enemy and attack with confidence. I may be mistaken, but I feel that our success over Lee's army is already insured."[72] Maybe Grant was correct in the long run, but his timing was off by almost eleven months.

There's no doubt that the Union attack at Cold Harbor was a miserable failure. So was the Confederate attack on the third day at Gettysburg. James McPherson, the Pulitzer Prize–winning Civil War historian, expressed bewilderment at how differently people remember the two failed attacks. At Cold Harbor, "Fifty thousand Union soldiers suffered seven thousand casualties, most of them in less than half an hour," wrote McPherson in *Hallowed Ground: A Walk at Gettysburg*, "For this mistake, which he admitted, Grant has been branded a 'butcher' careless of lives of his men, and Cold Harbor has become a symbol of mule-headed futility." McPherson points out that Lee's army also suffered around seven thousand casualties on July 3. "Yet this attack is perceived as an example of great courage and honor. This contrast speaks volumes about the comparative image of Grant and Lee, North and South, Union and Confederacy." [73]

I doubt Meade perceived much glory in either attack. In fact, by this point he believed Grant's relentless hammering at Lee had not worked and was becoming increasingly irritated by the way the general in chief eclipsed Meade's role in the campaign. "I feel a satisfaction in knowing that my record is clear, and that the results of this campaign are the clearest indications I could wish of my sound judgment, both at Williamsport and Mine Run," Meade wrote home on June 5. "In every instance that we have attacked the enemy in an entrenched position we have failed, except in the case of Hancock's attack at Spottsylvania [*sic*], which was a surprise discreditable to the enemy. So, likewise, whenever the enemy has attacked us in position, he has been repulsed. I think Grant has had his eyes opened, and is willing to admit now that Virginia and Lee's army is not Tennessee and Bragg's army. Whether the people will ever realize this fact remains to be seen."[74]

One problem with getting people to realize this, however, was that those people received word about such things from the newspapers, and Meade had poor relationships with the newspaper correspondents who followed the army. Lyman thought Meade's problem was "that he was too short with newspaper people to be popular, and not severe enough to be feared."[75] He was also thin-skinned about his coverage—or lack thereof—and often complained about the newspapers in his letters home. But it was during the Cold Harbor Campaign that Meade's dealings with the press suffered a blow that ultimately did him serious harm in the world of public opinion.

On June 2 an article by reporter Edward Crapsey appeared in the *Philadelphia Inquirer*. The unfortunately named Crapsey (often spelled Cropsey) was an experienced newspaperman. As a correspondent for Cincinnati papers, he had reported on Grant's successful Vicksburg Campaign and the fighting for Knoxville, Tennessee. By the time the Overland Campaign lurched into motion, he was reporting for the *Inquirer*. He had even been captured briefly by rebel cavalry near Rappahannock Station with two other reporters. The three newspapermen managed to escape when their captors got into a skirmish with some Union cavalrymen.[76]

In light of ensuing events, the irony was that the June 2 article was generally very positive about Meade's performance. "He is as much the commander of the Army of the Potomac as he ever was," it read. "GRANT plans and exercises a supervisory control over the army, but to MEADE belongs everything of detail. He is entitled to great credit for the magnificent movements of the army since we left Brandy, for they have been dictated by him. In battle he puts troops in action and controls their movements; in a word, he commands the army. General GRANT is here only because he deems the present campaign the vital one of the war, and wishes to decide on the spot all questions that would be referred to him as General-in-Chief."

If Crapsey had stopped there events would have taken a very different course. But unfortunately for all involved, he wrote more:

> History will record, but newspapers cannot, that on one eventful night during the present campaign GRANT's presence saved the army, and the nation too; not that General MEADE was on the point to commit a blunder unwittingly, but his devotion to his country made him loth to risk her last army on what he deemed a chance. GRANT assumed the responsibility and we are still
>
> On to Richmond.[77]

Meade wasn't quite clear what Crapsey meant by this, but he suspected the worst. He summoned the reporter to his tent for an explanation. Crapsey told him that the word throughout the army was that Meade had urged Grant to withdraw across the Rapidan after the Wilderness. Grant had refused, "and thus the country was saved the disgrace of a retreat."[78]

That accusation stung, especially with the stories circulating in Washington that Meade had intended to retreat from Gettysburg, the sense that Grant had to be present to keep the Army of the Potomac fighting, and the feeling that the newspapers—as well as Grant and the politicians in Washington—were unwilling to give Meade his due. Meade also worried that the article could cause his soldiers to lose confidence in their commander. This story in a paper from his hometown proved to be the last straw. He told Crapsey the account was "a base and wicked lie"[79] and decided to make an example of him. He ordered the reporter to be placed backward on a mule while wearing a sign around his neck that read, "Libeler of the press." Thus humiliated, Crapsey was drummed out of camp to the tune of the "Rogue's March."

This was not a wise media strategy.

Grant and Dana both tried to reassure Meade that the authorities in Washington would not believe the accusation. Dana even telegraphed Stanton about it. Stanton wired back, "Please say to General Meade that the lying report alluded to in your telegram was not even for a moment believed by the President or myself. We have the most perfect confidence in him. He could not wish a more exalted estimation of his ability, his firmness, and every quality of a commanding general than is entertained for him." By then, though, it was too late.[80] Meade probably felt he should take the soothing words of politicians with a grain of salt—especially when he heard rumors that the real source for Crapsey's story had been Congressman Eli Washburne, Grant's political mentor, who had been traveling with the army. If Meade got evidence to prove that charge, he told Margaret, he planned to show the congressman "no quarter."[81]

The newspaper reporters with the army reacted to Crapsey's punishment with outrage. "Major Gen. Meade may have the physical courage which bulls & bull dogs have; but he is as leprous with moral cowardice as the brute that kicks a helpless cripple in the street, or beats his wife at home," wrote Whitelaw Reid, the reporter who had written about Meade at Taneytown and Gettysburg."[82]

Sylvanus Cadwallader, then with the *Chicago Times*, was something of a favorite with Grant—or at least Grant was canny enough to make Cadwallader feel as if he were a favorite. "Every newspaper reporter in the Army of the Potomac, and in Washington City, had first an implied, and afterward an expressed understanding, to ignore Gen. Meade in every possible way and manner," Cadwallader reported. "The publishers shared their feelings to a considerable extent, and it was soon noticed that Gen. Meade's name never appeared in any army correspondence if it could be omitted." He became as forgotten, Cadwallader said, "as any dead hero of antiquity."[83] However, the press had been overlooking Meade even before the incident with Crapsey. On June 5, three days before Crapsey's humiliation, Charles Wainwright noted, "The newspaper correspondents speak of Grant doing this and that, hardly ever mentioning Meade's name. Here we see nothing of General Grant; I hardly heard his name mentioned."[84]

Meade was not the only person in the army who hated the press. In fact, if anything has remained consistent since the Civil War, it's that people in authority perceived the press as biased, dishonest, inaccurate, and an overall nuisance. Maj. James Biddle of Meade's staff called reporters "the scum of creation" and said "there is not one of them whom any gentleman would associate with."[85] The reporting of *New York Times* reporter William Swinton so outraged Burnside that he ordered him shot as a spy until Grant interceded. Grant later banished Swinton from the army after the reporter was discovered eavesdropping outside Meade's tent when the generals were conversing. A *New York Tribune* reporter named William H. Kent once wrote an article criticizing both Hancock and Meade, and

Hancock sent it to Meade, with the offending passages helpfully indicated. Meade suggested to Grant that Kent be arrested for publishing false information, but Kent managed to slip away before punishment could be meted out. It was probably just as well for both the reporter and the general.[86]

Charles Wainwright also disliked and distrusted the reporters who traveled with the army, but he correctly predicted that Meade's treatment of Crapsey would backfire. "I fear that the General will hurt himself by this, for these newspaper fellows stick very closely by one another when an outsider attacks them," Wainwright noted in his journal. "But I rejoice to see one of the rascals shown up, for they make more trouble than their heads are worth, with their lying accounts of affairs in the army; raising false hopes among the people, and almost always giving false ideas as to the merits of an officer, for they praise those who treat them, and ignore those who will have nothing to do with them. For my part, I should be glad if none were admitted to the army."[87]

As the relationship between Meade and the press soured, the one between the two enemy armies remained at a stubborn stalemate, with the soldiers on both sides living miserable, filthy existences within their trenches. Merely peeking over the breastworks tempted death, with sharpshooters lurking on each side to shoot anything that moved. The land around Cold Harbor became crisscrossed by vast networks of trenches, which reminded one Union soldier of the work of prairie dog colonies.[88]

It is eerie to see the earthworks that remain here today, knowing they had once provided the setting for scenes of bloodshed and horror and the deaths of hundreds of men whose names have been lost to history. At the same time, as I wander the battlefields and read the markers, I come across names that are familiar, almost like old friends. Upton's name pops up time and time again, and on one marker at Cold Harbor I find a quote from Wilbur Fisk, a Vermont soldier whose letters have been collected in a book called *Hard Marching Every Day*. "The breastworks against which I am leaning is not more than 200 yards from the enemy's lines, and in front of us are skirmishers and sharpshooters still nearer," he wrote on June 11. "Our line is just outside the edge of a woods, and theirs is partly in an open field, and partly covered by timber in our immediate front. The field is open between us, but it is a strip of land across which no man dare to pass. An attacking party from either side would be mown down like grass."[89]

On June 12 Meade ordered his staff to gather at his tent at 8:00. They had an appointment with photographer Mathew Brady and his cameramen. The group gathered for the cameras in front of the tent, Meade sitting in the center, Humphreys and provost marshal Marsena Patrick sitting to his right, the rest of the large group standing. "I doubt if it [will] prove a very good picture," Patrick grumped. The photographers also took photographs of Meade standing alone in front of his tent, his tall slouch hat pulled low over his eyes, one hand grasping his belt, one leg bent, and wearing big knee-high leather boots.[90] Meade thought that photo wasn't bad, but he believed the one of his staff was "the best picture I ever saw, each face being so distinct."[91]

But there were more important things to do on June 12 than photo sessions. Grant had finally realized the futility of attacking Lee's army in its entrenchments.

At Spotsylvania he had vowed to "fight it out on this line if it takes all summer," but apparently vows were meant to be broken. The man who had told Meade he wouldn't maneuver decided to maneuver once more. Grant made plans to cross the James River and move on to Petersburg, a vital railroad junction a little more than twenty miles south of Richmond. Two railroads crucial to the Confederates, the Weldon and the South Side, passed through Petersburg. If the Union could capture Petersburg, it would cut off the Confederate capital—and Lee's army—from its Southern supply lines.

Grant ordered Sheridan on another independent raid to destroy a third railroad, the Virginia Central, and break Richmond's supply line with the Shenandoah Valley to the north. Then, on June 12, Meade's army began to slip surreptitiously from its trenches and away from the killing fields of Cold Harbor. Grant and Meade left their headquarters that afternoon. They rode until 5:00 and established headquarters at a small house. Grant promptly lay down on a board with a bag for a pillow and went to sleep. The next day the army crossed the Chickahominy, the stream that had caused McClellan such trouble two years earlier. Now it was little more than "a wide ditch, partly choked with rotten logs, and full of brown, tepid, sickly-looking water, whose slow current would scarcely carry a straw along." The army, with its wagons and artillery trains, clattered across a pontoon bridge. Once over the sluggish water Barlow began marching his men so fast—with his provost guard spurring stragglers along at bayonet point—that Meade sent Lyman forward to tell him to slow down. Lyman found Barlow sitting, coatless, high up in the branches of a cherry tree. "By Jove!" came his voice from above Lyman's head. "I knew I wouldn't be here long before Meade's staff would be up. How do you do, Theodore? Won't you come up and take a few cherries?"

Later in the day Meade sent Lyman forward again to determine the lay of the land. He hadn't ridden far before he entered a clearing and got his first sight of the wide and placid James River. "To appreciate such a spectacle, you must pass five weeks in an almost unbroken wilderness, with no sights but weary, dusty troops, endless wagon-trains, convoys of poor wounded men, and hot, uncomfortable camps," he wrote. "Here was a noble river, a mile wide, with high green banks, studded with large plantation houses." A signal officer stood on the shore, waving a flag at the Union steamers in the river to let them know the Army of the Potomac had arrived. Meade established his headquarters at the birthplace of President John Tyler—"him of the big nose and small political principles," opined Lyman. Today the house, a long, low, white building, still stands off Route 5 but is privately owned. What most impressed Lyman about the place was that he got some green peas and milk there.[92]

I get my first glimpse of the James after my long, winding drive through Virginia Civil War history when I reach the end of the road leading to Lawrence Lewis Jr. Park. A wooden dock stretches out into the river here. At the end of it five men are fishing for catfish in the calm waters. A huge power transmission tower stands on the riverbank nearby, holding up wires that stretch far across the wide river to a sister tower on the opposite shore.

Like Aquia Creek this is a place whose complete stillness seems almost a rebuke to the intense activity that took place here during the war, but then faded away without even an echo remaining. In 1864 this was the site of Wilcox's Landing, originally established as a shipping point for tobacco. Once the Union engineers arrived here, they began rebuilding the wharves as the dirty and tired soldiers marched down to the water. On June 14 steamers shuttled members of the II Corps across the river from here while the engineers went to work three miles downstream and began laying a huge pontoon bridge, about thirteen feet wide and two thousand feet long (including its approaches) across a river eighty feet deep. It rested on about ninety-two pontoon boats.[94] Three schooners anchored by the bridge to help hold it in place. "The bridge and its approaches was, without question, one of the engineering feats of the war," said Lyman.[95] The engineers finished it in about twelve hours. Before they completed the span, steamers carrying Baldy Smith's XVIII Corps cruised past, on their way to rejoin Benjamin Butler's Army of the James and move on toward Petersburg. The entire army was across the James by the next day. It was a triumph of strategy and logistics that caught Lee unaware.

"And thus closed the wonderful campaign from the Rapidan to the James," wrote a soldier from the 20th Maine. "At its close, as we stood upon the opposite side of the James river and recalled it all, it seemed more like a fearful nightmare to us than a reality. . . . If there is a section of territory in all this Union that must forever remain sacred, it is that section of Virginia reaching from the Shenandoah valley to the James river, upon which was fought so many of the great battles of the war, and in whose bosom repose the ashes of so many thousand heroes."[96]

CHAPTER 16

Before Petersburg

Winfield Scott Hancock, seated, with his division commanders, from left:
Francis Barlow, David Birney, and John Gibbon
LIBRARY OF CONGRESS

• • •

The Petersburg National Military Park's visitors center looks like a large brick turret. It squats at the edge of the parking lot, brooding over the remains of some real fortifications from the Civil War. The grassy hummocks at the edge of the fields once belonged to Confederate Battery 5, part of the defenses around Petersburg that an engineer named Charles Dimmock laid out in 1862. Baldy Smith's men captured this portion of the line late in the day on June 15, 1864, and for a time almost nothing stood between the Union forces and the city beyond. Smith had the city in the palm of his hand, ripe for capture.

The visitors center is small but has some interesting items, such as two minié balls that collided in flight and flattened out to form something that looks a little like a sand dollar. Another display case has pieces of the fuse used to light the gunpowder that created the Crater, the park's star attraction. There's also a 12-pound bronze Napoleon cannon that the Confederates captured at the Battle of Reams Station on August 25, 1864, and then turned on its former owners. That fight, a humiliating defeat for Winfield Scott Hancock, was one of the many battles and skirmishes of the nearly eleven-month campaign around Petersburg.

That campaign might have been unnecessary had Baldy Smith pushed his advantage. The Federal sweep across the James River had been a complete success, leaving Lee unsure of Grant's intentions. Smith departed from the Army of the Potomac to rejoin the Army of the James at Bermuda Hundred, and on June 15 he set out with about sixteen thousand men to capitalize on Lee's uncertainty.

The defenses around Petersburg were under the command of the Confederate general with one of the best names in the Civil War: Pierre Gustave Toutant Beauregard. The Louisiana Creole had been in the thick of things since Fort Sumter, where he commanded the Confederate bombardment against his former West Point artillery instructor, Robert Anderson. Beauregard—a name that almost demands to be spoken in a Southern drawl—had been second in command under Joseph Johnston at First Bull Run, but his combustible personality and strained relations with President Jefferson Davis, as well as doubts about his actual ability on the battlefield, got him sent out west. When he returned east he took command of Charleston's defenses. Back in Virginia he thwarted Benjamin Butler's attempts to take Richmond, and then bottled up the Army of the James at Bermuda Hundred.

Beauregard had only a weak defense along the Dimmock Line. A mere twenty-four hundred men under former Virginia governor Henry Wise—who happened to be Meade's brother-in-law—and a cavalry brigade of about two thousand were all that stood between Smith and Petersburg. The Federals, among them two divisions of African American soldiers, pushed through the first line of defenses easily enough and captured several miles of entrenchments and fortifications. The prizes included Battery 5 and nearby Battery 8, now the second stop along the battlefield park's driving tour. Black soldiers of the United States Colored Troops (USCT) played important roles here, capturing forts and entrenchments that slaves had constructed for their Confederate masters. The efforts of these soldiers are commemorated with a small granite monument to the USCT at the third stop of the tour, near Battery 9.

And then Smith stopped. He evidently did not want to risk losing all his gains with a risky night attack. Hancock and the II Corps came up in support, arriving late after a fruitless wait for some promised rations. The delay wasn't Hancock's fault, though, because it seems Grant never told him or Meade that Smith would be attacking Petersburg's defenses or that he wanted the II Corps to help. When Hancock's soldiers arrived, Smith had them relieve some of his exhausted men in the captured lines instead of pushing them forward to renew the attack. It was yet another lost opportunity. Had Smith continued his advance, he could have pushed past the weak defenses and the town would have fallen, said Lyman, "like a rotten branch."[1]

Earlier that day Meade had arrived on the banks of the James to inspect the pontoon bridge. He received word of Smith's attack that evening and immediately ordered the IX Corps to hurry across the bridge and head toward Petersburg in Hancock's wake. The V Corps would follow the next day, with the VI taking up the rear guard.

The next morning Meade boarded a steamer with Humphreys, Lyman, and another aide for the hourlong trip to Grant's new headquarters at City Point, a peninsula at the junction of the James and Appomattox Rivers. There they mounted horses and began riding toward the front. They met Grant on his way back, and the general in chief appeared very pleased with developments. "Well, Smith has taken a line of works stronger than anything we have seen this campaign," he exulted. "If it is a possible thing, I want an assault made at 6 o'clock this evening." Meade's party continued on and soon caught up with Burnside's men, who were staggering with exhaustion, suffering from thirst and toiling through thick, choking dust. Meade spoke with Burnside and then rode forward in search of Hancock. He found him sitting under some pine trees at the edge of a field the Confederates had cleared in front of their works. "From a swell of land near by I got my first view of the spires of Petersburg, which I was destined to stare at for nearly ten months yet!" Lyman later recalled.[2]

Meade, Hancock, and officers from the II Corps conferred about the evening's attack. Humphreys and Barlow rode forward to examine the enemy's lines. Neither general wanted to be the first to suggest halting, so they continued until fire from enemy skirmishers demonstrated the wisdom of turning back. "You never saw such an old bird as General Humphreys!" wrote Lyman on another occasion. "I do like to see a brave man; but when a man goes out for the express purpose of getting shot at, he seems to me in the way of a maniac."[3]

An artillery barrage announced the start of the fighting at 6:00. Smith's XVIII Corps made a diversion on the right while the II Corps—Birney, Barlow, and some of Gibbon's men—made the main attack. "The cannonade was very grand, and, as the sun declined, the air, full of dust and powder smoke, gave a copper hue to the scene that was most striking," wrote Lyman. "The figures of the artillerymen sponging out and ramming down, and of the officers standing between the pieces, forcibly recalled those stiff, mezzo-tint engravings of Napoleon's battles that once were favorite ornaments of parlors."[4] The men of the II Corps moved ahead, but Southern reinforcements were already rushing forward to fill the enemy works, and the Union soldiers could not break their line.

Horace Porter arrived to find Meade near the edge of a field with some of his staff, directing the attacking forces. "His usual nervous energy was displayed in the intensity of his manner and the rapid and animated style of his conversation," said Porter. "He assured me that no additional orders could be given which could add to the vigor of the attack. He was acting with great earnestness, and doing his utmost to carry out the instructions which he had received."[5] Meade's forces made some headway, but they did not break the Confederate line.

Night fell and Meade sent Lyman back to City Point to report to Grant. Lyman found the lieutenant general in his tent, sitting on his cot in shirt and underwear. Grant was pleased, despite the attack's failure. "I think it is pretty well to get across a great river, and come up here, and attack Lee in his rear before he is ready for us!" he said.[6] Grant did not know that he had already lost his chance to capture Petersburg.

Meade launched more attacks on June 17 and 18, meeting with limited success. But Beauregard had moved back to a shorter defensive line and Lee's army finally began pouring into the entrenchments. On June 18 Grant remained behind at City Point while Meade led the attacks on Petersburg. "He showed himself the personification of earnest, vigorous action in rousing his subordinate commanders to superior exertions," Porter noted. His temper flared up on occasion, but Porter felt it helped spur on his subordinates. Pacing back and forth restlessly, Meade sent off dispatches in all directions and kept up a running commentary on the fighting. "His aquiline nose and piercing eyes gave him something of the eagle's look, and added to the interest of his personality," said Porter. "He had much to try him upon this occasion, and if he was severe in his reprimands and showed faults of temper, he certainly displayed no faults as a commander."[7]

As a Maine native, I'm intrigued by the monument to the 1st Maine Heavy Artillery. It lies at the end of a trail that runs across a field from the site of what the Federals later called Fort Stedman, named for a general who died here on August 6, 1864. Having your name attached to a Petersburg fort was an honor to avoid, because it meant you were dead. The driving tour also takes me to Forts Sedgwick and Haskell, both named after soldiers I have encountered in my readings. The forts are now little more than grassy humps on the roadsides, some of them with Civil War cannons inside.

A thick fog shrouds the fields around Fort Stedman when I park there early one morning. Cannons loom out of the mist, and I see the ghostlike figures of deer grazing in the fields. Ironically, the no-hunting regulations of the battlefield provide them with sanctuary during the hunting season. I find the monument to the regiment from the Pine Tree State surrounded, appropriately, by tall pine trees. Only a thin strip of woods separates it from a residential neighborhood, and I hear early-morning voices in one of the houses. Try as hard as you might, it's hard to avoid the twenty-first century on most Civil War battlefields.

The 1st Maine was one of the regiments summoned from the cushy assignment of the Washington defenses to fight as infantry against Lee's army. Lumbermen, sailors, farmers, and even some clerks and high school graduates had been recruited from the areas around Bangor and Penobscot Bay to form what had first been the 18th Maine Volunteer Infantry. On June 18 the Maine boys charged straight into hell here. "The earth was literally torn up with iron and lead," recalled a captain in the regiment. "The field became a burning, seething, crashing, hissing hell, in which human courage, flesh, and bone were struggling with an impossibility, either to succeed or to return with much hope of life." About nine hundred men went in; more than six hundred of them became casualties. The marker here says their losses were "more than any other regiment in any other single battle of the war." The next morning three members of the regiment crept forward to rescue their wounded under the cover of a dense fog, like the one that cloaks the battlefield when I visit this morning. But the fog quickly burned away, and they were forced to run for their lives as the enemy guns opened up. For days afterward the Union soldiers had to face the sight of the ground in front of them "strewn thick with the blue-coated bodies of those sterling sons of Maine, decomposing in the fierce rays of a Southern sun."[8]

All the attacks on Petersburg between June 15 and 18 had been characteristically bloody, with the Union forces suffering a total of nearly eleven thousand casualties.[9] Among those who fell wounded on June 18 was another son of the Pine Tree State, Joshua Lawrence Chamberlain, the hero of Little Round Top. Fearing that Chamberlain would die, Grant gave him a battlefield promotion to general.

Meade knew he had failed to overpower his outnumbered foe. "*I* should have taken Petersburg," he told Lyman. "The enemy had no defenses but what they had thrown up in a few hours; and I had 60,000 men to their 25,000." While acknowledging the truth of that, Lyman understood this was not the Army of the Potomac he had joined back in 1863. "The men who stormed the Rappahannock redoubts in November '63 would have walked over the breastworks and driven Beauregard into the Appomattox," he said; "but those men are [in] the ground between here and the Rapid Ann [*sic*], or fill the hospitals in the North. Put a man in a hole and a good battery on a hill behind him, and he will beat off three times his number, even if he is not a very good soldier."[10]

The next day, a Sunday, Meade dispatched Lyman on another mission to deliver a truce request so the army could recover the wounded between the lines. The experience was not as nerve-racking as the one at Cold Harbor, but it proved more frustrating. Beauregard wrote in reply to Meade's note that he had been unaware any fighting of consequence had taken place and therefore refused the request for a truce. If there had been a serious engagement, he said, he would be "glad to extend the courtesies of war." This infuriated Lyman. "He lied; for he knew full well that there had been heavy fighting and that we at least had lost some thousands. But he wished to show his dirty spite. Lee does not [do] such things."[11]

On June 18 Grant decided that headlong assaults against Petersburg's defenses would result only in useless bloodshed. He prepared to lay siege. "I am perfectly satisfied that all has been done that could be done, and that the assaults to-day were called for by all the appearances and information that could be obtained," he wrote in a message to Meade. "Now we will rest the men and use the spade for their protection until a new vein can be struck."[12]

One vein to try was the Weldon Railroad, one of the supply lines essential for the survival of Petersburg and Richmond. The first attempt, though, an operation conducted by the II and VI Corps on June 22, was a disaster, "perhaps the most humiliating episode in the experience of the Second Corps down to this time," wrote Francis Walker. With Hancock incapacitated by his Gettysburg wound, David Bell Birney had command of the II Corps. Meade had no love for Birney, who had maneuvered against him in Washington, but he did admire his abilities on the field. Here, though, Birney stumbled badly. As the Union forces advanced, Confederates managed to drive into the gap between the two Federal corps, forcing the II Corps back "in some disorder." Birney lost four guns and some seventeen hundred men as prisoner, more than the corps had lost at "Antietam, Fredericksburg, and Chancellorsville combined."[13]

The soldiers were showing the strain caused by weeks of bloodshed and death. "Their nerves had become so sensitive that the men would start at the slightest sound, and dodge at the flight of a bird or the sight of a pebble tossed past them," said Porter. Soldiers liked to contrive ways to make nervous comrades jump. They called the instinctive dodging "jack-knifing."[14]

"The feeling here in the army is that we have been absolutely butchered, that our lives have been periled to no purpose, and wasted," wrote Stephen Weld of the 56th Massachusetts. "In the Second Corps the feeling is so strong that the men say they will not charge any more works." Weld placed the blame on generals—"corps commanders and higher still"—"who have time and again recklessly and wickedly placed us in slaughter-pens."[15]

The soldiers had been bloodying themselves against Confederate entrenchments for more than two months, and they had endured enough. Although he was an artilleryman, Charles Wainwright was one officer who clearly saw the futility of storming rebel works. "It has been tried so often now and with such fearful losses that even the stupidest private now knows that it cannot succeed, and the natural consequence follows: the men will not try it," he wrote. "The very sight of a bank of fresh earth now brings them to a dead halt."[16]

On June 19 cavalry colonel Charles Francis Adams Jr. wrote to his father, the American ambassador to Great Britain, "We have assaulted the enemy's works repeatedly and lost many lives, but I cannot understand it. Why have these lives been sacrificed? Why is the Army kept continually fighting until its heart has sickened within it? I cannot tell. Doubtless Grant has his reasons and we must have faith; but, certainly, I have never seen the Army so haggard and worn, so worked out and fought out, so dispirited and hopeless, as now when the fall of Richmond is most likely. Grant has pushed his Army to the extreme limit of human endurance."[17]

The fighting had taken its toll on officers as well as the soldiers in the ranks. "Hancock's Corps has lost twenty brigade commanders, and the rest of the army is similarly situated," Meade noted. "We cannot replace the officers lost with experienced men, and there is no time for reorganization or careful selection."[18] The officers that remained were seriously worn down. Hancock and Gibbon, once close, had fallen out. Gibbon, that doughty warrior who had once led the Iron Brigade, had become nervous and jumpy. In the Wilderness Lyman had described Gibbon as a "tower of strength" who was "cool as a steel knife, always, and unmoved by anything and everything."[19] Now he reported that Gibbon's men had lost confidence in their commander and that his "former gallantry was all gone." His officers even tried to trick him into exposing himself to enemy fire as a joke.[20] Hancock wasn't the man he used to be either. His Gettysburg wound had reopened and bone fragments were working their way out, causing him considerable agony. He often had to ride in ambulances instead of commanding from horseback; on June 17 he had to temporarily relinquish command of the corps to Birney.[21] In the V Corps Warren showed signs of strain, becoming so short-tempered and surly that his artillery chief, Charles Wainwright, complained he "had a screw loose and is not quite accountable for all his freaks."[22]

As the campaign ground on, the stress had begun to affect the relationship between Meade and Warren. During the attacks on June 18 Meade fumed that Warren once again moved too slowly. The next day the two generals had a heated conversation. Warren exhibited "so much temper and bad feeling" that Meade sat down and wrote a long letter to Grant's chief of staff, John Rawlins, requesting that Warren be relieved. Despite Warren's good qualities—"No officer in the army exceeds Genl Warren in personal gallantry, in activity, in zeal and sleepless energy, or in devotion to his duties," Meade wrote—he suffered from a serious "defect," in which he often questioned orders rather than obey them. Such a defect, Meade wrote, "strikes at the root of all Military subordination, and it is entirely out of the question that I can command this Army," if each Corps Commander is to exercise a similar independence of action."[23]

Meade decided not to send the letter, but a month later he found an opportunity to discuss the matter. Warren asked Meade to officially deny a newspaper story that said Meade had preferred charges against Warren for his failure to obey orders. Meade told Warren he would deny the paper's statement, but he could not deny that there was bad feeling between the two generals. He had been irritated and wounded by Warren's talk, Meade said, and told Warren he had considering having him relieved.[24]

But the rift seemed beyond repair. "I believe Gen'l Meade is an august and unfeeling man and I dislike his personal character so much now that it is improbable we shall ever have again any friendly social relations," Warren wrote to his wife on July 24. "I have also lost all confidence in his ability as a general. He has quick perceptions but does not know how to act with patience and judgment. He would expect to hatch a chicken from the egg in the same time you would boil it."[25]

● ● ●

Late on July 5 Lyman heard the officer of the day enter Meade's tent and wake the general. "Very well, tell General Wright to send a good division," he heard Meade say. "I suppose it will be Ricketts." And then Meade went back to sleep.[26]

The occasion was an emergency to the north. While still at Cold Harbor, Lee had dispatched Jubal Early, his "bad old man," on a mission to redirect the Union's attention from Petersburg toward its own backyard. Early had marched north down the Shenandoah Valley, brushing aside Union resistance, and entered Maryland, where he battled outnumbered Federal defenders outside Frederick near the Monocacy River. He continued on until he reached Washington's outer defenses. This was precisely the scenario that Lincoln had long feared—that the Army of the Potomac would move so far south that it would leave the nation's capital wide open to a Confederate attack.

Grant ended up sending Wright and the VI Corps to defend Washington. Meade heard rumors that Grant would send him to Washington, too. That did not strike him as a pleasant prospect, considering the treatment he had received from the politicians there. However, Grant seemed confident that the troops he had sent, including the XIX Corps, which had been heading north from Louisiana, would be enough to handle the situation. If he had needed to send another corps, he said, he would order Meade to go with it. "I expect that after the rebels find Washington too strong for them, and they have done all the plundering they can, they will quietly slip across the Potomac and rush down here to reinforce Lee, who will then try to throw himself on us before our troops can get back," said Meade.[27]

The men who remained outside Petersburg sweltered through excruciating heat made even worse by the complete lack of rain between June 2 and July 19. Virginia seemed to be one big dust bowl. "This sacred soil of Virginia, on which we are at present trying to exist, seems made of dust," noted Chaplain Stewart of the 102nd Pennsylvania. "You see nothing but dust—you smell dust, you eat dust, you drink dust. Your clothes, blanket, tent, food, drink, are all permeated with dust. You walk in dust, you halt in dust, you lie down in dust, you sleep in dust, you wake in dust, you live in dust—you are emphatically dusty."[28]

Along with the dust came tedium, occasionally broken by sudden death. Rufus Dawes of the 6th Wisconsin found himself in the lines before Petersburg, sitting in a four-foot-deep hole, where he couldn't stick out his head without risking his life. When he did peer out, he could spy the steeples of Petersburg a mere two miles away. "We are completely holed, and ground-hogging for a steady living becomes very tedious," he wrote his wife on June 21. To pass the time one day Dawes taught a sergeant major Cicero's first oration against Catiline, in Latin. "The Calcutta black hole was not more disagreeable and the constant shower of rebel bullets are the chains that keep us imprisoned," he wrote. "Things look rather blue, I must confess, about Petersburg."[29]

Turmoil continued among the Union generals. On July 12 Meade informed Margaret that he and Baldy Smith were now "avowed antagonists," which he called "a much more comfortable position for me, than an attempt at friendly relations."[30] Smith was quite adept at creating friction. Over at the Army of the James, he, Grant, and Benjamin Butler became involved in a struggle for power. Grant longed to rid himself of Butler, a general who was much more skilled at politics than war. He contrived to have Smith take control of the Army of the James's field operations while Butler remained behind the lines in a strictly administrative role. Butler would have none of it. When the dust settled, Butler remained firmly in charge while Grant had sent Smith to New York. Smith later claimed that Butler gained the upper hand by blackmailing Grant over his drinking. The more likely scenario was that with the presidential election looming, the administration realized that this was no time to turn the politically connected General Butler into an enemy.

Replacing Smith at the head of the XVIII Corps was Maj. Gen. Edward Ord, the victor at the Battle of Dranesville back in December 1861. Afterward he had served out west under Grant, who came to appreciate his aggressive nature. Lyman, always ready with a pithy description, described Ord as "a tall man, with bushy eyebrows and a nervous manner, who looked like an eccentric Irishman who was about to tell a funny story."[31] The soldiers' nickname for E. O. C. Ord was "Old Alphabet."

On July 26 Meade told Margaret that the camp was full of rumor and intrigue. Hancock had informed Meade of one rumor—that Meade was going to be reassigned and Hancock would receive command of the Army of the Potomac. Charles Dana had also reported this to Stanton in one of the many gossipy telegrams he sent to the secretary of war from City Point.[32] At first Meade felt inclined to laugh at the story, but after thinking things over, he asked Grant about it. The general in chief said he had heard of no such thing.

Grant fueled more speculation when he asked Meade if he would be interested in taking over the Middle Division military department that included West Virginia, the Susquehanna, Baltimore, and Washington. Grant had wanted to appoint William Franklin, Meade's commander at Fredericksburg, but the administration wanted nothing to do with him. Grant suggested Meade instead. Meade told Grant he would accept any orders given to him. "So far as having an independent command, which the Army of the Potomac is not, I would like this change very well," he wrote to Margaret, but having to deal with the various commanders within the department as well as Lincoln, Stanton, and Halleck "will be a pretty trying position that no man in his senses could desire." He pronounced himself "indifferent" as to the end result, but it nagged at his ambitions. Before long the situation would explode in his face. First, though, there was a much bigger explosion to handle.[33]

◆ ◆ ◆

I have to admit that my first sight of the Petersburg crater leaves me a little disappointed. I wanted to see something like a hole a meteor would punch into the ground, the kind of crater you would find on the moon. I wanted to stand on the rim, peer into the depths, and get a sense of the terrible struggle that took place down there on July 30, 1864.

Instead, I find a grass-filled depression in the ground shaded by trees. The setting is too pastoral to be called a crater. If I had come across it in an ordinary field, I would probably pass by it without a second thought. I guess I expected more from the centerpiece of the Petersburg National Military Park and the inspiration for at least a dozen books, including a historical novel cowritten by former speaker of the house and presidential candidate Newt Gingrich.

Time heals all wounds. Visitors just after the war were probably more impressed when they stopped here. One of the historical markers includes a photo taken in 1867. It shows tourists standing at the bottom of the crater. There were no trees or grass back then, just a blasted landscape stripped of vegetation. And sitting in the dirt at the bottom of the crater was a human skull. Maybe the Park Service should scatter a few skulls and bones at the bottom of the crater today to set the mood.

The plan behind the crater was the brainchild of Lt. Col. Henry Pleasants of the IX Corps' 48th Pennsylvania. Like Meade, Pleasants had cosmopolitan origins, born in Buenos Aires of a Philadelphia Quaker and his Spanish bride. His regiment included many miners from Pennsylvania's coal country, men who knew a thing or two about digging. Some of them told Pleasants they could dig a tunnel beneath the Confederate breastworks, stuff it full of gunpowder, and blow a huge gap in the rebel defenses. Pleasants told his division commander, Brig. Gen. Robert B. Potter, about the idea. Potter told Burnside, who approved the scheme.

Meade entertained no great hopes for the idea; according to Pleasants, Meade told Burnside "it was all clap-trap and nonsense" and predicted that the tunnel would collapse or the men would suffocate. He also was not happy about the location, which would expose attackers to fire from the flank and rear as they moved forward. Meade could not summon any more enthusiasm when he summarized the plan for Grant. "I am not prepared to say the attempt would be hopeless" was the best he could manage.[34] Still, he allowed it to move forward, although Pleasants complained about the lack of support he received.

After scrounging what equipment they could, the Pennsylvania miners set to work on June 25. Over the next few weeks they dug a tunnel that stretched more than five hundred feet to a point beneath a Confederate fort in front of Burnside's position. At the end they dug two shorter tunnels to each side, one thirty-seven feet long and the other thirty-eight. The coal miners drew on all their experience not only to dig shafts to provide air to the men inside, but also to hide the dirt they removed so the Confederates would not suspect that something was going on beneath their feet. In fact, the rebels did suspect something but could not determine the tunnel's location. At the battlefield today you can still see the shallow depressions left behind by the countermines they dug.

What look like sandbags around the re-creation of the tunnel entrance today are actually clever concrete facsimiles. The little slant-sided entrance in the side of the hill below the crater is so low you would have to crouch to get in, and you'd have to keep crouching all the way to the end. Anyone who suffered from claustrophobia would have had some serious issues working here. Looking through the locked gate at the little mockup of the tunnel, with a painted backdrop at the other end to give the impression of depth, I realize that this was really quite an audacious enterprise. The audacity is one reason for the story's enduring popularity. The other is that the attack was such a complete and utter failure, "the saddest affair I have witnessed in the war," according to Grant.[35] Nothing seems to appeal to human nature as much as audacity crowned by disaster.

But the digging itself was a complete success. Trudging up the slope to the crater, I stop to read a marker about the ventilation system. A depression that still remains in the hillside indicates where the miners had dug a vertical shaft. At the bottom they lit a fire. That strikes me as completely counterintuitive, but these ex-miners knew what they were doing. They had also constructed a square wooden shaft that ran along the tunnel's floor from the entrance. When they sealed the entrance with a bit of airtight canvas, the fire drew the bad air out of the tunnel and up the vertical shaft; the resulting vacuum sucked in fresh air down the horizontal wooden shaft.

Excitement grew as it became more apparent that Pleasants's crackpot scheme might actually work. Grant had already made plans to have Hancock attack the

Confederates north of the James River, and he decided that movement would also provide a perfect way to draw troops from the site of the mine explosion. Burnside, in the meantime, prepared a plan of attack. He assigned Brig. Gen. Edward Ferrero's division of African American troops the mission of leading the assault on the enemy's lines after the explosion. Ferrero's men began training for their role.

Burnside preferred Ferrero's soldiers because, unlike the rest of the IX Corps, they had not seen any serious fighting, so they remained fresh. At the last minute, Meade decided that having the black soldiers lead the attack was not wise. He advised Grant that this was not a good time to give untested troops their first combat experience. Furthermore, Meade continued, if the attack should fail, it would be said "that we were shoving these people ahead to get killed because we did not care anything about them." Grant agreed. On the day before the mine explosion, Meade told Burnside to pick a different division to lead the attack.[36]

Rather than choosing the second-best men available, Burnside had his division commanders draw straws. The winner—or loser, depending on how you look at it—was Brig. Gen. James Ledlie. This was the same Ledlie who had been visibly intoxicated at the North Anna. ("Ledlie was a wretched, incapable drunkard, not fit to command a company, and was the ruin of his division," said Lyman.)[37] Meade also interfered with Burnside's tactics. Burnside wanted the first wave of attacking soldiers to swing left and right to roll up the Confederate lines on each side of the crater. Meade overruled him. He wanted the first troops to charge forward and take the high ground occupied by Blandford Cemetery, about four hundred yards away and off to the right. The divisions following would then turn to the sides to cover the leaders' flanks, with Ferrero's 4th Division taking up the rear. Ord's XVIII and Warren's V Corps would wait in support.

Soldiers quietly lugged bags of powder down the long, cramped tunnel and placed them in galleries along the lateral extensions at the end. Pleasants had planned to use twelve thousand pounds, but after consultation with his engineers, Meade decreed that eight thousand pounds would be sufficient. The miners strung a long, spliced-together fuse down the tunnel. The schedule called for the explosion to happen at 3:30 a.m. on July 30. In the predawn darkness Ledlie's division quietly filed down protected trenches to the front lines, and then they waited. The fuse was lit; time ticked by; the sky began lightening in the east; nerves were on edge as all ears strained for the sound of the explosion . . . and nothing happened.

Meade waited impatiently at IX Corps headquarters. Burnside had gone forward to observe from a gun battery, later named Fort Morton, but remained in communication with Meade by telegraph wire.

Grant arrived around 4:00. "What's the matter with the Mine?" he asked.

"Don't know," said Meade, but he figured rightly that the fuse had gone out.[38] Sgt. Henry Rees took on the unnerving duty of going into the tunnel to determine the problem and set things right. He found that the fuse had indeed been extinguished at one of the splices. With the help of Lt. Jacob Douty, he fixed the splice, relit the fuse, and hightailed it out of the tunnel.

The result was everything its planners hoped it would be. "The explosion was the grandest spectacle I ever saw," wrote Stephen Weld of the 56th Massachusetts, part of Ledlie's division. "The first I knew of it, was feeling the earth shaking. I looked up and saw a huge mass of earth and flame rising some 50 or 60 feet in the air, almost slowly and majestically, as if a volcano had just opened, followed by an immense volume of smoke rolling out in every direction." It looked as though the debris would rain down on the Union soldiers, and some of them broke and ran. It required twenty minutes or so to re-form the lines for the attack. (Imagine what would have happened had the mine used the full twelve thousand pounds of powder.) Then the men had to clamber over entrenchments and through abatis, further delaying them.

The explosion had created a crater indeed, one that was 60 feet wide, 170 feet long, and 30 feet deep. When Weld and his men reached the pit, he recalled, "The scene inside was horrible. Men were found half buried; some dead, some alive, some with their legs kicking in the air, some with the arms only exposed, and some with every bone in their bodies apparently broken."[39]

The Confederates had been surprised by the explosion, which wiped out some 150 feet of their defensive line. But the attacking troops seemed equally stunned. With Ledlie taking shelter behind the lines in a bombproof, drunk, there was no one in authority to spur the Union soldiers forward. The men moved into the crater and milled about in confusion as the defenders began to recover from the initial shock and turn to the business of killing their attackers. Back at IX Corps headquarters, Meade intercepted a message intended for Burnside that said the men would not advance. He telegraphed Burnside and demanded information. "I wish to know the truth and desire an immediate answer," he said.

Meade's implication enraged Burnside. "I have never in any report said anything different from what I conceived to be the truth," he telegraphed back. "Were it not insubordinate I would say that the latter remark of your note was unofficerlike and ungentlemanly."[40]

Meanwhile, the situation at the front was going from bad to worse. At 6:00 Meade told Burnside to push his entire command forward. Burnside interpreted that to mean he should order Ferrero's men to the crater, even though it was already crowded with soldiers who would not move forward. "It was a perfect pandemonium," Weld recalled. "The negroes charged into the mine, and we were packed in there like sardines in a box. I literally could not raise my arms from my side."[41] Some of the black soldiers did advance beyond the crater, but the intense Confederate fire soon drove them back in disorder.

The attack had clearly failed. Sometime before 10:00 Meade ordered Burnside to recall his men. Burnside rode over to protest in person. He said his troops could still take the hill. At the very least, he did not want to withdraw them until nightfall. Horace Porter described the encounter as "peppery" and said it "went far toward confirming one's belief in the wealth and flexibility of the English language as a medium of personal dispute."[42] Meade repeated his order for a withdrawal, but it remained unclear how the men could leave without being gunned down during the retreat. For hours the Union soldiers remained trapped within the crater under a sweltering sun, enemy fire making it impossible to move forward or backward. "It was a sickening sight," recalled one soldier: "men were dead and dying all around us; blood was streaming down the sides of the crater to the bottom, where it gathered in pools for a time before being absorbed by the hard red clay."[43]

Confederates under Brig. Gen. William Mahone finally charged to retake their lines. "Over the crest and into the crater they poured, and a hand-to-hand conflict ensued," recounted Maj. William H. Powell. "It was of short duration, however; crowded as our troops were, and without organization, resistance was vain."[44] Some of the Confederates were enraged to see the black soldiers and slaughtered them without mercy when they tried to surrender. Weld was standing next to a black soldier when they both were captured. "Shoot the nigger, but don't kill the white man," one of their captors yelled, and the rebels gunned down the black man. As Weld and the other prisoners climbed out of the crater, rebels shot another black man in front of him, killing the man after three shots.[45] Afterward A. P. Hill had the Union prisoners, white and black, marched through Petersburg so the residents could jeer and abuse them.

The attack had been a fiasco. Union casualties numbered around thirty-eight hundred, mostly from the IX Corps. Meade requested that Grant relieve Burnside from command. Grant did just that following a court of inquiry that parceled out the blame to Burnside, Ledlie, Ferrero, and others.

Ambrose Burnside left the Army of the Potomac on August 13. Officially he was on furlough, but his active role in the war was over. He later became the governor of Rhode Island and served in the U.S. Senate. Maj. Gen. John Parke, like Meade a Philadelphian and a West Point–trained engineer, took over command of the IX Corps.

There was plenty of blame to go around for the fiasco. Some must be attributed to Meade for interfering with Burnside's preparations at the last minute. Apparently he realized that. According to Col. Joshua Sigfried, "Had the original plan been adhered to, I am PERFECTLY satisfied Petersburg would have been in our possession before 10 o'clock. Generals Grant and Meade both admitted that to me afterwards."[46]

Why did Meade order Burnside to replace Ferrero's division? Was it because of their inexperience or their race? Lyman once noted that if Meade had a bias regarding black soldiers, "it is towards and not against them, and indeed it would go to the heart of the best Bob to see the punctilious way in which he returns their salutes." "The best Bob" referred to Lyman's Harvard friend Robert Gould Shaw, who took command of the 54th Massachusetts and died with the regiment's African American soldiers fighting to capture Battery Wagner outside Charleston. Matthew Broderick portrayed him in the 1989 movie *Glory*. "I can say with certainty," Lyman continued, "that there is not a General in this army from whom the nigs might expect a judicious helping hand more than from Meade."[47]

In a letter dated February 1863 Meade told his wife about a somewhat ambiguous encounter he had had in Washington. He had dropped by George McClellan's after dinner and found the ex-commander of the Army of the Potomac dining with a number of politicians and soldiers. One of them was Andrew Porter, a general who had served on McClellan's staff. For some reason he and Meade did not get along. Porter, apparently miffed over Meade's recent promotion to major general, decided to needle him. He said he had heard that Meade would receive command of "an *Army Corps of Niggers,*" as Meade related it. "I laughingly replied I had not been informed of the honor awaiting me, but one thing I begged to assure Porter, that if the niggers were going into the field and really could be brought heartily to fight, I was ready to command them, and should prefer such duty to others that might be assigned to me."[48] It was a polite thrust and parry, no doubt conducted behind tight smiles and with icy cordiality. We may find the language offensive today, but it was common parlance in 1863. Still, there is a mystery at the heart of this encounter. As a McClellanite, Porter certainly would have been opposed to waging a war of "servile insurrection," much less arming black soldiers. Meade was certainly no abolitionist, so I'm not sure whether he was expressing his real opinions or just saying something he knew would irritate Porter.

Meade was essentially conservative, as were many in the army, especially the officers who owed their positions to McClellan. It's probably not surprising that two of the generals with whom Meade had bad relationships were Birney and Doubleday, two men who sided with the abolitionists. Certainly he was not the only Union general who doubted the black soldiers' fighting abilities. H. Seymour Hall, who had served on the staff of the abolitionist Emory Upton before leaving to take command of the 43rd United States Colored Troops, noted that there was a "strong prejudice" against the use of African American soldiers. Said one general to Hall, "I am sorry to have you leave my command, and still more sorry that you are going to serve with negroes. I think it's a disgrace to the Army to make soldiers of them."[49]

Such attitudes were probably more common than otherwise. In July 1864 Grant suggested Andrew Humphreys for command of the X Corps in the Army of the James, which included African American soldiers. Although Humphreys was eager to receive a corps command, he declined this offer because he did not want to command blacks, telling Grant, "I confess that while I have the kindliest feelings for the negro race and gladly see anything done that promises to ameliorate their condition, yet as they are not my own people, nor my own race, I could not feel towards negro troops as I have always felt towards the troops I have commanded, that their character, their reputation, their honor was a part of mine, that the two were so intimately connected that they could not be separated."[50] And Lyman wrote, "I say, as I always have, that you never, in the long run, can make negroes fight with success against white men."[51]

By the end of the war, more than 186,000 African American men had joined the army to fight for the Union in a war that had started because of slavery and that Lincoln had turned into a war to end slavery. Great men rise above the accepted wisdom. When it came to the role of African American soldiers in his army, Meade, along with many of his fellow generals, fell short of greatness.

• • •

Strains began appearing in the relationship between Meade and Grant. Sheridan often proved the catalyst. In early August Meade read in the papers that Sheridan, whom Grant had sent north to deal with Jubal Early in the Shenandoah Valley, had received temporary command of the Middle Division, which Grant had

Petersburg

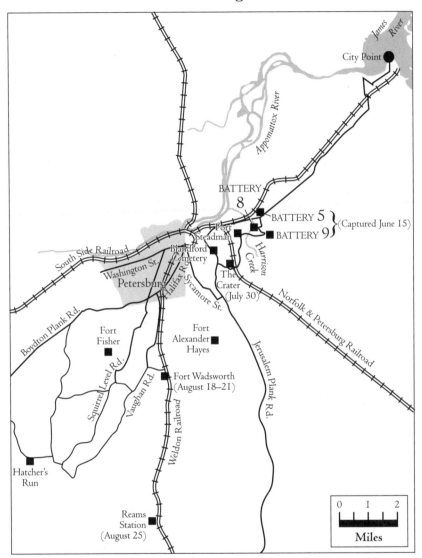

promised to Meade. Meade bristled at this perceived slight, but he hesitated to confront Grant "from a sense of self-respect, and from the fear I should not be able to restrain the indignation I hold to be natural at the duplicity some one has practiced."[52] When he finally did question Grant about it, the general in chief explained that Sheridan did not have command of the division, only of the soldiers gathered together from various departments to deal with Early. Meade agonized over whether Grant was being sincere or disingenuous.

If that weren't bad enough for Meade's state of mind, later that month he learned that Sherman, Hancock, and Sheridan all had received promotions, while his own promised advancement to major general in the Regular Army remained stalled. Meade fumed about the slight and once again confronted Grant. Grant told Meade he had asked Washington to hold back on the promotion because he did not want Meade to outrank Sherman. Meade would get his promotion when he received command of the Middle Division. The hitch, Grant explained, was that if he reassigned Meade there now, it would look like a slap at Sheridan. "Of course I could say nothing to this explanation," Meade complained to Margaret. "It is the same old story, an inability to appreciate the sensitiveness of a man of character and honor. Grant really thinks he is one of my best friends, and can't conceive why I should complain of a little delay in giving me what he tells me I am certainly to have."[53]

More than rank, it seems that Meade craved affirmation. He needed official "vindication" and validation that he had performed well.[54] Despite his repeated claims to Margaret that he was "indifferent" to such things, he wanted an official seal of approval that always seemed to evade him. Perhaps Meade would have had more success in advancing his cause if he had more nakedly lusted for glory and aggressively sought fame. He was more than willing to carp about the situation in his letters to his wife, but his son George edited most of these complaints out of the letters for publication. Publicly, though, Meade had an almost naïve—or perhaps idealistic is a better word—belief that true honors would come to those who deserved them.

For Phil Sheridan, fame and advancement were something to be pursued and taken. "Lying was just a part of his aggressive plan for advancing his own self-interest," Eric Wittenberg wrote in *Little Phil: A Reassessment of the Civil War Leadership of Gen. Philip H. Sheridan.* "He regularly lied to cover his mistakes at all costs. He seems to have been a congenital liar, and his perfidy often exposed him to public ridicule and criticism. Sheridan did not care. He lied anyway."[55] On this front Meade was clearly outmatched.

So it's really no surprise that Phil Sheridan received command of the newly formed Army of the Shenandoah. In part it was because Grant liked Sheridan and respected his aggressive nature. Meade's biographer Isaac Pennypacker, though, suggested another motive: "There was also undoubtedly a feeling among the men surrounding the lieutenant general that it would be inadvisable to place the victor at Gettysburg in a position to add in a marked way to the separate military renown which he had already won before the new element in the army appeared upon the scene."[56]

"Meade was a soldier and a gentleman, with no liking for intrigue and with no time for it, for he was busily engaged in a great work in a position of heavy responsibility," Pennypacker wrote. "He loved the truth. Indirection had no part in his mental methods, and what he himself was he was apt to think others were also."[57] That's true to a point. But when Meade was a brigade commander lusting after a division, he had Margaret see if her family's connections in Washington would help her husband's cause.

He remained baffled by Grant and the lieutenant general's attitude toward him. In a letter to Henry Cram, his wife's brother-in-law, Meade grappled with the subject without coming to any clear conclusions. "Grant is not a mighty genius, but he is a good soldier, of great force of character, honest and upright, of pure purposes, I think, without political aspirations, certainly not influenced by them," he wrote. "His prominent quality is unflinching tenacity of purpose, which blinds him to opposition and obstacles—certainly a great quality in a commander, when controlled by judgment, but a dangerous one otherwise. Grant is not without his faults and weaknesses. Among these is a want of sensibility, an almost too confident and sanguine disposition, and particularly a simple and guileless disposition, which is apt to put him, unknown to himself, under the influence of those who should not influence him, and desire to do so only for their own purposes." That proved to be a prescient view of Grant's presidency. Meade went on to tell Cram that he liked Grant and had good relations with him, even though Grant's arrival had meant that Meade felt largely set aside, almost as though he had been relieved of command. Grant, he said, didn't seem to understand this, which to Meade underscored the differences in their personalities: "I over-sensitive, and he deficient in sensibility." Grant never even perceived that his favoritism for Sheridan was unfair to Meade, "but when I called his attention to it, and explained how I thought it was unjust, he readily and frankly acknowledged I was right."[58]

Meade also had family concerns weighing on his mind. His oldest son, John Sergeant, was dying of tuberculosis. Meade managed to make a quick visit to see him in Philadelphia at the beginning of September, with a stop in Washington for visits to Stanton and Lincoln on the way back. "Both were very affable, apparently very glad to see me, and said many flattering things," he wrote to Margaret.[59] Stanton even offered the use of a government steamer if the couple wanted to take Sergeant to a better climate. Meade and his wife discussed the possibility of sending the sick young man to the island of Madeira, but they eventually decided he would not be up for the journey. His son's failing health was never far from Meade's mind during this time.

◆ ◆ ◆

The summer months crept into fall, and Grant and Meade continued to extend their reach westward, hoping to capture the railroads that supplied Petersburg and force Lee to abandon the city. I must admit I find this period to be a somewhat confusing and jumbled account of troop movements and inconclusive fighting, so I'm hoping that taking the Park Service's driving tours will help me obtain some clarity. The sixteen-mile route takes me to a number of forts the Union soldiers established as they reached farther and farther west, winning a battle here, suffering an embarrassing repulse there, but always whittling away at the enemy army and its ability to extend its lines to match the Union efforts.

From the crater site I exit the park property by turning onto South Crater Road. In 1864 this was the Jerusalem Plank Road, the name it still bears farther south, an important route right into the heart of Petersburg. Right now, though, I head south, away from town and into a land of forts named after dead soldiers.

Fort Davis, a small island of trees, humped remainders of earthworks, and swampy ditches surrounded by roads, marks the place where Union forces reached out and captured the Jerusalem Plank Road on June 21. The fort was originally called Fort Warren after the very-much-alive general but later received the name of Col. P. Stearns Davis, the surgeon for the 39th Massachusetts, who was killed here by a shell fragment on July 11.

Fort Alexander Hayes is a little farther on, a tangled mass of woods and swampy land just off the road. It bears the misspelled name of the general who fought so well at Gettysburg and died in the Wilderness. Poor Hays. It's bad enough to be dead, but even worse to have the people who name a fort after you get your name wrong.

Fort Wadsworth, more mounds of earth in a field at a crossroads, is the first official stop on the Western Front auto tour. It marks an important point in the campaign, when Meade's army finally severed the Weldon Railroad. Warren and the V Corps attacked here near a local landmark called Globe Tavern early on the morning of August 18, fighting off a Confederate counterattack to keep their grip on the railroad. The rebels counterattacked through a driving rain the next day. It was a close fight for a time, with the rebels overrunning Samuel Crawford's division of the V Corps, but the Union soldiers, reinforced by a division of the IX Corps, thrust the enemy back. The rebels attacked again on Sunday, August 21, but by then Warren had his men positioned behind entrenchments, and once again they repulsed the Confederate attack. This portion of the Weldon Railroad was now in Union hands, and the construction of Fort Wadsworth—named after the New York politician-turned-general who had fallen in the Wilderness—was built here to make sure the Confederates couldn't take it back. Now Confederate supplies coming to Petersburg could travel only as far as Stony Creek station, where they had to be unloaded, placed on wagons, and transported to Dinwiddie Court House and then up the Boydton Plank Road to the city.

I'm startled to see a field of white just across the road from Fort Wadsworth. It looks like snow, but suddenly I realize I'm looking at field full of cotton. I must be in the South! This is the first time I've ever seen cotton growing, and I can't resist the impulse to go over and pluck one of the soft white blossoms, which seems ready to be stuffed into an aspirin bottle. When I pick it, though, I can feel the hard cotton seeds inside the white fluff. Naturally that gets me thinking about Eli Whitney and the cotton gin. I recall some of the things I learned in school—that cotton production soared once Whitney's machine sped up the slow and tedious process of extracting the seeds, which in turn inflated the value of slavery for Southern plantations. Cotton production boomed, the number of slaveholding states increased with it, and before long the South and North were struggling in a great civil war. Simplistic? Perhaps, but there's a seed of truth in there.

On the grass next to Fort Wadsworth and across the street from the cotton field is a monument to Johnson Hagood's South Carolina brigade, which fought here on August 21 as part of William Mahone's division. "No prouder fate than theirs who gave their lives to liberty," say the words on the monument. I look at the monument and then over at the cotton field and think what kind of liberty the monument refers to.

Farther south, in a quiet field alongside the railroad, is the site of the Battle of Reams Station, a serious embarrassment for Hancock, who had returned to command on June 27, and the II Corps. Hancock's men were following up Warren's capture of the Weldon Railroad by moving south down the line and tearing up the rails, when they received word that elements of A. P. Hill's corps were heading their way. On August 25 the Federals managed to beat back the first attacks, but then their lines crumbled. The proud Hancock, humiliated by the behavior of his soldiers, told one of his staff officers, "Colonel, I do not care to die, but I pray to God I may never leave this field."[60] God must not have been listening, for Hancock was forced to retreat. Meade realized how his corps commander must have felt and sent him a dispatch. "I am satisfied you and your command have done all in your power," he wrote, "and though you have met with a reverse, the honor and escutcheon of the old Second is as bright as ever, and will, on some future occasion, prove it is only when enormous odds are brought against them that they can be moved.

"Don't let this matter worry you, because you have given me every satisfaction."[61]

Lyman noted that such setbacks never seemed to depress Meade; in fact, they seemed to "rouse and wind him up." Lyman mused that maybe after three years of war, there was something in his nature that needed such things, "just as some persons enjoy a daily portion of arsenic."[62]

As the two armies faced each other along the growing line of entrenchments protecting Petersburg, their soldiers often fell into unlikely camaraderie. Opposing pickets exchanged news and made trades. The Confederate soldiers had plenty of tobacco to barter, and they used it to obtain sugar, coffee, and other items such as needles and thread.[63] Lyman describes an incident when Gen. Crawford stood rather blatantly on the front lines and examined the rebel defenses through a telescope. A Confederate wrote out a note, wrapped it around a rock, and hurled it over to the Union side. "Tell the fellow with the spy-glass to clear out, or we shall have to shoot him," it read. Another time a rebel accidentally discharged his gun and nearly set off a general exchange. The rebels stood up and waved their hands. "Don't shoot!" they cried. "You'll see how we'll fix him." They made the guilty party place a rail over his shoulder in place of his weapon and march up and down in front of the Confederate defenses. When the Confederates did receive orders to open up on the other side, the rebels sometimes shouted out warnings or fired the first volley high to warn their opponents.[64]

Francis Barlow, "that eccentric officer," left the army in July. He had been "more like a dead than a living man" after learning that his wife had died of typhoid. Before the Battle of Reams Station he had been carried off the field on a stretcher.[65] David Birney had also left the II Corps when Hancock returned. Grant gave the cold and ambitious general command of the X Corps in the Army of the James. Birney died in Philadelphia of typhoid in October. Meade told Margaret that he had never liked the man personally but admired his abilities on the field. "General Birney is undoubtedly a loss to the army," Meade wrote. "He was a very good soldier, and very energetic in the performance of his duties. During the last campaign he had quite distinguished himself."[66]

Grant launched another offensive at the end of September, with the Army of the James assaulting the lines north of the James River and the Army of the Potomac operating south of it. Meade had a narrow escape during the resulting Battle of Peebles Farm, an unsuccessful attempt to extend the Union line farther west and sever the vital supply lines of the Boydton Plank Road and the South Side Railroad. Meade had ridden out to the field and was conversing with his generals when a Confederate shell nearly eliminated a good portion of the Union high command. It scraped the tail of Humphreys's horse, just missed Generals Griffin and Bartlett, grazed Meade's leg, and slammed into the ground among another group of officers, showering them with dirt. Meade felt the impact on his boot and hesitated to look down, fearing that he had lost his leg. He was relieved to find that the limb was still attached and surprised that he did not even get a bruise. "A more wonderful escape I never saw," he wrote to Margaret. "How would you like to have me back minus a leg and on crutches?" Lyman later went back to retrieve the shell so he could send it home.[67]

Meade had another narrow escape later that month during the Battle of Burgess's Mill on October 27. Once again Grant had Butler attack the Confederates north of the James, while Meade moved against the Confederate right in an attempt to capture the South Side Railroad. Hancock and the II Corps were to be the tip of the spear, supported by the V and IX Corps under Warren and Parke. Grant and Meade rode out to the front on the damp and dreary morning of October 27 to observe Hancock's position. The II Corps faced the Confederate right near Hatcher's Run at a spot called Burgess's Mill on the Boydton Plank Road. The fighting here was brisk, and a shell exploded near Meade—so close that Horace Porter thought it must have killed him. But again Meade emerged unscathed. Grant also had a close brush with a bursting shell, and then his horse got one leg tangled in a fallen telegraph line. An aide had to carefully free the horse's leg while Grant remained exposed to enemy fire.

By then it was apparent that the rebel entrenchments extended much farther to the west than anyone had anticipated, and Grant called off the attack. Hancock prepared to withdraw from his exposed position the next morning. The Confederates, as they often did, had different plans. Finding a weakness, William Mahone's men made a stealthy passage through swamp and forest toward the Union right. Hancock had thought Samuel Crawford's division was moving up to connect with him there; instead, the rebel forces swung around his flank and attacked. The Federals managed to recover from their surprise and force the Confederates back, but Hancock decided to withdraw his forces that night despite the rain and the darkness.

The Battle at Burgess's Mill finished the active campaigning for 1864—and it marked the end of Winfield Scott Hancock's time with the Army of the Potomac. He had been summoned back to Washington to raise a corps of veteran soldiers. The Petersburg Campaign had been one disappointment after another for Hancock, who seemingly had reached his own high-water mark at Gettysburg. One of his last actions was to make an official complaint to Meade about the reporting of Edward Crapsey, whom Meade had allowed to return to the army. Meade advised Hancock to write up charges and said he would have Crapsey tried by a commission.

With Hancock's departure, Humphreys took command of the II Corps. He had long been itching to get his own command, and when he finally did, a large contingent from Meade's staff escorted him to his new assignment, "for he is very popular," said Lyman, "for his bravery and urbanity."[68] His replacement as chief of staff was Alexander Stuart Webb, who had previously served in that position for Meade when he commanded the V Corps. Lyman called him "effervescent," "very jolly and pleasant, while, at the same time, he is a thorough soldier, wide-awake, quick and attentive to detail," although he "has a way of suddenly laughing in a convulsive manner."[69]

• • •

Another battle being waged that fall was the campaign for the White House, which pitted the incumbent President Lincoln against George Brinton McClellan. The army's former commander had accepted the Democratic nomination despite his misgivings over the party's antiwar plank. With the election essentially a referendum on the war effort, which was not going all that well, things did not look promising for Lincoln. The situation appeared so grim, in fact, that on August 23 the president wrote a letter stating that since it seemed "exceedingly probable that this Administration will not be re-elected," it would be his duty "to so co-operate with the President elect as to save the Union between the election and the inauguration; as he will have secured his election on such ground that he can not possibly save it afterwards."[70] He then had all the members of his cabinet endorse the letter without letting them read it.

The stalemate in the east was not helping Lincoln's chances, but when Sherman captured Atlanta on September 1, the good news immediately boosted his prospects.

Meade did not vote. The soldiers who did went overwhelmingly for Lincoln, with some 70 percent of the Army of the Potomac's votes going to the president.[71] The men still loved McClellan, but they felt betrayed by his association with a party platform built on the belief that the war effort had failed. "Yes, it was cruel in General McClellan to ask us to vote that our campaigns had all been failures, and that our comrades had all died in vain," wrote Theodore Gerrish of the 20th Maine. "And yet there were those who supposed that our love for him would cause us to do it."[72]

Meade had expected Lincoln to win, but shortly after the election he received some news that surprised him, and not pleasantly. Philip Sheridan had received promotion to major general in the Regular Army. Meade felt it was a slap in the face. Sheridan had advanced past him while his own long-promised promotion still languished. "*Every other officer* in this army, except myself, who has been recommended for promotion for services in this campaign has been promoted," he complained to Margaret. "It is rather hard I am to be the only exception to this rule."[73] Once again he confronted Grant, and once again Grant told him that no harm had been intended. He promised to straighten things out when he visited Washington and make sure that Meade's promotion was postdated before Sheridan's. Grant proved as good as his word, and Meade finally received his promotion to major general in the Regular Army dated to August 19, the day that Warren had captured the Weldon Railroad. He pronounced himself satisfied that justice had been done and gratified by "this evidence of Grant's truthfulness and sincerity."[73] However, the Senate still had to vote on the measure and did not do so until February 1, 1865.[74]

Shortly afterward, Meade's staff received brevet promotions—an honorary step up in rank with little real-world application. Lyman, being an unpaid volunteer, was not eligible. As the staff members had fun pinning new insignia to their uniforms, the newly promoted giving their old insignia to the men one rank below them, Meade watched in rare high spirits, having just received word of his own promotion. Lyman thought he looked "like Mephistopheles in good humor." "Now here's Lyman," Meade said. "He has no brevet, but I am going to write to the Governor of Massachusetts to make him a Field Marshal." Then he rubbed the side of his nose, which Lyman said was something Meade always did on those rare occasions when he laughed.[75]

CHAPTER 17

On to Appomattox

Philip Sheridan
LIBRARY OF CONGRESS

● ● ●

Dr. Christopher Stowe has brought me onto the grounds of Fort Lee, a U.S. Army base outside Petersburg, to show me where Meade had his headquarters during the campaign here. Stowe is an associate professor in the Department of Military History at the U.S. Army Command and General Staff College at Fort Lee, and he knows a thing or two about Meade. He wrote a master's thesis on the general's experiences with the Joint Committee on the Conduct of the War and a Ph.D. dissertation titled "A Philadelphia Gentleman: The Cultural, Institutional, and Political Socialization of George Gordon Meade." He's been laboring to turn his dissertation into a book, which will be published by Kent State University Press under the title *George Gordon Meade: A Nineteenth-Century Life*. Stowe also possesses an apparently encyclopedic knowledge of military history.

As we drive through Fort Lee, I remark on the irony that the site of Meade's headquarters is on an army base named after his defeated adversary. Stowe points out that there's less irony there than I think. In the years before World War I, he says, the army had a good reason for naming a base after Lee. "It was really more about sectional reconciliation and throwing these young boys a Confederate bone, so to speak, in order to get them into the military family again. It's a calculated move on the part of the Department of War."

Stowe bears a resemblance to the actor Stanley Tucci. He is tall and bespectacled, with some gray stubble on his nearly shaven head. He was the youngest of three boys. His father, whose enthusiasm about the Civil War was stoked by the centennial observances in the 1960s, took each boy on a trip to Gettysburg. "My chance came in '75," Stowe says. It struck a chord. He went for a second time and started visiting more battlefields. "After high school and some interludes—you know, girls, air guitar, things like that—I got back into it in university, in college." He wasn't a history major at Penn State, but he took enough courses to make it his minor. After an unsuccessful stint in sales, he followed the advice of a professor and considered an academic career.

We park the car and walk back to a green, weathered bronze marker on a concrete post by the side of the road. "Site of headquarters, Army of the Potomac," it reads, adding that Meade's headquarters was actually 275 yards to the west.

"There's another marker in the woods," Stowe says. "We'll go back there. It's a nice day. There are no chiggers, no poison ivy." Stowe, who has just come from work and is wearing a suit and tie, black overcoat, and nicely polished shoes, is hardly outfitted for a walk in the woods, but he gamely leads me through dried leaves, pine needles, and brambles. Deep trenches run in straight lines through the trees, but Stowe tells me they are not from the Civil War. These are training trenches U.S. soldiers dug during World War I.

Stowe hasn't been to this marker for three years or so, but he finds it pretty quickly. It's another bronze marker on a concrete post, and it looks as though someone attempted to scratch a swastika into it. A weather-beaten wooden bench sits beneath the shelter of a small tree nearby. Stowe tells me he used to come out here, sit on the bench, and read his copy of Meade's *Life and Letters*. "It's a cool place," he says.

In 1864 and 1865 the land here was stripped bare of trees and covered with tents and maybe wooden huts. It was a beehive of activity. "There would have been a small army of orderlies and headquarters guards," Stowe says. The provost general's headquarters was nearby. Meade Station, on the busy military railroad, was about one hundred yards away.

We get back in the car and drive across the base, and Stowe points out where soldiers formed to attack the Petersburg defenses on June 16, 1864. We pass a motor pool with long lines of Humvees parked behind a chain-link fence. That's probably the spot, Stowe tells me, where Abraham Lincoln stood with Meade as they watched Confederate prisoners being escorted to the rear after the IX Corps repulsed an attack on nearby Fort Stedman on March 25, 1865.

"I have just now a despatch from General Parke to show you," Meade said to the president.

Lincoln pointed to the lines of bedraggled Confederate prisoners. "Ah," he said, "*there* is the best despatch you can show me from General Parke!"[1]

I spend an enjoyable afternoon talking with Stowe about Meade. I pitch my theory that perhaps his prickly behavior over issues of rank and recognition stemmed from the way his family's privileged status disappeared when his father lost his fortune in Spain. Stowe politely tells me he thinks that's unlikely, since the young George Meade was only two years old when his mother brought him to the United States. Stowe sees a broader reason for Meade's behavior, rooted in the social structure in which he grew up "as a member of a kind of early-American gentry," a class with strict views of gender and masculinity. "Meade is that old gentleman who is to be honored and revered for the efforts that he has exerted on behalf of the Republic," Stowe says. His problems may have resulted when his superiors did not share his viewpoint.

"In some ways he's the victim, but in other ways I think he earned the reputation that he has, through some unfortunate mistakes," Stowe tells me. "I'm not talking necessarily military mistakes, though some of them are military." Stowe believes Meade's principal flaw as a commander was his idealization of the relationship between the military and political spheres. In Meade's ideal world, politicians devised the national strategies and then turned over the reins to the military professionals to achieve them. What made Grant a great general, Stowe explains, was his ability to conform his plans to the administration's national strategy without complaining about it. Meade, Stowe believes, was more passive-aggressive in his dealings with Washington. "When Lincoln and Halleck and Stanton are deliberating, Meade is pointing out obstacles rather than suggesting workarounds," Stowe says. "And if you're in the military chain of command, when you're given a shit sandwich, you have to find a way to eat it."

◆ ◆ ◆

New Year 1865 arrived and the Senate still had not confirmed Meade as a major general in the Regular Army, much to his displeasure. On January 23 Grant wrote to his political patron Eli Washburne, regarding the delay: "Gen. Meade is one of our truest men and ablest officers. He has been constantly with that Army confronting the strongest, best appointed and most confidant [*sic*] Army in the South. He therefore has not had the same opportunity of wining [*sic*] laurels so distinctively marked as have fallen to the lot of other Generals. But I defy any one to name a commander who could do more than he has done with the same chances. I am satisfied with a full knowledge of the man, what he has done, and the circumstances attending to all his Military acts, all objections would be removed."[2]

Meade fretted over the delay in his promotion, worried that some of his enemies in Washington were deliberately holding it back. But a much more serious concern was troubling him that winter: his oldest son was losing his battle against tuberculosis. Margaret kept him updated on John Sergeant's condition, and his letters to her are full of references to his son's health, a subject that preyed on his mind. When son George later edited the letters for publication, he cut out many of Meade's agonized passages about Sergeant's condition, but even the ones that remain indicate the depth of his pain and concern. His inability to be with his son troubled him greatly. "I think of him all the time, and feel at times like asking to be relieved, that I may go home and help you nurse him," he wrote to Margaret on February 7.[3]

Sergeant took a turn for the worse that month, prompting Margaret to send her husband several frantic telegrams. Meade felt torn between his family and duty to his army and country. He told Margaret that he could not go to Philadelphia unless he resigned his command. They would have to resign themselves to God's will. "Dear Margaret, let me rely on your exhibiting in this, the greatest trial you have had in life, true Christian fortitude," he wrote on February 21, 1864. "Bear up, in the consciousness that you have ever devoted all the energy of a tender mother's love to check and avert the fatal disease that is carrying off our first born; all that human power could do has been done. Our boy has had warning, and not only his good life, but the consciousness that he knew and was prepared for the change, should sustain us in that parting which had to be encountered one day, for we all must die in time."[4]

John Sergeant Meade's time came the day his father wrote that letter. He was twenty-three years old. Meade finally decided he could be spared from the army long enough for a trip home, but by the time he reached Philadelphia on February 23, his son was dead. Meade stayed long enough for the funeral, and then on February 26 Stanton summoned him to Washington for meetings. There was little time for grieving at a time when grief was engulfing families all over the divided nation.

For the Army of the Potomac, the mud and tedium of the winter encampment were punctuated by various entertainments. Lyman wrote home about attending a minstrel show at a theater the soldiers had built, as well as a musical program hosted by the 50th New York Engineers. Occasionally flocks of ladies, young and old, arrived in camp to get a sense of army life. One such entourage included a Miss Stanton, who Lyman eventually deduced was related to the secretary of war, and Julia Grant, the lieutenant general's wife. As she was leaving, Mrs. Grant announced, "General Meade, I would far rather command an army, as you do, than live at City Point and have the position of *Mr. Grant*!" Another party included the wife of chief of staff Webb. She hinted to Meade that she would like to stay the night in camp with her husband. That was strictly against orders, and Lyman reported that at the suggestion, Meade's "hooked nose became as a polite bit of flint unto any such proposition." Mrs. Webb sadly returned to City Point.[5]

On St. Patrick's Day the Irish Brigade put on an elaborate horse race complete with printed programs, a judge's stand, a band, and "a spacious refreshment room." Many generals, including Meade, showed up to observe the events, which the participants took as seriously as any battle. "Two or three accidents marred the pleasure of the day," reads a regimental history. One lieutenant died of a fractured skull, and a colonel was badly injured.[6]

Margaret Meade, accompanied by Lyman's wife, arrived on March 22. Margaret still would have been in mourning for her son, a process Victorian etiquette decreed should last up to a year. This was Lyman's first chance to size up the woman his chief had married, and he came away with mixed feelings. He noted that the general's wife "has a pleasant and still good looking face, for her age, and very fine hair," but she also had "a little of the languid, half southern way, and is wanting in force, somewhat."[7] For two days the women examined the Union frontlines and enjoyed trips up the James River from City Point. But then on March 25 Robert E. Lee had the bad manners to spoil their trip by launching what turned out to be his last offensive of the war.

● ● ●

A thick fog shrouds the fields around Fort Stedman in the early-morning hours when I visit. It's easy to pretend it's the smoky haze of gunpowder. I walk around the grassy hummocks that mark the fort's outlines and am pleased to find a quote from my old friend Lyman on one of the markers: "It is quite interesting to see a fort going up. The men work in the manner of bees. The mass throw the earth; the engineer soldiers do the 'rivetting,' that is, the interior facing the logs. The engineer sergeants run about with tapes and stakes, measuring busily; and the engineer officers look as wise as possible and superintend." Fort Stedman, named for a Connecticut general who died here on August 6, 1864, was one of the nicer bits of real estate along the Petersburg line. Its builders even left some trees standing inside the fortifications to give the soldiers a little relief from the battlefield's general air of bleak desolation.

Troops from the IX Corps defended this part of the line. The Confederates were only about three hundred yards away, off in the direction in which the 1st Maine had made its gallant but futile charge the previous year. Early in the morning on March 25, 1865, the rebels arrived from the opposite direction. First a group pretending to be deserters approached in the darkness and subdued the Union picket line. Behind them streamed some ten thousand men under the command of Gen. John B. Gordon, the fierce-looking fighter who had nearly undone Sedgwick's VI Corps with his flank attack in the Wilderness. The rebels charged across the fields and overwhelmed Stedman's defenders. Then they turned left and right and captured the batteries on each side.

Fort Haskell lay off to the left. On March 25 it was "a small field redoubt mounting six rifled guns and holding a feeble infantry garrison."[8] I walk over to the fort's site and look across a shallow ravine at Stedman. George Kilmer of the

14th New York Heavy Artillery was here during the fighting, as the Confederates opened up on Fort Haskell with Stedman's captured guns and from their own lines. A shell exploded within the fortifications, killing two men, shattering the thigh of another, and throwing a fourth into the air but leaving him unharmed. Another volley tore the arm off an artillery lieutenant.

Kilmer saw rebel infantry advancing across the ravine. The Federals here had just one cannon and fifty muskets to defend this side of the fort. The enemy came close enough to shout a demand for surrender before they charged. A well-aimed blast of canister from the cannon cut down the Confederates and drove them back.

Already the tide was turning. Brig. Gen. John Hartranft ("I'm not sure of the spelling of *his* name," said Lyman in a letter home) had thrown in enough troops from a reserve force to push the Confederates back and take many of them prisoner. "It was just the 'Mine,' turned the other way," said Lyman with satisfaction; "they got caught in there and could not get out."[9]

As the Confederates retreated, the Union guns turned the fields—the same quiet fields I look over on this peaceful morning, as the sun burns away the morning fog—into "a place of fearful slaughter," as Kilmer recalled. "My mind sickens at the memory of it—a real tragedy in war—for the victims had ceased fighting, and were now struggling between imprisonment on the one hand, and death or home on the other."[10]

Back at City Point, Meade was "greatly nettled" to be away from the army during such a crisis. Horace Porter watched as he paced up and down and dictated orders to chief of staff Webb "in tones which showed very forcibly the intensity of his feelings."[11] Meade hurried to the military railroad and reached the field by 11:30 that morning. A later military train brought Grant and his guest, President Lincoln, newly arrived from Washington. They rode over to join Meade and watched the Confederate prisoners filing past. As the president observed the prisoners, Lyman studied the commander in chief. "The President is, I think, the ugliest man I ever put my eyes on," he wrote; "there is also an expression of plebeian vulgarity in his face that is offensive (you recognize the recounter of coarse stories). On the other hand, he has the look of sense and wonderful shrewdness, while the heavy eyelids give him a mark almost of genius. He strikes me, too, as a very honest and kindly man; and, with all his vulgarity, I see no trace of low passions in his face. On the whole, he is such a mixture of all sorts, as only America brings forth. He is as much like a highly intellectual and benevolent Satyr as anything I can think of. I never wish to see him again, but, as humanity runs, I am well content to have him at the head of affairs. . . ."[12]

Lee's final offensive cut Margaret Meade's visit short, and she headed back to Philadelphia while her husband dealt with matters of war. "Your visit seems so like a dream I can hardly realize you have been here," he wrote her. "I expect we shall have stirring times before long. The fighting yesterday proved the enemy has still some spirit left in him, and Lee, having once begun, is likely to try his hand again; and if he don't, I suppose we shall have to take the matter in hand."[13] Winter was over. The spring campaign was about to begin, and everyone expected it would spell doom for the Army of Northern Virginia.

Appomattox Campaign

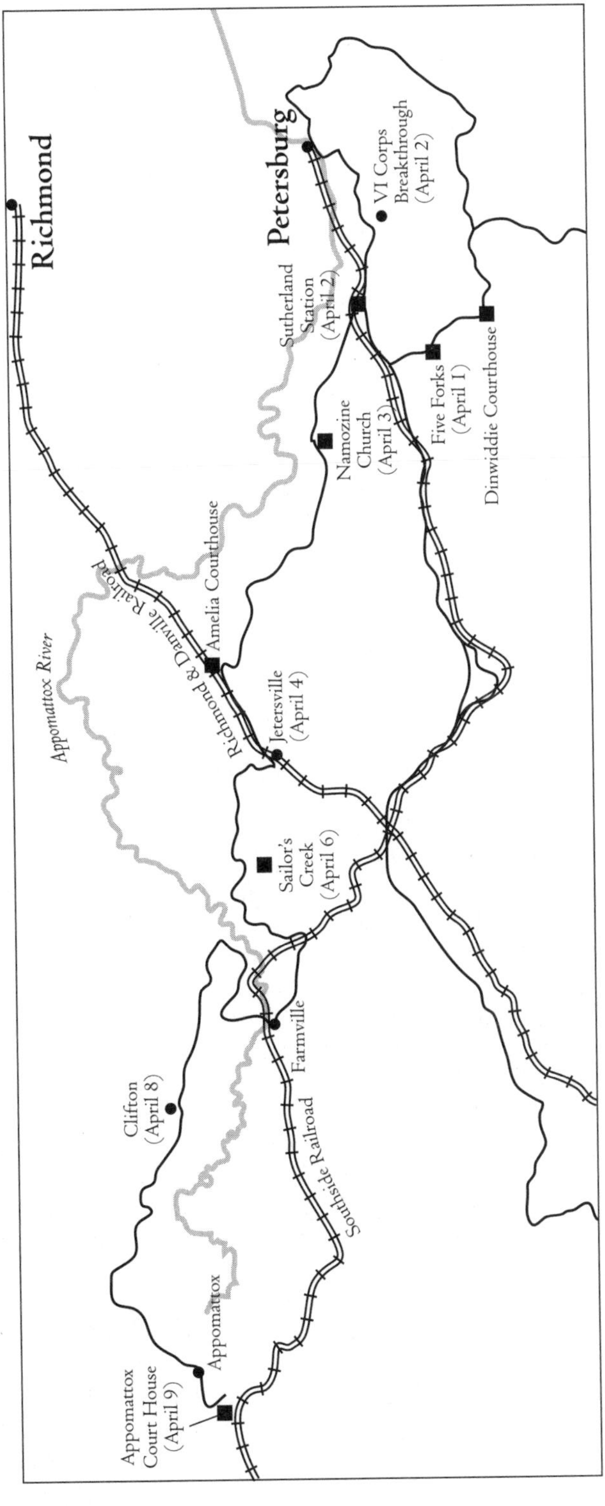

Richmond

Petersburg

VI Corps Breakthrough (April 2)

Sutherland Station (April 2)

Five Forks (April 1)

Dinwiddie Courthouse

Namozine Church (April 3)

Appomattox River

Amelia Courthouse

Richmond & Danville Railroad

Jetersville (April 4)

Sailor's Creek (April 6)

Farmville

Clifton (April 8)

Southside Railroad

Appomattox

Appomattox Court House (April 9)

The week started out dismally, with the kind of driving rain that turned the roads into runs and made it even more difficult than usual to maneuver the army. On March 30, amid the pouring rain and clinging mud, Warren and the V Corps fought a seesaw battle with Richard Anderson's division along the White Oak Road. The little battlefield here is another of the Civil War Trust's success stories and includes some trails that wind through the woods on both sides of the road, with markers among the trees that explain the action. Lee rode out here to supervise the fighting, knowing that the White Oak Road was an important supply line for his army. The rebels smashed into the Federal flank, forcing back the divisions of Romeyn Ayres and Samuel Crawford, but the Union soldiers counterattacked and pushed the rebels back to their earthworks. With the White Oak Road in Union hands, the Confederates off to the west around an intersection called Five Forks were now separated from the rest of the army.

• • •

It's pretty quiet today at the Five Forks battlefield. Except for the ranger behind the desk, I'm alone in the small visitors center. The only other person I see on the "battlefield" is a woman who has stopped her car to look at the markers at the intersection that gave Five Forks its name. I put "battlefield" in quotes because Five Forks today is more a collection of roadside markers than a place where you can walk around and follow the battle, as at Gettysburg or Antietam. The numbered stops on the driving tour don't even proceed in an easy-to-follow order. Heading down the White Oak Road, I hit stop number 2 first. To reach stop number 1, I continue on to the Five Forks intersection and then go south past the visitors center. Stop number 3 is back at the intersection. Number 4 is farther down the White Oak Road. To reach stop number 5, I have to reverse course again, drive back to the intersection, and turn north. It's all very confusing. As I discover, though, there was a fair amount of confusion here during the battle, too.

Grant had ordered a movement to get around Lee's right, with Sheridan's cavalry moving to Dinwiddie Court House, south of Five Forks, and operating in conjunction with Union infantry. The infantry Sheridan wanted was Horatio Wright's VI Corps, as he had worked well with Wright in the Shenandoah Valley. But the VI Corps was on the far side of the Petersburg lines, so Grant told Sheridan he would have to take Gouverneur Warren and the V Corps instead.

Sheridan and Warren didn't get along, apparently ever since Warren had complained about Sheridan's cavalry blocking his way en route to Spotsylvania Court House the previous spring. The relationship did not improve after one of Warren's divisions had to extricate Little Phil from difficulties with George Pickett's Confederates at Dinwiddie Court House on March 31. Sheridan did not like to admit he needed help from anyone, much less a cautious Army of the Potomac engineer like Warren.

Admittedly, Warren possessed a natural talent for irritating generals. Meade had reached the end of his patience with his onetime protégé. Grant, too, had tired of Warren's quirks and, like Meade, had discovered a "defect" in Warren's character: "He could see every danger at a glance before he had encountered it. He would not only make preparations to meet the danger which might occur, but he would inform his commanding officer what others should do while he was executing his move."[14] Grant told Sheridan he was free to relieve Warren and replace him if he felt it was necessary, thus sowing the seeds for Warren's downfall.

Sheridan wanted to attack the Confederate lines around Five Forks at noon on April 1. He fumed and fretted when Warren wasn't ready until 4:00. In later testimony Sheridan said he believed Warren was deliberately trying to delay the attack until it was too late to fight. That was an unfair accusation; "Warren's whole life is simply a refutation of this charge," wrote the author of an 1896 history of the V Corps.[15] But while he did not lack courage, Warren moved deliberately enough to infuriate the fiery and impatient Phil Sheridan.

Warren finally put his three divisions into motion, heading north toward the White Oak Road, but Sheridan had misinformed him about the enemy's position. Two divisions veered left to correct their advance, but Samuel Crawford's men kept marching straight ahead and missed the Confederate lines altogether. Warren rode off to find Crawford and get him back on track.

A soldier in the 20th Maine recalled the excitement as the other two divisions swept over the enemy's lines at the Angle, a spot where the rebel defenses bent back on themselves. "Sheridan went dashing past us, wild with the excitement of victory, shouting, as he swung his clenched hand through the air, 'Smash 'em! Smash 'em! We have a record to make before the sun goes down; we must have the Southside road.'"

In the meantime Warren found Crawford's men and got them heading the right way. In what turned out to be a great stroke of luck, their errant march had put them in a perfect position to attack the rebel flank and rear. Warren led the soldiers over the barricades and had his horse shot out from under him. "General Warren caught the corps flag from the hand of the man who carried it, and dashed across this field, leading on a column of soldiers he had hastily formed for the charge," the same soldier recalled. "It was the most gallant deed of the whole day's battle, and the whole rebel line was now in our possession."[16]

The Battle of Five Forks marked the beginning of the end for Lee's army—it was "the Waterloo of the Confederacy." The rebels had suffered a severe blow. Now that the Union army could move forward and sever the South Side Railroad, Petersburg and Richmond were doomed. Warren and the V Corps had delivered the blow that ensured the victory. Yet Sheridan, still livid over what he perceived as Warren's inexcusable slowness—and probably unwilling to share any credit for the victory—decided that Warren had not participated in the fighting at all. He ordered Charles Griffin to take over the V Corps and sent a note to Warren relieving him of command.

Warren was stunned. He rode to Sheridan and asked him to reconsider. "I don't reconsider my decisions!" Sheridan barked. "Obey the order!"[17]

Meade received word of the victory at Five Forks by telegram—but nothing about Warren. He sent a message to Grant. "I am truly delighted with the news from Sheridan," he said. "What part did Warren take? I take it for granted he was engaged."

"The Fifth Corps was in and did splendidly," Grant replied, "but Sheridan had to relieve Warren on the field after the fight began."[18]

The word of Warren's relief hit his subordinates like a thunderbolt. "I was astonished at this news and could not imagine what the trouble was," said Charles Wainwright. "The only thing that occurred to me was that Warren might have got into one of his ugly fits and said what he ought not to." Wainwright often used his journal to vent about Warren's ill temper, but he didn't agree with Sheridan's decision. "To me his removal at this time, and after the victory had been won, appears wrong and very cruel," he wrote.[19]

Warren reached Meade's headquarters around midnight, accompanied by only a single aide. Lyman, who had not yet heard what had happened, brought out some food. He noticed that Warren appeared strangely downcast. The aide whispered the news to him. Lyman had long believed that a corps command was too much for Warren, who always tried to do everything himself, "but this humiliation he did not deserve."[20]

Even people outside the army recognized Sheridan's ill treatment of Warren. On the back of a sketch he had made of Warren's attack at Five Forks, artist Alfred Waud wrote, "Sheridan and the ring he belongs to intends to grab all laurels no matter at the cost of what injustice."[21]

On two occasions Meade suggested to Grant that he reinstate Warren as commander of the V Corps. Grant did not respond. Nor did he make any efforts on Warren's part after he became president. Warren did not receive any kind of hearing until Rutherford B. Hayes reached the White House. When Warren finally got a court of inquiry to take on his case in 1879, it declared Sheridan's action unjustified, but Warren died before the court published its findings. His last words were "I die a disgraced soldier."[22] As William Henry Powell wrote in inimitable style in his V Corps history, "With the flush of victory on his brow, with the end of the struggle so near, with the faint rays of the dawn of peace already gleaming in the sanguinary sky, this noble warrior was brushed aside like a fly from a map and sent into what was an undeniable, if not apparently dishonorable, seclusion."[23]

● ● ●

Grant wanted to follow up the success at Five Forks with an assault all along the Confederate lines. "Meade was all activity, and so alive to the situation, and so anxious to carry out the orders of the general-in-chief, that he sent word that he was going to have the troops make a dash at the works without waiting to form assaulting columns," noted Porter. Grant sent a message back to Meade advising a little more prudence and suggesting he sound out the enemy with artillery and skirmishers first. In any event, the corps commanders reported that they wouldn't be ready to attack until morning. When they did, reported Horatio Wright, he expected the VI Corps would "make the fur fly." He added, "If the corps does half as well as I expect, we will have broken through the rebel lines in fifteen minutes from the word 'go.'"

"I like the way Wright talks; it argues success," said Grant. "I heartily approve."[24]

Brig. Gen. Lewis A. Grant of Getty's VI Corps division—the other General Grant, whose quotation I saw on the Vermont memorial in the Wilderness—examined the rebel lines on his front. He noticed a ravine that led toward the enemy's works and seemed weakly defended. He pointed it out to Getty, who rode out with Wright and Meade to examine the terrain. The generals determined to make this area the object of the VI Corps' attack. Grant's Vermont brigade would serve as the point of the spear.

Some fourteen thousand men of the VI Corps moved out from the area around the Union's Fort Fisher around 10:00 p.m. on April 1 to prepare for the assault on the Confederate entrenchments. These soldiers had attacked the rebels' defenses time and time again so they knew what awaited them. "Well, good-by, boys," some said. "This means death."[25] The soldiers spent what many believed—some correctly—would be their last hours shivering and miserable on the cold, damp ground, waiting in the dark. Artillery on both sides kept up fierce fire, and the Union pickets continued shooting into the darkness, perhaps to cover up the sound of the troops forming up behind them. Confederates returned the fire. "Every once in a while some one would get hit with a ball, and we could hear his cry of anguish as the lead tore through," recalled Col. Clinton Beckwith of the 121st New York. One of the wounded men was Vermont's General Grant, struck by a bullet in the head. Fortunately the wound wasn't mortal.

"Finally our men, by stopping their fire and crying, 'April Fool, Johnnies,' restored quiet, and for a long time we lay perfectly quiet, waiting for the time to come when we could move forward," recalled Beckwith. One soldier complained, "I would rather charge than lie here in this suspense and misery."[26]

The attack had been set for 4:00. The scheduled time arrived but the morning remained so dark and foggy that Wright decided to wait an additional forty-five minutes. As the sky lightened in the east, an artillery barrage from Fort Fisher announced the start of the attack. The cold and tired soldiers jumped to their feet and stumbled forward through the darkness, led by men with axes to cut away the tangled abatis in front of the Confederate fortifications. Artillerymen followed with their primers and rammers, ready to turn captured cannons on the rebels. The morning was still so black that the attackers used the flames from the enemy guns to find their way. As the dawning light improved visibility, some of the soldiers found a route through the rebel abatis and began climbing over the earthworks.

Capt. Charles Gould of the 5th Vermont was apparently the first man over. He clambered up on the works and found a Confederate musket pointing right at him. Fortunately the gun misfired. "I immediately jumped into the work, and my part in the engagement was soon over," Gould recalled. First he received a bayonet through his face. Despite the wound, he managed to kill his assailant. Another rebel slashed Gould in the head with a sword while a third stabbed him in the back with a bayonet. "This was the most severe wound of the three, the bayonet entering the spine and penetrating it nearly to the spinal cord," Gould said. "I have no distinct recollection of what followed, until I found myself at the parapet, trying to climb out of the work, but unable to do so." A private from the regiment grabbed Gould and dragged him to safety.[27] Gould later received the Medal of Honor for his actions on April 2.

This all took place on the grounds of what is now Pamplin Historical Park. "The engagement that occurred here is the literal trigger that sent the Army of Northern Virginia to its demise," says A. Wilson Greene, Pamplin Park's executive director. "You read any history that covers this part of the war," he tells me, "and

Five Forks will be the decisive battle. And April 2 and the breakthrough here, if it's mentioned at all, it's in half a sentence." Part of the reason for its relative obscurity, Greene says, is that VI Corps officers wrote few memoirs. On the other hand, Phil Sheridan *did* write about Five Forks ("a mixture of fact and fiction," Greene says), giving further prominence to that battle. Add the fact that the land where the breakthrough happened was privately owned and inaccessible until Pamplin Park opened in 1994, and you have a recipe for historical obscurity.

As the author of *Breaking the Backbone of the Rebellion: The Final Battles of the Petersburg Campaign* and through his work at Pamplin Park, Greene has done what he can to rescue the battles here from neglect. "Petersburg has not captured the imagination of American Civil War enthusiasts like most other parts of the war," he says. "Petersburg, for whatever reason, is not sexy. It's not a very well-understood campaign. It's huge, it's complicated, it covers vast amounts of ground, and there's this perception of a lack of contingency that robs the Petersburg Campaign of some popular interest. It's always been portrayed as a siege, which it wasn't, as a fait accompli, which it really wasn't until after the [presidential] election."

Greene hopes the park will continue to shine some light on Petersburg's role in the war. "Pamplin Historical Park was born from a preservation effort that I initiated in 1992," he tells me. Then president of the Association for the Preservation of Civil War Sites, the precursor to the Civil War Trust, Greene received word of a hundred-acre tract in Petersburg that had come on the market. A little research told him that Robert Pamplin Sr., a wealthy businessman and philanthropist in Oregon, was a descendant of the family that had owned the land during the war. Greene wrote to see if the family would make a matching grant for the land's purchase. Pamplin called back and said that the family had decided instead to buy the land outright and start a park. "About $42 million later, here we are, with a 422-acre campus, four museums, about four miles of interpretive trails, and four historic buildings on their original sites, three of which were generals' headquarters," Greene says with some pride. "We have twenty-seven structures under roof on the park, and it's quite an operation."

The park's centerpiece is the Museum of the Civil War Soldier, which examines the war from the viewpoint of the men in the trenches. After talking with Greene, I head over to check it out for myself. It's a quiet morning in January, and I'm one of the few people here today. I pick up a little audio player from a cheerful volunteer. I'll use it to hear short presentations on subjects related to soldiers' lives, from the games they played to the diseases that killed them. To personalize the experience, I can follow a representative soldier and hear some narrative about his experiences at stops along the way. I pick Pvt. George Washington Beidelman of Company C of the 71st Pennsylvania. A young man of Germanic descent, Beidelman hailed from Bloomsburg, Pennsylvania, and joined the army at age twenty-two.

Several large galleries re-create aspects of the soldiers' world. The first one shows a typical encampment—it could be Union or Confederate—from early in the war. A large, conical Sibley tent, big enough to accommodate eighteen sleeping soldiers in somewhat cramped conditions, dominates the room. Lifesize soldier mannequins lounge and play cards beneath a shelter made of tree branches.

Even the floor is constructed to look like dirt, impressed with many footprints. Another large gallery re-creates a typical winter encampment, with a wooden hut and even a crude little chapel and a sutler's tent. One of the items I see on the sutler's counter is a deck of "patriotic" playing cards—one of which, I am pleased to see, has a picture of Meade on it.

At an exhibit case about army bands, I write down the titles from the sheet music on display. They're not exactly feel-good tunes, with titles like "Weeping, Sad and Lonely," "Oh! I Wish the War Were Over," and "Just before the Battle, Mother." I also see an ode to McClellan called "Give Us Back Our Old Commander." It goes:

> Give us back our old commander,
> Let him manage, let him plan,
> With McClellan as our leader
> We can want no better man.

Like all Civil War museums, this one has plenty of weapons on display. The ones I appreciate most are those connected to specific individuals. One case holds a sword and scabbard that belonged to Lt. Andrew Dodds of the 91st New York. The scabbard is bent and twisted from a bullet that struck it and then ricocheted into Dodds's leg at the Battle of White Oak Road. He carried that bullet inside him until he died in 1910.

In the last gallery I learn Beidelman's fate. Wounded in both legs at Gettysburg, he recovered and began serving as a quartermaster sergeant at Fort William Penn outside Philadelphia, a training camp for colored troops. He had survived his combat experiences, but in a sad twist of irony, he died on March 14, 1864, after contracting what he thought was no more than a cold.

But it's too nice a day to spend it in a museum. I head outside to explore the rest of the park, starting with Tudor Hall Plantation. The Tudor House is a modest white building that dates from 1812. Confederate brigadier general Samuel McGowan used it as the headquarters for his brigade of South Carolinians from the fall of 1864 until only a few days before the Union soldiers stormed through on April 2. The plantation outbuildings are reconstructions, but they provide an example of what a middle-class farming operation would have been like—including a discussion of slavery, which is always a difficult topic.

The Battlefield Center is the park's original museum. Though it is not on the scale of the newer facility, it does include some films and exhibits, including information about Charles G. Gould. The picture of him here shows a round-faced young man with haunted eyes who bore scars on his face from his bayonet wound. A glass case holds the Medal of Honor that Sgt. John E. Buffington of the 6th Maryland won for his actions when he stormed the Confederate defenses farther down the line.

It's a beautiful day to walk the park's trails, which wind around and through extensive remains of Confederate breastworks. I pass a new monument, erected on April 2, 2011, to the 6th Maryland at the spot where they breached the defenses, John E. Buffington in the lead. The cleared fields at the nearby Hart Farm give a better idea of the naked terrain the Union soldiers had to cross on the dark morning of April 2.

I return to the still-quiet museum, where a staffer at the front desk gives me the access code to the Banks House, just a short drive away. On the way I pass a small monument to A. P. Hill, who was killed nearby on April 12 by a Union straggler he tried to capture. At the end of the driveway to the house, I punch in the code and the barrier silently swings open. The Banks House stands on a high point in the field ahead of me, a smallish white farmhouse with a smaller extension attached to it like a sidekick. Behind is a rare surviving example of a slave quarters, which also doubled as the plantation's kitchen.

Grant and his staff established headquarters here on April 2 in the wake of the VI Corps' attack. Horace Porter watched Grant come under fire as he sat under a tree near the house, concentrating so intently on the orders he was writing that he did not notice the enemy shells falling nearby or the increasingly insistent hints from his staff that he should move elsewhere.

Pamplin Park added the Banks House to its holdings as one of those compromises that so often drive Civil War preservation. Developers wanted to build a steel recycling mill nearby, Greene told me, so the developers donated the house, and the steel mill paid to have it restored. Greene also told me this was another example of how Petersburg remained below the preservation radar at the time. "That steel mill went on a battlefield property that was significant in three different engagements," he said. "Had it been proposed in Northern Virginia, there would have been a national news outcry."

Meade certainly understood the importance of what happened here on April 2. "Candor compels me to say that, in my opinion, the decisive moment of this campaign, which resulted in the capture of the Army of Northern Virginia, was the gallant and successful assault of the Sixth Corps on the morning of the 2nd of April," he told the soldiers a few days later.[28] Like a weakened dam that finally gave way, the Confederate defenses here collapsed and the Union soldiers rolled forward, some of them advancing all the way to the South Side Railroad. Wright then had his corps pivot to the left and advance as far as Hatcher's Run, then move back up the Boydton Plank Road toward Petersburg.

Farther to the right of the Union line, the IX Corps attacked in the area around Fort Sedgwick and the Crater, while Humphreys and the II Corps pushed forward on the left and broke the South Side Railroad at Sutherland Station. Meade and his staff rode forward to the Boydton Plank Road, deeply rutted by all the Confederate supply wagons that had passed this way after Warren severed the Weldon Railroad back in August. Union troops, recognizing Meade, cheered him as he passed by. At the Banks House, its grounds littered with the paperwork from the rebel ordnance sergeant who had been living there, Meade stopped to chat with Grant, who was sitting on the porch.

John Gibbon, who had taken command of the XXIV Corps in the Army of the James, experienced stiff resistance from Forts Gregg and Whitworth, and the Confederates there bought Lee enough time to prepare to evacuate Petersburg. That night the Confederates began pulling out of their works and crossing to the north side of the Appomattox River. From there they turned to the west. Lee's initial goal was to reach the town of Amelia Court House, where he expected to find supplies, and then move south to link up with Gen. Joseph E. Johnston, whose army was falling back through North Carolina before Sherman.

On April 3 Meade decided to ride into Petersburg and examine the prize his army had won at such a great cost. He and members of his staff passed through the now-empty Confederate entrenchments and into the town's outskirts. Local blacks happily greeted the Union troops while the poor whites who remained glowered at them from behind broken windows. The brick houses in the center of town reminded Lyman of Salem, "*plus* the southern shiftlessness and *minus* the Yankee thrift." Farther on they reached Cemetery Hill, the unobtainable objective of the Mine attack. They rode through the cemetery and down to the Crater. The Confederate defenses that had given them so much trouble were now silent and empty. Meade stood on the abandoned works and looked over toward the Union lines. "It was a sight only to be appreciated by those who have known the depression of waiting through summer, autumn and winter for so goodly an event!" wrote Lyman.[29]

From the Banks House, Grant, too, had ridden into Petersburg. He and Meade met on Market Street at the house of a lawyer named Thomas Wallace. Newly liberated slaves tried to sell the Union officers Confederate money. Meade and Lyman didn't tarry long and had departed before Abraham Lincoln arrived, accompanied by his young son Tad, Adm. David Porter, and a few others. His escort through the lines was his son Robert, who served on Grant's staff, and he was riding Grant's favorite horse, Cincinnati. The president dismounted and greeted the general in chief with joy. "I doubt whether Mr. Lincoln ever experienced a happier moment in his life," wrote Horace Porter.[30] Wallace, who had known Lincoln before the war, invited Grant and the president inside but they preferred to sit on the porch where Grant could smoke a cigar. Lincoln sat on a rocking chair Wallace brought out for him, his long legs dangling over the edge of the porch. The two men stayed there for about ninety minutes, hoping to receive word about the fall of Richmond.

Lincoln said he suspected Grant might have been planning to order Sherman up from the south to pitch in against Lee. Grant said he had considered that but "had a feeling that it would be better to let Lee's old antagonists give his army the final blow, and finish up the job." Grant added, "I have always felt confident that our troops here were amply able to handle Lee." He and Lincoln then talked a little about postwar concerns.[31] Finally, Grant could wait no longer. He mounted up and rode off to rejoin the army. Lincoln looked around Petersburg a little before returning to City Point.

Just a few weeks before my visit to Petersburg, Abraham Lincoln returned to the city, but this time in the person of actor Daniel Day-Lewis. He was here with director Steven Spielberg and a film crew to shoot scenes for *Lincoln*, an adaptation of Doris Kearns Goodwin's book *Team of Rivals*. The filmmakers dragged Petersburg's compact historic district back into the nineteenth century by covering the streets with dirt, disguising the modern storefronts with painted flats, and bringing in wagons to fill the streets. Christopher Stowe, who went into Petersburg with some friends for dinner while all this was going on, left quite impressed. "It was like we were walking in wartime Richmond," he told me. "It was remarkable."

Then the filmmakers packed up and Petersburg returned to its slightly woe-begone twenty-first-century self. There's something a little sad about downtown Petersburg, as though whole sections have the whiff of mothballs. It has a core of beautiful historic buildings, including the train station for the South Side Rail-road, which looks much as it did in 1865. It has cobblestone streets and historic storefronts and a scattering of newer and more upscale shops and restaurants. But a lot of the old buildings have fallen into disrepair, some of the "antique stores" lie more in the realm of "used furniture," and many of the businesses in the his-toric brick buildings are closed. It looks like a town on the verge of giving up.

One of the decaying old buildings is the Wallace House on South Market Street, a big red brick house behind a low iron fence and sheltered by two tow-ering trees. It has obviously seen better days. Through the windows I see scaf-folding, so it seems that major work is going on inside. When I asked Wil Greene about the Wallace House, he expressed bewilderment about its current state. "Here's a house where Grant and Lincoln met on April 3 to discuss the end of the Civil War," he said. "What a place! It should be a shrine!" Instead, it's privately owned, falling into disrepair, and with the exception of a new Civil War Trails sign on the opposite side of Market Street, it has never been treated as a place worthy of attention. "Why?" Greene asked. "Well, it's Petersburg. This is a Southern city. If it was Lee and Jefferson Davis who met there, it would be a mu-seum, but it's Lincoln and Grant."

Grant had rejoined Meade at Sutherland Station on the South Side Railroad when word arrived that Union troops had entered Richmond, a goal so long de-sired and so long out of reach. "Although the news was expected, there were loud shouts of rejoicing from the group who heard it read," said Porter.[32]

Meade managed to write a few lines to Margaret. "The telegraph will have conveyed to you, long before this reaches you, the joyful intelligence that Peters-burg and Richmond have fallen, and that Lee, broken and dispirited, has retreated towards Lynchburg and Danville," he said. "We are now moving after Lee, and if we are successful in striking him another blow before he can rally his troops, I think the Confederacy will be at an end."[33]

The struggle with the Army of Northern Virginia turned into a race. Lee's exhausted forces traced a westward course across the Virginia countryside, shed-ding men, equipment, and horses like a comet burning up in the atmosphere. They roughly followed the course of the Appomattox River on the north side, hoping to outdistance the Union forces so they could dart south and connect with Johnston's army. The Union army generally stayed to the south of the river while Sheridan's cavalry nipped at the enemy's heels and attacked its trains.

It's about one hundred miles from Petersburg to Appomattox Court House, and to get there I follow the Lee's Retreat map from the Virginia Civil War Trails. One of my first stops is at the tiny white Namozine Church, shaded in the trees by the side of Route 622 and looking as it did when it was a mute eyewitness to a cavalry battle here on the morning of April 3. Meade passed by the next day and

established his headquarters nearby. That night he fell very ill from a "severe bil-
ious catarrh," either a recurrence of malaria or a cold. Poor Meade! Perhaps the
war's strain was taking its toll even as he approached its end. He remained very
sick for the rest of the campaign, often forced to ride in an ambulance instead of
on horseback.

In his headquarters that night Meade received a message from Sheridan, who
had reached the town of Jetersville. With infantry support, Sheridan said, he could
capture the entire rebel army. The news stirred Meade to action—not necessarily
because he believed Sheridan's assessment, Lyman said, but because he feared
that Little Phil was merely maneuvering to grab all the credit in case of success
or transfer the blame in case of failure. Meade ordered the II and VI Corps to
Jetersville and issued an order asking his men to make every effort to defeat the
rebel army, even if they had to face starvation to do so. Lyman blamed the last
part of the "starvation order" on Meade's feverish condition, "which made his
language excited."[34]

Meade met Sheridan the next day at Jetersville. He gracefully declined to take
Sheridan's cavalry under his command, although he did resume responsibility for
the V Corps. Lyman said Meade behaved "very handsomely" toward Sheridan,
so he must have buried the feelings that erupted in a letter home a few days later.
"His determination to absorb the credit of everything done is so manifest as to
have attracted the attention of the whole army, and the truth will in time be made
known," he said of Little Phil. "His conduct towards me has been beneath contempt, and will most assuredly react against him in the minds of all just and fair-
minded persons."[35]

Lee had reached Amelia Court House, where he hoped to find supplies.
Today it's still a quiet little town, with a Civil War memorial in the middle of its
grassy central square, the statue of a rebel leaning on a musket and peering, I
assume, toward the south. When Lee reached here on April 5, he found only
disappointment. There were no supplies, and he lost a vital day waiting for them
to arrive and for his strung-out army to consolidate. Sheridan and Meade stood
between him and his escape route south to Johnston. He would have to continue
west. Even as Meade sent the II, VI, and IX Corps on their way toward Amelia
Court House, the Confederates were leaving. Meade pivoted his army west in
hot pursuit. They would catch up alongside a little waterway called Sailor's or
Sayler's Creek.

The tiny white Overton-Hillsman House is part of the Sailor's Creek Battlefield Historical State Park, which commemorates the fighting that took place
around here on April 6. It's not exactly in the *middle* of nowhere, but it's pretty
far from the edges. When I reach the house, I'm surprised to find a good number
of cars parked in the grass lot, a big turnout for a Sunday in December. I ask a
woman in eighteenth-century garb who stands by the steps what's going on.
"They've come to see Santa Claus," she says. I enter the tiny building to see Santa
for myself, but he's hidden away in a side room where excited little ones can't interfere with photo ops. Parents and children wait patiently in the house's main
room to get their time with him.

If I can't see Santa, I can at least hear some of the history that took place here. A young and enthusiastic Virginia State Parks staffer named Kira is happy to fill me in. On April 6, 1865, she tells me, this house was the property of James Moses Hillsman and his family. James had been fighting with the 44th Virginia and was captured at Spotsylvania, leaving his family to fend for themselves. His wife, mother, two children, and eight servants (probably slaves) were here when the armies arrived and pitched into each other. The civilians hid in the cellar during the battle. Surgeons treated the wounded on the first floor, and blood seeped through the ceiling. Kira tells me that the doctors probably used the little entrance room where we're standing as the surgery so they could operate in the light coming through the open door. Here and elsewhere, Plexiglas panels cover dark stains on the wood floors. Tradition says the dark patches are bloodstains. Just last year a forensics team came to the house and conducted tests in the basement, where they did indeed find old traces of blood.

We move outside and Kira points across the sloping field in front of us. Union soldiers of the VI Corps advanced down the field toward the creek. Ahead waited remnants of Lee's army, bolstered by a brigade of marines and naval personnel who had been manning Richmond's defenses—making Sailor's Creek a land battle that actually involved sailors. Wright's corps did the bulk of the fighting here, while Sheridan's cavalry assaulted the enemy's flanks.

More fighting raged upstream near the Lockett House, where two bridges crossed the creek. Humphreys's II Corps overwhelmed John Gordon's Confederates there late in the day as the rebels reached the bridges. The Lockett House, which also served as a hospital, is a private home today and still bears the scars of the fighting. The battle proved to be a disaster for the Army of Northern Virginia, which lost around eight thousand men. The tally included eight generals, among them Richard Ewell, who had been captured.

Meade passed this way, still sick and riding in the ambulance, on April 7. The road was strewn with debris from the battle, abandoned Confederate equipment filled the creekbed, and rebel paperwork from the adjutant general's wagons blew across the hillside opposite the creek, where a new visitors center stands today. Lyman was especially struck by the profusion of abandoned Dutch ovens. "You saw them lying about, with their little legs kicked up in the air, in a piteous manner!"[36]

After the battle, Meade received a dispatch from Sheridan, which he read with distaste. Lyman summarized it: "*I* attacked with two divisions of the 6th Corps. *I* captured many thousand prisoners, etc., etc. P. H. Sheridan."

"Oh," said Meade to the staff officer who had brought it, "so *General Wright wasn't there*."

"Oh, yes!" replied the officer, oblivious to Meade's sarcasm, "General Wright was there." Lyman thought he could have been talking about a mere brigade commander and not the head of the entire corps. Meade, infuriated, stalked off without another word.[37]

Lyman remained so incensed about Sheridan's credit grab that a month later he wrote a letter to the *Boston Advertiser* about it. It was Wright who attacked, he said, "and he was under the immediate orders of General Meade, and had nothing whatever to do with General Sheridan, whose entire command numbered not over 7000 mounted men, while the Second and Sixth Corps had together not less than 25,000 men actually in the fight."[38]

Meade biographer Isaac Pennypacker shared Lyman's poor opinion of Sheridan. A week after Sailor's Creek, Pennypacker reported, Sheridan demanded that Wright submit his report on the battle to him. Wright refused, stating that he was operating under Meade's orders that day, not Sheridan's, and he that he had already submitted his preliminary report to Meade's chief of staff. Grant, Pennypacker wrote, ordered Wright to submit the report to Sheridan. "To the public it was announced by the Secretary of War that Sheridan had attacked and routed Lee's army."[39]

At the town of Farmville the disintegrating Army of Northern Virginia crossed over to the north bank of the Appomattox, some of them using a bridge in town and the rest farther downstream at the tall High Bridge and a nearby wagon bridge. The Confederates attempted to burn the High Bridge after they had crossed to stymie their pursuers, but Francis Barlow, newly returned to the army, hurried his men forward in time to capture the span, while Col. Thomas Livermore of Humphreys's staff led a party to put out the fires.[40] The tall stone columns of the High Bridge still stand, as if at attention, in a line across the Appomattox, now supporting a newly repaired pedestrian bridge. The rebels also failed to destroy the nearby wagon bridge, a lucky break for the pursuing Federals and another stroke of bad luck for the Confederates. Once across the river, Barlow continued on toward Farmville, where he captured some Confederate wagons after spirited fighting. It was during this battle that Brig. Gen. Thomas Smyth, a former commander of the Irish Brigade, fell, mortally wounded by a rebel sniper. He was the last Union general killed during the war. "It would be impossible to picture the grief this unexpected calamity caused to his immediate command and to the Brigade, by whom he was almost idolized," read an Irish Brigade history.[41]

Grant reached Farmville on the afternoon of April 7 and set up his headquarters at a small brick hotel on the main street. Having heard from Sheridan that the captured General Ewell had said the Army of Virginia's situation was hopeless, he decided to send a message to Lee. "The results of the last week must convince you of the hopelessness of further resistance on the part of the Army of Northern Virginia in this struggle," Grant wrote. "I feel that it is so, and regard it as my duty to shift from myself the responsibility of any further effusion of blood by asking of you the surrender of that portion of the Confederate States army known as the Army of Northern Virginia." Grant gave the note to Seth Williams, who rode off toward Humphreys and the II Corps, which was hard on the heels of Lee's rear guard. Williams managed to get the note over to the Confederate lines despite riding into enemy fire that wounded his orderly.

Grant received Lee's reply at the hotel in Farmville sometime after midnight. "Though not entertaining the opinion you express of the hopelessness of further resistance on the part of the Army of Northern Virginia," Lee said, "I reciprocate your desire to avoid useless effusion of blood, and therefore, before considering your proposition, ask the terms you will offer on condition of its surrender." That night the VI Corps, sensing that the end was near, conducted an impromptu review through the town, lighting bonfires and carrying blazing torches, cheering, and singing as bands played "John Brown's Body."

Grant responded from Farmville on the morning of April 8. "In reply I would say that, peace being my great desire, there is but one condition I would insist upon—namely, that the men and officers surrendered shall be disqualified for taking up arms against the Government of the United States until properly exchanged. I will meet you, or will designate officers to meet any officers you may name for the same purpose, at any point agreeable to you, for the purpose, of arranging definitely the terms upon which the surrender of the Army of Northern Virginia will be received."[42]

April 8 dawned cold, with frost visible on the ground. Meade and his staff were up early and crossed the Appomattox near the partially burnt High Bridge. They found Humphreys, who told them about the communications between Grant and Lee. The fact that the messages had been passing both ways indicated that Lee was interested in discussing the prospect of surrender—"a most important fact!" in Lyman's view.[43]

Later that day Meade established his headquarters at Clifton, a medium-sized white house that now sits on the corner of Routes 15 and 636, across the street from a convenience store. When Grant reached here, he seemed to be in uncommonly good spirits. "How are you, old fellow?" he greeted Meade. Grant established himself in the house, then known as the Stutes House, and because Grant's headquarters wagon hadn't arrived, Meade treated him to a dinner provided by the Army of the Potomac.

The stress was taking its toll on Grant, too. Although suffering from a severe migraine, he didn't complain when some of his staffers began playing the piano at the Stutes House and singing. Grant went to bed upstairs, still suffering from a terrible headache. Their recital finally over, the staffers threw themselves down on the floors or on what little furniture remained to snatch a few hours sleep.

Sometime after midnight the occupants of the house heard the soldiers outside on guard duty challenge an approaching rider, followed by the sounds of spurs and the rattling of a saber from someone on the porch. It was a messenger with a reply from Lee. "I received at a late hour your note of to-day," it read. "In mine of yesterday I did not intend to propose the surrender of the Army of Northern Virginia, but to ask the terms of your proposition. To be frank, I do not think the emergency has arisen to call for the surrender of this army; but as the restoration of peace should be the sole object of all, I desired to know whether your proposals would lead to that end." Lee was saying he would not meet to surrender his army, but he would like to hear Grant's proposals.

Grant replied to Lee, keeping the delicate negotiations alive. He said a meeting would do no good, as he had no authority to discuss the general subject of peace. "I will state, however, general, that I am equally anxious for peace with yourself, and the whole North entertains the same feeling. The terms upon which peace can be had are well understood. By the South laying down their arms they will hasten that most desirable event, save thousands of human lives, and hundreds of millions of property not yet destroyed."[44]

Lee was running out of options. Whatever Sheridan's faults, the Union general had been driving himself and his men hard in pursuit of the retreating rebels. On April 8 a portion of his cavalry under George Custer had swung in front of the Confederates and captured a rich store of supplies at Appomattox Station, and Union cavalrymen blocked the road in front of Lee's army at Appomattox Court House. On the morning of April 9 John Gordon's men attacked the cavalry and seemed poised to break through—and then footsore soldiers of the V Corps and the Army of the James's XXIV Corps, some of them having marched thirty miles, came up on the double-quick and stabilized the Union lines. The rebels pulled back.

The end was near.

Grant had breakfast with Meade early that morning. It was Palm Sunday—the Easter holiday, with its promises of rebirth, was approaching. Breakfast ended, Grant left Meade and rode on to meet Sheridan. After the lieutenant general had departed, a messenger arrived with Lee's latest reply. Meade read it over. "I now request an interview, in accordance with the offer contained in your letter of yesterday, for that purpose," it said.[45]

Peace was almost at hand.

Meade sent one of his aides, Lt. Charles E. Pease, to take the letter to Grant. He then continued his own westward journey, still riding in an ambulance, with a bugler and chief of staff Webb riding in advance to shoo the soldiers off the road so the general could pass. Lyman noted the jocular comments the soldiers shouted out as the bigwigs clattered by. "Fish for sale!" one man called as he spied Meade's ambulance. "Yes, and a tarnation big one too!" another replied.

"That's Meade," a soldier remarked to a comrade.

"Is he sick?"

"I guess the old man hain't had much sleep lately."[46]

Meade caught up with Wright, and around noon he reached Humphreys. The II Corps had been pushing Lee relentlessly, having marched approximately twenty-six miles the previous day. They were now about four and a half miles from the little community of Appomattox Court House. Longstreet's men were arrayed before them. The VI Corps went into position on Humphreys's right, and the Federals prepared to attack.

An officer arrived with a note from Lee. Ord, now in command of the Army of the James, on the other side of the rebel army, had suspended hostilities. Lee wanted Meade to do the same. Meade announced that he had no authority for such a suspension and ordered Humphreys to push his skirmishers forward. Then a messenger arrived from Sheridan, who also urged a suspension. Meade agreed to postpone his attack until 2:00.

"We waited, not without excitement, for the appointed hour," wrote Lyman. The deadline passed without word of surrender. Meade pulled out his pocket watch to check the time. "Two o'clock—no answer—go forward," he ordered. Humphreys renewed his preparations for battle. Then one of Sheridan's staffers rode up, accompanied by a major from Lee's staff. They had a note from Grant telling Meade to suspend hostilities pending the outcome of the negotiations. Once again the army stood down and prepared to wait. The II Corps had captured a barrel of Confederate money, and Humphreys began handing out $100 bills to anyone who wanted a souvenir. [47]

Pease came riding up sometime around 5:00. "The Army of Northern Virginia has surrendered!" he announced. Webb led the men in three cheers, followed by three cheers for Meade. Meade mounted his horse and rode through the soldiers of the II and VI Corps. The men greeted him with pandemonium. Thomas Hyde, now commanding his own brigade in the VI Corps, called it "a saturnalia of joy."[48]

"Such a scene followed as I can never see again," wrote Lyman. "The soldiers rushed, perfectly crazy, to the roadside, and there crowding in dense masses, shouted, screamed, yelled, threw up their hats and hopped madly up and down! The batteries were run out and began firing, the bands played, the flags waved. The noise of the cheering was such that my very ears rang. And there was General Meade galloping about and waving his cap with the best of them!"[49] The victory over Lee at Gettysburg had not been enough to induce Meade to pull off his hat and wave it in the air. The surrender of Lee's army was.

◆ ◆ ◆

Meade missed the meeting between Grant and Lee, but I won't. My wife and I have traveled to Appomattox on the weekend of Palm Sunday to be here for the grand opening of the Museum of the Confederacy's first satellite museum. The day's events include a reenactment of the epochal surrender meeting.

This morning the *Richmond Times-Dispatch* is full of Civil War news. There's a story about Fort Monroe, recently decommissioned and just designated as a national monument, almost exactly 150 years after McClellan's army arrived there in 1862. There's also an item about a Richmond resident who found a Civil War cannonball, still fused, in a flowerbed, and another one about protests in Lexington, where both Robert E. Lee and most of Stonewall Jackson are buried, over the city's decision not to fly the Confederate flag. In addition, Pamplin Park is opening another trail today on ground from the April 2 breakthrough. What was it that William Faulkner said about the past not being dead? It's certainly alive and well in Virginia this weekend.

The gray skies are clearing, promising an afternoon of Union blue, as we reach the new museum, a low brick building with a green roof just a couple miles beyond Appomattox Court House National Historical Park. Hundreds of people have arrived for the event. We have to park in a nearby field and board a school bus the museum has borrowed from a Christian school—it has "Jesus" in the destination slot across the front—for the ride back to the museum. There we find a crowd gathered on the lot across the street, waving Confederate battle flags—the "Stars and Bars"— and holding banners. I approach two men who hold a sign with Grant's picture and the words "Gen. Grant: Yankee slave owner" and ask what the fuss is about. G. Ashleigh Moody of Petersburg, a thirty-five-year government employee and a onetime member of the North-South Skirmish Association, tells me the flag wavers are there to protest the museum's decision not to fly the Confederate flag out front. "It's all about Southern heritage," he tells me. In fact, he continues, "it's our *American* heritage—it's American heritage that's being obliterated."

•

The protest over the museum's decision was organized by the Sons of Confederate Veterans (SCV) and another group called the Virginia Flaggers. Participants include a large flag-waving contingent from the SCV's "mechanized cavalry," a.k.a. motorcyclists. Despite their somewhat threatening appearance, I approach them and chat with David Hoque, who tells me that not only won't the museum fly the Confederate flag, but he's heard it even displays a photograph of celebrity drag queen RuPaul wearing a dress made from the rebel banner. "That's just disrespectful," he says. Museum president S. Waite Rawls III explained the museum's thinking about not flying the flag to the *Richmond Times-Dispatch*: "Appomattox is a metaphor for the reunification of the country," he said. "To put the Confederate flag into that display would be a historical untruth."[50]

As the time for the opening ceremonies approaches, so do Robert E. Lee and Ulysses S. Grant impersonators, who ride up the drive and take positions on opposite sides of the Reunification Promenade in front of the museum. Lee is played by David Palmer and looks suitably weary. He is accompanied by several staff members as well as James Longstreet. Grant, played by Larry Clowers, is all by himself. His horse punctuates the ceremonies with occasional whinnies. I also spy John Cummings, who showed me around Spotsylvania, standing at attention with members of the 23rd USCT.

As Virginia lieutenant governor Bill Bolling speaks about the economic impact of heritage tourism, a buzzing from the sky begins to compete with his speech. Heads turn up to watch a small plane that begins to slowly circle the museum. It's towing a banner that includes a Confederate Stars and Bars and the words "Reunification by Bayonet SCV 1896." The plane, which I later learn has been jointly sponsored by the Sons of Confederate Veterans and the Virginia Flaggers, circles and circles during the ceremony, the drone of its engine almost drowning out the speakers, like an especially bothersome insect.

Today's keynote speaker is James Robertson Jr. He's a professor at Virginia Tech, the executive director of the school's Center for Civil War Studies, and author of more than twenty books, including an acclaimed biography of Stonewall Jackson. "The Civil War produced the nation we love and know," Robertson tells the assembled crowd. "Of course, the healing process would take time. Yet it was a healing process, not an ongoing bitterness that saps the very life out of a struggling young country." The plane continues to buzz in circles overhead, its banner betraying at least a hint of bitterness. "The past is the past," says Robertson. "It is what we do with the past that matters." He throws in a dig at New England by pointing out that a representative government met at Jamestown in 1619, "a year before the Massachusetts settlers spotted land," and another one at the "all-powerful, all-inclusive Federal government that watches over every action except the inertia of its own Congress." Both shots receive enthusiastic applause.

After the speeches the museum raises flags from the eleven states that seceded, plus Missouri, Kentucky, and Maryland, in the order they left the Union. But there is no Confederate flag. Then the lieutenant governor cuts the ribbon, and the throngs of visitors line up to make their way through the museum.

My wife and decide to visit the real Appomattox Court House while we wait for the crowds to die down a bit. We trudge back to the car and drive past the

Confederate flag wavers and onto Route 460. Appomattox Court House is just a couple miles down the road, in a bucolic setting of fields and trees. Visiting the park is like walking into 1865. There are homes and outbuildings, a tavern, the re-created courthouse (the original burned in 1892), a store, a jail (from 1867), and some slave quarters. The centerpiece is the McLean House, a re-creation of the building where Lee and Grant met on April 9, 1865.

Appomattox seems like a quiet, lazy kind of place from another era. It makes me want to lie back against a tree, tilt a hat over my eyes, and take a nap. Birds chirp and bees hum. The sense of midafternoon lethargy is so strong, in fact, that I find my eyelids slipping closed as I sit on a wooden bench beneath the trees and listen to an enthusiastic volunteer explain the sequence of events that brought Grant and Lee to this isolated spot.

It was the isolation that drew poor Wilmer McLean to this tiny village. In 1861 McLean had been living on what became the Bull Run battlefield. The battle there helped persuade him to pull up stakes and find a new home far from the war. On April 9 McLean just happened to be outside in the village when Lt. Col. Charles Marshall, a member of Lee's staff, rode up and asked him to recommend a place where the general could meet Grant. The building McLean initially recommended didn't have any furniture, so he offered the use of his own handsome brick house.

Lee, immaculately attired in his clean dress uniform, arrived first and waited in McLean's parlor with Marshall. Grant rode up later, wearing a private's coat with his insignia pinned on. After some small talk about the Mexican War (Lee somewhat passive-aggressively told Grant that, try as he might, he hadn't been able to remember a single feature of his), the two men got down to business. With a number of Union officers watching, including Sheridan, Ord, Custer, Porter, and Seth Williams, Grant wrote out a letter offering generous terms of surrender: parole for the soldiers upon their promise not to raise arms against the U.S. government until properly exchanged, with the officers keeping their sidearms, horses, and baggage. Lee pointed out that many of the men owned their own horses as well, so Grant said he would tell his men to allow any soldier who claimed ownership of a horse or mule to keep it. "This will have the best possible effect upon the men," said Lee. "It will be very gratifying, and will do much toward conciliating our people."[51]

Col. Ely Parker of Grant's staff, a full-blooded Seneca Indian, wrote out a clean copy of Grant's letter, and Lee had a formal letter of acceptance drafted. Lee told Grant his men lacked rations; Grant said he would make arrangements to have some delivered. Sheridan provided the only note of discord when he stepped forward and asked Lee to give him back some letters he had sent that morning complaining of truce violations. Lee handed them over. Then Grant and Lee signed their letters of agreement. Lee requested that Grant send a messenger to Meade with word of the surrender.

It was all over sometime around 4:00, and Lee bowed to the Union officers and left the house with Marshall. As Lee waited for his orderly to bring his horse, he stood on the steps and gazed sadly into the distance. "He thrice smote the palm of his left hand slowly with his right fist in an absent sort of way, seemed not to see the group of Union officers in the yard, who rose respectfully at his approach, and appeared unaware of everything about him," wrote Horace Porter. "All appreciated the sadness that overwhelmed him, and he had the personal sympathy of every one who beheld him at this supreme moment of trial. The approach of his horse seemed to recall him from his reverie, and he at once mounted. General Grant now stepped down from the porch, moving toward him, and saluted him by raising his hat. He was followed in this act of courtesy by all our officers present. Lee raised his hat respectfully, and rode off at a slow trot to break the sad news to the brave fellows whom he had so long commanded."[52]

Once the surrender was over, Union officers began looting McLean's property for souvenirs. Sheridan tossed McLean $20 and took the table that Grant had used. He gave it to Custer to give to his wife. Ord paid $40 for Lee's table. Others gave money to McLean for the other items of furniture in the house, whether he wanted to sell them or not. The entire house eventually fell victim to its fame. In 1893 a group bought it and had it disassembled so they could put it back together in Washington as a Civil War museum. But then they ran out of money, and the piles of house simply deteriorated. When the building was reconstructed on its original foundations in the 1940s, some fifty-five hundred bricks were all that remained. Two vases on the parlor's mantel and a horsehair sofa are the only original furnishings. The week before my visit, I saw the two chairs the generals sat in and the small table Grant used to write out his terms on display in the Smithsonian.

I hope the new museum won't be looted following today's events. We return to find a large crowd gathered around the side porch to watch a reenactment of the surrender. The crowd stirs as Grant and Lee appear from behind the building and ride up to wait behind us. Camera phones snap photos of the historic personages. Lee enters the porch first and sits, guided to position by John Cummings. (I ask him later if he was portraying a specific person. "No," he says, "I was just the only white guy wearing blue.") Grant pushes through the crowd to join Lee, and they reenact the moments that, though not officially ending the American Civil War, certainly made the end appear inevitable. The dialogue is largely taken from Horace Porter's account of the meeting, although I'm gratified when Lee asks about "my old friend, General Meade."

Afterward my wife and I make our way through the small museum. Lee's sword and dress coat, which we had seen at the Museum of the Confederacy in Richmond, are here now, sharing the space with an impressive array of documents, uniforms, weapons, and artifacts. Try as I might, though, I don't find that photo of RuPaul wearing a Confederate flag. I do find a *Dukes of Hazzard* tray, some Confederate flag boxer shorts, and other pop culture artifacts bearing the rebel banner, but no drag queens.

The museum also has plenty of information about the role slavery played in the war. In fact, earlier in the day I had been taken aback when looking at a "tree" that museum staffers use to explain the economic, political, and social causes of the Civil War to children. Among the causes displayed on the tree are that the South believed in states' rights while the North believed in a strong central government, and that the North was industrial while the South was agricultural. But I could see no mention of slavery among the leaves and branches. I asked a staff member about it. He smiled, reached down to the tree's roots, and pulled away a strip of plastic "grass." Beneath it was the word "slavery," the root cause of the conflict.

The day's events over, we drive back east past Appomattox Court House and pull into a small parking lot just a little ways beyond. We follow a path up a hill and into the woods to the site where Lee had set up his final headquarters as commander of the Army of Northern Virginia. About five hundred yards into the woods we find a large metal plaque and a wooden bench that indicate the exact spot. Someone has placed a little Confederate flag by the marker.

Meade brought Lyman, Webb, and his son George with him to this spot the day after the surrender, but Lee was out. The Union officers rode on. Before long they saw some men riding toward them. One of them had a gray beard and was wearing a blue military coat and a gray hat. It was Lee, followed by some of his staff. For long and bloody months Meade's army had been fighting and dying to defeat this man. Their contending armies had maneuvered and dueled across Virginia, leaving a trail of destruction in their wakes and putting tens of thousands of men into their graves. Lyman once compared Meade and Lee to "two exquisite swordsmen, each perfectly instructed, and never erring a hair in attack or in defence."[53] Now the duel had ended. Meade had won.

As his rival in arms approached, Meade removed his hat. "Good morning, General," he said.

Lee at first did not recognize him. When he did, he said, "But what are you doing with all that gray in your beard?"

"You have to answer for most of it!" Meade replied.

Lyman examined the Southern general closely. "Lee is, as all agree, a stately-looking man; tall, erect and strongly built, with a full chest," he wrote in a letter home. "His hair and closely trimmed beard, though thick, are now nearly white. He has a large and well-shaped head, with a brown, clear eye, of unusual depth. His face is sunburnt and rather florid. In manner he is exceedingly grave and dignified—this, I believe, he always has; but there was evidently added an extreme depression, which gave him the air of a man who kept up his pride to the last, but who was entirely overwhelmed. From his speech I judge he was inclined to wander in his thoughts."[54]

Meade introduced his staff officers, and Lee shook their hands. Lyman felt a sense of disbelief that he was shaking the hand of Robert E. Lee. Meade and Lee then moved off and had a long conversation in the rain, while Lyman and the other staff officers kept at a respectful distance by a fire. As the generals conversed, up rode an old, wrinkled man with a swept-back mane of white hair. He was wearing a battered felt hat and peered through spectacles. He had wrapped his legs in a blanket, making him look somewhat like a bandit. It was Henry A. Wise, the former governor of Virginia, the man who had signed John Brown's death warrant—and George Meade's brother-in-law. Meade had sent for him. He later wrote Margaret that Wise looked "old and feeble, said he was very sick, and had not a mouthful to eat." Meade had provisions sent over and arranged for an ambulance in which his brother-in-law could make his sad ride home.

Finally, Meade and his staff prepared to ride through the gray, wet, dreary weather back to their headquarters. "We left Lee, and kept on through the sad remnants of an army that has its place in history," Lyman wrote. "It would have looked a mighty host, if the ghosts of all its soldiers that now sleep between Gettysburg and Lynchburg could have stood there in the lines, beside the living."[55]

Meade's war with Robert E. Lee had ended, but he continued his battles against the press. "I have seen but few newspapers since this movement commenced," he wrote to Margaret on April 10, "and I don't want to see any more, for they are full of falsehood and of undue and exaggerated praise of certain individuals who take pains to be on the right side of the reporters. It cannot be remedied, and we should be resigned. I don't believe the truth ever will be known, and I have a great contempt for History. Only let the war be finished, and I returned to you and the dear children, and I will be satisfied."[56]

Yet the newspapers had softened in their treatment of Meade, or at least they stopped pretending he didn't exist. Two days after he wrote that screed to his wife, Meade noted with approval a note that appeared in the *New York Herald*. "The impression seems to have gotten out at the North that General Meade is not very popular with his army," the article said. "This is a great mistake, and has been fully verified in the past two days. I never saw so much enthusiasm displayed for any man as was for him after the surrender of Lee's army.

"Our troops were drawn up on either side of the road and when General Meade rode through they seemed nearly crazed with joy. Cheer followed cheer, and hats were thrown up in the air with apparent disregard of where they should land or what became of them. General Meade was equally excited. He seemed for the time to throw off his reserve and dignity and enter fully into the spirit of the occasion."[57]

The *Herald's* Sylvanus Cadwallader took credit for ending the reporters' unofficial boycott of Meade. In the fall Cadwallader had asked his correspondents to stop the "blockade." He sent his own paper a dispatch about Meade presenting medals to some of his soldiers and wrote to the general to call his attention to the coverage. Some weeks later Cadwallader was picking up passes at Meade's headquarters when assistant adjutant general Seth Williams insisted he meet with Meade. The general "threw aside all reserve at once," Cadwallader recounted, declared that he bore no ill will toward reporters "as a class," and admitted that perhaps Crapsey's punishment had been too harsh. Meade told Cadwallader that he had come to understand how mistakes could creep into newspaper accounts after his official report on Gettysburg aroused the ire of several officers who thought it didn't give them enough credit. "His confession was so full, free and spontaneous that I was disarmed at once," wrote Cadwallader, who said he kept up a relationship with Meade until the general's death.[58]

• • •

The joy of victory was short-lived, however. On April 15, a dreary rainy day, Meade was standing by a fire at his headquarters when he was handed a telegram. "Bless me!" he exclaimed. "This is terrible news!"[59] It was the announcement that President Lincoln had been assassinated in Washington. Meade issued a circular to break the news to the Army of the Potomac. "An honest man, a noble patriot, and sagacious statesman has fallen!" it read. "No greater loss, at this particular moment, could have befallen our Country. Whilst we bow with submission to the unfathomable and inscrutable decrees of Divine Providence, let us earnestly pray that God, in His infinite mercy, will so order, that this terrible calamity shall not interfere with the prosperity and happiness of our beloved Country!" Vice President Andrew Johnson became president.[60]

Although not on the same scale, Lyman's departure from the army on April 20 was another bit of bad news. He had been a loyal subordinate and Meade felt his loss keenly. "Lyman is such a good fellow, and has been so intimately connected personal with me, that I feel his separation as the loss of an old and valued friend," he said. He wrote Lyman a heartfelt letter and signed it, "Most truly your Friend." A few days later Margaret wrote that Lyman had paid her a visit in Philadelphia. "I am glad Lyman called to see you," he wrote back. "He is an honest man and a true friend. He has a healthy mental organization, which induces him to look on all matters in the most favorable light."[61]

More bad news arrived on April 22. Virginia had become part of the Military Division of the James, and Grant put the hated Henry Halleck in command. Meade poured out his feeling in an anguished letter to Margaret the next day. "This is the most cruel and humiliating indignity that has been put upon me," he wrote. He said he knew it was Grant's decision, made after the general in chief decided to base himself in Washington and realized Halleck would have to move elsewhere. Grant first suggested having Halleck replace Ord in the Department of Virginia and sending Ord to South Carolina. Meade assumed that Halleck had decided the position wasn't important enough for him. So now Halleck was coming to Richmond, and Meade would once again chafe beneath his command, this time without the benefit of distance.[62]

On May 3 Meade called on Robert E. Lee at his home on East Franklin Street in Richmond. The two generals had a long conversation. Meade tried to persuade Lee to take the oath of allegiance to the U.S. government—not just for himself but to set an example for other Confederates as well. Lee said he was willing but he wanted to see what the government's policy toward reconstruction would be. The two men also talked about the "status of the negro," which they agreed was "the great and formidable question of the day." When Meade left, he felt sad about his former adversary's diminished position.[63]

◆ ◆ ◆

Back in the dark autumn of 1862 some of McClellan's officers had suggested he take his army and march on Washington. He had declined. Now in May 1865 the Union armies were finally taking to the streets of the nation's capital. The days of defeat and dysfunction under McClellan were over; the soldiers were coming to celebrate not only their skill at war but also the peace they had secured. And they had come to receive the thanks of a grateful nation in a grand review.

Thousands of people poured into town to see the spectacle. "Never in the history of Washington had there been such an enormous influx of visitors as at that time," noted reporter Noah Brooks.[64] Visitors scrambled to find accommodations, and those who failed simply slept outdoors. The areas around the city became crowded with soldiers' camps. Workers began constructing reviewing stands in front of the White House, where the president and other notables would observe the passing troops. A wealthy man from Boston financed the construction of another stand for wounded veterans. Canny entrepreneurs began offering prime street-side seating locations for prices ranging from $10 for an hour to $50 for the entire day.

The review would take two days, with the Army of the Potomac marching on May 23 and the western armies on the second day. Washington's bars shut down the night before the review, and they remained closed until after the parades were over to keep overly lubricated spectators—and participants—from disrupting the celebrations. May 23 dawned with the promise of perfect weather, with just enough rain early in the morning to keep the dust down. The Army of the Potomac began forming around the Capitol building in the early hours. At 9:00 a cannon shot from Capitol Hill announced the parade's start, and the long blue lines of men began marching down Pennsylvania Avenue from the Capitol toward the White House, Meade astride his horse Blackie proudly at their head. "The plaudits of the multitude followed him along the entire line of march; flowers were strewn in his path, and garlands decked his person and his horse," wrote Porter.[65] His staff—minus Lyman, who was back in Boston—followed behind him. When he reached the reviewing stand in front of the White House, Meade turned, drew his sword, and saluted. He then joined the dignitaries to watch his army pass.

Sheridan was absent. Grant had sent him west to deal with matters there. However, Charles Wainwright suspected that Sheridan had left early because he did not want to appear in the Grand Review under Meade. Wesley Merritt led the cavalry in Sheridan's absence. When Custer passed the reviewing stand, a spectator tossed him a wreath, which made his horse bolt. Custer went galloping past before he could regain control and wheel back into position. Some people suspected that Custer was showing off for the crowd.

The cavalry followed Meade, then the IX, V, and II Corps. Cannons rumbled down Pennsylvania Avenue, and engineers hauled pontoon boats along the parade route. "The men preserved their alinement and distances with an ease which showed their years of training in the field," Porter noted with satisfaction. "Their movements were unfettered, their step was elastic, and the swaying of their bodies and the swinging of their arms were as measured as the vibrations of a pendulum. Their muskets shone like a wall of steel. The cannon rumbled peacefully over the paved street, banks of flowers almost concealing them."[66] No African American soldiers were in the parade, as the black units had gone west with Sheridan. The entire VI Corps was still in Virginia and unable to attend. But even with these absences, it took six hours for the eighty thousand men from the Army of the Potomac to pass in review.

Washington's residents had draped the buildings along the parade route with flags and banners, replacing the black symbols of mourning that had gone up following Lincoln's assassination. Charles Wainwright noticed one banner in particular: "The only debt we can never repay," it read; "what we owe to our gallant defenders." Wainwright eyed it cynically. "I could not help wondering whether, having made up their minds that they can never pay the debt, they will think it useless to try."[67]

But this was not a day for cynicism. "Everything went off to perfection," said Wainwright, who had his men shine their artillery until it gleamed and paid particular attention to the appearance of the horses. Of all the brigades in the army, Wainwright thought his artillery looked best.

It was Sherman's turn the next day. He rode in front of his men with Oliver O. Howard, who had become the commander of the Army of the Tennessee and now headed the new Freedman's Bureau. The main object of speculation was whether Sherman would shake Stanton's hand when he reached the reviewing stand. Stanton had publicly rebuked Sherman for the overly generous terms he had offered Joseph Johnston. Sherman had not forgiven the secretary of war for the insult—he did not shake his hand.

After the review ended, a woman told Wainwright that she preferred watching Sherman's men. "She said the Army of the Potomac marched past just like its commander (Meade), looking neither to the right nor the left, and only intent on passing the reviewing stand properly; while Sherman's officers and men were bowing on all sides and not half so stiff. I told her she had paid the greatest compliment to the Army of the Potomac I had heard."[68]

The Grand Review was over. Soon the Army of the Potomac, too, became a part of history. On June 28, 1865, George Gordon Meade issued a farewell address to the army he had taken over exactly two years earlier. "It is unnecessary to enumerate here all that has occurred in these two eventful years, from the grand and decisive Battle of Gettysburg, the turning point of the war, to the surrender of the Army of Northern Virginia at Appomattox Court House," he said. "Suffice it to say that history will do you justice, a grateful country will honor the living, cherish and support the disabled, and sincerely mourn the dead."[69]

The Army of the Potomac was no more.

CHAPTER 18

The Final Years

The last known picture of George Gordon Meade, taken in 1872
COURTESY DR. ANTHONY WASKIE

"When I tell people I spend New Year's Eve in a cemetery, they think I'm crazy," says Nancy Kelsey, a member of the General Meade Society of Philadelphia. This is indeed New Year's Eve—the afternoon of New Year's Eve, anyway—and, yes, Kelsey is in Philadelphia's historic Laurel Hill Cemetery, the last resting place for George Meade, members of his family, and a host of other dead people.

If Kelsey is crazy, she's not the only one. Several hundred people have gathered here to salute the victor of Gettysburg at his gravesite on what was not only his birthday but his wedding anniversary as well. It's a pleasantly warm sunny day, and the cemetery is free of snow. The paved area in front of the big columned gatehouse is already buzzing with activity. Andy Waskie is here, but not as Meade. He's engaged in energetic conversation with various people. In an example of life imitating . . . something, December 31 is Waskie's wedding anniversary, too. And he got married at Meade's gravesite in Laurel Hill. Jerry McCormick, wearing a Laurel Hill sweatshirt, bustles around as he helps prepare the buffet lunch. Living historians—I guess I shouldn't call them reenactors—mill about. A Zouave sports bright red leggings and a white turban, while a Civil War sailor looks like a daguerreotype come to life. There are plenty of civilians, too, the women wearing hoop skirts and the men with high top hats. Members of the Philadelphia Brigade Band sit around with their instruments. There are even a few Confederate officers. One of them, who looks like a Longstreet, puffs on a cigar, and the smell of the smoke permeates the air.

As it gets closer to noon, Waskie begins organizing the march down to the gravesite. The band takes the lead, living historians form up in their various units, nineteenth-century civilians are behind them, and the day's VIPs and military veterans follow. We regular, modern-day folk bring up the rear, and the procession winds its way through the cemetery to the Meade gravesite.

Laurel Hill Cemetery is truly a necropolis, a city of the dead. Founded in 1836 on heights overlooking the Schuylkill River, it's the nation's second-oldest Victorian garden cemetery. (Mount Auburn in Cambridge, Massachusetts, came first.) Its creators sought to make it not only a soothing place for the dead to spend an eternity, but also a pleasant one for the living to visit for walks and picnics. It's still a beautiful and fascinating place to spend some time.

A wealth of Victorian funerary ornamentation bedecks the cemetery's ninety-plus acres. There are broken columns, stone wreaths, and angels. Obelisks by the score point in the direction the people lying beneath them once hoped they'd go, while the truly wealthy provided themselves with ornate mausoleums. The latest big name interred here is Harry Kalas, the former broadcaster for the Philadelphia Phillies. His tombstone looks like a big microphone and has four stadium seats around it where fans can sit and consider their own mortality or the Phillies' chances.

On the way to Meade's grave, we pass the last resting place of his mother. She died in 1852, but her stone is one of the newest in the cemetery, installed just a year ago. A descendant, Maj. Charles Meade of San Antonio, Texas, had learned that this ancestor of his lacked a headstone, so he bought her one and came to the birthday ceremony last year to dedicate it.

Meade and his family reside on the edge of the hill overlooking the river, beneath modest stones at the base of a very large maple. His wife lies to one side of him, his daughter Margaret on the other. The gravesite gives me renewed respect for the "old goggle-eyed snapping turtle." Other monuments at Laurel Hill brazenly proclaim the importance of the dead people they commemorate; Meade was content with a simple stone that reads, "He did his work bravely and is at rest."

Waskie introduces all the various groups and organizations that have gathered for today's ceremony, including the Confederate representatives. "The war is over and we're all friends again," he says, and people in the crowd laugh. Champagne corks pop in the background as volunteers at a folding table a little ways uphill prepare for the toast. Down below us I see crew sculls on the Schuylkill, while a train makes a loud grating passage across the railroad bridge. It is a picturesque setting and not a bad place to spend eternity.

Waskie reads an excerpt from the letter Meade wrote to his wife 150 years ago on this very day, on his birthday and their anniversary. He was at an army camp in Virginia, still just a brigade commander but with his ambitions stirring. "Do you know, to-day is our wedding-day and my birthday," he wrote. "Twenty-one years ago we pledged our faith to each other, and I doubt if any other couple live who, with all the ups and downs of life, have had more happiness with each other than you and I. I trust a merciful Providence will spare us both to celebrate yet many returns of the day, and that we shall see our children advancing in life prosperously and happily."[1]

When the speeches and the wreath-layings are over, it's time for a twenty-one-gun salute fired by men in Civil War uniforms with period weapons. The guns roar and more than a few spectators jump. Throughout the ceremony, Meade Society members have been circulating through the crowd, pouring champagne into little paper cups. Waskie leads us in a toast to the victor of Gettysburg.

Afterward I strike up a conversation with the Zouave. He is Jeffrey Rodriguez, a photographer and artist from Winona, New Jersey. He has brought along a watercolor portrait of Meade that he has painted. He tells me he got interested in living history after reading an article in a photography magazine about how to shoot reenactments. He decided to go see one for himself. He took pictures the first day and joined a Civil War unit on the second. He's here today as a member of the 114th Pennsylvania, better known as Collis' Zouaves. For a time the 114th served as Meade's headquarters guard. Zouaves adopted colorful uniforms based on those worn by French Algerian troops, and Rodriguez is wearing their trademark bright red pants, white gaiters, red fez, and fancy embroidered coat. "I just have a thing for the past," Rodriguez says. "I'm drawn to Victorian times—I don't know, whatever kind of connection you want to call it. We do get those times when you're doing this and you have no modern things around you at all, and for a few seconds or a part of a second you feel you're back there."

"We call that a period rush," says Paul Leder, who is standing next to us.

"Yeah, or breaking the bubble or piercing the bubble, or something like that," says Rodriguez. Although, he adds, "after you've been doing it for twenty-two years, you don't reach it too often."

Waskie takes Rodriguez away for a photo opportunity, and I begin talking to Jim Cooke, a Meade descendant who spoke at the gravesite. He tells me a little bit about his family history, how his father's mother was one of George Meade Jr.'s children. "My dad was always proud of the Meade story, but he was also somewhat ashamed in that Meade was discredited for not following up right away after Gettysburg and smashing Lee and the Army of Northern Virginia and ending the conflict then," Cooke says. He mentions the letter of reprimand that Lincoln wrote but never sent after Lee crossed the Potomac. "Some of the lessons of his life and what he had to deal with, the adversity he dealt with, was remarkable," Cooke says. "The saddest thing about his life is that he did not write a book. He was an educated man; he could have written a beautiful, interesting history. He did not have a chance to tell his own story, so it's always told by others."

Back at the cemetery gatehouse, people line up for a buffet that includes Margaret Meade chicken, Oliver O. Howard cornbread, and other delights. People mill around outside eating their food and drinking beer. A group gathers around Waskie, who's going to lead an hourlong tour of Laurel Hill. He serves on its board of directors and knows a lot about the people buried here. Some are famous; most are not. One, at least, has been recently rescued from obscurity: Lt. Joseph Bonnell was a Philadelphia native who became a hero of Texas independence when he persuaded local tribes not to aid the Mexican Army. Bonnell was buried here in relative anonymity until a Texas historical society contacted the cemetery and explained his significance. Now the grave includes a marker that tells his story.

Waskie takes us to the gravesites of several notables. George Henry Boker was a cofounder of the Union League in Philadelphia. Thomas Sully was the nation's premier portrait painter in the early eighteenth century. The artist's son, Alfred Sully, was a Civil War general. Charles Ellet Jr. was a pioneering bridge builder who designed tinclad gunboats for the army in the Civil War (the navy, Waskie tells us, wasn't interested). Ellet was mortally wounded when his tinclads helped capture Memphis—in fact, Waskie says, he was the only Union casualty of the battle.

The tombstones here were supposed to preserve the memories of the deceased forever, but many have become cracked and weathered with age. Some of the sandstone ones are so worn that the names on them have become almost illegible. So it's not the stone markers that will keep these people alive for posterity; it's the sharing of knowledge by people such as Waskie that allow the dead to maintain at least a toehold on immortality.

We pause briefly at Meade's tomb and then continue on to the graves of people with connections to Meade. We stop at the stately tombstone of Adm. John Dahlgren, who served during the Civil War and developed the naval gun that bore his name. A small white stone next to his marks the resting place of his son, the unfortunate Ulric Dahlgren, killed in Kilpatrick's Richmond raid. Waskie tells us the strange and fascinating story of how Dahlgren's body got here. Enraged by the revelations that Dahlgren and his raiders planned to burn Richmond and execute President Jefferson Davis and his cabinet, Confederate authorities briefly put Dahlgren's body on display in the city before burying it in an unmarked grave. A Union spy named Elizabeth Van Lew arranged to have the body spirited away and buried on the property of a sympathetic farmer and Admiral Dahlgren recovered his son's remains after the war. A military guard brought the body back here, making stops for services in Washington, D.C., with a funeral oration by Henry Ward Beecher, and a day lying in state in Philadelphia's Independence Hall.

Admiral Dahlgren's widow later bought the old Stone House on South Mountain, where Meade once had his headquarters, and built the little Gothic chapel across the road. She intended to have the bodies of her husband and son reinterred there, but those plans never materialized. The same can't be said of Mrs. Dahlgren. Waskie tells us some people claim her ghost occasionally appears at the South Mountain Inn today.

Samuel Crawford's grave is nearby. He was an army surgeon who was at Fort Sumter when the war began in 1861. In 1865 he commanded a division of the V Corps at Appomattox Court House when Lee surrendered. In between, he led the Pennsylvania Reserves, Meade's old brigade, at Gettysburg. Waskie tells us that it was Crawford—not Joshua Chamberlain—who was the real savior of Little Round Top. I'll chalk that up to his Pennsylvania-centric way of thinking. But in one respect Crawford did save Little Round Top—he bought some of the land there after the war and had it deeded to the government when he died.

Horace Porter told a story about Meade and an officer who must have been Crawford, although Porter merely identified him as "an officer serving in the Army of the Potomac who had formerly been a surgeon." One day the officer arrived at Meade's headquarters "in a high state of indignation." As he had been riding over, some of the men had called him "Old Pills," and he thought that was a great affront to his dignity. "I would like to have it stopped," he said.

Meade put on his eyeglasses and glared through them at the complainer. "Well, what of that?" he demanded. "How can I prevent it? Why, I hear that, when I rode out the other day, some of the men called me a 'damned old goggle-eyed snapping-turtle,' and I can't even stop that!"[2] Now "Old Pills" and the "old goggle-eyed snapping-turtle" lie in the ground near each other, neighbors for eternity.

● ● ●

Meade had less than eight years left between the end of the war and his interment in Laurel Hill. They were interesting years, too. For a time he served the reconstruction effort in the South from a post in Georgia. He also spent a lot of time in Philadelphia, where he oversaw the layout of Fairmount Park. He helped subdue an army of Irishmen who tried to invade Canada. And he watched as other soldiers received promotions and positions he believed he deserved.

The main task after the war was the tricky one of reuniting a country torn apart by four years of bloody civil war. Meade played a role in that battle, too. It was a difficult task made even harder by a divided government. The Republicans in Congress pressed for a more draconian approach to the Southern states. They passed a series of reconstruction acts that required the Southern states to adopt new constitutions and pass the Fourteenth Amendment, giving citizenship to African Americans. President Andrew Johnson, a Democrat from Tennessee, was strongly opposed to black suffrage and fought for much more lenient terms for the Southern states. The president and Congress took opposite sides in an increasingly bitter struggle over reconstruction. The battles eventually led to Johnson's impeachment but not his removal from office.

"I am myself for conciliation, as the policy most likely to effect a speedy reunion," Meade noted shortly after Lee's surrender. "If we are going to punish treason, as perhaps strict justice would demand, we shall have to shed almost as much blood as has already been poured out in this terrible war. These are points, however, for others to adjust."[3] Those "others" were the politicians.

Meade realized the army would shoulder much of the responsibility for overseeing reconstruction, and that meant a military occupation of the South. In June 1865 the president directed that the country be divided into five military divisions, with states as separate departments within them. The Division of the Gulf went to Sheridan, George Thomas headed the Tennessee Division, Sherman got Mississippi, and Henry Halleck received command of the Military Division of the Pacific. No doubt many in Washington were glad to see Halleck pack his bags and relocate to California.

Meade received command of the largest division, the Atlantic, which included the territory from Maine through South Carolina. His headquarters were in Philadelphia. He had three Southern states under him, each commanded by a general—Alfred Terry in Virginia, John Schofield in North Carolina, and Quincy Gillmore in South Carolina. Meade, who still nursed his unrealistic expectations that the military should remain outside politics, did not relish his new responsibilities, which mixed the two. On August 28, 1867, Meade wrote to Regis de Trobriand, one of his former division commanders, complaining that his position required him to be both a soldier and a politician, "a part which I am sure both to you and me would be not only difficult but disagreeable."[4]

Some things were more agreeable, however. In July 1865 Meade visited Boston, where Lyman served as his host. He helped lay the cornerstone at Harvard's Memorial Hall and received an honorary degree during a week of dinners, appearances, receptions, and other festivities. One of the dinners was hosted by the father of Arthur Dehon, the aide who had been killed at Fredericksburg. Meade toasted his memory with "a few touching words."[5]

In August he toured Virginia and the Carolinas, the Southern states under his command. He reported that conditions were "on the whole satisfactory" and that the Southern people were recovering slowly from the effects of the war. The biggest issue was "the labor question," and Meade cautioned that it would take time for the Southern states to adapt to the end of slavery. Until they did, "it will undoubtedly be necessary to retain such military control as will compel mutual justice from both parties. This control should be exercised with judgment and discretion, and every effort made to convince both races that it is exercised only for their mutual benefit. Instructions were given to this effect to Department

Commanders, and I am satisfied there need be no apprehension of any improper interference of the military with the civil authorities."[6]

Surprisingly, though, it wasn't the Southern states that handed Meade his biggest crisis. Instead, it developed along the Canadian border and involved Irishmen, not Southerners. Now almost completely forgotten, the Fenian invasions provided a truly odd footnote to American history.

The Fenian Brotherhood was an Irish liberation movement named after Gaelic warriors from Ireland's pre-Christian era. At a convention in Chicago in 1863 its members took an oath to "labor with earnest zeal for the liberation of Ireland from the yoke of England."[7] Up to 175,000 Irishmen had fought for the Union in the Civil War, and the conflict served as a great training ground for future Fenian warriors who were willing to take up arms to throw off that English yoke. The Fenians did not overlook this fact. As the war drew to a close, Fenian representatives had begun a campaign to recruit soldiers for a Fenian army, offering bounties of up to 100 British pounds.

Thomas W. Sweeney didn't need the inducement of a bounty to join. Born in County Cork, Sweeney had immigrated to the United States at age twelve. He lost an arm fighting for the United States in Mexico, battled Indians out west, and fought bravely in the Civil War's Western Theater, where he received two wounds. He didn't fight all his battles against Confederates, either. Toward the end of the war Sweeney got into a drunken fracas with two of his fellow Union generals, one of whom had Sweeney arrested. A military court acquitted him. He joined the Fenian Brotherhood in August 1865 and was elected as the organization's secretary of war and commander in chief at a convention in Philadelphia that fall. "Fighting Tom" convinced the brotherhood that it should attack Canada, capture the northern provinces, and use them as a base from which to attack the hated Great Britain. Eventually, he reasoned, Britain would have to negotiate with the brotherhood and release Ireland from the Crown's grip.

Perhaps it sounded more realistic in 1865.

Fenian activity in the United States worried the British government so much that its minister in Washington approached Secretary of State William Seward about it. Seward appeared unconcerned. The Fenians also made overtures to Seward, hoping the United States, still nursing grievances over Britain's flirtations with the Confederacy, might aid their cause. Seward replied that the United States was not interested. North of the border, Canadians became concerned enough to call up militia companies and warn them to remain alert for invading Irishmen.

The invasion of Canada was much more than a pipe dream for Sweeney. All he needed, he said, was $450,000, and he and ten thousand men could launch attacks along the border from Illinois to Vermont. The Fenians even had a song:

We are the Fenian Brotherhood, skilled in the art of war,
And we're going to fight for Ireland, the land that we adore,
Many battles have we won, along with the boys in blue,
And we'll go and capture Canada for we've nothing else to do.[8]

When the Fenian invasion finally began to take shape, though, it was another wing of the often divided movement that moved first, and it aimed at maritime Canada, specifically the island of Campobello on the Maine–New Brunswick border. In March and April 1866 Maine residents noticed an unusual number of Irishmen drifting into the little coastal towns around the boundary with Canada. These new arrivals even made a few tentative raids into Canada, on one occasion capturing a British flag at a customs house and firing revolvers. In response, the British began concentrating their forces in the border regions, and when a ship loaded with weapons arrived in Eastport, Maine, on April 17, 1866, U.S. customs officials impounded the Fenians' arms.

When all this was happening, Meade was in St. Louis to serve with Sherman and George Thomas on a board to recommend brevet promotions. As soon as he received word of the Fenian activities, Meade immediately proceeded to Eastport, arriving there on April 19 with about 160 soldiers. He discovered that some three hundred Fenians were waiting expectantly in the area to see if the United States would release their impounded weapons. Meade dashed their hopes by having the arms hauled off to nearby Fort Stevens and warning the leaders that he would arrest anyone who violated the country's neutrality laws. Stymied by Meade's firm action, the Fenians began drifting off—but only after setting fire to a warehouse and a few woodpiles and jangling the nerves of the people across the border.

"It soon became evident to all that the thing was a miserable failure," read a contemporary history of the Fenians. "There were these few hundreds of repscallions [*sic*], without arms, food, or money to purchase it, about to attack the powers of Great Britain and the United States." [9] Poor Meade, however, fell ill while he was in Eastport and had to spend several weeks there recovering.

The Fenians weren't finished with their designs on Canada, though. Undeterred by the Campobello fizzle, Sweeney's branch of the movement remained determined to carry out attacks along the northern border of the United States. Whereas the Campobello debacle had an almost comical air about it, the next Fenian attempt to invade Canada drew blood.

Early on the morning of June 1 a Fenian force of about eight hundred men under Col. John O'Neill crossed the Niagara River on canal boats just north of Buffalo and landed on Canadian soil. Canadian authorities hastily raised a volunteer militia to counter the threat, while the USS *Michigan*, a U.S. gunboat, steamed up the Niagara River from Lake Erie to ensure that the Fenians could not receive any reinforcements from the U.S. side. The Fenians and the Canadian defenders clashed on the beautiful spring morning of June 2 near the town of Ridgeway. The Fenians, many of them experienced soldiers, routed the green Canadian militiamen, killing nine of them, but they soon realized they had bitten off considerably more than they could chew. The Irishmen withdrew back across the Niagara and straight into the arms of the U.S. soldiers aboard the *Michigan* and the steam tug USS *Harrison*.

By then Meade had reached Buffalo to deal with the crisis. He ordered the local commander to use whatever forces he had to prevent the Fenians from violating U.S. neutrality laws. On June 6 President Johnson, who had dithered because he worried about alienating the large Irish vote, belatedly issued a neutrality proclamation. Many Fenians took this as a betrayal. "We bought our rifles from your arsenals, and were given to understand that you would not interfere," one captured Irishman told Meade.[10]

Meade traveled along the frontier from Buffalo to St. Albans, Vermont, issuing orders to local commanders to confiscate any arms that might be intended for the invasion forces. After discussions with Buffalo's district attorney, he decided to parole all the captured enlisted men on their promise that they would not take up arms on U.S. territory again. Meade also suggested that the War Department provide funds for transportation home to any captured Fenians who could not afford a train ticket.

Sweeney and most of his staff were arrested in St. Albans on June 6, although one of his generals escaped and took a small force back into Canada for some minor pilfering. On June 8 a force of Canadian regulars and volunteers drove them back across the border and into the custody of waiting U.S. Army forces. The Fenian invasion of Canada had ended, not with a bang but with an embarrassing whimper.

After the crisis had passed, Stanton wrote Meade a letter to express his appreciation. "Your calm, patient and firm method of dealing with this matter, so as to avoid any possible collision or bloodshed, renders it needless to make any suggestions on the subject beyond approval of your actions," the secretary of war said.[11]

• • •

Politics had embroiled the Army of the Potomac during the war, and politics created more turbulence after the shooting stopped and the country wrestled with the complex issues of putting itself back together. Congress and the president engaged in an increasingly no-holds-barred fight over the best way to proceed, and the fight only intensified in 1866 when the November elections gave the Republicans dominance over Congress.

The political slugfests led to periodic shake-ups in the military organization behind Reconstruction. When Congress discontinued the Atlantic Division in August 1866, Meade took command of the Department of the East, with his headquarters still in Philadelphia. At the end of 1867 he became head of the Third Military District, with responsibility for Georgia, Alabama, and Florida. (In August 1868 the Second and Third Military Districts were combined to form the Department of the South, with Meade still in command. He added the two Carolinas to the states under his control.)

Meade's new headquarters were in Atlanta, where he replaced John Pope, whom Johnson suspected of having Radical Republican leanings. The more conservative Meade seemed to be a safer choice. One Georgia paper said that with Meade, "we may hope to escape from Negro bondage; with him it is not a crime to be white."[12] Meade, it appeared, hoped to be firm but fair. "It is not at all improbable that placed suddenly in so arduous and embarrassing a position, I may make errors of judgment to the regret and disappointment of former friends, and all I can say is that it is my intention, under the light I can get, to discharge my duty conscientiously and do only what I think is right."[13] On January 2, 1867, he departed for his new headquarters in Atlanta. This was not a post he desired, he wrote to a friend, because it "blended so intimately with the questions, not only of politics, but of party."[14] Meade reached Atlanta at a crucial period, as the Southern states were creating new constitutions so that they could be readmitted to the Union. The process involved plenty of local controversies over topics such as redistricting and questions about the military's role during the constitutional conventions.

Meade had the power to remove elected officials if he felt it necessary, but he preferred to exercise this power as little as possible. Sometimes he felt that he had no choice. He removed Georgia's governor and treasurer when the governor refused to approve the funds for the constitutional convention and the treasurer would not appropriate the money without the governor's approval. Meade said that his "only object in making the removals, was the execution of the Law, and that the same was free from any personal or political bias."[15]

Meade also faced another kind of situation as commander of the Third Military District, as exemplified in the case of the Ashburn murder. George W. Ashburn was a white North Carolinian who had opposed secession and served in the Union army. After the war, he moved to Columbus, Georgia, where he was a member of the state's constitutional convention and a political organizer for the local African American community. Around midnight on March 30–31, 1868, a group of up to thirty armed and masked men gathered near the seedy boardinghouse on Oglethorpe Street where Ashburn lived. Denied admittance, several members of this mob broke open the front door and stormed inside. Ashburn had a room in the back. When he opened the door to his room, several members of the party opened fire, shooting him dead. The murderers then disappeared into the night.

Once Meade received word of the crime, he ordered Capt. William Mills of the 16th Infantry, who was the senior officer in Columbus, to take charge. The local authorities, including Mayor F. W. Wilkins, promised to cooperate in the investigation but soon began dragging their feet. Meade used his authority to remove Wilkins and other members of the local government and install Mills as mayor. This turned out to be a wise move; later investigation discovered that after the murder, Mayor Wilkins had spontaneously offered one of the assailants, a soldier named Marshall, a $10 "loan" so he could leave the area on furlough. Mills reported that four policemen had seen the crowd gathering by Ashburn's house and even heard the cocking of their pistols, but they turned and went the other way. Mills arrested one of them, a man named Cash, who appeared to be good friends with the mayor. In addition, Mills heard reports that witnesses had seen the police chief and another officer disguising themselves on the night of the murder. There also were rumors that the newly formed Ku Klux Klan had been involved.

Meade requested that the War Department send down a detective, a Mr. Reed. In the meantime, Mills arrested ten men whom he suspected of being involved in the murder. Acting on the advice of another investigator named H. C. Whitely, Meade sent the suspects to Fort Pulaski in Savannah so they could be questioned without feeling threatened by the citizens of Columbus. Rumors spread that they were being tortured at the fort by being placed in a special box that slowly compressed them, with jets of hot steam adding to their discomfort. These tales, which apparently arose after someone overhead Meade joking with a child at a dinner party, affronted the general's sense of honor. Meade did have the suspects held in small and stifling cells in nearby Fort McPherson, and investigators threatened two black witnesses with having their heads shaved. Meade indignantly denied the rumors of torture but admitted there were "arbitrary measures resorted to, which in a different condition of society, and under a well ordered government, might seem to deserve reprobation."[16]

Since there seemed little chance of a fair trial from a local court, Meade wanted the suspects tried by a military commission. But in the end, Ashburn's killers remained free. When Georgia approved the Fourteenth Amendment in the summer of 1868, it paved the way for the state's readmittance to the Union and ended the military's jurisdiction in the case. Local authorities, of course, never bothered to take it up.

The town of Camilla, in southwestern Georgia, experienced trouble of a different sort. On September 19, 1868, a large group of up to four hundred freedmen approached the town to take part in a Republican rally. Sheriff Mumford Poore met the party outside town and told them they would not be allowed to bring in weapons. About half the group were armed, some only with walking sticks but many with guns loaded with birdshot. Republican congressional candidate William F. Pierce protested that the group had only peaceful intentions but would not give up their weapons. Poore galloped back to town and gathered a posse. When the freedmen entered town, a drunk and belligerent man named James Johns fired his gun at the wagon carrying the rally's musicians—accidentally, he said; on purpose, said others. In any event, the gunshot served to trigger a violent onslaught as Poore and his posse opened up on the Republicans, who fled town. Poore and his men systematically hunted them, killing at least nine and wounding up to thirty.

Meade sent the trustworthy Capt. William Mills to investigate but he did not send troops to pacify the town, explaining that he was able to intervene militarily only if civil authorities asked him, and they had not. In a long letter to the governor Meade attempted to parcel out blame to both the victims, who he said should have left their weapons behind when Poore asked them, and to the sheriff and his cronies, who spent hours hunting down and killing men who had attended the rally. "This is a grave and serious charge—almost too terrible to believe," Meade told the governor. Terrible it was, but nobody ever faced any charges for what happened at Camilla. Meade, who had been concentrating his scattered troops at distribution points throughout the state, faced criticism for not having soldiers in Camilla. He correctly pointed out that he had not been aware of the situation until it was too late. Even if his forces had not been concentrated, the closest soldiers would have been in Auburn, thirty miles away, too distant to do any good.[17]

Grant, back in Washington, had been continuing as general in chief. Although at first he attempted to remain above the bitter partisanship in Washington, he became increasingly alienated by President Johnson and more in tune with congressional Republicans. In May 1868 the Republican convention unanimously nominated him for president. He accepted the nomination with a letter that ended, "Let us have peace."[18]

Grant's election as president that fall meant he would have to vacate his position as general in the army. Sherman, the army's sole lieutenant general, would advance a grade to full general. Meade nursed not unrealistic hopes that he would be promoted to Sherman's now-vacant grade of lieutenant general, but previous history had certainly taught him not to get his hopes too high.

Before the inauguration Meade passed through Washington after a visit to Philadelphia. Troubled by rumors that Grant planned to bypass him, Meade stopped to visit the president-elect. The occasion must have stirred uncomfortable memories of the various meetings between the two men during the war, when Meade had come to Grant with issues concerning rank. Meade explained to the president-elect why he deserved the promotion. Grant remained silent, but his silence spoke volumes. Meade realized that once again he would be denied what he felt was his due. He was right. Grant promoted Sheridan instead.

"The blow has been struck and our worst fears realized," Meade wrote to Margaret from Atlanta on March 6, 1869. Meade received a letter from Sherman telling him return to Philadelphia and resume command of the Military Division of the Atlantic. He suspected that Sherman had sent the letter himself rather than have Meade face the indignity of receiving orders from Sheridan.

At least he would be back home, but that was small consolation for yet another betrayal by Grant. "My own sweet love, you can imagine the force of this blow," he wrote in an anguished letter to his wife, "but it is useless to repine over what cannot be remedied, and we must find consolation in the consciousness we have that it is the cruelest and meanest act of injustice, and the hope, if there is any sense of wrong or justice in the country, that the man who perpetrated it will some day be made to feel so." The perpetrator, of course, was President Ulysses S. Grant.[19]

Alexander McClure, a mover and shaker in Pennsylvania's Republican politics, said that after Sheridan's promotion, he saw Meade many times, "but always wearing the deep lines of sad disappointment in his finely-chiseled face. The Lieutenant-Generalship was obviously a forbidden topic with him, and he went down to his grave one of the sorrowing and unrewarded heroes of the war."[20]

• • •

There's a historical marker on the sidewalk on the corner of Delancey Place and Nineteenth Street in Philadelphia. "George Gordon Meade (1815–1872)," it reads. "Soldier, civil engineer. Major general, U.S. Army. Commander, victorious Army of the Potomac at Battle of Gettysburg, 1863. Philadelphia was his family's home; he died at No. 1836 here, in a house given to him for his service to the nation." On the lintel over the home's entrance on Nineteenth Street is carved a single word: "Meade." This is the building where the general spent his last years, although when he lived here the entrance (and the address) was on Delancey Place. The building, the last in a string of rowhouses, has been converted to apartments. It looks a little worse for wear and tear, although the rest of Delancey Place retains a nineteenth-century air of elegance.

Following the Battle of Gettysburg, the citizens of Philadelphia decided to raise money to buy this home for the victorious general. Meade wanted nothing to do with it, as he did not think it would be "proper." Should he die in the war, he told Margaret, then anything that could help his widow and orphans would be welcome. Otherwise, he said, "I don't think we would be comfortable in a house bought with our friends' money."[21] Margaret and her mother both wrote him back saying it was too late. Meade capitulated.

He lived here until his death. Sherman had assigned him to command of the Department of the Atlantic, with his headquarters in Philadelphia, so he returned home, where he resumed his duties as a commissioner for Fairmount Park. One of his greatest pleasures was riding through the park, sometimes on Old Baldy, planning its paths and landscapes.

On October 31, 1872, Meade and Margaret were taking their daily walk when the general complained of a pain in his side. He had suffered a near-fatal attack of pneumonia in April 1869, and his doctor diagnosed a return of the affliction. Meade apparently had a premonition that he was about to fight his last campaign, and he began making preparations for his demise. On November 6, 1872, George Gordon Meade died. He was fifty-six years old.

A "great conflagration" in Boston pushed Meade's funeral off the front page of the *Philadelphia Inquirer* for November 12, 1872, but the coverage filled up the majority of page 2. Old scores were forgotten as the paper paid flowery tribute to the late general. "More eloquently than could any volume or number of volumes speak in praise of what General Meade was while living, the demonstration yesterday spoke over the remains of the noble soldier and noble man," the paper said. "Public and private business was made to stand still for the time, that nothing should interfere to prevent fitting honor being bestowed upon the worthy remains. And nothing did prevent."

Police cleared the streets and roped them off in preparation for the expected crowds. By 8:00 that morning people began to gather in the streets around St. Mark's Church on Locust Street. The paper estimated that fifty thousand people filled the streets by 10:00, when President Grant arrived.

Back at the Meade home at Delancey Place, Generals Sheridan, Humphreys, Parke, and Wright helped carry the coffin to the hearse, which clattered through the streets to St. Mark's. They brought the coffin in through a side door and placed it in the center aisle. With Grant seated in one of the front pews, Bishop H. B. Whipple, who had conducted an Easter service for the Army of the Potomac on the eve of the Overland Campaign in 1864, gave a funeral address. "I have not come to bear tributes of respect to the great soldier who is dead," he said. "The city, the state, the nation—all have done this. Until longest time shall last, among the names which are inwrought in our country's history, his name will be a household word." Predicting the future apparently was not the bishop's strong suit.

Following the funeral services, the "immense funeral cortege" made its solemn way from the church and down Eighteenth Street through the city, past houses draped with black, flags at half staff, and citizens standing with their heads uncovered. Bands and military units marched in formation. Old Baldy, his saddle empty, followed the caisson. At a steamboat landing on the Schuylkill River, eight soldiers lifted the coffin from the hearse and carried it beneath a canopy of swords raised by members of the First City Troop and onto the steamer *Undine.* Three volleys from assembled soldiers and artillerymen shattered the silence. Then the *Undine,* draped in black, pulled away from the pier for the journey up the river to Laurel Hill Cemetery. More military units stood at intervals along the river's edge to fire volleys as the vessel passed.

More throngs awaited at the cemetery, with police stationed at each entrance to filter out the uninvited. The steamer soon hove into view and docked at a pier below the cemetery. The eight soldiers resumed their burden and carried the coffin to the gravesite for a reading of the Episcopalian burial service. And then George G. Meade was laid to rest.

The general's grave was beneath a dead oak tree wrapped tightly with ivy. The *Inquirer* writer found some symbolism here: "This is a beautiful symbol, for truly might Major-General Meade be likened unto a lifeless oak, and while this country has a history there will cling to loved memory twinings of tender affection and deep gratitude, whose brightness will ever remain fresher than even the green of ivy."[22]

● ● ●

Over the years, even as Meade's reputation declined, Robert E. Lee's rose. More than anyone else, Jubal Early was the man responsible for burnishing Lee's reputation after the war. During the war, Early had been one of Lee's subordinates and had even reached the outskirts of Washington in the summer of 1864. Peevish, eccentric, and high-strung, Early continued fighting the war on paper after it had ended. He embarked on a lifelong campaign to recast the Southern story in a truly heroic light by airbrushing slavery out of the picture and raising Lee and the Army of Northern Virginia to a suitably heroic pinnacle of greatness. Part of his motivation was to attach his own reputation to that of Lee's, and part no doubt was to remove some of the sting from the South's defeat. Other historians continued Early's work of buffing and polishing Lee's image, until he became, if not more than human, then at least "one of the greatest human beings of modern times," as biographer Douglas Southall Freeman put it.[23]

"Lee's image became larger than life," wrote Thomas L. Connelly in his book on the Confederate general. "He was the son who never disobeyed his mother, the perfect student, and the man of flawless character. He was the noble Lee of 1861, who supposedly loved the Union more than others who espoused the Confederate cause." In battle, "Lee was shaped as the god of war, compared favorably with Caesar, Frederick the Great, and Marlborough. He was the tactical genius who was seldom—if ever—defeated by mistakes of his own making."[24]

Then how does one explain Gettysburg, where George Gordon Meade and the Army of the Potomac beat Lee and the Army of Northern Virginia? One way Early and his confederates enhanced Lee's reputation was by tearing down those of his subordinates. If Lee was infallible, then his defeat must have been the fault of others—most notably, James Longstreet. Early became a vociferous critic of Longstreet and began trumpeting the story that Longstreet's tardiness in attacking on July 2 had cost Lee the battle and, by extension, lost the war for the South. Longstreet was an obvious target for Early's wrath. After the war Longstreet had done the unspeakable by criticizing Lee's actions at Gettysburg—and then he rubbed salt in the wounds by becoming a Republican. If the efforts of Early and others transformed Lee into the South's version of Christ, then Longstreet became the Confederacy's Judas. By the time Longstreet died in 1904, his legacy had become so tarnished that the Savannah chapter of United Daughters of the Confederacy refused to send flowers to his funeral and the United Confederate Veterans of Wilmington, North Carolina, would not send his family condolences.[25]

Meade never had such fervent supporters. It seems his reputation was being eclipsed even before the crowds attending his funeral could disperse. His son George set out to publish the general's collected letters, bridged by biographical passages, but he died before he could complete it. The general's grandson took up the task, and the two-volume *The Life and Letters of George Gordon Meade, Major-General United States Army*, came out in 1913, the fiftieth anniversary of Gettysburg. By then Meade had gone a long way toward slipping into obscurity. "For fifty years Meade has been set aside, ignored, depreciated, even insulted," wrote a Philadelphia poet named Charles Edward Moore when he reviewed *Life and Letters* for a magazine called *The Dial*. "Lee, in whose hand the South placed and kept its sword of command, will shine forth as the central figure of the strife. His audacities, his endurance, his resourcefulness, and his indomitable battle spirit, were longer tried and more triumphant than those of any other leader. But in Meade, though the latter had no such range of opportunity, no such unfettered command, we believe that Lee met his match. They were the two best soldiers of the war, and it was a fate propitious to the Republic which set them opposed in the battle that saved the Union."[26]

◆ ◆ ◆

George Meade is not completely forgotten in Philadelphia, and after our tour of Laurel Hill, my wife and I head into town in search of more Meades. We find two of them, both in Fairmount Park, the urban space that Meade helped create. One of them stands on a towering column that rears up above a somewhat odd collection of sculptures, columns, busts, balustrades, and engravings called the Smith Memorial Arch. Completed in 1912, this elaborate and towering tribute to Pennsylvania's Civil War notables owes its existence to a bequest from Richard Smith, who made type for printing presses. It's a strange and unlikely vision of excess that stands as a lonely gateway to West Fairmount Park. Meade's statue is the work of Daniel Chester French, whose most famous work is the statue in the Lincoln Memorial. His Meade stands so high atop its column I can't tell if it's any good. John Reynolds crowns the other column. On lower levels are equestrian statues of McClellan and Hancock, as well as busts of a couple men whose graves we have just visited, Samuel Crawford and John Dahlgren. The memorial in-cludes several other busts as well, while those worthies not important enough have their images immortalized had their names engraved. Richard Smith ponied up the money for this extravagance, which is why he has a statue here, a full-length figure titled "Type Founder." It's all very odd and reminds me a bit of the War Correspondents Arch down on South Mountain—a monument to oneself in the guise of commemorating others.

The other Meade is an equestrian statue by Alexander Milne Calder, whose huge William Penn stands atop the masonry tower of Philadelphia's City Hall. Calder's Meade has a much lonelier posting behind a sprawling Beaux-Arts style building called Memorial Hall. Calder created this Meade for $30,000 raised by the Fairmount Park Art Association and cast it with metal from captured Confederate cannons. "The design is a spirited one, and the execution all that could be desired," wrote a reporter for the *New York Times* when the statue was unveiled at a gala ceremony on October 18, 1887. The general's grandsons performed the actual unveiling "amid tumultuous cheering" from a crowd estimated at twenty thousand. John Gibbon was the featured speaker, and his listeners included Joshua Lawrence Chamberlain, now a former governor of Maine; Fitz John Porter, who had successfully challenged the court-martial over his actions at Second Bull Run; William Franklin, Meade's superior at Fredericksburg; and a number of other aging soldiers who had fought with the Army of the Potomac.

The cheers and speeches, as well as the soldiers, have long since faded away, replaced now by the rush of traffic from nearby I-76. Meade sits on his horse, a spirited steed that has its head down as it bites at its bridle, and he gazes in the direction of his grave up the Schuylkill. I agree with the *New York Times* assessment that the statue is a good likeness—better, I think, than the one at Gettysburg. Behind it a quiet and empty park stretches back to Memorial Hall, a behemoth constructed for the nation's centennial in 1876. It now houses the Please Touch Museum.

A few weeks later I return to Philadelphia to visit the Union League, the organization that George Boker, whose grave I saw at Laurel Hill, cofounded in 1862 so that Republicans would have a comfortable oasis in a city with strong secessionist tendencies. The league occupies a beautiful Beaux-Arts mansion on Broad Street. I had tried to visit once before. Wearing full tourist attire—shorts, sneakers, and backpack—I had climbed one of the spiral staircases that sweep up from Broad Street and peered through the windows of the front door. The concierge hurried out to head me off. He was polite but, I sensed, slightly pained as he informed me the Union League was a private club. No doubt I was violating the dress code on any number of points. Now slightly better dressed, I've shown up on a gray February day for an open house when I can finally tour the building.

This time I climb up the stairs at the less flashy Fifteenth Street entrance and enter the large Meade Room in a newer section of the building. When this large space opened in 1910, it housed pool tables. It was later a dining room, and in 1991 it was renamed after Meade. In a no doubt unintended irony, the original Meade Room is now the Sheridan Room. A number of tables are set up around the perimeter, and chairs are set out in front of a monitor that shows a video about the Union League.

Andy Waskie is here, too, this time in full Meade regalia. I'm talking with him when a man approaches. "Do you belong to Laurel Hill Cemetery?" he asks. Waskie straightens to his full height. He looks indignant. "Belong? Sir, I am *buried* there!" he thunders.

Today's tours go off with stopwatch precision. As my group ascends the stairs to the second floor, I spy a bust of Meade by Calder on the stairway and a large painting of Meade at Gettysburg by Philadelphia artist Daniel Ridgway Knight on a landing. In one of the library rooms, dominated by a large statue of Lincoln in a niche at one end, a bas-relief portrait of Meade appears in a row of generals (and one admiral) that runs along the wall. Throughout the mansion I spot representations of the generals that Meade knew, among them George McCall, Horatio Wright, Alexander Webb, and Ulysses S. Grant. One of the members shows us the tattered headquarters flag that Webb carried at the Battle of Gettysburg. There's also a huge equestrian painting of George Washington, done by Thomas Sully, one of Meade's neighbors in Laurel Hill.

It's a gorgeous building, full of paintings, sculpture, chandeliers, and antiques from a long-past gilded age, when the members were mayors, governors, and "captains of industry." Women were finally admitted in 1986, and the league's next president will be female. Yet as we move through on our carefully timed tours, I get a feeling that the Urban League is just a tad uneasy at having so many members of the hoi polloi wandering through the hallowed halls.

One part of the league is now regularly accessible to the general public. The Sir John Templeton Heritage Center, named after a financier and philanthropist with links to the league, opened in 2011 with a small museum that people can visit for a few hours on Tuesdays, Thursdays, and the second Saturday of each month. Currently it houses an exhibit about Philadelphia and the beginnings of the Civil War. A pike from John Brown's raid on Harpers Ferry hangs on one wall. Nearby, a glass case contains the flat gray hat that Abraham Lincoln wore when he hurried through Philadelphia on his way to Washington, D.C., for his inauguration in 1861. Rumors of assassination attempts had prompted the president-elect to travel into the capital city in the dead of night, wearing this hat as part of his disguise. The resulting ridicule made him regret his decision to make such an undignified arrival in Washington.

I see nothing about Meade here, although there is a turtle-shaped soup tureen in a display case about the league's elaborate entertainments. It was used to serve snapping turtle soup, so I consider that a tribute of sorts.

After the tour I make my way back to the Meade Room so I can ask Waskie about the Meade statue in Fairmount Park. I know the Meade Society has started a petition to have it moved to a place in front of Philadelphia's City Hall, where equestrian statues of McClellan and Reynolds already stand guard. "The monument was originally intended to be placed at City Hall," Waskie tells me. "It would have been an appropriate place to honor the greatest war hero in Philadelphia history." However, the family wanted the statue in Fairmount Park because of Meade's association with and love of the park. That was an appropriate place at the time, Waskie says, when thousands of people used Lansdowne Street every day. But as the years passed and the neighborhood declined, fewer people passed by. As long ago as 1913, says Waskie, the Grand Army of the Republic tried to have the statue moved. "It's even worse today," he says. "It's been vandalized and it's neglected and obscure, and it's really time to bring it back—if not to City Hall, then somewhere prominent in the city where he can be honored and remembered for his deeds."

Waskie has even found a mover who says he will relocate the statue for free. "It's just a matter of the will to do it," he says. "Now, the arts community is completely closed-minded about this. I've had meetings with them, and the first question I always get is, 'Who's Meade?' That's the first question. So right there it's an uphill battle." For the time being, like Meade himself, Calder's statue of the hero of Gettysburg will remain overlooked and nearly forgotten.

Notes

Preface

1. Isaac R. Pennypacker, *General Meade* (New York: D. Appleton, 1901), 7.

Introduction: Looking for Meade

1. George Meade, *The Life and Letters of George Gordon Meade, Major-General United States Army* (New York: Charles Scribner's Sons, 1913), Vol. I: 160.
2. Ibid., I: 347.
3. Horace Porter, *Campaigning with Grant* (New York: Century Company, 1907; reprint, Old Saybrook, CT: Konecky and Konecky, 1992), 83–84.
4. Theodore Lyman, *Meade's Army: The Private Notebooks of Lt. Col. Theodore Lyman*, ed. David W. Lowe (Kent, OH: Kent State University Press, 2007), 18.

Chapter 1: The Early Years

1. Charles S. Wainwright, *Diary of Battle: The Personal Journals of Colonel Charles S. Wainwright*, ed. Allan Nevins (New York: Harcourt, Brace and World, 1962), 215.
2. Meade, *Life and Letters*, I: 9.
3. Ibid., I: 262.
4. Stephen E. Ambrose, *Duty, Honor, Country: A History of West Point* (Baltimore: Johns Hopkins Press, 1966), 93.
5. Ibid., 102.
6. Meade, *Life and Letters*, I: 11.
7. Ambrose, *Duty, Honor, Country*, 117.
8. Meade, *Life and Letters*, I: 19.
9. Karla Zabludovsky, "Police Find 49 Bodies by a Highway in Mexico," *New York Times*, May 13, 2012. www.nytimes.com/2012/05/14/world/americas/police-find-49-bodies-by-a-highway-in-mexico.html?_r=1&hp.
10. Meade, *Life and Letters*, I: 154.
11. Luther Giddings, *Sketches of the Campaign in Northern Mexico in Eighteen Hundred Forty-Six and Seven* (New York: G. P. Putnam's Sons, 1853), 71–72.
12. John S. D. Eisenhower, *So Far from God: The U.S. War with Mexico, 1846–1848* (New York: Random House, 1989), 35–36.
13. Meade, *Life and Letters*, I: 26.
14. Ibid., I: 30.
15. Ibid., I: 36.
16. Ibid., I: 39.
17. Ibid., I: 48.
18. Quoted in Eisenhower, *So Far from God*, 65.

19. Quoted in Louis Fisher, "The Mexican War and Lincoln's 'Spot Resolutions,'" *Law Library of Congress*, April 18, 2009, http://loc.gov/law/help/usconlaw/pdf/Mexican.war.pdf. The House did not take any action on Lincoln's resolutions.

20. Ulysses S. Grant, *Personal Memoirs of U. S. Grant* (Cleveland: World Publishing Company, 1952; reprint, New York: Da Capo, 1982), 44.

21. George A. McCall, *Letters from the Frontiers: Written during a Period of Thirty Years' Service in the Army of the United States* (Philadelphia: J. B. Lippincott, 1868), 452.

22. Grant, *Memoirs*, 44.

23. Meade, *Life and Letters*, I: 80.

24. McCall, *Letters from the Frontiers*, 457.

25. Meade, *Life and Letters*, I: 81.

26. Quote from historical marker at Resaca de la Palma battlefield.

27. Meade, *Life and Letters*, I: 83.

28. Ibid., I: 94.

29. Ibid., I: 113.

30. Ibid., I: 107.

31. Ibid., I: 132.

32. Descriptions from Justin Harvey Smith, *The War with Mexico* (New York: The MacMillan Co., 1918), 239–246.

33. Meade, *Life and Letters*, I: 139.

34. Grant, *Memoirs*, 55–56.

35. Meade, *Life and Letters*, I: 132.

36. Grant, *Memoirs*, 57.

37. Meade, *Life and Letters*, I: 152.

38. Grant, *Memoirs*, 16.

39. Meade, *Life and Letters*, I: 158.

40. Ibid., I: 175.

41. Ibid., I: 187.

42. Ibid., I: 201.

43. Ibid., II: 184.

Chapter 2: War!

1. George B. McClellan, *The Civil War Papers of George B. McClellan: Selected Correspondence, 1860–1865*, ed. Stephen W. Sears (New York: Ticknor & Fields, 1989), 106.

2. Ibid., 269.

3. Ibid., 106.

4. Quoted in Stephen W. Sears, *George B. McClellan: The Young Napoleon* (New York: Ticknor and Fields, 1988), 6.

5. Ibid., 59.

6. Ibid., 26.

7. Ibid., 93.

8. McClellan, *Civil War Papers*, 70–71.

9. Ibid., 81.

10. Later in the war the Reserves received a second regimental number, which is why the 13th Pennsylvania Volunteers are also known as the 42nd Pennsylvania Volunteers.

11. A. F. Hill, *Our Boys: The Personal Experiences of a Soldier in the Army of the Potomac* (Philadelphia: John E. Potter, 1864), 139.

12. Steven M. Weld, *War Diary and Letters of Stephen Minot Weld, 1861–1865* (Cambridge, MA: Riverside Press, 1912), 230.

13. Edward J. Nichols, *Toward Gettysburg: A Biography of General John F. Reynolds* (University Park: Pennsylvania State University Press, 1958), 212.

14. Meade, *Life and Letters*, I: 218.

15. Ibid., I: 219.

16. Ibid., I: 225.
17. Sears, *George B. McClellan*, 122.
18. Ibid., 125.
19. Meade, *Life and Letters*, I: 229.
20. Ibid., I: 231.
21. Ibid., I: 234.
22. Ibid., I: 213.
23. Ibid., I: 247.
24. James M. McPherson, *Tried by War: Abraham Lincoln as Commander in Chief* (New York: Penguin Press, 2009), 63.
25. McClellan, *Civil War Papers*, 128.
26. Alexander S. Webb, *The Peninsula: McClellan's Campaign of 1862* (New York: C. Scribner's Sons, 1881; reprint, Edison, NJ: Castle Books, 2002), 29.
27. Sears, *George B. McClellan*, 171.
28. McClellan, *Civil War Papers*, 230.
29. David M. Jordan, *Winfield Scott Hancock: A Soldier's Life* (Bloomington: Indiana University Press, 1988), 444.
30. Ibid., 37.
31. Meade, *Life and Letters*, I: 266.
32. Ibid., I: 267.
33. Ibid., I: 269.
34. McClellan, *Civil War Papers*, 244.
35. Robert Underwood Johnson and Clarence Clough Buel, *Battles and Leaders of the Civil War: Being for the Most Part Contributions by Union and Confederate Officers* (New York: Century Company, 1887–1888; reprint, Secaucus, NJ: Castle Books, n.d.), II: 386.
36. Meade, *Life and Letters*, I: 274.
37. Ibid., I: 277.
38. Ibid., I: 278.
39. Johnson and Buel, *Battles and Leaders*, II: 352.
40. Quote is from the historical marker.
41. J. R. Sypher, *History of the Pennsylvania Reserve Corps* (Lancaster, PA: Elias Barr, 1865), 228.
42. Ibid., 231.
43. Johnson and Buel, *Battles and Leaders*, II: 337.
44. Hill, *Our Boys*, 299–300.
45. Ibid., 304–307.
46. Sypher, *Pennsylvania Reserve Corps*, 229.
47. Johnson and Buel, *Battles and Leaders*, II: 360.
48. McClellan, *Civil War Papers*, 322–323.
49. Sypher, *Pennsylvania Reserve Corps*, 248.
50. E. M. Woodward, *History of the Third Pennsylvania Reserve* (Trenton, NJ: MacCrellish and Quigley, 1883), 99.
51. R. Biddle Roberts to Col. George Meade, February 26, 1881, Meade Collection, reel 12, United States Army Heritage and Education Center (AHEC), Carlisle, PA.
52. Sypher, *Pennsylvania Reserve Corps*, 282.
53. Samuel P. Bates, *History of the Pennsylvania Volunteers, 1861–1865* (Harrisburg, PA: B. Singerly, 1869–1871), I: 638.
54. Pennypacker, *General Meade*, 47 and Meade, *Life and Letters*, I: 298.
55. Ibid., I: 299.
56. Ibid., I: 299–300.
57. William Swinton, *Campaigns of the Army of the Potomac* (New York: Charles B. Richardson, 1866; reprint, Secaucus, NJ: Blue and Gray Press, 1988), 163.
58. Johnson and Buel, *Battles and Leaders*, II: 394.
59. Stephen W. Sears, *To the Gates of Richmond: The Peninsula Campaign* (New York: Ticknor and Fields, 1992), 337.

60. United States War Department, *The War of the Rebellion: A Compilation of the Official Records of the Union and Confederate Armies* (Washington, DC: Government Printing Office, 1880–1901), Series I, Vol. XI, Pt. 2: 22 [hereafter *Official Records*].

61. Ibid., XI, II: 111.

62. Sypher, *Pennsylvania Reserve Corps*, 287.

63. Meade, *Life and Letters*, I: 297.

64. Johnson and Buel, *Battles and Leaders*, II: 405.

65. Meade, *Life and Letters*, I: 423.

66. Webb, *Peninsula*, 35.

Chapter 3: Civil War Redux

1. Paddy Griffith, *Battle Tactics of the Civil War* (New Haven, CT: Yale University Press, 2001), 85.

2. Ibid.

3. Johnson and Buel, *Battles and Leaders*, II: 511.

4. Quoted in Stephen Sears, *Landscape Turned Red: The Battle of Antietam* (New York: Mariner Books, 1993), 249.

5. Hill, *Our Boys*, 300–301.

6. Mark Adkin, *The Gettysburg Companion: The Complete Guide to America's Most Famous Battle* (Mechanicsburg, PA: Stackpole Books, 2008), 154.

7. Alexander K. McClure, *Abraham Lincoln and Men of War-Times: Some Personal Recollections of War and Politics during the Lincoln Administration* (Philadelphia: Times Publishing Co., 1892), 355–356.

Chapter 4: Back to Bull Run

1. John J. Hennessy, *Return to Bull Run: The Campaign and Battle of Second Manassas* (New York: Simon & Schuster, 1993), 182.

2. Johnson and Buel, *Battles and Leaders*, II: 493–494.

3. McClellan, *Civil War Papers*, 368.

4. Stephen W. Sears, *Controversies and Commanders: Dispatches from the Army of the Potomac* (New York: Houghton Mifflin, 1999), 54.

5. Herman Haupt, *Reminiscences of General Herman Haupt* (Milwaukee: Wright & Joys Co., 1901), 83.

6. Quoted in Stephen E. Ambrose, *Halleck: Lincoln's Chief of Staff* (Baton Rouge: Louisiana State University Press), 142.

7. Letter from George Gordon Meade to Margaret, August 20, 1862, Meade Collection, AHEC.

8. Meade, *Life and Letters*, I: 302.

9. McClellan, *Civil War Papers*, 344.

10. Letter from George Gordon Meade to Margaret, August 21, 1862, Meade Collection, AHEC.

11. This and preceding quote from Meade, *Life and Letters*, I: 303.

12. Meade, *Life and Letters*, I: 166.

13. Ibid., I: 305.

14. *Official Records*, I, XII, 2: 72.

15. Sears, *George B. McClellan*, 245.

16. Hennessy, *Return to Bull Run*, 242.

17. *Official Records*, I, XII, 2: 392.

18. Sypher, *Pennsylvania Reserve Corps*, 178–179.

19. Hill, *Our Boys*, 368.

20. Ibid., 370.

21. Ibid., 371.

22. Ibid., 373.

23. Meade, *Life and Letters*, I: 259.

24. James I. Robertson, *Stonewall Jackson: The Man, the Soldier, the Legend* (New York: MacMillan, 1997), 264.

25. Quote from a historical marker on the site.
26. Hennessy, *Return to Bull Run*, 360.
27. Hill, *Our Boys*, 384.
28. E. M. Woodward, *Our Campaigns; or, The Marches, Bivouacs, Battles, Incidents of Camp Life, and History of Our Regiment during Its Three Years Term of Service* (Philadelphia: John E. Potter, 1865), 186–187.
29. Hill, *Our Boys*, 385.
30. *Official Records*, I, XII, 2: 343.
31. Meade, *Life and Letters*, I: 306.
32. Ibid., I: 308.

Chapter 5: The Maryland Campaign

1. Johnson and Buel, *Battles and Leaders*, II: 550.
2. George W. Smalley, *Anglo-American Memories* (New York: G. P. Putnam's Sons, 1911), 143.
3. Seymour Hall, as recounted in Military Order of the Loyal Legion of the United States (MOLLUS), Kansas Commandery, *War Talks in Kansas* (Kansas City, MO: Franklin Hudson Publishing Co., 1906), 195 [hereafter MOLLUS, *War Talks in Kansas*].
4. Meade, *Life and Letters*, I: 304.
5. Morris Schaff, *The Battle of the Wilderness* (Boston: Houghton Mifflin Co., 1910), 226.
6. Hill, *Our Boys*, 391–392.
7. Meade, *Life and Letters*, I: 310.
8. Portions edited out of Meade's published letters. Letter from George Gordon Meade to Margaret, September 12, 1862, Meade Collection, AHEC.
9. John Gibbon, *Personal Recollections of the Civil War* (New York: G. P. Putnam's Sons, 1928), 73.
10. Henry Kyd Douglas, *I Rode with Stonewall* (Chapel Hill: University of North Carolina Press, 1940), 152.
11. Francis Adams Donaldson, *Inside the Army of the Potomac: The Civil War Experience of Captain Francis Adams Donaldson*, ed. J. Gregory Acken (Mechanicsburg, PA: Stackpole Books, 1998), 120.
12. Johnson and Buel, *Battles and Leaders*, II: 550.
13. Ibid., II: 564.
14. Joseph Gibbs, *Three Years in the Bloody Eleventh* (University Park: Pennsylvania State University Press, 2002), 174.
15. Henry Steele Commager, ed., *The Blue and the Gray* (Indianapolis: Bobbs-Merrill, 1950; reprint, New York: Fairfax Press, 1984), 205.
16. Bates, *Pennsylvania Volunteers*, 850.
17. Hill, *Our Boys*, 395–396.
18. Both quotes in this paragraph from Sypher, *Pennsylvania Reserve Corps*, 369.
19. Meade's report is in *Official Records*, XIX, 1: 266–268.
20. From Hooker's report in *Official Records*, XIX, 1: 213–216.
21. Johnson and Buel, *Battles and Leaders*, II: 631.
22. Osmund Rhodes Thomson and William H. Rauch, *History of the "Bucktails," Kane Rifle Regiment of the Pennsylvania Reserve Corps* (Philadelphia: Electric Printing Co., 1906), 210.
23. *Official Records*, I, XIX, 1: 218.
24. Ibid.
25. Sypher, *Pennsylvania Reserve Corps*, 382.
26. Hill, *Our Boys*, 403.
27. Ibid.
28. Holsinger's account is in MOLLUS, *War Talks in Kansas*, 290–304.
29. Johnson and Buel, *Battles and Leaders*, II: 668.
30. Meade, *Life and Letters*, I: 313.
31. Swinton, *Campaigns*, 89.
32. Johnson and Buel, *Battles and Leaders*, II: 643.
33. Sypher, *Pennsylvania Reserve Corps*, 385–386.

34. George F. Noyes, *The Bivouac and the Battlefield; or, Campaign Sketches in Virginia and Maryland* (New York: Harper & Brothers, 1863), 205.

35. Johnson and Buel, *Battles and Leaders*, II: 633.

36. Ibid., II: 650.

37. Thompson's account is from ibid., II: 662.

38. Donaldson, *Inside the Army of the Potomac*, 123.

39. Noyes, *Bivouac and Battlefield*, 196.

40. Commager, *The Blue and the Gray*, 209. Sears says this was at Porter's headquarters; see *George B. McClellan*, 307.

41. McClellan, *Civil War Papers*, 469.

42. Meade, *Life and Letters*, I: 310.

Chapter 6: Fredericksburg

1. Meade, *Life and Letters*, I: 315.

2. Ibid., I: 319.

3. Ibid., I: 317.

4. Wainwright, *Diary of Battle*, 116.

5. Ibid., 305–306.

6. McClellan, *Civil War Papers*, 516.

7. Ibid., 354.

8. Meade, *Life and Letters*, I: 325.

9. Donaldson, *Inside the Army of the Potomac*, 162.

10. Woodward, *Third Pennsylvania Reserve*, 225.

11. Meade, *Life and Letters*, I: 330. Meade wrote this on November 22, 1862.

12. Noah Brooks, *Washington in Lincoln's Time* (New York: Century Co., 1895), 46–47.

13. Meade, *Life and Letters*, I: 332.

14. Ibid., I: 325.

15. Ibid., I: 334.

16. Ibid.

17. A good description of Mansfield appears in Wainwright, *Diary of Battle*, 138–139.

18. Johnson and Buel, *Battles and Leaders*, III: 134.

19. See Wainwright, *Diary of Battle*, 143. This was Wainwright's account.

20. Simpson's report in *Official Records*, XXI: 513–515.

21. Woodward, *Third Pennsylvania Reserve*, 235; Bates, *Pennsylvania Volunteers*, II: 586.

22. William B. Strong, *History of the 121st Regiment Pennsylvania Volunteers* (Philadelphia: Catholic Standard and Times, 1906), 31.

23. Pennypacker, *General Meade*, 100.

24. Francis Augustín O'Reilly, *The Fredericksburg Campaign: Winter War on the Rappahannock* (Baton Rouge: Louisiana State University Press, 2003), 179.

25. Meade's report in *Official Records*, I, XXI: 509–513.

26. O'Reilly, *Fredericksburg Campaign*, 227.

27. Bates, *Pennsylvania Volunteers*, I: 851–852.

28. Theodore Lyman, *Meade's Headquarters, 1863–1865: Letters of Colonel Theodore Lyman from the Wilderness to Appomattox*, ed. George R. Agassiz (Boston: Massachusetts Historical Society, 1922), 266.

29. Sypher, *Pennsylvania Reserve Corps*, 415.

30. Frederick Lyman Hitchcock, *War from the Inside: The Story of the 132nd Regiment Pennsylvania Volunteer Infantry in the War for the Suppression of the Rebellion, 1862–1863* (Philadelphia: J. B. Lippincott Co, 1904), 134.

31. David Bell Birney Papers, United States Army Heritage and Education Center (AHEC), Carlisle, PA.

32. Francis Winthrop Palfrey, *The Antietam and Fredericksburg*, Vol. 5 of *Campaigns of the Civil War* (New York: Charles Scribner's Sons, 1912), 158.

33. See Pennypacker, *General Meade*, 106.

34. *Official Records*, I, XXI: 522.
35. Thomson and Rauch, *History of the "Bucktails"*, 236.
36. Quoted in Mark A. Snell, *From First to Last: The Life of Major General William B. Franklin* (New York: Fordham University Press, 2002), 222. Strangely, it was omitted from Meade, *Life and Letters*. I saw the actual letter on microfilm, which says that he and Reynolds had "a few little rubs during the latter part of our association," and that Reynolds seemed a little nettled by Meade's recent promotion, although that might have been Meade's imagination.
37. Meade, *Life and Letters*, I: 343.
38. Johnson and Buel, *Battles and Leaders*, III: 79.
39. Both soldiers quoted in O'Reilly, *Fredericksburg Campaign*, 269.
40. Johnson and Buel, *Battles and Leaders*, III: 113.
41. William McCarter, *My Life in the Irish Brigade: The Civil War Memoirs of Private William Mc-Carter, 116th Pennsylvania Infantry*, ed. Kevin O'Brien (Campbell, CA: Savas Publishing Co., 1996), vi.
42. O'Reilly, *Fredericksburg Campaign*, 313.
43. Ibid., 315.
44. McCarter, *My Life*, viii.
45. From Hooker's official report, quoted in Edward J. Stackpole, *The Fredericksburg Campaign*, 2nd ed. (Mechanicsburg, PA: Stackpole Books, 1991), 218.
46. Meade, *Life and Letters*, I: 337.
47. Ibid., I: 365.
48. Ibid., I: 339.
49. Ibid., I: 341.
50. Ibid., I: 341–342.
51. Ibid., I: 342.
52. Ibid., I: 345.
53. From John Davis Billings, *Hardtack and Coffee; or, The Unwritten Story of Army Life* (Boston: George M. Smith & Co., 1888), 72.
54. Meade, *Life and Letters*, I: 351.

Chapter 7: Chancellorsville

1. Jenn Rowell, "'Witness Tree' Falls at Ellwood: Civil War Tree at Ellwood Falls," *Freelance-Star*, September 18, 2006. http://fredericksburg.com/News/FLS/2006/092006/09182006/222337 (accessed June 19, 2012).
2. From information on display at Ellwood.
3. Meade, *Life and Letters*, I: 354.
4. Ibid., 352.
5. Smalley, *Anglo-American Memories*, 149.
6. Meade, *Life and Letters*, I: 354.
7. Ibid., I: 360.
8. Ibid., I: 364.
9. Ibid., I: 368.
10. Quoted by Seymour Hall in MOLLUS, *War Talks in Kansas*, 194.
11. Quoted in John Bigelow Jr., *Chancellorsville* (New York: Konecky & Konecky, 1995), 164. (Originally published as *The Campaign of Chancellorsville: A Strategic and Tactical Study*, New Haven, CT: Yale University Press, 1910.)
12. Survivors' Association, 118th (Corn Exchange) Regt. P.V., *History of the 118th Pennsylvania Volunteers, Corn Exchange Regiment* (Philadelphia: J. L. Smith, 1905), 166.
13. Bigelow, *Chancellorsville*, 199–200.
14. Survivors' Association, *118th Pennsylvania Volunteers*, 171.
15. Meade-Slocum exchange is from Bigelow, *Chancellorsville*, 221.
16. Ibid., 223.
17. Johnson and Buel, *Battles and Leaders*, III: 157.
18. Donaldson, *Inside the Army of the Potomac*, 233.

19. Alexander S. Webb, "Meade at Chancellorsville," in Military Historical Society of Massachusetts, *Campaigns in Virginia, Maryland and Pennsylvania, 1862-1863* (Boston: Griffith-Stillings Press, 1903), 229.

20. Survivors' Association, *118th Pennsylvania Volunteers*, 173–174.

21. Sykes's report in *Official Records*, I, XXV, 1: 525.

22. Francis A. Walker, *History of the Second Army Corps in the Army of the Potomac* (New York: Charles Scribner's Sons, 1886), 224.

23. Johnson and Buel, *Battles and Leaders*, III: 161.

24. Alpheus S. Williams, *From the Cannon's Mouth: The Civil War Letters of General Alpheus S. Williams*, ed. Milo M. Quaife (Detroit: Wayne State University Press, 1959), 180.

25. Johnson and Buel, *Battles and Leaders*, III: 219.

26. William Henry Powell, *The Fifth Army Corps (Army of the Potomac): A Record of Operations during the Civil War in the United States of America, 1861–1865* (New York: G. P. Putnam's Sons, 1896), 450.

27. Account of Jackson's wounding in Robertson, *Stonewall Jackson*, 726–729.

28. Lyman, *Meade's Headquarters*, 281.

29. Webb, "Meade at Chancellorsville," 229.

30. Bigelow, *Chancellorsville*, 326.

31. Quote from a marker at the Chancellorsville battlefield.

32. Webb, "Meade at Chancellorsville," 231.

33. National Park Service, Civil War Series: The Battle of Chancellorsville, www.nps.gov/history/history/online_books/civil_war_series/8/sec2.htm (accessed June 19, 2012).

34. Survivors' Association, *118th Pennsylvania Volunteers*, 189. See also Donaldson, *Inside the Army of the Potomac*, 246.

35. Bigelow, *Chancellorsville*, 371.

36. Johnson and Buel, *Battles and Leaders*, III: 169.

37. Elizabeth Meade Ingraham, *Leaves: The Diary of Elizabeth Meade Ingraham, the Rebel Sister of General George Meade*, eds. Sue Burns Moore and Rebecca Blackwell Drake (Raymond, MS: Champion Heritage Foundation, 2010), 55.

38. Abner Doubleday, *Chancellorsville and Gettysburg* (New York: Charles Scribner's Sons, 1882), 53.

39. These accounts are from Powell, *Fifth Army Corps*, 474–475; Johnson and Buel, *Battles and Leaders*, III: 171; and Bigelow, *Chancellorsville*, 420.

40. Powell, *Fifth Army Corps*, 472.

41. Wainwright, *Diary of Battle*, 200.

42. Webb, "Meade at Chancellorsville," 236.

43. Powell, *Fifth Army Corps*, 472.

44. Meade, *Life and Letters*, I: 370.

45. Wainwright, *Diary of Battle*, 202.

46. Powell, *Fifth Army Corps*, 479.

Chapter 8: Gettysburg

1. Meade, *Life and Letters*, I: 377.

2. Wainwright, *Diary of Battle*, 219.

3. Meade, *Life and Letters*, I: 381.

4. See J. Cutler Andrews, *The North Reports the Civil War* (Pittsburgh: University of Pittsburgh Press, 1955; reprint, 1985), 372–373; and Smalley, *Anglo-American Memories*, 159–160.

5. John Brown Gordon, *Reminiscences of the Civil War* (New York: Charles Scribner's Sons, 1904), 38.

6. Meade, *Life and Letters*, I: 388–389.

7. Johnson and Buel, *Battles and Leaders*, III: 243.

8. Bigelow, *Chancellorsville*, 31.

9. Halleck's orders quoted in Meade, *Life and Letters*, II: 3–4.

10. Meade, *Life and Letters*, I: 389.
11. Julia Lorrilard Butterfield. *A Biographical Memorial of General Daniel Butterfield, Including Many Addresses and Military Writings* (New York: The Grafton Press, 1904), 161.
12. Johnson and Buel, *Battles and Leaders*, III: 243.
13. Meade, *Life and Letters*, II: 2.
14. Johnson and Buel, *Battles and Leaders*, III: 243.
15. Charles Carleton Coffin, *Marching to Victory: The Second Period of the War of the Rebellion, Including the Year 1863* (New York: Harper & Brothers, 1888), 189.
16. Edwin B. Coddington, "The Strange Reputation of General Meade: A Lesson in Historiography," *The Historian* 23, no. 2 (1961): 153.
17. Quoted in Meade, *Life and Letters*, II: 5.
18. Gibbon, *Personal Recollections*, 128.
19. Wainwright, *Diary of Battle*, 229.
20. Frank A. Haskell, *The Battle of Gettysburg* (Madison: Wisconsin History Commission, 1908), 6.
21. Gibbs, *Three Years in the Bloody Eleventh*, 216.
22. John P. Nicholson, ed., *Pennsylvania at Gettysburg: Ceremonies at the Dedication of the Monuments Erected by the Commonwealth of Pennsylvania* (Harrisburg, PA: Wm. Stanley Ray, State Printer, 1904), I: 259.
23. Meade, *Life and Letters*, II: 14.
24. Nicholson, *Pennsylvania at Gettysburg*, I: 278.
25. Gary W. Gallagher, ed. *Two Witnesses at Gettysburg: The Personal Accounts of Whitelaw Reid and A. J. Fremantle*, 2nd ed. (Chichester, UK: Wiley-Blackwell, 2009), 16–17.
26. Edward Coddington, *The Gettysburg Campaign: A Study in Command* (New York: Charles Scribner's Sons, 1968), 225.
27. Meade, *Life and Letters*, II: 15–16.
28. Johnson and Buel, *Battles and Leaders*, III: 274.
29. Weld, *War Diary and Letters*, 232.
30. *Official Records*, I, XXVII, 1: 924.
31. Pennypacker, *General Meade*, 149.
32. Meade, *Life and Letters*, II: 315.
33. Meade, *Life and Letters*, II: 37.
34. MOLLUS, *War Talks in Kansas*, 284.
35. See Johnson and Buel, *Battles and Leaders*, III: 285; Oliver Otis Howard, *Autobiography of Oliver Otis Howard, Major General, United States Army* (New York: The Baker & Taylor Company, 1907), I: 418.
36. *Official Records*, I, XXVII: 1, 366.
37. Meade, *Life and Letters*, I: 349.
38. Wainwright, *Diary of Battle*, 233.
39. Howard, *Autobiography*, I: 423.
40. Carl Schurz, *The Reminiscences of Carl Schurz* (London: John Murray, 1909), III: 21.
41. MOLLUS, *War Talks in Kansas*, 253.
42. Pennypacker, *General Meade*, 151.
43. Powell, *Fifth Army Corps*, 513.
44. Meade, *Life and Letters*, II: 65–66.
45. Hunt's account is in Johnson and Buel, *Battles and Leaders*, III: 302.
46. Gibbon, *Personal Recollections*, 136.
47. Adkin, *Gettysburg Companion*, 402.
48. Stephen W. Sears, *Gettysburg* (New York: Houghton Mifflin, 2003), 305.
49. Adkin, *Gettysburg Companion*, 413.
50. Wainwright, *Diary of Battle*, 338.
51. Schaff, *Battle of the Wilderness*, 30.
52. New York State Military Museum and Veterans Research Center, Unit History Project: 140th Infantry Regiment, Civil War, http://dmna.state.ny.us/historic/reghist/civil/infantry/140thInf/140thInfMain.htm (accessed June 19, 2012).

53. Account from David L. Ladd and Audrey J. Ladd, eds., *The Bachelder Papers: Gettysburg in Their Own Words* (Dayton: Morningside Press, 1994–1995), II: 896.
54. Ibid., II: 920.
55. Coddington, *Gettysburg Campaign*, 423.
56. Meade, *Life and Letters*, II: 125.
57. Ibid., II: 89.
58. Meade Collection, AHEC, reel 12, 0760. Misspellings are from the original.
59. Sears, *Gettysburg*, 350.
60. Haskell, *Battle of Gettysburg*, 15.
61. Ibid., 34–36.
62. Gibbon's account in Johnson and Buel, *Battles and Leaders*, III: 313–314.
63. Doubleday, *Chancellorsville and Gettysburg*, 184.
64. Meade, *Life and Letters*, II: 97.
65. Gibbon, *Personal Recollections*, 145.
66. Haskell, *Battle of Gettysburg*, 43.
67. William Wheeler, *In Memoriam: Letters of William Wheeler of the Class of 1855, Y.C.* (Cambridge, MA: Privately printed by H.O. Houghton and Co., 1875), 14–15.
68. Gallagher, *Two Witnesses at Gettysburg*, 58.
69. Schurz, *Reminiscences*, III: 27.
70. Wainwright, *Diary of Battle*, 248.
71. Charles Carleton Coffin, *Four Years of Fighting: A Volume of Personal Observation with the Army and Navy, from the First Battle of Bull Run to the Fall of Richmond* (Boston: Ticknor and Fields, 1866), 293–294.
72. Ibid., 294.
73. Howard, *Autobiography*, 436–437.
74. Meade, *Life and Letters*, II: 107.
75. Ibid., II: 108, 125.
76. Johnson and Buel, *Battles and Leaders*, III: 343.
77. Ladd and Ladd, *Bachelder Papers*, II: 920–921.
78. This and the quote in the preceding paragraph are from ibid., I: 19.
79. Haskell, *Battle of Gettysburg*, 66.
80. Ladd and Ladd, *Bachelder Papers*, II: 854.
81. Ibid., I: 378–380, II: 852–858.
82. Ibid., I: 321, 389.
83. Haskell, *Battle of Gettysburg*, 69–70.
84. Charles Leonard Moore, "The Hero of Gettysburg." *The Dial* 55, no 13 (July 13, 1913): 13.

Chapter 9: The Old Brute

1. Meade, *Life and Letters*, I: 227.
2. Ibid., II: 132-3.
3. Ibid., II: 191 and 210.
4. Survivors' Association, *118th Pennsylvania Volunteers*, 209.
5. Lyman, *Meade's Headquarters*, 5–6.
6. Johnson and Buel, *Battles and Leaders*, III: 407.

Chapter 10: The Pursuit

1. Wittenberg also has a blog called "Rantings of a Civil War Historian," at http://civilwar cavalry.com.
2. McPherson, *Tried by War*, 185.
3. Kent Masterson Brown, *Retreat from Gettysburg: Lee, Logistics and the Pennsylvania Campaign* (Chapel Hill: University of North Carolina Press, 2005), 326.
4. Johnson and Buel, *Battles and Leaders*, III: 367.
5. Bill Hyde, ed., *The Union Generals Speak: The Meade Hearings on the Battle of Gettysburg* (Baton Rouge: Louisiana State University Press, 2003), 111.

6. Johnson and Buel, *Battles and Leaders*, III: 376.

7. Wainwright, *Diary of Battle*, 253.

8. Eric J. Wittenberg, David Petruzzi, and Michael F. Nugent, *One Continuous Fight: The Retreat from Gettysburg and the Pursuit of Lee's Army of Northern Virginia, July 4–14, 1863* (New York: Savas Beatie, 2008; reprint, Philadelphia: Casemate Publishers, 2011), 27.

9. Swinton, *Campaigns of the Army of the Potomac*, 364.

10. Donaldson, *Inside the Army of the Potomac*, 312.

11. Schurz, *Reminiscences*, III: 35.

12. *Official Records*, I, XXVII, 1: 78.

13. Coddington, *Gettysburg Campaign*, 536.

14. McPherson, *Tried by War*, 182.

15. Hyde, *Union Generals Speak*, 260–261.

16. George T. Stevens, *Three Years in the Sixth Corps* (Albany, NY: S. R. Gray, 1866; reprint, Bedford, MA: Applewood Books, 2008), 253.

17. Meade, *Life and Letters*, II: 125.

18. Schaff, *Battle of the Wilderness*, 43–44.

19. Charles A. Dana, *Recollections of the Civil War with the Leaders at Washington and in the Field in the Sixties* (New York: D. Appleton and Co., 1913), 192.

20. Haupt, *Reminiscences*, 221.

21. Ibid, 224.

22. For these cavalry movements, see Brown, *Retreat from Gettysburg*, 125–126.

23. Samuel J. Martin, *Kill-Cavalry: The Life of Union General Hugh Judson Kilpatrick* (Mechanicsburg, PA: Stackpole Books, 2000), 12.

24. *New York Times*, March 15, 1896.

25. Eric J. Wittenberg, "Ulric Dahlgren in the Gettysburg Campaign," *Gettysburg Magazine* 22 (January 2000): 96–111; online at www.gdg.org/GettysburgMagazine/dahlgren.html (accessed June 19, 2012).

26. Craig Swaim, "The Leg of Colonel Ulric Dahlgren," Historical Marker Database, July 2010, www.hmdb.org/marker.asp?marker=32629 (accessed June 24, 2012).

27. Meade, *Life and Letters*, II: 132.

28. Ibid.

29. The communications between Halleck and Meade are from a website where they are all compiled, www.civilwarhome.com/aftergettysburgor.htm.

30. Meade, *Life and Letters*, II: 132.

31. Wittenberg et al., *One Continuous Fight*, 148.

32. Donaldson, *Inside the Army of the Potomac*, 313.

33. The communications between Halleck and Meade in this and the preceding paragraphs are all taken from www.civilwarhome.com/aftergettysburgor.htm.

34. Donaldson, *Inside the Army of the Potomac*, 314.

35. Meade's wire and Halleck's response are from www.civilwarhome.com/aftergettysburgor.htm.

36. Coffin, *Four Years of Fighting*, 302–305.

37. Wittenberg et al., *One Continuous Fight*, 161. Brown, *Retreat from Gettysburg*, 90–92, describes the destruction of the bridge.

38. Wittenberg et al., *One Continuous Fight*, 242. However, Brown, *Retreat from Gettysburg*, 321, attributes it to a Private Casler of the 33rd Virginia.

39. Wittenberg et al., *One Continuous Fight*, 161, 284.

40. Account from Evelyn Page, "After Gettysburg: Frederick Law Olmsted on the Escape of Lee," *Pennsylvania Magazine of History and Biography* 75, no. 4 (October 1951): 436–446.

41. Meade and Halleck correspondence quoted in Meade, *Life and Letters*, II: 311–312. Meade letter to Margaret, ibid., 135.

42. Ibid., II: 312.

43. Sears, *Gettysburg*, 494.

44. Stevens, *Three Years in the Sixth Corps*, 265.

45. Wainwright, *Diary of Battle*, 261.

46. See Hyde, *Union Generals Speak*, 200–201.
47. Johnson and Buel, *Battles and Leaders*, III: 383.
48. Rufus Dawes, *Service with the Sixth Wisconsin Volunteers* (Marietta, OH: K. R. Aldeman & Sons, 1890), 192.
49. Meade, *Life and Letters*, II: 134.
50. Donaldson, *Inside the Army of the Potomac*, 318.

Chapter 11: Back to Virginia

1. Alexander Morrison Stewart, *Camp, March and Battle-field; or, Three Years and a Half with the Army of the Potomac* (Philadelphia: Jas. B. Rodgers, Printer, 1865), 353.
2. *Official Records*, I, XXVII, 1: 99.
3. Ibid., 108.
4. Jeffrey D. Wert, *The Sword of Lincoln: The Army of the Potomac* (New York: Simon & Schuster, 2005), 311
5. Meade, *Life and Letters*, II: 138.
6. *Official Records*, I, XXVII, 1: 104–105.
7. Ibid., 109.
8. Meade, *Life and Letters*, I: 366.
9. Ibid., II: 145
10. Wainwright, *Diary of Battle*, 277.
11. Pennypacker, *General Meade*, 257.
12. Meade, *Life and Letters*, II: 146.
13. Donaldson, *Inside the Army of the Potomac*, 333–336, note on 473.
14. Meade, *Life and Letters*, II: 146.
15. For his Washington experiences, see Meade, *Life and Letters*, II: 150–151; figure is from Donaldson, *Inside the Army of the Potomac*, 357.
16. Lyman, *Meade's Headquarters*, xviii.
17. Lyman, *Meade's Army*, 11.
18. Ibid., 103.
19. Lyman, *Meade's Headquarters*, 17.
20. Ibid., 21.
21. Ibid., 10.
22. Wert, *Sword of Lincoln*, 320.
23. Lyman, *Meade's Headquarters*, 26.
24. Lyman, *Meade's Army*, 176, 123.
25. Stewart, *Camp, March, and Battle-field*, 349.
26. Ibid., 351.
27. Lyman, *Meade's Headquarters*, 29–30.
28. Ibid., 31.
29. Stewart, *Camp, March, and Battle-field*, 350.
30. Ibid., 351.
31. Donaldson, *Inside the Army of the Potomac*, 368.
32. Correspondence between Meade and Halleck from *Official Records*, XXIX, 2: 346.
33. Lyman, *Meade's Headquarters*, 36.
34. Walker, *History of the Second Army Corps*, 344.
35. Ibid., 349.
36. Ibid.
37. Figures from Civil War Trust, "Bristoe Station," 2011, www.civilwar.org/battlefields/bristoe-station.html (accessed June 25, 2012).
38. Gordon C. Rhea, *To the North Anna River: Grant and Lee, May 13–25, 1864* (Baton Rouge: Louisiana State University Press, 2000), 317.
39. Walker, *History of the Second Army Corps*, 363.
40. Stewart, *Camp, March, and Battle-field*, 352.
41. Meade, *Life and Letters*, II: 154–155.

42. Donaldson, *Inside the Army of the Potomac*, 371.
43. Department of the Army, *The Medal of Honor of the United States Army*, http://www.army .mil/medalofhonor/.
44. Stewart, *Camp, March, and Battle-field*, 356.
45. Meade, *Life and Letters*, II: 156.
46. This exchange is from Johnson and Buel, *Battles and Leaders*, IV: 186; Russell's class rank is from Larry Tagg, *The Generals of Gettysburg* (El Dorado Hills, CA: Savas Beatie, 1998; reprint, Cambridge, MA: Da Capo Press, 2003), 110.
47. Donaldson, *Inside the Army of the Potomac*, 385.
48. Johnson and Buel, *Battles and Leaders*, IV: 87.
49. Stewart, *Camp, March, and Battle-field*, 357.
50. Ibid., 358.
51. Meade, *Life and Letters*, II: 156.
52. Survivors' Association, *118th Pennsylvania Volunteers*, 347.
53. James F. Rusling, *Men and Things I Saw in Civil War Days* (New York: Eaton & Mains, 1899), 73.
54. Andrew A. Humphreys, *From Gettysburg to the Rapidan: The Army of the Potomac July 1863 to April 1864* (New York: Charles Scribner's Sons, 1883), 50.
55. Warren's report in *Official Records*, I, XXIX, 1: 695.
56. Humphreys, *From Gettysburg to the Rapidan*, 63.
57. Lyman, *Meade's Headquarters*, 56.
58. Ibid., 57.
59. Stewart, *Camp, March, and Battle-field*, 364–365.
60. Walker, *History of the Second Army Corps*, 383.
61. Wilbur Fisk, *Hard Marching Every Day: The Civil War Letters of Private Wilbur Fisk, 1861–1865*, eds. Emil Rosenblatt and Ruth Rosenblatt (Lawrence: University Press of Kansas, 1983), 171.
62. Meade, *Life and Letters*, II: 156–157.
63. Lyman, *Meade's Headquarters*, 57–58.
64. Humpreys, *From Gettysburg to the Rapidan*, 68.

Chapter 12: Troubles in Washington

1. James A. Hessler, *Sickles at Gettysburg: The Controversial Civil War General Who Committed Murder, Abandoned Little Round Top, and Declared Himself the Hero of Gettysburg* (New York: Savas Beatie, 2009), 382, 393.
2. Coddington, *Gettysburg Campaign*, 347.
3. Webb, *Peninsula*, 16–17.
4. Meade, *Life and Letters*, I: 340.
5. Hyde, *Union Generals Speak*, 4; Bruce Tap, *Over Lincoln's Shoulder: The Committee on the Conduct of the War* (Lawrence: University Press of Kansas, 1998), 124, 154.
6. Sears, "The Ordeal of General Stone," *Controversies and Commanders*, 27–50.
7. Meade, *Life and Letters*, I: 245.
8. Hyde, *Union Generals Speak*, 74.
9. Coddington, "Strange Reputation of General Meade," 159.
10. Hyde, *Union Generals Speak*, 95.
11. Freeman Cleaves, *Meade of Gettysburg* (Norman: University of Oklahoma Press, 1960), 216–217.
12. Hyde, *Union Generals Speak*, 106.
13. Ibid., 109.
14. Meade, *Life and Letters*, II: 169–170.
15. Wainwright, *Diary of Battle*, 325.
16. Hyde, *Union Generals Speak*, 134–135.
17. See also Alfred Pleasonton, "The Campaign of Gettysburg," in *The Annals of the War: Written by Leading Participants, North and South*, edited by Alexander Kelly McClure (Philadelphia: Times Publishing Company, 1879), 455.

18. Richard A. Sauers, *A Caspian Sea of Ink: The Meade-Sickles Controversy* (Baltimore: Butternut and Blue, 1989), 135.
19. Birney Letters, AHEC. For Birney's statements, see Hyde, *Union Generals Speak*, 400.
20. Hyde, *Union Generals Speak*, 201.
21. Ibid., 225.
22. Coddington, *Gettysburg Campaign*, 219.
23. Hyde, *Union Generals Speak*, 256.
24. Letter to the Editor from "Historicus," *New York Herald*, March 12, 1864.
25. Meade, *Life and Letters*, II: 335–336.
26. Letter to the Editor from "Historicus," *New York Herald*, April 4, 1864.
27. Hyde, *Union Generals Speak*, 294.
28. Ibid., 408.
29. Coddington, "Strange Reputation of General Meade," 147.
30. Kathryn Allamong Jacob, *Testament to Union: Civil War Monuments in Washington, D.C.* (Baltimore: Johns Hopkins University Press, 1998), 56–57.

Chapter 14: The New Boss

1. Ladd and Ladd, *Bachelder Papers*, III: 1906.
2. Lyman, *Meade's Headquarters*, 89.
3. Roy Morris Jr., *Sheridan: The Life & Wars of General Phil Sheridan* (New York: Vintage, 1993), 3.
4. Meade, *Life and Letters*, II: 167–168.
5. Ibid., II: 190–191.
6. Schaff, *Battle of the Wilderness*, 42.
7. Lyman, *Meade's Headquarters*, 82.
8. Letter from Birney to George I. Gott, April 5, 1864, Birney Letters, AHEC.
9. Meade, *Life and Letters*, II: 190.
10. Letter from Birney to George I. Gott, April 18, 1864, Birney Letters, AHEC.
11. Lyman, *Meade's Headquarters*, 102.
12. Porter, *Campaigning with Grant*, 14.
13. Meade, *Life and Letters*, II: 162.
14. Grant, *Memoirs*, 359.
15. Meade, *Life and Letters*, II: 178, 181, 191.
16. Ibid., II: 189.
17. Johnson and Buel, *Battles and Leaders*, IV: 98.
18. Schaff, *Battle of the Wilderness*, 47.
19. Lyman, *Meade's Headquarters*, 81.
20. Pennypacker, *General Meade*, 263.
21. Walker, *History of the Second Army Corps*, 417.
22. Meade, *Life and Letters*, II: 192–193.
23. Wainwright, *Diary of Battle*, 348.
24. Porter, *Campaigning with Grant*, 42.
25. Schaff, *Battle of the Wilderness*, 84.
26. Lyman, *Meade's Army*, 132.
27. Johnson and Buel, *Battles and Leaders*, IV: 145.
28. Exchange from Schaff, *Battle of the Wilderness*, 128.
29. Swinton, *Campaigns*, 421.
30. Johnson and Buel, *Battles and Leaders*, IV: 97.
31. Schaff, *Battle of the Wilderness*, 129.
32. Thomas W. Hyde, *Following the Greek Cross; or, Memories of the Sixth Army Corps* (Boston: Houghton, Mifflin and Company, 1894), 182–184.
33. Ibid.
34. Ibid., 185.
35. Theodore Gerrish, *Army Life: A Private's Reminiscences of the Civil War* (Portland, ME: Hoyt, Fogg & Donham, 1882), 161–162.

36. Gouverneur K. Warren, *Journal, May 4–June 12, 1864: Campaign from the Rapidan to the James River, Va.* Available at www.civilwarhome.com/warrenwilderness.htm (accessed July 5, 2012).
37. Schaff, *Battle of the Wilderness*, 165–166.
38. Ibid., 80.
39. Lyman, *Meade's Headquarters*, 90–91.
40. Schaff, *Battle of the Wilderness*, 245.
41. Lyman, *Meade's Headquarters*, 92–93.
42. Gordon C. Rhea, *The Battle of the Wilderness, May 5–6, 1864* (Baton Rouge: Louisiana State University Press, 1994), 184.
43. Gary W. Gallagher, ed., *The Wilderness Campaign* (Chapel Hill: University of North Carolina Press, 1997), 94.
44. Lyman, *Meade's Army*, 136.
45. *Official Records*, I, XLVII, 1: 325.
46. Schaff, *Battle of the Wilderness*, 272.
47. Lyman, *Meade's Headquarters*, 95–96.
48. Dawes, *Service with the Sixth Wisconsin Volunteers*, 262.
49. Deborah Fitts, "Vermont Brigade Monument Is Readied for the Wilderness," *Civil War News*, December 2005, www.civilwarnews.com/archive/articles/vtmonument.htm (accessed June 19, 2012).
50. Josiah Marshall Favill, *The Diary of a Young Officer Serving with the Armies of the United Sates during the War of the Rebellion* (Chicago: R. R. Donnelley & Sons Co., 1909), 290.
51. Ibid., 291.
52. Gerrish, *Army Life*, 165.
53. Schaff, *Battle of the Wilderness*, 318–319.
54. Porter, *Campaigning with Grant*, 70.
55. Ibid., 73.
56. Lyman, *Meade's Army*, 141.
57. Rhea, *Battle of the Wilderness*, 26; Porter, *Campaigning with Grant*, 71.

Chapter 15: On to Richmond

1. Porter, *Campaigning with Grant*, 79.
2. Robert S. Robertson, "The Escape of Grant and Meade," *Magazine of American History* 19 (1888), 248–251.
3. Porter, *Campaigning with Grant*, 81.
4. Account in ibid., 83–84; Johnson and Buel, *Battles and Leaders*, IV: 189.
5. See Lyman, *Meade's Army*, 147; Johnson and Buel, *Battles and Leaders*, IV: 175.
6. Hyde, *Following the Greek Cross*, 193.
7. Lyman, *Meade's Army*, 148.
8. Samuel Wheelock Fiske, *Mr. Dunn Browne's Experiences in the Army* (Boston: Nichols and Noyes, 1866), 327.
9. Isaac Oliver Best, *History of the 121st New York State Infantry* (Chicago: Lieut. Jas. H. Smith, 1921), 129.
10. *Official Records*, I, XXXVI, 1: 668.
11. Lyman, *Meade's Headquarters*, 110–111; Porter, *Campaigning with Grant*, 103–104.
12. Favill, *Diary of a Young Officer*, 298.
13. Walker, *History of the Second Army Corps*, 470, 473.
14. Lyman, *Meade's Headquarters*, 111; Lyman, *Meade's Army*, 154.
15. Dawes, *Service with the Sixth Wisconsin Volunteers*, 266–268; Porter, *Campaigning with Grant*, 110.
16. See description in Johnson and Buel, *Battles and Leaders*, IV: 174.
17. Porter, *Campaigning with Grant*, 110–111.
18. Dawes, *Service with the Sixth Wisconsin Volunteers*, 269.
19. Johnson and Buel, *Battles and Leaders*, IV: 174.
20. Meade, *Life and Letters*, II: 195.

21. Ibid., 196.
22. Porter, *Campaigning with Grant*, 114–115.
23. Ibid., 115–116.
24. Lyman, *Meade's Headquarters*, 115. Different descriptions appear in Lyman, *Meade's Army*, 161.
25. Meade, *Life and Letters*, II: 197.
26. Ibid., 190, 197–198.
27. Gordon C. Rhea, *The Battles for Spotsylvania Court House and the Road to Yellow Tavern, May 7– 12, 1864* (Baton Rouge: Louisiana State University Press, 1997), 318.
28. Carl Sandburg, *Abraham Lincoln: The Prairie Years and The War Years* (New York: Harcourt, 2002), 328.
29. Henry Livermore Abbott, *Fallen Leaves: The Civil War Letters of Major Henry Livermore Abbott*, ed. Robert Garth Scott (Kent, OH: Kent State University Press, 1991), 246.
30. Rhea, *To the North Anna River*, 86–87; Lyman, *Meade's Army*, 159.
31. John F. Cummings III, "Your Husband's Noble Self-Sacrifice." *North and South: The Official Magazine of the Civil War Society* 7, no. 14, (June 2004): 75–79.
32. Lyman, *Meade's Headquarters*, 126.
33. Lyman, *Meade's Army*, 156.
34. Ibid., 142.
35. Dana, *Recollections of the Civil War*, 189–190.
36. Porter, *Campaigning with Grant*, 133.
37. Lyman, *Meade's Headquarters*, 120.
38. Porter, *Campaigning with Grant*, 138–139.
39. Col. Theodore Rodenbough of the 18th Pennsylvania Cavalry in Johnson and Buel, *Battles and Leaders*, IV: 191.
40. Meade, *Life and Letters*, II: 198.
41. Lyman, *Meade's Headquarters*, 122.
42. Lyman, *Meade's Army*, 173; Lyman, *Meade's Headquarters*, 126.
43. Lyman, *Meade's Army*, 442.
44. Quotes on panel at the site.
45. Lyman, *Meade's Headquarters*, 126–127.
46. See Lyman, *Meade's Headquarters*, 129; Lyman, *Meade's Army*, 177.
47. Lyman, *Meade's Army*, 179.
48. Frank Wilkeson, *Recollections of a Private Soldier in the Army of the Potomac* (New York: G. P. Putnam's Sons, 1887), 124.
49. Lyman, *Meade's Army*, 179.
50. Ibid., 182.
51. Gerrish, *Army Life*, 193.
52. Lyman, *Meade's Headquarters*, 122.
53. Ibid., 140.
54. James Harrison Wilson, *Heroes of the great conflict: Life and Services of William Farrar Smith, Major General, United States Volunteers in the Civil War* (Wilmington, DE: The John Rogers Press, 1904), 112.
55. Lyman, *Meade's Headquarters*, 138; *Official Records* XXXVI, 1: 1000.
56. Stevens, *Three Years in the Sixth Corps*, 349.
57. Emory Upton, *The Life and Letters of Emory Upton, Colonel of the Fourth Regiment of Artillery, and Brevet Major-General, U.S. Army*, ed. Peter S. Michie (New York: D. Appleton and Company, 1885), 109.
58. Lyman, *Meade's Headquarters*, 138.
59. Porter, *Campaigning with Grant*, 174.
60. Johnson and Buel, *Battles and Leaders*, IV: 217.
61. Haskell, *Battle of Gettysburg*, xvi–xix.
62. Walker, *History of the Second Army Corps*, 515.
63. *Official Records* I, XXXVI, 3: 525.
64. Ibid., 525–526.

65. Lyman, *Meade's Headquarters*, 147–148.
66. Most of the account from Ibid., 149–153, and Lyman, *Meade's Army*, 192–194.
67. Walker, *History of the Second Army Corps*, 518.
68. *Official Records* I, XXXVI, 3: 524, and Porter, *Campaigning with Grant*, 179.
69. Upton, *Life and Letters of Emory Upton*, 108.
70. Johnson and Buel, *Battles and Leaders*, IV: 228.
71. Wainwright, *Diary of Battle*, 405.
72. *Official Records* I, XXXVI, 1: 206.
73. James McPherson, *Hallowed Ground: A Walk at Gettysburg* (New York: Crown Publishers, 2003), 124.
74. Meade, *Life and Letters*, II: 201.
75. Lyman, *Meade's Army*, 196.
76. Andrews, *The North Reports the Civil War*, 547–548.
77. *Philadelphia Inquirer*, June 2, 1864.
78. Meade, *Life and Letters*, II: 202.
79. Ibid.
80. Porter, *Campaigning with Grant*, 190–191.
81. From the original letter to Margaret, June 9, 1864, seen on microfilm at AHEC.
82. Andrews, *The North Reports the Civil War*, 547–548.
83. Sylvanus Cadwallader, *Three Years with Grant, as Recalled by War Correspondent Sylvanus Cadwallader*, ed. Benjamin P. Thomas (New York: Alfred A. Knopf, 1955; reprint Lincoln, NE: Bison Books, 1996), 208.
84. Wainwright, *Diary of Battle*, 406.
85. Ernest B. Furgursson, *Not War But Murder: Cold Harbor 1864* (New York: Alfred A Knopf, 2000), 42.
86. Andrews, *The North Reports the Civil War*, 551.
87. Wainwright, *Diary of Battle*, 409.
88. Stevens, *Three Years in the Sixth Corps*, 354.
89. Fisk, *Hard Marching Every Day*, 225.
90. William A. Frassanito, *Grant and Lee: The Virginia Campaigns, 1864–1865* (New York: MacMillan, 1983), 194–195.
91. Letter to Margaret Meade, July 23, 1864, AHEC.
92. Account from Theodore Lyman, "Operations of the Army of the Potomac, June 5–15, 1864," in *Papers of the Military Historical Society of Massachusetts* (Boston: The Military Historical Society of Massachusetts, 1906), Vol. 5 (*Petersburg, Chancellorsville, Gettysburg*): 18–24.
94. Porter, *Campaigning with Grant*, 101.
95. Lyman, "Operations of the Army of the Potomac," 22.
96. Gerrish, *Army Life*, 197.

Chapter 16: Before Petersburg

1. Lyman, *Meade's Headquarters*, 162.
2. Theodore Lyman, "Crossing of the James and Advance on Petersburg, June 13–16, 1864," in *Papers of the Military Historical Society of Massachusetts* (Boston: The Military Historical Society of Massachusetts, 1906), Vol. 5 (*Petersburg, Chancellorsville, Gettysburg*): 29.3. Lyman, *Meade's Headquarters*, 108.
4. Lyman, "Crossing of the James, June 13–16, 1864," 30.
5. Porter, *Campaigning with Grant*, 206.
6. Lyman, "Crossing of the James, June 13–16, 1864," 31.
7. Porter, *Campaigning with Grant*, 209.
8. Horace J. Shaw, *The First Maine Heavy Artillery, 1862–1865* (Portland, ME: publisher unknown, 1903), 122–123.
9. Pennypacker, *General Meade*, 326.
10. Lyman, *Meade's Headquarters*, 224.
11. Lyman, *Meade's Army*, 217.

12. Powell, *Fifth Army Corps*, 702.
13. Walker, *History of the Second Army Corps*, 544.
14. Porter, *Campaigning with Grant*, 140.
15. Weld, *War Diary and Letters*, 318.
16. Wainwright, *Diary of Battle*, 425.
17. Worthington Chauncey Ford, ed., *A Cycle of Adams Letters, 1861–1865*, vol. 2 (Boston: Houghton Mifflin Company, 1920), 154.
18. Meade, *Life and Letters*, II: 207.
19. Lyman, *Meade's Headquarters*, 102.
20. Lyman, *Meade's Army*, 227.
21. See Walker, *History of the Second Army Corps*, 533, 539.
22. Wainwright, *Diary of Battle*, 436.
23. Ulysses S. Grant, *The Papers of Ulysses S. Grant*, edited by John Y. Simon (Carbondale and Edwardsville IL: Southern Illinois University Press, 1985), XI: 104–105.
24. *Official Records* I, XL, 3: 393–394.
25. Lyman, *Meade's Army*, 455.
26. Ibid., 230.
27. Meade, *Life and Letters*, II: 213.
28. Stewart, *Camp, March, and Battle-field*, 398–399.
29. Dawes, *Service with the Sixth Wisconsin Volunteers*, 291.
30. Letter of July 12, 1864, to Margaret, Meade Collection, AHEC.
31. Lyman, *Meade's Army*, 230.
32. *Official Records* I, XL, 1: 36.
33. Meade, *Life and Letters*, II: 216.
34. Johnson and Buel, *Battles and Leaders*, IV: 545, and *Official Records* I, XL, 1: 131.
35. Ibid. (*Official Records*), 17.
36. Johnson and Buel, *Battles and Leaders*, IV: 548.
37. Lyman, *Meade's Army*, 241.
38. Ibid., 240.
39. Weld, *War Diary and Letters*, 353.
40. For correspondence, see *Official Records* I, XL, 3: 660.
41. Weld, *War Diary and Letters*, 356.
42. Porter, *Campaigning with Grant*, 267.
43. Johnson and Buel, *Battles and Leaders*, IV: 562.
44. Ibid., 558.
45. Weld, *War Diary and Letters*, 356–357.
46. Quoted by H. Seymour Hall in MOLLUS, *War Talks in Kansas*, 243.
47. Lyman, *Meade's Headquarters*, 256.
48. Meade, *Life and Letters*, I: 355–356.
49. MOLLUS, *War Talks in Kansas*, 216.
50. Grant, *Papers of Ulysses S. Grant*, XI: 260.
51. Lyman, *Meade's Headquarters*, 214.
52. Meade, *Life and Letters*, II: 220.
53. Ibid., II: 224.
54. Ibid.
55. Eric J. Wittenberg, *Little Phil: A Reassessment of the Civil War Leadership of Gen. Philip H. Sheridan* (Washington, DC: Potomac Books, 2002), 135.
56. Pennypacker, *General Meade*, 334.
57. Ibid., 335.
58. Meade, *Life and Letters*, II: 246.
59. Ibid., 227.
60. Walker, *History of the Second Army Corps*, 559.
61. Ibid., 601–602.
62. Lyman, *Meade's Headquarters*, 225.

63. Walker, *History of the Second Army Corps*, 744.
64. Lyman, *Meade's Headquarters*, 181–182.
65. Walker, *History of the Second Army Corps*, 578.
66. Meade, *Life and Letters*, II: 235.
67. Lyman, *Meade's Headquarters*, 232; Meade, *Life and Letters*, II: 231.
68. Lyman, *Meade's Army*, 298.
69. Lyman, *Meade's Headquarters*, 307.
70. McPherson, *Tried by War*, 240.
71. Ibid., 386.
72. Gerrish, *Army Life*, 209.
73. Meade, *Life and Letters*, II: 244.
74. Ibid., 247.
74. Pennypacker, *General Meade*, 346.
75. Lyman, *Meade's Headquarters*, 290–291.

Chapter 17: On to Appomattox

1. Lyman, *Meade's Headquarters*, 324–325.
2. Grant, *Papers of Ulysses S. Grant*, XIII: 299.
3. Meade, *Life and Letters*, II: 261.
4. Ibid., 283.
5. Lyman, *Meade's Headquarters*, 316–317.
6. David Power Conyngham, *Irish Brigade and Its Campaigns* (New York: Fordham University Press, 1994), 514–515.
7. Lyman, *Meade's Army*, 348.
8. Johnson and Buel, *Battles and Leaders*, IV: 579–580.
9. Lyman, *Meade's Headquarters*, 323.
10. Johnson and Buel, *Battles and Leaders*, IV: 583.
11. Porter, *Campaigning with Grant*, 404.
12. Lyman, *Meade's Headquarters*, 324–325.
13. Meade, *Life and Letters*, II: 267–268.
14. Grant, *Memoirs*, 534.
15. Powell, *Fifth Army Corps*, 803.
16. Gerrish, *Army Life*, 244–245.
17. See Sears, *Controversies and Commanders*, 281.
18. *Official Records* I, XLVI, 3: 398–399.
19. Wainwright, *Diary of Battle*, 513–514.
20. Lyman, *Meade's Army*, 356.
21. William Marvel, *Lee's Last Retreat: The Flight to Appomattox* (Chapel Hill: University of North Carolina, 2002), 16.
22. Sears, *Controversies and Commanders*, 284.
23. Powell, *Fifth Army Corps*, 809.
24. Porter, *Campaigning with Grant*, 444.
25. George Grenville Benedict, *Vermont in the Civil War: A History of the Part Taken by the Vermont Soldiers and Sailors in the War for the Union, 1861–5* (Burlington, VT: Free Press Association, 1886), 584.
26. Best, *History of the 121st New York State Infantry*, 209–210.
27. Benedict, *Vermont in the Civil War*, 594–595.
28. Pennypacker, *General Meade*, 363.
29. Lyman, *Meade's Headquarters*, 341.
30. Porter, *Campaigning with Grant*, 450.
31. Porter, *Campaigning with Grant*, 450–451. Also details from A. Wilson Greene, *Civil War Petersburg: Confederate City in the Crucible of War* (Charlottesville: University of Virginia Press, 2006), 260.
32. Porter, *Campaigning with Grant*, 452.

33. Meade, *Life and Letters*, II: 269.
34. Lyman, *Meade's Army*, 361.
35. Meade, *Life and Letters*, II: 271.
36. Lyman, *Meade's Headquarters*, 351.
37. Ibid.
38. Lyman, *Meade's Army*, 395.
39. Pennypacker, *General Meade*, 380.
40. Walker, *History of the Second Army Corps*, 682.
41. Conyngham, *The Irish Brigade*, 524.
42. Grant and Lee correspondence quoted in Grant, *Memoirs*, 550.
43. Lyman, *Meade's Army*, 367.
44. Lee to Grant in *Official Records*, I, LVIII, 3: 641: Grant to Lee, ibid., 664.
45. Ibid.
46. Lyman, *Meade's Headquarters*, 356.
47. Ibid., 357, and Lyman, *Meade's Army*, 369.
48. Hyde, *Following the Greek Cross*, 256.
49. Lyman, *Meade's Headquarters*, 358.
50. *Richmond Times-Dispatch*, April 1, 2012, B2.
51. Porter, *Campaigning with Grant*, 479–480.
52. Ibid., 485–486.
53. Lyman, *Meade's Headquarters*, 271.
54. Lyman, *Meade's Headquarters*, 360.55. Accounts in Lyman, *Meade's Headquarters*, 359–362; Meade, *Life and Letters*, II: 269.
56. Meade, *Life and Letters*, II: 271.
57. Ibid., II: 350.
58. Account in Cadwallader, *Three Years with Grant*, 257–258.
59. Lyman, *Meade's Army*, 373.
60. Meade, *Life and Letters*, II: 274.
61. Ibid.; Lyman, *Meade's Headquarters*, 362; Meade, *Life and Letters*, II: 276
62. Meade, *Life and Letters*, II: 275–276.
63. See Meade, *Life and Letters*, II: 278–279.
64. Brooks, *Washington in Lincoln's Time*, 308.
65. Porter, *Campaigning with Grant*, 507.
66. Ibid., 508.
67. Wainwright, *Diary of Battle*, 527.
68. Ibid., 530.
69. Meade, *Life and Letters*, II: 282.

Chapter 18: The Final Years

1. Meade, *Life and Letters*, I: 241.
2. Porter, *Campaigning with Grant*, 247–248.
3. Meade, *Life and Letters*, II: 283.
4. James E. Sefton, *The United States Army and Reconstruction, 1865–1877* (Baton Rouge: Louisiana State University Press, 1967), 8.
5. Account in Lyman, *Meade's Army*, 388–392.
6. Meade, *Life and Letters*, II: 284.
7. W. S. Neidhardt, *Fenianism in North America* (University Park: Pennsylvania State University Press, 1975), 12.
8. Ibid., 35.
9. W. C. Chewett and Co., *The Fenian Raid at Fort Erie, June the First and Second, 1866: With a Map of the Niagara Peninsula, Shewing the Route of the Troops; and a Plan of the Lime Ridge Battle Ground* (Toronto: W. C. Chewett and Co., 1866), 18.
10. Neidhardt, *Fenianism in North America*, 72; Mabel Gregory Walker, *The Fenian Movement* (Colorado Springs: Ralph Myles Publisher, 1969), 102.

11. Meade, *Life and Letters*, II: 288.

12. Sefton, *United States Army and Reconstruction*, 169.

13. Ibid., 170.

14. Meade, *Life and Letters*, II: 290.

15. George Gordon Meade, *Report of Major General Meade's Military Operations and Administration of Civil Affairs in the Third Military District and Department of the South for the Year 1868, with Accompanying Documents* (Atlanta: Assistant Adjutant General's Office, Department of the South, 1868), 4

16. Ibid., 10.

17. Ibid., 81.

18. Jean Edward Smith, *Grant* (New York: Touchstone, 2001), 457.

19. Meade, *Life and Letters*, II: 299.

20. McClure, *Abraham Lincoln and Men of War-Times*, 362.

21. Meade, *Life and Letters*, II: 197.

22. *Philadelphia Inquirer*, November 12, 1872.

23. Quoted in Thomas L. Connelly, *The Marble Man: Robert E. Lee and His Image in American Society* (Baton Rouge: Louisiana State University Press, 1978), 146.

24. Ibid., 3.

25. Ibid., 64.

26. Charles Leonard Moore, "The Hero of Gettysburg." *The Dial* 55, no 13 (July 13, 1913): 14.

Bibliography

Papers and Collections

George Gordon Meade Collection, United States Army Heritage and Education Center (AHEC), Carlisle, PA.
George Gordon Meade Collection, The Historical Society of Pennsylvania, Philadelphia.
David Bell Birney Papers, United States Army Heritage and Education Center (AHEC), Carlisle, PA.

Books

Abbott, Henry Livermore. *Fallen Leaves: The Civil War Letters of Major Henry Livermore Abbott*. Edited by Robert Garth Scott. Kent, OH: Kent State University Press, 1991.

Adkin, Mark. *The Gettysburg Companion: The Complete Guide to America's Most Famous Battle*. Mechanicsburg, PA: Stackpole Books, 2008.

Alexander, Ted. *The Battle of Antietam: The Bloodiest Day*. Charleston, SC: History Press, 2011.

Ambrose, Stephen E. *Duty, Honor, Country: A History of West Point*. Baltimore: Johns Hopkins Press, 1966.

———. *Halleck: Lincoln's Chief of Staff*. Baton Rouge: Louisiana State University Press, 1962.

Andrews, J. Cutler. *The North Reports the Civil War*. Pittsburgh: University of Pittsburgh Press, 1955; reprint, 1985.

Axelrod, Alan. *The Horrid Pit: The Battle of the Crater, the Civil War's Cruelest Mission*. New York: Carrol & Graf, 2007.

Bache, Richard Meade. *Life of General George Gordon Meade, Commander of the Army of the Potomac*. Philadelphia: Henry T. Coates & Co., 1897.

Bates, Samuel P. *History of the Pennsylvania Volunteers, 1861–1865*. 5 vols. Harrisburg, PA: B. Singerly, 1869–1871.

Benedict, George Grenville. *Vermont in the Civil War: A History of the Part Taken by the Vermont Soldiers and Sailors in the War for the Union, 1861–5*. Burlington, VT: Free Press Association, 1886.

Best, Isaac Oliver. *History of the 121st New York State Infantry*. Chicago: Lt. Jas. H. Smith, 1921.

Beyer, W. F., and O. F. Keydel. *Deeds of Valor: How America's Civil War Heroes Won the Congressional Medal of Honor*. New York: Smithmark Publishers, 2000.

Bigelow, John Jr. *Chancellorsville*. New York: Konecky & Konecky, 1995. Originally published as *The Campaign of Chancellorsville: A Strategic and Tactical Study*. New Haven, CT: Yale University Press, 1910.

Billings, John Davis. *Hardtack and Coffee; or, The Unwritten Story of Army Life*. Boston: George M. Smith & Co., 1888.

Borit, Gabor S., ed. *Lincoln's Generals*. New York: Oxford University Press, 1994.

Brooks, Noah. *Washington in Lincoln's Time*. New York: Century Co., 1895.

Brown, Kent Masterson. *Retreat from Gettysburg: Lee, Logistics and the Pennsylvania Campaign*. Chapel Hill: University of North Carolina Press, 2005.

Butterfield, Julia Lorrilard Safford. *A Biographical Memorial of General Daniel Butterfield, Including Many Addresses and Military Writings*. New York: The Grafton Press, 1904.

Cadwallader, Sylvanus. *Three Years with Grant, as Recalled by War Correspondent Sylvanus Cadwallader*. Edited by Benjamin P. Thomas. New York: Alfred A. Knopf, 1955; reprint Lincoln, NE: Bison Books, 1996.

Catton, Bruce. *Grant Takes Command*. New York: Little, Brown, 1969.

Chewett, W. C., and Co. *The Fenian Raid at Fort Erie, June the First and Second, 1866: With a Map of the Niagara Peninsula, Shewing the Route of the Troops; and a Plan of the Lime Ridge Battle Ground.* Toronto: W. C. Chewett and Co., 1866.

Cleaves, Freeman. *Meade of Gettysburg.* Norman: University of Oklahoma Press, 1960.

Coddington, Edward. *The Gettysburg Campaign: A Study in Command.* New York: Charles Scribner's Sons, 1968.

Coffin, Charles Carleton. *The Boys of '61; or, Four Years of Fighting.* Boston: Estes and Lauriat, 1881.

———. *Four Years of Fighting: A Volume of Personal Observation with the Army and Navy, from the First Battle of Bull Run to the Fall of Richmond.* Boston: Ticknor and Fields, 1866.

———. *Marching to Victory: The Second Period of the War of the Rebellion, Including the Year 1863.* New York: Harper & Brothers, 1888.

Commager, Henry Steele, ed. *The Blue and the Gray.* 2 vols. Indianapolis: Bobbs-Merrill, 1950; reprint, New York: Fairfax Press, 1984.

Connelly, Thomas L. *The Marble Man: Robert E. Lee and His Image in American Society.* Baton Rouge: Louisiana State University Press, 1978.

Conyngham, David Power. *The Irish Brigade and Its Campaigns* (edited, with an introduction by Lawrence Frederick Kohl). New York: Fordham University Press, 1994.

Dana, Charles A. *Recollections of the Civil War with the Leaders at Washington and in the Field in the Sixties.* New York: D Appleton and Co., 1913.

Dawes, Rufus. *Service with the Sixth Wisconsin Volunteers.* Marietta, OH: K. R. Aldeman & Sons, 1890.

Department of the Army. *The Medal of Honor of the United States Army.* Washington, DC: United States Government Printing Office, 1948.

Donaldson, Francis Adams. *Inside the Army of the Potomac: The Civil War Experience of Captain Francis Adams Donaldson.* Edited by Gregory J. Acken. Mechanicsburg, PA: Stackpole Books, 1998.

Doubleday, Abner. *Chancellorsville and Gettysburg.* New York: Charles Scribner's Sons, 1882.

Douglas, Henry Kyd. *I Rode with Stonewall.* Chapel Hill: University of North Carolina Press, 1940.

Dugard, Martin. *The Training Ground: Grant, Lee, Sherman, and Davis in the Mexican War, 1846–1848.* New York: Little, Brown and Co, 2008.

Eisenhower, John S. D. *So Far from God: The U.S. War with Mexico, 1846–1848.* New York: Random House, 1989.

Evelyn, Douglas, and Paul Dickson. *On This Spot: Pinpointing the Past in Washington, D.C.* Washington, DC: Farragut Publishing Co., 1992.

Fairmount Park Art Association. *Unveiling of the Equestrian Statue of Major-General George Gordon Meade, Fairmount Park, Philadelphia.* Philadelphia: Allen, Lane & Scott, 1887.

Faust, Patricia L., ed. *Historical Times Illustrated Encyclopedia of the Civil War.* New York: Harper & Row, 1986; reprint, 1991.

Favill, Josiah Marshall. *The Diary of a Young Officer Serving with the Armies of the United States during the War of the Rebellion.* Chicago: R. R. Donnelley & Sons Co., 1909.

Fisk, Wilbur. *Hard Marching Every Day: The Civil War Letters of Private Wilbur Fisk, 1861–1865.* Edited by Emil Rosenblatt and Ruth Rosenblatt. Lawrence: University Press of Kansas, 1983.

Fiske, Samuel Wheelock. *Mr. Dunn Browne's Experiences in the Army.* Boston: Nichols and Noyes, 1866.

Ford, Worthington Chauncey, ed. *A Cycle of Adams Letters, 1861–1865.* Vol. 2. Boston: Houghton Mifflin, 1920.

Frassanito, William A. *Grant and Lee: The Virginia Campaigns, 1864–1865.* New York: MacMillan Publishing Co., 1983.

Furgurson, Ernest B. *Not War But Murder: Cold Harbor 1864.* New York: Alfred A. Knopf, 2000.

Gallagher, Gary W., ed. *Two Witnesses at Gettysburg: The Personal Accounts of Whitelaw Reid and A. J. Fremantle.* 2nd ed. Chichester, UK: Wiley-Blackwell, 2009.

———. *The Wilderness Campaign.* Chapel Hill: University of North Carolina Press, 1997.

Gerrish, Theodore. *Army Life: A Private's Reminiscences of the Civil War.* Portland, ME: Hoyt, Fogg & Donham, 1882.

Gibbon, John. *Personal Recollections of the Civil War.* New York: G. P. Putnam's Sons, 1928.

Gibbs, Joseph. *Three Years in the Bloody Eleventh.* University Park: Pennsylvania State University Press, 2002.

Giddings, Luther. *Sketches of the Campaign in Northern Mexico in Eighteen Hundred Forty-Six and Seven.* New York: G. P. Putnam's Sons, 1853.

Gordon, John Brown. *Reminiscences of the Civil War.* New York: Charles Scribner's Sons, 1904.

Grant, Ulysses S. *The Papers of Ulysses S. Grant.* Edited by John Y. Simon. Carbondale and Edwardsville: Southern Illinois University Press, 1985.

———. *Personal Memoirs of U. S. Grant.* Cleveland: World Publishing Company, 1952; reprint, New York: Da Capo, 1982.

Greene, A. Wilson. *Breaking the Backbone of the Rebellion: The Final Battles of the Petersburg Campaign.* Mason City, IA: Savas Publishing Co., 2000.

———. *Civil War Petersburg: Confederate City in the Crucible of War.* Charlottesville: University of Virginia Press, 2006.

Griffith, Paddy. *Battle Tactics of the Civil War.* New Haven, CT: Yale University Press, 1989; reprint, 2001.

Haskell, Frank A. *The Battle of Gettysburg.* Madison: Wisconsin History Commission, 1908; reprint, Boston: Houghton-Mifflin, 1969.

Haupt, Herman. *Reminiscences of General Herman Haupt.* Milwaukee: Wright & Joys Co., 1901.

Hennessy, John J. *Return to Bull Run: The Campaign and Battle of Second Manassas.* New York: Simon & Schuster, 1993.

Hessler, James A. *Sickles at Gettysburg: The Controversial Civil War General Who Committed Murder, Abandoned Little Round Top, and Declared Himself the Hero of Gettysburg.* New York: Savas Beatie, 2009.

Hill, A. F. *Our Boys: The Personal Experiences of a Soldier in the Army of the Potomac.* Philadelphia: John E. Potter, 1864.

Hitchcock, Frederick Lyman. *War from the Inside: The Story of the 132nd Regiment Pennsylvania Volunteer Infantry in the War for the Suppression of the Rebellion, 1862–1863.* Philadelphia: J. B. Lippincott Co., 1904.

Howard, Oliver Otis. *Autobiography of Oliver Otis Howard, Major General, United States Army,* Volume 1. New York: The Baker & Taylor Company, 1907.

Humphreys, Andrew A. *From Gettysburg to the Rapidan: The Army of the Potomac July 1863 to April 1864.* New York: Charles Scribner's Sons, 1883.

———. *The Virginia Campaign of '64 and '65.* New York: Charles Scribner's Sons, 1883.

Hyde, Bill, ed. *The Union Generals Speak: The Meade Hearings on the Battle of Gettysburg.* Baton Rouge: Louisiana State University Press, 2003.

Hyde, Thomas W. *Following the Greek Cross; or, Memories of the Sixth Army Corps.* Boston: Houghton, Mifflin, 1894.

Ingraham, Elizabeth Meade. *Leaves: The Diary of Elizabeth Meade Ingraham, the Rebel Sister of General George Meade.* Edited by Sue Burns Moore and Rebecca Blackwell Drake. Raymond, MS: Champion Heritage Foundation, 2010.

Jacob, Kathryn Allamong. *Testament to Union: Civil War Monuments in Washington, D.C.* Baltimore: Johns Hopkins University Press, 1998.

Johnson, Robert Underwood, and Clarence Clough Buel. *Battles and Leaders of the Civil War: Being for the Most Part Contributions by Union and Confederate Officers.* 4 vols. New York: Century Company, 1887–1888; reprint, Secaucus, NJ: Castle Books, n.d.

Jones, Wilmer L. *Generals in Blue and Gray.* Vol. 1, *Lincoln's Generals.* Westport, CT: Greenwood Publishing Group, 2004.

———. *Generals in Blue and Gray.* Vol. 2, *Davis's Generals.* Westport, CT: Greenwood Publishing Group, 2006.

Jordan, David M. *Happiness Is Not My Companion: The Life of General G. K. Warren.* Bloomington: Indiana University Press, 2001.

———. *Winfield Scott Hancock: A Soldier's Life.* Bloomington: Indiana University Press, 1988.

Ladd, David L., and Audrey J. Ladd, eds. *The Bachelder Papers: Gettysburg in Their Own Words.* 3 vols. Dayton: Morningside Press, 1994–1995.

Longacre, Edward G. *General Ulysses S. Grant: The Soldier and the Man.* Cambridge, MA: Da Capo Press, 2006.

Lyman, Theodore. *Meade's Headquarters, 1863–1865: Letters of Colonel Theodore Lyman from the Wilderness to Appomattox.* Edited by George R. Agassiz. Boston: Massachusetts Historical Society, 1922.

———. *Meade's Army: The Private Notebooks of Lt. Col. Theodore Lyman.* Edited by David W. Lowe. Kent, OH: Kent State University Press, 2007.

Marszalek, George, ed. *The Grand Review: The Civil War Continues to Shape America.* York, PA: Bold Print, 2000.

Martin, Samuel J. *Kill-Cavalry: The Life of Union General Hugh Judson Kilpatrick.* Mechanicsburg, PA: Stackpole Books, 2000.

Marvel, William. *Lee's Last Retreat: The Flight to Appomattox.* Chapel Hill: University of North Carolina, 2002.

McCall, George A. *Letters from the Frontiers: Written during a Period of Thirty Years' Service in the Army of the United States.* Philadelphia: J. B. Lippincott, 1868.

McCarter, William. *My Life in the Irish Brigade: The Civil War Memoirs of Private William McCarter, 116th Pennsylvania Infantry.* Edited by Kevin E. O'Brien. Campbell, CA: Savas Publishing Co., 1996.

McClellan, Carswell. *The Personal Memoirs and Military History of U.S. Grant versus the Record of the Army of the Potomac.* Boston: Houghton, Mifflin, 1887.

McClellan, George B. *The Civil War Papers of George B. McClellan: Selected Correspondence, 1860–1865.* Edited by Stephen W. Sears. New York: Ticknor and Fields, 1989.

McClure, Alexander K. *Abraham Lincoln and Men of War-Times: Some Personal Recollections of War and Politics during the Lincoln Administration.* Philadelphia: Times Publishing Co., 1892.

McPherson, James M.. *Hallowed Ground: A Walk at Gettysburg.* New York: Crown Publishers, 2003.

———. *Tried by War: Abraham Lincoln as Commander in Chief.* New York: Penguin Press, 2009.

Meade, George. *The Life and Letters of George Gordon Meade, Major-General United States Army.* 2 vols. New York: Charles Scribner's Sons, 1913.

Meade, George Gordon. *Report of Major General Meade's Military Operations and Administration of Civil Affairs in the Third Military District and Department of the South for the Year 1868, with Accompanying Documents.* Atlanta: Assistant Adjutant General's Office, Department of the South, 1868.

Military Order of the Loyal Legion of the United States (MOLLUS), Kansas Commandery. *War Talks in Kansas.* Kansas City, MO: Franklin Hudson Publishing Co., 1906.

Morris, Roy Jr. *Sheridan: The Life & Wars of General Phil Sheridan.* New York: Vintage, 1993.

Neidhardt, W. S. *Fenianism in North America.* University Park: Pennsylvania State University Press, 1975.

Nichols, Edward J. *Toward Gettysburg: A Biography of General John F. Reynolds.* University Park: Pennsylvania State University Press, 1958.

Nicholson, John P., ed. *Pennsylvania at Gettysburg: Ceremonies at the Dedication of the Monuments Erected by the Commonwealth of Pennsylvania.* 2 vols. Harrisburg, PA: Wm. Stanley Ray, State Printer, 1904.

Noyes, George F. *The Bivouac and the Battlefield; or, Campaign Sketches in Virginia and Maryland.* New York: Harper & Brothers, 1863.

O'Reilly, Francis Augustín. *The Fredericksburg Campaign: Winter War on the Rappahannock.* Baton Rouge: Louisiana State University Press, 2003.

Palfrey, Francis Winthrop. *The Antietam and Fredericksburg.* Vol. 5 of *Campaigns of the Civil War.* New York: Charles Scribner's Sons, 1912.

Pennypacker, Isaac R. *General Meade.* New York: D. Appleton, 1901.

Pleasonton, Alfred. "The Campaign of Gettysburg." In *The Annals of the War: Written by Leading Participants, North and South,* edited by Alexander Kelly McClure, 447–459. Philadelphia: Times Publishing Company, 1879.

Porter, Horace. *Campaigning with Grant.* New York: Century Company, 1907; reprint, Old Saybrook, CT: Konecky and Konecky, 1992.

Powell, William Henry. *The Fifth Army Corps (Army of the Potomac): A Record of Operations during the Civil War in the United States of America, 1861–1865*. New York: G. P. Putnam's Sons, 1896.

———. *Officers of the Volunteer Army and Navy Who Served in the Civil War*. Philadelphia: L. R. Hamersly & Co., 1893.

Priest, John M. *Antietam: The Soldiers' Battle*. Shippensburg, PA: White Mane Publishing Co., 1989.

Rafuse, Ethan S. *George Gordon Meade and the War in the East*. Abilene, TX: McWhiney Foundation Press, 2003.

Rhea, Gordon C. *The Battle of the Wilderness, May 5–6, 1864*. Baton Rouge: Louisiana State University Press, 1994.

———. *The Battles for Spotsylvania Court House and the Road to Yellow Tavern, May 7–12, 1864*. Baton Rouge: Louisiana State University Press, 1997.

———. *To the North Anna River: Grant and Lee, May 13–25, 1864*. Baton Rouge: Louisiana State University Press, 2000.

Robertson, James I. *Stonewall Jackson: The Man, the Soldier, the Legend*. New York: MacMillan, 1997.

Rusling, James F. *Men and Things I Saw in Civil War Days*. New York: Eaton & Mains, 1899.

Sandburg, Carl. *Abraham Lincoln: The Prairie Years and The War Years*. New York: Harcourt, 2002.

Sauers, Richard A. *A Caspian Sea of Ink: The Meade-Sickles Controversy*. Baltimore: Butternut and Blue, 1989.

———. *Meade: Victor of Gettysburg*. Dulles, VA: Brassey's, 2003.

Schaff, Morris. *The Battle of the Wilderness*. Boston: Houghton Mifflin, 1910.

Schurz, Carl. *The Reminiscences of Carl Schurz*, 3 vols. London: John Murray, 1909.

Sears, Stephen W. *Chancellorsville*. New York: Houghton Mifflin, 1996.

———. *Controversies and Commanders: Dispatches from the Army of the Potomac*. New York: Houghton Mifflin, 1999.

———. *George B. McClellan: The Young Napoleon*. New York: Ticknor and Fields, 1988.

———. *Gettysburg*. New York: Houghton Mifflin, 2003.

———. *Landscape Turned Red: The Battle of Antietam*. New York: Mariner Books, 1993.

———. *To the Gates of Richmond: The Peninsula Campaign*. New York: Ticknor and Fields, 1992.

Sedgwick, John, and George William Curtis. *Correspondence of John Sedgwick, Major-General*. Vol. 2. New York: Printed for Carl and Ellen Battelle Stoeckel by the De Vinne Press, 1903.

Sefton, James E. *The United States Army and Reconstruction, 1865–1877*. Baton Rouge: Louisiana State University Press, 1967.

Shaw, Horace J. *The First Maine Heavy Artillery, 1862–1865*. Portland, ME, 1903.

Smalley, George W. *Anglo-American Memories*. New York, G. P. Putnam's Sons, 1911.

Smith, Jean Edward. *Grant*. New York: Touchstone, 2002.

Smith, Justin Harvey. *The War with Mexico*. New York: The MacMillan Co., 1918.

Snell, Mark A. *From First to Last: The Life of Major General William B. Franklin*. New York: Fordham University Press, 2002.

Stackpole, Edward J. *The Fredericksburg Campaign*. 2nd ed. Mechanicsburg, PA: Stackpole Books, 1991.

———. *From Cedar Mountain to Antietam*. 2nd ed. Mechanicsburg, PA: Stackpole Books, 1993.

———. *They Met at Gettysburg*. 3rd ed. Mechanicsburg, PA: Stackpole Books, 1982.

Stevens, George T. *Three Years in the Sixth Corps*. Albany, NY: S. R. Gray, 1866; reprint, Bedford, MA: Applewood Books, 2008.

Stewart, Alexander Morrison. *Camp, March and Battle-field; or, Three Years and a Half with the Army of the Potomac*. Philadelphia: Jas. B. Rodgers, Printer, 1865.

Strong, William B. *History of the 121st Regiment Pennsylvania Volunteers*. Philadelphia: Catholic Standard and Times, 1906.

Survivors' Association, 118th (Corn Exchange) Regt. P.V. *History of the 118th Pennsylvania Volunteers, Corn Exchange Regiment*. Philadelphia: J. L. Smith, 1905.

Swinton, William. *Campaigns of the Army of the Potomac*. New York: Charles B. Richardson, 1866; reprint, Secaucus, NJ: Blue and Gray Press, 1988.

Sypher, J. R. *History of the Pennsylvania Reserve Corps*. Lancaster, PA: Elias Barr, 1865.

Tagg, Larry. *The Generals of Gettysburg*. El Dorado Hills, CA: Savas Beatie, 1998; reprint, Cambridge, MA: Da Capo Press, 2003.

Tap, Bruce. *Over Lincoln's Shoulder: The Committee on the Conduct of the War*. Lawrence: University Press of Kansas, 1998.

Thomson, Osmund Rhodes, and William H. Rauch. *History of the "Bucktails," Kane Rifle Regiment of the Pennsylvania Reserve Corps*. Philadelphia: Electric Printing Co., 1906.

Trudeau, Noah Andrew. *The Last Citadel: Petersburg, Virginia, June 1864–April 1865*. Baton Rouge: Louisiana State University Press, 1993.

United States Army, Department of the South, and George Gordon Meade. *Major General Meade's Report on the Ashburn Murder*. Atlanta, 1868.

United States War Department. *The War of the Rebellion: A Compilation of the Official Records of the Union and Confederate Armies*. Washington, DC: Government Printing Office, 1880–1901.

Upton, Emory. *The Life and Letters of Emory Upton, Colonel of the Fourth Regiment of Artillery, and Brevet Major-General, U.S. Army*. Edited by Peter S. Michie. New York, D. Appleton and Company, 1885.

Wainwright, Charles S. *Diary of Battle: The Personal Journals of Colonel Charles S. Wainwright*, edited by Allan Nevins. New York: Harcourt, Brace and World, 1962.

Walker, Francis A. *History of the Second Army Corps in the Army of the Potomac*. New York: Charles Scribner's Sons, 1886.

Walker, Mabel Gregory. *The Fenian Movement*. Colorado Springs: Ralph Myles Publisher, 1969.

Waskie, Anthony. *Philadelphia and the Civil War: Arsenal of the Union*. Charleston, SC: History Press, 2011.

Webb, Alexander S. *The Peninsula: McClellan's Campaign of 1862*. New York: C. Scribner's Sons, 1881; reprint, Edison, NJ: Castle Books, 2002.

Weld, Steven M. *War Diary and Letters of Stephen Minot Weld, 1861–1865*. Cambridge, MA: Riverside Press, 1912.

Wert, Jeffrey D. *The Sword of Lincoln: The Army of the Potomac*. New York: Simon & Schuster, 2005.

Wheeler, William. *In Memoriam: Letters of William Wheeler of the Class of 1855, Y.C.* Cambridge, MA: Privately printed by H. O. Houghton and Co., 1875.

Wilkeson, Frank. *Recollections of a Private Soldier in the Army of the Potomac*. New York: G. P. Putnam's Sons, 1887.

Williams, Alpheus S. *From the Cannon's Mouth: The Civil War Letters of General Alpheus S. Williams*. Edited by Milo M. Quaife. Detroit: Wayne State University Press, 1959.

Wilson, James Harrison. *Heroes of the great conflict: Life and Services of William Farrar Smith, Major General, United States Volunteers in the Civil War*. Wilmington, DE: The John Rogers Press, 1904.

Wittenberg, Eric J. *Little Phil: A Reassessment of the Civil War Leadership of Gen. Philip H. Sheridan*. Washington, DC: Potomac Books, 2002.

Wittenberg, Eric J., David Petruzzi, and Michael F. Nugent. *One Continuous Fight: The Retreat from Gettysburg and the Pursuit of Lee's Army of Northern Virginia, July 4–14, 1863*. New York: Savas Beatie, 2008; reprint, Philadelphia: Casemate Publishers, 2011.

Woodbury, Augustus. *Major General Ambrose E. Burnside and the Ninth Army Corps: A Narrative of Campaigns in North Carolina, Maryland, Virginia, Ohio, Kentucky, Mississippi and Tennessee, during the War for the Preservation of the Republic*. Providence: Sidney S. Rider & Brother, 1867.

Woodward, E. M. *History of the Third Pennsylvania Reserve*. Trenton, NJ: MacCrellish and Quigley, 1883.

———. *Our Campaigns; or, The Marches, Bivouacs, Battles, Incidents of Camp Life, and History of Our Regiment during Its Three Years Term of Service*. Philadelphia: John E. Potter, 1865.

Articles

Civil War Trust. "Bristoe Station." 2011. www.civilwar.org/battlefields/bristoe-station.html (accessed June 25, 2012).

Coddington, Edwin B. "The Strange Reputation of General Meade: A Lesson in Historiography." *The Historian* Vol. 23, no. 2 (1961): 145–166.

Cummings, John F. III. "Your Husband's Noble Self-Sacrifice." *North and South: The Official Magazine of the Civil War Society* 7, no. 4 (June 2004): 75.

Fisher, Louis. "The Mexican War and Lincoln's 'Spot Resolutions.'" Law Library of Congress, April 18, 2009. http://loc.gov/law/help/usconlaw/pdf/Mexican.war.pdf (accessed July 15, 2012).

Fitts, Deborah. "Vermont Brigade Monument Is Readied for the Wilderness." *Civil War News*, December 2005. www.civilwarnews.com/archive/articles/vtmonument.htm (accessed June 19, 2012).

"Historicus." Letter to the Editor. *New York Herald*, March 12, 1864. Available at www.civilwarhome.com/historicusarticle.htm (accessed June 27, 2012).

Lyman, Theodore. "Operations of the Army of the Potomac, June 5–15, 1864" and "Crossing of the James and Advance on Petersburg," *Papers of the Military Historical Society of Massachusetts* (Boston, 1906), Vol. 5 (*Petersburg, Chancellorsville, Gettysburg*), 1–24 and 25–32.

Moore, Charles Leonard. "The Hero of Gettysburg." *The Dial* 55, no 13 (July 13, 1913): 13–15.

National Park Service. "Civil War Series: The Battle of Chancellorsville." www.nps.gov/history/history/online_books/civil_war_series/8/sec2.htm (accessed June 19, 2012).

New York State Military Museum and Veterans Research Center. "Unit History Project: 140th Infantry Regiment, Civil War." http://dmna.state.ny.us/historic/reghist/civil/infantry/140thInf/140thInfMain.htm (accessed June 19, 2012).

Page, Evelyn. "After Gettysburg: Frederick Law Olmsted on the Escape of Lee." *Pennsylvania Magazine of History and Biography* 75, no. 4 (October 1951): 436–446.

Robertson, Robert S. "The Escape of Grant and Meade." *Magazine of American History* 19 (1888): 248–251.

Rowell, Jenn. "'Witness Tree' Falls at Ellwood: Civil War Tree at Ellwood Falls." *Freelance-Star* (Fredericksburg, VA), September 18, 2006. Available at http://fredericksburg.com/News/FLS/2006/092006/09182006/222337 (accessed June 19, 2012).

Swaim, Craig. "The Leg of Colonel Ulric Dahlgren." Historical Marker Database, July 2010. www.hmdb.org/marker.asp?marker=32629 (accessed June 24, 2012).

Warren, Gouverneur K. *Journal, May 4–June 12, 1864: Campaign from the Rapidan to the James River, Va.* Available at www.civilwarhome.com/warrenwilderness.htm (accessed July 5, 2012).

Webb, Alexander S. "Meade at Chancellorsville" in Military Historical Society of Massachusetts, *Campaigns in Virginia, Maryland and Pennsylvania, 1862–1863.* Boston: Griffith-Stillings Press, 1903.

Weeks, James. "The Civil War's Greatest Scoop." *American Heritage* 40, no. 5 (July–August 1989): 100.

Wittenberg, Eric J. "Ulric Dahlgren in the Gettysburg Campaign." *Gettysburg Magazine* 22 (January 2000): 96–111. Available at www.gdg.org/GettysburgMagazine/dahlgren.html (accessed June 19, 2012).

Zabludovsky, Karla. "Police Find 49 Bodies by a Highway in Mexico." *New York Times*, May 13, 2012. Available at www.nytimes.com/2012/05/14/world/americas/police-find-49-bodies-by-a-highway-in-mexico.html?_r=1&hp (accessed June 19, 2012).

Index

Page numbers in *italics* indicates illustrations.